2016 EDITION

CODING WITH CONFIDENCE: THE "GO TO" GUIDE FOR CDT 2016

Dramatically Cut Coding Errors and Boost Legitimate Reimbursement

Charles Blair, DDS – EDITOR

Published by:
Dr. Charles Blair & Associates, Inc.

(866) 858-7596
www.practicebooster.com
85 Catawba Street
P.O. Box 986
Belmont, NC 28012-0986

©2015 Dr. Charles Blair & Associates, Inc. All rights reserved.
This manual utilizes Predictive Error Correction℠ technology.

IMPORTANT! REGISTER YOUR 2016 EDITION

BOOK REGISTRATION - CODING WITH CONFIDENCE

NAME: _____

ADDRESS: _____
_____

TELEPHONE: _____ EMAIL: _____

PLEASE FAX TO: (855) 825-3960   EMAIL/SCAN TO: info@practicebooster.com
OR MAIL TO: DR. CHARLES BLAIR & ASSOCIATES, INC.
P.O. BOX 986, BELMONT, NC 28012-0986

THANK YOU FOR REGISTERING!

COMMENTS

IF YOU WOULD LIKE TO PROVIDE A TESTIMONIAL, SUGGESTION, OR FIND AN ERROR IN THIS BOOK, PLEASE COMPLETE THE FORM BELOW.

NAME: _____

ADDRESS: _____
_____

TELEPHONE: _____ EMAIL: _____

PLEASE CHECK ONE OF THE FOLLOWING:

☐ TESTIMONIAL   ☐ SUGGESTION   ☐ ERROR (Please indicate the code and page number)

COMMENTS

_____
_____
_____
_____
_____

email: info@drcharlesblair.com   fax: (855) 825-3960

THANK YOU FOR YOUR CONTRIBUTION!

COPYRIGHT

©2015 Dr. Charles Blair & Associates, Inc. All rights reserved. No portion of this manual may be reproduced or transmitted in any form or by any means, electronic or mechanical, including photocopying or information storage and retrieval without written permission from the publisher. Unauthorized reproduction, in whole or part, is a violation of U.S. Copyright Law. This manual may not be used for any purpose other than reference without the express written permission of the publisher.

The Code On Dental Procedures and Nomenclature is published in *Current Dental Terminology* (CDT), copyright © 2015 American Dental Association (ADA). All rights reserved. Used with permission of ADA. A royalty is paid to the ADA for the use of the codes.

Certain portions or phrases incorporated herein are licensed from American Dental Support, LLC and Practicebooster, LLC.

This manual's learning system utilizes Predictive Error Correction℠ technology and associated learning systems.

TRADEMARK/SERVICE MARK

All marks, whether of words, phrases or graphics, regardless if distinguished by ®, "TM", "SM" or neither, are specific trademarks of Dr. Charles Blair & Associates, Inc., the editor, or of their respective owners.

DISCLAIMER

By purchasing, reading, or referring to this manual, you (the reader, purchaser, or recipient of this book) agree to the following terms, conditions and disclaimers:

Substantial effort was made to ensure the accuracy of the information contained herein.
However:

- Interpretations can be difficult due to the variability of interpretation and application of CDT (Current Dental Terminology) codes.
- Within the dental profession and insurance industry there is a degree of disagreement on the uses and application of various codes.
- Third-party contract language dictates reimbursement from an insurance company.

By using this manual you, the purchaser, user or recipient of this manual, agree that interpretation and application of each code is made by the individual dentist and his/her supporting staff. The author, editor, or publisher is in no way responsible for any interpretation or final judgment made in conjunction using the information contained in this book.

Also, be aware insurance codes and code interpretations are constantly changing, with CDT updates updated every year. Always rely on the most recent CDT version when reporting any dental procedure. Each CDT update includes new, deleted, and revised procedure codes. It is necessary that the practice reports exactly "what you do" and adhere to the current CDT code set. Historically, insurance companies have not been consistent in code interpretations, and UCR (usual, customary and reasonable) or MPA (maximum plan allowance) fees vary widely among payers and from contract to contract. The level of reimbursement is determined by the plan purchased and the reimbursement schedule. There are endless variations from contract to contract, and payer to payer. Please contact each individual insurance company or the employer of the patient for specific contract information if you are unsure of its policies, reimbursement, or exclusions. Additionally, benefits coverage is becoming increasingly more difficult to predict due to numerous and subtle exclusions, limitations, and alternative benefits designed to correspond with the employer's desire to reduce the premium level, or to limit a current premium increase. The bottom line is that employees will be paying more, out-of-pocket, for both dental and medical coverage in the future.

The editor and publisher specifically assume no liability, responsibility, or guarantee for specific adjudication of a claim, results of an audit by an insurance company or government entity, acceptability of a narrative, or any code reported. The publisher and editor have attempted to verify the information contained herein, but assume no responsibility for omissions, inaccuracies, or errors. In addition, no representations or warranties are made regarding the use of the manual or any associated updates. The user is solely responsible for the use of this book (including updates) and for full compliance with any state or federal laws, or restrictions of any third party contract. This publication is a reference and not intended to offer legal advice; as always, you should always seek the review of an attorney where applicable. Furthermore, the manual user should periodically monitor the applicability of any error correction updates as follows on the next page.

CODING WITH CONFIDENCE ERROR CORRECTION UPDATES

The publisher requests errors be identified when discovered by readers. With every code set release, there is some disagreement among various industry experts and pundits on the interpretation of the language of a given code, nomenclature, and its descriptor.

If, as a reader, you feel any recognized dental authority is at issue with the interpretations in this manual, please contact Dr. Charles Blair at (866) 858-7596, or fax your concerns to (855) 825-3960. The publisher's intent is for this manual to be as accurate as possible. As errors are identified, revisions and updates may be available for registered users. Each copy of this manual should be registered.

This manual will be revised every year to reflect the most current information available, and to coincide with annual CDT code revisions. This manual is time sensitive and current through 2016. This edition of the manual becomes obsolete January 1, 2017.

NOTICE TO END USER

As the recipient of this publication, you the END USER, agree that you will not:

1. Alter, amend, or modify the Code or other portions of the CDT (Current Dental Terminology© developed by and all rights reserved by the American Dental Association);

2. Resell, transmit, or distribute copies of the Code or other portions of the CDT or any electronic files or printed documents that contain the Code or other portions of the CDT and that are generated by Dr. Charles Blair & Associates, Inc., pursuant to that agreement between the ADA and Dr. Charles Blair & Associates, Inc.;

3. Print copies, download, or store on End User's electronic media the Code or other portions of the CDT as reproduced in electronic publication(s). This manual is intended for the End User's private individual use and not for resale or redistribution;

4. Remove any CDT copyright or other proprietary notices, labels, or marks for the Code or other portions of the CDT; or

5. Use this publication to provide consulting, application service provider, or outsourcing services or to act as a service bureau operation. Any use of the Code or CDT outside this publication by the End User requires a valid CDT license from the American Dental Association (ADA).

TABLE OF CONTENTS

Copyright/Disclaimer	Preface
Table of Contents	Preface
Introduction	1
Why this Manual is Different	1
Philosophy of Publication	1
New, Revised and Deleted Procedures for CDT 2016	2
Explanation of the Use of Legends	7
CDT 2016 Codes with Explanations	8
Glossary	383
Code Index	387
Coding Compliance	435
The Four Levels of Coding Compliance	435
Why Compliance Can Be Painful	436
Why Compliance Can Be Profitable	436
Surviving an Audit: The Importance of Good Records and Documentation	436
Insurance Issues	437
Why the Insurance Companies "March to the Beat of a Different Drummer"	437
Do not Try to "Get Back" at the Insurance Company	437
The Insurance-Independent Practice	437
Coding and Explanations In this Manual	438
The "F" Word (Fraud!)	438
The Importance of Using Current CDT Codes and the Future	438
A Simple Guide to Using this Manual to Search for a Given CDT Code	438
Acknowledgements	439
About the Author and Author's Services	439

NOTES

Go to www.practicebooster.com to learn about the Revenue Enhancement Program, a coding and fee positioning consultation for you and your staff.
Cut coding errors and maximize legitimate reimbursement!
Tel: (866) 858-7596; Fax: (855) 825-3960; info@drcharlesblair.com

INTRODUCTION

There are several useful references available regarding CDT 2016 coding and dental terminology in the marketplace, cross-coding references, and other coding-related topics. You may very well have a library filled with them in your office. So why buy or use another manual like this one?

Why this Manual is Different

This manual is different in that it was written to specifically predict, and therefore prevent the typical coding errors, misuse, and common coding mistakes made by dental practices.

In this manual Dr. Charles Blair applies the use and application of **Predictive Error Correction**[SM] technology. Dr. Blair developed **Predictive Error Correction**[SM] technology as the end result of the clinical protocol, code reporting, clinical procedure count and fee analyses of thousands of dental practices across the country. In addition to his analysis of this vast amount of practice data, his study also included seminars with thousands of doctors and front office staff. This resulted in the emergence of utilization patterns which were then reverse-engineered, allowing him to write this manual to assist you in dramatically preventing coding errors and to maximize legitimate insurance reimbursement.

As experienced business staff and dentists know, the *Current Dental Terminology* (CDT) system was designed to establish standardized codes and descriptions to report dental procedures. However, guidance as to the specific application of many of these codes is limited. In particular, there is not a publication that is designed to correct common coding errors. This manual provides that "missing link," with guidance and strategies for proper application and reporting of the current CDT 2016 codes, while greatly decreasing code reporting errors. This manual contains an exhaustive Index starting on page 387. This manual's information is targeted to reduce errors and it is highly recommended to purchase the ADA's manual on *Current Dental Terminology 2016* book. Go to www.ada.org to order it. Your staff needs both tools.

Philosophy of Publication

As a consultant with experience in assisting thousands of dental practices become more profitable and productive, Dr. Charles Blair has "seen it all." He shares his vast experience and expertise with the dental community through this seventh manual, ***Coding with Confidence: The "Go To" Guide for CDT 2016***, which has been specifically designed to:

- Provide extensive information regarding the proper use of reporting CDT 2016 codes.

- Offer advice and strategy to prevent coding errors, to encourage proper reporting, and to streamline clinical protocols using **Predictive Error Correction**[SM] technology.

- Provide supplemental information to the additions, revisions, and deletions in CDT 2016.

- Offer guidance on how to implement proper documentation and proven clinical protocols in the practice.

- Present strategies regarding fee positioning, practice management, and other finance-related matters.

Take action today to REDUCE coding errors, prevent costly mistakes, limit audit exposure and improve legitimate reimbursement. Discover what you are doing well, but could be doing better, as well as what you should NOT be doing at all. Finally, learn how to implement this information to maximize long-term profitability and productivity, and to report codes and documentation accurately.

NEW, REVISED, AND DELETED PROCEDURES FOR CDT 2016

This book outlines nineteen new procedures, fifty-one code revisions and eight deletions in CDT 2016. It is recommended that the reader quickly scan all of the code changes in this section to determine if any apply to your particular practice. The page numbers for these codes have been provided. Turn to the proper page for the code changes. The subject code will be highlighted in red as "**deleted**", "**revised**", or "**new procedure**." Read, in depth, the modifications, additions, and deletions of codes that apply to your practice. Refer to code tabs in the manual to locate these new procedures, code revisions, and deletions. Some codes, particularly important, may NOT appear in numerical order because this is the order they are listed in CDT 2016.

NEW PROCEDURES (NINETEEN)

CODE		PAGE
D0251	EXTRA-ORAL POSTERIOR DENTAL RADIOGRAPHIC IMAGE – Image limited to exposure of complete posterior teeth in both dental arches. This is a unique image that is not derived from another image.	23
D0422	COLLECTION AND PREPARATION OF GENETIC SAMPLE MATERIAL FOR LABORATORY ANALYSIS AND REPORT	41
D0423	GENETIC TEST FOR SUSCEPTIBILITY TO DISEASES – SPECIMEN ANALYSIS – Certified laboratory analysis to detect specific genetic variations associated with increased susceptibility for diseases.	42
D1354	INTERIM CARIES ARRESTING MEDICAMENT APPLICATION – Conservative treatment of an active, non-symptomatic carious lesion by topical application of a caries arresting or inhibiting medicament and without mechanical removal of sound tooth structure.	59
D4283	AUTOGENOUS CONNECTIVE TISSUE GRAFT PROCEDURE (INCLUDING DONOR AND RECIPIENT SURGICAL SITES) – EACH ADDITIONAL CONTIGUOUS TOOTH, IMPLANT OR EDENTULOUS TOOTH POSITION IN SAME GRAFT SITE – Used in conjunction with D4273.	166
D4285	NON-AUTOGENOUS CONNECTIVE TISSUE GRAFT PROCEDURE (INCLUDING RECIPIENT SURGICAL SITE AND DONOR MATERIAL) – EACH ADDITIONAL CONTIGUOUS TOOTH, IMPLANT OR EDENTULOUS TOOTH POSITION IN SAME GRAFT SITE – Used in conjunction with D4275.	167
D5221	IMMEDIATE MAXILLARY PARTIAL DENTURE – RESIN BASE (INCLUDING ANY CONVENTIONAL CLASPS, RESTS AND TEETH) – Includes limited follow-up care only; does not include future rebasing / relining procedure(s).	193
D5222	IMMEDIATE MANDIBULAR PARTIAL DENTURE – RESIN BASE (INCLUDING ANY CONVENTIONAL CLASPS, RESTS AND TEETH) – Includes limited follow-up care only; does not include future rebasing / relining procedure(s).	194
D5223	IMMEDIATE MAXILLARY PARTIAL DENTURE – CAST METAL FRAMEWORK WITH RESIN DENTURE BASES (INCLUDING ANY CONVENTIONAL CLASPS, RESTS AND TEETH) – Includes limited follow-up care only; does not include future rebasing / relining procedure(s).	195
D5224	IMMEDIATE MANDIBULAR PARTIAL DENTURE – CAST METAL FRAMEWORK WITH RESIN DENTURE BASES (INCLUDING ANY CONVENTIONAL CLASPS, RESTS AND TEETH) – Includes limited follow-up care only; does not include future rebasing / relining procedure(s).	196
D7881	OCCLUSAL ORTHOTIC DEVICE ADJUSTMENT	329
D8681	REMOVABLE ORTHODONTIC RETAINER ADJUSTMENT	350
D9223	DEEP SEDATION/GENERAL ANESTHESIA – EACH 15 MINUTE INCREMENT – Anesthesia time begins when the doctor administering the anesthetic agent initiates the appropriate anesthesia and non-invasive monitoring protocol and remains in continuous attendance of the patient. Anesthesia services are considered completed when the patient may be safely left under the observation of trained personnel and the doctor may safely leave the room to attend to other patients or duties. The level of anesthesia is determined by the anesthesia provider's documentation of the anesthetics effects upon the central nervous system and not dependent upon the route of administration.	359
D9243	INTRAVENOUS MODERATE (CONSCIOUS) SEDATION/ANALGESIA – EACH 15 MINUTE INCREMENT – Anesthesia time begins when the doctor administering the anesthetic agent initiates the appropriate anesthesia and non-invasive monitoring protocol and remains in continuous attendance of the patient. Anesthesia services are considered completed when the patient may be safely left under the observation of trained personnel and the doctor may safely leave the room to attend to other patients or duties. The level of anesthesia is determined by the anesthesia provider's documentation of the anesthetics effects upon the central nervous system and not dependent upon the route of administration.	361
D9932	CLEANING AND INSPECTION OF REMOVABLE COMPLETE DENTURE, MAXILLARY – This procedure does not include any adjustments.	371
D9933	CLEANING AND INSPECTION OF REMOVABLE COMPLETE DENTURE, MANDIBULAR – This procedure does not include any adjustments.	371

Code	Description	Page
D9934	CLEANING AND INSPECTION OF REMOVABLE PARTIAL DENTURE, MAXILLARY – This procedure does not include any adjustments.	372
D9935	CLEANING AND INSPECTION OF REMOVABLE PARTIAL DENTURE, MANDIBULAR – This procedure does not include any adjustments.	372
D9943	OCCLUSAL GUARD ADJUSTMENT	375

REVISED (FIFTY-ONE) THE FOLLOWING CODE REVISIONS INCLUDE SUBSTANTIVE AND EDITORIAL REVISIONS

CODE		PAGE
D0250	EXTRA-ORAL – 2D PROJECTION RADIOGRAPHIC IMAGE CREATED USING A STATIONARY RADIATION SOURCE, AND DETECTOR – These images include, but are not limited to: Lateral Skull; Posterior-Anterior Skull; Submentovertex; Waters; Reverse Tomes; Oblique Mandibular Body; Lateral Ramus.	23
D0340	2D CEPHALOMETRIC RADIOGRAPHIC IMAGE – ACQUISITION, MEASUREMENT AND ANALYSIS – Image of the head made using a cephalostat to standardize anatomic positioning, and with reproducible x-ray beam geometry.	31
D1999	UNSPECIFIED PREVENTIVE PROCEDURE, BY REPORT – Used for procedure that is not adequately described by another CDT code. Describe procedure.	63
D2712	CROWN – ¾ RESIN-BASED COMPOSITE (INDIRECT) – This procedure does not include facial veneers.	88
D2783	CROWN – ¾ PORCELAIN/CERAMIC – This procedure does not include facial veneers.	94
D4273	AUTOGENOUS CONNECTIVE TISSUE GRAFT PROCEDURE (INCLUDING DONOR AND RECIPIENT SURGICAL SITES) FIRST TOOTH, IMPLANT, OR EDENTULOUS TOOTH POSITION IN GRAFT – There are two surgical sites. The recipient site utilizes a split thickness incision, retaining the overlapping flap of gingiva and/or mucosa. The connective tissue is dissected from a separate donor site leaving an epithelialized flap for closure.	161
D4275	NON-AUTOGENOUS CONNECTIVE TISSUE GRAFT (INCLUDING RECIPIENT SITE AND DONOR MATERIAL) FIRST TOOTH, IMPLANT, OR EDENTULOUS TOOTH POSITION IN GRAFT – There is only a recipient surgical site utilizing split thickness incision, retaining the overlaying flap of gingiva and/or mucosa. A donor surgical site is not present.	163
D4277	FREE SOFT TISSUE GRAFT PROCEDURE (INCLUDING RECIPIENT AND DONOR SURGICAL SITES) FIRST TOOTH, IMPLANT OR EDENTULOUS TOOTH POSITION IN GRAFT	164
D4278	FREE SOFT TISSUE GRAFT PROCEDURE (INCLUDING RECIPIENT AND DONOR SURGICAL SITES) EACH ADDITIONAL CONTIGUOUS TOOTH, IMPLANT OR EDENTULOUS TOOTH POSITION IN SAME GRAFT SITE – Used in conjunction with D4277.	165
D5130	IMMEDIATE DENTURE – MAXILLARY – Includes limited follow-up care only; does not include required future rebasing / relining procedure(s).	185
D5140	IMMEDIATE DENTURE – MANDIBULAR – Includes limited follow-up care only; does not include required future rebasing / relining procedure(s).	187
D5630	REPAIR OR REPLACE BROKEN CLASP – PER TOOTH	202
D5660	ADD CLASP TO EXISTING PARTIAL DENTURE – PER TOOTH	203
D5875	MODIFICATION OF REMOVABLE PROSTHESIS FOLLOWING IMPLANT SURGERY – Attachment assemblies are reported using separate codes.	221
D5993	MAINTENANCE AND CLEANING OF A MAXILLOFACIAL PROSTHESIS (EXTRA-OR INTRA-ORAL) OTHER THAN REQUIRED ADJUSTMENTS, BY REPORT	228
D6103	BONE GRAFT FOR REPAIR OF PERI-IMPLANT DEFECT – DOES NOT INCLUDE FLAP ENTRY AND CLOSURE – Placement of a barrier membrane or biologic materials to aid in osseous regeneration are reported separately.	240
D6600	RETAINER INLAY – PORCELAIN/CERAMIC, TWO SURFACES	274
D6601	RETAINER INLAY – PORCELAIN/CERAMIC, THREE OR MORE SURFACES	274
D6602	RETAINER INLAY – CAST HIGH NOBLE METAL, TWO SURFACES	275
D6603	RETAINER INLAY – CAST HIGH NOBLE METAL, THREE OR MORE SURFACES	275
D6604	RETAINER INLAY – CAST PREDOMINANTLY BASE METAL, TWO SURFACES	276
D6605	RETAINER INLAY – CAST PREDOMINANTLY BASE METAL, THREE OR MORE SURFACES	276
D6606	RETAINER INLAY – CAST NOBLE METAL, TWO SURFACES	277

Code	Description	Page
D6607	RETAINER INLAY – CAST NOBLE METAL, THREE OR MORE SURFACES	277
D6608	RETAINER ONLAY – PORCELAIN/CERAMIC, TWO SURFACES	278
D6609	RETAINER ONLAY – PORCELAIN/CERAMIC, THREE OR MORE SURFACES	279
D6610	RETAINER ONLAY – CAST HIGH NOBLE METAL, TWO SURFACES	279
D6611	RETAINER ONLAY – CAST HIGH NOBLE METAL, THREE OR MORE SURFACES	280
D6612	RETAINER ONLAY – CAST PREDOMINANTLY BASE METAL, TWO SURFACES	281
D6613	RETAINER ONLAY – CAST PREDOMINANTLY BASE METAL, THREE OR MORE SURFACES	281
D6614	RETAINER ONLAY – CAST NOBLE METAL, TWO SURFACES	282
D6615	RETAINER ONLAY – CAST NOBLE METAL, THREE OR MORE SURFACES	283
D6624	RETAINER INLAY – TITANIUM	277/283
D6634	RETAINER ONLAY – TITANIUM	284
D6710	RETAINER CROWN – INDIRECT RESIN BASED COMPOSITE – Not to be used as a temporary or provisional prosthesis.	285
D6720	RETAINER CROWN – RESIN WITH HIGH NOBLE METAL	285
D6721	RETAINER CROWN – RESIN WITH PREDOMINANTLY BASE METAL	286
D6722	RETAINER CROWN – RESIN WITH NOBLE METAL	286
D6740	RETAINER CROWN – PORCELAIN/CERAMIC	287
D6750	RETAINER CROWN – PORCELAIN FUSED TO HIGH NOBLE METAL	287
D6751	RETAINER CROWN – PORCELAIN FUSED TO PREDOMINANTLY BASE METAL	288
D6752	RETAINER CROWN – PORCELAIN FUSED TO NOBLE METAL	288
D6780	RETAINER CROWN – ¾ CAST HIGH NOBLE METAL	288
D6781	RETAINER CROWN – ¾ CAST PREDOMINANTLY BASE METAL	289
D6782	RETAINER CROWN – ¾ CAST NOBLE METAL	289
D6783	RETAINER CROWN – ¾ PORCELAIN/CERAMIC	290
D6790	RETAINER CROWN – FULL CAST HIGH NOBLE METAL	290
D6791	RETAINER CROWN – FULL CAST PREDOMINANTLY BASE METAL	291
D6792	RETAINER CROWN – FULL CAST NOBLE METAL	291
D6794	RETAINER CROWN – TITANIUM	292/293
D9248	NON-INTRAVENOUS CONSCIOUS SEDATION – This includes non-IV minimal and moderate sedation. A medically controlled state of depressed consciousness while maintaining the patient's airway, protective reflexes and the ability to respond to stimulation or verbal commands. It includes non-intravenous administration of sedative and/or analgesic agent(s) and appropriate monitoring. The level of anesthesia is determined by the anesthesia provider's documentation of the anesthetic's effects upon the central nervous system and not dependent upon the route of administration.	362

ADDITIONAL EDITORIAL REVISIONS MADE TO CDT 2016 ARE AS FOLLOWS:

Classification of Materials

Resin – Refers to any resin-based composite, including fiber or ceramic reinforced polymer compounds and glass ionomers.

Glass ionomer was added to the classification of materials for CDT 2016.

D6200 – D6999 IX. Prosthodontics, fixed

The term "fixed partial denture" or FPD is synonymous with fixed bridge or bridgework.

This revision for CDT 2016 clarifies that "Fixed partial denture" or "FPD" is synonymous with "fixed bridge" or "bridgework", because these are common terms still used in dentistry.

DELETED (EIGHT)

CODE		PAGE
D0260	EXTRAORAL – EACH ADDITIONAL RADIOGRAPHIC IMAGE	24
D0421	GENETIC TEST FOR SUSCEPTIBILITY TO ORAL DISEASES – Sample collection for the purpose of certified laboratory analysis to detect specific genetic variations associated with increased susceptibility for oral diseases such as severe periodontal disease.	41
D2970	TEMPORARY CROWN (FRACTURED TOOTH) – Usually a preformed artificial crown, which is fitted over a damaged tooth as an immediate protective device. This is not to be used as temporization during crown fabrication.	110
D9220	DEEP SEDATION/GENERAL ANESTHESIA – FIRST 30 MINUTES – Anesthesia time begins when the doctor administering the anesthetic agent initiates the appropriate anesthesia and non-invasive monitoring protocol and remains in continuous attendance of the patient. Anesthesia services are considered completed when the patient may be safely left under the observation of trained personnel and the doctor may safely leave the room to attend to other patients or duties. The level of anesthesia is determined by the anesthesia provider's documentation of the anesthetic's effects upon the central nervous system and not dependent upon the route of administration.	359
D9221	DEEP SEDATION/GENERAL ANESTHESIA – EACH ADDITIONAL 15 MINUTES	359
D9241	INTRAVENOUS MODERATE (CONSCIOUS) SEDATION/ANALGESIA – FIRST 30 MINUTES – Anesthesia time begins when the doctor administering the anesthetic agent initiates the appropriate anesthesia and non-invasive monitoring protocol and remains in continuous attendance of the patient. Anesthesia services are considered completed when the patient may be safely left under the observation of trained personnel and the doctor may safely leave the room to attend to other patients or duties. The level of anesthesia is determined by the anesthesia provider's documentation of the anesthetic's effects upon the central nervous system and not dependent upon the route of administration.	360
D9242	INTRAVENOUS MODERATE (CONSCIOUS) SEDATION/ANALGESIA – EACH ADDITIONAL 15 MINUTES	361
D9931	CLEANING AND INSPECTION OF A REMOVABLE APPLIANCE – This procedure does not include any required adjustments.	371

NOTES

Go to www.practicebooster.com to learn about the Revenue Enhancement Program,
a coding and fee positioning consultation for you and your staff.
Cut coding errors and maximize legitimate reimbursement!
Tel: (866) 858-7596; Fax: (855) 825-3960; info@drcharlesblair.com

EXPLANATION OF THE USE OF THE LEGENDS

Throughout the CDT 2016 Code section of this manual, you will find Coding Correction Warning, Watch, and Match legends depicting many common mistakes, as well as specific Comments/Limitations, Tips, Narratives, Photos, and Clinical Flow Chart legends. In addition, Revised, New Procedure, Deleted Code, Previously Deleted Code and the Author's Comments comprise the other legends. Each legend's description and purpose is as follows:

LEGENDS	DESCRIPTIONS
CDT 2016	This legend designates the official CDT 2016 code, nomenclature, and descriptor. The Code and nomenclature is always enclosed in a solid "bar", plus a "box", if applicable, which contains the descriptor. Current Dental Terminology (CDT) ©2015 American Dental Association. All rights reserved.
REVISIONS	This legend offers the exact revision to the nomenclature and descriptor as applicable.
Coding Correction WARNING	This legend signifies a serious misuse of reporting the code, which could be considered fraudulent (if intentional) or at the minimum, misleading. If discovered, the result could be loss of license, fine, or worse; at the least, repayment or restitution by the practice could be required. The legend's description may offer correct, alternative coding and in some cases offer another legitimate approach for better reimbursement.
Coding Correction WATCH	This legend can signify a misuse of reporting the code. The economic result of the misuse may be financially positive in the short term, but misuse is always costly in the long run. In most cases, the correct or alternate code is listed for reference.
Coding Correction MATCH	This legend identifies a code which is a "match" for an associated or complimentary code. For instance, this legend would illustrate the proper code match for the pontic and retainer crown of a bridge.
COMMENTS	The "Comments" legend offers commentary and information about the code.
LIMITATIONS	The "Limitations" legend spells out common limitations and exclusions of the use of this code in insurance contract language.
TIPS	The "Tips" legend signifies a legitimate approach that may result in improved benefit coverage.
NARRATIVES	The "Narratives" legend offers suggestions regarding narratives and documentation.
CLINICAL FLOW CHART	This legend illustrates a scenario in which the code is used in a proper clinical sequence associated with other procedures.
REVISED	This legend identifies a substantive or editorial revision in the nomenclature and/or the descriptor of a code. Be sure to read the entire description of the revised code. There are fifty-one code revisions in CDT 2016.
NEW PROCEDURE	This legend identifies a new procedure code. There are nineteen new procedure codes in CDT 2016.
DELETED CODE	This legend identifies a procedure code that was deleted. There are eight deleted codes in CDT 2016.
PREVIOUSLY DELETED CODE	This legend identifies a procedure code that was previously deleted. The manual continues to carry previously deleted codes for reference and to guide the reader to a current code, if applicable.
PHOTO	This legend identifies a photograph of an appliance, restoration, implant, model, or radiographic image.
AUTHOR'S COMMENTS	This legend identifies the author's general comments at the beginning of a code section.

CODE ON DENTAL PROCEDURES AND NOMENCLATURE

D0100-D0999 I. DIAGNOSTIC

CLINICAL ORAL EVALUATIONS — CDT 2016

The codes in this section recognize the cognitive skills necessary for patient evaluation. The collection and recording of some data and components of the dental examination may be delegated; however, the evaluation, which includes diagnosis and treatment planning, is the responsibility of the dentist. As with all ADA procedure codes, there is no distinction made between the evaluations provided by general practitioners and specialists. Report additional diagnostic and/or definitive procedures separately.

D0120 PERIODIC ORAL EVALUATION – ESTABLISHED PATIENT — CDT 2016

An evaluation performed on a patient of record to determine any changes in the patient's dental and medical health status since a previous comprehensive or periodic evaluation. This includes an oral cancer evaluation and periodontal screening, where indicated, and may require interpretation of information acquired through additional diagnostic procedures. Report additional diagnostic procedures separately.

1. It is improper to report a periodic oral evaluation (D0120) or any other evaluation unless *the doctor* completed the clinical exam and did the evaluation. A hygienist can *screen* but not *diagnose* unless specifically permitted by law.
2. It is improper to charge insurance patients for a periodic oral evaluation (D0120), while the evaluation is "free" for non-insured patients. Treatment and fee protocols should be identical for both insured *and* non-insured patients.
3. The periodic oral evaluation (D0120) code includes an oral cancer evaluation (OCE), *where indicated. The fact that the oral cancer evaluation was done and any significant findings* should be documented in the clinical notes. OCE is conducted "where indicated."
4. D0120 is billed only for established patients.

1. Some offices *do not* report periodic oral evaluation (D0120) or the comprehensive periodontal evaluation (D0180) in conjunction with periodontal maintenance (D4910). Oral evaluations are *not* included in D4910. Oral evaluations may be reported in addition to D4910, periodontal maintenance, when completed. The clinician may choose to perform an oral evaluation every other visit for a three-month periodontal recall patient, twice per year, or as deemed necessary.
2. The reimbursement frequency for D0120 may be limited. See limitations below.
3. Do not report a new patient child comprehensive oral evaluation (D0145) using a lower fee periodic oral evaluation (D0120). See Tip #6 below.
4. If the child is *less* than three years of age, see D0145 to report an oral evaluation. Counseling with a primary caregiver is required to report D0145.

LIMITATIONS

1. D0120 is typically subject to the "two evaluations per year" or "one per six months" limitation, as established by the plan. However, some payers will reimburse for a *third* evaluation when performed in a different office or if there is an *additional* problem focused oral evaluation during the limitation period. To control costs, some employers are choosing plans that have the "one evaluation per year" limitation.
2. Periodontal maintenance (D4910) does not include any type of oral evaluation. Most doctors perform and report two periodic oral evaluations (D0120) per year for both periodontal and non-periodontal patients. The comprehensive periodontal evaluation (D0180) may also be used to describe a periodontal evaluation for an established periodontal patient under certain circumstances, particularly in conjunction with D4910. See D0180 for specific reporting requirements and patient criteria. Note that some new contracts are trending toward the global "one evaluation per year" limitation.
3. Some payers process orthodontic consultations as D0120, D0150, D0160, D8660, or D9310. These codes are generally subject to the overall "two evaluations per year" limitation. The maximum plan allowance (MPA) fee may be applied to the periodic oral evaluation (D0120) fee, regardless of the *specific* evaluation code submitted. If a *third* evaluation is reimbursable in a different office, the orthodontic evaluation may be reimbursed. This reimbursement, when paid, may or may not be processed under a separate orthodontic maximum. In some cases, consultation (D9310) whether by a specialist or general practitioner is reimbursed in addition to the "one" per six months or "two" oral evaluations per year. See D9310.

Note: Either D0150 or D0180 may be reported for comprehensive oral evaluations of *established* patients under *specific* circumstances. However, some payers will reimburse these comprehensive evaluations at the lower periodic oral evaluation (D0120) maximum plan allowance (MPA) fee. See D0150/D0180 for specific details for their limited use with *established* patients.

TIPS

1. The periodic oral evaluation (D0120) includes "periodontal screening, where indicated." A periodontal screening may be performed at a D0120 visit. This does not mean periodontal probing and full charting is required at each periodic oral evaluation in order to report the periodic oral evaluation code. There is no separate (stand-alone) code for full mouth periodontal probing and it is included (when performed) in all oral evaluation procedures. If a full mouth probing and charting is performed on a separate, stand-alone visit, see both D0180 and D4999 for reporting. Some patients may not require a periodontal screening (e.g., young children or edentulous patients).

2. The periodic oral evaluation (D0120) includes an "oral cancer evaluation, where indicated." This does not mean the oral cancer evaluation is mandatory at a given visit. It would be considered the standard of care to perform an oral cancer evaluation where indicated. Generally the oral cancer evaluation is done at the periodic oral evaluation (D0120) visit on patients on an annual basis, provided the patient does not have additional risk factors.

3. If the need for active periodontal treatment (SRP or osseous surgery) is diagnosed at the periodic oral evaluation, a comprehensive periodontal evaluation and full probing and charting should be performed to document the necessity of treatment for SRP. This evaluation should be reported as D0180 (provided a full mouth probing and charting is performed), but the reimbursement level may be limited to the D0120 fee.

4. If the doctor's productivity is suffering due to interruption for hygiene check oral evaluations, consider a periodic oral evaluation (D0120) of the low-risk patient *once* per year, if permitted by state law.

5. For low-risk hygiene patients, consider extending the routine six-month prophylaxis interval to seven-nine months. This would help to open hygiene time for more productive periodontal hygiene appointments.

6. Some offices *erroneously* report a *periodic* oral evaluation (D0120) rather than a *comprehensive* oral evaluation performed on children who are new patients (D0150) in an effort to hold down the initial comprehensive oral evaluation fee. This is a common error. The child evaluation is simpler (quicker) and prophylaxis, fluoride, and diagnostic images are typically performed on the same service date. The total visit fee could be priced appropriately. Doctors should establish two consistent fees (adult and child) for code D0150. To distinguish between the two, use D0150A (child) and D0150B (adult), or similar coding to distinguish the fee structure within your software program. The computer software will not post the "A" or "B" code for reporting purposes on the walk-out statement or electronic claim form. With this approach, the reimbursement UCR will be higher for the child comprehensive evaluation (D0150) while the proper code is reported.

7. An oral evaluation (either initial or recall) for a child under three years of age must include counseling with a caregiver if reporting D0145. If the periodic oral evaluation for a child under three years of age does not include counseling with the caregiver, report D0120.

8. Additional diagnostic procedures should be reported separately. Although not covered by some dental plans, it is appropriate to bill pulp vitality tests (D0460), caries susceptibility tests (D0425), viral cultures (D0416), etc., separately.

D0140 LIMITED ORAL EVALUATION – PROBLEM FOCUSED   CDT 2016

An evaluation limited to a specific oral health problem or complaint. This may require interpretation of information acquired through additional diagnostic procedures. Report additional diagnostic procedures separately. Definitive procedures may be required on the same date as the evaluation.

Typically, patients receiving this type of evaluation present with a specific problem and/or dental emergencies, trauma, acute infections, etc.

1. Limited oral evaluation – problem focused (D0140) should not be used to report a routine periodic hygiene evaluation (D0120); however, should a routine periodic oral evaluation turn into a more complex problem focused evaluation requiring *additional* diagnostic time, then D0140 may be reported rather than D0120.

2. Reporting a single bitewing (BWX) image taken at the D0140 appointment may potentially exhaust the annual "once per year" BWX allowance. Periapical (PA) diagnostic images exposed at the *emergency* evaluation typically do not count against the annual BWX limitation. PAs are considered separate *stand-alone procedures*. Periapicals may have a deductible and a maximum fee limitation applied if multiple periapical films are exposed on the same service date or if multiple PAs or a Full Mouth Series (FMX) have been taken within the plan's limitation period.

3. The consultation (diagnostic service provided by dentist or physician after another dentist or physician referred the patient) D9310 should not be reported for the patient who *self-refers* for a second opinion. D9310, if reimbursed, may be subject to the "two evaluations per year" limitation. Some payers consider D9310 for reimbursement on a case-by-case basis. Payers may look more favorably on referrals to specialists rather than referrals to another general dentist. D9310 is reported by a dentist when either rendering a second opinion or providing clinical treatment for the patient as referred specifically by another dentist or physician.

4. Consider D0140 for new patient evaluations when a self-referring patient requests a second opinion related to a problem focused complaint. Consider a D0150/D0180 oral evaluation if the self-referred patient has been provided a comprehensive treatment plan by another dentist and the patient is seeking a second opinion.

5. Some doctors perform a *minor procedure* at the emergency visit, but erroneously report this procedure as a problem focused limited oral evaluation (D0140). D0140 is an oral evaluation code, not a treatment code. If a minor *procedure* was performed due to discomfort, sensitivity, or pain, D9110 may be reported (see palliative (D9110) for further details). In many cases, D9110 and D0140 are not reimbursed if reported on the same service date. Likewise, the problem focused oral evaluation (D0140) is typically denied if reported on the same service date that definitive treatment is performed. Some practices do not use D0140 but save the evaluation allowance for the comprehensive oral evaluation (D0150/D0180). This billing/coding decision is sometimes influenced by the fact that the D0150 and D0180 have a higher UCR (usual, customary and reasonable) fee. However, D0140 is a stand-alone code and may be reported in *addition* to any other treatment procedures rendered on the same service date, i.e., extraction, filling, or palliative (D9110), etc., but remember it may be subject to the plan's limitations.

6. Do not report case presentation (D9450) for the initial evaluation of self-referred patients. Instead, report D9450 for case presentations that follow the patient's comprehensive oral evaluation (D0150/D0180) date.

COMMENTS The limited oral evaluation – problem focused (D0140) is used to evaluate *one* problem or complaint (emergency). Specialists may also report D0140. A periodontist could report this evaluation code for a limited evaluation in association with a crown lengthening or a bone graft procedure. An endodontist may report D0140 in association with an evaluation for a single procedure root canal. Specialists may also report consultation (D9310) rather than the D0140. The use of and reimbursement for D0140 in these examples is highly variable.

LIMITATIONS
1. Many payers limit evaluations (of any type) to "two evaluations per year/12 months" or "one per six months." This type of evaluation (D0140) is often denied as an "extra" evaluation. There are exceptions to this general rule. Some payers will reimburse a problem focused evaluation (D0140) or evaluation with a specialist in *addition* to the two annual periodic oral evaluation visits per year. In addition, there are a few plans that allow up to three limited oral evaluations per year. Some plans have no frequency limitations. Sometimes a consultation (D9310) is reimbursed for a visit to a specialist in addition to the typical "two oral evaluations per year." Thus, the reimbursement for D0140 is highly variable.

2. Some payers will not reimburse D0140 in conjunction with a definitive procedure (e.g., extractions, fillings, etc.) on the same service date. For example, the extraction and periapical diagnostic images are typically reimbursed, while D0140 performed on the same service date may be denied. D0140 *is a stand-alone* code and may be charged in *addition* to the clinical procedure provided. If the doctor is out-of-network, the patient can be expected to pay out-of-pocket for the D0140 evaluation under this scenario.

TIPS
1. Some offices charge for D0140 in conjunction with an extraction when the patient is not a patient of record as the new emergency patient requires additional time and effort to process. This being the case, the office policy and protocol should be *consistent* for both insured and non-insured patients.

2. Palliative (D9110) and periapical diagnostic images (D0220/D0230) go *hand-in-hand* for emergency evaluations when the situation involves a minor (not definitive) procedure. Conversely, any bitewing image reported/billed at the problem focused evaluation (D0140) or emergency visit may apply toward the typical "once per year" BWX limitation. See D0272/D0273/D0274 for further details. Even so, always report what you do; never change a code for reporting purposes or to gain higher reimbursement.

3. Pulp vitality test (D0460) is a *stand-alone* code. The UCR fee for D0460 is often below D0140. Some payers limit the benefits to *either* D0140 or the pulp vitality test (D0460) reported on the same service date. *When the "two evaluations per year" are exhausted, D0460 may be reimbursed on a "stand-alone" basis. See D0460 for further details on reporting this code on a "stand-alone" basis.*

4. Consider limiting the use of problem focused limited oral evaluations (D0140) as they often count toward the "one evaluation per six months" or "two evaluations per year/12 months" limitation. Consider reporting palliative treatment of dental pain (D9110) along with any necessary periapical radiographic images as an alternative, when a minor procedure is performed to relieve the pain. See D9110 for comments about the proper usage of the palliative code, D9110. D0140 can *always* be reported in conjunction with D9110, but payers may have limits that apply to the payment of D0140.

NARRATIVES Separate diagnostic procedures may be reported in addition to, and apart from, D0140. Radiographs and viral cultures (D0416) are examples of services that may be reported separately. The additional procedures must be deemed necessary by the doctor to evaluate the specific problem/complaint and supported by a narrative.

D0145 — ORAL EVALUATION FOR A PATIENT UNDER THREE YEARS OF AGE AND COUNSELING WITH PRIMARY CAREGIVER — CDT 2016

Diagnostic services performed for a child under the age of three, preferably within the first six months of the eruption of the first primary tooth, including recording the oral and physical health history, evaluation of caries susceptibility, development of an appropriate preventive oral health regimen and communication with and counseling of the child's parent, legal guardian and/or primary caregiver.

COMMENTS

1. Key elements of D0145:
   a. The goal is early intervention/development of a prevention plan – performed on patients under three years of age.
   b. Includes diagnostic services:
      i. Recording the oral and physical health history.
      ii. Evaluation of caries susceptibility (risk assessment).
      iii. Does the child have developmental problems?
      iv. Does the primary caregiver have active caries?
      v. Development of a plan to reduce the child's risk of caries.
   c. Includes counseling with the child's primary caregiver:
      i. Instructions for cleaning child's teeth.
      ii. Fluoride recommendations.
      iii. Diet recommendations.
      iv. Recommendations to reduce transmission of bacteria (e.g., antibacterial rinses, xylitol, saliva substitutes, etc.).

2. D0145 was a new oral evaluation code under CDT 2007/2008 for the child patient who has not reached the age of three and includes counseling with the primary caregiver. Note that the oral evaluation is not identified as either "comprehensive" or "periodic." It appears that D0145 would be reported for the initial oral evaluation and may be used for subsequent oral evaluation visits so long as the child remains under the age of three and *counseling* is provided each visit. The code specifically includes preventive counseling for the primary caregiver.

3. Once the child reaches three years of age the periodic oral evaluation (D0120) would be reported. If the child is under three years of age at the time of the periodic oral evaluation, consider D0120 if *no counseling* is provided to the primary caregiver.

LIMITATIONS

1. When the child reaches three years of age or older report the comprehensive oral evaluation (D0150) at the first visit, or periodic oral evaluation (D0120), whichever applies to the child's current evaluation status. If D0145 has been reported previously, a *comprehensive* evaluation has not been performed. If D0150 has been reported previously for the patient, some payers may provide the alternate benefit of D0120.

2. D0145 may be subject to the "one evaluation per six months" or "two evaluations per year" contract limitation.

TIPS

1. The descriptor for D0145 is an evaluation code and does not prevent one from reporting a prophylaxis (D1120) separately when performed on the same day as an oral evaluation of a patient under three years of age. If plaque is removed from a child's teeth, regardless of the technique, it can be reported as D1120. Likewise, if topical fluoride treatment (any type, except fluoride varnish) is applied, regardless of the number of teeth, report D1208. Report D1206 if fluoride varnish is applied. Thus, preventive procedures such as toothbrush deplaquing and fluoride applications can be reported separately when performed on the same day as D0145.

2. D0145 may be reimbursed at the D0120 fee level by some payers. However, in most cases the reimbursement for D0145 is higher than D0120. Note that in some states Medicaid reimburses D0145 at a higher Maximum Plan Allowance (MPA) level than D0150. The practice fee charged should be a consistent fee for Medicaid and non-Medicaid patients.

D0150 COMPREHENSIVE ORAL EVALUATION – NEW OR ESTABLISHED PATIENT   CDT 2016

Used by a general dentist and/or a specialist when evaluating a patient comprehensively. This applies to new patients; established patients who have had a significant change in health conditions or other unusual circumstances, by report, or established patients who have been absent from active treatment for three or more years. It is a thorough evaluation and recording of the extraoral and intraoral hard and soft tissues. It may require interpretation of information acquired through additional diagnostic procedures. Additional diagnostic procedures should be reported separately.

This includes an evaluation for oral cancer where indicated, the evaluation and recording of the patient's dental and medical history and a general health assessment. It may include the evaluation and recording of dental caries, missing or unerupted teeth, restorations, existing prosthesis, occlusal relationships, periodontal conditions (including periodontal screening and/or charting), hard and soft tissue anomalies, etc.

1. It is improper to report a comprehensive oral evaluation (D0150) or any other oral evaluation unless the doctor has physically examined *(hands in mouth!)* and evaluated the patient.

2. It is improper to charge insured patients for a comprehensive oral evaluation (D0150) while the evaluation is "free" for non-insured patients. Treatment and fee protocols should be identical for insured and non-insured patients. Otherwise, this practice may be considered "discriminatory" and can be deemed "overbilling" by payers, and may be considered a fraudulent act.

1. The consultation code (diagnostic service provided by a dentist or physician other than practitioner providing treatment – D9310) should not be reported for evaluations for the self-referring patient seeking a second opinion from the general practitioner. D9310 may be subject to the "two evaluations per year" limitation. Some payers reimburse D9310 to *specialists* in addition to the typical two evaluations. D9310 may be reported when rendering a second opinion by a provider. The second provider may or may not provide the indicated treatment. For general practices, consider D0140 for new patient evaluations when a *self-referring* patient requests a second opinion related to a limited complaint. Consider reporting D0150/D0180 when the *self-referring* patient has already been treatment planned by a previous dentist for *comprehensive* treatment.

2. D0150 should *not* be reported on the same service date as gross debridement to enable comprehensive evaluation (D4355). D4355 *enables* D0150, comprehensive oral evaluation, to be performed (after a healing period). D0150 should follow D4355 by 10-14 days later to allow some healing of the tissues to occur; however, nothing in the descriptor of D4355 prohibits a comprehensive oral evaluation (D0150) or even D0140 from being performed on the same service date. However, most payers will not benefit D4355 if any type of oral evaluation is completed on the same service date. (See D4355 for reporting details.)

LIMITATIONS

1. The comprehensive oral evaluation (D0150) is *comprehensive* and extensive in nature and *may* include periodontal screening and/or charting, depending on the age/circumstances of the patient. The comprehensive evaluation includes a visual evaluation for oral cancer, where indicated. The general dentist would report D0150 for most new patients since this exam by definition is all encompassing and extensive. A periodontist would generally use D0180 for the new and established patient if he/she exhibit signs and symptoms, or is at greater risk of periodontal disease. Nothing precludes the general practitioner from using D0180 for the new and established patient, provided the patient has signs and symptoms of periodontal disease or risk factors such as smoking or diabetes. If a D0180 is reported, a mandatory full mouth (six points/tooth) probing and charting is necessary and should be completed on the day D0180 is reported. D0150 applies to both new child and adult patients. (For a child less than three years of age, see D0145 for an oral evaluation.) The benefit for the comprehensive oral evaluation (D0150) is generally subject to the "one per six months" or "two evaluations per year" limitation. Some payers will reimburse a third evaluation within the limitation period when a specialist performs the oral evaluation in a different office or if the evaluation is a problem focused oral evaluation (D0140) or a consultation.

2. D0150 may be reported for an extensive evaluation of an *established* patient in *very limited* circumstances. Generally, this requires a significant change in health status (these can include, but are not limited to, a new diagnosis of cancer, HIV/AIDS, diabetes, Sjogren's disease, GERD, bulimia, epilepsy, heart disease, asthma, etc.) or absence from *active* treatment for three years or more. In spite of this, many payers still remap D0150 to D0120, at the lower fee. The payer may consider D0150 to be "once per lifetime" per office. Others use an every "three" or "five" year reimbursement rule for D0150. Some payers reimburse consultation (D9310) on a case-by-case basis to specialists. D9310 should generally be reported when rendering a consultation by a specialist or general practitioner who may or may not provide treatment. See "consultation" (D9310) for further reporting details.

3. Some payers reimburse orthodontic evaluations (consultations) as either D0120 or D0150 and limit the reimbursement to the lower UCR fee. These evaluations are generally subject to the "one per six months" or "two evaluations per year" limitation. In some cases, a third oral evaluation may be reimbursed if it is provided by a different office or a specialist.

TIPS

1. Most payers reimburse the *same* fee for a comprehensive oral evaluation (D0150), whether for child or adult. The first visit for a child the age of 3 years and above may include the comprehensive oral evaluation (D0150), as well as a prophylaxis, fluoride, and diagnostic radiographic images. Some practices charge less for the child's comprehensive oral evaluation (D0150). Practices may establish two fees (child and adult) for D0150. To distinguish between the two scenarios, establish separate in office codes with different fees. The office may establish "in house" codes of D0150A (child) and D0150B (adult) with different fees. Using this approach, the corresponding code is reported (D0150A, child or D0150B, adult). By implementing this system, the reimbursement level will typically be higher for the D0150B, child evaluation, than the periodic oral evaluation (D0120). This will allow the fee for the child comprehensive evaluation to be less than the adult comprehensive evaluation. If configured correctly, the computer software will reference the "A" or "B" from the code when assigning the fee but remove the "A" or "B" from the code when posting the procedure on the claim form. For a child less than three years of age, see D0145 for reporting an oral evaluation. Note that counseling must be provided to the primary caregiver at the D0145 visit.

2. A comprehensive oral evaluation typically includes a periodontal screening and/or charting:

    a. Periodontal screening includes selected six-points-per-tooth probing, the words "may include" in the descriptor, simply acknowledges that some patients may not require a periodontal screening or charting (e.g., young children or edentulous patients).

    b. Periodontal charting includes, but is not limited to recording six-points-per-tooth pocket depths, recessions, furcations, areas of mobility, bleeding points, minimal attached gingiva notations, suppuration, etc.

        i. A dentist "may" determine a full periodontal charting is not necessary if the periodontal screening was within normal limits.

        ii. A dentist "may" decide not to perform a full periodontal charting if he/she intends to refer the patient to a periodontist based on the results of the periodontal screening.

3. Additional diagnostic procedures should be reported separately such as radiographs, pulp vitality tests, caries susceptibility tests, genetic tests, viral cultures, diagnostic casts, etc.

NARRATIVES If a comprehensive oral evaluation is performed on an established patient, list the significant change(s) in health status or the number of years the patient has been absent from active treatment (must be three years or more).

FLOW CHARTS Typical new patient scenario (assuming that calculus/debris still permits the comprehensive oral evaluation (D0150) at the initial visit):

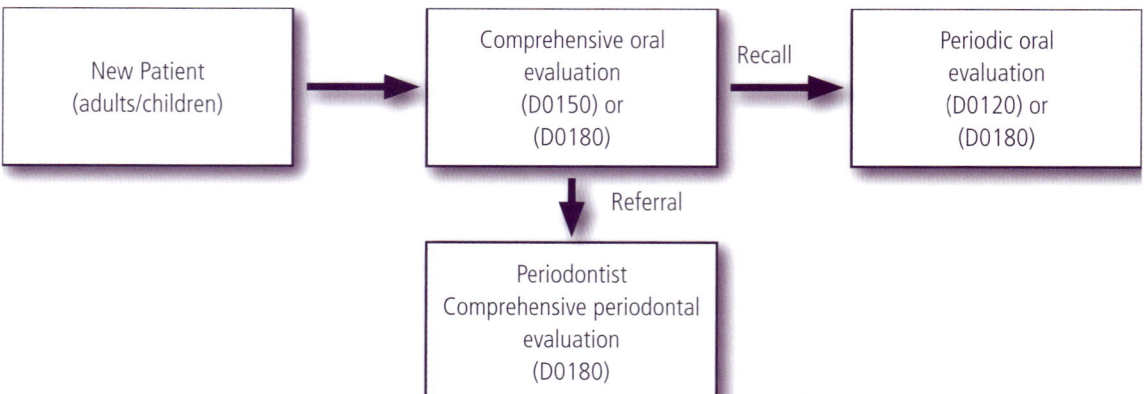

Note: If a comprehensive oral evaluation (D0150) *cannot* be accomplished due to excessive calculus and plaque, then proceed to gross debridement (D4355). D0150 would generally follow (next visit after an appropriate period of resolution) subsequent to the initial D4355 visit. See D4355 for further details and flow chart. Nothing precludes the general dentist from using D0180 for the new patient evaluation provided the new patient has "signs and symptoms or risk factors of periodontal disease," *and* a full mouth probing and charting is performed on the same service date.

D0160 DETAILED AND EXTENSIVE ORAL EVALUATION – PROBLEM FOCUSED, BY REPORT
CDT 2016

A detailed and extensive problem focused evaluation entails extensive diagnostic and cognitive modalities based on the findings of a comprehensive oral evaluation. Integration of more extensive diagnostic modalities to develop a treatment plan for a specific problem is required. The condition requiring this type of evaluation should be described and documented.

Examples of conditions requiring this type of evaluation may include dentofacial anomalies, complicated perio-prosthetic conditions, complex temporomandibular dysfunction, facial pain of unknown origin, conditions requiring multi-disciplinary consultation, etc.

COMMENTS
1. The detailed and extensive oral evaluation – problem focused, by report (D0160) may follow the comprehensive oral evaluation (D0150) or comprehensive periodontal evaluation (D0180) on a subsequent visit date. For instance, if a complex TMJ or periodontal-restorative problem is discovered at the initial comprehensive oral evaluation (D0150/D0180), a detailed and extensive follow-up oral evaluation (D0160) may be indicated. If the D0160 is for TMJ or other *non-covered* procedures, the TMJ evaluation will often be *excluded* for reimbursement by dental insurance. D0160 may also be used for the new patient presenting with complex treatment such as multi-implant placement by a periodontist or oral surgeon.
2. If covered, D0160 is typically reimbursed at a higher fee level than D0150/D0120 with some payers. The first comprehensive oral evaluation visit can be reimbursed as a D0150 (higher fee), and the *subsequent* D0160 or other visit as a D0120 (lower fee). So, reimbursement varies widely.
3. D0160 should not be considered a *routine* procedure that follows the D0150/D0180 comprehensive oral evaluation.
4. D0160 may also report an orthodontic evaluation. The orthodontist's detailed and extensive oral evaluation code reported would be D0160 following a previously reported D0150/D0180 (provided at a prior visit) by the referring general dentist. Pre-orthodontic treatment visit (D8660) and consultation (D9310) may better describe the service and be used for reporting the specialist's evaluation. See D8660 and D9310.

LIMITATIONS
1. Many payers limit oral evaluations of any type to "two evaluations per year" or "one per six months." D0160, as all oral evaluation codes, is typically subject to the oral evaluation limitation.
2. D0160 requires a report/copy of the complex diagnosis.
3. D0160 requires the use of more extensive diagnostic modalities, and treatment is usually performed over an extended length of time.
4. Frequency limitations for D0160 vary widely. Some dental plans provide a benefit once per provider. Some apply it to their D0150 frequency limit. Others consider it part of the plan's exam limitation policy. Most plans require a report whenever D0160 is submitted while others only request a report if they feel the code is being abused. Note: Some plans require the evaluation history of the patient that may include the date(s) of previous comprehensive oral evaluation(s) (D0150/D0180) before paying for D0160.
5. Consultation (D9310) may also be reimbursed to specialists by some payers. See Consultation (D9310).
6. If the patient's case presentation does not occur on the same day as the evaluation, D9450 (case presentation, detailed and extensive treatment planning) can be reported separately since D0160 requires the use of more extensive diagnostic modalities. Also note, however, that most payers do not pay for D9450 and most dentists do not charge for the visit.

NARRATIVES Provide a complete narrative for D0160 that supports the need for this detailed and extensive evaluation. History of the comprehensive oral evaluation (D0150/D0180) may be required prior to reporting D0160 for reimbursement.

FLOW CHARTS Detailed and extensive oral evaluation, problem focused (D0160) scenario:

The patient presents at a second evaluation appointment with *extensive* problems based on the findings of an initial comprehensive oral or periodontal evaluation (D0150/D0180). An example of a condition not fully covered in the routine comprehensive oral evaluation would be a complex TMJ case. An in-depth, detailed, and extensive oral evaluation (D0160) is necessary to *further evaluate* a *previously* discovered condition at a previous evaluation appointment.

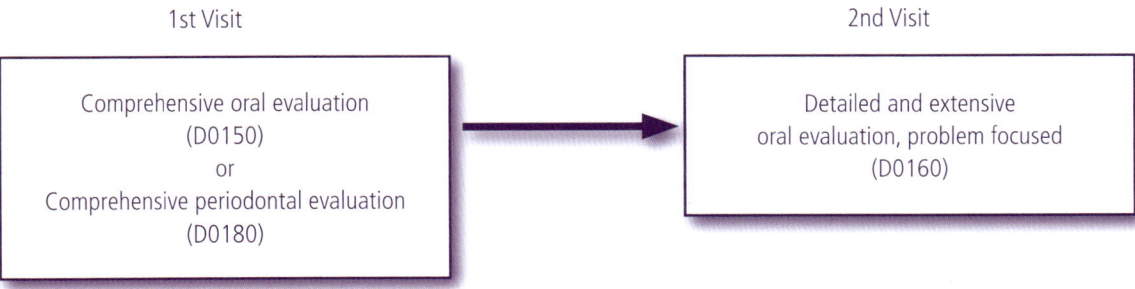

1st Visit: Comprehensive oral evaluation (D0150) or Comprehensive periodontal evaluation (D0180)

2nd Visit: Detailed and extensive oral evaluation, problem focused (D0160)

Notes: The detailed and extensive oral evaluation (D0160) must be preceded by a comprehensive oral evaluation (D0150 or D0180). D0160 is a *detailed* and *extensive* oral evaluation following the *discovery* of a complex periodontal, TMJ, restorative, etc. condition. Write a complete report and document time spent in determining the diagnosis and treatment plan. However, some payers continue to reimburse D0160 at the lower subsequent periodic oral evaluation (D0120) fee subject to any frequency limitations and availability.

D0170 RE-EVALUATION – LIMITED, PROBLEM FOCUSED (ESTABLISHED PATIENT; NOT POST-OPERATIVE VISIT) — CDT 2016

Assessing the status of a previously existing condition. For example: A traumatic injury where no treatment was rendered but patient needs follow-up monitoring; evaluation for undiagnosed continuing pain; soft tissue lesion requiring follow-up evaluation.

1. D0170 should be reported when "assessing the status of a previously existing condition," such as lesions requiring a *follow-up* evaluation. Typically, D0170 would be *preceded* by the comprehensive oral evaluation (D0150), comprehensive periodontal evaluation (D0180), the limited oral evaluation – problem focused (D0140) visit, or periodic oral evaluation (D0120).

2. From the nomenclature and descriptor language, the re-evaluation – limited, problem focused (D0170) should not be reported following definitive treatment (i.e., periodontal, root canal, extraction post-op). The fee for any initial periodontal treatment, such as scaling and root planing (SRP), usually includes any post-operative evaluation associated with said procedure. Likewise, a post-operative (within thirty days) routine evaluation after oral surgery would generally be considered inclusive in the surgery fee. However, an extensive infection following surgery, for instance, could be reported separately. See treatment of complications (post-surgical), D9930.

3. D0170 should not be used to report a post-operative re-evaluation. In other words, it should not be used when re-evaluating a patient following surgical extraction, root canal, implant surgery, etc. D0171 could report re-evaluation – post operative office visit (D0171). Both D0170 and D0171 could not be reported on the same service date.

4. D0170 should not be used to report a periodontal re-evaluation of charting and probing. The nomenclature of D0170 specifically indicates it is *not* for a post-operative visit. Currently, there is no *specific* code to report a stand-alone periodontal re-evaluation by a hygienist, so unspecified periodontal procedure, by report (D4999) could be used to report this procedure, if done by a hygienist. However, D4999 is rarely reimbursed. Those doctors who do not participate in the patient's dental plan may hold the patient responsible for payment of the unspecified D4999. If a comprehensive periodontal evaluation is performed *by the dentist* including complete charting and probing, D0180 could be reported. However, D0180 would be subject to any reimbursement limitations. Also see D0171.

COMMENTS

1. Key elements of D0170:
   a. Involves the re-evaluation of an established patient for a specific problem in which definitive treatment has not been rendered.
   b. Typically used to report the monitoring of soft tissue abnormalities, such as an aphthous ulcer, leukoplakia, erythroplakia, etc.
   c. Can also be used to report follow-up appointments to monitor/evaluate trauma to soft tissue or teeth following an accident, root development after apexogenesis, and continuing undiagnosed pain.

2. Consider limiting the use of re-evaluation – limited, problem focused (D0170), since the UCR fee is generally *lower* than other evaluations. This procedure generally is subject to the "two evaluations per year/12 months" or "one evaluation per six months" limitation. Occasionally payers will reimburse a third evaluation, if the evaluation occurs in a *different* billing office or the patient sees a specialist. See the palliative (D9110), consultation (D9310), and re-evaluation – post-operative office visit (D0171) codes for other reporting options that might be applicable.

LIMITATIONS

1. All periodontal, endodontic, and oral surgery procedure codes generally include any routine follow up (to check healing, etc.) within thirty days of initial treatment (six months if a prosthesis) as a policy limitation. A follow-up visit due to extensive infection and complications, for instance, could be reported separately. See treatment of complications (D9930). However, D9930 generally is not paid as a separate procedure by payers. This post-op evaluation is considered a part of the treatment procedure unless provided by a different billing entity.

2. The fee for D0170 may be excluded by payers if reported in conjunction with other procedures on the same service date. However, D0170 is a "stand-alone" oral evaluation code and may always be reported separately.

3. Many plans consider D0170 part of the patient's two exams per year allowance. However, some plans will consider payment for D0170 if a narrative verifies that it was not a post-operative re-evaluation.

NARRATIVES

A narrative for D0170 could state, "This evaluation was conducted to complete a more in depth, thorough exam of a soft tissue lesion adjacent to #3. Patient was last examined for this condition on mm/dd/yy."

FLOW CHARTS

Re-evaluation, limited problem focused (D0170) scenario:

Scenario: On the playground a child's tooth is "bumped." The mother takes the child to the office for an evaluation. The doctor examines the child (D0140) and takes necessary diagnostic radiographs. Six weeks later the child returns for a *follow-up* re-evaluation visit with the dentist (D0170), including a periapical diagnostic image (D0220). Everything looks okay, the child is dismissed and instructed to return for his/her routine periodic check-up. This second follow-up visit would be reported as re-evaluation, limited problem focused (D0170) and periapical first film (D0220).

```
┌─────────────────────────┐              ┌─────────────────────────┐
│ Limited oral evaluation-│              │   Re-evaluation –       │
│    problem focused      │              │ limited, problem focused│
│      (D0140)            │  Six Weeks   │ (established patient);  │
│ and intraoral periapical│ Follow-up    │   not post – operative  │
│  first radiographic     │ re-evaluation│     visit (D0170)       │
│    image (D0220)        │   ═══════▶   │periapical first radio-  │
│                         │              │  graphic image (D0220)  │
└─────────────────────────┘              └─────────────────────────┘
```

D0171   RE-EVALUATION – POST OPERATIVE OFFICE VISIT   CDT 2016

1. D0171 could be reported when "assessing the status of a previously performed procedure," such as grafts, oral surgery, periodontal surgery, and endodontics which require a *follow-up* post-operative visit.

2. From the nomenclature language, the re-evaluation – post-operative visit (D0171) could be reported following definitive treatment (i.e., periodontal, graft, root canal, extraction post-op) or palliative D9110 treatment. The fee for any initial periodontal treatment, such as scaling and root planing (SRP), usually includes any post-operative evaluation associated with said procedure. Likewise, a post-operative (within thirty days) routine evaluation after oral surgery would generally be considered inclusive in the surgery fee.

3. D0171 could be used to report a periodontal re-evaluation that includes charting and probing. The nomenclature of D0171 specifically indicates it is for a post-operative visit. Currently, there is no *specific* code to report a stand-alone periodontal re-evaluation by a hygienist, so unspecified periodontal procedure, by report (D4999) could be used to report this procedure. D4999 is rarely reimbursed. Those doctors who do not participate in the patient's dental plan may hold the patient responsible for payment of the unspecified procedure, D4999. However, if a comprehensive periodontal evaluation is performed by the dentist including complete charting and probing, D0180 could be reported, which should have a higher fee than D0171. However, D0180 (just like D0171) would be subject to any frequency limitations.

LIMITATIONS

1. All periodontal, endodontic, and oral surgery procedure codes generally include any routine follow up (to check healing, etc.) within thirty days of initial treatment (six months if a prosthesis) as a policy limitation, so D0171 will probably not be reimbursed.

2. Many plans will consider D0171 part of the patient's two evaluations per year allowance or one evaluation per six months.

3. The fee for D0171 may be excluded by payers if reported in conjunction with other definitive procedures on the same service date. However, D0171 is a "stand-alone" oral evaluation code and may always be reported separately.

TIPS

1. Consider limiting the use of re-evaluation – post-operative visit (D0171), since the UCR fee will be *lower* than other evaluations. This procedure generally is subject to the "two evaluations per year/12 months" or "one evaluation per six months" limitation. Occasionally payers will reimburse a third evaluation, if the evaluation occurs in a *different* billing office or the patient sees a specialist. See the palliative (D9110) and consultation (D9310) codes for other reporting options that might be applicable.

2. A follow-up visit due to extensive infection and complications, for instance, could be reported separately. See treatment of complications (D9930). However, D9930 generally is not paid as a separate procedure by payers unless a different office (provider) performs the service. This evaluation is considered a part of the treatment procedure unless provided by a different billing entity.

D0180   COMPREHENSIVE PERIODONTAL EVALUATION – NEW OR ESTABLISHED PATIENT
CDT 2016

This procedure is indicated for patients showing signs or symptoms of periodontal disease and for patients with risk factors such as smoking or diabetes. It includes evaluation of periodontal conditions, probing and charting, evaluation and recording of the patient's dental and medical history and general health assessment. It may include the evaluation and recording of dental caries, missing or unerupted teeth, restorations, occlusal relationships and oral cancer evaluation.

1. Do not report D0180 in *addition* to the comprehensive oral evaluation (D0150) on the *same* service date. However, the general practitioner can report D0180 provided the patient exhibits signs and symptoms (or periodontal risk factors) of periodontal disease, and the dentist performs a detailed full mouth periodontal charting with six points/tooth probing on the same evaluation date.

2. D0180 is not used to report a periodontal screening record (PSR) since *periodontal screening*, where indicated, is now specifically described as a component of periodic oral evaluation (D0120). D0180 is more detailed and includes " six point per tooth probing (full mouth) and charting," and also identifies furcations, wear facets, abraction lesions, areas of mobility, bleeding on probing, areas and amounts of recession, amounts of remaining attached gingiva, etc. D0180 may be used for both new and established patients. See comments and limitations below.

COMMENTS

1. Key elements of D0180:
   a. Reported when performing a comprehensive periodontal evaluation only on a "qualified" patient showing signs, symptoms, or risk factors such as smoking and diabetes for periodontal disease.
      i. May be performed on both new or established patients.
      ii. May be reported by general dentists or periodontists as all codes are available to any dentist practicing within his/her scope of license.
   b. Requires the components of a comprehensive oral evaluation (D0150) plus a complete and comprehensive periodontal charting.
      i. D0150 gives the option of periodontal screening or charting, as deemed necessary.
      ii. D0180 requires complete periodontal charting, which includes, but is not necessarily limited to six-points-per-tooth pocket depths, recessions, furcations, areas of mobility, bleeding points, purulent discharge, minimal attachments, (i.e., amount of remaining attached gingiva) and/or a periodontal diagnosis.

2. The comprehensive periodontal evaluation (D0180) may be reported for *new* or *established* periodontal patients presenting with signs, symptoms, and risk factors (such as smoking or diabetes) of periodontal disease at the *initial* evaluation. D0180 "may include" an oral cancer evaluation.

3. The comprehensive periodontal evaluation (D0180) is not specialty-specific. The general practitioner can report it, as with any CDT code. However, the general practitioner would generally report more of the comprehensive, extensive, and all-encompassing comprehensive oral evaluations (D0150) for the new patient. D0180 may be reported for the *qualified* periodontal patient and the Maximum Plan Allowance (MPA) may be higher for it than for D0150.

4. This comprehensive periodontal evaluation (D0180) is indicated for patients showing signs/symptoms of periodontal disease, or for patients with risk factors such as smoking or diabetes. If evident, list these signs/symptoms and/or risk factors in the patient chart. Reporting the D0180 code indicates that extra time and effort were spent in making an in-depth evaluation of the overall periodontal condition, including charting and "full mouth" probing. D0180 may be reported for the initial (comprehensive) new patient evaluation or for the recall visit. However, D0180 is typically subject to the "two evaluations per year/12 months" or "one per six months" limitation. Some payers will reimburse a third evaluation, if the evaluation occurs in a different office or with a specialist. Some payers will "downcode" D0180 or "remap" it to the D0150 or D0120 fee for reimbursement.

LIMITATIONS

1. D0180 may be reported for the established periodontal patient or patient with periodontal risk factors and requires that a *full*, complete, and detailed periodontal evaluation be completed. Reimbursement for D0180 is typically *remapped* and *limited* by many payers to the D0120 lower fee for established patients.

2. Some general practice and periodontal offices establish two *consistent* fee levels for D0180. The higher fee is charged for the *new* patient comprehensive periodontal evaluation (taking more time). A lower fee is charged for the *established* patient's annual periodontal oral evaluation at the periodontal maintenance (D4910) visit. Some offices *alternate* the D0120 and D0180 evaluations each six months to differentiate the more extensive periodontal workup done once per year. D0180 reported at recall may be *remapped* and *limited* by some payers to the lower fee D0120 as reimbursed for established patients.

3. Some payers reimburse D0180 every 12 or 24 months, others every three to five years, and some once in a "lifetime." Reimbursement for D0180 varies widely. D0180 may be reimbursed only "once" per lifetime (like D0150) per doctor by *some* payers.

4. D0180 may be reported on the same service date as active periodontal maintenance therapy (D4910), but is subject to the "one per six months" or "two evaluations per year/12 months" limitation. In some cases, reimbursement will be made at the lower D0120 fee. Some plans occasionally reimburse at a higher fee. Some offices perform a detailed and extensive *annual* evaluation on the *established* periodontal patient and report the more extensive D0180 once per year. D0180 encompasses all elements of the comprehensive periodontal evaluation and must include mandatory full mouth probing with extensive periodontal charting and a comprehensive periodontal evaluation by the dentist.

NARRATIVES List the patient's sign(s) or symptom(s) of periodontal disease and/or risk factors (e.g., smoking or diabetes) in the patient's chart. Generally a narrative on the claim form is not required.

PRE-DIAGNOSTIC SERVICES — CDT 2016

D0190 SCREENING OF A PATIENT — CDT 2016

A screening, including state or federally mandated screening, to determine an individual's need to be seen by a dentist for diagnosis.

COMMENTS
1. While diagnosis and treatment are the responsibilities of the dentist, a dental screening may be performed by other medical or dental professionals who are acting within the scope of their state licenses (i.e., mid-level provider, hygienist, physician, physician's assistant, nurse, or other authorized personnel). A dental screening typically involves a brief oral examination (with a tongue depressor) to check for decay, injury, pain, developmental problems, and other abnormal oral conditions or risk factors (i.e., poor oral home care) that require evaluation by a dentist.
2. A dental screening may or may not lead to a referral to a dentist.

D0191 ASSESSMENT OF A PATIENT — CDT 2016

A limited clinical inspection that is performed to identify possible signs of oral or systemic disease, malformation, or injury, and the potential need for referral for diagnosis and treatment.

COMMENTS
1. An oral assessment commonly includes a review and documentation of the patient's medical and dental history, a limited clinical examination (recording dental restorations and conditions that should be called to the attention of a dentist), and collection of other oral health data to assist in the development of a professional treatment plan if a referral to a dentist for diagnosis and treatment is necessary.
2. A dental assessment involves a limited clinical examination typically by an independent hygienist or other mid-level provider acting within the scope of his/her state license.
3. A dental assessment is distinct from oral evaluations in that it does not involve interpretation or diagnosis and is performed to determine if the patient needs to be referred to a dentist for diagnosis and treatment.

DIAGNOSTIC IMAGING — CDT 2016

Should be taken only for clinical reasons as determined by the patient's dentist. Should be of diagnostic quality and properly identified and dated. Is a part of the patient's clinical record and the original images should be retained by the dentist. Originals should not be used to fulfill requests made by patients or third-parties for copies of records.

IMAGE CAPTURE WITH INTERPRETATION — CDT 2016

D0210   INTRAORAL – COMPLETE SERIES OF RADIOGRAPHIC IMAGES   CDT 2016

A radiographic survey of the whole mouth, usually consisting of 14-22 periapical and posterior bitewing images intended to display the crowns and roots of all teeth, periapical areas and alveolar bone.

1. It is misleading to report an extraoral panoramic radiographic image (D0330) and bitewing images (D0272/D0273/D0274) as an intraoral complete series (D0210). The dental office should not combine these two procedures (panoramic film and bitewings) and report as an intraoral complete series. A panoramic image is *extraoral*, not intraoral. Always report exactly what you do and only date the service the day the service is performed. **Note: It is not illegal or improper for an insurance company to "remap" a submitted code to another code for *payment* purposes.** This modification is in accordance with the *contract language*. Payers routinely convert the extraoral panoramic images and intraoral bitewing images to a complete series (D0210) for reimbursement purposes. See (D0330) for further details. However, the frequency of (D0210) or any other radiographic imaging is always determined by the dentist based on the needs of the patient.

2. Note that the word "usually" in the descriptor indicates that the exact number of periapical and posterior images is not as important as the need to "display the crowns and roots of *all* teeth, periapical areas and alveolar bone."

COMMENTS

1. A complete series (D0210) is *inclusive* of bitewings, but bitewings are not necessarily required. The complete series is intraoral.

2. A complete series (D0210) is most often taken *after* the evaluation of the new patient by the dentist at the comprehensive oral evaluation (D0150) or (D0180). Radiographic images are ordered by the dentist per the needs of the patient. A complete series (D0210) helps to determine a diagnostic baseline. The complete series is repeated on a three to five-year basis per the needs of the patient. Many payers are trending toward a five-year reimbursement limitation rather than the more traditional three-year benefit exclusion. This limitation period varies among plans.

3. The type and sequence of diagnostic images should be determined and ordered by the doctor on a patient-by-patient basis. This determination is based on risk assessment, observation, and medical necessity. Images should not be taken based on the patient's plan benefits or limitations. Patient documentation should contain the dentist's written evaluation of the diagnostic images taken. If there is no documentation of the radiographic evaluation in the chart, the payer may deny payment of the claim or ask for reimbursement in the event of an audit.

LIMITATIONS

1. A complete series *usually* consists of 14-22 periapical and posterior bitewing images. A pediatric complete series may consist of 8-9 periapical diagnostic images and either two or four bitewing images. The pediatric full series should display the crowns and roots of all teeth. Note: Some payers require a specific number of diagnostic images to qualify as a complete series.

2. If a number of periapicals and bitewing images are taken on the same service date and the fee for those images is equal to or greater than the complete series, the fee reimbursed by third parties may be limited to that of the complete series. The payment of the complete series will trigger the "once every three to five-year limitation." If a complete series is reimbursed, a notation should be made in the patient's billing record for future reference.

3. If either a complete series (D0210) *or* panoramic image (D0330) is taken and then a new complete series and/or panoramic image is taken during the exclusion period (typically three or five years), the second radiographic image service will not be reimbursed. Both services are usually subject to the same three to five-year limitation.

4. Many plans have a one-year limitation exclusion for bitewing radiographic images taken *after the service date* of a complete series (D0210) or a panoramic radiographic image (D0330).

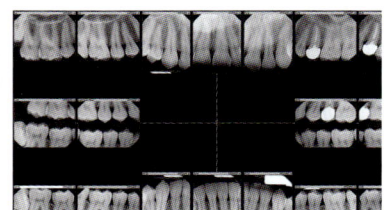

This is a complete series (including bitewings).

Courtesy DEXIS, LLC and DEXIS®

D0220 INTRAORAL – PERIAPICAL FIRST RADIOGRAPHIC IMAGE — CDT 2016

COMMENTS
1. D0220 is only for the first periapical (PA) radiograph taken on any date of service.
2. Report D0230 for each *additional* periapical radiographic image taken *after* the first image on the same service date.
3. Periapicals associated with an endodontic *diagnosis* on a date prior to definitive treatment are typically reimbursed. "Working and post-treatment" images associated with endodontic treatment are part of the global endodontic fee. Diagnostic images taken of the treated tooth within 30 days of the completion of a root canal are typically included in the overall endodontic fee.
4. The type and sequence of diagnostic images should be determined and ordered by the dentist based on the patient needs. This determination is based on risk assessment, observation, and dental necessity. Images should not be taken based on the patient's plan benefits or limitations. Patient documentation should contain the dentist's written evaluation of the diagnostic images taken. If there is no documentation of the dentist's radiographic evaluation in the chart, the payer may deny payment of the claim or ask for reimbursement in the event of an audit.

LIMITATIONS
1. Periapical radiographic images at emergency visits are routinely reimbursed. However, periapicals at checkups may require a narrative (required more and more). A caries risk assessment (D0601, D0602, and D0603) may help justify periapicals at a checkup taken in conjunction with bitewings.
2. If a number of periapicals and bitewing radiographic images are taken on the same service date and the fee for those images is equal to or greater than the complete series, the fee reimbursed will be limited to that of the complete series. The payment of the complete series will trigger the "once every three to five-year limitation." If a complete series is reimbursed, a notation should be made in the patient's billing record for future reference.
3. Reimbursement for periapical images, if reported in conjunction with bitewing images, may be limited.

TIPS
1. One, two, or three periapical images may be reimbursed on a problem focused evaluation (D0140) service date. Periapical images taken at the problem focused visit typically do not affect the "once per year/12 months" limitations for *bitewing* images associated with recall visits.
2. Intraoral periapical first image (D0220) and an additional periapical image(s) (D0230) are often payable at any visit (including recall), if medically necessary. At an emergency, problem focused oral evaluation (D0140) or periodic oral evaluation (D0120) recall visit, the periapical image reimbursement may be subject to a deductible as well as the maximum fee limitation for multiple diagnostic images.
3. Periapicals, particularly at different "angles," are often necessary to provide alternate views of the anatomy of an area for a complete diagnosis. Periapicals are a better choice at the emergency visit from a reimbursement perspective as well as from the clinical perspective.

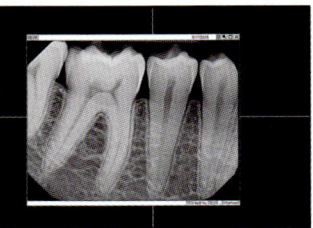

This is a periapical radiographic image.

Courtesy DEXIS, LLC and DEXIS®

D0230   INTRAORAL – PERIAPICAL EACH ADDITIONAL RADIOGRAPHIC IMAGE   CDT 2016

The use of a dual pack (two images at once) is not reported as an *additional* radiograph.

COMMENTS
1. Report D0230 for each additional periapical radiographic image taken *after* the first image on the same service date.
2. Periapicals associated with an endodontic *diagnosis* on a date prior to definitive treatment are typically reimbursed. If the diagnostic PA is taken on the day endodontic treatment is started, report the PA periapical radiograph as it still may be reimbursed. "Working and post-treatment" images associated with endodontic treatment are part of the global endodontic fee. Diagnostic images taken of the treated tooth within 30 days of the completion of a root canal are typically included in the overall endodontic fee.
3. The type and sequence of diagnostic images should be determined and ordered by the dentist based on the patient's needs. This determination is based on risk assessment, observation, and dental necessity. Images should not be taken based on the patient's plan benefits or limitations. Patient documentation should contain the dentist's written evaluation of the diagnostic images taken.

LIMITATIONS
1. Periapical radiographic images at emergency visits are routinely reimbursed. However, periapicals at checkups may require a narrative (required more and more). A caries risk assessment (D0601, D0602, and D0603) may help justify periapicals at checkup taken in conjunction with bitewings.
2. If a number of periapicals and bitewing radiographic images are taken on the same service date and the fee for those images is equal to or greater than the complete series, the fee reimbursed will be limited to that of the complete series. The payment of the complete series will trigger the "once every 3-5 year limitation." If a complete series is reimbursed, a notation should be made in the patient's billing record for future reference.
3. Reimbursement for periapical images, if reported in conjunction with bitewing images, may be limited.

TIPS
1. One, two, or three periapical images may be reimbursed on a problem focused evaluation (D0140) service date. Periapical images taken at the problem focused visit typically do not affect the "once per year/12 months" limitations for *bitewing* images associated with recall visits.
2. Intraoral periapical first image (D0220) and an additional periapical image(s) (D0230) are often payable at *any* visit (including recall), if medically necessary. At an emergency, problem focused oral evaluation (D0140) or periodic oral evaluation (D0120) recall visit, the periapical image reimbursement may be subject to a deductible as well as the maximum fee limitation for multiple diagnostic images. Some plans limit reimbursement for periapical images taken in conjunction with bitewing images.
3. Periapicals, particularly at different "angles," are often necessary to provide alternate views of the anatomy of an area for a complete diagnosis. Periapicals may be a better choice at the emergency visit from a reimbursement perspective as well as from the clinical perspective.

D0240   INTRAORAL – OCCLUSAL RADIOGRAPHIC IMAGE   CDT 2016

COMMENTS
1. Intraoral – occlusal radiographic image (D0240) is also taken on young children (at the initial new patient evaluation) and later as needed for a full arch or anterior segment view and may be taken in conjunction with bitewing radiographic images. At the initial visit, typically two PAs are taken, one of the maxillary teeth and one of the mandibular teeth.
2. The type and sequence of diagnostic images should be determined and ordered by the dentist based on the patient's needs. This determination is based on risk assessment, observation, and medical necessity. Films should not be taken based on the patient's plan benefits or limitations. Patient documentation should contain the dentist's written evaluation of the diagnostic radiograph(s).

LIMITATIONS

1. D0240 is typically reimbursed and is limited to the complete series (D0210) UCR fee and by the complete series limitations. If an occlusal radiographic image (D0240) and a number of other images are taken on the same service date, and the fee for those images is equal to or greater than the complete series, the fee reimbursed will be limited to that of the complete series. The payment of the complete series will trigger the "once every 3-5 year limitation." If a complete series is reimbursed, a notation should be made in the patient's chart for future reference.

2. Typically, an occlusal radiographic image (D0240) plus two bitewing images (D0272) are reimbursed as submitted. Note: The total fee reimbursed for all images reported in a period determined by the payer may be subject to the fee and frequency limitations placed on the complete series (D0210).

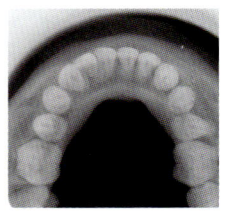

This is an occlusal radiographic image.

Courtesy Gendex Dental Systems and DenOptix®

D0250 REVISED EXTRA-ORAL 2D PROJECTION RADIOGRAPHIC IMAGE CREATED USING A STATIONARY RADIATION SOURCE, AND DETECTOR — CDT 2016

These images include, but are not limited to: Lateral Skull; Posterior-Anterior Skull; Submentovertex; Waters; Reverse Tomes; Oblique Mandibular Body; Lateral Ramus.

REVISIONS

EXTRA-ORAL ~~FIRST~~ 2D PROJECTION RADIOGRAPHIC IMAGE CREATED USING A STATIONARY RADIATION SOURCE AND DETECTOR

These images include, but are not limited to: Lateral Skull; Posterior-Anterior Skull; Submentovertex; Waters; Reverse Tomes; Oblique Mandibular Body; Lateral Ramus.

With the extraoral – radiographic image (D0250), the radiographic image/sensor/film is positioned *outside* the oral cavity when the radiograph is taken. The image must now be created using a stationary radiation source and detector. Note that extraoral – each additional radiographic image (D0260) is a deleted code.

LIMITATIONS

1. If existing oral conditions suggest the need for D0250, the service may be reimbursed; however, this reimbursement is subject to the plan's limitations. Conditions relating to trauma or suspected pathology could justify the dental necessity of this service.

2. The type and sequence of diagnostic radiographic images should be determined and ordered by the dentist based on the patient's needs. This determination is based on risk assessment, observation, and medical necessity. Images should not be taken based on the patient's plan benefits or limitations. Patient documentation should contain the dentist's written evaluation of the diagnostic radiograph(s).

NARRATIVES

1. For reporting multiple images on the same service date enter the quantity in Box 29b. If your software will not accept the entry, then enter each image on a separate line. Provide a narrative.

2. Conditions relating to trauma or suspected pathology could justify the medical necessity of this service. The narrative should include the specific observations made by the provider that made this radiograph necessary to diagnose the pathology.

D0251 NEW PROCEDURE EXTRA-ORAL POSTERIOR DENTAL RADIOGRAPHIC IMAGE — CDT 2016

Image limited to exposure of complete posterior teeth in both dental arches. This is a unique image that is not derived from another image.

CODING WATCH CORRECTION

1. D0250 reports an extra-oral – 2D radiographic image created using a stationary radiation source and detector without specifically referencing the area of the mouth viewed. D0250 is non-specific as to the area of exposure.

2. D0251 is used to describe an extra-oral posterior dental radiograph that produces an image of the posterior teeth area of both dental arches. This D0251 image is not to be derived from another image. D0251 describes an image that is unique and not produced from, or a duplicate produced from, another existing image (e.g., not produced from cone beam CT reconstruction of the data captured in the scan).

COMMENTS D0251 reports a posterior radiographic image of both the upper and lower jaws of the posterior area of the mouth. If both right and left images are produced, report D0251 twice and identify the right or left side represented by each image.

LIMITATIONS Because this is a new code, many existing plans will not provide reimbursement.

D0260 — DELETED CODE EXTRAORAL – EACH ADDITIONAL RADIOGRAPHIC IMAGE CDT 2016

This is a deleted code. See D0250 for further details.

D0270 — BITEWING – SINGLE RADIOGRAPHIC IMAGE CDT 2016

COMMENTS Also see D0272/D0273/D0274 for further details.

LIMITATIONS If a single bitewing (BW) image is reported at a given recall or emergency visit, subsequent bitewing images *may be denied. Be aware that any number of bitewings taken at any particular visit may "trigger"* the "once per year/12 months" limitation by most plans. One bitewing, two bitewings, three bitewings, or four bitewings taken at a particular visit date could be subject to the plan's bitewing frequency limitation. Be careful to report the number and date of diagnostic images accurately. The reimbursement for bitewings, according to the limitations of different plans is highly variable.

TIPS

1. For diagnostic purposes, two periapical (D0220/D0230) radiographs taken at different angulations or views are most often the preferred choice at the problem focused oral evaluation (D0140) or emergency visit.

2. Some dentists will choose to take both a periapical and a bitewing radiographic image at the D1040 visit. This is determined and ordered by the doctor. Note that the reporting of a single bitewing image may trigger the "once per year" bitewing image limitation and render the bitewings taken at a subsequent recall visit non-reimbursable. Also refer to periapical radiographic image D0220 for certain limitations in combination with bitewing radiographic images.

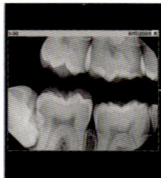

This is a bitewing – single image.

Courtesy DEXIS, LLC and DEXIS®

D0272 — BITEWINGS – TWO RADIOGRAPHIC IMAGES CDT 2016

CODING WARNING CORRECTION

1. Unless a patient has recent *history* of caries or other factors, such as *progressing* periodontal disease, routine six-month or annual bitewing images may be considered unnecessary. Some payers have requested refunds for the bitewings, stating the diagnostic images were "medically unnecessary" when documentation does not support the medical necessity of taking the images. When bitewings are taken at six-month intervals, be careful to document the reason the images were taken such as caries risk assessment, *recent* decay or other caries *risk* factors. A caries risk assessment (D0601, D0602, and D0603) should be reported (often at "zero" fee) to support six-month intervals. Documentation supporting the need for bitewings taken in 12-24 month intervals should be made as well. Diagnostic image guidelines for radiographic images may be found at www.ada.org/2760.aspx.

2. It is misleading to report panoramic radiographic images (D0330) and bitewing images (D0272, D0273 or D0274) as a complete series (D0210). Always report the panoramic/bitewing images *separately*. The payer may "remap" this radiograph combination to a complete (D0210) series as an alternate benefit. This remapping typically occurs as a result of policy limitations and exclusions in the contract language. For further information on reimbursement policies, see panoramic image (D0330).

COMMENTS

1. Many offices do not establish, maintain, and adhere to proper bitewing radiographic image protocol as determined and prescribed by the dentist.

2. Most offices take bitewing radiographic images every 12 months. The most common clinical protocol is to take two bitewing images (D0272) for children, three bitewing images (D0273) or four bitewing images (D0274) for adults (second molars erupted).

3. When the dentist orders a six-month bitewing image interval on a given patient, be careful to document the presence of decay, history of caries, or other risk factors. A caries risk assessment (D0601, D0602, and D0603) should be reported (often at "zero" fee) to support six-month intervals. The type, sequence, and frequency of diagnostic radiographic images should be determined by the dentist for each individual patient based on risk assessment and need, not based on the patient's plan benefits or limitations. Clinical notation in the patient's chart should reflect the dentist's evaluation of images taken.

LIMITATIONS

1. There is generally an *annual* limitation for bitewing reimbursement; however, some payers will further limit bitewing image reimbursement to once every 24 months. Some payers may reimburse bitewing images twice annually for high-risk children under 13 years old. The allowances are more generous for children as they are generally at a higher risk for caries. Reimbursement is dictated by the type of plan purchased by the employer and by dental necessity.

2. Many plans limit reimbursement for bitewings taken after complete series (D0120) to at least 12 months after the complete series.

3. Bitewing images are generally reimbursed as a preventive service at 100% of the UCR fee. Some payers reimburse bitewing images as basic (80% of the UCR fee).

TIPS

1. Some policies reimburse for a number of periapical diagnostic radiographic images in addition to two bitewing images (D0272), three bitewing images (D0273), or four bitewing images (D0274) at the recall visit. Some offices report two bitewing images (D0272), three bitewing images (D0273) or four bitewing images (D0274) in addition to several periapicals in order to monitor anterior areas for caries and/or periodontal disease. More payers are requiring narratives and caries risk assessment to support taking periapicals with bitewings. See D0220 for further details.

2. If the second molars have erupted, consider four bitewing images (D0274). There is often no *age limitation* for reimbursement for three or four bitewing images. If an adult has missing posterior teeth, 2BWX (D0272) or 3BWX (D0273) may be appropriate.

3. Periapical (D0220/D0230) diagnostic radiographic images are most often the best clinical choice for an emergency evaluation. If a single bitewing image is taken at the *emergency* evaluation visit, bitewing images *may be denied* at the next recall service date due to the "once per year/12 months" plan limitation. Note: This limitation may not apply when only *one* bitewing image is reported.

4. To monitor the bitewing frequency, if 20% of the practice's prophys are child prophys, approximately 20% of total bitewing radiographic images should be two bitewing radiographic images.

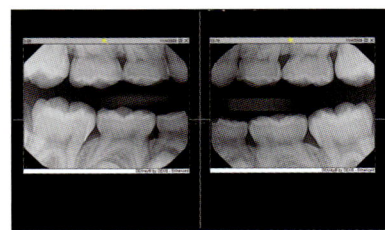

These are bitewings – two images.

Courtesy DEXIS, LLC and DEXIS®

D0273 BITEWINGS – THREE RADIOGRAPHIC IMAGES — CDT 2016

1. Unless a patient has recent *history* of caries or other factors, such as *progressing* periodontal disease, routine six-month or annual bitewing radiographic images may be considered medically unnecessary. Some payers have requested reimbursement for the bitewings, stating the diagnostic radiographic images were "medically unnecessary" when documentation does not support the dental necessity. When bitewings are taken at six-month intervals, be careful to document any contributing factors such as *recent* decay or other caries *risk* factors. A caries risk assessment (D0601, D0602, and D0603) should be reported (often at "zero" fee) to support six-month intervals. Documentation supporting the exposure of 12 to 24 month bitewing radiographic images should be made as well. Diagnostic image guidelines for radiographs may be found at www.ada.org/2760.aspx.
2. It is misleading to report panoramic radiographic images (D0330) and bitewing radiographs (D0272, D0273 or D0274) as a complete series (D0210). Always report the panoramic/ bitewing radiographic images *separately*. The payer may "remap" this radiographic combination to a complete (D0210) series as an alternative payment. This remapping typically occurs as a result of policy limitations and exclusions. For further information on reimbursement policies, also see panoramic radiographic image (D0330).

COMMENTS

1. Bitewing – three radiographic images (D0273) code could report one bitewing on one side (missing teeth) and two bitewings taken on the other side of the mouth.
2. Many offices do not establish, maintain and *enforce* proper bitewing image protocol as determined and *prescribed* by the dentist.
3. Most offices take bitewing radiographic images every 12-24 months; bitewing radiographic images – two radiographic images (D0272) for children and either bitewings – three radiographic images (D0273) or bitewings – four radiographic images (D0274) for adults (second molars erupted) as an adjunct to diagnosis at the recall visit. This is the most *common* clinical protocol.
4. Generally, age is *not* an issue for reimbursement of either three (D0273) or four (D0274) bitewing radiographic images. However, frequency limits may also be age limited with some payers.
5. When the dentist orders a six-month bitewing radiographic image interval on a given patient, be sure to document the presence of decay, history of caries, or other high-risk factors. A caries risk assessment (D0601, D0602, and D0603) should be reported (often at "zero" fee) to support six-month intervals. The type, sequence, and frequency of diagnostic images should be determined by the dentist for each individual patient, based on diagnosis, not based on the patient's plan benefits or limitations. Clinical notation in the patient's chart should reflect the dentist's diagnosis. For updated diagnostic image guidelines, go to www.ada.org/2760.aspx.

LIMITATIONS

1. There is generally an *annual* limitation for bitewing image reimbursement; however, some payers will further limit bitewing image reimbursement to once every 24 months. Some payers will reimburse bitewing images twice annually for high-risk children under 13 years old. The allowances are more generous for children, as they are generally at a higher risk for caries. Reimbursement is dictated by the type of plan purchased by the employer and by dental necessity.
2. Many plans limit reimbursement for bitewings taken after a complete series (D0210) to at least 12 months after the complete series.
3. Bitewing images are generally reimbursed as a preventive service at 100% of the UCR fee. Some payers reimburse bitewing images as basic (80% of the UCR fee).

TIPS

1. Some policies reimburse for a number of periapical diagnostic images in addition to two bitewing images (D0272), three bitewing images (D0273), or four bitewing images (D0274) at the recall visit. Some offices report two bitewing images (D0272), three bitewing images (D0273), or four bitewing images (D0274) in addition to several periapicals in order to monitor anterior areas for caries and/or periodontal disease. More payers are requiring narratives and caries risk assessment (D0601, D0602, and D0603) to support taking periapicals with bitewings. See D0220 for further details.
2. If the second molars have erupted, consider taking four bitewing images (D0274). There is often *no age limitation* for reimbursement for three or four bitewing images. If an adult has missing posterior teeth, 2BWX (D0272) or 3BWX (D0273) may be appropriate.

3. Periapical (D0220/D0230) diagnostic radiographic images are most often the best clinical choice for an emergency evaluation. If a single bitewing image is taken at the *emergency* evaluation visit, bitewing images *may be denied* at the next recall service date due to the "once per year/12 months" plan limitation. Note: This limitation may not apply when only *one* bitewing image is reported.

4. See gross debridement to enable comprehensive evaluation (D4355) for diagnostic image sequence options.

5. To monitor bitewing frequency, if 80% of the practice's prophys are adult prophys, approximately 80% of total bitewing radiographic images should be three or four bitewing radiographic images.

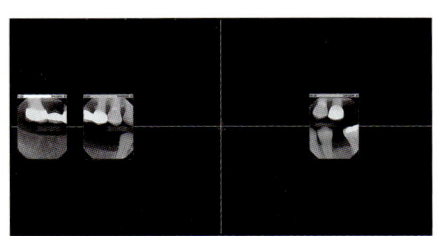

These are bitewings – three images.

Courtesy DEXIS, LLC and DEXIS®

D0274 BITEWINGS – FOUR RADIOGRAPHIC IMAGES CDT 2016

1. Unless a patient has recent *history* of caries or other factors, such as *progressing* periodontal disease, routine six-month or annual bitewing radiographic images may be considered dentally unnecessary. Some payers have requested reimbursement for the bitewings, stating the diagnostic radiographic images were "medically unnecessary" when documentation does not support the medical necessity of taking the images. When bitewings are taken at six-month intervals, be careful to document the reason(s) the images are taken such as *recent* decay or other caries *risk* factors. A caries risk assessment (D0601, D0602, and D0603) should be reported (often at "zero" fee) to support six-month intervals. Documentation supporting the exposure of 12 to 24 month bitewing radiographic images should be made as well. Diagnostic image guidelines for radiographic images may be found at www.ada.org/2760.aspx and are fairly conservative.

2. It is misleading to report extraoral panoramic radiographic image (D0330) and intraoral bitewing radiographic images (D0272, D0273 or D0274) as a complete series (D0210). Always report the panoramic/bitewing radiographic images *separately* as *taken*. The payer may "remap" this radiographic image combination to a complete (D0210) series as an alternative payment. This remapping typically occurs as a result of policy limitations and exclusions in the contract language. For further information on reimbursement policies, also see panoramic radiographic image (D0330).

COMMENTS

1. Many offices do not establish, maintain, and *enforce* proper bitewing image protocol as determined and *prescribed* by the dentist.

2. Most offices take bitewing radiographic images every 12-24 months; bitewings – two radiographic images (D0272) for children and bitewings – three radiographic images (D0273) or bitewing radiographic images – four radiographic images (D0274) for adults (second molars erupted) as an adjunct to diagnosis at the recall visit. This is the most *common* clinical protocol but no matter the protocol, the dentist must evaluate each patient and then prescribe which radiographic images, if any, should be taken.

3. Generally, age is *not* an issue for reimbursement of either three (D0273) or four (D0274) bitewing radiographic images. However, frequency limits may be age limited with some payers.

4. When the dentist orders a six-month bitewing image interval on a given patient, be sure to document the reason for taking the images (e.g., the presence of decay, history of caries, or other high-risk factors). The type, sequence, and frequency of diagnostic images should be determined by the dentist for each individual patient based on diagnosis, not based on the patient's plan benefits or limitations. Clinical notation in the patient's chart should reflect the dentist's diagnosis. For updated diagnostic image guidelines, go to www.ada.org/2760.aspx.

LIMITATIONS

1. There is generally an *annual* limitation for bitewing image reimbursement; however, some payers will further limit bitewing radiographic image reimbursement to once every 24 months. Some payers will reimburse bitewing radiographs twice annually for high risk children under 13 years old. The allowances are more generous for children as they are generally at a higher risk for caries. This determination is based on the plan purchased by the employer and by established dental necessity for the patient.

2. Many plans have a 12-month limitation exclusion for bitewing radiographic images after the exposure of a complete series (D0210).
3. Bitewing radiographic images are generally reimbursed as a preventive service at 100% of the UCR fee. A few payers reimburse as basic (80% of the UCR fee).

TIPS

1. Some policies reimburse for several periapical diagnostic radiographic images in *addition* to the three bitewing radiographic images (D0273) or four bitewing radiographic images (D0274) at the recall visit. Some offices report three bitewing radiographic images (D0273) or four bitewing radiographic images (D0274) in addition to several periapicals in order to monitor anterior areas of caries and/or periodontal disease. A caries risk assessment (D0601, D0602, and D0603) should be reported (often at "zero" fee) to support six-month intervals.
2. If the second molars have erupted for a child, consider four bitewing radiographic images (D0274).
3. Periapical (D0220/D0230) diagnostic radiographic images are most often the clinical choice at an emergency evaluation. If a bitewing image is reported on an *emergency* evaluation service date, bitewing radiographic images *may be denied* at the next recall service date, due to the "once per year/12 months" limitation, generally in effect for bitewing diagnostic radiographic images. However, this may not be true in all cases or when only *one* bitewing image is reported.
4. See gross debridement to enable comprehensive evaluation (D4355) for diagnostic image sequence options.
5. If 80% of prophylaxis counts are adults, then it would follow that approximately 80% of total bitewings would be three and/or four bitewing radiographic images.
6. Bitewings – three radiographic images (D0273) may be appropriate for the adult patient who is missing posterior teeth on one or both sides.

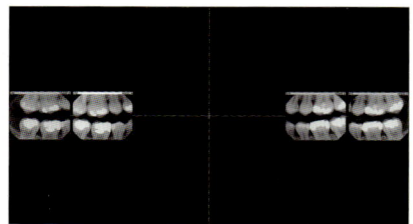

These are bitewings – four images.

Courtesy DEXIS, LLC and DEXIS®

D0277 VERTICAL BITEWINGS – 7 TO 8 RADIOGRAPHIC IMAGES — CDT 2016

This does not constitute a full mouth intraoral radiographic series.

LIMITATIONS

1. Vertical bitewing radiographic images (D0277) may be subject to the *complete series* (D0210) *limitation*, i.e., once per three to five years.
2. D0277 may be reimbursed as 4BWX (D0274) at a lower fee and subject to the contract benefit limitations (generally "once per year").
3. Vertical bitewing radiographic images (D0277) may be re-mapped by payers to a complete series (D0210) for reimbursement. Note that D0277 may be reimbursed at 80% of the full series UCR fee. Although the descriptor for D0277 states, "this does not constitute a full mouth intraoral radiographic series," payers may re-map this service. If this remapping occurs, include a copy of the D0277 code description with the appeal for documentation.
4. If D0277 is reported at a periodic oral evaluation (D0120) visit, this may reset the "three to five-year" limitation for reimbursement of a complete series (D0210). This reset occurs most often if the D0277 fee is 75-80% or more of the complete series (D0210) UCR fee.
5. There is generally an annual limitation for bitewing radiographic image reimbursement; however, some payers limit reimbursement for D0277 to once per 24-month period.
6. Reimbursement is highly variable.
7. If D0277 is reported within six months of full series (D0210), payers may *disallow* the charge considering it a part of the previous full mouth series.

TIPS

1. Some contracts reimburse for several periapical diagnostic radiographic images in *addition* to three bitewing radiographic images (D0273) or four bitewing radiographic images (D0274) at the recall visit. Some offices report four bitewing radiographic images (D0274) in addition to several periapicals in order to monitor specific anterior caries and/or periodontal disease areas. A caries risk assessment (D0601, D0602, and D0603) should be reported (often at "zero" fee) to support six-month intervals.

2. Some offices alternate four *posterior* vertical bitewings and three or four *anterior* vertical bitewings year to year for periodontal patients. This protocol provides complete diagnostic imaging on a two-year basis (more in line with ADA radiographic frequency guidelines) and is generally reimbursed without triggering contract limitation for either service.

3. The type, sequence, and frequency of diagnostic radiographic images must be ordered by the dentist, based on risk assessment and specific need, *not* based on the patient's plan benefits or limitations. Clinical need should be established and recorded in the clinical record, as well as the written assessment of the image(s) after they are taken.

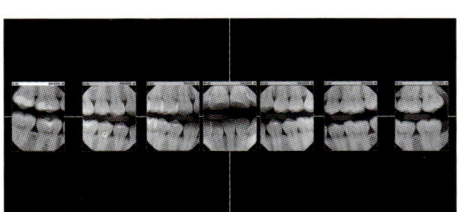

These are vertical bitewings – 7 images.

Courtesy DEXIS, LLC and DEXIS®

D0290 — POSTERIOR-ANTERIOR OR LATERAL SKULL AND FACIAL BONE SURVEY RADIOGRAPHIC IMAGE — CDT 2016

COMMENTS Posterior-anterior or lateral skull and facial bone survey radiographic images (D0290) may be payable under certain dental related conditions. Contact payer for specific policy requirements.

TIPS D0290 is sometimes reimbursed under "orthodontic records." However, the reimbursement may be deducted from either the patient's lifetime orthodontic benefits or general dental benefits. The claim form question, "Is this for orthodontics?" must be answered "yes" to be considered for orthodontic reimbursement.

NARRATIVES A narrative should be submitted with D0290.

D0310 — SIALOGRAPHY — CDT 2016

LIMITATIONS Sialography (D0310) is not typically reimbursed through dental benefits, but may be considered for reimbursement through medical insurance.

D0320 — TEMPOROMANDIBULAR JOINT ARTHROGRAM, INCLUDING INTERPRETATION — CDT 2016

LIMITATIONS Temporomandibular joint (TMJ) arthrogram (D0320) treatment services or diagnostic services are not typically reimbursed through dental benefits, but they may be considered for reimbursement through medical insurance.

D0321 — OTHER TEMPOROMANDIBULAR JOINT RADIOGRAPHIC IMAGES, BY REPORT — CDT 2016

LIMITATIONS Other TMJ radiographic images D0321 are not typically reimbursed through dental benefits, but they may possibly be considered for reimbursement through medical insurance.

D0322 TOMOGRAPHIC SURVEY — CDT 2016

LIMITATIONS Tomographic surveys are not typically reimbursed through dental benefits, but they may be considered for reimbursement through medical insurance.

D0330 PANORAMIC RADIOGRAPHIC IMAGE — CDT 2016

1. It is misleading to report or "upcode" an extraoral panoramic radiographic image (D0330) and bitewing images (D0272/D0273/D0274) to an intraoral complete series (D0210) if performed on the same service date. Although payers may "remap" or reimburse at a complete series fee level, the provider should not report a procedure that was not performed. If both (D0330) and (D0272/D0273 or D0274) are taken on the same service date, report the procedures separately. Report the procedure(s) performed on the date the service was performed. Note: It is not illegal or improper for an insurance company to reimburse a submitted code at a rate assigned another code. These alternate benefit reimbursements are explained in that plan's *contract language*. Payers routinely convert separately coded extraoral panoramic image and intraoral bitewing radiographic images to the lower, global complete series (D0210) UCR fee.

2. A panoramic radiographic image (D0330) is *extraoral*, not intraoral. A full series (D0210) is *intraoral*.

1. Practices should not have a protocol in place to delineate a specific time interval for the panoramic radiographic image (D0330). The panorex interval should be *individually* prescribed and ordered by the dentist. (D0330 is typically reimbursed every three to five years if deemed dentally necessary.)

2. Do not convert or "upcode" a radiographic image (D0330) and bitewing radiographic image (D0272, D0273 or D0274) to a complete series (D0210). A panoramic radiographic image is an extraoral radiographic image, not intraoral. A full series (D0210) is a set of intraoral radiographic images. It is improper/misleading to report a panorex and bitewings as a full mouth series. Report D0330 and D0274/D0273 or D0274 separately, as actually performed. The payer is allowed to re-map individual diagnostic images to a complete series code as an alternate reimbursement. The dental practice is not. The payer may do this in accordance with specific policy limitations and exclusions of the contract. The contract may allow:

    a. Conversion or re-mapping a panorex and bitewings to a complete radiographic image series (D0210) UCR fee. (A complete series is typically reimbursed at a lower fee than the panorex and bitewings reimbursed separately.)

    b. Reimbursement for the bitewing radiographic images and panoramic radiographic images *separately*. The best result.

    c. Reimbursement for a panoramic radiographic image only and *nothing* for the bitewing radiographic images. This is the worst result.

LIMITATIONS

1. Panoramic radiographic images (D0330) are typically reimbursed and payable every three to five years, depending on the specific policy limitations. The trend for many contracts is to reimburse the procedure every five years. If D0330 is taken in conjunction with bitewing images on the *same* service date, it is often converted or "re-mapped" by the payer to a complete series (D0210) and paid at the UCR fee for a complete series. The fee is generally lower than the combined UCR fee for D0330 and D0272/D0273/D0274 when filed *separately*. Some payers will reimburse D0330, while rejecting payment for the bitewing radiographic images performed on the *same* service date. Some payers will reimburse the full UCR fee for *each* procedure D0330 and D0272/D0273/D0274 *separately*, yielding the best result.

2. Most payers will reimburse either D0330 or D0210 during the limitation period, not both.

3. Panoramic image (D0330) may be considered to be a part of the orthodontic records. There are no specific codes for orthodontic records. D0330 may be reimbursed under "orthodontic records;" however, the reimbursement may be deducted from either the patient's lifetime orthodontic benefits or general dental benefits. The claim form question, "Is this for orthodontics?" must be answered "yes" to be considered a part of the orthodontic records.

4. There may be an age limitation applicable to the reimbursement for panoramic radiographic image (D0330). Some payers may require that a child be a minimum of five, six or seven years old to provide benefits for this service.

TIPS

1. Some offices take bitewing radiographic images on children at the comprehensive oral evaluation (D0150) and a panoramic radiographic image (D0330) (for growth and development studies) at either a subsequent operative visit or on a later recall service date, as determined by the dentist.

2. Reimbursement for a panoramic radiographic image (D0330) may be better when taken *alone* on a given service date than when taken in *conjunction* with bitewing films on the same service date.

3. Some offices establish a standard panoramic radiographic image (D0330) fee for two clinical situations. A lower standard fee for the panoramic radiographic image taken at the comprehensive oral *evaluation* (D0150) appointment in conjunction with bitewing diagnostic radiographic images. A higher standard fee for the panoramic radiographic image is established for a stand-alone panoramic image. (Set up a D0330A and D0330B fee to reflect whether the panoramic image is stand-alone or in conjunction with bitewings).

4. See gross debridement to enable comprehensive oral evaluation and diagnosis (D4355) for diagnostic radiographic image protocol options.

ADDITIONAL INFORMATION

1. Diagnostic images are *adjunctive* to the diagnosis process, and must be medically *necessary*.

2. Diagnostic images should be *individually* ordered by the doctor, following evaluation of the patient and performed for a *specific* reason(s). The justification for the radiographic image(s) should be documented in the chart.

3. Diagnostic radiographic images should be evaluated and *interpreted* by the doctor, and the indications *documented* in the patient's chart.

4. Read FDA/ADA diagnostic image guidelines at www.ada.org/2760.aspx or www.fda.gov/downloads/Radiation-EmittingProducts/RadiationEmittingProductsandProcedures/MedicalImaging/MedicalX-Rays/ucm116507.pdf. Important!

5. Poor and/or non-existing *documentation* of the dental necessity for diagnostic radiographic images may result in a demand for repayment of benefits for radiographs taken if audited by the payer, even though the diagnostic radiographic images were taken!

6. Radiographs of diagnostic quality should be dated and labeled in the patient's record.

7. Be careful to note the location, left and right (upper/lower), if not otherwise indicated by the radiograph to avoid review errors.

D0340 REVISED 2D CEPHALOMETRIC RADIOGRAPHIC IMAGE – ACQUISITION, MEASUREMENT AND ANALYSIS — CDT 2016

Image of the head made using a cephalostat to standardize anatomic positioning, and with reproducible x-ray beam geometry.

REVISIONS 2D CEPHALOMETRIC RADIOGRAPHIC IMAGE – ACQUISITION, MEASUREMENT AND ANALYSIS
Image of the head made using a cephalostat to standardize anatomic positioning, and with reproducible x-ray beam geometry.

Cephalometric radiographic image (D0340) is considered to be a *component* of orthodontic records. There are no global or specific codes to report *orthodontic* records. See also photographic images (D0350) and diagnostic casts (D0470). These procedures, added to the cephalometric image, typically constitute orthodontic records.

COMMENTS

1. WARNING! A cephalometric cannot be reported by a cone beam CT (CBCT). D0340 requires that the image of the head is made using a cephalostat to standardize anatomic positioning.

2. Cephalometric image (D0340) is often payable as a component of orthodontic records. For reimbursement of this code check "yes" in the box asking "Is this for orthodontics?" on the claim form. Also see diagnostic casts (D0470) and photographic images (D0350), which, together with a cephalometric image, are typically the components of the orthodontic records.

LIMITATIONS Reimbursement for cephalometric image (D0340) may be deducted from the lifetime orthodontic benefit. If orthodontic benefits are available the cephalometric image is typically reimbursed at 50% of the UCR fee. Sometimes the general dental benefit component of the plan will reimburse for orthodontic records separate from the orthodontic benefit. If reimbursed as part of the general dental benefits, D0340 may be paid at 50%, 80%, or 100% of the UCR fee.

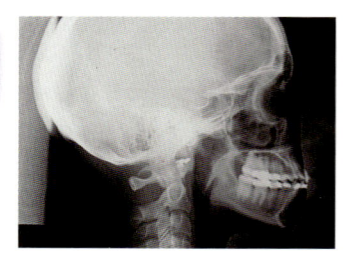

This is a cephalometric image.

D0350 — 2D ORAL/FACIAL PHOTOGRAPHIC IMAGE OBTAINED INTRA-ORALLY OR EXTRA-ORALLY

CDT 2016

CODING MATCH CORRECTION Each component of orthodontic records is reported separately. There are no global or specific code(s) to report orthodontic records. Oral/facial photographic images (D0350) are considered to be a *component* of orthodontic records. See also cephalometric radiographic images (D0340) and diagnostic casts (D0470), which are common components of orthodontic records.

COMMENTS
1. There are no global or specific code(s) for orthodontic records.
2. 2D oral/facial photographic images (D0350) are not typically reimbursed except as a component of orthodontic records.
3. D0350 includes both traditional photographs and images obtained by intraoral cameras. These 2D images are a part of the patient's clinical record. D0350 describes 2D oral and/or facial photographic images.
4. For 3D oral/facial photographic images, see D0351.

LIMITATIONS
1. The claim form question, "Is this for orthodontics?" must be answered "yes" to be considered a part of the orthodontic records. D0350 is considered to be a part of orthodontic records/workup and is typically reimbursed *once* per lifetime. See cephalometric radiographic image (D0340) and diagnostic casts (D0470) for further orthodontic record component details.
2. Reimbursement for 2D oral/facial photographic images (D0350) may reduce the lifetime orthodontic benefit. If orthodontic benefits are available these photographic images are typically reimbursed at 50% of the UCR fee. Sometimes the general dental benefit component of the plan will reimburse for photographic images separate from the orthodontic benefit. If reimbursed as part of the general dental benefits, D0350 may be paid at 50%, 80%, or 100% of the UCR fee.

TIPS
1. While payers do not generally reimburse 2D oral photographic images (D0350), practices can add "value" by charging a "zero" fee.
2. Intraoral photographs often provide documentation that is helpful in documenting claims. In particular, photographs can be helpful in documenting the need for soft and connective tissue grafts, crowns and onlays, core buildups, labial veneers, frenectomies, and apically repositioned flaps. If the problem is not obvious on a radiographic image but is seen on the photograph, by all means, send it.

NARRATIVES Photos are helpful to document cusp fractures, missing and undermined cusps, and cracks for onlays and crowns. Use a dye to emphasize the crack. Photos can also illustrate pocket depths (with probe in place) for periodontal documentation. Example narrative: "The photograph demonstrates a fractured mesio-buccal cusp that is not visible on the diagnostic film. Crown/onlay coverage is necessary."

D0351   3D PHOTOGRAPHIC IMAGE   CDT 2016

This procedure is for dental or maxillofacial diagnostic purposes. Not applicable for a CAD-CAM procedure.

CODING MATCH CORRECTION: There is no global or specific code(s) for orthodontic records. Each component of orthodontic records is reported separately. 3D oral/facial photographic images (D0351) could possibly be considered a *component* of orthodontic records. Also see 2D photographic image (D0350), cephalometric radiographic image (D0340), and diagnostic casts (D0470), which are common components of orthodontic records. 3D photographic image (D0351) might be used in orthodontic or some other diagnosis.

COMMENTS

1. D0351 can be used to document a dimensionally accurate 3D photographic intraoral or extraoral image constructed by the integration of multiple photographic images or laser scan.

2. There has been no specific CDT code for 3D visible light images previously. Such images are used independently or in conjunction with other diagnostic modalities D0393 (treatment simulation using 3D image volume) or D0395 (fusion of two or more 3D image volumes of one or more modalities). 3D photographic images may also substitute for images made using ionizing radiation for evaluation of facial appearance over time, especially following orthodontic or orthognathic treatment.

LIMITATIONS

1. 3D photographic image (D0351) is not typically reimbursed, but may be as a component of orthodontic records.

2. The claim form question, "Is this for orthodontics?" must be answered "yes" to be considered a part of the orthodontic records. D0351 might be considered to be a part of orthodontic records/workup and might be reimbursed *once* per lifetime. See 2D oral/facial photographic image (D0350), cephalometric radiographic image (D0340), and diagnostic casts (D0470) for further orthodontic record component details.

3. Reimbursement for 3D photographic image (D0351) may reduce the lifetime orthodontic benefit. If orthodontic benefits are available these photographic images are typically reimbursed at 50% of the UCR fee. Sometimes the general dental benefit component of the plan will reimburse for photographic images separate from the orthodontic benefit. If reimbursed as part of the general dental benefits, D0351 may be paid at 50%, 80%, or 100% of the UCR fee.

TIPS

1. While payers do not generally reimburse 3D photographic image (D0351), practices can add "value" by charging a "zero" fee.

2. A 3D photographic image may provide documentation that is helpful in documenting claims. In particular, 2D and 3D photographs can be helpful in documenting the need for soft and connective tissue grafts, crowns and onlays, core buildups, labial veneers, frenectomies, and apically repositioned flaps. If the problem is not obvious on a radiographic image, but is seen on the photograph, send it.

NARRATIVES 3D photos are helpful to document cusp fractures, missing and undermined cusps, and cracks for onlays and crowns. Use a dye to emphasize the crack. Photos can also illustrate pocket depths (with probe in place) for periodontal documentation. Example narrative: "The photograph demonstrates a fractured mesio-buccal cusp that is not visible on the diagnostic image. Crown/onlay coverage is necessary."

COMMENTS REGARDING CONE BEAM CT (CBCT)   AUTHOR'S COMMENTS

1. Cone Beam CT (CBCT) is a relatively new 3D imaging technology that provides a method to evaluate the anatomical positions of teeth and the makeup of the bone in a 3D image. An imaging unit (similar in size to a Panorex machine) has an arm that revolves around the patient's head in about 20 seconds. The CT acquires the axial, coronal, and sagittal data. The patient is exposed to radiation as the data is collected. An actual image is not produced. The data is captured and is stored, collated and compiled into a 2D or 3D data pack. This data may be retrieved, assimilated, and viewed at a later time.

2. 3D imaging allows a dentist to evaluate the exact position of impacted teeth, the position of third molars and their relationship to the inferior alveolar nerve or maxillary sinus, the osseous structure of the TMJ region, etc. While it has endless applications, it is the ultimate diagnostic tool for implant dentistry since the bony architecture and density of edentulous spaces can be clearly visualized.
3. Cone Beam CT scanning technology with 2D or 3D renderings allows the doctor to "see" critical anatomic structures for implant placement, oral surgery, orthodontic, periodontal, and TMJ procedures.
4. Even when listed as a benefit, coverage is determined by clinical necessity.
5. Situations where Cone Beam CT may be covered include:
    a. Impacted third molars positioned close to the inferior alveolar nerve.
    b. Proposed implant placement close to the inferior alveolar nerve or sinus.
    c. Proposed implant placement where there may be inadequate bone.
    d. TMJ abnormalities/pathology.
6. Reimbursement for Cone Beam CT's is highly variable.

D0360 — PREVIOUSLY DELETED CODE CONE BEAM CT – CRANIOFACIAL DATA CAPTURE

This is a previously deleted code. See other CBCT codes in this section.

D0362 — PREVIOUSLY DELETED CODE CONE BEAM – TWO-DIMENSIONAL IMAGE RECONSTRUCTION USING EXISTING DATA, INCLUDES MULTIPLE IMAGES

This is a previously deleted code. See other CBCT codes in this section.

D0363 — PREVIOUSLY DELETED CODE CONE BEAM – THREE-DIMENSIONAL IMAGE RECONSTRUCTION USING EXISTING DATA, INCLUDES MULTIPLE IMAGES

This is a previously deleted code. See other CBCT codes in this section.

D0364 — CONE BEAM CT CAPTURE AND INTERPRETATION WITH LIMITED FIELD OF VIEW – LESS THAN ONE WHOLE JAW — CDT 2016

COMMENTS D0364 reports both the Cone Beam CT *capture* and *interpretation* with a limited field of view – less than one whole jaw.

ADDITIONAL INFORMATION Important! See Author's Cone Beam Comments prior to code D0360.

D0365 — CONE BEAM CT CAPTURE AND INTERPRETATION WITH FIELD OF VIEW OF ONE FULL DENTAL ARCH – MANDIBLE — CDT 2016

COMMENTS D0365 reports both Cone Beam CT *capture* and *interpretation* with a field of view of one full dental arch – mandible.

ADDITIONAL INFORMATION IMPORTANT: See Author's Cone Beam Comments prior to code D0360.

D0366 — CONE BEAM CT CAPTURE AND INTERPRETATION WITH FIELD OF VIEW OF ONE FULL DENTAL ARCH – MAXILLA, WITH OR WITHOUT CRANIUM — CDT 2016

COMMENTS D0366 reports Cone Beam CT *capture* and *interpretation* with a limited field of view of one full dental arch – maxilla, with or without cranium.

ADDITIONAL INFORMATION IMPORTANT: See Author's Cone Beam Comments prior to code D0360.

D0367 CONE BEAM CT CAPTURE AND INTERPRETATION WITH FIELD OF VIEW OF BOTH JAWS, WITH OR WITHOUT CRANIUM — CDT 2016

COMMENTS D0367 reports both Cone Beam CT *capture* and *interpretation* with a field of view of both jaws, with or without cranium.

ADDITIONAL INFORMATION IMPORTANT: See Author's Cone Beam Comments prior to code D0360.

D0368 CONE BEAM CT CAPTURE AND INTERPRETATION FOR TMJ SERIES INCLUDING TWO OR MORE EXPOSURES — CDT 2016

COMMENTS D0368 reports both Cone Beam CT *capture* and *interpretation* for TMJ series including two or more exposures.

ADDITIONAL INFORMATION IMPORTANT: See Author's Cone Beam Comments prior to code D0360.

D0369 MAXILLOFACIAL MRI CAPTURE AND INTERPRETATION — CDT 2016

COMMENTS
1. D0369 reports both the *capture* and the *interpretation* of a maxillofacial MRI (magnetic resonance imaging).
2. MRI is a well-established FDA approved imaging modality that is used to obtain accurate depiction of soft tissues. Within dentistry, maxillofacial MRI can be used to examine the soft tissues in and around the temporomandibular joint and for evaluation of certain oral pathology conditions that may have soft tissue components. In some cases, both the capture and interpretation may be performed by staff at a hospital or radiology clinic. However, in some cases, the MRI capture may be performed at the hospital or radiology clinic and the interpretation may be made by a separate practitioner who has DICOM reading software.

D0370 MAXILLOFACIAL ULTRASOUND CAPTURE AND INTERPRETATION — CDT 2016

COMMENTS
1. D0370 reports maxillofacial ultrasound *capture* and includes *interpretation*. It is often performed in hospitals and radiology clinics.
2. Maxillofacial ultrasonograms may be used to evaluate salivary glands, swollen head and neck soft tissues, zygomatic arch fractures, and salivary gland function/Sjogren's syndrome. In addition, ultrasonography can be used to detect and view boundaries of soft tissue pathology and used for guidance of fine needle aspiration biopsies. They are often performed in hospitals and radiology clinics, but not necessarily so; however, reimbursement is not based on where the procedure is performed.

D0371 SIALOENDOSCOPY CAPTURE AND INTERPRETATION — CDT 2016

COMMENTS
1. D0371 reports both the *capture* and the *interpretation* of a sialoendoscopy.
2. Sialoendoscopy is an FDA approved method for examining the salivary gland duct structures. It requires special equipment which enables direct visualization of the salivary gland using visible light rather than ionizing radiation. It is used for diagnosis and as a surgical guide.

IMAGE CAPTURE ONLY — CDT 2016

Capture by a Practitioner not associated with Interpretation and Report

D0380 — CONE BEAM CT IMAGE CAPTURE WITH LIMITED FIELD OF VIEW – LESS THAN ONE WHOLE JAW
CDT 2016

COMMENTS
1. D0380 reports the Cone Beam CT image *capture* (only) with limited field of view – less than one whole jaw.
2. The interpretation and report is performed by a practitioner not associated with the capture.
3. The interpretation and report by another practitioner is reported by D0391.

ADDITIONAL INFORMATION IMPORTANT: See Author's Cone Beam Comments prior to code D0360.

D0381 — CONE BEAM CT IMAGE CAPTURE WITH FIELD OF VIEW OF ONE FULL DENTAL ARCH – MANDIBLE
CDT 2016

COMMENTS
1. D0381 reports the Cone Beam CT image *capture* (only) with a field of view of one full dental arch – mandible.
2. The interpretation and report is performed by a practitioner not associated with the capture.
3. The interpretation and report by another practitioner is reported by D0391.

ADDITIONAL INFORMATION IMPORTANT: See Author's Cone Beam Comments prior to code D0360.

D0382 — CONE BEAM CT IMAGE CAPTURE WITH FIELD OF VIEW OF ONE FULL DENTAL ARCH – MAXILLA, WITH OR WITHOUT CRANIUM
CDT 2016

COMMENTS
1. D0382 reports the Cone Beam CT image *capture* (only) with a field of view of one full dental arch – maxilla, with or without cranium.
2. The interpretation and report is performed by a practitioner not associated with the capture.
3. The interpretation and report by another practitioner is reported by D0391.

ADDITIONAL INFORMATION IMPORTANT: See Author's Cone Beam Comments prior to code D0360.

D0383 — CONE BEAM CT IMAGE CAPTURE WITH FIELD OF VIEW OF BOTH JAWS, WITH OR WITHOUT CRANIUM
CDT 2016

COMMENTS
1. D0383 reports the Cone Beam CT image *capture* (only) with a field of view both jaws, with or without cranium.
2. The interpretation and report is performed by a practitioner not associated with the capture.
3. The interpretation and report by another practitioner is reported by D0391.

ADDITIONAL INFORMATION IMPORTANT: See Author's Cone Beam Comments prior to code D0360.

D0384 — CONE BEAM CT IMAGE CAPTURE FOR TMJ SERIES INCLUDING TWO OR MORE EXPOSURES
CDT 2016

COMMENTS
1. D0384 reports the Cone Beam CT image *capture* (only) with a field of view for TMJ series including two or more exposures.
2. The interpretation and report are performed by a practitioner not associated with the capture.
3. The interpretation and report by another practitioner are reported by D0391.

ADDITIONAL INFORMATION IMPORTANT: See Author's Cone Beam Comments prior to code D0360.

D0385 MAXILLOFACIAL MRI IMAGE CAPTURE — CDT 2016

COMMENTS
1. D0385 reports the maxillofacial MRI image *capture* (only).
2. MRI is a well-established FDA-approved imaging modality that is used to obtain accurate depiction of soft tissues. Within dentistry, maxillofacial MRI can be used to examine the soft tissues in and around the temporomandibular joint and for evaluation of certain oral pathology conditions that may have soft tissue components. In some cases, both the capture and interpretation may be performed by staff at a hospital or radiology clinic. However, in some cases, the MRI capture may be performed at the hospital or radiology clinic and the interpretation may be made by a separate practitioner who has DICOM reading software.
3. Bill D0385 when capturing the MRI image only and sending it to another practitioner at a different location for interpretation and report.

D0386 MAXILLOFACIAL ULTRASOUND IMAGE CAPTURE — CDT 2016

COMMENTS
1. D0386 reports the maxillofacial ultrasound image *capture* (only).
2. Maxillofacial ultrasonograms may be used to evaluate salivary glands, swollen head and neck soft tissues, zygomatic arch fractures, and salivary gland function/Sjogren's syndrome. In addition, ultrasonography can be used to detect and view boundaries of soft tissue pathology and for guidance of fine needle aspiration biopsies. These are often performed in hospitals and radiology clinics, but not always.
3. D0386 should not be reported if the same provider performs the ultrasound and interprets the image. See D0370.

INTERPRETATION AND REPORT ONLY — CDT 2016

Interpretation and Report by a Practitioner not associated with Image Capture

D0391 INTERPRETATION OF DIAGNOSTIC IMAGE BY A PRACTITIONER NOT ASSOCIATED WITH CAPTURE OF THE IMAGE, INCLUDING REPORT — CDT 2016

COMMENTS
1. D0391 reports the interpretation of *any type of* diagnostic image by a practitioner not associated with the capture of the image.
2. A written report (i.e., record of findings) must be written and sent to the referring doctor to confirm the interpretation of the diagnostic images.

POST PROCESSING OF IMAGE OR IMAGE SETS — CDT 2016

D0393 TREATMENT SIMULATION USING 3D IMAGE VOLUME — CDT 2016

The use of 3D image volumes for simulation of treatment, including, but not limited to, dental implant placement, orthognathic surgery and orthodontic tooth movement.

COMMENTS
1. D0393 describes the use of the 3D image to simulate treatment for the dental patient.

2. Cone Beam CT is a relatively new 3D imaging technology that provides a method to evaluate the anatomical positions of teeth and the makeup of the bone in a 3D image. An imaging unit (similar in size to a Panorex machine) has an arm that revolves around the patient's head in 20 seconds. The CT acquires the axial, coronal, and sagittal data. The patient is exposed to radiation as the data is collected. An actual image is not produced. The data is captured and is stored, collated and compiled into a 2D or 3D data pack. This data may be retrieved, assimilated and viewed at a later time and place. When Cone Beam technology is used to produce a 3D image, that image may be used to simulate treatment. D0393 describes the use of the 3D image to simulate treatment for the dental patient. The technology allows the user to place implants virtually into the 3D image to help determine the size and position of that implant best suited for the application and to identify and avoid any challenges that may exist such as nerves, blood vessels, and any other unfavorable anatomy. Likewise, the 3D image provides the surgeon information about the position and location of structures that may be impacted during orthognathic surgery thus maximizing the end result while minimizing the possible risks by avoiding vital structures. Orthodontists may use the 3D image to maximize the result from appliance placement.

3. D0393, 3D image(s) to simulate treatment may be used:

   a. In the planning placement of dental implants to optimize biomechanics and to avoid damaging anatomic structures. In planning orthognathic surgery by stimulating the range of possible outcome esthetics.

   b. In planning orthognathic surgery by simulating the range of possible esthetic outcomes.

   c. To assess potential outcomes and to plan necessary surgical templates, stents, and retaining devices to expedite treatment and reduce the likelihood of complications.

4. Placing appliances, implants, and other prosthetic devises in the 3D imaging allows a dentist to evaluate that appliance in relation to the inferior alveolar nerve or maxillary sinus, the osseous structure of the TMJ region, etc. While it has endless applications, the CBCT image is the ultimate diagnostic tool for implant dentistry as the bony architecture and density of edentulous spaces can be clearly visualized. The procedure may be used to demonstrate soft tissue details of the skin surface in relation to underlying bony anatomy, or to demonstrate muscles of mastication from MRI images in relation to their points of insertion in the jaws and surrounding tissues, as shown by CBCT or multislice computed tomography (MSCT). It can also be used to fuse optical images to CBCT to have higher resolution and to avoid radiographic images artifacts, or the skin surface to CBCT, MSCT, or MRI volumes.

LIMITATIONS

1. Reimbursement for Cone Beam CT images is highly variable and may be limited to applications of a medical (not dental) nature. Even when listed as a benefit, coverage is determined by clinical necessity.

2. Situations where Cone Beam CT may be covered include:

   a. Impacted third molars positioned close to the inferior alveolar nerve.

   b. Proposed implant placement close to the inferior alveolar nerve or sinus.

   c. Proposed implant placement where there may be inadequate bone.

   d. TMJ abnormalities/pathology.

   e. Reconstructive or cosmetic surgery.

D0394 — DIGITAL SUBTRACTION OF TWO OR MORE IMAGES OR IMAGE VOLUMES OF THE SAME MODALITY — CDT 2016

To demonstrate changes that have occurred over time.

COMMENTS

1. Cone Beam technology allows the de-construction of an image by subtracting two or more image volumes. D0394 describes this "subtraction" process. When two or more images or image volumes are combined, see D0395. By systematically removing (subtracting) selected images or images volumes from the "hybrid" image produced by the fusing of two or more images or image volumes, the doctor can more accurately assess changes in the structures that may have occurred over a period of time. This information can be particularly important when determining the progression of periodontal disease, growth or reduction in the size of a lesion, or the status of site healing after surgery.

2. The procedure may be used to demonstrate soft tissue changes of the skin surface in relation to underlying bony anatomy, or to demonstrate muscles of mastication from MRI images in relation to their points of insertion in the jaws and surrounding tissues (shown by CBCT or MSCT).

3. D0394, subtraction of two or more 3D images of one or more modalities, may also be used to demonstrate changes during growth or subsequent to treatment. It can be used to assess the changes in facial appearance, jaw position, and also for measurement of airway effects from placement of a mandibular advancement device to treat sleep apnea.

LIMITATIONS
1. Reimbursement for Cone Beam CT images is highly variable and may be limited to applications of a medical (not dental) nature. Even when listed as a benefit, coverage is determined by clinical necessity.

2. Situations where Cone Beam CT may be covered include:
   a. Impacted third molars positioned close to the inferior alveolar nerve.
   b. Proposed implant placement close to the inferior alveolar nerve or sinus.
   c. Proposed implant placement where there may be inadequate bone.
   d. TMJ abnormalities/pathology.
   e. Reconstructive or cosmetic surgery.

D0395 FUSION OF TWO OR MORE 3D IMAGE VOLUMES OF ONE OR MORE MODALITIES
CDT 2016

COMMENTS
1. D0395, fusion of two or more 3D of one or more modalities, involves combining two 3D images of different modalities (i.e., CBCT data with MRI data) into a single image. Examples of use include precise registration of photographic images to Cone Beam CT volumes or fusion of CBCT volumes to MRI volumes to demonstrate soft tissue and hard tissue anatomy simultaneously. D0395 describes the use of Cone Beam technology to fuse two or more images or image volumes. The "hybrid layered" image can be used to evaluate the differences between the images or image volumes. By systematically adding (D0395) or removing (subtracting D0394) selected images or image volumes from the "hybrid layered," the dentist can more accurately assess changes in the structures that may have occurred over a period of time. This information can be particularly important when determining the progression of periodontal disease, growth or reduction in the size of a lesion, or the status of site healing after surgery.

2. D0395 describes the combining of two 3D images of different modalities (i.e., CBCT data with MRI data). Examples of use include the fusion of CBCT volumes to MRI volumes to simultaneously demonstrate soft tissue and hard tissue anatomy.

3. The fusion of images (D0395) may be used to demonstrate soft tissue details of the skin surface in relation to underlying bony anatomy or to demonstrate muscles of mastication from MRI images in relation to their points of insertion in the jaws and surrounding tissues (shown by CBCT or MSCT). It can also be used to fuse optical images to CBCT to have higher resolution and to avoid radiographic image artifacts, or the skin surface to CBCT, MSCT, or MRI volumes.

4. D0395, fusion of two or more 3D images of one or more modalities may also be used to demonstrate changes during growth or subsequent to treatment. It can be used for facial appearance, jaw position, and for measurement of airway effects from placement of a mandibular advancement device to treat sleep apnea.

LIMITATIONS
1. Reimbursement for Cone Beam CT images is highly variable and may be limited to applications of a medical (not dental) nature. Even when listed as a benefit, coverage is determined by clinical necessity.

2. Situations where Cone Beam CT may be covered include:
   a. Impacted third molars positioned close to the inferior alveolar nerve.
   b. Proposed implant placement close to the inferior alveolar nerve or sinus.
   c. Proposed implant placement where there may be inadequate bone.
   d. TMJ abnormalities/pathology.
   e. Reconstructive or cosmetic surgery.

TESTS AND EXAMINATIONS — CDT 2016

D0415 — COLLECTION OF MICROORGANISMS FOR CULTURE AND SENSITIVITY — CDT 2016

LIMITATIONS Collection of microorganisms for culture and sensitivity (D0415) is reported when testing the type and concentration of bacteria. For instance, D0415 helps confirm the endpoint of periodontal therapy, but it is rarely reimbursed.

TIPS Consider providing this test at a low fee as a value-added service to the patient.

NARRATIVES A narrative should always be submitted when reporting D0415.

D0416 — VIRAL CULTURE — CDT 2016

A diagnostic test to identify viral organisms, most often herpes virus.

COMMENTS
1. Viral culture (D0416) is not typically reimbursed by dental insurance.
2. D0416 may possibly be reimbursed by medical insurance.

TIPS Consider D0416 for OraRisk® HPV.

OralDNA® Labs
Innovations in Salivary Diagnostics
A Quest Diagnostics Company

D0417 — COLLECTION AND PREPARATION OF SALIVA SAMPLE FOR LABORATORY DIAGNOSTIC TESTING — CDT 2016

COMMENTS
1. Saliva sample (D0417) is for the *collection* and *preparation* of a saliva sample for laboratory diagnostic testing.
2. Saliva testing is currently being used to check hormone levels, cholesterol levels, drug levels, etc. Several new studies suggest that saliva proteins may also be used to detect oral cancer, HIV infection, and a host of other diseases beyond the oral cavity. D0417 can be used to report the collection and preparation of a saliva sample for laboratory analysis when it involves a technique-sensitive collection and preparation procedure.
3. For example, consider D0417 for: MyPerioPath℠, MyPerioID®, OraRisk® HPV tests.

LIMITATIONS Saliva sample (D0417) reimbursement is presently limited to reimbursement by the patient's medical plan. It is recommended that the claim be submitted to dental insurance, nonetheless, in an effort to encourage future reimbursement by dental plans.

NARRATIVES
1. Describe the purpose of the saliva sample and analysis to be done.
2. Attach diagnosis to claim. Do not file claim until diagnosis is confirmed.

| **D0418** | **ANALYSIS OF SALIVA SAMPLE** | **CDT 2016** |

Chemical or biological analysis of saliva sample for diagnostic purposes.

COMMENTS
1. Analysis of saliva sample (D0418) describes the chemical or biological analysis of a saliva sample for diagnostic purposes.
2. Several chairside saliva testing kits are now available to help dentists determine if the quality or quantity of a patient's saliva is a caries risk factor (e.g., GC America's Saliva-Check, Ivoclar's CRT Buffer Test, etc.). These saliva tests typically measure both resting and stimulated saliva production, saliva consistency/viscosity, resting and stimulated saliva pH, and saliva buffering capacity. These tests usually take about 10-15 minutes and are typically performed during the patient's routine oral evaluation. The results are immediate. D0418 can be used to report the use of these in-office saliva analysis kits.
3. D0425 may also be used to report saliva testing to measure caries susceptibility. D0425 differs from D0418 in that D0418 may be applied in a much broader context as D0418 includes the analysis of saliva for conditions other than caries. Historically, D0425 has not been reimbursed by most dental plans; however, some insurance industry insiders believe this is largely because claim submissions for caries susceptibility tests have been few in number. As more dental payers move toward a "preventive" dental reimbursement model rather than the traditional "restorative" reimbursement model, some believe that dental plans will be more likely to provide a benefit for a saliva-based caries risk test under code D0425 in the near future.
4. For example, consider D0418 for OraRisk® HPV.

NARRATIVES
1. Describe the chemical or biological analysis and the diagnosis.
2. The analysis report should be attached to D0418.

| **D0421** | **DELETED CODE GENETIC TEST FOR SUSCEPTIBILITY TO ORAL DISEASES** | **CDT 2016** |

This is a deleted code. See D0422 and D0423.

| **D0422** | **NEW PROCEDURE COLLECTION AND PREPARATION OF GENETIC SAMPLE MATERIAL FOR LABORATORY ANALYSIS AND REPORT** | **CDT 2016** |

1. The *collection and preparation* of the genetic sample are reported as D0422, separately from the analysis.
2. The *analysis* of a genetic sample is reported as D0423.

LIMITATIONS
1. Because D0422 is a new code and a relatively new service, many existing plans will not reimburse the procedure.
2. Payers that provide reimbursement for genetic testing may provide reimbursement for the collection and preparation of the sample while others may only provide reimbursement for the laboratory analysis. D0423 reports analysis.

NARRATIVES
1. Describe the purpose of the genetic sample and the analysis to be performed.
2. The analysis report should be attached to D0422.

D0423 — NEW PROCEDURE GENETIC TEST FOR SUSCEPTIBILITY TO DISEASES – SPECIMEN ANALYSIS   CDT 2016

Certified laboratory analysis to detect specific genetic variations associated with increased susceptibility for diseases.

CODING WARNING CORRECTION
1. The *collection and preparation* of the genetic sample are reported as D0422.
2. The laboratory *analysis* is reported separately as D0423.

COMMENTS
1. D0422 reports the collection and preparation of the sample.
2. D0423 (specimen analysis) is reported separately from the D0422 (collection and preparation) and may be performed by either the same practice or a different entity.
3. Genetic tests for susceptibility include: EasyDNA, MyPerioID®, DNA DrugMap™, etc.

LIMITATIONS
1. Because D0423 is a new code and a relatively new service many existing plans will not reimburse this procedure.
2. Payers that provide reimbursement for genetic testing may provide reimbursement for the collection and preparation of the sample (D0422) while others may only provide reimbursement for the laboratory analysis. D0423 reports analysis.

NARRATIVES
1. Describe the purpose of the specimen analysis.
2. Attach the analysis report.

D0425 — CARIES SUSCEPTIBILITY TESTS   CDT 2016

Not to be used for carious dentin staining.

CODING WATCH CORRECTION
Some practices erroneously report the caries susceptibility test (D0425) to describe a staining test for carious lesions; however, D0425 is a diagnostic test for the susceptibility of caries, not a stain to indicate the presence of caries.

COMMENTS
1. D0425 describes a diagnostic test that tests conditions like dry mouth syndrome or determines the patient's saliva pH using a litmus strip. This type of testing is typically not reimbursed.
2. Several chairside saliva testing kits are available to help dentists determine if the quality or quantity of a patient's saliva is a caries risk factor (tests are available from GC America's Saliva-Check®, Ivoclar's CRT Buffer Test®, etc.). These saliva tests measure both resting and stimulated saliva production, saliva consistency/viscosity, resting and stimulated saliva pH, and saliva buffering capacity. These tests usually take about 10-15 minutes and are typically performed during the patient's routine oral evaluation. The results are immediate.

3. D0425 may also be used to report saliva testing to measure caries susceptibility. D0425 differs from D0418 in that D0418 may be applied in a much broader context as D0418 includes the analysis of saliva for conditions other than caries. Historically, D0425 has not been reimbursed by most dental plans; however, some insurance industry insiders believe this is largely because claim submissions for caries susceptibility tests have been few in number. As more dental payers move toward a "preventive" dental reimbursement model rather than the traditional "restorative" reimbursement model, some believe that dental plans will be more likely to provide a benefit for a saliva-based caries risk test under code D0425 in the near future.

LIMITATIONS This type of test is typically not reimbursed.

TIPS In limited circumstances, such as presence of rampant caries, a caries susceptibility test (D0425) is sometimes reimbursed if the test immediately follows restorative care.

D0431 ADJUNCTIVE PRE-DIAGNOSTIC TEST THAT AIDS IN DETECTION OF MUCOSAL ABNORMALITIES INCLUDING PREMALIGNANT AND MALIGNANT LESIONS, NOT TO INCLUDE CYTOLOGY OR BIOPSY PROCEDURES
CDT 2016

CODING CORRECTION WATCH

1. Some practices confuse the adjunctive pre-diagnostic test (D0431) with oral brush biopsy (D7288, OralCDx®); however, D0431 is a visual cancer detection screening test, *not* a biopsy.
2. D7288 reports the separate brush biopsy which harvests transepithelial cells.

COMMENTS
1. A basic oral cancer screening includes a visual and physical evaluation. During a visual exam the dentist looks for abnormal color and texture. During a physical exam the dentist feels for abnormal lumps and bumps.
2. An enhanced oral cancer examination involves additional methods to detect mucosal abnormalities. VELscope® uses a special blue light to cause tissue fluorescence, which allows the dentist to differentiate between healthy and abnormal oral tissue responses. ViziLite® Plus with TBlue630® uses a chemiluminescent light source to improve the identification of lesions and uses a blue dye to temporarily mark them. The use of VELscope® and/or ViziLite® Plus with TBlue630® could be reported using code D0431.
3. This code also reports the use of staining (toluidine blue) as an adjunctive test. Codes are not brand-name or product-specific. Codes are procedure specific.

LIMITATIONS D0431 enhanced cancer screening (not diagnosis) tests are reimbursed by few payers.

TIPS If the result of D0431 is positive, the dentist may consider a brush biopsy (D7288), an excisional biopsy of oral tissue (D7286), or may refer the patient to an oral surgeon for further evaluation.

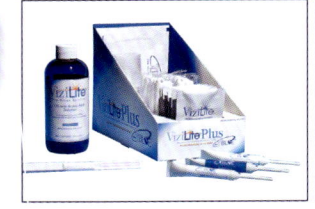

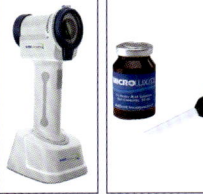

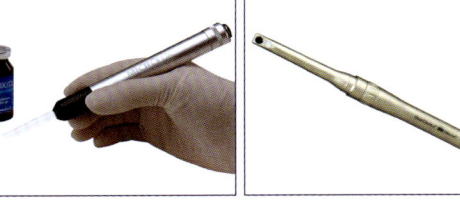

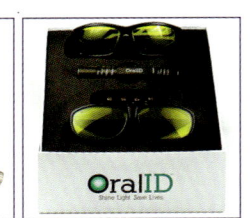

1. Vizilite® Plus — Courtesy Zila Pharmaceuticals, Inc.
2. VELscope® — Courtesy LED Dental Inc.
3. Microlux DL — Courtesy AdDent, Inc.
4. Identafi® — Courtesy StarDental
5. OralID™ — Courtesy Forward Science

D0460 PULP VITALITY TESTS — CDT 2016

Includes multiple teeth and contralateral comparison(s), as indicated.

CODING WARNING CORRECTION

It is considered abusive to report a pulp vitality test with crown preparation. The pulp vitality test should be performed when medically necessary.

COMMENTS D0460 includes the testing of multiple teeth and contralateral comparisons, and should be reported on a "*per visit*" basis, not a "*per tooth*" basis. Pulp vitality test (D0460) is a stand-alone diagnostic code.

LIMITATIONS
1. The pulp vitality test (D0460) may be reimbursed at an emergency visit when a problem focused oral evaluation (D0140) is *not* reported. Many payers will not reimburse for *both* D0460 and the problem focused oral evaluation (D0140) on the same service date. Many payers consider pulp vitality test (D0460) a component of the problem focused evaluation (D0140).
2. Some payers do reimburse pulp vitality test (D0460) in *conjunction* with emergency procedures on the same service date, such as palliative (D9110). Other payers consider D0460 *integral* to all services. Some payers classify the pulp vitality test as a basic procedure (which may be subject to a deductible). Some payers classify the pulp vitality test as a preventive procedure, and others consider it a component of the oral evaluation. Reimbursement for D0460 is highly variable.
3. If a definitive procedure is performed on the same service date as the pulp vitality test (D0460), the pulp vitality test is often considered to be a part of the global fee for the definitive procedure.

TIPS
1. Some payers consider a pulp vitality test (D0460) included with the palliative (D9110) procedure. Generally, only *one* of three codes (D9110, D0140 and D0460) is payable on the same service date with any related diagnostic images.
2. Regardless of reimbursement issues, D0460 is a *stand-alone* diagnostic code that can be reported *in addition* to other procedures performed.

NARRATIVES
1. When the "two evaluations per year" limitation has been met, pulp vitality test (D0460) may be reimbursed at the emergency visit as a stand-alone service.
2. Some payers require a narrative that identifies the suspect tooth and its symptoms, the teeth and contra lateral side tested, the methods used, and the results before considering payment for D0460.

D0470 DIAGNOSTIC CASTS — CDT 2016

Also known as diagnostic models or study models.

CODING WARNING CORRECTION

It could be considered fraudulent to report diagnostic casts (D0470) in order to gain reimbursement for an athletic mouthguard, tooth whitening trays, splint, or other appliance.

CODING MATCH CORRECTION

Diagnostic casts (D0470) are considered an individual component of orthodontic records. There is/are no global code(s) to describe orthodontic records. Report the individual components that make up the orthodontic record separately with individual codes. Orthodontic records could include photographs (D0350), diagnostic casts (D0470), and a cephalometric radiographic image (D0340).

COMMENTS
1. For an occlusal analysis of a mounted case, report D9950 in addition to diagnostic casts D0470.
2. For an occlusal adjustment, see both Occlusal Adjustment-Limited (D9951) and Occlusal Adjustment-Complete (D9952).

LIMITATIONS
1. Diagnostic casts (D0470) are not typically reimbursed and are generally considered *integral* to most procedures other than orthodontic records.
2. Reimbursement for orthodontic records may be applied to the patient's general dental benefits. These orthodontic records may include the diagnostic casts (D0470) and may be paid at 50% of the UCR fee. For reimbursement of this code check "yes" in the box asking "Is this for orthodontics?" on the claim form. Diagnostic casts (D0470) and photographic images (D0350), together with a cephalometric image (D0340), are typically the components of an orthodontic record. If reimbursed, diagnostic casts (D0470) are typically payable "once per case," per lifetime, in conjunction with orthodontic benefits.

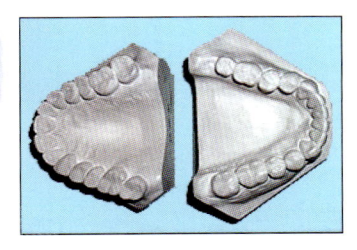

These are known as study models, diagnostic casts and diagnostic models.

D0601 CARIES RISK ASSESSMENT AND DOCUMENTATION, WITH A FINDING OF LOW RISK — CDT 2016

Using recognized assessment tools.

COMMENTS D0601 (low risk assessment) is used to describe the process of determining and recording the caries risk assessment of an individual during the evaluation process. Risk assessment is now considered a distinct/separate procedure and is described using codes D0601 (low caries risk), D0602 (moderate caries risk), and D0603 (high caries risk). A risk assessment tool is used during an examination of a new patient or of an established patient who has any of the following attributes:

1. Has not presented for periodic evaluations.
2. Has had a significant change in health conditions.
3. Manifests a risk of caries activity.

The ADA and other organizations have published information on caries risk assessment and have developed separate forms for dentists to use with child and adult patients. Although there are a variety of risk classification models, most recognize low, moderate, and high risk categories. The addition of risk assessment codes provides a means to record the service in a machine readable format that supports patient record keeping and transmission to third party payers and/or other providers.

Caries risk assessment includes the recording of clinical conditions, general health conditions and contributing conditions present, and evaluation of the overall risk status of the patient based on these conditions. It also includes the development of an appropriate preventive oral health regimen based on the overall assessment of caries risk. According to the National CAMBRA Coalition and American Dental Education Association Cariology Section, 100% of dental schools surveyed reported teaching caries risk assessment.

Some third party payers believe that risk assessment is part of an oral evaluation and do not plan to reimburse the procedure separately.

Recognized assessment tools include those established by the ADA and the AAPD and may be found by searching their websites. See: www.ada.org and search: caries risk assessment.

Conditions that affect caries risk may include:

- Poor oral hygiene (visible plaque).
- High titers of cariogenic bacteria.
- Prolonged nursing (bottle/breast).
- Poor family dental health or dental history.
- Genetic abnormality of teeth.
- Chemo/radiation therapy.
- Many multisurface restorations.
- Eating disorders.
- Drug or alcohol abuse.
- Smokeless tobacco use.
- Irregular dental care.
- High sucrose diet.
- Active orthodontic treatment.
- Exposed root surfaces.
- Overhangs and open margins.
- Physical or mental disability.
- Low socioeconomic status.
- Inadequate fluoride exposure.
- Medication or disease-induced xerostomia.

Caries risk assessment may ultimately be used to help determine the type and frequency of treatment allowed. The higher the caries risk, the more frequent the preventive schedule and more aggressive the treatment indicated.

LIMITATIONS
1. Most third party payers believe that risk assessment is part of a comprehensive oral evaluation (D0150/D0180) or periodic oral evaluation and do not reimburse the procedure separately.
2. A caries risk assessment code (D0601, D0602, and D0603) can be reported (typically at "zero" fee) when performed to establish medical necessity for reporting radiographic image frequency, adult fluoride, preventive resin restorations, and other procedures.

NARRATIVES Include a copy of a completed approved assessment form (attachment) with the claim. Submit D0601 where the caries risk assessment has a finding of low risk.

D0602 CARIES RISK ASSESSMENT AND DOCUMENTATION, WITH A FINDING OF MODERATE RISK — CDT 2016

Using recognized assessment tools.

COMMENTS D0602 describes the completion of the caries risk assessment for a patient resulting in a finding of moderate caries risk.

LIMITATIONS
1. Most third-party payers believe that risk assessment is part of a comprehensive oral evaluation (D0150/D0180) or periodic oral evaluation (D0120) and do not plan to reimburse the procedure separately.
2. A caries risk assessment code (D0601, D0602, and D0603) can be reported (typically at "zero" fee) when performed to establish medical necessity for reporting radiographic image frequency, adult fluoride, preventive resin restorations, and other procedures.

NARRATIVES Include a copy of a completed approved assessment form (attachment) with the claim. Submit D0602 where the caries risk assessment has a finding of moderate risk.

See D0601 for further explanation of the caries risk assessment process.

D0603 CARIES RISK ASSESSMENT AND DOCUMENTATION, WITH A FINDING OF HIGH RISK — CDT 2016

Using recognized assessment tools.

COMMENTS D0603 describes the completion of the caries risk assessment for a patient resulting in a finding of high risk.

LIMITATIONS
1. Most third party payers believe that risk assessment is part of a comprehensive oral evaluation (D0150/D0180) or periodic oral evaluation (D0120) and do not plan to reimburse the procedure separately.
2. A caries risk assessment code (D0601, D0602, and D0603) can be reported (typically at "zero" fee) when performed to establish medical necessity for reporting radiographic image frequency, adult fluoride, preventive resin restorations, and other procedures.

NARRATIVES Include a copy of a completed approved assessment form (attachment) with the claim. Submit D0603 where the caries risk assessment has a finding of high risk.

See D0601 for further explanation of the caries risk assessment process.

WARNING! Many of the Oral Pathology codes are positioned out of numerical order by CDT in the next section – Oral Pathology Laboratory. However, they are in the correct order.

ORAL PATHOLOGY LABORATORY (USE CODES D0472-D0502) — CDT 2016

These procedures do not include collection of the tissue sample, which is documented separately.

D0472 ACCESSION OF TISSUE, GROSS EXAMINATION, PREPARATION AND TRANSMISSION OF WRITTEN REPORT — CDT 2016

To be used in reporting architecturally intact tissue obtained by invasive means.

LIMITATIONS This procedure is typically not a covered dental benefit; it may be considered for reimbursement through medical insurance.

D0473 ACCESSION OF TISSUE, GROSS AND MICROSCOPIC EXAMINATION, PREPARATION AND TRANSMISSION OF WRITTEN REPORT — CDT 2016

To be used in reporting architecturally intact tissue obtained by invasive means.

LIMITATIONS This procedure is typically not a covered dental benefit; it may be considered for reimbursement through medical insurance.

D0474 ACCESSION OF TISSUE, GROSS AND MICROSCOPIC EXAMINATION, INCLUDING ASSESSMENT OF SURGICAL MARGINS FOR PRESENCE OF DISEASE, PREPARATION AND TRANSMISSION OF WRITTEN REPORT — CDT 2016

To be used in reporting architecturally intact tissue obtained by invasive means.

LIMITATIONS This procedure is typically not a covered dental benefit; it may be considered for reimbursement through medical insurance.

D0480 — ACCESSION OF EXFOLIATIVE CYTOLOGIC SMEARS, MICROSCOPIC EXAMINATION, PREPARATION AND TRANSMISSION OF WRITTEN REPORT — CDT 2016

To be used in reporting disaggregated, non-transepithelial cell cytology sample via mild scraping of the oral mucosa.

LIMITATIONS This procedure is typically not a covered dental benefit; it may be considered for reimbursement through medical insurance.

D0486 — ACCESSION OF TRANSEPITHELIAL CYTOLOGIC SAMPLE, MICROSCOPIC EXAMINATION, PREPARATION AND TRANSMISSION OF WRITTEN REPORT — CDT 2016

Analysis, and written report of findings, of cytologic sample of disaggregated transepithelial cells.

CODING WATCH CORRECTION This code does **NOT** report brush biopsy collection. See D7288 for the brush biopsy transepithelial sample *collection* procedure.

COMMENTS
1. D0486 reports the microscopic examination, preparation, and transmission of a written report based on transepithelial, disaggregated cell samples which could be obtained by brush biopsy or by another technique.
2. This analytical procedure, with the associated written report, generally is performed in a pathology laboratory and *does not* include the procedure for removal of the sample tissue.
3. This procedure is seldom performed by the dental provider, nor is the cytological study normally done in the dental office.

LIMITATIONS This procedure is typically not a covered dental benefit; it may be considered for reimbursement through medical insurance. When the service is provided by a laboratory, the lab submits the claim to the medical payer. The dentist only submits a claim for the cell/tissue collection.

D0475 — DECALCIFICATION PROCEDURE — CDT 2016

Procedure in which hard tissue is processed in order to allow sectioning and subsequent microscopic examination.

LIMITATIONS This procedure is typically not a covered dental benefit; it may be considered for reimbursement through medical insurance.

D0476 — SPECIAL STAINS FOR MICROORGANISMS — CDT 2016

Procedure in which additional stains are applied to a biopsy or surgical specimen in order to identify microorganisms.

LIMITATIONS This procedure is typically not a covered dental benefit; it may be considered for reimbursement through medical insurance.

D0477 — SPECIAL STAINS, NOT FOR MICROORGANISMS — CDT 2016

Procedure in which additional stains are applied to a biopsy or surgical specimen in order to identify such things as melanin, mucin, iron, glycogen, etc.

LIMITATIONS This procedure is typically not a covered dental benefit; it may be considered for reimbursement through medical insurance.

| **D0478** | **IMMUNOHISTOCHEMICAL STAINS** | **CDT 2016** |

A procedure in which specific antibody based reagents are applied to tissue samples in order to facilitate diagnosis.

LIMITATIONS This procedure is typically not a covered dental benefit; it may be considered for reimbursement through medical insurance.

| **D0479** | **TISSUE IN-SITU HYBRIDIZATION, INCLUDING INTERPRETATION** | **CDT 2016** |

A procedure that allows for the identification of nucleic acids, DNA and RNA, in the tissue sample in order to aid in the diagnosis of microorganisms and tumors.

LIMITATIONS This procedure is typically not a covered dental benefit; it may be considered for reimbursement through medical insurance.

| **D0481** | **ELECTRON MICROSCOPY** | **CDT 2016** |

LIMITATIONS This procedure is typically not a covered dental benefit; it may be considered for reimbursement through medical insurance.

| **D0482** | **DIRECT IMMUNOFLUORESCENCE** | **CDT 2016** |

A technique used to identify immunoreactants that are localized to the patient's skin or mucous membranes.

LIMITATIONS This procedure is typically not a covered dental benefit; it may be considered for reimbursement through medical insurance.

| **D0483** | **INDIRECT IMMUNOFLUORESCENCE** | **CDT 2016** |

A technique used to identify circulating immunoreactants.

LIMITATIONS This procedure is typically not a covered dental benefit; it may be considered for reimbursement through medical insurance.

| **D0484** | **CONSULTATION ON SLIDES PREPARED ELSEWHERE** | **CDT 2016** |

A service provided in which microscopic slides of a biopsy specimen prepared at another laboratory are evaluated to aid in the diagnosis of a difficult case or to offer a consultative opinion at the patient's request. The findings are delivered by written report.

LIMITATIONS This procedure is typically not a covered dental benefit; it may be considered for reimbursement through medical insurance.

TIPS Consultation on slides prepared elsewhere (D0484) may be considered and reimbursed as a consultation (D9310) in some circumstances.

NARRATIVES D0484 is by written report and requires a narrative. Include the written report with the claim to document the service.

| **D0485** | **CONSULTATION, INCLUDING PREPARATION OF SLIDES FROM BIOPSY MATERIAL SUPPLIED BY REFERRING SOURCE** | **CDT 2016** |

A service that requires the consulting pathologist to prepare the slides as well as render a written report. The slides are evaluated to aid in the diagnosis of a difficult case or to offer a consultative opinion at the patient's request.

LIMITATIONS This procedure is typically not a covered dental benefit; it may be considered for reimbursement through medical insurance.

TIPS Consultation (D9310), including preparation of slides from biopsy material supplied by a referring source (D0485), may be considered for reimbursement in some circumstances.

NARRATIVES D0485 is by written report and requires a narrative. Include the written report with the claim to document the service.

D0502 OTHER ORAL PATHOLOGY PROCEDURES, BY REPORT — CDT 2016

NARRATIVES D0502 is a by report code. A written report/narrative **must** accompany the claim.

D0999 UNSPECIFIED DIAGNOSTIC PROCEDURE, BY REPORT — CDT 2016

Used for procedure that is not adequately described by a code. Describe procedure.

NARRATIVES There is no code for a caries detectability test. Use D0999, by report. D0999 is a by report code; a report/narrative must accompany the claim.

D1000-D1999 II. PREVENTIVE

DENTAL PROPHYLAXIS

D1110   PROPHYLAXIS – ADULT

Removal of plaque, calculus and stains from the tooth structures in the permanent and transitional dentition. It is intended to control local irritational factors.

CODING WATCH CORRECTION

1. If gross debridement (D4355) is *necessary* to enable a comprehensive oral evaluation, the prophy (D1110), if applicable, should *follow* on a separate service date. See D4355 for details.
2. Full mouth debridement to enable comprehensive oral evaluation (D4355) will generally not be reimbursed if it follows prophylaxis (D1110) in sequence. See D4355.
3. If the patient requires *both an* adult prophylaxis (D1110) as well as a few teeth scaled and root planed (D4342), consider providing the adult prophylaxis at the *first* visit, then provide the D4342 on a subsequent visit.
4. There is no code to report a "difficult" prophylaxis. Modify the fee accordingly and report a D1110 if the visit is longer or perform two separate prophylaxis visits. Prophylaxis is the treatment for gingivitis.

COMMENTS

1. The D1110 descriptor includes the statement to "control local irritational factors." This procedure is to treat gingival inflammation (gingivitis) caused by irritational factors. If the periodontal tissue is healthy or has some level of gingivitis with *no significant loss* of connective tissue or bone loss, a prophylaxis (D1110) is indicated. Gingivitis is the first stage of periodontal disease and *may, or may not,* progress to periodontitis.
2. Adult prophylaxis (D1110) is *preventive* in nature and includes scaling and polishing of tooth structures with the removal of plaque, calculus and stains. The removal of all calculus and plaque above the CEJ is part of a prophylaxis. "Pseudo" pockets may be present, but there should not be bone loss or loss of attachment. If bone loss is evident and the root has access, see scaling and root planing (D4341/D4342). Instrumentation of the root with SRP is only possible when there is bone loss.
3. Do not report prophylaxis (D1110) for cleaning and inspection of partial and complete dentures. See D9932, D9933, D9934, and D9935.
4. A prophylaxis performed on a child having lost *all* his/her deciduous teeth should be reported as *adult* prophylaxis (D1110), regardless of age. The D1110 fee for a child who has no "baby teeth" may be adjusted to the lower child prophylaxis fee if deemed appropriate by the dentist.
5. Adult prophylaxis (D1110) does not include the application of topical fluoride. Report adult fluoride treatments, when applied separately from the prophylaxis paste, using either code D1208 or D1206. D1206 specifically requires topical application of fluoride varnish. D1208 would include any prescription strength fluoride product, excluding varnish (swish, trays, isolate, and paint-on). Fluoride must be applied separately from prophylaxis paste. See D1206 and D1208 for additional information and how to increase the odds of adult fluoride reimbursement.

LIMITATIONS

1. Adult prophylaxis (D1110) includes both *transitional* (mixed) and *permanent* dentition. Transitional dentition refers to a mixed dentition. Transitional dentition begins with the appearance of the permanent tooth and ends with the exfoliation (loss) of the last deciduous tooth. Permanent dentition refers to the permanent or adult teeth in the dental arch. Accordingly, *any* transitional dentition may be reported as an adult prophylaxis (D1110) regardless of age. Many payers will apply an arbitrary age limitation (typically at least fourteen years of age) before considering reimbursement at the adult prophylaxis fee level.
2. The ADA's House of Delegates has, in the past, addressed the "age issue" and has passed two resolutions that address this issue:

Age of "Child" (1991:635)

Resolved, that when dental plans differentiate coverage based on the child or adult status of the patient, this determination should be based on clinical development of the patient's dentition, and be it further resolved, that where administrative constraints of a dental plan preclude the use of clinical development so that chronological age must be used to determine child or adult status, the plan defines a patient as an adult beginning at age 12 with the exclusion of treatment for orthodontics and sealants.

3. Adult prophylaxis (D1110) is *not* reimbursed in *conjunction* with ongoing periodontal maintenance (D4910) or full mouth debridement (D4355) when provided on the same service date.

4. Adult prophylaxis (D1110) is typically reimbursed either on a "one per six months" (to the day!) **or** on a "two per year" basis. Please note that other exceptions can apply to the reimbursement of D1110.

5. See periodontal scaling and root planing – one to three teeth per quadrant (D4342) regarding the reporting of prophylaxis (D1110) and SRP (D4342) on the same service date.

TIPS
1. An adult prophylaxis (D1110) provided for a patient with *transitional* (mixed) dentition may be reported no matter the child's age, as long as there is at least one permanent tooth in the mouth. For example, an eleven-year-old boy with braces has "challenging" hygiene. In this scenario, the service may be reported as an adult prophylaxis (D1110); however, contract age limitations may be applied by payers. Alternately, the child prophy (D1120) may be reported in this situation and the fee adjusted accordingly. The plan limitations and reimbursement may vary widely from plan to plan.

2. The prophylaxis codes are dentition specific rather than age specific. When a single permanent tooth erupts into the patient's mouth, the adult prophy (D1110) code could be used to describe the prophylaxis service provided. The reimbursement, however, is usually subject to contractual age limitations.

NARRATIVES
1. Reimbursement for adult prophylaxis (D1110) is typically age specific and is determined by the terms of the insurance plan. Most payers set the "adult" age threshold at "14 or above." Some will begin recognizing the patient as an adult at "12 or above." A few payers begin to reimburse an adult prophy for those patients "16" years of age and older. A narrative stating "permanent dentition only" may help with the reimbursement process for patients who do not fall within the recognized "norms."

2. If the patient requires extra time (i.e., an orthodontic patient presenting with calculus, cements and bonding agents remaining after the removal of braces, etc.), report adult prophylaxis (D1110), in addition to an unspecified orthodontic procedure (D8999), with a narrative. PPOs will not reimburse for D8999, but some will allow the dentist to charge the additional unspecified D8999 fee directly to the patient under these circumstances. Review the contract language and the PPO's Processing Policy Manual to understand the limitations/exclusions.

FLOW CHARTS
1. There is no specific code to report a "difficult" prophylaxis. If a patient requires additional time or is extremely "challenging", perform one prophylaxis (higher fee and longer appointment) or schedule *two* prophys on separate service dates. With this approach the patient, if not part of a PPO, would generally pay out of pocket for the higher fee prophylaxis costs.

2. Some patients will present with heavy calculus and debris (but no bone loss) and will require more time than a standard prophylaxis. They are often referred to as a "difficult" prophylaxis. There is no code to report this type of prophylaxis. You may choose to provide a *single* extended prophylaxis (D1110) or two *separate* prophylaxis (D1110) visits. If two prophylaxis visits are required, inform the patient that only one will generally be reimbursed. Option #1 and #2 below describe the "difficult prophylaxis" scenario:

Option #1

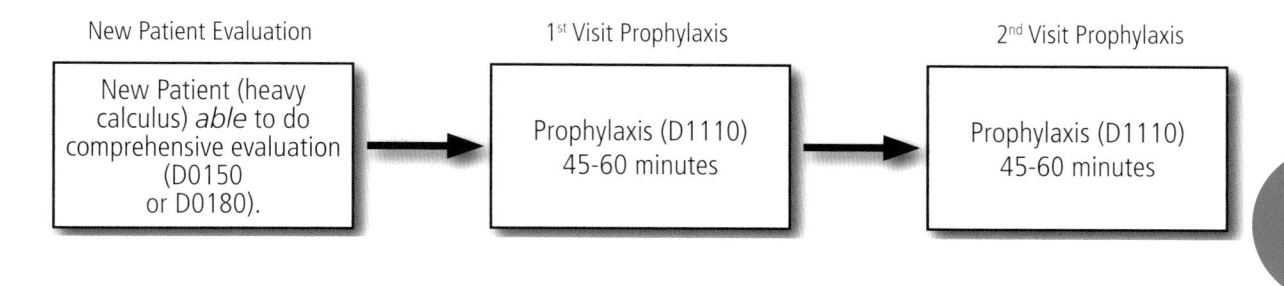

New Patient Evaluation → 1st Visit Prophylaxis → 2nd Visit Prophylaxis

- New Patient (heavy calculus) *able* to do comprehensive evaluation (D0150 or D0180).
- Prophylaxis (D1110) 45-60 minutes
- Prophylaxis (D1110) 45-60 minutes

Option #2

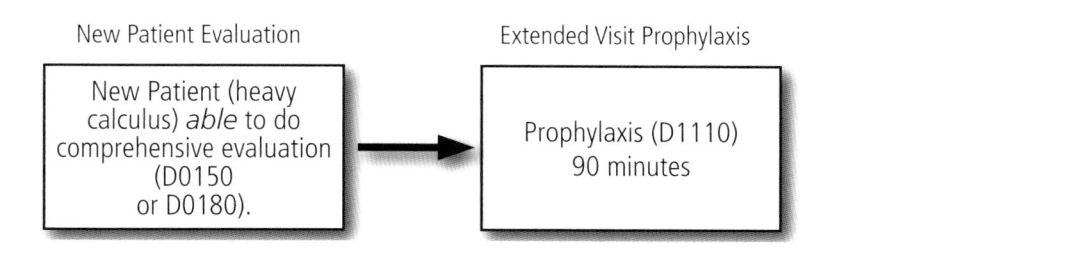

New Patient Evaluation → Extended Visit Prophylaxis

- New Patient (heavy calculus) *able* to do comprehensive evaluation (D0150 or D0180).
- Prophylaxis (D1110) 90 minutes

Notes:

1. If a comprehensive oral evaluation (D0150/D0180) *can* be performed, with heavy calculus and debris present, *two* adult prophylaxis (D1110) visits or *one* extended-visit (higher fee) prophylaxis may be required. The adult prophylaxis (D1110) fee may be reimbursed at the lower, contracted fee if the patient is covered by *a third-party contract (PPO)*, even though an extended appointment was required to provide the service.

2. If a comprehensive oral evaluation (D0150/D0180) is *not* possible due to excess calculus and debris, see full mouth debridement (D4355) which is performed to enable a comprehensive evaluation and diagnosis. This full mouth debridement is a *preliminary* procedure to enable the doctor to do an oral evaluation and is provided *prior* to the comprehensive oral evaluation (D0150 or D0180). See D4355 for details.

3. Adult prophylaxis (D1110) should not follow periodontal scaling and root planing – one to three teeth (D4342). If the patient requires *both* prophylaxis and a *few* teeth scaled and root planed (D4342), then consider the adult prophylaxis (D1110) for the *first* visit and the D4342 at a subsequent visit. Note: Some payers will not reimburse D1110 or D4910 within a 90-day period following D4341/D4342. See D4342 for further details and the flow chart below:

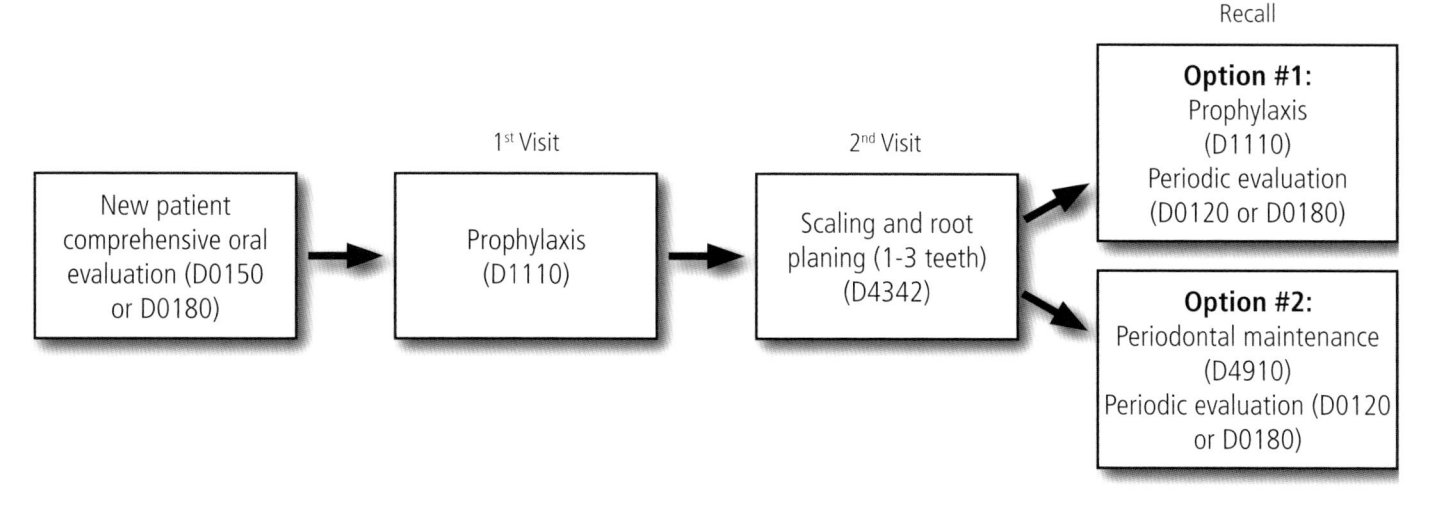

Recall

New patient comprehensive oral evaluation (D0150 or D0180) → 1st Visit: Prophylaxis (D1110) → 2nd Visit: Scaling and root planing (1-3 teeth) (D4342) →

Option #1: Prophylaxis (D1110) Periodic evaluation (D0120 or D0180)

Option #2: Periodontal maintenance (D4910) Periodic evaluation (D0120 or D0180)

Notes:

1. Following a single SRP (D4342) visit, if *very limited* pockets are involved, the doctor has the latitude to provide adult prophylaxis (D1110) for recall maintenance (should be more often than two per year). Be sure and document in the patient's clinical notes the isolated root planing (by tooth) at the adult prophylaxis (D1110) appointment and keep the patient informed of the "limited" periodontal treatment. On the other hand, ongoing periodontal maintenance (D4910) will most often be appropriate. Keep in mind that some payers will not recognize D4910 for reimbursement if less than two initial quadrants (D4341/D4342) were scaled and root planed (SRP). Sometimes D4342 does not qualify for recall perio maintenance (D4910).

2. Adult prophylaxis (D1110) will have a "one per six months" or "two per year" benefit limitation.
3. Be sure to read SRP 1-3 teeth (D4342) for additional details and how it relates to the adult prophylaxis (D1110).

D1120 PROPHYLAXIS – CHILD — CDT 2016

Removal of plaque, calculus, and stains from the tooth structures in the primary and transitional dentition. It is intended to control local irritational factors.

COMMENTS
1. Primary dentition refers to the first set of teeth. These are also called baby teeth, or deciduous teeth. Transitional dentition begins with the appearance of the first permanent tooth and ends with the exfoliation (loss) of the last deciduous tooth.
2. Child prophylaxis (D1120) may be used to report a prophylaxis of both *primary* and *transitional* (mixed) dentitions. On the other hand, an adult prophylaxis (D1110) reports both *permanent* and *transitional* (mixed) dentitions. See D1110 for further comments in reporting transitional (mixed) dentitions as an adult prophylaxis.
3. Child prophylaxis (D1120) does not include the topical application of fluoride. Report fluoride treatments, when applied separately from the prophylaxis paste, using either code D1208 topical application of fluoride or D1206, if fluoride varnish is applied. D1208 would include any prescription strength fluoride products excluding varnish (swish, trays, isolate and paint on). D1206 specifically requires application of fluoride varnish. Fluoride must be applied separately from the prophylaxis paste. See D1206 and D1208 for additional information.
4. Fluoride codes D1203 and D1204 are deleted. See D1206 and D1208.

LIMITATIONS
1. There are generally no age limitations for reporting child prophylaxis (D1120).
2. Child prophylaxis (D1120) may be reimbursed on either a "one per six months" (to the day!) **or** on a "two per year" basis.

TIPS If a patient with a *transitional* dentition presents with "challenging" prophylaxis, regardless of age, consider reporting adult prophylaxis (D1110). See D1110 for details of this scenario as it applies to the transitional dentition.

TOPICAL FLUORIDE TREATMENT (OFFICE PROCEDURE) — CDT 2016

Prescription strength fluoride product designed solely for use in the dental office, delivered to the dentition under the direct supervision of a dental professional. Fluoride must be applied separately from prophylaxis paste.

D1201 PREVIOUSLY DELETED CODE TOPICAL APPLICATION OF FLUORIDE (INCLUDING PROPHYLAXIS) – CHILD

This is a previously deleted code. See D1206 (fluoride varnish) and D1208 to report topical application of fluoride.

D1203 PREVIOUSLY DELETED CODE TOPICAL APPLICATION OF FLUORIDE – CHILD

This is a previously deleted code. See D1206 (fluoride varnish) and D1208 to report topical application of fluoride.

D1204 PREVIOUSLY DELETED CODE TOPICAL APPLICATION OF FLUORIDE – ADULT

This is a previously deleted code. See D1206 (fluoride varnish) and D1208 to report topical application of fluoride.

D1205 — PREVIOUSLY DELETED CODE — TOPICAL APPLICATION OF FLUORIDE (INCLUDING PROPHYLAXIS) – ADULT

This is a previously deleted code. See D1206 (fluoride varnish) and D1208 to report topical application of fluoride.

D1206 — TOPICAL APPLICATION OF FLUORIDE VARNISH — CDT 2016

CODING WARNING CORRECTION

1. Some practices erroneously report fluoride application when the prophylaxis paste contains fluoride. For reimbursement, fluoride varnish application must be applied separately from the prophylaxis paste.
2. Fluoride for home use should not be reported as D1206. See D9630 to report certain take-home products and see D1999 for unspecified preventive procedure.
3. D1206 should not be used to report desensitization. See D9910 for generalized desensitization procedure.

COMMENTS

1. D1206 reports topical fluoride varnish.
2. D1206 reports the therapeutic application of topical fluoride varnish delivered throughout the entire oral cavity in a single visit. The technique used for application is not specified, but *fluoride varnish* application is required to report D1206.
3. The fluoride varnish procedure may be reported in addition to a related prophylaxis (child or adult) or on a stand-alone basis. Fluoride varnish (D1206) may be applied and reported without having provided a prophylaxis.
4. D1206 is applicable to *both* children and adults.

LIMITATIONS

1. Fluoride varnish application, if a covered benefit, is often reimbursed twice per year; however, the reimbursement *trend* is once per year. Patients age 16 and older are generally not covered. In some cases, the limitation begins at 15 years.
2. In the past D1206 required that the patient have a moderate to high risk for caries. The code has been revised and a caries risk status is no longer required. However, some payers require a moderate to high caries risk to reimburse for adult varnish application.
3. D1206 may be reimbursed at a higher fee than D1208 with some plans.

NARRATIVES Some contracts may reimburse fluoride varnish (D1206) specifically for ages above 18, particularly if the patient is moderate or high caries risk. Be sure to note "high caries risk" in the remarks section of the claim form for adults. Confirm that a caries risk assessment has been done and is part of the patient's chart, and report D0602 or some other risk assessment code on the claim form. The D0602 moderate caries assessment code may be "no charge to the patient" and reported as no charge on the claim form. There is no "special" narrative for adult fluoride coverage. Fluoride is either covered or not in the plan document (15% of time).

D1208 — TOPICAL APPLICATION OF FLUORIDE – EXCLUDING VARNISH — CDT 2016

CODING WARNING CORRECTION

1. Some practices erroneously report fluoride application when the prophylaxis is provided using a paste containing fluoride. For proper reporting, fluoride must be applied to the teeth in a *separate* procedure afterward, apart from the prophylaxis paste.
2. Fluoride preparations dispensed for home use should not be reported as D1208. See D9630 for take home fluoride application and D1999 for fluoride toothpaste, toothbrushes, etc.
3. D1208 should not be used to report desensitization. See D9910 to report generalized desensitization.

CODING WATCH CORRECTION

The D1208 code does not specify the *specific* type of fluoride formulation or technique used for the topical application, but it does *exclude* fluoride varnish. For fluoride varnish, see D1206 to report topical application of fluoride varnish.

COMMENTS
1. Topical application of fluoride – excluding varnish (D1208) reports *any* fluoride application using prescription strength swish, trays, isolate and paint-on. The specific delivery mechanism is not important. The topical application of fluoride must be applied as a separate procedure apart from the prophylaxis. The fluoride formulation and application technique is not specified in this code description but it is assumed that the fluoride used must be prescription strength. However, the nomenclature of D1208 specifically excludes fluoride varnish.
2. If therapeutic topical fluoride varnish is applied, report D1206.

LIMITATIONS
1. Fluoride application, if a covered benefit, is often reimbursed twice per year. However, the reimbursement trend is once per year. Patients age 16 and older are generally not covered. In some cases, the limitation begins at 15 years.
2. D1206 may be reimbursed at a higher fee than D1208 with some plans. D1206 might be covered for certain plans whereas D1208 is not. On the other hand, D1208 might be covered for certain plans whereas D1206 is not. See D1206.
3. D1206 may be required for adult coverage, where covered in certain circumstances. See D1206.

OTHER PREVENTIVE SERVICES — CDT 2016

D1310 NUTRITIONAL COUNSELING FOR CONTROL OF DENTAL DISEASE — CDT 2016

Counseling on food selection and dietary habits as a part of treatment and control of periodontal disease and caries.

LIMITATIONS Nutritional counseling (D1310) is not typically reimbursed.

D1320 TOBACCO COUNSELING FOR THE CONTROL AND PREVENTION OF ORAL DISEASE — CDT 2016

Tobacco prevention and cessation services reduce patient risks of developing tobacco-related oral diseases and conditions and improves prognosis for certain dental therapies.

LIMITATIONS Tobacco counseling (D1320) is not typically reimbursed.

D1330 ORAL HYGIENE INSTRUCTIONS — CDT 2016

This may include instructions for home care. Examples include tooth brushing technique, flossing, and use of special oral hygiene aids.

LIMITATIONS
1. Oral hygiene instruction (D1330) is not typically reimbursed.
2. Some Medicaid programs may reimburse D1330.

TIPS
1. While payers don't generally reimburse D1330, the practice can "add value" by charging out the regular fee and then adjusting the fee to *zero* using a "professional courtesy" adjustment.
2. For legal and documentation purposes, make a note in the clinical record that, "oral hygiene instruction" was provided even if no fee is charged for the service.

D1351 SEALANT – PER TOOTH — CDT 2016

Mechanically and/or chemically prepared enamel surface sealed to prevent decay.

COMMENTS The differences between a sealant (D1351), preventive resin restoration (D1352), and resin-based composite restoration (D2391) are:

1. Sealant (D1351): Mechanically and/or chemically prepared enamel surface sealed to prevent decay. *The enamel surface is non-carious.* The global fee for a sealant includes a fissurotomy, as a part of the procedure.

2. Preventive Resin Restoration (D1352): Conservative restoration of an *active cavitated lesion* in a pit or fissure of a permanent tooth which *does not extend into the dentin*; also includes placing a sealant in any radiating non-carious fissures or pits. Patient must be moderate to high caries risk.

3. Resin-based composite-One surface, posterior (D2391): This is a resin restoration where the caries and preparation *extends into the dentin* or a deeply eroded area *into the dentin*.

LIMITATIONS

1. Reimbursement of sealants is generally limited to the occlusal surface of the permanent first and second molars. Some plans will provide reimbursement for sealants provided for permanent bicuspids; however, this is quite rare. There may be exclusions for sealants if the tooth has been previously restored with an occlusal restoration or if caries is present. Sealants are reported on a "per tooth" basis.

2. The sealant replacement exclusion varies from two to five years or to the lifetime of the insured. For sealant repair, per tooth, see D1353.

3. Sealant coverage for permanent molars varies, and may cover the period from eruption to 15 to 18 years of age. Some plans cover first molars only from age 6-10. Most payers have an age limit. The reimbursement for sealants is highly variable. It is recommended that sealant coverage be verified prior to placement.

4. Sealants typically are reimbursed as a preventive procedure. Most plans cover preventive procedures at 100% of the UCR allowance. Other payers consider sealants a basic service and some consider sealants under the "major" category of benefits. If considered a basic or major benefit, the reimbursement will be less than a 100% UCR fee, per the plan's benefit structure. There may be waiting periods, co-payments, deductibles, or other limitations that apply to sealant services. The reimbursement for sealants is highly variable.

5. If amalgams/composites are performed along with sealants on the same tooth, on the same service date, then the sealants are usually considered a part of the global amalgam/composite procedure.

6. Sealants may be applied to primary teeth but typically are not reimbursed.

7. Sealants are not generally covered for adults.

D1352 — PREVENTIVE RESIN RESTORATION IN A MODERATE TO HIGH CARIES RISK PATIENT – PERMANENT TOOTH — CDT 2016

Conservative restoration of an active cavitated lesion in a pit or fissure that does not extend into dentin; includes placement of a sealant in any radiating non-carious fissures or pits.

CODING WARNING CORRECTION

1. Do not report this preventive type resin *restoration* (PRR) if there is no active cavitated lesion (no active decay) in the enamel. See Sealant (D1351) for sealing the enamel surface and any radiating non-carious fissures and pits.

2. Do not report this preventive type resin restoration if the preparation and decay extends into the dentin. See D2391 for a routine resin-based one surface composite restoration where preparation and caries extends into the dentin or a deeply eroded area *into the dentin*.

3. Do not report this preventive resin restoration for a primary tooth. D1352 reports only a permanent tooth and the patient is a moderate to high caries risk patient.

CODING WATCH CORRECTION

1. The preventive resin restoration (D1352) requires that the patient be in the moderate to high caries risk category. The patient should have had a risk assessment performed and documented and classified as a moderate to high caries risk patient.

2. D1352 is a preventive resin (not amalgam) restoration restricted to the treatment of a permanent tooth. A PRR is used to restore a cavitated lesion in a pit or fissure that does not extend into the dentin or a deeply eroded area *into the dentin*.

3. The preventive resin restoration procedure also includes the placement of a sealant in any radiating non-carious fissures or pits of the treated tooth.

COMMENTS The differences between a sealant (D1351), preventive resin restoration (D1352), and resin-based composite restoration (D2391) are:

1. Sealant (D1351): Mechanically and/or chemically prepared enamel surface sealed to prevent decay. *The enamel surface is non-carious.* The global fee for a sealant includes a fissurotomy as part of the procedure, if it is needed. D1352 can only be reported for permanent teeth.

2. Preventive Resin Restoration (D1352): Conservative restoration of an *active cavitated lesion* in a pit or fissure of a permanent tooth which *does not extend into the dentin*; also includes placing a sealant in any radiating non-carious fissures or pits. The patient must have moderate to high caries risk.

3. Resin-based composite-One surface, posterior (D2391): This is a resin restoration where the caries and preparation *extends into the dentin* or a deeply eroded area *into the dentin*.

LIMITATIONS
1. Some plans will pay an alternate benefit of a sealant, while others will pay more than a sealant (up to twice the fee) but generally less than a one-surface posterior composite restoration (D2391).

2. If a PRR is denied, appeal by asking for the alternate benefit of a sealant, D1351.

NARRATIVES "Tooth #X had active cavitated lesion that did not extend into dentin." (Make sure a caries risk assessment form is in the patient's chart. The payer may request it or you may wish to attach a copy of it to the claim form).

D1353 SEALANT REPAIR – PER TOOTH — CDT 2016

COMMENTS
1. According to the American Academy of Pediatric Dentistry (AAPD), sealant maintenance and repair are an essential part of an effective caries-control protocol for susceptible teeth and moderate to high-risk populations. "Dental sealants may fail completely (i.e., no sealant material remains bonded to the tooth surface), but most fail incrementally, with partial loss of sealant material. When either occurs, reapplication of sealant material to the now unprotected caries-susceptible pits and fissures is indicated."

   This is consistent with accepted clinical sealant guidelines, including that of the AAPD, which states that sealant maintenance or repair is a clinical procedure distinct from initial sealant placement and which should be separately reported so that the clinical record remains accurate.

2. Electronic health records (EHR) necessitate that dentists have a way to document the services they perform whether dental plans provide a benefit or not. Some payers think the sealant code (D1351) should be reported whether a sealant is repaired or replaced since frequency limits will apply either way. Although many dentists tend not to charge for repairing sealants within a given time frame, the Code Maintenance Committee (CMC) determined that it is important to have a specific code that accurately documents the procedure performed.

3. D1353 provides a way for dentists to document and track sealant repairs separate from new sealants in their practice management system even if they repair them free of charge. This code allows dentists to track sealant repairs without skewing UCR fee data for sealants (D1351).

LIMITATIONS
1. The sealant *replacement* exclusion varies from two to five years or to the lifetime of the insured. If paid, a sealant *repair* may trigger the sealant replacement exclusion.

2. The same frequency limits for replacement will more than likely also apply to sealant repair (D1353). Expect poor reimbursement coverage for sealant repairs.

ADDITIONAL INFORMATION As an example of when D1353 could be reported: One year after placing dental sealants on the occlusal surfaces of the patient's four first permanent molars, clinical examination reveals that part of the sealant material bonded to the maxillary right first molar has been lost, exposing the pits and fissures to bacteria, oral fluids, and oxygen. The tooth is isolated, existing sealant material that is not well bonded is removed, the enamel surfaces are conditioned by acid etching, and the new sealant material is applied to the caries-susceptible pits and fissures.

D1354 — NEW PROCEDURE INTERIM CARIES ARRESTING MEDICAMENT APPLICATION — CDT 2016

Conservative treatment of an active, non-symptomatic carious lesion by topical application of a caries arresting or inhibiting medicament and without mechanical removal of sound tooth structure.

CODING WATCH CORRECTION

1. Report topical fluoride or fluoride varnish with codes D1208 and D1206, *not* D1354.
2. Resin infiltration of an incipient smooth surface lesion is reported as D2990. This is not reported as D1354.

COMMENTS D1354 reports the application and/or treatment of early non-symptomatic carious lesions using topical medicaments that either arrest or inhibit the progression of the lesion. The area treated would not be prepared (drilled) during this procedure. Caries arresting or inhibiting treatments of this type may include Ozone, Silver Diamine, etc.

LIMITATIONS
1. As with all new codes, coverage will vary among dental plans. Some government-funded plans (Medicaid) may provide reimbursement for this treatment.
2. This procedure oftentimes involves multiple visits. Dental plans may include all medicament application visits in the global fee of the procedure.
3. Reimbursement may be limited to treatment of primary teeth.
4. Some payers may require a moderate to high caries risk for reimbursement of D1354. If so, report D0602 (moderate caries risk) or D0603 (high caries risk). Typically, the fee for D0602/D0603 is zero.
5. Reimbursement of these treatments may preclude reimbursement for subsequent definitive restorations placed on the same tooth.
6. Some plans could pay an alternate benefit of fluoride varnish (D1206).

NARRATIVES "Tooth X had a non-symptomatic carious lesion." It should also be noted why D1354 was provided rather than a definitive restoration. The clinical record should clearly document the caries diagnosis, indicating an active, non-symptomatic carious lesion. Include the caries risk assessment determination. Some payers may require a copy of this form and the appropriate caries risk code (D0601, D0602, and D0603) on the claim.

SPACE MAINTENANCE (PASSIVE APPLIANCES) — CDT 2016

Passive appliances are designed to prevent tooth movement.

D1510 — SPACE MAINTAINER – FIXED – UNILATERAL — CDT 2016

COMMENTS
1. A space maintainer is considered a *passive* (not active) appliance. No teeth are moved or space regained with a space maintainer. Space is held, not gained by this type of "holding" fixed appliance.
2. Any stainless steel crown or orthodontic band that is part of a fixed space maintainer is generally included in the space maintainer fee.
3. When a unilateral space maintainer is re-cemented, see D1550.
4. To report a fixed *bilateral* space maintainer, see D1515.

LIMITATIONS
1. Passive space maintainers often have an age limitation from 14-18 years.

2. *Removal* of the fixed – unilateral space maintainer (D1510) is not typically reimbursed for the doctor (or office) who initially placed the space maintainer. If the space maintainer is removed by a different office, the service may be payable. To report removal of a fixed unilateral space maintainer, see D1555.

3. Repair or replacement of a fixed unilateral space maintainer (D1510) is not typically reimbursed.

4. The space maintainer – fixed – unilateral (D1510) is often referred to as a "band and loop" or "crown and loop" fixed appliance. D1510 is generally not reimbursed to maintain space solely for missing primary centrals/laterals/canines. Reimbursement for space maintenance generally requires missing primary first or secondary molars (or permanent molars).

5. D1510 is typically reimbursed on a "once per quadrant" per lifetime basis. If reimbursed, the procedure is typically considered preventive in nature and is reimbursed at 100% of UCR allowance and not subject to the plan's deductible.

NARRATIVES The quadrant should be documented on the claim form, along with the missing tooth number(s).

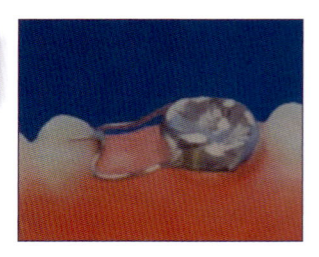

1. This is a fixed, unilateral space maintainer.
2. This fixed type of space maintainer is commonly referred to as a "crown and loop."

Courtesy Space Maintainers Lab

D1515 SPACE MAINTAINER – FIXED – BILATERAL   CDT 2016

CODING WARNING CORRECTION It is misleading to report a fixed pediatric cosmetic partial (with anterior teeth) as a space maintainer – fixed-bilateral (D1515), without a narrative disclosing the true nature of the cosmetic service. See D6985 for further details concerning a fixed pediatric partial placed for cosmetic purposes.

COMMENTS
1. A space maintainer is considered a *passive* (not active) appliance. No teeth are moved or space regained with a space maintainer. Space is held, not gained by this type of "holding" fixed appliance.
2. Any stainless steel crown or orthodontic band that is a part of a fixed space maintainer is generally included in the space maintainer fee.
3. When a fixed bilateral space maintainer is re-cemented, see D1550.
4. To report a fixed *unilateral* space maintainer, see D1510.

LIMITATIONS
1. Passive space maintainers often have an age limitation from 14-18 years.
2. *Removal* of the fixed – bilateral space maintainer (D1515) is not typically reimbursed for the doctor (or office) who initially placed the space maintainer. If the space maintainer is removed by a different office, the service may be payable. For removal of a fixed bilateral space maintainer, see D1555.
3. Repair or replacement of a fixed bilateral space maintainer (D1515) is not typically reimbursed.
4. D1515 is often referred to as a "lingual arch" fixed bilateral space maintainer. D1515 is generally not reimbursed to maintain space solely for missing primary centrals/laterals/canines. Reimbursement for space maintenance generally requires missing primary first or secondary molars (or permanent molars).
5. D1515 is typically reimbursed on a "once per arch" per lifetime basis. If reimbursed, the procedure is typically considered preventive in nature and is reimbursed at 100% of the UCR allowance and not subject to the plan's deductible..

NARRATIVES The arch (upper or lower) should be identified on the claim form, along with the missing tooth number(s).

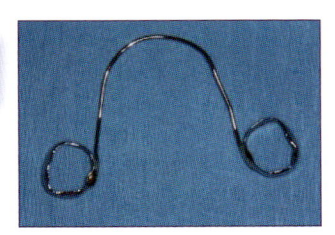

1. This is a fixed bilateral space maintainer.
2. This fixed type of space maintainer is commonly referred to as a "lingual arch."

Courtesy Dr. Jill Spurlin

D1520 — SPACE MAINTAINER – REMOVABLE – UNILATERAL — CDT 2016

COMMENTS
1. A space maintainer is considered a *passive* (not active) appliance. No teeth are moved or space regained with a space maintainer. Space is held, not gained by this type of passive appliance.
2. A removable space maintainer could be placed in an adult (to stop the shifting of teeth) but would generally not be reimbursed.

LIMITATIONS
1. Passive space maintainers often have an age limitation from 14-18 years. To be reimbursed, either the primary first or second molar, or permanent first molar must generally be missing. A missing primary central, lateral incisor or cuspid will often not be reimbursed per plan limitations.
2. *Repair or replacement* of a removable unilateral space maintainer (D1520) is not typically reimbursed.
3. Space maintainers are typically a one-time only benefit. The space maintainer – removable – unilateral (D1520) is typically reimbursed on a "once per quadrant" per lifetime basis.
4. If reimbursed, the removable space maintainer service is typically considered preventive in nature and is reimbursed at 100% of the UCR allowance and not subject to the plans deductible.

NARRATIVES The quadrant should be documented on the claim form, along with the missing tooth number(s).

D1525 — SPACE MAINTAINER – REMOVABLE – BILATERAL — CDT 2016

COMMENTS
1. A space maintainer is considered a *passive* (not active) appliance. No teeth are moved or space regained with a space maintainer. Space is held, not gained by this type of passive appliance.
2. A removable space maintainer could be placed in an adult (to stop the shifting of teeth) but would generally not be reimbursed.

LIMITATIONS
1. Passive space maintainers often have an age limitation from 14-18 years. To be reimbursed, either the primary first or second molar, or permanent first molar must generally be missing. A missing primary central, lateral incisor or cuspid will often not be reimbursed per plan limitations.
2. *Repair or replacement* of a removable space maintainer (D1525) is not typically reimbursed.
3. Space maintainers are typically a one-time only benefit. The space maintainer – removable – bilateral (D1525) is typically reimbursed on a "once per quadrant" per lifetime basis.
4. If reimbursed, the removable space maintainer service is typically considered preventive in nature and is reimbursed at 100% of the UCR allowance and is not subject to the plan's deductible.

NARRATIVES The arch (upper or lower) should be documented on the claim form, along with the missing tooth number(s).

D1550 — RE-CEMENT OR RE-BOND SPACE MAINTAINER — CDT 2016

CODING MATCH CORRECTION

Re-cement or re-bond space maintainer (D1550) describes the re-cementation or re-bonding of a *fixed* unilateral space maintainer (D1510) or a *fixed* bilateral space maintainer (D1515).

LIMITATIONS
1. Reimbursement for D1550, re-cementation or re-bonding of a space maintainer may be limited to a period of more than six months after the original placement date. Reimbursement for the re-cement or re-bond of a space maintainer (D1550) may be made to the same doctor or office who originally placed the space maintainer if the appliance is re-cemented or re-bonded at some interval six months after the original placement date.
2. If a different office re-cements or re-bonds a space maintainer, the exclusion period from the original placement date might be waived.

NARRATIVES
1. The narrative should include the initial placement date, who placed the space maintainer and the reason for the re-cement or re-bond.
2. Re-cement or re-bond space maintainer (D1550) is typically reimbursed if performed by a different doctor (in a different office) by some payers. The narrative should state that the office who re-cemented or re-bonded the space maintainer is a different office than the one who originally provided the space maintainer.

D1555 — REMOVAL OF FIXED SPACE MAINTAINER — CDT 2016

Procedure delivered by a dentist who did not originally place the appliance, or by the practice where the appliance was originally delivered to the patient.

CODING WATCH CORRECTION

1. Removal of fixed space maintainer (D1555) may be reimbursed if removed by a provider/practice other than the provider/practice who originally placed the space maintainer.
2. Removal of fixed space maintainer (D1555) may be used to report the removal of:
   a. A fixed bilateral space maintainer (D1515).
   b. A fixed unilateral space maintainer (D1510).
   c. Orthodontic fixed retention appliances.

COMMENTS D1555 describes the removal of a bonded or cemented, fixed unilateral (D1510) or bilateral space maintainer (D1515) by a dentist (or practice) who did not originally place the appliance.

LIMITATIONS
1. Removal of a fixed space maintainer may not be reimbursed if removed by the same dentist or practice who originally delivered and cemented the appliance. Only a different dentist (not in the same office) or practice should report this procedure.
2. Removal of fixed space maintainer is considered as part of the overall fee for the space maintainer if removed by the dentist/practice who placed the space maintainer.

NARRATIVES
1. If D1555 is denied when a dentist/practice other than the dentist/practice who placed the spacer removes the appliance, and the removal occurred at an emergency visit, appeal and ask for an alternate benefit, palliative (D9110). See D9110 for further details.
2. The narrative should include the initial placement date, who placed the space maintainer, and the reason for the removal by a practice other than who placed it.

D1999 — REVISED UNSPECIFIED PREVENTIVE PROCEDURE, BY REPORT — CDT 2016

Used for procedure that is not adequately described by another CDT Code. Describe procedure.

REVISIONS Used for procedure that is not adequately described by another CDT Code. Describe procedure.

COMMENTS
1. D1999 is an unspecified code used to describe any preventive procedure that is not described by an existing preventive code.
2. The following is a list of unspecified preventive procedures that do not have an existing code to describe them. Report D1999, by report. The list is not exhaustive but may include:
   a. Distribution of prescription-strength fluoride toothpaste.
   b. Distribution of xylitol products and floss.
   c. Distribution of cleaning devices such as tooth brushes, inter-dental cleaners, and floss threaders.
3. For oral antibiotics, oral analgesics, and prescription-strength topical fluoride dispensed in the office for home use, report D9630. Since D9630 is for other drugs and/or medicaments, by report, then D9630 can also be used to report take home chlorhexidine and Peridex®.
4. To report an in-office treatment for root sensitivity in conjunction with SRP or prophylaxis procedures, see D9910 which reports an application of desensitizing medicament for a single tooth, or up to the whole mouth.
5. Chlorhexidine used for gingival irrigation-per quadrant should be reported as D4921. See D4921.

LIMITATIONS D1999, Unspecified preventive procedure, by report will not generally be reimbursed. Most states require a sales tax on products sold separately from dental services. See Sales Tax (D9985).

NOTES

Go to www.practicebooster.com to learn about the Revenue Enhancement Program, a coding and fee positioning consultation for you and your staff.
Cut coding errors and maximize legitimate reimbursement!
Tel: (866) 858-7596; Fax: (855) 825-3960; info@drcharlesblair.com

D2000-D2999 III. RESTORATIVE — CDT 2016

Local anesthesia is usually considered to be part of Restorative procedures.

EXPLANATION OF RESTORATIONS — CDT 2016

Anterior 1-Surface – Placed on one of the following five surface classifications – Mesial, Distal, Incisal, Lingual, or Labial.

Anterior 2-Surface – Placed, without interruption, on two of the five surface classifications – e.g., Mesial-Lingual.

Anterior 3-Surface – Placed, without interruption, on three of the five surface classifications – e.g., Lingual-Mesial-Labial.

Anterior 4 or more-Surface – Placed, without interruption, on four or more of the five surface classifications – e.g., Mesial-Incisal-Lingual-Labial.

Posterior 1-Surface – Placed on one of the following five surface classifications – Mesial, Distal, Occlusal, Lingual, or Buccal.

Posterior 2-Surface – Placed, without interruption, on two of the five surface classifications – e.g., Mesial-Occlusal.

Posterior 3-Surface – Placed, without interruption, on three of the five surface classifications – e.g., Lingual-Occlusal-Distal.

Posterior 4 or more-Surface – Placed, without interruption, on four or more of the five surface classifications – e.g., Mesial-Occlusal-Lingual-Distal.

AMALGAM RESTORATIONS (INCLUDING POLISHING) — CDT 2016

Tooth preparation, all adhesives (including amalgam bonding agents), liners and bases are included as part of the restoration. If pins are used, they should be reported separately (see D2951).

D2140 AMALGAM – ONE SURFACE, PRIMARY OR PERMANENT — CDT 2016

1. It is misleading to report an amalgam restoration as a filling if the *caries* and *preparation do not* extend into the *dentin* and/or fracture is not involved. Restoration of an active cavitated lesion where the filling material is placed in *enamel* only (not extending into the dentin) is considered a preventive resin restoration (D1352).

2. All bases, liners, adhesives, etching, polishing, contact and occlusal adjustments, and the use of caries detection agents are included in the overall amalgam restoration fee. If a pulp cap (D3110/D3120) is reported with an amalgam restoration placed on the same date of service, payers consider the pulp cap (as a base or liner) part of the restoration procedure. A pulp cap's purpose (promotion of *healing* and *repair*) is to assist in the formation of secondary dentin and may be billed separately. A routine base or liner decreases sensitivity and protects the pulp. Pulp caps promote healing (secondary dentin) and repair. (See D3110/D3120 for further details.)

3. It is necessary to disclose the reason for a restoration if its purpose is to treat abfraction, erosion, wear, abrasion, attrition, or to improve esthetics/cosmetics. These situations are addressed in, and limited by, most third-party contracts. Most payers require that *decay* and/or *fracture* be present to justify reimbursement for a restoration.

4. It is misleading to report amalgam restorations built to full contour as core buildups (D2950). Core buildups (after the tooth is fully prepared) are justified when they are necessary for the *retention* of the crown. A core buildup is followed by a temporary crown placement or final restoration.

5. When two or more separate restorations are performed on the same tooth on the same date of service, report each restoration *separately*. Reporting separate restorations on the same tooth is *not* considered unbundling. Always "report what you do." Note that many payers will limit reimbursement for restorations placed on the same tooth surface on the same service date.

COMMENTS
1. Cervical restorations that extend into the dentin are typically considered a one surface restoration.
2. Report pins separately. See D2951. For pulp caps, see D3110 or D3120.

LIMITATIONS 1. The exclusion period for replacement of amalgam restorations is typically 24 to 36 months, depending on the contract. In some circumstances involving accidents, new caries, or radiation therapy the typical limitations may not apply. Should one of these situations exist and the reimbursement for the replaced restoration denied, appeal with a written narrative explaining the dental necessity. If a restoration is replaced within the limitation period by a different provider, the new provider may be reimbursed. This, however, is dependent upon contract language.

2. Reimbursement for removing and replacing defective restorations may require that the treated tooth have decay, open margins, and/or fracture.

TIPS Report D2140 when restoring an endodontic access opening or the access opening for the internal bleaching (D9974) of a natural tooth. Do not report core buildup (D2950) or prefabricated post and core when restoring and closing an endodontic access opening. Core buildups and prefabricated post and core are reimbursable when they are necessary for the *retention* of the crown, not for closure of an endodontic access opening. Do not report crown repair necessitated by material failure either. If the crown is *removed* first then core buildup/prefabricated post and core can be reported.

NARRATIVES A crown placed after an amalgam restoration may be fully reimbursed (without the payer deducting the restoration fee from the crown fee) if an unexpected fracture of that tooth or failure of the restoration placed on that tooth is involved. Should this be the case, a narrative and/or appeal may be necessary to prevent the restoration fee from being deducted from the crown fee. Some payers deduct the fee for the restoration (in addition to patient co-pay) from the subsequent crown procedure if the restoration was placed within 12 to 24 months prior to the crown being seated.

D2150 AMALGAM – TWO SURFACES, PRIMARY OR PERMANENT — CDT 2016

1. It is misleading to report an amalgam restoration as a filling if the *caries* and *preparation do not* extend into the *dentin* and/or fracture is not involved. Restoration of an active cavitated lesion where the filling material is placed in *enamel* only (not extending into the dentin) is considered a preventive resin restoration (D1352).

2. All bases, liners, adhesives, etching, polishing, contact and occlusal adjustments, and the use of caries detection agents are included in the overall amalgam restoration fee. If a pulp cap (D3110/D3120) is reported with an amalgam restoration placed on the same date of service, payers consider the pulp cap (as a base or liner) part of the restoration procedure. A pulp cap's purpose (promotion of *healing* and *repair*) is to assist in the formation of secondary dentin and may be billed separately. A routine base or liner decreases sensitivity and protects the pulp. Pulp caps promote healing (secondary dentin) and repair. (See D3110/D3120 for further details.)

3. It is necessary to disclose the reason for a restoration if its purpose is to treat abfraction, erosion, wear, abrasion, attrition, or to improve esthetics/cosmetics. These situations are addressed in, and limited by most third party contracts. Most payers require that *decay* and/or *fracture* be present to justify reimbursement for a restoration.

4. It is misleading to report amalgam restorations built to full contour as core buildups (D2950). Core buildups (after the tooth is fully prepared) are justified when they are necessary for the *retention* of the crown. A core buildup is followed by a temporary crown placement or final restoration.

5. When two or more separate restorations are performed on the same tooth on the same date of service, report each restoration *separately*. Reporting separate restorations on the same tooth is *not* considered unbundling. Always "report what you do." Note that many payers will limit reimbursement for restorations placed on the same tooth surface on the same service date.

COMMENTS Report pins separately. See D2951. For pulp caps see D3110 or D3120.

LIMITATIONS 1. The exclusion period for replacement of amalgam restorations is typically 24 to 36 months, depending on the contract. In some circumstances involving accidents, new caries, or radiation therapy the typical limitations may not apply. Should one of these situations exist and the reimbursement for the replaced restoration denied, appeal with a written narrative explaining the dental necessity. If a restoration is replaced within the limitation period by a different provider, the new provider may be reimbursed. This is, however, dependent on contract language.

2. Reimbursement for removing and replacing defective restorations may require that the treated tooth have decay, open margins, and/or fracture.

NARRATIVES A crown placed after an amalgam restoration may be fully reimbursed (without the payer deducting the restoration fee from the crown fee) if an unexpected fracture of that tooth or failure of the restoration placed on that tooth is involved. Should this be the case, a narrative and/or appeal may be necessary to prevent the restoration fee from being deducted from the crown fee. Some payers deduct the fee for the restoration (in addition to patient co-pay) from the subsequent crown procedure if the restoration was placed within 12 to 24 months prior to the crown being seated.

D2160	AMALGAM – THREE SURFACES, PRIMARY OR PERMANENT	CDT 2016

1. It is misleading to report an amalgam restoration as a filling if the *caries* and *preparation do not* extend into the *dentin* and/or fracture is not involved. Restoration of an active cavitated lesion where the filling material is placed in *enamel* only (not extending into the dentin) is considered a preventive resin restoration (D1352).

2. All bases, liners, adhesives, etching, polishing, contact and occlusal adjustments, and the use of caries detection agents are included in the overall amalgam restoration fee. If a pulp cap (D3110/D3120) is reported with an amalgam restoration placed on the same date of service, payers consider the pulp cap (as a base or liner) part of the restoration procedure. A pulp cap's purpose (promotion of *healing* and *repair*) is to assist in the formation of secondary dentin and may be billed separately. A routine base or liner decreases sensitivity and protects the pulp. Pulp caps promote healing (secondary dentin) and repair. (See D3110/D3120 for further details.)

3. It is necessary to disclose the reason for a restoration if its purpose is to treat abfraction, erosion, wear, abrasion, attrition, or to improve esthetics/cosmetics. These situations are addressed in, and limited by most third party contract(s). Most payers require that *decay* and/or *fracture* be present to justify reimbursement for a restoration.

4. It is misleading to report amalgam restorations built to full contour as core buildups (D2950). Core buildups (after the tooth is fully prepared) are justified when they are necessary for the *retention* of the crown. A core buildup is followed by a temporary crown placement or final restoration.

5. When two or more separate restorations are performed on the same tooth on the same date of service, report each restoration *separately*. Reporting separate restorations on the same tooth is *not* considered unbundling. Always "report what you do." Note that many payers will limit reimbursement for restorations placed on the same tooth surface on the same service date.

COMMENTS Report pins separately. See D2951. For pulp caps, see D3110 or D3120.

LIMITATIONS
1. The exclusion period for replacement of amalgam restorations is typically 24 to 36 months, depending on the contract. In some circumstances involving accidents, new caries, or radiation therapy the typical limitations may not apply. Should one of these situations exist and the reimbursement for the replaced restoration denied, appeal with a written narrative explaining the dental necessity. If a restoration is replaced within the limitation period by a different provider, the new provider may be reimbursed. This is, however, dependent on contract language.

2. Reimbursement for removing and replacing defective restorations may require that the treated tooth have decay, open margins, and/or fracture.

NARRATIVES A crown placed after an amalgam restoration may be fully reimbursed (without the payer deducting the restoration fee from the crown fee) if an unexpected fracture of that tooth or failure of the restoration placed on that tooth is involved. Should this be the case, a narrative and/or appeal may be necessary to prevent the restoration fee from being deducted from the crown fee. Some payers deduct the fee for the restoration (in addition to patient co-pay) from the subsequent crown procedure if the restoration was placed within 12 to 24 months prior to the crown being seated.

D2161	AMALGAM – FOUR OR MORE SURFACES, PRIMARY OR PERMANENT	CDT 2016

1. It is misleading to report an amalgam restoration as a filling if the *caries* and *preparation do not* extend into the *dentin* and/or fracture is not involved. Restoration of an active cavitated lesion where the filling material is placed in *enamel* only (not extending into the dentin) is considered a preventive resin restoration (D1352).

2. All bases, liners, adhesives, etching, polishing, contact and occlusal adjustments, and the use of caries detection agents are included in the overall amalgam restoration fee. If a pulp cap (D3110/D3120) is reported with an amalgam restoration placed on the same date of service, payers consider the pulp cap (as a base or liner) part of the restoration procedure. A pulp cap's purpose (promotion of *healing* and *repair*) is to assist in the formation of secondary dentin and may be billed separately. A routine base or liner decreases sensitivity and protects the pulp. Pulp caps promote healing (secondary dentin) and repair. (See D3110/D3120 for further details.)

3. It is necessary to disclose the reason for a restoration if its purpose is to treat abfraction, erosion, wear, abrasion, attrition, or to improve esthetics/cosmetics. These situations are addressed in, and limited by most third party contracts. Most payers require that *decay* and/or *fracture* be present to justify reimbursement for a restoration.

4. It is misleading to report amalgam restorations built to full contour as core buildups (D2950). Core buildups (after the tooth is prepared) are justified when they are necessary for the *retention* of the crown. A core buildup is followed by a temporary crown placement or final restoration.

5. When two or more separate restorations are performed on the same tooth on the same date of service, report each restoration *separately*. Reporting separate restorations on the same tooth is *not* considered unbundling. Always "report what you do." Note that many payers will limit reimbursement for restorations placed on the same tooth surface on the same service date.

COMMENTS Report pins separately. See D2951. For pulp caps, see D3110 or D3210.

LIMITATIONS
1. The exclusion period for replacement of amalgam restorations is typically 24 to 36 months, depending on the contract. In some circumstances involving accidents, new caries, or radiation therapy the typical limitations may not apply. Should one of these situations exist and the reimbursement for the replaced restoration denied, appeal with a written narrative explaining the dental necessity. If a restoration is replaced within the limitation period by a different provider, the new provider may be reimbursed. This is, however, dependent on contract language.

2. Reimbursement for removing and replacing defective restorations may require that the treated tooth have decay, open margins, and/or fracture.

NARRATIVES A crown placed after an amalgam restoration may be fully reimbursed (without the payer deducting the restoration fee from the crown fee) if an unexpected fracture of that tooth or failure of the restoration placed on that tooth is involved. Should this be the case, a narrative and/or appeal may be necessary to prevent the restoration fee from being deducted from the crown fee. Some payers deduct the fee for the restoration (in addition to patient co-pay) from the subsequent crown procedure if the restoration was placed within 12 to 24 months prior to the crown being seated.

RESIN-BASED COMPOSITE RESTORATIONS – DIRECT   CDT 2016

Resin-based composite refers to a broad category of materials including but not limited to composites. May include bonded composite, light-cured composite, etc. Tooth preparation, acid etching, adhesives (including resin bonding agents), liners and bases and curing are included as part of the restoration. Glass ionomers, when used as restorations, should be reported with these codes. If pins are used, they should be reported separately (see D2951).

D2330   RESIN-BASED COMPOSITE – ONE SURFACE, ANTERIOR   CDT 2016

1. It is misleading to report *individual* composite restorations (D2330-D2335) for "splinting" of anterior teeth for periodontal reasons. D4320/D4321 are used to report splints for treatment of periodontally involved teeth. For splints associated with the stabilization of *traumatic* injury, see D7270.

2. It is necessary to disclose the reason for a restoration if its purpose is to close a diastema or to improve esthetics/cosmetics where caries and/or fracture is *not* involved. These situations are addressed in, and limited by, third party contracts. Most payers require that *decay* and/or *fracture* be present to justify reimbursement. To provide a cosmetic service and report them as anterior composites restorations (D2330-D2335) to gain reimbursement could be considered fraud.

3. It is misleading to report composite restorations built to full contour as core buildups (D2950). Core buildups (after the tooth is prepared) are justified when they are necessary for the *retention* of the crown.

4. When two or more separate restorations are performed on the same tooth on the same date of service, report the restorations *separately*. Reporting separate restorations on the same tooth is *not* considered unbundling. Always "report what you do." Note that many payers will limit reimbursement for restorations placed on the same tooth surface on the same service date.

CODING WATCH CORRECTION

D2330 reports the one surface restored incisal "edge," not the multi-surface incisal "angle." For incisal "angle" (the corner of an anterior tooth), see D2335. D2335 describes a composite restoration involving four or more surfaces or the incisal "angle" of the anterior tooth.

COMMENTS
1. Pins, if placed in an anterior restoration, are billed separately. See D2951.
2. All composite codes include light curing, bonding, and any acid etching in the overall restoration fee. The composite restoration codes also include any bases, liners, polishing, and occlusal adjustment provided for the tooth being restored.

LIMITATIONS
1. Resin-based composite (D2330) for an anterior tooth is reimbursed when *decay* and/or *fracture* are present in one surface of an anterior tooth (primary or permanent).
2. Pulp caps (D3110/D3120), when provided, are typically considered a part of, and are included in, the composite restoration fee. Note: there is a difference between a base/liner (which decreases sensitivity and protects the pulp) and a pulp cap. A pulp cap may be used to promote *healing* and *repair of the pulpal tissue,* and may assist in the formation of secondary dentin. If the service provided is a base or liner as a part of an amalgam or composite, do not submit a pulp cap for reimbursement. See D3110/D3120 for further details.
3. Class V restorations are typically reimbursed as single surface facial or lingual restorations.
4. Glass ionomers, when used as restorations are reported as resin-based composites.
5. Reimbursement for removing and replacing defective restorations may require that the treated tooth have decay, open margins, and/or fracture.

TIPS
Report D2330 when restoring an endodontic access opening or the access opening for the internal bleaching (D9974) of a natural tooth. Do not report core buildup (D2950) or prefabricated post and core when restoring and closing an endodontic access opening. Core buildups and prefabricated post and core are reimbursable when they are necessary for the *retention* of the crown, not for closure of an endodontic access opening. Do not report crown repair necessitated by material failure either. If the crown is *removed* first then core buildup/prefabricated post and core can be reported.

NARRATIVES
A crown placed after a composite restoration may be fully reimbursed (without the payer deducting the restoration fee from the crown fee) if an unexpected fracture of that tooth or failure of the restoration placed on that tooth is involved. Should this be the case, a narrative and/or appeal may be necessary to prevent the restoration fee from being deducted from the crown fee. Some payers deduct the fee for the restoration (in addition to patient co-pay) from the subsequent crown procedure if the restoration was placed within 12 to 24 months prior to the crown being seated.

D2331 RESIN-BASED COMPOSITE – TWO SURFACES, ANTERIOR — CDT 2016

CODING WARNING CORRECTION

1. It is misleading to report *individual* composite restorations (D2330-D2335) for "splinting" of anterior teeth for periodontal reasons. D4320/D4321 report splints for treatment of periodontally-involved teeth. For splints used in the stabilization of *traumatic* injury, see D7270.

2. It is necessary to disclose the reason for a restoration if its purpose is to close a diastema or to improve esthetics/cosmetics where caries and/or fracture is *not* involved. These situations are addressed in, and limited by, third party contracts. Most payers require that *decay* and/or *fracture* be present to justify reimbursement. To provide a cosmetic service and report them as anterior composite restorations (D2330-D2335) to gain reimbursement could be considered fraud.

3. It is misleading to report composite restorations built to full contour as core buildups (D2950). Core buildups (after the tooth is prepared) are justified when they are necessary for the *retention* of the crown.

4. When two or more separate restorations are performed on the same tooth on the same date of service, report the restorations *separately*. Reporting separate restorations on the same tooth is *not* considered unbundling. Always "report what you do." Note that many payers will limit reimbursement for restorations placed on the same tooth surface on the same service date.

CODING WATCH CORRECTION

1. Certain payers may not reimburse anterior multi-surface composite codes, but convert them to a one-surface composite (D2330) for reimbursement. Always report the correct multi-surface code and let the payer re-map for reimbursement purposes.

2. D2331 is used to report a two surface restoration. One of the surfaces may be the incisal "edge." For incisal "angle" (the corner of an anterior tooth), see D2335. D2335 describes a composite restoration involving 4 or more surfaces or the incisal "angle" of the anterior tooth.

COMMENTS

1. Pins, if placed in an anterior restoration, are billed separately. See D2951.

2. All composite codes include light curing, bonding, and any acid etching in the overall restoration fee. The composite restoration codes also include any bases, liners, polishing, and occlusal adjustment provided for the tooth being restored.

LIMITATIONS

1. Resin-based composite (D2331) for an anterior tooth is reimbursed when *decay* and/or *fracture* are present in two surfaces of an anterior tooth (primary or permanent).

2. Pulp caps (D3110/D3120), when provided, are typically considered a part of, and are included in, the composite restoration fee. Note: there is a difference between a base/liner (which decreases sensitivity and protects the pulp) and a pulp cap. A pulp cap may be used to promote *healing* and *repair of the pulpal tissue*, and may assist in the formation of secondary dentin. If the service provided is a base or liner as a part of an amalgam or composite, do not submit a pulp cap for reimbursement. See D3110/D3120 for further details.

3. Glass ionomers, when used as restorations, are reported as resin-based composites.

4. Reimbursement for removing and replacing defective restorations may require that the treated tooth have decay, open margins, and/or fracture.

NARRATIVES

A crown placed after a composite restoration may be fully reimbursed (without the payer deducting the restoration fee from the crown fee) if an unexpected fracture of that tooth or failure of the restoration placed on that tooth is involved. Should this be the case, a narrative and/or appeal may be necessary to prevent the restoration fee from being deducted from the crown fee. Some payers deduct the fee for the restoration (in addition to patient co-pay) from the subsequent crown procedure if the restoration was placed within 12 to 24 months prior to the crown being seated.

D2332 RESIN-BASED COMPOSITE – THREE SURFACES, ANTERIOR CDT 2016

CODING WARNING CORRECTION

1. It is misleading to report *individual* composite restorations (D2330-D2335) for "splinting" of anterior teeth for periodontal reasons. D4320/D4321 are used to report splints for treatment of periodontally involved teeth. For splints used in the stabilization of *traumatic* injury, see D7270.

2. It is necessary to disclose the reason for a restoration if its purpose is to close a diastema or to improve esthetics/cosmetics where caries and/or fracture is *not* involved. These situations are addressed in, and limited by, third party contracts. Most payers require that *decay* and/or *fracture* be present to justify reimbursement. To provide a cosmetic service and report them as anterior composites restorations (D2330-D2335) to gain reimbursement could be considered fraud.

3. It is misleading to report composite restorations built to full contour as core buildups (D2950). Core buildups (after the tooth is prepared) are justified when they are necessary for the retention of the crown.

4. When two or more separate restorations are performed on the same tooth on the same date of service, report the restorations *separately*. Reporting separate restorations on the same tooth is *not* considered unbundling. Always "report what you do." Note that many payers will limit reimbursement for restorations placed on the same tooth surface on the same service date.

CODING WATCH CORRECTION

1. Certain payers may not reimburse anterior multi-surface composite codes, but convert them to a one-surface composite (D2330) for reimbursement. Always report the correct multi-surface code and let the payer re-map for reimbursement purposes.
2. D2332 is used to report a three surface restoration. One of the surfaces may be the incisal "edge." For incisal "angle" (the corner of an anterior tooth), see D2335. D2335 describes a composite restoration involving four or more surfaces or the incisal "angle" of the anterior tooth.

COMMENTS

1. Pins, if placed in an anterior restoration, are billed separately. See D2951.
2. All composite codes include light curing, bonding, and any acid etching in the overall restoration fee. The composite restoration codes also include any bases, liners, polishing, and occlusal adjustment provided for the tooth being restored.

LIMITATIONS

1. Resin-based composite (D2332) for an anterior tooth is reimbursed when *decay* and/or *fracture* are present in three surfaces of an anterior tooth (primary or permanent).
2. Pulp caps (D3110/D3120), when provided, are typically considered a part of, and are included in, the composite restoration fee. Note: there is a difference between a base/liner (which decreases sensitivity and protects the pulp) and a pulp cap. A pulp cap may be used to promote *healing* and *repair of the pulpal tissue,* and may assist in the formation of secondary dentin. If the service provided is a base or liner as a part of an amalgam or composite, do not submit a pulp cap for reimbursement. See D3110/D3120 for further details
3. Glass ionomers, when used as restorations, are reported as resin-based composites.
4. Reimbursement for removing and replacing defective restorations may require that the treated tooth have decay, open margins, and/or fracture.

NARRATIVES

A crown placed after a composite restoration may be fully reimbursed (without the payer deducting the restoration fee from the crown fee) if an unexpected fracture of that tooth or failure of the restoration placed on that tooth is involved. Should this be the case, a narrative and/or appeal may be necessary to prevent the restoration fee from being deducted from the crown fee. Some payers deduct the fee for the restoration (in addition to patient co-pay) from the subsequent crown procedure if the restoration was placed within 12 to 24 months prior to the crown being seated.

D2335 RESIN-BASED COMPOSITE – FOUR OR MORE SURFACES OR INVOLVING INCISAL ANGLE (ANTERIOR) CDT 2016

Incisal angle to be defined as one of the angles formed by the junction of the incisal and the mesial or distal surface of an anterior tooth.

CODING WARNING CORRECTION

1. It is misleading to report *individual* composite restorations (D2330-D2335) for "splinting" of anterior teeth for periodontal reasons. D4320/D4321 are used to report splints for treatment of periodontally-involved teeth. For splints used in the stabilization of *traumatic* injury, see D7270.
2. It is necessary to disclose the reason for a restoration if its purpose is to close a diastema or to improve esthetics/cosmetics where caries and/or fracture is *not* involved. These situations are addressed in, and limited by, third party contracts. Most payers require that *decay* and/or *fracture* to be present to justify reimbursement. To provide a cosmetic service and report them as anterior composites restorations (D2330-D2335) to gain reimbursement could be considered fraud.
3. It is misleading to report composite restorations built to full contour as core buildups (D2950). Core buildups (after the tooth is prepared) are justified when they are necessary for the *retention* of the crown.
4. When two or more separate restorations are performed on the same tooth on the same date of service, report the restorations *separately*. Reporting separate restorations on the same tooth is *not* considered unbundling. Always "report what you do." Note that many payers will limit reimbursement for restorations placed on the same tooth surface on the same service date.

CODING CORRECTION WATCH

1. Certain payers may not reimburse anterior multi-surface composite codes, but convert them to a one-surface composite (D2330) for reimbursement. Always report the correct multi-surface code and let the payer re-map for reimbursement purposes.
2. D2335 describes a composite restoration involving four or more surfaces of the anterior tooth or a multi-surface incisal "angle" restoration.

COMMENTS

1. All composite codes include light curing, bonding, and any acid etching in the overall restoration fee. The composite restoration codes also include any bases, liners, polishing, and occlusal adjustment provided for the tooth being restored.
2. Pins, if placed in an anterior restoration, are billed separately. See (D2951).

LIMITATIONS

1. Resin-based composite (D2335) is reimbursed when *decay* and/or *fracture* are present in four or more surfaces or involving incise/angle of an anterior tooth (primary or permanent)..
2. Pulp caps (D3110/D3120), when provided, are typically considered a part of, and are included in, the composite restoration fee. Note: there is a difference between a base/liner (which decreases sensitivity and protects the pulp) and a pulp cap. A pulp cap may be used to promote *healing* and *repair of the pulpal tissue*, and may assist in the formation of secondary dentin. If the service provided is a base or liner as a part of an amalgam or composite, do not submit a pulp cap for reimbursement. See D3110/D3120 for further details.
3. Glass ionomers, when used as restorations, are reported as resin-based composites.
4. Reimbursement for removing and replacing defective restorations may require that the treated tooth have decay, open margins, and/or fracture.

TIPS

Failing to use D2335 to describe anterior restorations *involving the incisal angle* is a common error. The incisal "angle" restoration is reported using code D2335, not D2331 or D2332, composite restoration two surfaces/composite restoration three surfaces. Use four surfaces (MIFL or DILF) to report an incisal "angle" restoration. D2330, D2331, or D2332 may describe an incisal "edge" restoration depending on the location of the restoration.

NARRATIVES

1. Enclose a copy of a radiographic image which demonstrates and documents the incisal "angle" is missing (the incisal corner of the tooth). Also, a photograph of the broken incisal angle can verify that the "angle" is broken.
2. A crown placed after a composite restoration may be fully reimbursed (without the payer deducting the restoration fee from the crown fee) if an unexpected fracture of that tooth or failure of the restoration placed on that tooth is involved. Should this be the case, a narrative and/or appeal may be necessary to prevent the restoration fee from being deducted from the crown fee. Some payers deduct the fee for the restoration (in addition to patient co-pay) from the subsequent crown procedure if the restoration was placed within 12 to 24 months prior to the crown being seated.

D2390 RESIN-BASED COMPOSITE CROWN, ANTERIOR CDT 2016

Full resin-based composite coverage of tooth.

COMMENTS

1. D2390 reports a direct composite anterior "crown" restoration that covers all five surfaces of an anterior tooth MIFLD. It is fabricated using composite resins or glass ionomers. This procedure is typically reimbursed.
2. All composite codes include light curing, adhesive, and any acid etching in the overall restoration fee. The composite restoration codes also include any bases, liners, polishing, and occlusal adjustment provided for the tooth being restored.
3. Pins, if placed in an anterior restoration, are billed separately. See (D2951).

LIMITATIONS

1. Pulp caps (D3110/D3120), when provided, are typically considered a part of, and are included in, the composite restoration fee. Note: there is a difference between a base/liner (which decreases sensitivity and protects the pulp) and a pulp cap. A pulp cap may be used to promote *healing* and *repair of the pulpal tissue,* and may assist in the formation of secondary dentin. If the service provided is a base or liner as a part of an amalgam or composite, do not submit a pulp cap for reimbursement. See D3110/D3120 for further details.

2. Some payers may classify a direct composite "crown" as a *major* procedure for reimbursement (50% of the UCR fee), rather than a *basic* restorative procedure (80% of the UCR fee) for reimbursement purposes.

NARRATIVES

1. If a (direct) composite crown has been performed on a tooth and the procedure reimbursed by the payer, a crown limitation period may apply. The previously reimbursed composite crown fee may be subtracted from the subsequent crown reimbursement fee or the subsequent crown may be denied completely if the crown limitation period applies. If the direct composite crown fractures and/or recurrent caries is present, the limitation may not apply. Use a narrative when reporting a replacement crown and include a diagnostic radiographic image. A different provider may be fully reimbursed for a subsequent crown.

2. The exclusion period for composite restorations is typically 24 to 36 months; however, if the tooth fractures after the restoration is placed, or if new caries is present, the limitation may *not* apply. Use a narrative when reporting a replacement indirect crown and include a diagnostic image. A different provider may be fully reimbursed for a subsequent crown. If denied, appeal.

D2391 — RESIN-BASED COMPOSITE – ONE SURFACE, POSTERIOR — CDT 2016

Used to restore a carious lesion into the dentin or a deeply eroded area into the dentin. Not a preventive procedure.

CODING WARNING CORRECTION

1. It is misleading to report a resin-based composite restoration where air abrasion or fissurotomy is done without an active cavitated lesion present that extends into dentin. A diagnostic radiographic image or other documentation (photo/narrative) should be a part of the patient's record to support the presence of caries. It is misleading to report D2391 if occlusal caries and the preparation remain in the *enamel*. To report D2391, occlusal caries and *preparation* must extend *into* the *dentin* and/or a fracture *into* the *dentin* and is repaired by the restoration.

2. It is misleading to report composite restorations as core buildups (D2950). Composite restorations are built to full contour and have occlusion, anatomy and depending on the restoration often has proximal contacts. Core buildups on a prepared tooth are necessary if there is insufficient retention for a separate extracoronal restorative procedure, e.g., a crown.

CODING WATCH CORRECTION

1. A "preventive" resin-based composite procedure can be erroneously reported as a resin-based composite. A posterior composite code is used to describe the restoration of a carious lesion that extends *into* the *dentin* and/or where fracture is involved. If the occlusal caries and *preparation* are limited to the cavitated pits and fissures of a permanent tooth, not extending to the dentin, the restoration is considered a preventative resin restoration (D1352). Pits and fissures adjacent to the PRR that are sealed are considered a part of the D1352 procedure. If the enamel *surface* is sealed with a resin, and there is no active cavitated lesion in the tooth, the resin is a sealant (D1351). See D1351 and D1352.

2. If two or more separate restorations are performed on the same tooth, on the same service date, report the restorations separately. Reporting separate restorations on the same tooth *is not* considered unbundling. Always "report what you do" but note that some payers may restrict coverage for more than one restoration on the same surface on the same service date.

COMMENTS

1. All composite codes include light curing, bonding, acid etching, bases, liners, polishing, and occlusal adjustment in the overall restoration fee.

2. Pulp caps (D3110/D3120), when provided, are typically considered a part of, and are included in, the composite restoration fee. Note: there is a difference between a base/liner (which decreases sensitivity and protects the pulp) and a pulp cap. A pulp cap may be used to promote *healing* and *repair of the pulpal tissue,* and may assist in the formation of secondary dentin. If the service provided is a base or liner as a part of an amalgam or composite, do not submit a pulp cap for reimbursement. See D3110/D3120 for further details.

3. Pins, if placed in a posterior composite restoration, are billed separately. See D2951.

4. Report D2391 when restoring an endodontic access opening or the access opening for the internal bleaching (D9974) of a natural tooth. Do not report core buildup (D2950) or prefabricated post and core when restoring and closing an endodontic access opening. Core buildups and prefabricated post and core are reimbursable when they are necessary for the *retention* of the crown, not for closure of an endodontic access opening. Do not report crown repair necessitated by material failure either. If the crown is *removed* first then core buildup/prefabricated post and core can be reported.

TIPS Sealants (D1351), preventive resin restorations (D1352), and resin-based composite restorations (D2391) differ as follows:

1. Sealant (D1351): Mechanically and/or chemically prepared enamel surface sealed to prevent decay. The enamel surface is non-carious.

2. Preventive Resin Restoration (D1352): Conservative restoration of an active cavitated lesion in a pit or fissure of a permanent tooth which does not extend into the dentin. Also includes placing a sealant in any radiating noncarious pits or fissures. Patient must be moderate to high caries risk.

3. Resin-based composite – one surface, posterior (D2391): This is a posterior resin restoration where the caries and preparation extends into the dentin or a deeply eroded area into the dentin.

NARRATIVES
1. If decay is not clearly visible on the diagnostic image, clinical documentation supporting the need for treatment is strongly recommended in the event of third party review. The clinical record might note: "Caries not evident on diagnostic image; however, was «sticky» to the explorer. Caries and preparation extend into the dentin." Also include any Diagnodent® /SoproLIFE® readings or photo(s) where applicable.

2. The exclusion period for replacement of composite restorations is typically 12 to 36 months; but, if the tooth fractures after the restoration is placed, or if new caries is present, the limitation may *not* apply. If replacement is necessary, a narrative plus diagnostic image(s) should be submitted when reporting D2391 again for the same tooth. If denied, appeal. A different provider than the one who placed the original restoration may be reimbursed.

3. If a posterior composite restoration has been placed and reimbursed on a tooth that later requires a crown, a limitation may apply (if within a 24 to 36 month period). The previously reimbursed composite restoration fee may be subtracted from the subsequent crown reimbursement fee. If the posterior composite fractures and/or new caries is present, the limitation may not apply. Use a narrative when reporting the need for the crown and include a diagnostic image. A different provider for a subsequent crown may be fully reimbursed.

D2392 — RESIN-BASED COMPOSITE – TWO SURFACES, POSTERIOR — CDT 2016

CODING WARNING CORRECTION
It is misleading to report composite restorations as core buildup (D2950). Composite restorations are built to full contour and have occlusion, anatomy and depending on the restoration, often has proximal contacts. Core buildups on a prepared tooth are necessary if there is insufficient retention for a separate extracoronal restorative procedure, e.g., a crown.

CODING WATCH CORRECTION
1. A "preventive" resin-based composite procedure can be erroneously reported as a resin-based composite. A posterior composite code is used to describe the restoration of a carious lesion that extends *into* the *dentin* and/or where fracture is involved. If the caries and *preparation* are limited to the cavitated pits and fissures of a permanent tooth, not extending to the dentin, the restoration is considered a preventive resin restoration (D1352). Pits and fissures adjacent to the PRR that are sealed are considered a part of D1352. If the enamel *surface* is sealed with a resin, and there is no cavitated lesion in the tooth, the resin is a sealant (D1351). See D1351 and D1352.

2. If two or more separate restorations are performed on the same tooth, on the same service date, report the restorations separately. Reporting separate restorations on the same tooth *is not* considered unbundling. Always "report what you do" but note that some payers may restrict coverage for more than one restoration on the same surface on the same service date.

COMMENTS
1. All composite codes include light curing, bonding, acid etching, bases, liners, polishing, and occlusal adjustment in the overall restoration fee.

2. Pulp caps (D3110/D3120), when provided, are typically considered a part of, and are included in, the composite restoration fee. Note: there is a difference between a base/liner (which decreases sensitivity and protects the pulp) and a pulp cap. A pulp cap may be used to promote *healing* and *repair of the pulpal tissue,* and may assist in the formation of secondary dentin. If the service provided is a base or liner as a part of an amalgam or composite, do not submit a pulp cap for reimbursement. See D3110/D3120 for further details.
3. Pins, if placed in a posterior composite restoration, are billed separately. See D2951.

NARRATIVES

1. If decay is not clearly visible on the diagnostic image, clinical documentation supporting the need for treatment is strongly recommended in the event of third party review. The clinical record might note: "Caries not evident on diagnostic image; however, was "sticky" to the explorer. Caries and preparation extend into the dentin." Also include any Diagnodent® /SoproLIFE® readings or photo(s) where applicable.
2. The exclusion period for replacement of composite restorations is typically 12 to 36 months; but, if the tooth fractures after the restoration is placed, or if new caries is present, the limitation may *not* apply. If replacement is necessary, a narrative plus diagnostic image(s) should be submitted when reporting D2392 again for the same tooth. If denied, appeal. A different provider than the one who placed the original restoration may be reimbursed.
3. If a posterior composite restoration has been placed and reimbursed on a tooth that later requires a crown, a limitation may apply (if within a 24 to 36 month period). The previously reimbursed composite restoration fee may be subtracted from the subsequent crown reimbursement fee. If the posterior composite fractures and/or recurrent caries is present, the limitation may not apply. Use a narrative when reporting the need for the crown and include a diagnostic image. A different provider may be fully reimbursed for a subsequent crown.

D2393 — RESIN-BASED COMPOSITE – THREE SURFACES, POSTERIOR — CDT 2016

It is misleading to report composite restorations as core buildups (D2950). Composite restorations are built to full contour and have occlusion, anatomy and depending on the restoration often has proximal contacts. Core buildups on a prepared tooth are necessary if there is insufficient retention for a separate extracoronal restorative procedure, e.g., a crown.

1. A "preventive" resin-based composite procedure can be erroneously reported as a resin-based composite. A posterior composite code is used to describe the restoration of a carious lesion that extends *into* the *dentin* and/or where fracture is involved. If the caries and *preparation* are limited to the cavitated pits and fissures of a permanent tooth, not extending to the dentin, the restoration is considered a preventive resin restoration (D1352). Pits and fissures adjacent to the PRR that are sealed are considered a part of D1352. If the enamel *surface* is sealed with a resin and there is no cavitated lesion in the tooth, the resin is a sealant (D1351). See D1351 and D1352.
2. If two or more separate restorations are performed on the same tooth, on the same service date, report the restorations separately. Reporting separate restorations on the same tooth *is not* considered unbundling. Always "report what you do" but note that some payers may restrict coverage for more than one restoration on the same surface on the same service date.
3. Some offices are not aware of the resin-based composite (D2394), which is available for reporting four or more surfaces on a posterior tooth. They think the maximum number of surfaces to report is limited to three surfaces. See D2394 to report four or more surfaces.

COMMENTS

1. All composite codes include light curing, bonding, acid etching, bases, liners, polishing, and occlusal adjustment in the overall restoration fee.
2. Pulp caps (D3110/D3120), when provided, are typically considered a part of, and are included in, the composite restoration fee. Note: there is a difference between a base/liner (which decreases sensitivity and protects the pulp) and a pulp cap. A pulp cap may be used to promote *healing* and *repair of the pulpal tissue,* and may assist in the formation of secondary dentin. If the service provided is a base or liner as a part of an amalgam or composite, do not submit a pulp cap for reimbursement. See D3110/D3120 for further details.
3. Pins, if placed in a posterior composite restoration, are billed separately. See D2951.

NARRATIVES

1. If decay is not clearly visible on the diagnostic image, clinical documentation supporting the need for treatment is strongly recommended in the event of third party review. The clinical record might note: "Caries not evident on diagnostic image; however, was "sticky" to the explorer. Caries and preparation extend into the dentin." Also include any Diagnodent® /SoproLIFE® readings or photo(s) where applicable.

2. The exclusion period for replacement of composite restorations is typically 12 to 36 months; but, if the tooth fractures after the restoration is placed, or if new caries is present, the limitation may *not* apply. If replacement is necessary, a narrative plus diagnostic image(s) should be submitted when reporting D2393 again for the same tooth. If denied, appeal. A different provider than the one who placed the original restoration may be reimbursed.

3. If a posterior composite restoration has been placed and reimbursed on a tooth that later requires a crown, a limitation may apply (if within a 24 to 36 month period). The previously reimbursed composite restoration fee may be subtracted from the subsequent crown reimbursement fee. If the posterior composite fractures and/or new caries is present, the limitation may not apply. Use a narrative when reporting the need for the crown and include a diagnostic image. A different provider may be fully reimbursed for a subsequent crown.

D2394 — RESIN-BASED COMPOSITE – FOUR OR MORE SURFACES, POSTERIOR — CDT 2016

CODING CORRECTION WARNING

It is misleading to report composite restorations as core buildups (D2950). Composite restorations are built to full contour and have occlusion, anatomy and depending on the restoration, often have proximal contacts. Core buildups on a prepared tooth are necessary if there is insufficient retention for a separate extracoronal restorative procedure, e.g., a crown.

CODING CORRECTION WATCH

If two or more separate restorations are performed on the same tooth, on the same service date, report the restorations separately. Reporting separate restorations on the same tooth *is not* considered unbundling. Always "report what you do" but note that some payers may restrict coverage for more than one restoration on the same surface on the same service date.

COMMENTS

1. All composite codes include light curing, bonding, acid etching, bases, liners, polishing, and occlusal adjustment in the overall restoration fee.

2. Pulp caps (D3110/D3120), when provided, are typically considered a part of, and are included in, the composite restoration fee. Note: there is a difference between a base/liner (which decreases sensitivity and protects the pulp) and a pulp cap. A pulp cap may be used to promote *healing* and *repair of the pulpal tissue*, and may assist in the formation of secondary dentin. If the service provided is a base or liner as a part of an amalgam or composite, do not submit a pulp cap for reimbursement. See D3110/D3120 for further details.

3. Pins, if placed in a posterior composite restoration, are billed separately. See D2951.

4. (D2394), reports *four or more* surfaces on a posterior tooth.

NARRATIVES

1. If decay is not clearly visible on the diagnostic image, clinical documentation supporting the need for treatment is strongly recommended in the event of third party review. The clinical record might note: "Caries not evident on diagnostic image; however, was "sticky" to the explorer. Caries and preparation extend into the dentin." Also include any Diagnodent® /SoproLIFE® readings or photos where applicable.

2. The exclusion period for replacement of composite restorations is typically 12 to 36 months; but, if the tooth fractures after the restoration is placed, or if new caries is present, the limitation may *not* apply. If replacement is necessary, a narrative plus diagnostic image(s) should be submitted when reporting D2394 again for the same tooth. If denied, appeal. A different provider than the one who placed the original restoration may be reimbursed.

3. If a posterior composite restoration has been placed and reimbursed on a tooth that later requires a crown, a limitation may apply (if within a 24 to 36 month period). The previously reimbursed composite restoration fee may be subtracted from the subsequent crown reimbursement fee. If the posterior composite fractures and/or new caries is present, the limitation may not apply. Use a narrative when reporting the need for the crown and include a diagnostic image. A different provider may be fully reimbursed for a subsequent crown.

GOLD FOIL RESTORATIONS — CDT 2016

D2410 — GOLD FOIL – ONE SURFACE — CDT 2016

LIMITATIONS
1. Gold foil (D2410) is not typically reimbursed.
2. Some payers may provide an alternate benefit of an amalgam/composite restoration.

D2420 — GOLD FOIL – TWO SURFACES — CDT 2016

LIMITATIONS
1. Gold foil (D2420) is not typically reimbursed.
2. Some payers may provide an alternate benefit of an amalgam/composite restoration.

D2430 — GOLD FOIL – THREE SURFACES — CDT 2016

LIMITATIONS
1. Gold foil (D2430) is typically not reimbursed.
2. Some payers may provide an alternate benefit of an amalgam/composite restoration.

INLAY/ONLAY RESTORATIONS — CDT 2016

Inlay: An intra-coronal dental restoration, made outside the oral cavity to conform to the prepared cavity, which does not restore any cusp tips.

Onlay: A dental restoration made outside the oral cavity that covers one or more cusp tips and adjoining occlusal surfaces, but not the entire external surface.

D2510 — INLAY – METALLIC – ONE SURFACE — CDT 2016

LIMITATIONS
1. Inlay-metallic-one surface reports *any* type of cast metal.
2. Inlays are rarely reimbursed. However, an alternate benefit is often reimbursed (amalgam/composite restoration).
3. If the practice participates in PPOs, reimbursement may be restricted to the fee schedule applicable to the inlay by the PPO (third-party) although the PPO reimburses the alternate benefit of an amalgam/composite restoration.

D2520 — INLAY – METALLIC – TWO SURFACES — CDT 2016

LIMITATIONS
1. Inlay-metallic-two surfaces reports *any* type of cast metal.
2. Inlays are rarely reimbursed. However, an alternate benefit is often reimbursed (amalgam/composite restoration).
3. If the practice participates in PPOs, reimbursement may be restricted to the fee schedule applicable to the inlay by the PPO (third-party) although the PPO reimburses the alternate benefit of an amalgam/composite restoration.

D2530 — INLAY – METALLIC – THREE OR MORE SURFACES — CDT 2016

LIMITATIONS
1. Inlay-metallic – three or more surfaces reports *any* type of cast metal.
2. Inlays are rarely reimbursed. However, an alternate benefit is often reimbursed (amalgam/composite restoration).
3. If the practice participates in PPOs, reimbursement may be restricted to the fee schedule applicable to the inlay by the PPO (third-party) although the PPO reimburses the alternate benefit of an amalgam/composite restoration.

GENERAL COMMENTS FOR ONLAY SERVICES — AUTHOR'S COMMENTS

CODING WARNING CORRECTION

1. It is misleading to report an onlay if at least one cusp is not "capped" or "shoed." An onlay requires "capping one or more cusps." Going up the incline more than ½ of the distance from fossa to cusp tip is not an onlay, according to the CDT glossary. Also see the Journal of Prosthodontic Dentistry; the Glossary of Prosthodontic Terms; July 2005, page 57.

2. It is misleading to report a core buildup (D2950) in conjunction with an inlay or onlay. The sole purpose of a core build-up is for crown retention of the tooth. D2950 should only be used to report a core buildup for crown retention, not in conjunction with an onlay.

COMMENTS

1. Gold and ceramic onlay materials are the most often reimbursed. A small number of payers exclude reimbursement for laboratory fabricated resin-based onlays; or when reimbursed, the UCR fee is substantially lower than the comparable gold/ceramic onlay reimbursement.

2. Some payers have an age limitation of 13 years and older for reimbursement of onlays and/or crowns.

3. An onlay is determined by the onlay's buccal and/or lingual surfaces extending only to above the height of contour. A crown is determined when the surfaces of the restoration extend below the height of contour.

4. Trauma requiring a new onlay may nullify the five to 10 year common replacement exclusion for most policies.

5. A small number of payers require that all cusps be capped in order to obtain reimbursement for an onlay. Buccal and/or lingual surfaces, as appropriate, must be entered on the claim form for reimbursement of an onlay. An MOD does not describe an onlay. An MOF, MOL, DOF, DOL, MODL, MODF or MODFL does describe an onlay.

6. Onlay restorations may be excluded (for reimbursement) for esthetic, periodontal (splinting), abrasion, or erosion-related procedures.

TIPS

1. To receive reimbursement for an onlay, the tooth must generally meet the criteria for a crown (missing a cusp, undermined cusp, fractured cusp and breakdown), necessitated by fracture or decay. Onlays are usually reimbursed when reported with full documentation (proper narrative, beginning diagnostic radiographic image/photograph). A narrative should be used when reporting an onlay stating that the onlay is a "conservative option to a full crown, while capping and replacing the cusp(s)." Buccal and/or lingual surfaces, as appropriate, must be entered on the claim form for reimbursement.

2. Belleglass®, Targis®, Vectris®, Sculpture®, ArtGlass®, Concept® and Cristobel® are classified as indirect resin-based composite. Report this type of restoration using resin-based codes (D2662–D2664).

3. Porcelain/ceramics would include Empress®, Procera®, InCeram®, Lava®, Lava Ultimate®, Finesse®, Cerinate®, and Opc®. Report onlays made of these materials with D2642-D2644.

4. Unfortunately, resin-based (indirect) composites are denied as a material by some contracts. Furthermore, the resin-based composite UCR fee allowance may be 30-40% below the same gold or ceramic restoration fee.

D2542 ONLAY – METALLIC – TWO SURFACES — CDT 2016

CODING WARNING CORRECTION

1. It is misleading to report an onlay if at least one cusp is not "capped" or "shoed." An onlay requires "capping one or more cusps and adjoining occlusal surfaces or the entire occlusal surface" per the glossary of dental terms in the ADA coding manual. A cusp tip must be covered for the restoration to be considered an onlay. Going up the incline "nearly" to the cusp *does not* restore the cusp.

2. It is misleading to report a core buildup (D2950) in conjunction with an inlay or an onlay. A core buildup D2950 should only be used in conjunction with a *crown*.

COMMENTS An onlay has buccal and/or lingual surfaces that terminate above the height of contour and restores/covers at least one cusp.

LIMITATIONS
1. Some payers have an age limitation of 13 years and older for reimbursement of onlays and/or crowns.
2. Trauma requiring a new onlay may override the five to 10 year replacement exclusion contained in most policies.
3. Some payers require that *all* cusps be included in order to obtain reimbursement for an onlay.
4. Onlay restorations may be excluded (for reimbursement) for esthetic, periodontal (splinting), abrasion, or erosion related reasons.

NARRATIVES
1. To receive reimbursement for an onlay, the tooth must meet the same criteria that justifies payment for a crown. Those criteria include, but may not be limited to, missing a cusp, undermined cusp, fractured tooth or related breakdown and/or in conjunction with decay. Onlays are typically reimbursed when reported with adequately supporting documentation. That documentation should include a narrative, pretreatment diagnostic radiographic image and/or photograph and a photograph of the prepared tooth. The narrative should state that the onlay was a "conservative alternative to a full crown used to replace the defective cusp(s)."
2. *Be careful to report a buccal and/or lingual surface in association with the onlay coding.* An MOD *does not* describe an onlay. An MO*F*, MO*L*, DO*F,* DO*L* MOD*L,* MOD*F* or MOD*FL* describes an onlay.
3. "See attached radiographic image" (if tooth has RCT, send PA radiographic image).
4. List any missing cusps.
5. State the estimated percentage of healthy tooth structure left after fracture, caries and/or any previous restoration removed. If the tooth is diagnosed with cracked tooth syndrome – state method of diagnosis, e.g. Tooth Slooth™ positive on MF cusp.
6. State if tooth has existing or planned RCT (root canal therapy).
7. State if tooth has circumferential decay and amount of decay, e.g. circumferential decay on M, L and D encompassing 270 degrees of tooth.
8. State endodontic and periodontal prognosis for tooth.
9. If this is a replacement onlay, state date that the previous onlay was seated and reason(s) the new onlay is required.
10. If replacing an existing onlay, state the reason for replacement, e.g., tooth has caries, margins are open, porcelain is fractured off, poor contacts are causing food impactions, etc.

D2543 ONLAY – METALLIC – THREE SURFACES CDT 2016

CODING WARNING CORRECTION
1. It is misleading to report an onlay if at least one cusp is not "capped" or "shoed." An onlay requires "capping one or more cusps and adjoining occlusal surfaces or the entire occlusal surface" per the glossary of dental terms in the ADA coding manual. A cusp tip must be covered for the restoration to be considered an onlay. Going up the incline "nearly" to the cusp *does not* restore the cusp.
2. It is misleading to report a core buildup (D2950) in conjunction with an inlay or an onlay. A core buildup D2950 should only be used in conjunction with a *crown*.

COMMENTS An onlay has buccal and/or lingual surfaces that terminate above the height of contour and restores/covers at least one cusp.

LIMITATIONS
1. Some payers have an age limitation of 13 years and older for reimbursement of onlays and/or crowns.
2. Trauma requiring a new onlay may override the five to 10 year replacement exclusion contained in most policies.
3. Some payers require that *all* cusps be restored in order to obtain reimbursement for an onlay.
4. Onlay restorations may be excluded (for reimbursement) for esthetic, periodontal (splinting), abrasion, or erosion related reasons.

NARRATIVES **IMPORTANT!** See D2542 for onlay narratives/recommendations.

D2544 — ONLAY – METALLIC – FOUR OR MORE SURFACES — CDT 2016

CODING CORRECTION WARNING

1. It is misleading to report an onlay if at least one cusp is not "capped" or "shoed." An onlay requires "capping one or more cusps and adjoining occlusal surfaces or the entire occlusal surface" per the glossary of dental terms in the ADA coding manual. A cusp tip must be covered for the restoration to be considered an onlay. Going up the incline "nearly" to the cusp *does not* restore the cusp.
2. It is misleading to report a core buildup (D2950) in conjunction with an inlay or an onlay. A core buildup D2950 should only be used in conjunction with the retention of a *crown*.

COMMENTS An onlay has buccal and/or lingual surfaces that terminate above the height of contour and restores/covers at least one cusp tip.

LIMITATIONS
1. Some payers have an age limitation of 13 years and older for reimbursement of onlays and/or crowns.
2. Trauma requiring a new onlay may override the five to 10 year replacement exclusion contained in most policies.
3. Some payers require that *all* cusps be restored in order to obtain reimbursement for an onlay.
4. Onlay restorations may be excluded (for reimbursement) for esthetic, periodontal (splinting), abrasion, or erosion related reasons.

NARRATIVES **IMPORTANT**! See D2542 for onlay narrative recommendations.

PORCELAIN/CERAMIC INLAYS/ONLAYS INCLUDE ALL INDIRECT CERAMIC AND PORCELAIN TYPE INLAYS/ONLAYS — CDT 2016

D2610 — INLAY – PORCELAIN/CERAMIC – ONE SURFACE — CDT 2016

CODING CORRECTION WARNING

It is misleading to report a *resin-based* inlay for this code. D2610 reports a *porcelain/ceramic* one-surface inlay.

LIMITATIONS
1. Inlays are not typically reimbursed; however, an alternate benefit is often reimbursed (amalgam/composite restoration).
2. If the practice is a PPO provider, reimbursement may be restricted to the inlay fee schedule of the PPO (third party), even though the PPO reimburses only the alternate benefit of an amalgam/composite restoration.
3. Porcelain/ceramics would include materials as Vita®, ProCad®, Lava Ultimate®, Empress®, Procera®, InCeram®, Lava®, Finesse®, Cerinate®, and Opc®. They *do not* include Cristobel®, Artglass®, Belleglass®, Targis®, Vectris®, Concept®, and similar materials.

TIPS Inlay (D2610) would also be used to report a CAD/CAM porcelain/ceramic restoration with one surface.

D2620 — INLAY – PORCELAIN/CERAMIC – TWO SURFACES — CDT 2016

CODING CORRECTION WARNING

It is misleading to report a *resin-based* inlay for this code. D2620 reports a porcelain/ceramic two surface inlay.

LIMITATIONS
1. Inlays are not typically reimbursed. However, an alternate benefit is often reimbursed (amalgam/composite restoration).
2. If the practice is a PPO provider, reimbursement may be restricted to the inlay fee schedule of the PPO (third-party), even though the PPO reimburses only the alternate benefit of an amalgam/composite.
3. Porcelain/ceramics would include materials as Vita®, ProCad®, Lava Ultimate®, Empress®, Procera®, InCeram®, Lava®, Finesse®, Cerinate®, and Opc®. They *do not* include Cristobel®, Artglass®, Belleglass®, Targis®, Vectris®, Concept®, and similar materials.

TIPS Inlay (D2620) would also be used to report a CAD/CAM porcelain/ceramic restoration with two surfaces.

D2630 INLAY – PORCELAIN/CERAMIC – THREE OR MORE SURFACES — CDT 2016

CODING WARNING CORRECTION
It is misleading to report a *resin-based* inlay for this code. D2630 reports a porcelain/ceramic three or more surface inlay.

LIMITATIONS
1. Inlays are not typically reimbursed. However, an alternate benefit is often reimbursed (amalgam/composite restoration).
2. If the practice is a PPO provider, reimbursement may be restricted to the inlay fee schedule of the PPO (third-party), even though the PPO reimburses only the alternate benefit of an amalgam/composite.
3. Porcelain/ceramics would include materials as Vita®, ProCad®, Lava Ultimate®, Empress®, Procera®, InCeram®, Lava®, Finesse®, Cerinate®, and Opc®. They *do not* include Cristobel®, Artglass®, Belleglass®, Targis®, Vectris®, Concept®, and similar materials.

TIPS Inlay (D2630) would also be used to report a CAD/CAM porcelain/ceramic restoration with three or more surfaces.

D2642 ONLAY – PORCELAIN/CERAMIC – TWO SURFACES — CDT 2016

CODING WARNING CORRECTION
1. It is misleading to report an onlay if at least one cusp is not "capped" or "shoed." An onlay requires "capping one or more cusps and adjoining occlusal surfaces or the entire occlusal surface" per the glossary of dental terms in the ADA coding manual. A cusp tip must be covered for the restoration to be considered an onlay. Going up the incline "nearly" to the cusp *does not* restore the cusp.
2. It is misleading to report a core buildup (D2950) in conjunction with an inlay or an onlay. A core buildup D2950 should only be used in conjunction with a *crown* (required for crown retention).
3. It is misleading to report a *resin-based* onlay code when a porcelain/ceramic material is used. This code reports a two surface porcelain/ceramic onlay.

COMMENTS An onlay must include a portion of the buccal and/or lingual surfaces and restores/covers at least one cusp. The margin of the onlay terminates above the height of contour on the buccal and/or lingual surface.

LIMITATIONS
1. Some payers have an age limitation of 13 years and older for reimbursement of onlays and/or crowns.
2. Trauma requiring a new onlay may override the five to 10 year replacement exclusion contained in most policies.
3. Some payers require that *all* cusps be restored in the restoration in order to obtain reimbursement for an onlay.
4. Onlay restorations may be excluded (for reimbursement) for esthetic, periodontal (splinting), abrasion, or erosion related reasons.

5. Porcelain/ceramics would include materials such as Vita®, ProCad®, Empress®, Lava Ultimate®, Procera®, InCeram®, Lava®, Finesse®, Cerinate®, and Opc®. They *do not* include resin-based Cristobel®, Artglass®, Belleglass®, Targis®, Vectris®, Concept®, and similar materials.

6. Gold and ceramic are the most commonly reimbursed onlay *materials*. A small number of payers *exclude* reimbursement for lab-made or CAD/CAM *resin-based* onlays. Some payers have a UCR for onlays that is much lower than the comparable gold/ceramic onlay's reimbursement.

TIPS Onlay (D2642) would also be used to report a CAD/CAM porcelain/ceramic-type restoration with two surfaces.

NARRATIVES **IMPORTANT!** See D2542 for onlay narrative recommendations.

D2643 — ONLAY – PORCELAIN/CERAMIC – THREE SURFACES — CDT 2016

1. It is misleading to report an onlay if at least one cusp is not "capped" or "shoed." An onlay requires "capping one or more cusps and adjoining occlusal surfaces or the entire occlusal surface" per the glossary of dental terms in the ADA coding manual. A cusp tip must be covered for the restoration to be considered an onlay. Going up the incline "nearly" to the cusp *does not* restore the cusp.

2. It is misleading to report a core buildup (D2950) in conjunction with an inlay or an onlay. A core buildup D2950 should only be used in conjunction with a *crown*.

3. It is misleading to report a *resin-based* onlay code when a porcelain/ceramic material is used. This code reports a three surface porcelain/ceramic onlay.

COMMENTS An onlay must include a portion of the buccal and/or lingual surfaces and restore/cover at least one cusp. The margin of the onlay terminates above the height of contour on the buccal and/or lingual surface.

LIMITATIONS
1. Some payers have an age limitation of 13 years and older for reimbursement of onlays and/or crowns.
2. Trauma requiring a new onlay may override the five to 10 year replacement exclusion contained in most policies.
3. Some payers require that *all* cusps be restored in the restoration in order to obtain reimbursement for an onlay.
4. Onlay restorations may be excluded (for reimbursement) for esthetic, periodontal (splinting), abrasion, or erosion related reasons.
5. Porcelain/ceramics would include materials as Vita®, ProCad®, Empress®, Lava Ultimate®, Procera®, InCeram®, Lava®, Finesse®, Cerinate®, and Opc®. They *do not* include resin-based Cristobel®, Artglass®, Belleglass®, Targis®, Vectris®, Concept®, and similar materials.
6. Gold and ceramic are the most commonly reimbursed onlay *materials*. A small number of payers *exclude* reimbursement for laboratory made or CAD/CAM resin-based onlays. Some payers have a UCR fee for resin-based onlays that is much lower than the comparable gold/ceramic onlays' reimbursement.

TIPS Onlay (D2643) would also be used to report a CAD/CAM porcelain/ceramic restoration with three surfaces.

NARRATIVES **IMPORTANT!** See D2542 for onlay narrative recommendations.

D2644 — ONLAY – PORCELAIN/CERAMIC – FOUR OR MORE SURFACES — CDT 2016

CODING WARNING CORRECTION

1. It is misleading to report an onlay if at least one cusp is not "capped" or "shoed." An onlay requires "capping one or more cusps and adjoining occlusal surfaces or the entire occlusal surface" per the glossary of dental terms in the ADA coding manual. A cusp tip must be covered for the restoration to be considered an onlay. Going up the incline "nearly" to the cusp *does not* restore the cusp.
2. It is misleading to report a core buildup (D2950) in conjunction with an inlay or an onlay. A core buildup D2950 should only be used in conjunction with a *crown*.
3. It is misleading to report a *resin-based* onlay code when a porcelain/ceramic material is used. This code reports a four or more surface porcelain/ceramic onlay.

COMMENTS An onlay must include a portion of the buccal and/or lingual surfaces and restores/covers the cusp. The margin of the onlay terminates above the height of contour on the buccal and/or lingual surface.

LIMITATIONS
1. Some payers have an age limitation of 13 years and older for reimbursement of onlays and/or crowns.
2. Trauma requiring a new onlay may override the five to 10 year replacement exclusion contained in most policies.
3. Some payers require that *all* cusps be restored in the restoration in order to obtain reimbursement for an onlay.
4. Onlay restorations may be excluded (for reimbursement) for esthetic, periodontal (splinting), abrasion, or erosion related reasons.
5. Porcelain/ceramics would include materials as Vita®, ProCad®, Empress®, Lava Ultimate®, Procera®, InCeram®, Lava®, Finesse®, Cerinate®, and Opc®. They *do not* include resin-based Cristobel®, Artglass®, Belleglass®, Targis®, Vectris®, Concept®, and similar materials.
6. Gold and ceramic are the most commonly reimbursed onlay *materials*. A small number of payers *exclude* reimbursement for laboratory made or CAD/CAM resin-based onlays. Some payers have a UCR fee for resin-based composite onlays that is much lower than the comparable gold/ceramic onlays' reimbursement.

TIPS Onlay (D2644) would also be used to report a CAD/CAM porcelain/ceramic-type restoration with four or more surfaces.

NARRATIVES **IMPORTANT!** See D2542 for onlay narrative recommendations.

RESIN-BASED COMPOSITE INLAYS/ONLAYS MUST UTILIZE INDIRECT TECHNIQUE — CDT 2016

D2650 — INLAY – RESIN-BASED COMPOSITE – ONE SURFACE — CDT 2016

CODING WARNING CORRECTION

It is misleading to report inlays fabricated from Cristobel®, Artglass®, Belleglass® and similar resin-based materials using the ceramic codes (D2610-D2630). Reporting a resin inlay as a ceramic inlay for reimbursement is improper and misleading. Use D2650 to report an indirect (laboratory made) *resin* inlay.

LIMITATIONS
1. Inlays are rarely reimbursed. However, an alternate benefit may be reimbursed (amalgam/composite restoration).
2. If the practice participates in PPOs, reimbursement may be restricted by the PPO (third-party). The PPO may reimburse the alternate benefit of an amalgam/composite restoration.
3. Resin-based composites include Cristobel®, Artglass®, Belleglass®, Targis®, Vectris®, Concept®, and similar materials.

TIPS Inlay (D2650) would also be used to report a CAD/CAM *resin-based* material with one surface.

D2651 — INLAY – RESIN-BASED COMPOSITE – TWO SURFACES — CDT 2016

CODING WARNING CORRECTION

It is misleading to report inlays fabricated from Cristobel®, Artglass®, Belleglass®, and similar resin-based materials using the ceramic codes (D2610-D2630). Reporting a resin inlay as a ceramic inlay for reimbursement is improper and misleading. Use D2651 to report an indirect (lab-made) *resin* inlay, two surfaces.

LIMITATIONS
1. Inlays are rarely reimbursed. However, an alternate benefit may be reimbursed (amalgam/composite restoration).
2. If the practice participates in PPOs, reimbursement may be restricted by the PPO (third-party). The PPO may reimburse the alternate benefit of an amalgam/composite restoration.
3. Resin-based composites include Cristobel®, Artglass®, Belleglass®, Targis®, Vectris®, Concept®, and similar materials.

TIPS Inlay (D2651) would also be used to report a CAD/CAM *resin-based* material with two surfaces.

D2652 — INLAY – RESIN-BASED COMPOSITE – THREE OR MORE SURFACES — CDT 2016

CODING WARNING CORRECTION

It is misleading to report inlays fabricated from Cristobel®, Artglass®, Belleglass®, and similar resin-based materials using the ceramic codes (D2610-D2630). Reporting a resin inlay as a ceramic inlay for reimbursement is improper and misleading. Use D2652 to report an indirect (lab-made) *resin* inlay, three or more surfaces.

LIMITATIONS
1. Inlays are rarely reimbursed. However, an alternate benefit may be reimbursed (amalgam/composite restoration).
2. If the practice participates in PPOs, reimbursement may be restricted by the PPO (third-party). The PPO may reimburse the alternate benefit of an amalgam/composite restoration.
3. Resin-based composites include Cristobel®, Artglass®, Belleglass®, Targis®, Vectris®, Concept®, and similar materials.

TIPS Inlay (D2652) would also be used to report a CAD/CAM *resin-based* material with three or more surfaces.

D2662 — ONLAY – RESIN-BASED COMPOSITE – TWO SURFACES — CDT 2016

CODING WARNING CORRECTION

1. It is misleading to report an onlay if at least one cusp is not "capped" or "shoed." An onlay requires "capping one or more cusps and adjoining occlusal surfaces or the entire occlusal surface" per the glossary of dental terms in the ADA coding manual. A cusp tip must be covered for the restoration to be considered an onlay. Going up the incline "nearly" to the cusp *does not* restore the cusp.
2. It is misleading to report a core buildup (D2950) in conjunction with an inlay or an onlay. A core buildup D2950 should only be used in conjunction with a *crown* (required for crown retention).
3. Some practices erroneously report Cristobel®, Artglass®, Belleglass® and similar materials using the ceramic code D2642. Report this resin-based composite restoration as an "indirect" (laboratory made) or CAD/CAM resin, D2662. Reporting a ceramic code for reimbursement when using this resin-based material is improper and misleading.

COMMENTS An onlay must include a portion of the buccal and/or lingual surfaces and restore/cover at least one cusp. The margin of the onlay terminates above the height of contour on the buccal and/or lingual surface.

LIMITATIONS
1. Some payers have an age limitation of 13 years and older for reimbursement of onlays and/or crowns.

2. Trauma requiring a new onlay may override the five to 10 year replacement exclusion contained in most policies.

3. Some payers require that *all* cusps be restored in the restoration in order to obtain reimbursement for an onlay.

4. Onlay restorations may be excluded (for reimbursement) for esthetic, periodontal (splinting), abrasion, or erosion related reasons.

5. Gold and ceramic are the most commonly reimbursed onlay *materials*. A small number of payers *exclude* reimbursement for laboratory made or CAD/CAM resin-based onlays. Some payers have a UCR fee for resin-based composite onlays that is much lower than the comparable gold/ceramic onlay.

6. *Be careful to report a buccal and/or lingual surface in association with the onlay coding.* An MOD *does not* describe an onlay. An MO*F*, MO*L*, DO*F,* DO*L*, MOD*L*, MOD*F* or MOD*FL* describes an onlay.

TIPS   Onlay (D2642) would be used to report a CAD/CAM *porcelain/ceramic* restoration with two surfaces. See D2642.

NARRATIVES   **IMPORTANT!** See D2542 for onlay narrative recommendations.

D2663   ONLAY – RESIN-BASED COMPOSITE – THREE SURFACES   CDT 2016

CODING WARNING CORRECTION

1. It is misleading to report an onlay if at least one cusp is not "capped" or "shoed." An onlay requires "capping one or more cusps and adjoining occlusal surfaces or the entire occlusal surface" per the glossary of dental terms in the ADA coding manual. A cusp tip must be covered for the restoration to be considered an onlay. Going up the incline "nearly" to the cusp *does not* restore the cusp.

2. It is misleading to report a core buildup (D2950) in conjunction with an inlay or an onlay. A core buildup D2950 should only be used in conjunction with a *crown* (required for crown retention).

3. Some practices erroneously report Cristobel®, Artglass®, Belleglass® and similar materials using the ceramic code D2643. Report this resin-based composite restoration as an "indirect" (laboratory made) or CAD/CAM resin, D2663. Reporting ceramic coding for reimbursement with this resin material is improper and misleading.

COMMENTS   An onlay must include a portion of the buccal and/or lingual surfaces and restores/covers at least one cusp. The margin of the onlay terminates above the height of contour on the buccal and/or lingual surface.

LIMITATIONS
1. Some payers have an age limitation of 13 years and older for reimbursement of onlays and/or crowns.

2. Trauma requiring a new onlay may override the five to 10 year replacement exclusion contained in most policies.

3. Some payers require that *all* cusps be restored in the restoration in order to obtain reimbursement for an onlay.

4. Onlay restorations may be excluded (for reimbursement) for esthetic, periodontal (splinting), abrasion, or erosion related reasons.

5. Gold and ceramic are the most commonly reimbursed onlay *materials*. A small number of payers *exclude* reimbursement for lab-made or CAD/CAM resin-based onlays. Some payers have a UCR fee for resin-based composite onlays that is much lower than the comparable gold/ceramic onlays' reimbursement.

6. Be careful to report a buccal and/or lingual surface in association with the onlay coding. MOD does not describe an onlay. An MO*F*, MO*L*, DO*F*, DO*L*, MOD*L*, MOD*F* or MOD*FL* describes an onlay.

TIPS   Onlay (D2643) would be used to report a CAD/CAM *porcelain/ceramic* type restoration with three surfaces. See D2643.

NARRATIVES   **IMPORTANT!** See D2542 for onlay narrative recommendations.

| **D2664** | **ONLAY – RESIN-BASED COMPOSITE – FOUR OR MORE SURFACES** | **CDT 2016** |

CODING WARNING CORRECTION

1. It is misleading to report an onlay if at least one cusp is not "capped" or "shoed." An onlay requires "capping one or more cusps and adjoining occlusal surfaces or the entire occlusal surface" per the glossary of dental terms in the ADA coding manual. A cusp tip must be covered for the restoration to be considered an onlay. Going up the incline "nearly" to the cusp *does not* restore the cusp.
2. It is misleading to report a core buildup (D2950) in conjunction with an inlay or an onlay. A core buildup D2950 should only be used in conjunction with a crown (required for *crown* retention).
3. Some practices erroneously report Cristobel®, Artglass®, Belleglass® and similar materials using the ceramic code D2644. Report this resin-based composite restoration as an "indirect" (laboratory made) or CAD/CAM resin, D2664. Reporting ceramic coding for reimbursement with this resin material is improper and misleading.

COMMENTS An onlay must include a portion of the buccal and/or lingual surfaces and restore/cover at least one cusp. The margin of the onlay terminates above the height of contour on the buccal and/or lingual surface.

LIMITATIONS
1. Some payers have an age limitation of 13 years and older for reimbursement of onlays and/or crowns.
2. Trauma requiring a new onlay may override the five to 10 year replacement exclusion contained in most policies.
3. Some payers require that *all* cusps be restored in the restoration in order to obtain reimbursement for an onlay.
4. Onlay restorations may be excluded (for reimbursement) for esthetic, periodontal (splinting), abrasion, or erosion related reasons.
5. Gold and ceramic are the most commonly reimbursed onlay *materials*. A small number of payers *exclude* reimbursement for laboratory made or CAD/CAM resin-based onlays. Some payers have a UCR fee for resin-based composite onlays that is much lower than the comparable gold/ceramic onlays' reimbursement.
6. Be careful to report a buccal and/or lingual surface in association with the onlay coding. MOD does not describe an onlay. An MO*F*, MO*L*, DO*F*, DO*L*, MOD*L*, MOD*F* or MOD*FL* describes an onlay.

TIPS Onlay (D2644) would be used to report a CAD/CAM *porcelain/ceramic* restoration with four or more surfaces. See D2644.

NARRATIVES IMPORTANT! See D2542 for onlay narrative recommendations.

| **CROWNS – SINGLE RESTORATIONS ONLY** | **CDT 2016** |

| **CLASSIFICATION OF MATERIALS** | **CDT 2016** |

Classification of Metals (Source: ADA Council on Scientific Affairs – online at ADA.org/2190.aspx**)**

The noble metal classification system has been adopted as a more precise method of reporting various alloys used in dentistry. The alloys are defined on the basis of the percentage of metal content:

high noble alloys - noble metal content >= 60% (gold+platinum group) and gold >= 40%;

titanium and titanium alloys – Titanium >= 85%;

noble alloys - noble metal content >= 25% (gold+platinum group);

predominantly base alloys - noble metal content < 25% (gold+platinum group);

*metals of the platinum group are platinum, palladium, rhodium, iridium, osmium and ruthenium.

Porcelain/ceramic - Refers to pressed, fired, polished or milled materials containing predominantly inorganic refractory compounds including porcelains, glasses, ceramics and glass-ceramics.

Resin - Refers to any resin-based composite, including fiber or ceramic reinforced polymer compounds, and glass ionomers.

GENERAL COMMENTS FOR CROWN SERVICES — AUTHOR'S COMMENTS

CODING WARNING CORRECTION

1. It is misleading to report natural tooth crowns if the restoration is a crown on an implant. Select the appropriate code from the implant services (D6000-D6199) section.

2. It is misleading to report retainer crowns of a fixed bridge as a single crown to receive a higher reimbursement 80% of the UCR fee rather than a 50% UCR fee for a bridge retainer. The reimbursement level, if different, is set by contract.

3. It is misleading to report Cristobel®, Artglass®, Belleglass®, and similar materials using the porcelain/ceramic codes, rather than the correct "indirect" (laboratory processed) resin codes. Cristobel®, Artglass®, and Belleglass® are considered laboratory processed indirect resins, not porcelain/ceramics. Porcelain materials could include Vita®, ProCad®, Empress®, Procera®, InCeram®, Lava®, Lava Ultimate®, Finesse®, Cerinate®, and Opc®.

CODING WATCH CORRECTION

Many practices commonly miscode the type of metal used in a crown (high noble, noble, base, etc.). The treatment plan and laboratory slip should always document the type of metal. With this information, the correct code can easily be chosen.

COMMENTS

1. Crown replacement clause exclusions vary from five to 10 years, with the trend moving towards 10 years, or even lifetime! However, trauma requiring a new crown may nullify the replacement exclusion.

2. Most payers have an age limitation exclusion. They will not reimburse a permanent crown unless the patient is at least 12-13 years old. If the patient is under 18, always determine if there is an age exclusion before starting treatment.

TIPS

1. It is essential to include clear, readable (diagnostic) radiographic images and a narrative (even though some payers do not require one) when reporting a crown to reduce delays and/or claim denials. Note and comment on the existence of caries or other pathology; condition and size of prior restoration; and the remaining tooth structure. Mention missing cusps, fractured cusps and undermined cusps. Comment on any patient symptoms. If fracture is the reason for the crown, document how the fracture was diagnosed, e.g., MB cusp positive to tooth sleuth.

2. Use the term "bridge retainer," not "bridge abutment." Abutments are placed on implants and support abutment-supported implant crowns.

3. If a tooth to be crowned has a root canal, send a periapical radiograph to verify adequate endodontic treatment.

D2710 CROWN – RESIN-BASED COMPOSITE (INDIRECT) — CDT 2016

CODING WARNING CORRECTION

1. It is misleading to report a crown placed on a *natural* tooth if the restoration is an *implant supported* crown.

2. It is misleading to report retainer crowns of a fixed bridge as single crowns in order to receive a higher reimbursement. (Single unit crowns may be reimbursed at 80% of the UCR fee whereas a retainer crown may be reimbursed at 50% of the UCR fee.)

3. It is misleading to report Cristobel®, Artglass®, Belleglass® and similar materials using the porcelain/ceramic codes, rather than the "indirect" (laboratory processed) or CAD/CAM resin-based composite codes. Cristobel®, Artglass®, and Belleglass® are considered laboratory processed indirect resin-based composites, not porcelain/ceramics. Porcelain materials could include Vita®, ProCad®, Empress®, Lava Ultimate®, Procera®, InCeram®, Lava®, Finesse®, Cerinate®, and Opc®.

COMMENTS D2710 is used to report Cristobel®, Artglass®, Fibrecor®, Targis®, Vectris®, Concept®, and Belleglass® type restorations. The UCR fee is often lower for an indirect resin-based composite than for porcelain/ceramic restorations.

LIMITATIONS

1. Most payers have an age limitation exclusion. They will not reimburse a permanent crown unless the patient is at least 12-13 years old. If the patient is under 18, always determine if there is an age used exclusion before starting treatment.

2. Crown replacement may be limited by the plan and can vary from five to 10 years after the prior placement. The trend is moving toward 10 years. Trauma requiring a new crown may override this replacement exclusion.

TIPS
1. The code used to report the restoration should properly reflect the material (resin) used for the restoration. The material used should be the same as recorded in the treatment plan, on the lab slip, and the insurance claim form.
2. D2710 would also be used to report a *resin-based* CAD/CAM crown when using a resin block to mill the restoration.

NARRATIVES
1. When submitting a crown claim it is essential that a narrative be included to avoid delays and/or claim denials. The narrative should address the existence of caries or other pathology, condition and size of prior restoration, and the condition of the remaining tooth structure. Make note of any undermined, fractured or missing cusps and any symptoms the patient may be experiencing with the affected tooth.
2. If treating cracked tooth syndrome, indicate how the diagnosis was made, e.g., MF cusp positive to Tooth Slooth™.
3. "See attached radiographic image" (if tooth has RCT, send PA radiographic image).
4. List any missing cusps.
5. State the estimated percentage of healthy tooth structure left after fracture, caries and/or any previous restoration is removed.
6. State if tooth has existing or planned RCT (root canal therapy).
7. State if tooth has circumferential decay and amount of decay, e.g. circumferential decay on M, L and D encompassing 270 degrees of tooth.
8. State endodontic and periodontal prognosis for tooth.
9. If this is a replacement crown, state date that the previous crown was seated.
10. If replacing an existing crown, state reason for replacement, e.g., tooth has caries, margins are open, porcelain is fractured off, poor contacts are causing food impactions, etc.

D2712   REVISED CROWN – 3/4 RESIN-BASED COMPOSITE (INDIRECT)   CDT 2016

This procedure does not include facial veneers.

REVISIONS   This ~~code~~ procedure does not include facial veneers.

CODING WARNING CORRECTION
1. It is misleading to report a crown placed on a *natural* tooth if the restoration is an *implant supported* crown.
2. It is misleading to report retainer crowns of a fixed bridge as a single crown(s) in order to receive a higher reimbursement. (Single unit crowns may be reimbursed at 80% of the UCR fee whereas a retainer crown may be reimbursed at 50% of the UCR fee.)
3. It is misleading to report Cristobel®, Artglass®, Belleglass® and similar materials using the porcelain/ceramic codes, rather than the "indirect" (laboratory processed) or CAD/CAM resin codes. Cristobel®, Artglass®, and Belleglass® are considered lab processed indirect resins, not porcelain/ceramics. Porcelain materials could include Vita®, ProCad®, Empress®, Procera®, InCeram®, Lava®, Lava Ultimate®, Finesse®, Cerinate®, and Opc®.

COMMENTS   3/4 Crown (D2712) is used to report Cristobel®, Artglass®, Fibrecor®, Targis®, Vectris®, Concept®, and Belleglass® type restorations. The UCR fee is often lower for an indirect resin-based composite than for porcelain/ceramic restorations.

LIMITATIONS
1. Most payers have an age limitation exclusion. They will not reimburse a permanent crown unless the patient is at least 12-13 years old. If the patient is under 18, always determine if there is an age used exclusion before starting treatment.
2. Crown replacement may be limited by the plan and can vary from five to 10 years after the prior placement. The trend is moving toward 10 years. Trauma requiring a new crown may override this replacement exclusion.

TIPS

1. The code used to report the restoration should properly reflect the material (resin) used for the restoration. The material used should be the same as recorded in the treatment plan, on the lab slip, and the insurance claim form.
2. D2712 would also be used to report a *resin-based* CAD/CAM crown when using a resin block to mill the restoration.

NARRATIVES   **IMPORTANT!** See D2710 for crown narrative recommendations.

D2720   CROWN – RESIN WITH HIGH NOBLE METAL   CDT 2016

CODING WARNING CORRECTION

1. It is misleading to report a crown placed on a *natural* tooth if the restoration is an *implant supported* crown.
2. It is misleading to report retainer crowns of a fixed bridge as a single crown(s) in order to receive a higher reimbursement. (Single unit crowns may be reimbursed at 80% of the UCR fee, whereas a retainer crown may be reimbursed at 50% of the UCR fee.)
3. It is misleading to report Cristobel®, Artglass®, Belleglass®, and similar materials using the porcelain/ceramic codes, rather than the "indirect" (lab-processed) or CAD/CAM resin codes. Cristobel®, Artglass®, and Belleglass® are considered lab processed indirect resins, not porcelain/ceramics. Porcelain materials could include Vita®, ProCad®, Empress®, Procera®, InCeram®, Lava®, Lava Ultimate®, Finesse®, Cerinate®, and Opc®.

COMMENTS

1. D2720 is used to report a crown using high noble metal and covered by a resin material such as Cristobel®, Artglass®, Fibrecor®, Targis®, Vectris®, Concept®, and Belleglass®. The UCR fee may be lower for an indirect resin-based composite coating, than for porcelain/ceramic coated restorations.
2. The code used to report the restoration should properly reflect the material (resin with high noble metal) used for the restoration. The material used should be the same as recorded in the treatment plan, on the lab slip, and the insurance claim form.

LIMITATIONS

1. Most payers have an age limitation exclusion. They will not reimburse a permanent crown unless the patient is at least 12-13 years old. If the patient is under 18, always determine if there is an age used exclusion before starting treatment.
2. Crown replacement may be limited by the plan and can vary from five to 10 years after the prior placement. The trend is moving toward 10 years. Trauma requiring a new crown may override this replacement exclusion.

NARRATIVES   **IMPORTANT!** See D2710 for crown narrative recommendations.

D2721   CROWN – RESIN WITH PREDOMINANTLY BASE METAL   CDT 2016

CODING WARNING CORRECTION

1. It is misleading to report a crown placed on a *natural* tooth if the restoration is an *implant supported* crown.
2. It is misleading to report retainer crowns of a fixed bridge as a single crown(s) in order to receive a higher reimbursement. (Single unit crowns may be reimbursed at 80% of the UCR fee whereas a retainer crown may be reimbursed at 50% of the UCR fee.)
3. It is misleading to report Cristobel®, Artglass®, Belleglass®, and similar materials using the porcelain/ceramic codes, rather than the "indirect" (lab-processed) or CAD/CAM resin codes. Cristobel®, Artglass®, and Belleglass® are considered lab processed indirect resins, not porcelain/ceramics. Porcelain materials could include Vita®, ProCad®, Empress®, Procera®, InCeram®, Lava®, Finesse®, Lava Ultimate®, Cerinate®, and Opc®.

COMMENTS

1. D2721 is used to report a *base metal* crown coated with materials such as Cristobel®, Artglass®, Fibrecor®, Targis®, Vectris®, Concept®, and Belleglass®. The UCR fee may be lower for an indirect resin-based composite coating than for porcelain/ceramic coated restorations.
2. The code used to report the restoration should properly reflect the material (resin with predominantly base metal) used for the restoration. The material used should be the same as recorded in the treatment plan, on the lab slip, and the insurance claim form.

LIMITATIONS
1. Most payers have an age limitation exclusion. They will not reimburse a permanent crown unless the patient is at least 12-13 years old. If the patient is under 18, always determine if there is an age used exclusion before starting treatment.
2. Crown replacement may be limited by the plan and can vary from five to 10 years after the prior placement. (The trend is moving toward 10 years). Trauma requiring a new crown may override this replacement exclusion.

NARRATIVES **IMPORTANT!** See D2710 for crown narrative recommendations.

D2722 CROWN – RESIN WITH NOBLE METAL CDT 2016

CODING WARNING CORRECTION
1. It is misleading to report a crown placed on a *natural* tooth if the restoration is an *implant supported* crown.
2. It is misleading to report retainer crowns of a fixed bridge as a single crown(s) in order to receive a higher reimbursement. (Single unit crowns may be reimbursed at 80% of the UCR fee, whereas a retainer crown may be reimbursed at 50% of the UCR fee.)
3. It is misleading to report Cristobel®, Artglass®, Belleglass®, and similar materials using the porcelain/ceramic codes, rather than the "indirect" (lab-processed) or CAD/CAM resin codes. Cristobel®, Artglass®, and Belleglass® are considered lab processed indirect resins, not porcelain/ceramics. Porcelain materials could include Vita®, ProCad®, Empress®, Procera®, InCeram®, Lava®, Finesse®, Cerinate®, and Opc®.

COMMENTS
1. D2722 is used to report a noble *metal* crown coated with materials such as Cristobel®, Artglass®, Fibrecor®, Targis®, Vectris®, Concept®, and Belleglass®. The UCR fee may be lower for an indirect resin-based composite coating than for porcelain/ceramic coated restorations.
2. The code used to report the restoration should properly reflect the material (resin with noble metal) used for the restoration. The material used should be the same as recorded in the treatment plan, on the lab slip, and the insurance claim form.

LIMITATIONS
1. Most payers have an age limitation exclusion. They will not reimburse a permanent crown unless the patient is at least 12-13 years old. If the patient is under 18, always determine if there is an age used exclusion before starting treatment.
2. Crown replacement may be limited by the plan and can vary from five to 10 years after the prior placement. (The trend is moving toward 10 years). Trauma requiring a new crown may override this replacement exclusion.

NARRATIVES **IMPORTANT!** See D2710 for crown narrative recommendations.

D2740 CROWN – PORCELAIN/CERAMIC SUBSTRATE CDT 2016

CODING WARNING CORRECTION
1. It is misleading to report a crown placed on a *natural* tooth if the restoration is an *implant supported* crown.
2. It is misleading to report retainer crowns of a fixed bridge as a single crown(s) in order to receive a higher reimbursement. (Single unit crowns may be reimbursed at 80% of the UCR fee whereas a retainer crown may be reimbursed at 50% of the UCR fee.)
3. Porcelain materials could include Vita®, Lava Ultimate®, ProCad®, Empress®, Procera®, InCeram®, Lava®, Finesse®, Cerinate®, Zirconia®, BruxZir®, Opc®, e-max®

COMMENTS Empress®, Procera®, Inceram®, Lava Ultimate®, Finesse®, Cerestore®, Cerinate®, Zirconia®, BruxZir® and Opc® are porcelain/ceramic materials.

LIMITATIONS
1. Porcelain/ceramic crown (D2740) should not be used to describe facial veneers.
2. Most payers have an age limitation exclusion. They will not reimburse a permanent crown unless the patient is at least 12-13 years old. If the patient is under 18, always determine if there is an age used exclusion before starting treatment.

3. Reimbursement for crown replacement may be limited by the plan and can vary from five to 10 years after the prior placement. (The trend is moving toward 10 years). Trauma requiring a new crown may override this replacement exclusion.
4. D2740 may be reimbursed as a porcelain fused to metal crown, or gold metal crown as an alternate benefit.
5. The code used to report the restoration should properly reflect the material (porcelain/ceramic substrate) used for the restoration. The material used should be the same as recorded in the treatment plan, on the lab slip, and the insurance claim form.

TIPS D2740 would be used to report a CAD/CAM porcelain/ceramic crown restoration milled from a Vita®/Procad® block.

NARRATIVES **IMPORTANT!** See D2710 for crown narrative recommendations.

The image depicts a porcelain/ceramic crown (D2740).

Courtesy of Keller Dental Lab

D2750 CROWN – PORCELAIN FUSED TO HIGH NOBLE METAL — CDT 2016

1. It is misleading to report a crown placed on a *natural* tooth if the restoration is an *implant supported* crown.
2. It is misleading to report retainer crowns of a fixed bridge as a single crown(s) in order to receive a higher reimbursement. (Single unit crowns may be reimbursed at 80% of the UCR fee, whereas a retainer crown may be reimbursed at 50% of the UCR fee.)
3. Porcelain materials could include Vita®, Lava Ultimate®, ProCad®, Empress®, Procera®, InCeram®, Lava®, Finesse®, Cerinate®, Zirconia®, BruxZir® and Opc®.

LIMITATIONS
1. Most payers have an age limitation exclusion. They will not reimburse a permanent crown unless the patient is at least 12-13 years old. If the patient is under 18, always determine if there is an age used exclusion before starting treatment.
2. Reimbursement for crown replacement may be limited by the plan and can vary from five to 10 years after the prior placement. The trend is moving toward 10 years. Trauma requiring a new crown may override this replacement exclusion.
3. The code used to report the restoration should properly reflect the material (porcelain fused to high noble) used for the restoration. The material used should be the same as recorded in the treatment plan, on the lab slip, and the insurance claim form.

TIPS
1. D2750 may also be used to report a PFM high noble Captek® crown and Gramm crowns. A Gramm crown is a PFM high noble crown that has a thin 24K gold coping.
2. Porcelain/ceramic materials include Empress®, Procera®, Inceram®, Lava®, Finesse®, Cerestore®, Cerinate®, and Opc®.

NARRATIVES **IMPORTANT!** See D2710 for crown narrative recommendations.

D2751   CROWN – PORCELAIN FUSED TO PREDOMINANTLY BASE METAL   CDT 2016

CODING WARNING CORRECTION

1. It is misleading to report a crown placed on a *natural* tooth if the restoration is an *implant supported* crown.
2. It is misleading to report retainer crowns of a fixed bridge as a single crown(s) in order to receive a higher reimbursement. (Single unit crowns may be reimbursed at 80% of the UCR fee whereas a retainer crown may be reimbursed at 50% of the UCR fee.)
3. Porcelain materials could include Vita®, ProCad®, Empress®, Procera®, InCeram®, Lava®, Finesse®, Cerinate®, and Opc®.

LIMITATIONS

1. Most payers have an age limitation exclusion. They will not reimburse a permanent crown unless the patient is at least 12-13 years old. If the patient is under 18, always determine if there is an age used exclusion before starting treatment.
2. Reimbursement for crown replacement may be limited by the plan and can vary from five to 10 years after the prior placement. (The trend is moving toward 10 years). Trauma requiring a new crown may override this replacement exclusion.
3. The code used to report the restoration should properly reflect the material (porcelain fused to predominantly base metal) used for the restoration. The material used should be the same as recorded in the treatment plan, on the lab slip, and the insurance claim form.

TIPS   Porcelain/ceramic materials include Empress®, Procera®, Inceram®, Lava®, Lava Ultimate®, Finesse®, Cerestore®, Cerinate®, and Opc®.

NARRATIVES   **IMPORTANT!** See D2710 for crown narrative recommendations.

D2752   CROWN – PORCELAIN FUSED TO NOBLE METAL   CDT 2016

CODING WARNING CORRECTION

1. It is misleading to report a crown placed on a *natural* tooth if the restoration is an *implant supported* crown.
2. It is misleading to report retainer crowns of a fixed bridge as a single crown(s) in order to receive a higher reimbursement. (Single unit crowns may be reimbursed at 80% of the UCR fee whereas a retainer crown may be reimbursed at 50% of the UCR fee.)
3. Porcelain materials could include Vita®, ProCad®, Empress®, Procera®, InCeram®, Lava®, Finesse®, Cerinate®, and Opc®.

LIMITATIONS

1. Most payers have an age limitation exclusion. They will not reimburse a permanent crown unless the patient is at least 12-13 years old. If the patient is under 18, always determine if there is an age used exclusion before starting treatment.
2. Reimbursement for crown replacement may be limited by the plan and can vary from five to 10 years after the prior placement. (The trend is moving toward 10 years). Trauma requiring a new crown may override this replacement exclusion.
3. The code used to report the restoration should properly reflect the material (porcelain fused to noble metal) used for the restoration. The material used should be the same as recorded in the treatment plan, on the lab slip, and the insurance claim form.

TIPS   Porcelain/ceramic materials include Empress®, Procera®, Inceram®, Lava®, Lava Ultimate®, Finesse®, Cerestore®, Cerinate®, and Opc®.

NARRATIVES   **IMPORTANT!** See D2710 for crown narrative recommendations.

D2780 CROWN – 3/4 CAST HIGH NOBLE METAL — CDT 2016

CODING WARNING CORRECTION

1. It is misleading to report a crown placed on a *natural* tooth if the restoration is an *implant supported* crown.
2. It is misleading to report retainer crowns of a fixed bridge as a single crown(s) in order to receive a higher reimbursement. (Single unit crowns may be reimbursed at 80% of the UCR fee whereas a retainer crown may be reimbursed at 50% of the UCR fee.)

COMMENTS

1. D2780 is used to report a ¾ cast *high noble metal* crown.
2. ¾ crown (D2780) is typically a restoration on the upper first molar, but can be done on any tooth. This type of crown is sometimes designed to leave the mesio-buccal cusp intact for esthetics.
3. ¾ crown (D2780) covers the occlusal and 3 to 4 of the molar cusps and extends beyond the height of contour of either the facial or lingual surface.
4. The code used to report the restoration should properly reflect the material (high noble metal) used for the restoration. The material used should be the same as recorded in the treatment plan, on the lab slip, and the insurance claim form.

LIMITATIONS

1. Most payers have an age limitation exclusion. They will not reimburse a permanent crown unless the patient is at least 12-13 years old. If the patient is under 18, always determine if there is an age used exclusion before starting treatment.
2. Reimbursement for crown replacement may be limited by the plan and can vary from five to 10 years after the prior placement. (The trend is moving toward 10 years). Trauma requiring a new crown may override this replacement exclusion.

NARRATIVES   **IMPORTANT!** See D2710 for crown narrative recommendations.

D2781 CROWN – 3/4 CAST PREDOMINANTLY BASE METAL — CDT 2016

CODING WARNING CORRECTION

1. It is misleading to report a crown placed on a *natural* tooth if the restoration is an *implant supported* crown.
2. It is misleading to report retainer crowns of a fixed bridge as a single crown in order to receive a higher reimbursement. (Single unit crowns may be reimbursed at 80% of the UCR, whereas a retainer crown may be reimbursed at 50% of the UCR fee.)

COMMENTS

1. ¾ crown (D2781) is used to report a ¾ cast predominately base metal crown.
2. ¾ crown (D2781) is typically a restoration on the upper first molar, but can be done on any tooth. This type of crown is sometimes designed to leave the mesio-buccal cusp intact for esthetics.
3. ¾ crown (D2781) covers the occlusal and 3 to 4 of the molar cusps and extends beyond the height of contour of either the facial or lingual surface.
4. The code used to report the restoration should properly reflect the material (predominantly base metal) used for the restoration. The material used should be the same as recorded in the treatment plan, on the lab slip, and the insurance claim form.

LIMITATIONS

1. Most payers have an age limitation exclusion. They will not reimburse a permanent crown unless the patient is at least 12-13 years old. If the patient is under 18, always determine if there is an age used exclusion before starting treatment.
2. Reimbursement for crown replacement may be limited by the plan and can vary from five to 10 years after the prior placement. (The trend is moving toward 10 years). Trauma requiring a new crown may override this replacement exclusion.

NARRATIVES   **IMPORTANT!** See D2710 for crown narrative recommendations.

D2782 — CROWN – 3/4 CAST NOBLE METAL — CDT 2016

CODING WARNING / CORRECTION

1. It is misleading to report a crown placed on a *natural* tooth if the restoration is an *implant supported* crown.
2. It is misleading to report retainer crowns of a fixed bridge as a single crown(s) in order to receive a higher reimbursement. (Single unit crowns may be reimbursed at 80% of the UCR fee, whereas a retainer crown may be reimbursed at 50% of the UCR fee.)

COMMENTS

1. ¾ crown (D2782) is used to report a ¾ cast predominately noble metal crown.
2. ¾ crown (D2782) is typically a restoration on the upper first molar, but can be any tooth. This type of crown is used to leave the mesio-buccal cusp intact for esthetics.
3. ¾ crown (D2782) covers the occlusal and 3 to 4 of the molar cusps and extends beyond the height of contour of either the facial or lingual surface.
4. The code used to report the restoration should properly reflect the material (noble metal) used for the restoration. The material used should be the same as recorded in the treatment plan, on the lab slip, and the insurance claim form.

LIMITATIONS

1. Most payers have an age limitation exclusion. They will not reimburse a permanent crown unless the patient is at least 12-13 years old. If the patient is under 18, always determine if there is an age used exclusion before starting treatment.
2. Reimbursement for crown replacement may be limited by the plan and can vary from five to 10 years after the prior placement. (The trend is moving toward 10 years). Trauma requiring a new crown may override this replacement exclusion.

NARRATIVES **IMPORTANT!** See D2710 for crown narrative recommendations.

D2783 — REVISED CROWN – 3/4 PORCELAIN/CERAMIC — CDT 2016

This procedure does not include facial veneers.

REVISIONS This ~~code~~ procedure does not include facial veneers.

CODING WARNING / CORRECTION

1. It is misleading to report a crown placed on a *natural* tooth if the restoration is an *implant supported* crown.
2. It is misleading to report retainer crowns of a fixed bridge as a single crown(s) in order to receive a higher reimbursement. (Single unit crowns may be reimbursed at 80% of the UCR, whereas a retainer crown may be reimbursed at 50% of the UCR fee.)
3. Porcelain material could include Vita®, ProCad®, Empress®, Procera®, InCeram®, Lava®, Lava Ultimate®, Finesse®, Cerinate®, and Opc®.

CODING WATCH / CORRECTION

It is improper to report ¾ crown (D2783) when a labial veneer (D2962) was placed. The descriptor of the porcelain veneer code (D2962) includes "the extension of the restoration interproximally and/or covering the incisal edge." See D2962 for porcelain laminate veneers.

COMMENTS

1. ¾ crown (D2783) is not synonymous (or interchangeable) with porcelain veneer (D2962). A ¾ porcelain crown (D2783) may be reimbursed. Porcelain veneers (D2962) are generally considered cosmetic in nature and not reimbursed.
2. The porcelain veneer (D2962) descriptor states that a veneer preparation "extends interproximally and/or covers the incisal edge." An anterior ¾ porcelain crown (D2783) involves the mesial, facial and distal surfaces. The lingual portion of the tooth remains intact – in essence, a "reverse ¾ crown."

3. ¾ Crown (D2783) porcelain/ceramic would include materials such as Empress®, Procera®, Inceram®, Lava®, Lava Ultimate®, Finesse®, Cerinate®, and Opc®.

4. D2783 would be used to report a CAD/CAM *porcelain/ceramic* crown restoration milled from a Vita®/Procad® block.

5. The code used to report the restoration should properly reflect the material (porcelain/ceramic) used for the restoration. The material used should be the same as recorded in the treatment plan, on the lab slip, and the insurance claim form.

LIMITATIONS

1. The ¾ ceramic crown (D2783), along with other crowns, may be payable when used to correct significant pathology such as failing restorations, caries and/or fractures, and undermined, fractured or missing cusps.

2. Most payers have an age limitation exclusion. They will not reimburse a permanent crown unless the patient is at least 12-13 years old. If the patient is under 18, always determine if there is an age used exclusion before starting treatment.

3. Reimbursement for crown replacement may be limited by the plan and can vary from five to 10 years after the prior placement. (The trend is moving toward 10 years). Trauma requiring a new crown may override this replacement exclusion.

NARRATIVES

1. The ¾ crown (D2783) is often reimbursed when supported with full documentation. Include a proper narrative, diagnostic radiographic images, and photographs (pretreatment and postpreparation). To be considered for reimbursement of D2783, some payers require a large pre-existing restoration and/or fracture and/or caries. D2783 would not typically be reimbursed if performed on a virgin anterior tooth.

2. **IMPORTANT!** See D2710 for crown narrative recommendations.

D2790 CROWN – FULL CAST HIGH NOBLE METAL — CDT 2016

CODING WARNING CORRECTION

1. It is misleading to report a crown placed on a *natural* tooth if the restoration is an *implant supported* crown.

2. It is misleading to report retainer crowns of a fixed bridge as a single crown(s) in order to receive a higher reimbursement. (Single unit crowns may be reimbursed at 80% of the UCR fee, whereas a retainer crown may be reimbursed at 50% of the UCR fee.)

LIMITATIONS

1. Most payers have an age limitation exclusion. They will not reimburse a permanent crown unless the patient is at least 12-13 years old. If the patient is under 18, always determine if there is an age used exclusion before starting treatment.

2. Reimbursement for crown replacement may be limited by the plan and can vary from five to 10 years after the prior placement. The trend is moving toward 10 years. Trauma requiring a new crown may override this replacement exclusion.

3. The code used to report the restoration should properly reflect the material (high noble metal) used for the restoration. The material used should be the same as recorded in the treatment plan, on the lab slip, and the insurance claim form.

NARRATIVES **IMPORTANT!** See D2710 for crown narrative recommendations.

D2791 CROWN – FULL CAST PREDOMINANTLY BASE METAL — CDT 2016

CODING WARNING CORRECTION

1. It is misleading to report a crown placed on a *natural* tooth if the restoration is an *implant supported* crown.

2. It is misleading to report retainer crowns of a fixed bridge as a single crown(s) in order to receive a higher reimbursement. (Single unit crowns may be reimbursed at 80% of the UCR fee, whereas a retainer crown may be reimbursed at 50% of the UCR fee.)

LIMITATIONS

1. Most payers have an age limitation exclusion. They will not reimburse a permanent crown unless the patient is at least 12-13 years old. If the patient is under 18, always determine if there is an age used exclusion before starting treatment.

2. Reimbursement for crown replacement may be limited by the plan and can vary from five to 10 years after the prior placement. The trend is moving toward 10 years. Trauma requiring a new crown may override this replacement exclusion.

3. The code used to report the restoration should properly reflect the material (predominantly base metal) used for the restoration. The material used should be the same as recorded in the treatment plan, on the lab slip, and the insurance claim form.

NARRATIVES **IMPORTANT!** See D2710 for crown narrative recommendations.

D2792 CROWN – FULL CAST NOBLE METAL   CDT 2016

CODING WARNING CORRECTION

1. It is misleading to report a crown placed on a *natural* tooth if the restoration is an *implant supported* crown.
2. It is misleading to report retainer crowns of a fixed bridge as a single crown(s) in order to receive a higher reimbursement. (Single unit crowns may be reimbursed at 80% of the UCR fee, whereas a retainer crown may be reimbursed at 50% of the UCR fee.)

LIMITATIONS
1. Most payers have an age limitation exclusion. They will not reimburse a permanent crown unless the patient is at least 12-13 years old. If the patient is under 18, always determine if there is an age used exclusion before starting treatment.
2. Reimbursement for crown replacement may be limited by the plan and can vary from five to 10 years after the prior placement. The trend is moving toward 10 years. Trauma may override this replacement exclusion.
3. The code used to report the restoration should properly reflect the material (noble metal) used for the restoration. The material used should be the same as recorded in the treatment plan, on the lab slip, and the insurance claim form.

NARRATIVES **IMPORTANT!** See D2710 for crown narrative recommendations.

D2794 CROWN – TITANIUM   CDT 2016

CODING WARNING CORRECTION

1. It is misleading to report a crown placed on a *natural* tooth if the restoration is an implant *supported* crown.
2. It is misleading to report retainer crowns of a fixed bridge as a single crown(s) in order to receive a higher reimbursement. (Single unit crowns may be reimbursed at 80% of the UCR fee, whereas a retainer crown may be reimbursed at 50% of the UCR fee.)

COMMENTS
1. The nomenclature for D2794 – titanium is very *broad*, and reports *any* type of titanium crown. D2794 includes full metallic titanium crowns, as well crowns with a titanium coping and other materials covering all or part of the crown's surface.
2. D2794 also reports porcelain fused to titanium crown.
3. The code used to report the restoration should properly reflect the material (titanium metal) used for the restoration. The material used should be the same as recorded in the treatment plan, on the lab slip, and the insurance claim form.

LIMITATIONS
1. Most payers have an age limitation exclusion. They will not reimburse a permanent crown unless the patient is at least 12-13 years old. If the patient is under 18, always determine if there is an age used exclusion before starting treatment.
2. Reimbursement for crown replacement may be limited by the plan and can vary from five to 10 years after the prior placement. The trend is moving toward 10 years. Trauma requiring a new crown may override this replacement exclusion.

NARRATIVES **IMPORTANT!** See D2710 for crown narrative recommendations.

D2799 — PROVISIONAL CROWN-FURTHER TREATMENT OR COMPLETION OF DIAGNOSIS NECESSARY PRIOR TO FINAL IMPRESSION — CDT 2016

Not to be used as a temporary crown for a routine prosthetic restoration.

CODING WARNING CORRECTION

Do not report provisional crown (D2799) as a temporary crown for routine crown restorations.

CODING WATCH CORRECTION

1. D2799 reports a single unit *provisional* crown of any duration.
2. See D6253/D6793 for a *multi-unit* provisional bridge of any duration.

COMMENTS

1. D2799 reports a provisional restoration. This type of provisional restoration allows time for healing or completion of other procedures, prior to the fabrication of the final definitive restoration. This includes a provisional crown placed over an implant abutment.
2. Provisional restorations may be used to change the vertical dimension, complete periodontal therapy, diagnose cracked tooth syndrome, etc.
3. A provisional crown (D2799) can be placed on a fractured tooth.

LIMITATIONS

1. A provisional crown (D2799) is placed as an interim restoration and allows time for healing or completion of other procedures. A provisional bridge (D6253/D6793) functions in like manner. Most dental plans exclude provisional procedures but these restorations are utilized as needed and can impact payment of the final prosthesis. This "interim" principal also applies to interim partial dentures (D5820/D5821), e.g., flippers, stayplates, etc., and interim complete dentures (D5810/D5811). Although CDT does not specify a minimum or a maximum amount of time these removable procedures must be in place, be aware that contracts often limit reimbursement based on how long the provisional restoration is in the mouth. Some plans may consider the provisional restoration a permanent restoration/prosthesis from the reimbursement perspective if the restoration/prosthesis is in place for 12 months or longer. (Some plans consider a provisional to be permanent after six months.) This means that a provisional crown (D2799), bridge, partial, or full denture can be subject to a plan's prosthetic replacement limitation. The submission of a claim for a provisional restoration/prosthesis may prevent the patient from receiving coverage on the permanent restoration for up to 10 years depending on the contract's language.
2. D2799 is reimbursed in limited circumstances. D2799 may apply in multi-staged treatment situations or where the provisional restoration is being used to diagnose a tooth fracture or some other pathology.
3. Reimbursement for D2799 is highly variable among payers.

TIPS

Use D6253 to report a provisional pontic and D6793 to report a provisional retainer crown of any duration.

NARRATIVES

1. State necessity for a provisional crown, e.g., completing periodontal therapy, cracked tooth syndrome. If diagnosis is cracked tooth syndrome, state method of diagnosis, e.g., Tooth Slooth™ positive on MF cusp. "See attached radiographic image." If tooth has RCT, send PA radiographic image.
2. State how long the crown will be utilized as an interim restoration.

OTHER RESTORATIVE SERVICES

D2990 — RESIN INFILTRATION OF INCIPIENT SMOOTH SURFACE LESIONS

Placement of an infiltrating resin restoration for strengthening, stabilizing and/or limiting the progression of the lesion.

Note: D2990 appears here correctly but is not in numerical order.

COMMENTS
1. D2990 reports the resin infiltration of incipient smooth surface lesions.
2. Historically, only two choices have been available with incipient caries: fluoride therapy or a restoration.
3. The DMG Icon® product is a treatment for incipient lesions or white spot lesions. The infiltrant is applied to arrest caries on smooth surfaces, including proximal surfaces. Resin infiltration allows for the treatment of incipient lesions prior to cavitation taking place. It cannot be used to treat advanced decay of the enamel into the dentin.

LIMITATIONS
1. As a fairly new code, D2990 is seldom reimbursed, and if reimbursed, the UCR fee may be poor. Ask for an alternate benefit of a two surface posterior composite (D2392) or a two surface anterior composite (D2331) should D2990 benefits not be available.
2. Enter service date and tooth number and area of infiltration.

D2910 — RE-CEMENT OR RE-BOND INLAY, ONLAY, VENEER OR PARTIAL COVERAGE RESTORATION

COMMENTS
1. D2910 reports re-cementing or re-bonding an inlay, onlay, veneer, or partial coverage restoration.
2. See D2920 for re-cementing or re-bonding a ¾ *crown or full crown.*

LIMITATIONS
1. Re-cementation or re-bonding is typically not reimbursed until six to 12 months following initial placement of the restoration.
2. If the re-cementation or re-bonding of the restoration is performed in a *different* office within the exclusion period, it may be reimbursed.

TIPS The fee for D2910 is comparable to the fee for re-cementing a ¾ or full crown.

D2915 — RE-CEMENT OR RE-BOND INDIRECTLY FABRICATED OR PREFABRICATED POST AND CORE

COMMENTS D2915 reports re-cementing or re-bonding an indirectly fabricated or prefabricated post and core as a stand-alone procedure.

LIMITATIONS
1. The re-cement or re-bond is typically not reimbursed until six to 12 months following initial placement of the post and core.
2. If re-cement or re-bond is performed in a *different* office within the exclusion period, it might be reimbursed.

NARRATIVES If re-cementation or re-bonding occurs in an office by a dentist that did not originally place the crown, note this in a brief narrative.

D2920 RE-CEMENT OR RE-BOND CROWN — CDT 2016

CODING CORRECTION — WATCH: It is improper to use re-cement or re-bond crown (D2920) to report a re-cementation or re-bonding of an inlay, onlay, or veneer. See D2910 to report the re-cementation or re-bonding of an inlay, onlay, veneer, or partial coverage restoration.

CODING CORRECTION — MATCH:
1. *Do not* use this code to report re-cementing or re-bonding an implant or abutment supported crown, report D6092.
2. *Do not* use this code to report re-cementing or re-bonding an implant or abutment supported fixed partial denture (bridge). See D6093.
3. *Do not* use this code to report re-cementing or re-bonding a fixed partial denture (bridge). See D6930.

LIMITATIONS
1. Re-cementation or re-bonding is typically not reimbursed until six to 12 months following initial placement of the restoration.
2. If re-cementation or re-bonding is performed in a *different* office within the exclusion period, it might be reimbursed.

TIPS
1. Re-cement or re-bond crown (D2920) reports re-cementing or re-bonding a *¾ or full coverage* crown.
2. Re-cement or re-bond crown (D2920) also reports re-cementing or re-bonding a stainless steel or prefabricated resin crown.
3. See D2910 to report re-cementing or re-bonding a *partial coverage* restoration, such as inlay, onlay, or veneer.
4. See D6930 to report re-cementing or re-bonding a fixed partial denture (bridge).
5. See D6092 to report re-cementing or re-bonding an implant or abutment supported crown.
6. See D6093 to report re-cementing or re-bonding an implant or abutment supported fixed partial denture (bridge).

D2921 REATTACHMENT OF TOOTH FRAGMENT, INCISAL EDGE OR CUSP — CDT 2016

COMMENTS D2921 is used to describe the bonding of a broken fragment from a fractured tooth back into place rather than restoring the tooth with composite material.

LIMITATIONS The reimbursement for this type of procedure is uncertain. It is unlikely that payers will provide reimbursement for the procedure until time for assessment of the utilization and efficacy of the procedure has been determined.

NARRATIVES An alternate benefit of a one or two surface composite could be requested, upon appeal.

D2929 PREFABRICATED PORCELAIN/CERAMIC CROWN – PRIMARY TOOTH — CDT 2016

CODING CORRECTION — WARNING: Reports *primary tooth* ceramic crown, not for a permanent tooth.

COMMENTS
1. D2929 reports a prefabricated ceramic/porcelain primary crown for a *primary* anterior or posterior tooth. It is individually milled to a generic tooth preparation model, rather than to a finished tooth preparation.
2. Choices in the past for primary tooth restorations have been a primary stainless steel crown (D2930), exterior esthetic-coated stainless steel crown (D2934), or prefabricated stainless steel crown with resin window (D2933).

LIMITATIONS Payers may re-map D2929 to either D2930, D2933, or D2934.

D2930 — PREFABRICATED STAINLESS STEEL CROWN – PRIMARY TOOTH — CDT 2016

COMMENTS
1. Prefabricated stainless steel crown (D2930) reports a stainless steel crown for both anterior and posterior *primary* teeth.
2. See (D2931) which reports a stainless steel crown for a *permanent* tooth.

LIMITATIONS D2930 often has a lifetime exclusion, i.e., it is only reimbursed once per tooth. Some plans have a 24-month exclusion. The exclusion for D2930 varies among payers.

This is a prefabricated stainless steel crown for a primary tooth.

Courtesy 3M

D2931 — PREFABRICATED STAINLESS STEEL CROWN – PERMANENT TOOTH — CDT 2016

COMMENTS Prefabricated stainless steel crown (D2931) reports a stainless steel crown for a *permanent* tooth.

LIMITATIONS
1. An age limitation may apply (thirteen to fourteen years).
2. D2931 may have a 2-5 year exclusion or with some plans a 10 year exclusion. The exclusions/limitations for this code are variable among payers.

TIPS A core buildup (D2950), if necessary for the *retention* of a permanent tooth stainless steel crown, may be reimbursed. See D2950.

This is a prefabricated stainless steel crown for a primary tooth.

Courtesy 3M

D2932 — PREFABRICATED RESIN CROWN — CDT 2016

CODING WATCH CORRECTION This is not a lab processed indirect crown. It is a *prefabricated* resin crown.

COMMENTS D2932 reports a *prefabricated resin* crown for *either* a primary or permanent tooth.

LIMITATIONS 1. Some payers have a lifetime exclusion if performed on a primary tooth or an age limitation (under thirteen-fourteen) if for a permanent tooth.

2. Limitations may not apply when the replacement is a result of an accident or injury.

NARRATIVES 1. An alternate benefit of a stainless steel crown may be reimbursed for D2932. Reimbursement among payers is highly variable for D2932. It is recommended that coverage be verified with the payer prior to rendering treatment. The narrative should outline the conditions that exist to justify the placement of a prefabricated crown along as an estimate of the period of the crown's use.

2. The narrative should clearly describe any accident and/or injury involving the tooth treated with the prefabricated resin crown D2932.

D2933 PREFABRICATED STAINLESS STEEL CROWN WITH RESIN WINDOW — CDT 2016

Open-face stainless steel crown with aesthetic resin facing or veneer.

COMMENTS 1. Prefabricated stainless steel crown with resin window (D2933) is generally reimbursed when placed on anterior primary teeth. When placed on posterior primary teeth the service may be considered cosmetic and an alternate benefit of a primary stainless steel crown (D2930) may be reimbursed or (D2931) if placed on a permanent tooth.

2. Prefabricated stainless steel crown with resin window (D2933) may be placed on primary or permanent teeth.

LIMITATIONS 1. Replacement for prefabricated stainless steel crown with resin window (D2933) may be limited to 24 months on *permanent* teeth. For patients thirteen-fourteen years and younger there is often a two to five year exclusion when the prefabricated stainless steel crown with resin window is performed on an anterior permanent tooth. Reimbursement among payers is highly variable for this procedure. It is recommended that the coverage is verified with the payer prior to rendering the treatment.

2. Reimbursement for prefabricated stainless steel crown with resin window (D2933) is typically once per lifetime when performed on an anterior *primary* tooth.

D2934 PREFABRICATED ESTHETIC COATED STAINLESS STEEL CROWN – PRIMARY TOOTH — CDT 2016

Stainless steel primary crown with exterior esthetic coating.

COMMENTS 1. Prefabricated esthetic coated stainless steel crown (D2934) reports a prefabricated, esthetic coated, stainless steel crown for a *primary* anterior or posterior tooth.

2. It is misleading to use (D2934) to describe a prefabricated esthetic coated stainless steel crown placed on a *permanent* tooth.

LIMITATIONS 1. D2934 may be subject to a 24-month or up to a lifetime exclusion. Exclusions among payers for this code are highly variable. It is recommended that coverage be verified with the payer before rendering treatment.

2. D2934 may be reimbursed when performed on *primary* anterior teeth. D2934 may be reimbursed by payers with an alternate benefit of stainless steel crown (D2930) on a primary tooth.

3. For posterior *primary* teeth, an alternate benefit, primary stainless steel crown (D2930), may be reimbursed. Reimbursement among payers is highly variable for this code; verify coverage with the payer before rendering treatment.

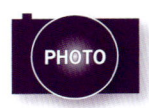

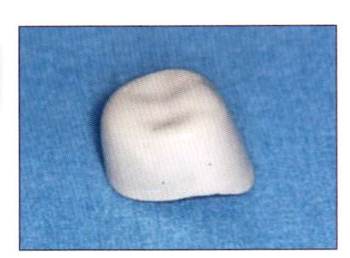

This is a prefabricated esthetic coated stainless steel crown primary tooth.

Courtesy Java Crown, Inc.

D2940 PROTECTIVE RESTORATION — CDT 2016

Direct placement of a restorative material to protect tooth and/or tissue form. This procedure may be used to relieve pain, promote healing, or prevent further deterioration. Not to be used for endodontic access closure, or as a base or liner under a restoration.

CODING WARNING CORRECTION

1. D2940 should *not* be reported as a base or liner in conjunction with an amalgam/composite restoration or any other type of restoration.
2. D2940 should *not* be reported for endodontic access closure. Use D2140, D2330 or D2391.
3. D2940 should *not* be reported in conjunction with palliative (D9110) on the same service date.
4. D2940 should *not* be used to report root desensitization. See application of desensitizing resin for cervical and/or root surface sensitivity (D9911).

CODING WATCH CORRECTION

1. The protective restoration (D2940) was *formerly* termed a "sedative filling."
2. D2940 is sometimes used to report a restoration placed at an emergency *evaluation* appointment associated with a fractured tooth. See also palliative (D9110).
3. D2940 should *not* be reported in conjunction with palliative D9110 on the same service date.
4. D2940 should *not* be reported in conjunction with pulp cap (D3110 or D3120). Report either D2940 or a pulp cap, not both on the same service date. See D3110/D3120.
5. D2940 should not be reported as an interim therapeutic restoration. See D2941.

LIMITATIONS

1. Protective restoration (D2940) is an *interim* treatment to protect the tooth, relieve dental pain, and/or promote healing. While some payers may exclude reimbursement for this procedure, others may "re-map" it to palliative (D9110) for reimbursement when performed to relieve discomfort or to temporarily "fill a hole" at an emergency visit. Reimbursement among payers is highly variable.
2. Payers may subtract the fee previously reimbursed for D2940 from the reimbursement fee for the final restoration, such as a crown or filling if performed within the exclusion period. That exclusion period is typically thirty days to six months. When applicable, D2940 may be considered a "take-back" code. Reimbursement among payers is highly variable.
3. A separate fee for a pulp cap (direct or indirect) plus a protective restoration (D2940) is not typically reimbursed if both are reported on the same service date. See D3110/D3120.
4. Reimbursement for the protective restoration (D2940) is highly variable among payers when the procedure is performed on the same tooth on multiple dates. The reimbursement may be limited to once per lifetime per tooth.
5. Some payers limit reimbursement for D2940 to situations where the protective restoration relieves acute pain. Palliative (D9110) may be reimbursed by some payers for the relief of minor discomfort/sensitivity/pain when "filling a hole" at an emergency visit. The procedure may consist of caries excavation and IRM (immediate restorative material) placement. Some payers "re-map" D2940 to D9110 for reimbursement if the protective restoration is performed at an *emergency visit*. Palliative (D9110) is not generally a "take-back" code, but the UCR fee may be lower for palliative than a protective restoration. This is often true of a PPO fee controlled plan.

D2941 — INTERIM THERAPEUTIC RESTORATION – PRIMARY DENTITION — CDT 2016

Placement of an adhesive restorative material following caries debridement by hand or other method for the management of early childhood caries. Not considered a definitive restoration.

COMMENTS

1. An Interim Therapeutic Restoration (ITR) is a provisional technique used to restore and prevent dental caries in young patients, uncooperative patients, or patients with special healthcare needs for whom traditional cavity preparation and/or placement of traditional dental restorations are not feasible. ITR may be used for caries control in children with multiple carious lesions prior to definitive restoration of teeth. In addition, D2941 may be used to describe the removal of grossly carious tooth structure and placement of an interim therapeutic restoration in the primary dentition to "manage" the disease process. The procedure is provided to reduce the impact of an active carious lesion by removing the grossly carious component of the lesion and then sealing the area in an attempt to arrest the progression of the disease process without violating the pulp by removing the entire lesion. D2941 is not a definitive treatment. D2941 should be followed by a definitive treatment procedure to permanently remove diseased primary tooth structure and restore the resulting defect.

2. While there are similarities to D2940 (protective restoration), the interim therapeutic restoration (ITR) for primary teeth, used in a program of Early Childhood Caries (ECC) management differs in several important respects:
   - The ITR for primary teeth is a specific procedure with specific indications and technique (often performed in the parent's lap) for a specific age-related population.
   - The ITR is taught as a distinct clinical entity in dental schools in the U.S. at the pre-doctoral and post-doctoral levels as part of early childhood caries management.
   - The mechanics of the procedure (caries debridement by hand or slow-speed rotary instrumentation without local anesthesia) differs significantly from cavity preparation in the adult dentition. It also differs for the adult dental patient for placement of a protective filling material as part of a temporization strategy during oral rehabilitation or as a treatment response to an emergency or urgent dental condition.

3. A 2012 article on community-based oral health care delivery systems published in the Journal of the California Dental Association refers to the specific procedure of the ITR as a "minimally invasive treatment modality that…uses only hand instrumentation to remove markedly demineralized (softened) carious enamel and dentin, and then restores the cavitation with an adhesive restorative material."

LIMITATIONS

As a new code, the reimbursement for this procedure is uncertain. It is unlikely that payers will provide reimbursement for the procedure until time for assessment of the utilization and efficacy of the procedure has been determined.

ADDITIONAL INFORMATION

Typical scenario for D2941: A patient, 30 months of age, presents with several small carious lesions penetrating into the dentin on the facial surfaces of the maxillary central and lateral incisors. Incipient (non-cavitated) enamel lesions are present on other aspects of these teeth. After consideration of the venues of available pharmacologic behavior and anxiety management, the dentist and the parents agree upon an approach of caries arrestment by ITR, fluoride therapy, dietary modification, and plaque management that will avoid the necessity of pharmacologic intervention. With the patient in his mother's lap in a knee-to-knee position, caries debridement of the active lesions is accomplished by the dentist with hand instrumentation, and the teeth are restored with a fluoride releasing adhesive restorative material such as self-setting or resin-modified glass ionomer cement. A fluoride varnish is applied and the patient is re-appointed for follow-up evaluation of plaque management and another fluoride varnish application in eight weeks.

D2949 — RESTORATIVE FOUNDATION FOR AN INDIRECT RESTORATION — CDT 2016

Placement of restorative material to yield a more ideal form, including elimination of undercuts.

CODING WARNING CORRECTION

1. Do not report D2950, core buildup, when placing a restorative foundation to aid in the fabrication of an indirect restoration. D2950 should only be reported when the restoration is necessary for the *retention* of the indirect restoration.

2. D2949 describes the placement of a "filler" to eliminate undercuts and/or to provide an ideal contour.

COMMENTS D2949 is used to describe the placement of a restorative material in a tooth to prepare for the ultimate placement of a crown, bridge, inlay, onlay, veneer and or other type of fixed indirect restoration. D2949 is used to provide a more ideal form for the processing and adaptation of the final indirect restoration. The restorative foundation, described by D2949 is provided to establish a more ideal form and/or to eliminate undercuts. Report D2950 when a buildup is necessary for the *retention* of the final indirect restoration.

LIMITATIONS It is unlikely that D2949 will be reimbursed. Most payers have determined that a restorative foundation is a part of the reimbursement provided for the indirect restoration. Even so, it is recommended that the procedure be reported as it will provide utilization information for the payers to consider for possible future reimbursement.

D2950 CORE BUILDUP, INCLUDING ANY PINS WHEN REQUIRED — CDT 2016

Refers to building up of coronal structure when there is insufficient retention for a separate extracoronal restorative procedure. A core buildup is not a filler to eliminate any undercut, box form, or concave irregularity in a preparation.

CODING CORRECTION — WARNING

1. It is misleading to report a core buildup (D2950) when the affected tooth after preparation would be retentive enough to support a crown without the core buildup. Core buildups placed to improve "box-form," eliminate "concave irregularity" or "undercuts" and "fillers" should not be submitted for reimbursement. A core buildup must be *necessary* for crown *retention* to be considered a core buildup. The core buildup should rebuild the *internal anatomy* of the tooth structure as prepared for a crown.

2. It is misleading to report a one-piece Cerec® or E4D® fabricated crown, as a crown (D2740) *and* a core buildup. A core buildup is a separate component apart and separate from the CAD/CAM crown. Cerec 3D® or E4D® users may report unspecified restorative procedure, by report (D2999) for a *one-piece* "endo-crown." *Do not expect an alternate reimbursement for both a core buildup and crown.* Expect only the alternate benefit of a crown.

3. It is misleading to report a core buildup as a direct amalgam/composite restoration. A restoration is built to *occlusion*, with normal *anatomy*, proximal *contacts*, and is in full *function*. A filling restores the tooth to full form and function. Amalgams and composites reported shortly before the crown preparation may be *deducted* from the subsequent crown reimbursement amount. The restoration is a "take back" procedure if placed just prior to placing a crown. The "take back" provision may vary according to the time period between the restorative procedure and the crown.

4. It is misleading to report a core buildup with an inlay or onlay. A core buildup is only justified when placed in a tooth to allow for the *retention* of the extracoronal restorative procedure.

CODING CORRECTION — WATCH

1. D2950 also reports a core buildup placed under a retainer crown of a bridge. There is no separate code to report a core buildup under a retainer crown.

2. It is unnecessary to report pin retention (D2951) in *addition* to a core buildup. The core buildup includes *any* pin placement when required.

3. Report D2330 when restoring an endodontic access opening or the access opening for the internal bleaching (D9974) of a natural tooth. Do not report core buildup (D2950) or prefabricated post and core when restoring and closing an endodontic access opening. Core buildups and prefabricated post and core are reimbursable when they are necessary for the *retention* of the crown, not for closure of an endodontic access opening. Do not report crown repair necessitated by material failure either. If the crown is *removed* first then core buildup/prefabricated post and core can be reported.

LIMITATIONS

1. A core buildup (D2950) may be reimbursed when its *necessity* is objectively determined and properly documented. Some payers will not reimburse a core buildup on a vital tooth. These payers indicate that the core buildup is a part of the crown preparation. If a payer denies reimbursement for this reason, have the patient request a copy of their specific dental insurance contract from their Human Resources department at work. Use the contract to verify the contract language for the specific exclusion of a core buildup.

2. While core buildups may be performed on vital teeth, coverage may be limited to non-vital posterior teeth. Core buildups performed on non-vital teeth are generally covered, especially if associated with a posterior tooth.

TIPS

1. Some payers require a certain "date sequence" to justify the core buildup (D2950). Report the core buildup (D2950) when performed. Note that *some* payers will not reimburse the core buildup unless a predetermination has been submitted for the planned crown or until the crown has been seated (on a subsequent date). Note: Per the ADA, procedures may be reported either at the *start date*, or at the *completion date*. (See the current language at the bottom of the ADA claim form.) The claim form states "I hereby certify that the procedures as indicated by date are in *progress* (for procedures that require multiple visits) or have been *completed*." Note: The third-party contract (PPO) may dictate that the doctor report the crown on either the *start* or *completion* date. Generally the reporting date should be the *completion* date according to most PPO contracts. Refer to the contract language for the proper coding/billing.

2. Some practices file a "paper" claim form on the preparation date with the "predetermination" and "statement of actual services" blocks checked (at the top of the form). Enter the core buildup with fee and date. Next, enter the proposed crown to be placed with the date area empty but the fee entered. Many payers will consider the core buildup claim as they have been alerted that the crown is planned and will follow the core buildup. Note: The core buildup (D2950) must be necessary for retention of the crown.

NARRATIVES

1. Always include a narrative when reporting core buildup (D2950), for example, "a core buildup is *necessary for the retention of the crown*." The narrative should identify the actual percentage of missing tooth structure, e.g., 60% of the tooth was missing. Some payers require that 50% or *more* of the tooth be missing for reimbursement. When less than 50% of the tooth is missing, some payers consider the procedure a "filler." Some payers require that less than a 2mm-3mm "collar" (tooth height structure) remain. A supporting diagnostic radiographic film/photograph should be included in the documentation for the core buildup. Pretreatment radiographic and photographic images are recommended to document the need for the core buildup.

2. A narrative is especially important when reporting core buildup associated with an endodontically treated tooth. Some payers reimburse core buildups on non-vital (endodontic) teeth, but *exclude* reimbursement for vital teeth. When reporting a core buildup placed on an endodontically treated tooth, submit the narrative: *"The core buildup was necessary for the retention of the crown. This is an endodontically treated tooth. Endodontics completed mm/dd/yy."* Enclose a diagnostic image (periapical) showing the tooth has received adequate endodontic treatment. If D2950 is rejected for an endodontically treated tooth, submit a paper claim form with narrative, "This is an endodontically treated tooth."

3. The payer may refuse reimbursement for a core buildup unless/until the crown has been placed. If a patient has the core buildup but does not have the crown placed (due to finances or loss of commitment), re-file the claim with an explanation explaining why the patient did not complete the treatment. Request an alternate be*nefit* for a four surface composite restoration (D2335, D2394, or a four surface amalgam D2161). In this situation the restoration may be reimbursed.

4. Core buildups (D2950) are typically limited to cast or milled crowns. In some limited circumstances, stainless steel crowns on *permanent* teeth provided to a child may require a buildup for *retention* of the stainless steel crown and may be reimbursed. The claim should include a full narrative with diagnostic images as documentation. Payers seldom reimburse a core buildup required for the retention of *primary* tooth due to contract limitations.

5. In summary, the narrative could say:

    a. "See attached radiographic image." (If tooth has RCT, send PA radiographic image).

    b. List any missing cusps. Estimate and state percentage of healthy tooth structure left after fracture, caries and/or any previous restoration is removed.

    c. Document any existing circumferential caries at gingival margin and extensive caries detectable by explorer under existing crown. State if tooth has existing or planned RCT (root canal therapy).

    d. State endodontic and periodontal prognosis for tooth.

    e. If there is less than 2mm of vertical height remaining of the tooth, state that and also state the number of degrees of circumference of the tooth where this exists, e.g., "only 1mm of vertical tooth height remains around 270 degrees of tooth circumference."

D2951 — PIN RETENTION – PER TOOTH, IN ADDITION TO RESTORATION — CDT 2016

CODING WARNING CORRECTION

1. It is misleading to *routinely* report pin retention (D2951) in every amalgam/composite restoration when the need is not justified.
2. Do not charge pins in addition to core buildup (D2950), per the nomenclature for D2950. If pins are placed they are considered a part of the core buildup procedure.

LIMITATIONS
1. Pin reimbursement is generally excluded for *primary* teeth.
2. Pins placed to aid in the retention of an amalgam/composite restoration are generally reimbursed. Pins are reported on a "per tooth" basis. There could be *several* pins placed in any given restoration.

NARRATIVES Report the number of pins placed. (For example, "three pins placed in the amalgam/composite restoration," tooth #3.)

D2952 — POST AND CORE IN ADDITION TO CROWN, INDIRECTLY FABRICATED — CDT 2016

Post and core are custom fabricated as a single unit.

CODING WARNING CORRECTION

It is inappropriate to report the prefabricated post and core (D2954) as an indirectly fabricated or cast post and core (D2952).

CODING WATCH CORRECTION

The same code reports a post and core, indirectly fabricated (D2952) under *either* a single crown **or** retainer crown of a bridge.

LIMITATIONS
1. Some payers may reimburse the *alternate benefit* of a prefabricated post and core (D2954) for the indirectly fabricated post and core (D2952).
2. For *anterior* teeth with root canals, documentation of insufficient tooth structure to support a crown may be required to justify reimbursement. See D2950 for narratives and further details.

NARRATIVES
1. The indirectly fabricated post and core (D2952) is generally reimbursed for a *posterior* tooth. The reimbursement for an indirectly fabricated post and core (D2952) is typically higher than for a core buildup (D2950) or the prefabricated post and core (D2954). A narrative may not be required when performed on a posterior tooth as it is assumed that the indirectly fabricated post and core is performed on an endodontically treated tooth. The indirect cast post procedure is used less frequently than the prefabricated post and core (D2954). A diagnostic image of the endodontically treated tooth should be submitted. Photographs may be helpful to document need. Payers generally require the endodontic treatment be clinically acceptable and the tooth free of pathology (endodontic and periodontic).
2. If tooth does not have existing RCT (root canal therapy), state when RCT will be done.
3. Estimate and state percentage of healthy tooth structure left after fracture, caries and/or any previous restoration is removed. "See attached radiographic image." (Send PA radiographic image).

D2953 — EACH ADDITIONAL INDIRECTLY FABRICATED POST – SAME TOOTH — CDT 2016

To be used with D2952.

COMMENTS D2953 is used to report each *additional* indirectly fabricated post – same tooth. Report this code in *conjunction* with D2952 for the same tooth. See D2952 for further details.

LIMITATIONS Most payers consider D2953 a part of the indirectly fabricated post and core procedure (D2952) and do not provide additional reimbursement for the D2953 placement.

NARRATIVES
1. If the tooth does not have an existing RCT (root canal therapy), state when RCT will be done.
2. Estimate and state the percentage of healthy tooth structure left after fracture, caries and/or any previous restoration is removed. "See attached radiographic image." (Send PA radiographic image).

D2954	PREFABRICATED POST AND CORE IN ADDITION TO CROWN	CDT 2016

Core is built around a prefabricated post. This procedure includes the core material.

CODING WARNING CORRECTION
1. It is misleading to report a prefabricated post and core (D2954) as an indirectly fabricated post and core (D2952), or vice versa.
2. By definition, prefabricated post and core in addition to crown (D2954) *includes* the core material placed *around* a prefabricated post. Do not report core buildup (D2950) in addition to D2954. When placing a prefabricated post and core in addition to crown, report *only* D2954.
3. It is inappropriate to report the canal preparation and fitting of the post (D3950) if the *same* provider will place the prefabricated post and core in addition to crown (D2954).

CODING WATCH CORRECTION

The reporting of a post and core associated with the retainer crown of a bridge utilizes the same code. Report D2954 to describe a prefabricated post and core for either a single *crown or retainer crown* of a bridge.

TIPS If a post and core is placed in an endodontically treated tooth access hole and a filling (amalgam/composite) is placed rather than a crown placed, report D2999 to describe the placement of the post and core and the restoration.

NARRATIVES
1. For *anterior* teeth, documentation of insufficient tooth structure to support the crown is sometimes required for reimbursement. Provide a narrative similar to the one for a core buildup. See D2950 for further details.
2. The prefabricated post and core (D2954) is generally reimbursed when used to restore an endodontically treated tooth. The reimbursement for D2954 is higher than a core buildup (D2950) and lower than a post and core in addition to crown, indirectly fabricated (D2952). A narrative may not be required for a posterior tooth. It is assumed that the buildup has been performed on an endodontically treated tooth. Many doctors routinely use prefabricated post and core (D2954) on endodontically treated teeth. The carbon Fibercor® post is frequently used as a prefabricated post. A diagnostic image of the endodontically treated tooth should be submitted to document the need for the prefabricated post and core. Photographs may be helpful to justify the need for a prefabricated post and core. Payers generally require that the endodontic treatment be clinically acceptable and the tooth free of pathology (endodontic and periodontic).
3. If tooth does not have existing RCT (root canal therapy), state when RCT will be done.
4. Estimate and state percentage of healthy tooth structure left after fracture, caries and/or any previous restoration is removed. "See attached radiographic image." (Send PA radiographic image).

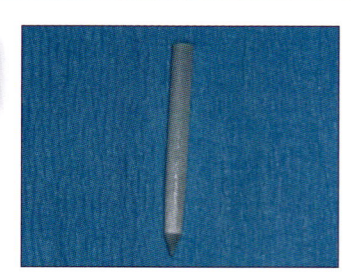

This is a prefabricated post which is placed in an endodontically treated tooth. After placement of the post a core is built around it.

Courtesy Ultradent®

D2955 POST REMOVAL — CDT 2016

CODING WATCH CORRECTION

1. D2955 reports a *stand-alone* post removal. Post removal is not part of retreatment of a previous root canal therapy.
2. D2955 may be reported *separately* from endodontic treatment.
3. If the post is loose or easy to remove, requiring little time, do not report D2955.

LIMITATIONS
1. The post removal procedure is generally considered *inclusive* by third-party payers for root canal retreatment (D3346, D3347, and D3348).
2. D2955 might be reimbursed if the same billing provider does not perform *both* post removal and the endodontic retreatment procedure. Reimbursement may be made when the general practitioner removes the post while the endodontist (different practitioner and office) provides the retreatment.

NARRATIVES
1. It is recommended that a narrative be included with a claim for D2955. The narrative should describe the complexity, depth of post, and extra time required for removal.
2. Describe if the same billing provider does not perform both post removal and the endodontic procedure. This may improve the odds for reimbursement.

D2957 EACH ADDITIONAL PREFABRICATED POST – SAME TOOTH — CDT 2016

To be used with D2954.

CODING MATCH CORRECTION

D2957 is used to report each *additional* prefabricated post and core for the same tooth. This procedure code would only be reported in addition to prefabricated post and core (D2954). See D2954 for further details.

LIMITATIONS Most payers consider D2957 to be integral to the basic prefabricated post and core (D2954) procedure, and do not provide additional reimbursement for each additional prefabricated post(s) placed in the same tooth.

NARRATIVES
1. If tooth does not have existing RCT (root canal therapy), state when RCT will be done.
2. Estimate and state percentage of healthy tooth structure left after fracture, caries and/or any previous restoration is removed. "See attached radiographic image." (Send PA radiographic image).

D2960 LABIAL VENEER (RESIN LAMINATE) – CHAIRSIDE — CDT 2016

Refers to labial/facial direct resin bonded veneers.

LIMITATIONS
1. Plan limitations and reimbursements are highly variable for this chairside direct procedure.

2. If the plan has a special policy rider, reimbursement may be provided for this procedure. To be considered for reimbursement, the procedure would treat severe fluorosis, tetracycline staining, pegged laterals, amelogenesis imperfecta, or some other type of pathology.

NARRATIVES
1. D2960 reports a "free hand" chairside resin-bonded veneer. This procedure is generally considered *cosmetic* in nature. If decay has been diagnosed or if the procedure is provided to replace a defective restoration with decayed margins, it may be a covered benefit.
2. Photographs, diagnostic images, and a narrative should be submitted with the claim.

D2961 — LABIAL VENEER (RESIN LAMINATE) – LABORATORY — CDT 2016

Refers to labial/facial indirect resin bonded veneers.

CODING CORRECTION WATCH: Do not report D2961 for laboratory made or CAD/CAM *porcelain/ceramic* veneers. See D2962 for further details regarding a *porcelain/ceramic* laminate that is indirectly fabricated.

COMMENTS D2961 reports Belleglass®, Cristobal®, Artglass®, Concept®, and Targis/Vectris® resin-type materials. D2961 should not be used to report porcelain/ceramic-type veneers. If reporting a *porcelain* laminate material, see D2962 for further details.

LIMITATIONS
1. Plan limitations for veneers are highly variable.
2. If the employer opts to purchases a special policy rider, reimbursement may be provided for this procedure. To be considered for reimbursement, the procedure would be used to treat severe fluorosis, tetracycline staining, pegged laterals, amelogenesis imperfecta, or some other type of pathology.

TIPS Fees charged for labial veneers should reflect the time, laboratory expense and skill required to perform this tedious anterior cosmetic procedure. Although the preparation for a veneer is generally faster than for a crown, temporization and seating is much more difficult. Consider setting a fee for a resin laminate veneer (D2961) comparable to that of a porcelain/ceramic crown (D2740). Consider setting a higher fee than for a *routine* porcelain fused to metal crown.

NARRATIVES
1. A resin laminate veneer is generally considered a *cosmetic* procedure and is generally not reimbursed. In some limited circumstances, payers may reimburse veneers if the veneer is used to treat decay, cracks or other pathology. Diagnostic images and diagnostic photographs should be submitted with the claim, along with a narrative. Often, a veneer must be appealed to receive reimbursement, even if used to treat pathology. Ask the patient to obtain a copy of the full dental coverage contract from their Human Resources department at work. Review the policy to determine if there is veneer coverage. If veneers are excluded, ask for an alternate benefit.
2. In limited circumstances (with a cosmetic rider), payers may reimburse veneers to correct severe congenital or developmental anomalies. Plan limitations and exclusions vary widely between policies and payers. It is recommended that when veneers are placed, a brief narrative and supporting documentation accompany the claim.
3. Documentation should state; "see attached radiographic image." Identify the surfaces of the tooth that are fractured, have caries and/or have existing restorations that are failing or leaking. If fractured, state how fracture occurred.

D2962 — LABIAL VENEER (PORCELAIN LAMINATE) – LABORATORY — CDT 2016

Refers also to facial veneers that extend interproximally and/or cover the incisal edge. Porcelain/ceramic veneers presently include all ceramic and porcelain veneers.

CODING WARNING CORRECTION

It is misleading to report anterior porcelain veneers on *virgin* teeth as "reverse" ¾ porcelain/ceramic crowns (D2783). The descriptor for D2962 states that the porcelain veneer code (D2962) now includes prepping and "extending interproximally and/or covering the incisal edge." The "reverse" ¾ porcelain crown preparation is more aggressive, with less lingual enamel remaining. The tooth might have had previous interproximal restorations. See D2783 for further details regarding reporting a ¾ porcelain crown.

LIMITATIONS

1. The descriptor of a veneer has been expanded to include prepping into the mesial and distal (interproximally) and/or covering the incisal edge. On a virgin tooth, a veneer (D2962) is more appropriate to report, if it only extends interproximally, rather than a reverse ¾ porcelain crown (D2783).
2. Plan limitations for veneers are highly variable.
3. If the employer purchases a policy rider in addition to the basic policy, reimbursement may be provided for veneers used to treat severe fluorosis, tetracycline staining, pegged laterals, amelogenesis imperfecta, and other types of pathology.

TIPS

Fees charged for laboratory labial veneers should reflect the time, laboratory expense and skill required to perform this tedious anterior cosmetic procedure. Although the preparation for a veneer is generally faster, temporization and seating is much more difficult. Consider setting a fee for a porcelain labial veneer (D2962) comparable to that of a porcelain/ceramic crown (D2740). Consider setting a higher fee than for a *routine* porcelain fused to metal crown.

NARRATIVES

1. A porcelain veneer is generally considered a *cosmetic* procedure and is generally not reimbursed. In some limited circumstances, payers may reimburse veneers if the veneer is used to treat decay, cracks or other pathology. Diagnostic images and diagnostic photographs should be submitted with the claim, along with a narrative.
2. Often, a veneer must be appealed to receive reimbursement, even if used to treat pathology. Ask the patient to obtain a copy of the full dental coverage contract (plan document) from their Human Resources department at work. Review the plan document to determine if there is veneer coverage. If veneers are excluded, ask for an alternate benefit. If veneers are not excluded, appeal the denial with the necessary documentation.
3. In limited circumstances (with a cosmetic rider), payers may reimburse veneers to correct severe congenital or developmental anomalies. Plan limitations and exclusions vary widely between policies and payers. It is recommended that when veneers are placed, a brief narrative and supporting documentation accompany the claim.
4. Documentation should state, "see attached radiographic image." Identify the surfaces of the tooth that are fractured, have caries and/or have existing restorations that are failing or leaking. If fractured, state how fracture occurred.

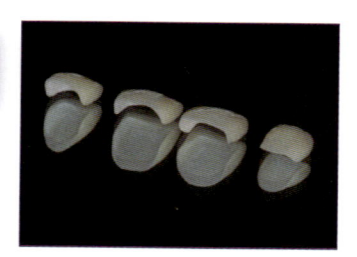

PHOTO

This is a photograph of four porcelain veneers sitting on a reflective surface.

Courtesy Drake Dental Lab

D2970 — DELETED CODE TEMPORARY CROWN (FRACTURED TOOTH) — CDT 2016

This is a deleted code. See Provisional Crown, D2799.

D2971 — ADDITIONAL PROCEDURES TO CONSTRUCT NEW CROWN UNDER EXISTING PARTIAL DENTURE FRAMEWORK — CDT 2016

To be reported in addition to a crown code.

CODING MATCH CORRECTION — When placing a crown on a tooth that currently supports a partial denture, use this code to describe the additional work necessary to fabricate a new crown that is made to fit the clasp/rest of the existing partial denture framework. Report this procedure in conjunction with the crown fabrication. Report the crown separately.

COMMENTS
1. D2971 reports the additional laboratory and chairside procedures required to construct a new crown under an *existing* partial denture framework.
2. If the crown is a survey crown for a new partial (to be fabricated in the future), see D2999.

LIMITATIONS D2971 may be reimbursed once per tooth, subject to the same five to 10 year limitation period for a replacement crown. *Report the crown separately*.

TIPS
1. Fabricating a new crown to fit under an *existing* partial denture framework's clasp is challenging. Extra laboratory steps, cost, and time are involved. In addition, extra chairside time is typically required at delivery to properly adjust the new crown to the existing partial framework. List *both* the appropriate crown code plus code D2971 as two separate line items, with two separate distinct fees on the claim form. D2971 requires a tooth number for reimbursement.
2. Report D2971 and the crown as separate codes and submit them on the seat date to eliminate any possible confusion, delays, or denials.

NARRATIVES Include a short narrative describing the additional procedures necessary to construct a new crown under an existing cast partial framework and attach a copy of the lab bill reflecting the extra charge.

D2975 COPING CDT 2016

A thin covering of the coronal portion of a tooth, usually devoid of anatomic contour, that can be used as a definitive restoration.

COMMENTS
1. D2975 reports a definitive (final) restoration over the remaining natural tooth. As an example, a removable prosthesis (overdenture) fits over two separate and *independent* canine coping abutments. There is no connecting bar and both copings are reported independently as D2975.
2. If a bar connects the copings, each connected coping is reported as D2975. See D6920 to report the connector bar. Note that D6975 has been deleted and that D2975 reports all copings.
3. A telescopic crown (D27xx) may be indicated to provide more ideal alignment and support for removable or fixed partial denture cases involving teeth that are badly broken, malpositioned, or tipped. Sometimes referred to as a "double crown retained prostheses," Telescopic retainers appear to have a crown on a crown. The first "crown" is actually a metal coping that is cemented to the prepped tooth and reported as D2975. The second crown-like piece (D27xx), is fabricated to fit over the coping (D2975). It is the definitive restoration.

LIMITATIONS D2975 is not typically reimbursed unless an alternate benefit is available. However, an alternate benefit is unlikely. This procedure, in all likelihood, will be a patient responsibility.

D2980 CROWN REPAIR NECESSITATED BY RESTORATIVE MATERIAL FAILURE CDT 2016

CODING WARNING CORRECTION
1. A crown repair (D2980) requires a restorative material failure (fracture). It includes any part of the crown. If a filling is needed to repair decay below the crown's margins, report the appropriate amalgam or composite code. Include a narrative indicating there was facial decay below the crown's margins.
2. It is misleading to report a core buildup (D2950) in conjunction with crown repair (D2980) when the crown has not been removed.

LIMITATIONS
1. A crown repair (D2980) may be subject to the five to 10 year limitation for a replacement crown and if performed may limit the replacement of that crown by the same term. If reimbursed, the amount may be 50% of the UCR fee.

2. For endodontic access closure (through an existing cemented or bonded crown), consider a single surface amalgam (D2140) or composite (D2391) to report this type of service. These procedures are typically reimbursed at 80% of the UCR fee. However, a few payers could require that D2980 be reported for closure of an intentional endodontic access opening made through an existing crown.

NARRATIVES A brief narrative should describe the crown repair procedure. The fee reimbursed may be based on the time necessary to perform the service and amount of the laboratory bill, if applicable. It is suggested that the time spent be included in the narrative and a copy of the laboratory bill be attached.

D2981 INLAY REPAIR NECESSITATED BY RESTORATIVE MATERIAL FAILURE — CDT 2016

COMMENTS D2981 requires a restorative material failure (fracture) of the inlay. It includes any part of the inlay restoration. A composite filling that may be required at the inlay's margin to address decay and is reported as a composite restoration.

LIMITATIONS
1. An inlay repair (D2981) requires a restorative material failure (fracture). It is suggested that the coverage be verified for this procedure before submitting a claim.

2. An inlay repair (D2981) may be subject to the five to 10 year limitation for a replacement inlay and if performed may limit the replacement of that inlay by the same term. If reimbursed, the amount is typically 50% of the UCR fee.

3. Plan limitations are generally highly variable, and some may have an exclusion of one tooth per 12 months for inlay repair.

4. For endodontic access closure (through an existing cemented or bonded inlay), consider a single surface amalgam (D2140) or composite (D2330 or D2391). These procedures are typically reimbursed at 80% of the UCR fee. However, a few payers could possibly require that you report inlay repair necessitated by restorative material failure (D2981) for closure of an intentional endodontic access opening made through an existing inlay. The inlay repair may be reimbursed at 50% of the UCR fee.

NARRATIVES A brief narrative should describe the inlay repair procedure when reporting this procedure. The fee reimbursed may be based on time necessary to perform the service and amount of the laboratory bill. It is suggested that the time spent be included in the narrative and a copy of the laboratory bill (if applicable) be attached.

D2982 ONLAY REPAIR NECESSITATED BY RESTORATIVE MATERIAL FAILURE — CDT 2016

COMMENTS D2982 requires a restorative material failure (fracture) of the onlay. It includes any part of the onlay restoration. A composite filling that may be required below the onlay's margin to address decay would be reported as a composite restoration. Include a narrative indicating there was facial decay below the onlay's margins.

LIMITATIONS
1. An onlay repair (D2982) requires a restorative material failure (fracture). It is suggested that coverage be verified for this procedure before submitting a claim.

2. An onlay repair (D2982) may be subject to the five to 10 year limitation for a replacement onlay and if performed may limit the replacement of that onlay by the same term. If reimbursed, the amount is typically 50% of the UCR fee.

3. Plan limitations are highly variable, and some may have an exclusion of one tooth per 12 months for onlay repair.

4. For endodontic access closure (through an existing cemented or bonded onlay), consider a single surface amalgam (D2140) or composite (D2330 or D2391). These procedures are typically reimbursed at 80% of the UCR fee. However, a few payers could possibly require that you report onlay repair necessitated by restorative material failure (D2982) for closure of an intentional endodontic access opening made through an existing onlay. The onlay repair may be reimbursed at 50% of the UCR fee.

NARRATIVES A brief narrative should describe the onlay repair procedure when reporting this procedure. The fee reimbursed may be based on time necessary to perform the service and amount of the laboratory bill. It is suggested that the time spent and a copy of the laboratory bill (if applicable) be included in the narrative.

D2983   VENEER REPAIR NECESSITATED BY RESTORATIVE MATERIAL FAILURE   CDT 2016

COMMENTS D2983 requires a restorative material failure (fracture) of the veneer. It includes any part of the veneer restoration, but does not include a composite filling placed at the margin that may be required to treat decay. Include a narrative indicating there was facial decay at the veneer's margins.

LIMITATIONS
1. A veneer repair (D2983) requires a restorative material failure (fracture). It is suggested that coverage be verified for this procedure before submitting a claim.
2. A veneer repair (D2983) may be subject to the five to 10 year limitation for a replacement veneer and if performed may limit the replacement of that veneer by the same term. If reimbursed, the amount is typically 50% of the UCR fee.
3. Plan limitations are highly variable, and some may have an exclusion of one tooth per 12 months for veneer repair.

NARRATIVES A narrative should describe the veneer repair procedure when reporting this procedure. The fee reimbursed may be based on time necessary to perform the service and amount of the laboratory bill, if applicable. It is suggested that the time spent and a copy of the laboratory bill (if applicable) be included in the narrative.

D2990   RESIN INFILTRATION OF INCIPIENT SMOOTH SURFACE LESIONS   CDT 2016

Placement of an infiltrating resin restoration for strengthening, stabilizing and/or limiting the progression of the lesion.

This code appears here in numerical order. However, it appears prior to D2910 according to CDT.

COMMENTS
1. D2990 reports the resin infiltration of incipient smooth surface lesions.
2. Historically, only two choices have been available with incipient caries; either fluoride therapy or a restoration.
3. The DMG Icon® product is a treatment for incipient lesions or white spot lesions. The infiltrant is applied to arrest caries on smooth surfaces, including proximal surfaces. Resin infiltration allows for the treatment of incipient lesions prior to cavitation taking place. It cannot be used to treat advanced decay of the enamel into the dentin.

LIMITATIONS
1. As a fairly new code, D2990 is seldom reimbursed, and if reimbursed, the UCR fee may be poor. Ask for an alternate benefit of a two surface posterior composite (D2392) or a two surface anterior composite (D2331) should D2990 benefits not be available.
2. Enter service date and tooth number and area of infiltration.

D2999   UNSPECIFIED RESTORATIVE PROCEDURE, BY REPORT   CDT 2016

Use for procedure that is not adequately described by a code. Describe procedure.

COMMENTS D2999 may be used to report the following restorative procedures as well as any other restorative procedure, which is not described by any other restorative code(s):
1. An amalgam/composite restoration that is placed over a prefabricated post and core (D2954), not a crown.
2. A restoration placed over a core buildup (D2950), not a crown.
3. A CEREC 3D®, Planscan® or E4D® milled one-piece "endo-crown" used to restore an endodontically treated tooth. These one-piece crowns typically extend into the chamber area with a "foot." Expect no additional reimbursement beyond the alternate benefit of a crown UCR fee. Report this crown procedure as D2999.

4. Custom staining of a crown with the patient presenting personally to the outside laboratory. Report the fee for custom staining separately as D2999. For PPO plans, check the Processing Policy Manual as to protocol for billing an optional service.

5. Sealing the endodontic access hole may be reported as a restorative code (amalgam or composite). Only use D2999 as a last resort.

6. A survey crown, which involves extra procedures to contour a new crown to receive the clasp assembly of a new (future) partial denture framework. The diagnostic cast (and often the crown itself) is placed on a surveyor and designed so the crown will have minimal interference with the seating and removal of the new partial (to be fabricated). The extra process of surveying a crown increases the laboratory fee. Currently, the process of surveying a crown to fit a new partial should be submitted "by report" using D2999. Use D2999 to describe the process of surveying a *new* crown (an extra charge in addition to crown) so that the new crown is ready to accept a clasp assembly of a planned partial denture. For PPO plans, check the Processing Policy Manual as to protocol for billing an optional service.

7. Custom ceramic margin.

8. A coping "first component" under a telescopic crown would be reported as D2975. The crown is then reported, separately.

9. D2999 could report creating a partial framework rest in a natural tooth.

NARRATIVES Always use a brief narrative to describe D2999 unspecified restorative procedure, by report.

NOTES

Go to www.practicebooster.com to learn about the Revenue Enhancement Program, a coding and fee positioning consultation for you and your staff.
Cut coding errors and maximize legitimate reimbursement!
Tel: (866) 858-7596; Fax: (855) 825-3960; info@drcharlesblair.com

D3000-D3999 IV. ENDODONTICS

CDT 2016

Local anesthesia is usually considered to be part of Endodontic procedures.

PULP CAPPING

CDT 2016

D3110 PULP CAP – DIRECT (EXCLUDING FINAL RESTORATION)

CDT 2016

Procedure in which the exposed pulp is covered with a dressing or cement that protects the pulp and promotes healing and repair.

LIMITATIONS
1. All adhesives, liners and bases (thermal protection) are *included* in the restorative (amalgam/composite) description and included in the *global* fee for a restoration. Many payers consider a direct pulp cap performed on the same service date to be a part of the restorative global fee. A direct pulp cap is an additional procedure where the *exposed* pulp is covered with a dressing or cement that seals and *protects the pulp and promotes healing and repair* of the pulp. There is nothing in the descriptor that prevents a direct pulp cap from being reported in *addition* to the restoration on the same date of service.

2. It is appropriate to report D3110 when the pulp is directly exposed and a dressing material is placed while the tooth heals and repairs for several months. A final restoration may or may not be placed on the same treatment date. In either case, the pulp cap is a stand-alone procedure. Do not report D3110 in conjunction with a protective restoration (D2940) on the same service date. A protective restoration (D2940) is a temporary restoration to relieve pain. Reimbursement is highly variable for D3110, direct pulp cap and D2940, protective restoration. Reporting D3110 may result in a better reimbursement than reporting a protective restoration (D2940). D2940 is often not payable or is a "take-back" code (meaning the fee reimbursed for the protective restoration, will be subtracted from the final restoration fee reimbursement if placed on a subsequent treatment date). There may be a time limitation/exclusion for the subsequent restoration. See D2940 for further details.

NARRATIVES
1. Direct pulp cap procedures may be reported in addition to the restoration on the same service date but the direct pulp cap may not be reimbursed. If the direct pulp cap is denied, some payers may pay upon appeal if a radiographic image and narrative support the need for the direct pulp cap. The patient would be responsible for payment of the procedure out of pocket if the doctor is not subject to a third party contract. Participating dentists are often required to write off the fee for the direct pulp cap procedure.

2. "See attached radiographic image." State if pulp exposed due to caries or due to fracture. State endodontic prognosis for tooth.

D3120 PULP CAP – INDIRECT (EXCLUDING FINAL RESTORATION)

CDT 2016

Procedure in which the nearly exposed pulp is covered with a protective dressing to protect the pulp from additional injury and to promote healing and repair via formation of secondary dentin. This code is not to be used for bases and liners when all caries have been removed.

CODING WATCH CORRECTION
1. The indirect pulp cap code is *not* to be reported to describe a base and liner when *all* caries has been removed.
2. All adhesives, liners and bases (thermal protection) are *included* in the restorative code descriptors and included in the global fee of a restoration. The global fee for the restoration may be increased if a base (after removal of deep caries) is required, but the base may not be separately charged. The higher fee will not be permitted by PPOs.

LIMITATIONS
1. It is appropriate to report an indirect pulp cap (D3120) when caries removal is close to the pulp leaving some decay to prevent exposure and a protective material is placed sealing in the decay and allowing the tooth to heal (via formation of secondary dentin). The indirect pulp cap may be left in place for several months prior to completing the final restoration as a separate treatment procedure. After a healing period and adequate secondary dentin formation, the dressing material and any remaining caries would be removed. A new base or liner would be placed and the tooth would then be restored.

2. Do not report D3120 in conjunction with a protective restoration (D2940) on the same service date. A protective restoration is a temporary restoration to relieve pain. A protective restoration (D2940) or IRM is considered a part of the indirect pulp cap and is reimbursed as part of the global fee for the procedure. In some cases, the payer may reimburse the protective restoration (if reported), but not the indirect pulp cap procedure. Reimbursement for this procedure is highly variable. See D2940 for further details.

TIPS The CDT descriptor indicates that D3120 should not be used to describe bases and liners when *all caries has been removed*. The CDT does not state that the restoration cannot be performed on the same day as the indirect pulp cap. There are two methods of indirect pulp capping:

1. The first method involves leaving a thin layer of caries (to avoid exposing the pulp) and placing a temporary filling. The tooth is reentered several months later, the temporary filling and remaining demineralized dentin are removed, and a permanent restoration is placed. (If all caries were removed, at the first appointment, a protective restoration (sedative filling – D2940) should have been reported instead of D3120).

2. The second method typically involves treating the tooth with stannous fluoride, a calcium hydroxide base and/or IRM, and placing the permanent restoration at the same visit. Dentists often do not want to unnecessarily traumatize the tooth by reentering it a second time, and it is less efficient.

D3120 can be used to report either method as long as all the caries were not removed. Note that few dental plans pay for an indirect pulp cap when performed on the same day as the final restoration. Third party contracts may prohibit reporting D3120 on the same service date as a restoration.

NARRATIVES "See attached radiographic image. Pulp nearly exposed due to deep caries; some caries were left and indirect pulp cap was placed."

PULPOTOMY   CDT 2016

D3220 **THERAPEUTIC PULPOTOMY (EXCLUDING FINAL RESTORATION) – REMOVAL OF PULP CORONAL TO THE DENTINOCEMENTAL JUNCTION AND APPLICATION OF MEDICAMENT**   CDT 2016

Pulpotomy is the surgical removal of a portion of the pulp with the aim of maintaining the vitality of the remaining portion by means of an adequate dressing. To be performed on primary or permanent teeth. This is not to be construed as the first stage of root canal therapy. Not to be used for apexogenesis.

CODING WATCH CORRECTION

1. Pulpotomy is "not to be construed as the first stage of root canal therapy."

2. This code does not describe apexogenesis. Apexogenesis is vital pulp therapy performed to encourage continued physiological formation and development of the tooth root, according to the ADA Glossary. See D3222 for *partial* pulpotomy for apexogenesis. D3222, not D3220 would be performed to save a permanent tooth.

3. It is erroneous to open the tooth (remove all pulpal tissue) to relieve acute pain *prior* to root canal treatment, and report it as a pulpotomy (D3220). The purpose of a pulpotomy is to "maintain the *vitality*" of the remaining pulpal tissue in the root(s) of the tooth. A pulpotomy is typically performed when caries removal or trauma results in pulp exposure of a primary tooth. Do not report D3220 *prior* to endodontic therapy. If opening a tooth to relieve acute pain at an emergency visit, see pulpal debridement, primary and permanent teeth (D3221), and palliative (D9110) for further details.

4. Billing *separately* for a protective restoration (D2940) and pulpotomy (D3220) on the same date of service could be considered overbilling. D2940 is not a part of the pulpotomy procedure. A protective restoration (D2940) is a stand-alone temporary restoration to relieve pain. A pulpotomy is a separate procedure performed to remove the affected pulpal tissue and maintain the tooth. The access opening made during the pulpotomy procedure may be sealed by IRM or other material prior to the subsequent restoration.

5. Typically, a pulpotomy is performed on *vital* primary teeth. Other pulpal therapies (D3230 or D3240) are performed on *necrotic* primary teeth. D3230 and D3240 involve the placement of a resorbable filling placed down the canals, similar to a root canal procedure. The UCR fee is sometimes higher for D3230 or D3240 than for D3220, so report these codes appropriately when providing pulpal therapy rather than a pulpotomy.

COMMENTS

1. If an anterior or posterior primary tooth is necrotic, perform and bill (D3230 or D3240) pulpal therapy. Pulpal therapy is similar to a root canal procedure for a permanent tooth with the difference being that it is done on a primary tooth and resorbable material is used in the obturated canals.

2. Report the final restoration (e.g., stainless steel crown, amalgam, or composite) separately.

3. If a permanent tooth is opened and active endodontic procedures started (a sequence of file measurements and instrumentation), endodontic codes (D3310, D3320, D3330) should be reported. Thus, endodontic therapy has been *initiated*. If endodontic therapy has been initiated do not report a pulpotomy (D3220).

4. To report a Cvek pulpotomy, see D3222.

LIMITATIONS

1. The therapeutic pulpotomy (D3220) is generally reported on primary teeth, and is usually reimbursed. The pulpotomy procedure is meant to "maintain the *vitality*" of the remaining pulpal tissue in the roots of the primary tooth. The primary tooth remains as a space maintainer, prior to exfoliation.

2. The pulpotomy is often followed by a restoration such as stainless steel crown, amalgam, or composite. Some payers limit the reimbursement of a pulpotomy to *primary* teeth, even though the code descriptor indicates that it can be performed on a primary or permanent tooth.

TIPS

1. When performed on permanent teeth, the pulpotomy may be reimbursed in some cases, but note that the fee reimbursed for the pulpotomy may be subtracted from the subsequent endodontic reimbursement. This take-back generally applies if the endodontic therapy is performed by either a specialist or general practitioner. Do not report D3220 *prior* to root canal therapy.

2. If the permanent tooth is "opened" to relieve acute pain (removing pulpal tissue) prior to the definitive RCT at an emergency visit, consider using the pulpal debridement (D3221) code to describe the procedure. Also consider using palliative (D9110) to describe a partial debridement procedure if performed at an emergency visit.

3. If the primary tooth does not have a succedaneous permanent tooth successor, then a traditional gutta-percha filled (or other non-resorbable material) root canal (D3310 or D3330) could be performed. Write a narrative explaining the reason for the gutta-percha procedure and ask for the root canal (D3310 or D3330) benefit. See D3310 and D3330.

D3221 PULPAL DEBRIDEMENT, PRIMARY AND PERMANENT TEETH — CDT 2016

Pulpal debridement for the relief of acute pain prior to conventional root canal therapy. This procedure is not to be used when endodontic treatment is completed on the same day.

CODING WARNING CORRECTION

1. It is misleading to report D3221 on the *same* service date, *in conjunction* with routine endodontic therapy. D3221 reports relief (open, remove pulpal tissue and drain) of acute pain *prior* to completing root canal therapy at a *subsequent* visit.

2. It is misleading to report D3221 at the first visit of a two appointment visit root canal technique.

COMMENTS

1. D3221 reports opening and debriding the pulp for relief of acute pain, *prior* to completing endodontic treatment. The emergency patient "interrupts" the dentist's schedule. After the pulpal debridement, the patient is then referred to an endodontist or the patient's dentist of record for completion of root canal therapy. If a covered benefit, pulpal debridement (D3221) may command a *higher* allowable fee than the palliative (D9110). Note that some payers "remap" and reimburse the pulpal debridement at the lower palliative (D9110) fee.

2. The CDT 2015 companion indicates that a protective restoration (D2940) could be reported in conjunction with D3221 on the same service date prior to starting endodontic treatment at the next visit. However, the payer would most likely refuse reimbursement for D2940 in conjunction with D3221.

LIMITATIONS

1. D3221 may be a "take-back" code if *the same provider or office* who performs D3221 performs the subsequent completion of endodontic treatment. If "taken-back," the previous reimbursement for D3221 is subtracted from the final endodontic reimbursement. If an endodontist at a *different* office (different taxpayer ID) does the endodontic treatment (even on the same service date), it generally is not a "take-back" procedure. Reimbursement for pulpal debridement among payers is highly variable. In some cases, the payer simply "remaps" D3221 to a lower-fee palliative (D9110) code for reimbursement.

2. If the patient presents for an emergency visit and endodontic treatment has been *initiated* (a sequence of file measurements and instrumentation), D3221 can be reported. The emergency visit would be followed by a subsequent visit for *completion* of endodontic treatments (D3310, D3320, D3330). D3221 should not be reported for the scheduled multi-appointment endodontic treatment but rather the unscheduled emergency visit for the relief of acute pain. Definitive endodontic treatment may be reported on the initiation date, upon the completion date of therapy, or as established by any third party contract provisions. The ADA Policy Eligibility and Payment Dates for Endodontic Treatment (1994:674) encourages the completion date as the date of service.

NARRATIVES
1. If the *same* office performs the endodontic treatment on a subsequent service date, following the emergency visit, palliative (D9110) may apply. Submit a narrative reporting exactly what was performed at the D9110 emergency visit. If definitive endodontic treatment was not initiated and *complete* pulpal debridement was not accomplished, consider D9110. If D9110 is reimbursed, full benefits remain available for endodontic treatment of the tooth at a later service date. See D9110.
2. If substantial time was spent on *instrumentation* prior to the fill, but the *patient does not return* to complete the root canal, report D3999. Indicate that the root canal was partially completed. Explain the time taken and the treatment provided. Be careful to document in the chart and report to the payer any cancellations and attempts to reschedule the patient for this treatment. The reimbursement fee may be higher for D3999 than D3221. See D3999 for further details.

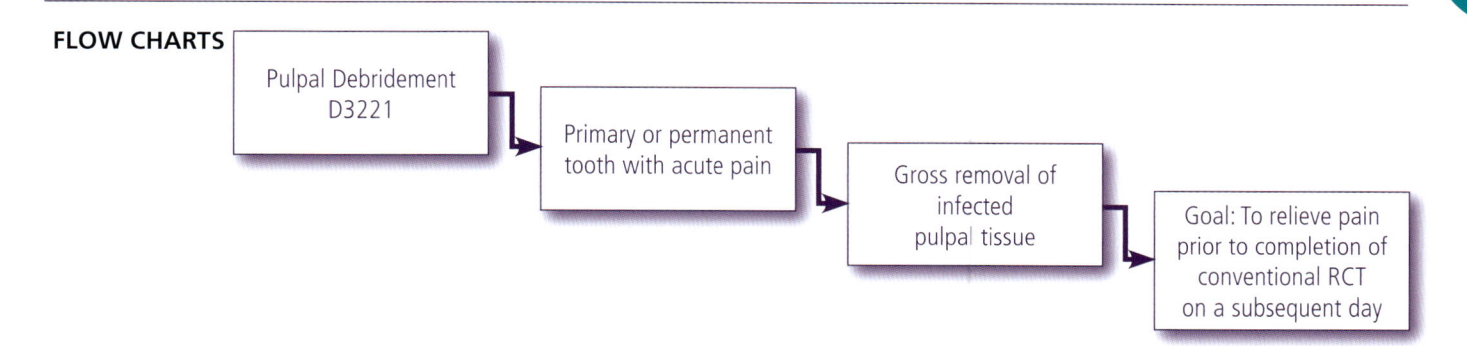

FLOW CHARTS

Pulpal Debridement D3221 → Primary or permanent tooth with acute pain → Gross removal of infected pulpal tissue → Goal: To relieve pain prior to completion of conventional RCT on a subsequent day

D3222 PARTIAL PULPOTOMY FOR APEXOGENESIS – PERMANENT TOOTH WITH INCOMPLETE ROOT DEVELOPMENT — CDT 2016

Removal of a portion of the pulp and application of a medicament with the aim of maintaining the vitality of the remaining portion to encourage continued physiological development and formation of the root. This procedure is not to be construed as the first stage of root canal therapy.

COMMENTS
1. D3222 reports a *partial* pulpotomy (vital pulp tissue remains in pulpal chamber) on a *permanent* tooth for *apexogenesis*. Apexogenesis is performed on an immature permanent tooth with a pulp exposure due to caries or trauma. The procedure involves removing only the infected part of the pulp from the pulp chamber (partial pulpotomy) with the goal of obtaining normal maturation and formation of the root. Apexogenesis encourages the continued development and formation of the root.
2. Report as D3999, by report, when performed on a primary tooth that has no permanent successor.
3. For a *pulpal regeneration* of an *immature permanent tooth* with a *necrotic* pulp, see the pulpal regeneration treatment sequence of D3355, D3356 and D3357. For *pulpotomy*, see D3220.
4. Report D3222 to describe Cvek pulpotomy, performed due to trauma.

ENDODONTIC THERAPY ON PRIMARY TEETH — CDT 2016

Endodontic therapy on primary teeth with succedaneous teeth and placement of resorbable filling. This includes pulpectomy, cleaning, and filling of canals with resorbable material.

D3230 — PULPAL THERAPY (RESORBABLE FILLING) – ANTERIOR, PRIMARY TOOTH (EXCLUDING FINAL RESTORATION) — CDT 2016

Primary incisors and cuspids.

CODING WATCH CORRECTION: It is inappropriate to report pulpal therapy – anterior, primary tooth (D3230) on *necrotic* anterior primary teeth as a pulpotomy (D3220). A pulpotomy is performed on a *vital* tooth, while pulpal therapy (D3230) is generally performed on *necrotic* primary teeth when *resorbable* material is used to fill the canals. Pulpal therapy (D3230) is similar to a conventional "root canal" but is used to treat necrotic *anterior primary teeth*. The UCR fee is sometimes higher for D3230 than pulpotomy (D3220).

COMMENTS: Report D3230 when the pulpal tissue is removed completely. D3230 includes instrumentation and placement of some type of *resorbable* root canal filling material in the canal of the anterior primary tooth. It is similar to a root canal but resorbable filling material is used in a primary tooth.

LIMITATIONS:
1. Pulpal therapy (D3230) is typically reimbursed once per primary anterior tooth, per lifetime. Benefits may be available for primary incisors (centrals and laterals) up to age six and primary cuspids up to age 11.
2. Some payers reimburse the lower vital pulpotomy (D3220) UCR fee as an *alternate b*enefit, rather than the higher UCR fee of pulpal therapy (D3230).

TIPS: If the pulp is necrotic *and* a resorbable material is placed into the canal after instrumentation, report pulpal therapy; anterior (D3230). D3230 should have a higher UCR fee than a therapeutic (vital) pulpotomy (D3220). D3230 is a more time-consuming procedure as the canals are instrumented and then filled with a resorbable filling material.

NARRATIVES: If the anterior primary tooth *has no permanent tooth to follow*, then the endodontic treatment should be reported as a *conventional* root canal if a non-resorbable material (gutta-percha) is used. For a primary anterior tooth (without a succedaneous tooth), report an anterior root canal (D3310). Be advised that some payers exclude a primary *anterior* tooth from conventional endodontic treatment reimbursement. Write a narrative explaining what was done and why the D3310 procedure was necessary.

D3240 — PULPAL THERAPY (RESORBABLE FILLING) – POSTERIOR, PRIMARY TOOTH (EXCLUDING FINAL RESTORATION) — CDT 2016

Primary first and second molars.

CODING WATCH CORRECTION: Do not report pulpal therapy – posterior, primary (D3240) on posterior primary first and second molar teeth that are vital. Pulpotomies are performed on *vital* teeth. Pulpal therapy (D3240) is performed on *necrotic* primary first and second molars when resorbable material is used to seal the canals. Pulpal therapy (D3240) is similar to a conventional "root canal" but is used to treat necrotic posterior *primary teeth*. The UCR fee is sometimes higher for D3240 than pulpotomy (D3220).

COMMENTS: Report D3240 when all the pulpal tissue is removed. D3240 includes instrumentation of canals and placement of some type of resorbable filling material in the canal of the posterior primary tooth.

LIMITATIONS:
1. Pulpal therapy (D3240) is typically reimbursed once per primary posterior tooth, per lifetime.
2. Some payers reimburse the lower vital pulpotomy (D3220) UCR fee as an *alternate b*enefit, rather than the higher UCR fee of D3240.

TIPS: If the primary posterior tooth pulp is non-vital and if a resorbable material is placed into the canal after instrumentation, report pulpal therapy – posterior (D3240). D3240 should have a higher UCR fee than a therapeutic (vital) pulpotomy (D3220). D3240 is a more time consuming procedure as the canals are instrumented and then filled with a resorbable filling.

NARRATIVES If the posterior primary tooth *has no permanent succedaneous tooth to follow*, then the endodontic treatment should be reported as a *conventional* root canal if a non-resorbable material, (e.g., gutta-percha) is used. For a primary posterior tooth (without a succedaneous tooth), report a posterior root canal (D3330). Be advised that some payers exclude a primary *posterior* tooth from conventional endodontic treatment reimbursement. Write a narrative explaining what was done and why this procedure was necessary. Send both pre- and post-op periapical radiographs of the tooth treated.

ENDODONTIC THERAPY (INCLUDING TREATMENT PLAN, CLINICAL PROCEDURES AND FOLLOW-UP CARE) — CDT 2016

Includes primary teeth without succedaneous teeth and permanent teeth. Complete root canal therapy: Pulpectomy is part of root canal therapy.

Includes all appointments necessary to complete treatment; also includes intra-operative radiographs. Does not include diagnostic evaluation and necessary radiographs/diagnostic images.

D3310 ENDODONTIC THERAPY, ANTERIOR TOOTH (EXCLUDING FINAL RESTORATION) — CDT 2016

CODING WARNING CORRECTION

1. It is inappropriate to report pulpal debridement (D3221) or palliative (D9110) at the initial, regularly-scheduled root canal visit to receive a higher overall reimbursement. If a root canal is initiated (the length determined and the instrumentation of the canal begun), the root canal codes (D3310, D3320, or D3330) should be used to report the service. Although the terminology used on the current ADA claim form permits reporting of the root canal on the start date, third party payers may require the root canal be submitted using the completion date. Also, the ADA's Coding Companion encourages reporting the completion date as the date of service.

2. For treatment to alleviate acute pain at an emergency visit by debriding the pulpal tissue, consider the use of the palliative (D9110) or pulpal debridement (D3221) code to describe this emergency procedure. See both pulpal debridement (D3221) and palliative (D9110) codes for further details. Obturation can be started. The root canal would be completed on a subsequent date.

3. If an endodontic access opening is done through a crown which is already permanently cemented/bonded, it is inappropriate to report restoration of the endodontic *access opening* as a core buildup (D2950). The purpose of a core buildup, reported as D2950, is for retention of a crown. Report a one surface amalgam or composite (see comments below, Narrative #2) to describe the access opening hole closure restorative procedure.

4. A root canal procedure performed to allow the placement of an overdenture attachment in the tooth is an "elective" procedure. An "elective" root canal procedure completed to aid in the delivery of another more "specialized" procedure, like an overdenture, should be submitted, but is generally not reimbursed.

5. For a routine, regularly-scheduled visit, do not report D3221 at the first visit of a two appointment root canal.

CODING WATCH CORRECTION

It is inappropriate to report endodontic therapy, anterior (D3310) for a one canal bicuspid. It should be reported as D3320. The determination of the endodontic code that describes the endodontic procedure provided is based on the tooth type rather than the number of canals treated. Report D3320 to describe a root canal provided for a bicuspid, regardless of the *number* of canals treated.

COMMENTS

1. Report a root amputation (D3450) separately.

2. An oral evaluation and diagnostic radiograph(s) should be reported separately from the root canal procedure. An oral evaluation would not be reported if the need for treatment had been previously diagnosed. Only the initial diagnostic radiograph(s) should be reported, not working radiographs. Working radiographs are considered part of the endodontic procedure. If multiple visits are necessary, the diagnostic radiographic images should be reported prior to, or on the first visit.

LIMITATIONS

1. "Working" or intraoperative radiographs and post-treatment images (within thirty days of treatment) are considered a part of the root canal global fee. Note: *diagnostic* images done *prior* to initiation of endodontic treatment are considered a separate diagnostic procedure and may be reimbursed. A problem focused evaluation (D0140) may be submitted at the evaluation appointment; however, plan limitations may limit reimbursement. See D0140.

2. Reimbursement for an under filled or over filled root canal may be denied.

3. D3310 could be used to report a root canal on an anterior *primary* tooth in a patient who is missing the permanent tooth when the primary tooth is sealed using a non-resorbable (gutta-percha type) material.

4. A pulpal debridement (D3221) or palliative (D9110) procedure may be reported when performed to relieve *acute* pain if endodontic treatment is not initiated on the same service date by the same office. "Starting" an endodontic procedure involves establishing working length and beginning the using of a sequence of files to instrument and enlarge the canal. Some payers "re-map" D3221 to a pulpotomy (D3220) or palliative (D9110) for reimbursement.

NARRATIVES

1. A root canal submitted for reimbursement and paid based on the start date that is never completed may be considered overbilling and is subject to a fee adjustment by the third party payer. A refund may be requested by the payer for all or part of the fee. Any cancellations and attempts to reschedule the patient for completion of treatment must be noted in the clinical record. Notify the payer that the root canal was not completed. Submit a request for the alternate benefit D3999, unspecified procedure, by report, to recoup for the time and materials used. The ADA *recommends* the root canal completion date be used when reporting endodontic therapy; however, state law and/or contract language could indicate or require otherwise.

2. The closure of an endodontic access hole is reported as a *separate* procedure. Use codes such as a one surface amalgam or composite to report the restoration for access hole closure. Restorations to seal the access opening are generally reimbursed at 80% of the UCR fee. Some third party contracts include access closure in the *global* fee for the endodontic procedures. It is recommended that a brief narrative be included with the claim that describes the restoration technique used and reason for the procedure. "An occlusal composite was placed for access hole closure." The payer may have tracked the tooth with a crown and may reject the composite restoration without a narrative.

3. The D2980 crown repair code now reports "necessitated by restorative failure" in its nomenclature so now either a one surface amalgam or composite is the code to use to report access hole closure, not crown repair.

4. If documentation is requested: "See attached pre- and post-op radiographic images."

5. If diagnostic radiographic images are denied, submit a narrative stating they were taken prior to initiation of endodontic therapy and are not "working" or intraoperative radiographs.

D3320 ENDODONTIC THERAPY, BICUSPID TOOTH (EXCLUDING FINAL RESTORATION)
CDT 2016

CODING WARNING CORRECTION

1. It is inappropriate to report pulpal debridement (D3221) or palliative (D9110) at the initial regularly scheduled root canal visit to receive a higher overall reimbursement. If a root canal is initiated (the length determined and the regularly-scheduled instrumentation of the canal begun), the root canal codes (D3310, D3320, or D3330) should be used to report the service. Although the terminology used on the current ADA claim form permits reporting of the root canal on the start date, third party payers may require the root canal be submitted using the completion date. Also, the ADA's Coding Companion (page 55) encourages reporting the completion date as the date of service.

2. For treatment to alleviate acute pain at an emergency visit by debriding and removing the pulpal tissue, consider the use of the palliative (D9110) or pulpal debridement (D3221) code to describe this emergency procedure. See both pulpal debridement (D3221) and palliative (D9110) for further details. Obturation could be started. The root canal would be completed on a subsequent visit.

3. It is inappropriate to report restoration of the endodontic access opening as a core buildup (D2950). The purpose of a core buildup, reported as D2950 is for retention. Report a one surface amalgam or composite (see comments below, Narrative #2) to describe the access opening hole closure restorative procedure.

4. A root canal procedure performed to allow the placement of an overdenture attachment in the tooth is an "elective" procedure. An "elective" root canal procedure completed to aid in the delivery of another more "specialized" procedure, like an overdenture, should be submitted, but is generally not reimbursed.

5. For a routine, regularly-scheduled visit, do not report D3221 at the first visit of a two appointment visit technique.

CODING WATCH CORRECTION

The determination of the endodontic code that describes the endodontic procedure provided is based on the tooth type rather than the number of canals treated. Report D3320 to describe a root canal provided to a bicuspid, regardless of the *number* of canals treated.

COMMENTS
1. Report the root amputation (D3450) or hemisection (D3920) separately.
2. Report D3320 for root canals performed on bicuspids, regardless of the number of canals. Fees vary and dentists may charge an additional $100-$200 fee for a two or three canal bicuspid, vs. a one canal bicuspid.
3. An oral evaluation and diagnostic radiograph(s) should be reported separately from the root canal procedure. An evaluation would not be reported if the need for treatment had been previously diagnosed. The initial diagnostic radiograph(s) should be reported, not working radiographs. Working and intraoperative radiographs are considered part of the endodontic procedure. If multiple visits are necessary, the diagnostic test(s) should be reported prior to, or on the first visit.

LIMITATIONS
1. "Working" or intraoperative radiographs and post-treatment images (within thirty days of treatment) are considered a part of the root canal global fee. Note: *Diagnostic* images done *prior* to initiation of endodontic treatment are considered a separate diagnostic procedure and may be reimbursed. A problem focused oral evaluation (D0140) may be submitted at the evaluation appointment; however, plan limitations may limit reimbursement. See D0140.
2. Reimbursement for an under filled or over filled root canal may be denied.
3. A pulpal debridement (D3221) or palliative (D9110) procedure may be reported when performed to relieve *acute* pain. "Starting" an endodontic procedure involves establishing working length and beginning the use of a sequence of files to instrument and enlarge the canal. This is permitted at the emergency visit. Some payers "re-map" D3221 to a pulpotomy (D3220) or palliative (D9110) for reimbursement.

NARRATIVES
1. A root canal submitted for reimbursement and paid based on the start date that is never completed is considered overbilling and is subject to adjustment by the third party payer. A refund may be requested by the payer for all or part of the fee. Any cancellations and attempts to reschedule the patient for completion of treatment must be noted in the clinical record. Notify the payer that the root canal was not completed. Submit a request for the alternate benefit D3999, unspecified procedure, by report, to recoup for the time and materials used. The ADA *recommends* the root canal completion date be used when reporting endodontic therapy; however, state law and/or contract language could indicate or require otherwise.
2. The closure of an endodontic access hole is reported as a *separate* procedure. Use codes such as a one surface amalgam or composite to report the restoration for access hole closure. Restorations to seal the access opening are generally reimbursed at 80% of the UCR fee. Some third party contracts include access closure in the *global* fee for the endodontic procedures. It is recommended that a brief narrative be included with the claim that describes the restoration technique used and reason for the procedure. "An occlusal composite was placed for access hole closure." The payer may have tracked the tooth with a crown and may reject the composite restoration without a narrative.
3. The D2980 crown repair code now reports "necessitated by restorative failure" in its nomenclature so now either a one surface amalgam or composite is the code to use to report endodontic access hole closure, not crown repair.
4. If documentation is requested: "See attached pre- and post-op radiographic images."
5. If diagnostic radiographic images are denied, submit a narrative stating they were taken prior to initiation of endodontic therapy and are not "working" or intraoperative radiographs.

D3330 ENDODONTIC THERAPY, MOLAR (EXCLUDING FINAL RESTORATION) — CDT 2016

CODING WARNING/CORRECTION

1. It is inappropriate to report pulpal debridement (D3221) or palliative (D9110) at the initial, regularly-scheduled root canal visit to receive a higher overall reimbursement. If a root canal is initiated (the length determined and the instrumentation of the canal begun), the root canal codes (D3310, D3320, or D3330) should be used to report the service. Although the terminology used on the current ADA claim form permits reporting of the root canal on the start date, the third party payer may require that the root canal be submitted using the completion date. Also, the ADA's Coding Companion (page 55) encourages reporting the completion date as the date of service.

2. For treatment to alleviate acute pain at an emergency visit by debriding and removing the pulpal tissue, consider the use of the palliative (D9110) or pulpal debridement (D3221) code to describe this emergency procedure. See both pulpal debridement (D3221) and palliative (D9110) for further details. Obturation could be started. The root canal would be completed on a subsequent visit.

3. If an endodontic access opening is done through a crown which is already permanently cemented/bonded, it is inappropriate to report restoration of the endodontic *access opening* as a core buildup (D2950). The purpose of a core buildup, reported as D2950, is for retention of the crown. Report a one surface amalgam or composite (see comments below, Narrative #2) to describe the access opening hole closure restorative procedure.

4. A root canal procedure performed to allow the placement of an overdenture attachment in the tooth is an "elective" procedure. An "elective" root canal procedure completed to aid in the delivery of another more "specialized" procedure, like an overdenture, should be submitted, but is generally not reimbursed.

5. For a routine, regularly-scheduled visit, do not report D3221 at the first visit of a two appointment visit technique.

COMMENTS

1. Report a root amputation (D3450) or hemisection (D3920) separately.

2. Report D3330 for all molar root canals, regardless of the number of canals. Note: Some dentists charge an additional $100-$200 for a four canal molar vs. a three canal molar.

3. D3330 may be used to report a root canal completed on a first or second *primary* molar tooth when the corresponding permanent tooth is not present. In this case the canals must be obturated and filled with a non-resorbable, gutta-percha like material.

4. An oral evaluation, diagnostic radiograph(s), and pulp vitality test (may not be reimbursed) should be reported separately from the root canal. An oral evaluation would not be reported if the problem had been previously diagnosed. Only the initial diagnostic radiograph(s) can be reported, not working radiographs. If multiple visits are necessary, the diagnostic test(s) should be reported on the first visit and the root canal procedure upon completion, at the last visit.

LIMITATIONS

1. "Working" or intraoperative radiographs and post-treatment images (within thirty days of treatment) are considered as part of the root canal global fee. Note: *Diagnostic* images done *prior* to initiation of endodontic treatment are considered a separate diagnostic procedure and may be reimbursed. A problem focused oral evaluation (D0140) may be submitted at the evaluation appointment; however, plan limitations may limit reimbursement. See D0140.

2. Reimbursement for an under filled or over filled root canal may be denied.

3. A pulpal debridement (D3221) or palliative (D9110) code may be reported when performed to relieve *acute* pain. "Starting" an endodontic procedure involves establishing working length and beginning the use of a sequence of files to instrument and enlarge the canal. This is permitted at the emergency visit. Some payers "re-map" D3221 to a pulpotomy (D3220) or palliative (D9110), for reimbursement.

NARRATIVES

1. A root canal submitted for reimbursement and paid based on the start date, but never completed, is considered overbilling and is subject to adjustment by the third party payer. A refund may be requested for all or part of the fee. Any cancellations and attempts to reschedule the patient for completion of treatment must be noted in the clinical record. Notify the payer that the root canal was not completed. Submit a request for the alternate benefit of D3999, unspecified procedure, by report, to recoup for the time and materials used. The ADA *recommends* the root canal completion date be used when reporting endodontic therapy; however, state law and/or contract language could indicate or require otherwise.

2. The closure of an endodontic access hole is reported as a *separate* procedure. Use codes such as a one surface amalgam or composite to report the restoration for access hole closure. Restorations to seal the access opening are generally reimbursed at 80% of the UCR fee. Some third party contracts include access closure in the *global* fee for the endodontic procedures. It is recommended that a brief narrative be included with the claim that describes the restoration technique used and reason for the procedure. "An occlusal composite was placed for access hole closure." The payer may have tracked the tooth with a crown and may reject the composite restoration without a narrative.

3. The D2980 crown repair code now reports "necessitated by restorative failure" in its nomenclature so now either a one surface amalgam or composite reports endodontic access hole closure, not crown repair.

4. If documentation is requested: "See attached pre- and post-op radiographic images."

5. If diagnostic radiographic images are denied, submit a narrative stating they were taken prior to initiation of endodontic therapy and are not "working" or intraoperative radiographs.

D3331 TREATMENT OF ROOT CANAL OBSTRUCTION; NON-SURGICAL ACCESS — CDT 2016

In lieu of surgery, the formation of a pathway to achieve an apical seal without surgical intervention because of a non-negotiable root canal blocked by foreign bodies, including but not limited to separated instruments, broken posts or calcification of 50% or more of the length of the tooth root.

COMMENTS

1. If the obstruction is iatrogenic, (caused inadvertently by the dentist), it is not appropriate for the dentist causing the obstruction to report D3331.

2. The descriptor for D3331 indicates separated instruments and broken posts are examples of foreign bodies that can prevent a dentist from negotiating a canal. According to the American Association of Endodontists (AAE) coding recommendations, D3331 is intended for use in cases where there is complete calcification of 50% or more of the canal length (not diameter) and to report the removal of separated files or other obstructions left in the root canal by another practitioner.

LIMITATIONS

1. D3331 may be reported in *addition* to the treatment or retreatment of root canals. Note that even though D3331 may be reported with the root canal, D3331 may be considered a part of the global root canal procedure by payers and may not be reimbursed.

2. Reimbursement for D3331, if available, often requires documentation with pretreatment and mid-treatment diagnostic images. It is important to maintain complete records that document the treatment provided.

NARRATIVES

1. Treatment of root canal obstruction (D3331) is not generally reimbursed to the provider who obstructs the canal, but may be reimbursed to a *different* provider overcoming the obstruction. Pretreatment and mid-treatment diagnostic images and a narrative are required for reimbursement by most payers. Also, indicate the *additional* time required to complete the root canal. It is important to maintain complete records that document the need for the D3221 treatment provided.

2. "See attached radiographic image." State why the root canal was non-negotiable/blocked, e.g., canal blocked by separated instrument, broken post or calcification of 50% or more of the length of the root.

D3332 INCOMPLETE ENDODONTIC THERAPY; INOPERABLE, UNRESTORABLE OR FRACTURED TOOTH — CDT 2016

Considerable time is necessary to determine diagnosis and/or provide initial treatment before the fracture makes the tooth unretainable.

CODING WARNING CORRECTION

D3332 should not be used to describe a situation where the patient fails to return for the completion of root canal therapy. See D3999, by report, to report an incomplete root canal.

COMMENTS
1. D3332 reports a situation where endodontic therapy is initiated but then terminated when it is determined the tooth is inoperable, unrestorable, or fractured. Occasionally, the initial clinical evaluation and diagnostic radiographs appear to indicate a tooth can be treated successfully with root canal therapy, but once treatment begins, the situation is deemed hopeless. The problem may be due to extensive decay, calcifications, divergences, obstructed canals, or vertical root fractures that were not evident on radiographs or clinically evident. Once the dentist determines that root canal therapy cannot be completed, D3332 may be reported to reimburse for the time invested and the work that was performed.
2. Use D3221 to describe the pulpal debridement of a tooth at an emergency visit when the initial provider determines that they cannot complete treatment and that the patient must be referred to an endodontist to complete the root canal therapy.
3. Use D3332 to describe a flap that is laid to diagnose a fracture prior to the start of endodontic therapy and where the patient is referred back to the GP or to a specialist for an extraction.

LIMITATIONS
1. For reimbursement, D3332 often requires pretreatment and mid-treatment diagnostic radiographic images.
2. Some dental plans do not provide a benefit for D3332. Some payers will reimburse for the alternate benefit of palliative treatment (D9110) when incomplete root canal therapy is reported using D3332, at an emergency visit.

NARRATIVES
1. If a patient *voluntarily* discontinues endodontic treatment, D3332 should *not* be reported. Consider reporting an endodontic unspecified procedure (D3999) with a narrative when the patient fails to return for completion of root canal therapy. See D3999, by report, for further details or consider D3221 or D9110 to possibly describe this scenario.
2. D3332 is a *stand-alone* code and may be reimbursed when a significant amount of time, energy, and effort is spent prior to discovering a fracture or pathology that cannot be resolved. Plan limitations for D3332 are highly variable. It is recommended that a brief narrative be included when reporting D3332. In the narrative, indicate the diagnosis and reason why root canal therapy was not completed.
3. D3332, if reimbursed, is paid at 30-50% of the allowable root canal fee. Payers typically require a narrative that includes any diagnostic findings, radiographs before and during treatment as well as an explanation of why the root canal procedure was not completed. The narrative should include documentation of the time spent in treatment and number of treatment appointments provided before determining that the tooth was inoperable, unrestorable, or fractured. The extraction should be reported separately from D3332 and can be reported on the same date at a different office or on a subsequent appointment date.

D3333   INTERNAL ROOT REPAIR OF PERFORATION DEFECTS   CDT 2016

Non-surgical seal of perforation caused by resorption and/or decay but not iatrogenic by provider filing claim.

COMMENTS
1. D3333 reports the non-surgical seal of a perforation caused by resorption and/or decay not caused by the provider performing an endodontic procedure. Payers deny the claim if the perforation was caused by the provider (iatrogenic).

LIMITATIONS
1. For reimbursement, some payers require obturation, not just removal of decay.
2. Payers may require four to six months healing, with no pathology evident, prior to performing definitive root canal treatment.
3. D3333 is typically not reimbursed in conjunction with an apicoectomy/retrograde filling performed by the same dentist or by the same dental office.

NARRATIVES A detailed narrative with pre-operative and post-operative radiographs may be required for reimbursement. Evidence of healing four to six months after the repair of the perforation may be necessary for RCT reimbursement.

ENDODONTIC RETREATMENT — CDT 2016

D3346 — RETREATMENT OF PREVIOUS ROOT CANAL THERAPY – ANTERIOR — CDT 2016

COMMENTS
1. The 2980 crown repair code reports "necessitated by restorative failure" in its nomenclature so now either a one surface amalgam or composite is the code to report an endodontic access hole closure, not crown repair.
2. **IMPORTANT!** See D3310 for additional information regarding the anterior root canal.

LIMITATIONS
1. Payers consider retreatment of a previous anterior root canal (D3346) to include removal of post, pin(s), old root canal filling material, as well as the finished, re-treated root canal therapy. The fee for D3346 is typically several hundred dollars higher than the comparable anterior root canal (D3310).
2. To be reimbursed, most payers require that the retreatment be performed more than six months after the original root canal. Some payers require more than 24 months to have elapsed after the original root canal for the retreatment service to be reimbursed. Time limitations vary.
3. The time limitation may not apply when the retreatment service is performed by a different office.

NARRATIVES
1. The narrative should include the approximate date of the previously completed root canal therapy. The narrative should include what portion of the root canal failed, why the overall endo failed, and how retreatment corrected the problem. It is important to include a diagnostic radiographic image taken before the re-treatment and a post-treatment periapical radiographic image.
2. The closure of an endodontic access hole is reported as a *separate* procedure. Use codes such as a one surface amalgam or composite to report the restoration of the access opening. Restorations to seal the access opening are generally reimbursed at 80% of the UCR fee. Some third party contracts include access closure in the *global* fee for the endodontic procedures. It is recommended that a brief narrative be included with the claim that describes the access hole closure restoration technique used and reason for the procedure.
3. "See attached pre- and post-op radiographic images." State the date that the initial/previous root canal was completed.

D3347 — RETREATMENT OF PREVIOUS ROOT CANAL THERAPY – BICUSPID — CDT 2016

COMMENTS
1. The D2980 crown repair code now reports "necessitated by restorative failure" in its nomenclature so now either a one surface amalgam or composite is the code to report an endodontic access hole closure, not crown repair.
2. **IMPORTANT!** See D3320 for additional information regarding the bicuspid root canal.

LIMITATIONS
1. Payers consider retreatment of a previous bicuspid root canal (D3347) to include removal of post, pin(s), old root canal filling material, as well as the finished, retreated root canal therapy. The fee for D3347 is typically several hundred dollars higher than the comparable bicuspid root canal (D3320).
2. To be reimbursed, most payers require that the retreatment be performed more than six months after the original root canal. Some payers require more than 24 months to have elapsed after the original root canal for the retreatment service to be reimbursed. Time limitations vary.
3. The time limitation may not apply when the retreatment service is performed by a different office.

NARRATIVES
1. The narrative should include the approximate date of the previously completed root canal therapy. The narrative should include what portion of the root canal failed, why the overall endo failed, and how retreatment corrected the problem. It is important to include a diagnostic radiographic image taken before the retreatment and a post-treatment periapical radiographic image.

2. The closure of an endodontic access hole is reported as a *separate* procedure. Use codes such as a one surface amalgam or composite to report the restoration of the access openings. Restorations to seal the access opening are generally reimbursed at 80% of the UCR fee. Some third party contracts include access closure in the *global* fee for the endodontic procedures. It is recommended that a brief narrative be included with the claim that describes the access hole closure restoration technique used and reason for the procedure

3. "See attached pre- and post-op radiographic images." State the date that the initial/previous root canal was completed.

D3348 — RETREATMENT OF PREVIOUS ROOT CANAL THERAPY – MOLAR — CDT 2016

COMMENTS
1. The D2980 crown repair code now reports "necessitated by restorative failure" in its nomenclature so now either a one surface amalgam or composite is the code to report an endodontic access hole closure, not crown repair.
2. **IMPORTANT!** See D3330 for additional information regarding the molar root canal.

LIMITATIONS
1. Payers consider retreatment of a previous molar root canal (D3348) to include removal of post, pin(s), old root canal filling material, as well as the finished, retreated root canal therapy. The fee for D3348 is typically several hundred dollars higher than the comparable molar root canal (D3330).
2. To be reimbursed, most payers require that the retreatment be performed more than six months after the original root canal. Some payers require more than 24 months to have elapsed after the original root canal for the retreatment service to be reimbursed. Time limitations vary.
3. The time limitation may not apply when the retreatment service is performed by a different office.

NARRATIVES
1. The narrative should include the approximate date of the previously completed root canal therapy. The narrative should include what portion of the root canal failed, why the endo failed, and how retreatment corrected the problem. It is important to include a diagnostic radiographic image taken before the retreatment and a post-treatment periapical radiographic image.
2. The closure of an endodontic access hole is reported as a *separate* procedure. Use codes such as a one surface amalgam or composite to report the restoration of the access opening. Restorations to seal the access opening are generally reimbursed at 80% of the UCR fee. Some third party contracts include access closure in the *global* fee for the endodontic procedures. It is recommended that a brief narrative be included with the claim that describes the access hole closure restoration technique used and reason for the procedure.
3. "See attached pre- and post-op radiographic images." State the date that the initial/previous root canal was completed.

APEXIFICATION/RECALCIFICATION — CDT 2016

D3351 — APEXIFICATION/RECALCIFICATION – INITIAL VISIT (APICAL CLOSURE/ CALCIFIC REPAIR OF PERFORATIONS, ROOT RESORPTION, ETC.) — CDT 2016

Includes opening tooth, preparation of canal spaces, first placement of medication and necessary radiographs. (This procedure may include first phase of complete root canal therapy.)

If the pulpal tissue is non-vital, use the pulpal regeneration procedures for continued root development. The necrotic pulpal regeneration treatment sequence is: D3355 for initial pulpal regeneration treatment, D3356 for interim pulpal regeneration treatment (may require multiple visits), and D3357 for the final stage of pulpal regenerative treatment. Working radiographs are a part of the treatment and should not be submitted for reimbursement. The final stage of pulpal regeneration includes placement of a seal at the coronal (crown) portion of the root canal system, however, per the descriptor for D3357, it does not include the final restoration. Conventional root canal treatment *is not* performed with pulpal regeneration, D3357.

CODING MATCH CORRECTION

If the pulpal tissue is *vital*, the apexification procedures are used to encourage continued root development. The apexification treatment sequence is: D3351 for initial treatment, D3352 for interim treatment (may require multiple visits), and D3353 for the final stage of apexification. The final apexification treatment stage includes obturation and placement of root canal filling material.

COMMENTS
1. The goal of apexification/recalcification is to induce root maturation and closing of the root apex.
2. Apexogenesis is a *partial* pulpotomy of a *vital* tooth performed to encourage and allow for the development of the tooth root. See D3222.
3. Report D3351 for the *initial* visit for apexification/recalcification which includes any working radiographs.

LIMITATIONS
1. D3351 only pertains to the permanent dentition.
2. Some payers withhold reimbursement until the *completion* of the apexification and recalcification process. This process may include root canal obturation when required as part of the procedure. Under this scenario, one all-inclusive fee reimburses all visits. It is suggested that the reimbursement policy of the payer be verified *prior* to initiating treatment.
3. Some payers limit reimbursement for the multi stage treatment (and for all treatment visits) to the fee paid for the "regular" root canal performed on that tooth.
4. Working radiographs are included in the treatment fees and should not be submitted separately.

TIPS The initial diagnostic radiographs may be submitted for reimbursement separately up front, while working radiographs are included in the treatment fees.

NARRATIVES It is recommended that a comprehensive narrative with the diagnostic radiograph(s) be submitted with the claim form. Any working radiograph(s) can be sent for documentation purposes, but should not be submitted for reimbursement.

D3352 APEXIFICATION/RECALCIFICATION – INTERIM MEDICATION REPLACEMENT (APICAL CLOSURE/CALCIFIC REPAIR OF PERFORATIONS, ROOT RESORPTION, PULP SPACE DISINFECTION, ETC.) CDT 2016

For visits in which the intra-canal medication is replaced with new medication. Includes any necessary radiographs.

CODING WARNING CORRECTION

If the pulpal tissue is non-vital, use the pulpal regeneration procedures for continued root development. The necrotic pulpal regeneration treatment sequence is: D3355 for initial pulpal regeneration treatment, D3356 for interim pulpal regeneration treatment (may require multiple visits), and D3357 for the final stage of pulpal regeneration treatment. Working radiographs are a part of the treatment and should not be submitted for reimbursement. The final stage of pulpal regeneration includes placement of a seal at the coronal (crown) portion of the root canal system, however, per the descriptor for D3357, it does not include the final restoration. Conventional root canal treatment *is not* performed with pulpal regeneration, D3357.

CODING MATCH CORRECTION

If the pulpal tissue is *vital*, the apexification procedures are used to encourage continued root development. The apexification treatment sequence is: D3351 for initial treatment, D3352 for interim treatment (may require multiple visits), and D3353 for the final stage of apexification. The final apexification treatment stage includes obturation and placement of root canal filling material.

COMMENTS
1. The goal of apexification/recalcification is to induce development of the root apex.
2. Apexogenesis is a *partial* pulpotomy of a *vital* tooth performed to encourage and allow for the development of the tooth root. See D3222.
3. Report apexification/recalcification (D3352) for an *interim* visit for apexification/recalcification, when a new medication is placed. D3352 includes any working (intra-operative) radiographs.

4. There may be several visits for *interim* medication replacement over a period of months or years.

LIMITATIONS
1. D3352 only pertains to the permanent dentition.
2. Some payers withhold reimbursement until the *completion* of the apexification, recalcification or pulpal regeneration process. This process may include root canal obturation when required as part of the procedure. Under this scenario one all-inclusive fee reimburses all visits. It is suggested that the reimbursement policy of the payer be verified *prior* to initiating treatment.
3. Some payers limit reimbursement for the multi stage treatment (and for all treatment visits) to the fee paid for the "regular" root canal performed on that tooth, depending on the anatomic type of tooth, not the number of canals.
4. Working radiographs are included in the treatment fees and should not be submitted separately.

NARRATIVES It is recommended to send a brief narrative and periodic working radiographs to document the progress of treatment. Working radiographic images are not submitted for reimbursement.

D3353 APEXIFICATION/RECALCIFICATION – FINAL VISIT (INCLUDES COMPLETED ROOT CANAL THERAPY – APICAL CLOSURE/CALCIFIC REPAIR OF PERFORATIONS, ROOT RESORPTION, ETC.)   CDT 2016

Includes removal of intra-canal medication and procedures necessary to place final root canal filling material including necessary radiographs. (This procedure includes last phase of complete root canal therapy.)

CODING WARNING CORRECTION
If the pulpal tissue is non-vital, use the pulpal regeneration procedures for continued root development. The necrotic pulpal regeneration treatment sequence is: D3355 for initial pulpal regeneration treatment, D3356 for interim pulpal regeneration treatment (may require multiple visits), and D3357 for the final stage of pulpal regeneration treatment. Working radiographs are a part of the treatment and should not be submitted for reimbursement. The final stage of pulpal regeneration includes placement of a seal at the coronal (crown) portion of the root canal system, however, per the descriptor for D3357, it does not include the final restoration. Conventional root canal treatment *is not* performed with pulpal regeneration, D3357.

CODING MATCH CORRECTION
If the pulpal tissue is *vital*, the apexification procedures are used to encourage continued root development. The apexification treatment sequence is: D3351 for initial treatment, D3352 for interim treatment (may require multiple visits), and D3353 for the final stage of apexification. The final apexification treatment stage includes obturation and placement of root canal filling material.

COMMENTS
1. The goal of apexification and recalcification is to induce development of a root apex.
2. Apexogenesis is a *partial* pulpotomy of a *vital* tooth performed to encourage and allow for the development of the tooth root. See D3222.
3. Report D3353 for the final visit for apexification/recalcification, which includes completed root canal therapy (last phase). This visit includes any working (intra-operative) radiographs.
4. The fee for the apexification or recalcification final visit (assuming reimbursement for D3351 or D3352 previously) should be about 80-100% of the root canal fee. If the preliminary procedures, D3351/D3352 were not previously reimbursed for initial and interim steps, consider a higher fee for the apexification final visit (D3353) than for the typical root canal fee for the tooth.

LIMITATIONS
1. D3353 only pertains to the permanent dentition. Some payers withhold reimbursement until the *completion* of the apexification, recalcification or pulpal regeneration process. This process may include root canal obturation when required as part of the procedure. Under this scenario, one all-inclusive fee reimburses all visits. It is suggested that the reimbursement policy of the payer be verified *prior* to initiating treatment.

2. Some payers limit reimbursement for the multistage treatment (for all apexification or recalcification visits) to the regular endodontic root canal fee reimbursement, depending on the anatomic type of tooth, not the number of canals.

3. Working radiographs are included in the treatment fees.

TIPS This procedure does not include the final restoration of the tooth. Report the final restoration separately.

NARRATIVES It is recommended to send a brief narrative and periodic working radiographs to document the progress and completion of the apexification treatment.

D3354 — PREVIOUSLY DELETED CODE PULPAL REGENERATION – (COMPLETION OF REGENERATIVE TREATMENT IN AN IMMATURE PERMANENT TOOTH WITH A NECROTIC PULP); DOES NOT INCLUDE FINAL RESTORATION

This is a previously deleted code. See D3357 for further details.

PULPAL REGENERATION — CDT 2016

D3355 PULPAL REGENERATION – INITIAL VISIT — CDT 2016

Includes opening tooth, preparation of canal spaces, placement of medication.

Important: See D3357 comments.

CODING WARNING CORRECTION — If the pulpal tissue is *vital*, the apexification procedures are used to encourage continued root development. The apexification treatment sequence is: D3351 for initial apexification/recalcification treatment, D3352 for interim apexification/recalcification treatment (may require multiple visits), and D3353 for the final stage of apexification/recalcification treatment. The final apexification/recalcification treatment stage includes obturation and placement of root canal filling material.

CODING MATCH CORRECTION — If the pulpal tissue is non-vital, use the pulpal regeneration procedures for continued root development. The necrotic pulpal regeneration treatment sequence is D3355 for initial pulpal regeneration treatment, D3356 for interim pulpal regeneration treatment (may require multiple visits), and D3357 for the final stage of pulpal regenerative treatment.

COMMENTS
1. The goal of pulpal regeneration (regenerative treatment in an immature permanent tooth with a necrotic pulp) is to induce development of the root apex. Report D3355 for the *initial* visit for pulpal regeneration which includes any working radiographs. Report D3356 for an *interim* visit for pulpal regeneration.

2. The final stage of pulpal regeneration (D3357) includes placement of a seal at the coronal (crown) portion of the root canal system. The final restoration is billed separately. Conventional root canal treatment *is not* performed with pulpal regeneration.

LIMITATIONS
1. D3355 only pertains to the permanent dentition.

2. Some payers withhold reimbursement until the *completion* of the pulpal regeneration process. Under this scenario one all-inclusive fee reimburses all visits. It is suggested that the reimbursement policy of the payer be verified *prior* to initiating treatment.

3. Some payers limit reimbursement for the multistage treatment (and for all treatment visits including pulpal regeneration) to the fee paid for the "regular" root canal performed on that tooth.

CODING WATCH CORRECTION

1. The removal of a nonodontogenic cyst or tumor (D7460/D7461) and apicoectomy – anterior may be reported concurrently. It is improper/misleading to report (D7460/D7461), removal of a nonodontogenic cyst or tumor, and D3410, apicoectomy, concurrently if the apicoectomy is not performed.

2. Biopsy of oral tissue – hard (D7285) and biopsy of oral tissue – soft (D7286) prohibits their reporting with apicoectomy/periradicular surgery codes, (D3410, D3421, D3425, D3426 or D3427).

COMMENTS

1. D3410 reports the amputation of the apex (tip) of the root of the previously endodontically treated *anterior* tooth. An apicoectomy is performed when:
   a. It is impossible to do conventional root canal therapy because the canal(s) can't be negotiated, or
   b. Root canal therapy was completed, but it was unsuccessful.

2. A retrograde filling (D3430) is necessary to seal the end of the tooth root when the apex has been surgically amputated, (i.e., an apicoectomy has been done).

3. This procedure includes exploratory curettage to look for root fractures. For periradicular surgery without apicoectomy, see D3427.

LIMITATIONS

1. The retrograde filling (D3430) is a separate procedure. Note, the retrograde filling is often combined with the apicoectomy for reimbursement. See D3430 for further details.

2. Apicoectomy treatment may not be reimbursed if performed on a tooth less than 24 months after the completion of the root canal. Time limitations vary.

3. If the apicoectomy is performed on the same service date as a root canal, only a portion of the apicoectomy fee may be reimbursed.

4. Reimbursement for D3410 is highly variable.

D3421 APICOECTOMY – BICUSPID (FIRST ROOT) CDT 2016

For surgery on one root of a bicuspid. Does not include placement of retrograde filling material. If more than one root is treated, see D3426.

CODING WATCH CORRECTION

1. The removal of a nonodontogenic cyst or tumor (D7460/D7461) and apicoectomy – bicuspid may be reported concurrently. It is improper/misleading to report (D7460/D7461), removal of a nonodontogenic cyst or tumor, and D3421 apicoectomy, concurrently, if the apicoectomy is not performed.

2. Biopsy of oral tissue – hard (D7285) and biopsy of oral tissue – soft (D7286) prohibits their reporting with apicoectomy/periradicular surgery codes, (D3410, D3421, D3425, D3426 or D3427).

COMMENTS

1. D3421 reports the amputation of the apex (tip) of the root of the previously endodontically treated *bicuspid* tooth. If more than one root is treated, see D3426. An apicoectomy is performed when:
   a. It is impossible to do conventional root canal therapy because the canal(s) can't be negotiated, or
   b. Root canal therapy was completed, but it was unsuccessful.

2. A retrograde filling (D3430) is necessary to seal the end of the tooth root when the apex has been surgically amputated, (i.e., an apicoectomy has been done)

3. This procedure includes exploratory curettage to look for root fractures. For periradicular surgery without apicoectomy, see D3427.

LIMITATIONS

1. The retrograde filling (D3430) is a separate procedure. Note, the retrograde filling is often combined with the apicoectomy for reimbursement. See D3430 for further details.

2. Apicoectomy treatment may not be reimbursed if performed on a tooth less than 24 months after the completion of the root canal. Time limitations vary.

3. If the apicoectomy is performed on the same service date as a root canal, only a portion of the apicoectomy fee may be reimbursed.

4. Reimbursement for D3421 is highly variable.

D3425 APICOECTOMY – MOLAR (FIRST ROOT) CDT 2016

For surgery on one root of a molar tooth. Does not include placement of retrograde filling material. If more than one root is treated, see D3426.

CODING WATCH CORRECTION

1. The removal of a nonodontogenic cyst or tumor (D7460/D7461) and apicoectomy – molar may be reported concurrently. It is improper/misleading to report (D7460/D7461), removal of a nonodontogenic cyst or tumor, and D3425 apicoectomy, concurrently, if the apicoectomy is not performed.

2. Biopsy of oral tissue – hard (D7285) and biopsy of oral tissue – soft (D7286) prohibits their reporting with apicoectomy/periradicular surgery codes, (D3410, D3421, D3425, D3426 or D3427).

COMMENTS

1. D3425 reports the amputation of the apex (tip) of the root of the previously endodontically-treated *molar* tooth. If more than one root is treated, see D3426. An apicoectomy is performed when:

   a. It is impossible to do conventional root canal therapy because the canal(s) can't be negotiated, or

   b. Root canal therapy was completed, but it was unsuccessful.

2. A retrograde filling (D3430) is necessary to seal the end of the tooth root when the apex has been surgically amputated, (i.e., an apicoectomy has been done).

3. This procedure includes exploratory curettage to diagnose root fractures. For periradicular surgery without apicoectomy, see D3427.

LIMITATIONS

1. The retrograde filling (D3430) is a separate procedure. Note, the retrograde filling is often combined with the apicoectomy for reimbursement by payers. See D3430 for further details.

2. Apicoectomy treatment may not be reimbursed if performed on a tooth in less than 24 months after the completion of the root canal. Time limitations vary.

3. If the apicoectomy is performed on the same service date as a root canal, only a portion of the apicoectomy fee may be reimbursed.

4. Reimbursement for D3425 is highly variable.

D3426 APICOECTOMY (EACH ADDITIONAL ROOT) CDT 2016

Typically used for bicuspids and molar surgeries when more than one root is treated during the same procedure. This does not include retrograde filling material placement.

CODING WATCH CORRECTION

1. The removal of a nonodontogenic cyst or tumor (D7460/D7461) and apicoectomy (each additional root) – molar may be reported concurrently. It is improper/misleading to report (D7460/D7461), removal of a nonodontogenic cyst or tumor, and D3426 apicoectomy, concurrently, if the apicoectomy is not performed.

2. Biopsy of oral tissue – hard (D7285) and biopsy of oral tissue – soft (D7286) prohibits their reporting with apicoectomy/periradicular surgery codes, (D3410, D3421, D3425, D3426 or D3427).

COMMENTS D3426 reports the amputation of the apex of an *additional* root in addition to first root of a previously endodontically treated tooth. (It is rare but an anterior tooth can have more than one root).

LIMITATIONS

1. The retrograde filling (D3430) is a separate procedure. Note, the retrograde filling is often combined with the apicoectomy for reimbursement by payers. See D3430 for further details.

2. Apicoectomy treatment may not be reimbursed if performed on a tooth less than 24 months after the completion of the root canal. Time limitations vary.

3. If the apicoectomy is performed on the same service date as a root canal, only a portion of the apicoectomy fee may be reimbursed.

4. Reimbursement for D3426 is highly variable.

D3427 PERIRADICULAR SURGERY WITHOUT APICOECTOMY — CDT 2016

CODING CORRECTION WATCH

1. The removal of a nonodontogenic cyst or tumor (D7460/D7461) and periradicular surgery without apicoectomy (D3427) should not be reported concurrently. Use the code that best describes the procedure performed. Do not use D3427, periradicular surgery without apicoectomy when a cyst or tumor is involved. It is improper/misleading to report D7460/D7461 removal of a nonodontogenic cyst or tumor *and* D3427 periradicular surgery without apicoectomy concurrently unless the surgery is intended to treat separate and discrete condition(s).

2. Biopsy of oral tissue – hard (D7285) and biopsy of oral tissue – soft (D7286) prohibits their reporting with apicoectomy/periradicular surgery codes, (D3410, D3421, D3425, D3426 or D3427).

3. Periradicular surgery (D3427) would be reported when doing surgery on a resorptive lesion that does not touch the apex.

COMMENTS

1. Periradicular surgery can be performed without an apicoectomy. This code allows for an accurate description reporting D3427.

2. Report D3427 to describe surgery performed in the periradicular area without performing an apicoectomy. When biologic materials are used to aid in soft and osseous tissue regeneration in conjunction with periradicular surgery, report D3431. When providing guided tissue regeneration, resorbable barrier, per site, in conjunction with periradicular surgery, report D3432.

LIMITATIONS

1. The reimbursement may be limited for periradicular surgery without apicoectomy (D3427).

2. If D3427 is performed on the same service date as a root canal, only a portion of the periradicular surgery fee may be reimbursed.

3. Reimbursement for D3427 is highly variable.

D3428 BONE GRAFT IN CONJUNCTION WITH PERIRADICULAR SURGERY – PER TOOTH, SINGLE SITE — CDT 2016

Includes non-autogenous graft material.

CODING CORRECTION WARNING

Bone graft in conjunction with periradicular surgery – per tooth, single site (D3428) is used to describe a bone graft placed during periradicular surgery. Do not use periodontal osseous surgery bone replacement grafts codes (D4263 or D4264) to report a bone graft in conjunction with periradicular surgery without apicoectomy (D3427).

COMMENTS

1. An osseous autograft, allograft or non-osseous graft is placed in a periradicular defect at the time of the periradicular surgery to preserve the alveolar (bone) integrity and to aid in the healing process.

2. Periradicular surgery requires bone removal to access the root area being treated. This type of surgery can remove a significant amount of bone structure and can hinder the long term stability of the tooth. A bone graft placed to augment the bony defect can enhance the healing process and may benefit the overall result. D3428 should be reported when performing a bone graft in conjunction with periradicular surgery – per tooth, single site at the time of the periradicular surgery. D3428 includes any non-autogenous graft material. Separately, biologic materials to aid in soft and osseous tissue regeneration in conjunction with periradicular surgery (D3431) and guided tissue regeneration, resorbable barrier, per site, in conjunction with periradicular surgery (D3432), when placed, are reported separately.

3. If a membrane is placed, the resorbable membrane would be reported separately as guided tissue regeneration procedure (D3432). Thus, guided tissue regeneration is also reported in conjunction with a periradicular surgery. The reimbursement is subject to the plan's limitations.

4. Although the same materials are often used, this endodontic procedure (D3428) is reported with a different code from a bone graft performed to correct deformities caused by *periodontal* disease. This endodontic procedure involves the use of osseous grafts, osseous allografts, or non-osseous grafts to stimulate bone growth when periradicular pathosis has led to a deformity of the bone.

5. Only non-autogenous bone graft material is included in reporting D3428. The harvesting of autogenous graft material should be reported as D7295. Typically, autogenous graft material is used less than 1% of the time.

6. D3429, bone graft in conjunction with periradicular surgery-each additional contiguous tooth in the same surgical site, cannot be reported for another site on the same tooth reported for D3428. D3429 can only be used for a tooth contiguous to the tooth reported in D3428.

LIMITATIONS
1. Reimbursement for this procedure in addition to the periradicular surgery is limited and seldom reimbursed.

2. Some contracts stipulate that only one regenerative procedure will be paid per periradicular area. For example, D3428 or D3429 may be paid following periradicular surgery but the biologic materials (D3431) denied. Additionally, payment for GTR is often limited to two sites per quadrant. Note: D3429 would not be paid unless D3428 had already been paid. If they pay only one regenerative procedure per periradicular area, D3429 would probably never be paid.

TIPS
1. The material cost of bone grafts varies widely. The fee charged should be the actual material's cost of the graft plus a "labor" charge, plus the GTR resorbable membrane barrier (D3432) fee, if placed. Don't overprice the combination of procedures – keep the total time of all the procedures (plus materials) in mind.

2. D3432, guided tissue regeneration, if done in conjunction with D3428, is reported separately.

3. Terms you should know:

   Allogenic graft – usually freeze-dried cells (from another human being) that are used to repair a defect or supplement a deficiency. Demineralized bone graft products are an example of this (allograft bone material).

   Alloplastic – refers to man-made materials used for tissue grafting and augmentation. Hydroxylapatite bone graft is an example of this type of graft (e.g., OsteoGraft®, etc.).

   Autogenous – a graft taken from one part of a patient's body and transferred to another. Chin, hip, and rib grafts would be examples of an autogenous graft.

   Xenograft – bone graft tissue from another species, such as bovine bone (Bio-oss®).

   Guided tissue regeneration – used to enhance and promote bone growth by placing a resorbable barrier membrane D3432 under gingival tissue and over remaining bone (e.g., Gore-tex®, BioMend®, etc.). GTR is placed to inhibit fast growing soft tissue from filling in the graft area while allowing slower growing bone to fill in the defect.

   Reimbursement is subject to the need and benefit availability. Reimbursement for a bone graft is inconsistent. Payers require the bone graft be done on the same service date as the periradicular surgery.

NARRATIVES It is recommended that the payer be contacted for specific coverage information/limitations and supporting documentation required for consideration. Most payers request periodontal charting even though pocket depths are irrelevant in terms of endodontic indications for the periradicular surgery procedure.

D3429	BONE GRAFT IN CONJUNCTION WITH PERIRADICULAR SURGERY – EACH ADDITIONAL CONTIGUOUS TOOTH IN THE SAME SURGICAL SITE	CDT 2016

Includes non-autogenous graft material.

COMMENTS 1. Bone graft in conjunction with periradicular surgery – each additional contiguous tooth in the same surgical site (D3429) is used to describe an additional bone graft placed in a tooth contiguous to the tooth reported in D3428. D3429 cannot be reported for another site on the same tooth reported for D3428.

2. See D3428 for additional information regarding a bone graft in conjunction with periradicular surgery.

LIMITATIONS Some contracts stipulate that only one regenerative procedure will be paid per periradicular area. For example, D3428 or D3429 may be paid following periradicular surgery but the biologic materials (D3431) denied. Additionally, payment for GTR is often limited to two sites per quadrant. Note: D3429 would not be paid unless D3428 had already been paid. If they pay only one regenerative procedure per periradicular area, D3429 would probably never be paid.

D3430   RETROGRADE FILLING – PER ROOT   CDT 2016

For placement of retrograde filling material during periradicular surgery procedures. If more than one filling is placed in one root – report as D3999 and describe.

COMMENTS 1. Retrograde filling (D3430) reports a retrograde filling which seals the root apex of an endodontically treated tooth, that has had an apicoectomy

2. D3430 is reported on a *per root* basis.

NARRATIVES If more than one filling is placed in the same root, report as D3999 and provide a brief narrative that describes the procedure.

D3431   BIOLOGIC MATERIALS TO AID IN SOFT AND OSSEOUS TISSUE REGENERATION IN CONJUNCTION WITH PERIRADICULAR SURGERY   CDT 2016

COMMENTS 1. Biologic materials may be used alone or with other regenerative substrates such as bone and barrier membranes, depending upon their formulation and the presentation of the periradicular defect. This procedure (D3431) does not include surgical entry and closure, wound debridement, osseous contouring, or the placement of graft materials and/or barrier membranes. Other separate procedures may be required in conjunction with D3431 and should be reported using their own unique codes.

2. During periradicular surgery, biologic materials may be placed in a bony defect to aid in the regeneration of soft and osseous tissue. These materials may include bone morphogenetic protein 2 (BMP-2), Emdogain®, etc. Bone graft materials (D3428/D3429) and/or GTR barrier membranes (D3432) may also be placed at the same time and should be reported separately.

LIMITATIONS 1. Reimbursement for biologic materials used to aid in soft and osseous tissue regeneration in conjunction with periradicular surgery (D3431) may be limited to the surgical portion of the overall periradicular procedure.

2. Some contracts stipulate that only one regenerative procedure will be paid per periradicular area. For example, D3428 or D3429 may be paid following periradicular surgery but the biologic materials (D3431) denied. Additionally, payment for GTR is often limited to two sites per quadrant.

Note: D3429 would not be paid unless D3428 had already been paid. If they pay only one regenerative procedure per periradicular area, D3429 would probably never be paid.

3. Fibrin Glue®, PepGen®, Gem 21®, and Emdogain® are all examples of biologic materials. Some payers limit reimbursement to specific materials such as Emdogain®. In addition, Plasma Rich Protein (PRP) is also considered a biologic material. When using PRP (also known as autologous blood concentrate product), report D7921.

4. D3431 is seldom reimbursed by payers. This procedure requires consultant review prior to reimbursement.

5. Should payers reimburse D3431, the amount reimbursed for D3431 may be limited to the cost of the materials used.

TIPS Associated procedures that may be provided along with D3431 may include but are not limited to D3410, D3421, D3425, D3426, and D3427.

NARRATIVES A narrative is required to document this procedure. The narrative should clearly describe the condition of the surgical area being treated by the biologic material and why the treatment was needed. The narrative should identify the material used for regenerative purposes.

D3432 GUIDED TISSUE REGENERATION, RESORBABLE BARRIER, PER SITE, IN CONJUNCTION WITH PERIRADICULAR SURGERY — CDT 2016

COMMENTS
1. This procedure does not include other procedures provided in conjunction with periradicular surgery, including apicoectomy, retrograde filling, grafting, cyst removal, biopsy, or the use of biologic materials to aid in healing. D3432 is used for regeneration of tissue associated with periradicular surgery and is reported as a stand-alone procedure.
2. The process of healing after periradicular surgery is important to the long term success of the periradicular procedure. Bone requires more time to regenerate and mature than soft tissue. A barrier membrane is placed to stabilize the surgery site so that the new bone can mature & heal without interference from the healing soft tissue. The resorbable membrane (D3432) is integrated into the regeneration site and resorbed or broken down by the body in the healing process. This type of barrier membrane does not require a second surgery for removal.
3. A bone graft is not always required when a barrier membrane is used. Some regeneration techniques encourage bone regrowth without an associated bone graft. Guided Tissue Regeneration (GTR) inhibits faster growing soft tissue from filling in the site, allowing the slower growing bone to fill in the site first.
4. Other procedures may be performed with D3432 and should be reported separately using their unique codes.

LIMITATIONS
1. Guided tissue regeneration, resorbable barrier, per site, in conjunction with periradicular surgery (D3432) should be reported separately when placed in association with other periradicular procedures. Barrier membranes should be reported separately when placed in concert with bone grafts D3428 and D3429. Tooth number, surface/site, radiographic images (pre- and post-treatment) and clinical notes are typically required to be reported for reimbursement.
2. Some contracts stipulate that only one regenerative procedure will be paid per periradicular area. For example, D3428 or D3429 may be paid following periradicular surgery but the biologic materials (D3431) denied. Additionally, payment for GTR is often limited to two sites per quadrant. Note: D3429 would not be paid unless D3428 had already been paid. If they pay only one regenerative procedure per periradicular area, D3429 would probably never be paid.

D3450 ROOT AMPUTATION – PER ROOT — CDT 2016

Root resection of a multi-rooted tooth while leaving the crown. If the crown is sectioned, see D3920.

CODING CORRECTION WARNING: If the crown is sectioned, *do not* report D3450. See hemisection (D3920) for further details.

COMMENTS
1. The word "crown" in the descriptor does not refer to a restorative crown, but to the anatomical crown portion of the natural tooth.
2. The natural crown is left intact while one of the roots is removed of a multi-rooted tooth.
3. Any endodontic treatment provided is reported separately.
4. Any restorative treatment provided is reported separately.

LIMITATIONS If an apicoectomy is performed, the root amputation is often considered a part of the apicoectomy procedure and not reimbursed.

NARRATIVES
1. State necessity for root amputation. Also send a pre-operative periodontal chart and pre-operative radiographic image(s).
2. State endodontic and periodontal prognosis for remaining part of tooth.

D3460 ENDODONTIC ENDOSSEOUS IMPLANT — CDT 2016

Placement of implant material, which extends from a pulpal space into the bone beyond the end of the root.

COMMENTS
1. Endodontic endosseous implant (D3460) reports an endodontic implant, which extends through the pulpal space of the tooth beyond the end of the root. This code is often used in association with a natural tooth overdenture and the related metallic coping.
2. Conventional implants are more often indicated than the endodontic endosseous implant (D3460). This procedure is seldom performed and is considered obsolete.

LIMITATIONS D3460 is not typically reimbursed.

D3470 INTENTIONAL REIMPLANTATION (INCLUDING NECESSARY SPLINTING) — CDT 2016

For the intentional removal, inspection and treatment of the root and replacement of a tooth into its own socket. This does not include necessary retrograde filling material placement.

CODING CORRECTION WATCH
1. It is erroneous to report D3470 for an accident related reimplantation. If reimplantation follows an accident, see D7270 for appropriate coding.
2. It is inappropriate to report D3470 for tooth transplantation (D7272). Transplantation (D7272) describes a situation where a tooth is removed and repositioned in a second tooth's socket. See D7272.

COMMENTS Intentional reimplantation (D3470) reports extracting a tooth and then replacing it in the same socket. D3470 does not include a retrograde filling (D3430) performed on the extracted tooth while in hand. Report the retrograde filling (D3430) procedure separately.

LIMITATIONS The intentional reimplantation (D3470) procedure is not typically reimbursed.

OTHER ENDODONTIC PROCEDURES — CDT 2016

D3910 SURGICAL PROCEDURE FOR ISOLATION OF TOOTH WITH RUBBER DAM — CDT 2016

COMMENTS D3910 should only be billed when the dentist uses a scalpel, laser or electrosurgery to surgically recontour the *soft tissue* in order to have access to more tooth structure to support a rubber dam clamp. For example, if the palatal cusp of tooth #5 has fractured off 1-2mm beneath the gingival margin, soft tissue surgical recontouring may be necessary, which then justifies billing D3910.

LIMITATIONS
1. Surgical procedure for isolation of tooth with rubber dam (D3910) which is done on the same day as a root canal or gross pulpal debridement (D3221) is not typically reimbursed. D3910 is considered a part of the global fee by most payers.

2. D3910 may be reimbursed if the isolation is necessary to treat trauma. For example, after a traumatic fracture, D3910 might be required for the isolation of a tooth with rubber dam to treat the fracture and might be reimbursed.

NARRATIVES Write a narrative describing why the soft tissue surgical procedure was required for the isolation of the tooth with rubber dam.

D3920 — HEMISECTION (INCLUDING ANY ROOT REMOVAL), NOT INCLUDING ROOT CANAL THERAPY — CDT 2016

Includes separation of a multi-rooted tooth into separate sections containing the root and the overlying portion of the crown. It may also include the removal of one or more of those sections.

COMMENTS
1. The word "crown" in the descriptor does not refer to a restorative crown, but to the anatomical crown portion of a tooth.
2. Before D3920 is done, the tooth has already had root canal treatment.
3. D3920 reports the *sectioning* of the multi-rooted tooth in preparation for the placement of a crown. These sections may contain the roots only. Or they may contain the separate root(s) with their portion of the anatomic crown.
4. D3920 may be used to describe the sectioning of a tooth with the removal of a root or when each part of the tooth is restored.
5. Any restorative treatment provided is reported separately.

NARRATIVES Write a narrative describing the procedure.

D3950 — CANAL PREPARATION AND FITTING OF PREFORMED DOWEL OR POST — CDT 2016

Should not be reported in conjunction with D2952, D2953, D2954 or D2957 by the same practitioner.

CODING WATCH CORRECTION
1. It is inappropriate to report canal preparation and fitting of preformed dowel or post (D3950) if the practitioner providing the root canal treatment is also restoring the tooth.
2. D3950 could be reported by the endodontist who provides the root canal treatment if another dentist restores the tooth.

COMMENTS D3950 is used to report the preparation of the canal for a preformed dowel or post. This service is typically provided by an endodontist after completing a root canal. This allows the restorative dentist to place the preformed post or dowel to restore the endodontically treated tooth. This procedure provides space to accommodate the placement of the preformed dowel or post.

LIMITATIONS
1. D3950 is often considered a part of the placement procedure of the prefabricated post and core procedure. D3950 is not typically reimbursed.
2. D2952 is reported by the restorative dentist when placing a cast post and core. This procedure is global and includes the canal preparation and seating of a cast post and core.
3. D2954 is reported by the restorative dentist when placing a prefabricated post and core. This procedure is global and includes the canal preparation and fitting of a preformed dowel or post.
4. If a dentist is placing a post in a filling (as a final restoration), and not completing a post and buildup in *preparation* for a crown, report D2999, by report, to describe the post.

NARRATIVES It is important to include a narrative with this procedure that explains that the doctor providing D3950 is not the provider who subsequently will place the post and core.

D3960	PREVIOUSLY DELETED CODE INTERNAL BLEACHING

This is a previously deleted code. See D9974 for further details.

D3999	UNSPECIFIED ENDODONTIC PROCEDURE, BY REPORT	CDT 2016

Used for procedure that is not adequately described by a code. Describe procedure.

NARRATIVES D3999, by report, may be used to describe the following endodontic and other related procedures. These procedures, at this time, have no specific code to describe the procedure:

1. When a patient does not return to complete endodontic treatment, a payer may reimburse up to one-third of the root canal fee. This reimbursement is highly variable. The payer may re-map the reimbursement level to coincide with the pulpal debridement (D3221) or palliative (D9110) UCR fee. For reimbursement it is important to include a narrative with the claim. Document any cancellations, no shows, and attempts to reschedule the patient.
2. Removal of a broken instrument. Write a narrative. Plan limitations are highly variable.
3. Removal of pulp stones. Write a narrative. Plan limitations are highly variable.
4. Calcified canals that are less than 50%. Write a narrative. Plan limitations are highly variable.
5. Retrograde filling – *more* than one filling is placed in one root. Write a narrative and describe. Also, see D3430.

D4000-D4999 GENERAL COMMENTS FOR PERIODONTAL SERVICES — AUTHOR'S COMMENTS

1. The old periodontal classification (1989 AAP system), type I, II, III, IV, V is used in this section for purposes of illustration. Dental practices and the insurance industry continue to use this system. The current system was developed in 1999 with 8 categories. Many payers still ask for the type I-V description. To learn more about the current classification system go to http://dent.osu.edu/d3_case_presentations/pdf/classificationpd.pdf.

2. The definition of "quadrant" requires "four or more contiguous teeth or tooth bound spaces per quadrant." The codes specifying "four or more contiguous teeth or tooth bound spaces per quadrant" are gingivectomy or gingivoplasty (D4210), gingival flap procedure, including root planing (D4240), and osseous surgery (including flap entry and closure) (D4260).

   Note: The definition of periodontal scaling and root planing (D4341) *differs* from the other periodontal codes. D4341 describes scaling and root planing provided "for four or more teeth per quadrant" with no reference to the teeth being "contiguous" or to "tooth bound spaces." Simply put, D4341 requires a count of four or more qualified and treated teeth per quadrant.

3. Many periodontal codes apply to "one to three contiguous teeth or tooth bound spaces per quadrant." The codes specifying "one to three contiguous teeth or tooth bound spaces per quadrant" are gingivectomy or gingivoplasty (D4211), gingival flap procedure, including root planing (D4241), and osseous surgery (including flap entry and closure) (D4261).

   Note: The definition of periodontal scaling and root planing (D4342) differs from the other periodontal codes. D4342 describes scaling and root planing provided "for one to three teeth per quadrant" with no reference to the teeth being "contiguous" or to "tooth bound spaces." Simply put, D4342 requires a count of one to three qualified and treated teeth per quadrant.

4. If more than one periodontal procedure is provided (in the same area/quadrant/) on the same day, only the most complicated procedure is usually reimbursed.

5. Reimbursements for periodontal procedures are typically limited to procedures provided to natural teeth.

LANAP® CODING RECOMMENDATIONS

There continues to be controversy about the coding for the Laser Assisted New Attachment Procedure (LANAP®). To better understand the coding of LANAP® a look at the codes and the procedure itself should help establish the coding criterion for LANAP®. Codes D4260/D4261 were revised in CDT 2015 to be more specific in their description of the mandatory procedures performed. The ADA's Code Maintenance Committee was clear in that the procedure must now include:

A full thickness flap be laid.

As well as these requirements:

- Modification of the bony support of the teeth by reshaping the alveolar process to achieve a more physiologic form **during** the surgical procedure.
- The bony reshaping must include removal of supporting bone (ostectomy) and/or non-supporting bone (osteoplasty).

There have been a number of indications, per the FDA for the effective use of the PerioLaseNd:YAG Dental laser system. None of these indications involve:

- Modification of the bony support of the teeth by reshaping the alveolar process to achieve a more physiologic form during the surgical procedure.
- The bony reshaping must include removal of supporting bone (ostectomy) and/or non-supporting bone (osteoplasty).

Can the PerioLaseNd:YAG Dental laser system lay a full thickness flap? If used properly, the laser can be used to lay a full thickness flap.

So, where does all this information lead? Because codes D4260 and 4261 require:

- Modification of the bony support of the teeth by reshaping the alveolar process to achieve a more physiologic form **during** the surgical procedure.
- The bony reshaping must include removal of supporting bone (ostectomy) and/or non-supporting bone (osteoplasty), during the procedure.

The LANAP® procedure does not modify bone during the procedure and although the laser can (in theory) lay a full thickness flap the LANAP® procedure should not be described using codes D4260/D4261.

Conclusion: The official LANAP® procedure is best reported using either code D4341/D4342 (based on the number of teeth treated in a quadrant) and should not be described using the current D4260 or D4261. D4240/D4241 may be performed during LANAP® and may be reported in conjunction with and separately from D4341/D4342.

D4000-D4999 V. PERIODONTICS — CDT 2016

Local anesthesia is usually considered to be part of Periodontal procedures.

SURGICAL SERVICES (INCLUDING USUAL POSTOPERATIVE CARE) — CDT 2016

Site: A term used to describe a single area, position, or locus. The word "site" is frequently used to indicate an area of soft tissue recession on a single tooth or an osseous defect adjacent to a single tooth; also used to indicate soft tissue defects and/or osseous defects in edentulous tooth positions.

- If two contiguous teeth have areas of soft tissue recession, each area of recession is a single site.
- If two contiguous teeth have adjacent but separate osseous defects, each defect is a single site.
- If two contiguous teeth have a communicating interproximal osseous defect, it should be considered a single site.
- All non-communicating osseous defects are single sites.
- All edentulous non-contiguous tooth positions are single sites.
- Depending on the dimensions of the defect, up to two contiguous edentulous tooth positions may be considered a single site.

Tooth Bounded Space: A space created by one or more missing teeth that has a tooth on each side.

D4210 GINGIVECTOMY OR GINGIVOPLASTY – FOUR OR MORE CONTIGUOUS TEETH OR TOOTH BOUNDED SPACES PER QUADRANT — CDT 2016

It is performed to eliminate suprabony pockets, or to restore normal architecture when gingival enlargements or asymmetrical or unaesthetic topography is evident with normal bony configuration.

CODING CORRECTION WARNING

1. It is misleading to report gingivectomies or gingivoplasties (D4210) performed to improve esthetics without a narrative disclosing the cosmetic nature of the procedure.
2. To report a gingivectomy performed to allow access for a restorative procedure, see D4212.
3. When removing inflamed or hypertrophied tissue around *partially* erupted or impacted teeth, report excision of pericoronal gingiva (D7971), also known as an operculectomy.

COMMENTS

1. A *gingivectomy* involves the excision of gingiva to reduce gingival hypertrophy or to improve asymmetrical or unaesthetic gingival topography. A *gingivoplasty* is surgically reshaping the gingiva.
2. Pockets deeper than 3mm are difficult to clean and the patient may benefit from the surgical reduction of pocket depths. Gum tissue removed to reduce pocket depths around teeth make the area easier for the patient to maintain/keep clean. The gingivectomy is performed to treat suprabony pockets (pockets that are coronal to the bone level).
3. If the gingival overgrowth is caused by a medication, report the gingivectomy procedure to the *medical* insurance payer for reimbursement.
4. For anatomical crown exposure, removing both gingival tissue *and* supporting bone, see D4230 and D4231.

LIMITATIONS

1. Gingivectomies are generally paid when performed as part of periodontal therapy, or for patients currently taking Dilantin, cyclosporine medication or several types of calcium channel blocking agents. Calcium channel blocking agents are often prescribed for patients with hypertension and/or coronary artery disease. Dental plans typically require a current periodontal charting and related diagnosis for reimbursement. Some payers will cover a gingivectomy if the patient is diagnosed as case type II (early periodontitis). Other payers limit reimbursement for periodontal case types III or IV (moderate to severe periodontitis). If SRP (D4341/D4342) is performed in the same quadrant within four weeks of gingivectomy (D4210/D4211), the SRP may be denied as part of the gingivectomy for reimbursement purposes. Some payers consider D4341/D4342 a part of postoperative care (if done within three months) and as well as a part of any additional periodontal surgery for three years post gingivectomy.

2. There is typically a 24 to 36 month exclusion period when providing the same D4210 procedure to the same area of the mouth.

3. A gingivectomy is not generally reimbursed in association with scaling and root planing (SRP), or osseous surgery if performed on the same service date. The gingivectomy is considered to be a part of the SRP or osseous surgery procedure.

4. A gingivectomy performed with a distal wedge (D4274) or frenectomy procedure (D7960) is typically considered a part of that procedure. A gingivectomy performed to allow access for a restorative procedure should be reported as D4212.

5. A gingivectomy performed to allow access for a restorative procedure should be reported as D4212, per tooth.

TIPS

1. A gingivectomy may be indicated to treat a type II periodontal treatment case.

2. D4210 may be performed using a variety of methods: laser, electrosurgery, or scalpel. There is no special code for using a laser to perform this procedure. Payers reimburse for the specific procedure performed and are not concerned about the technique or technology used to accomplish the procedure.

NARRATIVES

1. Submit a current dated, pre-operative periodontal chart. Most payers require full periodontal probing and charting within the last ninety days and a corresponding periodontal *diagnosis* to approve reimbursement. If the gingivectomy is related to pathology (not cosmetic) it may be reimbursed. To qualify for reimbursement a 4mm or 5mm pocket must be noted on each tooth surgically treated. A gingivoplasty is surgically reshaping the gingiva. Photographs of the probe in place are helpful in obtaining reimbursement. Document that the procedure is not cosmetic related. When gingivectomy/gingivoplasty is performed some payers require thirty days healing prior to a crown preparation visit.

2. If the hyperplastic tissue is caused/aggravated by orthodontic treatment include a narrative that identifies the cause. There typically would be no reimbursement in this case, but it still should be reported.

3. "See attached periodontal chart." State necessity for gingivectomy or gingivoplasty, e.g., to eliminate suprabony pockets, to allow access for restorative dentistry in the presence of suprabony pockets, or to restore normal architecture when gingival enlargements or asymmetrical or unaesthetic topography is evident with normal bony configuration.

4. Treatment for gingival hypertrophy caused by a medication should be billed to the patient's medical plan. Medical plans often cover dental conditions that are either caused by, or exacerbated by, a patient's medication.

D4211 GINGIVECTOMY OR GINGIVOPLASTY – ONE TO THREE CONTIGUOUS TEETH OR TOOTH BOUNDED SPACES PER QUADRANT — CDT 2016

It is performed to eliminate suprabony pockets, or to restore normal architecture when gingival enlargements or asymmetrical or unaesthetic topography is evident with normal bony configuration.

CODING WARNING CORRECTION

1. It is misleading to report gingivectomies or gingivoplasties (D4211) performed to improve esthetics without a narrative disclosing the cosmetic nature of the procedure.

2. To report a gingivectomy performed to allow access for a restorative procedure, see D4212.

3. When removing inflamed or hypertrophied tissue around *partially* erupted or impacted teeth, report excision of pericoronal gingiva (D7971), also known as an operculectomy.

COMMENTS
1. A *gingivectomy* involves the excision of gingiva to reduce gingival hypertrophy or to improve asymmetrical or unaesthetic gingival topography. A *gingivoplasty* is surgically reshaping the gingiva.
2. Pockets deeper than 3mm are difficult to clean and the patient may benefit from the surgical reduction of pocket depths. Gum tissue removed to reduce pocket depths around teeth make the area easier for patient to maintain/keep cleaner. The gingivectomy is performed to treat suprabony pockets (pockets that are coronal to the bone level).
3. If the gingival overgrowth is caused by a medication, report the gingivectomy procedure to the *medical* insurance payer for reimbursement.
4. For anatomical crown exposure, removing both gingival tissue *and* supporting bone, see D4230 and D4231.

LIMITATIONS
1. Gingivectomies are generally paid when performed as part of periodontal therapy, or for patients currently taking Dilantin, cyclosporine medication or several types of calcium channel blocking agents. Calcium channel blocking agents are often prescribed for patients with hypertension and/or coronary artery disease. Dental plans typically require a current periodontal charting and related diagnosis for reimbursement. Some payers will cover a gingivectomy if the patient is diagnosed as case type II (early periodontitis). Other payers limit reimbursement for periodontal case types III or IV (moderate to severe periodontitis). If SRP (D4341/D4342) is performed in the same quadrant within four weeks of gingivectomy (D4210/D4211), the SRP may be denied as part of the gingivectomy for reimbursement purposes. Some payers consider D4341/D4342 a part of postoperative care (if done within three months) and as well as a part of any additional periodontal surgery for three years post gingivectomy.
2. When reimbursed, D4211 is typically reimbursed at 50-60% UCR fee of D4210.
3. There is typically a 24 to 36 month exclusion period when providing the same D4210 procedure to the same area of the mouth.
4. A gingivectomy is not generally reimbursed in association with scaling and root planing (SRP), or osseous surgery if performed on the same service date. It is considered a part of SRP.
5. A gingivectomy performed with a distal wedge (D4274) or frenectomy procedure (D7960) is typically considered a part of that procedure.
6. A gingivectomy performed to allow access for a restorative procedure should be reported as D4212, per tooth.

TIPS
1. A gingivectomy may be indicated to treat a type II periodontal treatment case.
2. D4211 may be performed using a variety of methods: laser, electrosurgery, or scalpel. There is no special code for reporting a laser used to perform this procedure. Payers reimburse for the specific procedure performed and are not concerned about the technique or technology used to accomplish the procedure.

NARRATIVES
1. Submit a current dated, pre-operative periodontal chart. Most payers require full periodontal probing and charting within the last ninety days and a corresponding periodontal *diagnosis* to approve reimbursement. If the gingivectomy is related to pathology (not cosmetic) it may be reimbursed. To qualify for reimbursement a 4mm or 5mm pocket must be noted for each tooth surgically treated. A gingivoplasty is surgically reshaping the gingiva. Photographs of the probe in place are helpful in obtaining reimbursement. Document that the procedure is not cosmetic related. When gingivectomy/gingivoplasty is performed some payers require thirty days healing prior to a crown preparation visit.
2. If the hyperplastic tissue is caused/aggravated by orthodontic treatment include a narrative that identifies the cause. There typically would be no reimbursement in this case, but it still should be reported.
3. "See attached periodontal chart." State necessity for gingivectomy or gingivoplasty, e.g., to eliminate suprabony pockets, to allow access for restorative dentistry in the presence of suprabony pockets, or to restore normal architecture when gingival enlargements or asymmetrical or unaesthetic topography is evident with normal bony configuration.
4. Treatment for gingival hypertrophy caused by a medication should be billed to the patient's medical plan. Medical plans often cover dental conditions that are either caused by, or exacerbated by, a patient's medication.

D4212 — GINGIVECTOMY OR GINGIVOPLASTY TO ALLOW ACCESS FOR RESTORATIVE PROCEDURE, PER TOOTH — CDT 2016

CODING CORRECTION (WARNING)

1. Gingivectomy or gingivoplasty – four or more contiguous teeth or tooth bounded spaces per quadrant (D4210) and gingivectomy or gingivoplasty – one to three contiguous teeth or tooth bounded spaces per quadrant (D4211) report *periodontal* related procedures. Do not report D4210 or D4211 for restorative access, only for periodontal treatment.
2. The D4212 procedure is to allow access for a restorative procedure, and is reported "per tooth."
3. When removing inflamed or hypertrophied tissue around *partially* erupted or impacted teeth, report excision of pericoronal gingiva (D7971), also known as an operculectomy.

COMMENTS

1. D4212 reports gingivectomy or gingivoplasty which provides access during a restorative procedure. *The D4212 gingivectomy removes gingival tissue to provide access to the margins of a crown preparation or cavity preparation and may aid in placing a restoration or to improve the isolation of the preparation while taking an impression.*
2. Gingivectomy D4212 is reported on a "per tooth" basis.
3. During the gingivectomy procedure (D4212) healthy gum tissue is removed to reduce pocket depths around teeth making the area easier to access and restore or to take an impression. The gingivectomy is performed to access and restore suprabony pockets (pockets that are coronal to the bone level).
4. For anatomical crown exposure, removing both gingival tissue *and* supporting bone, see D4230 and D4231.
5. For gingivectomy to treat purely periodontal conditions, see D4210 or D4211.
6. For clinical crown lengthening – hard tissue, see D4249.

LIMITATIONS

1. Most payers include "all soft tissue management procedures" in the global restorative fee. Gingivectomies to allow access for restorative procedures (D4212) are not typically reimbursed in conjunction with routine crown preparations or other restorative procedures. Gingivectomies may be considered a part of the crown procedure (soft tissue management or periodontal management) or restorative procedure by most payers when performed on the same day as the preparation of the crown or restorative procedure.
2. Gingivectomy D4212 for restorative access is silent regarding how tissue is removed. It may be removed by a variety of methods, including scalpel, electrosurgery, laser, etc.

TIPS

Gingivectomies for restorative access should ideally be followed by an appropriate healing period. Failure to allow for an adequate healing period may result in the denial of the gingivectomy for restorative access (D4212) with many payers. Many payers will deny D4212 even if the restoration is done on a subsequent date.

D4230 — ANATOMICAL CROWN EXPOSURE – FOUR OR MORE CONTIGUOUS TEETH PER QUADRANT — CDT 2016

This procedure is utilized in an otherwise periodontally healthy area to remove enlarged gingival tissue and supporting bone (ostectomy) to provide an anatomically correct gingival relationship.

CODING CORRECTION (WATCH)

It is an error to report anatomical crown exposure (D4230) to describe crown lengthening. Clinical crown lengthening (D4249) is used to report bony recontouring to apically reposition the crest of bone and overlying tissue. The result is a more favorable positioning (proper biologic width) of bone and gingival attachment to provide for a proper biologic width.

COMMENTS

1. Anatomical crown exposure (D4230) reports the removal of both enlarged gingival tissue *and* supporting bone. This code reports a quadrant (four or more contiguous teeth). The treatment area is periodontally healthy prior to treatment.

2. Note: There are several periodontal procedures not related to the treatment of periodontal disease. D4230 describes a procedure where both bone and gum tissue are removed. Anatomical crown exposure is indicated to provide an anatomically correct gingival relationship. Removing both bone and excess gum tissue leads to the repositioning of the remaining gum tissue to a more anatomically acceptable position. If gum tissue only is removed without bone being removed, the appropriate code to describe the procedure is gingivectomy D4210 or D4211.

3. If the procedure involves soft tissue management, i.e., bony recontouring is not involved, see gingivectomy (D4210) for a quadrant (four or more teeth).

4. This procedure does not require a flap. A soft and/or hard tissue laser may also be utilized in helping to accomplish this procedure.

LIMITATIONS Current periodontal charting and a detailed narrative regarding the necessity for treatment may be required. Dental payers generally consider anatomic crown exposure (D4230) to be cosmetic in nature and not reimbursable.

NARRATIVES "Bone and enlarged gingival tissue were/will be removed to provide an anatomically correct gingival relationship. See attached periodontal chart."

D4231 ANATOMICAL CROWN EXPOSURE – ONE TO THREE TEETH PER QUADRANT CDT 2016

This procedure is utilized in an otherwise periodontally healthy area to remove enlarged gingival tissue and supporting bone (ostectomy) to provide an anatomically correct gingival relationship.

CODING WATCH CORRECTION

It is an error to report anatomical crown exposure (D4231) to describe crown lengthening. Clinical crown lengthening (D4249) is used to report bony recontouring to apically reposition the crest of bone and overlying tissue. The result is a more favorable positioning (proper biologic width) of bone and gingival attachment to provide for a proper biologic width.

COMMENTS
1. Anatomical crown exposure (D4231) reports the removal of both enlarged gingival tissue *and* supporting bone. This code reports one to three teeth. The treatment area is periodontally healthy prior to treatment.

2. Note: There are several periodontal procedures not related to the treatment of periodontal disease. D4230 describes a procedure where both bone and gum tissue are removed. Anatomical crown exposure is indicated to provide an anatomically correct gingival relationship. Removing both bone and excess gum tissue leads to the repositioning of the remaining gum tissue to a more anatomically acceptable position. If gum tissue *only* is removed without bone being removed, the appropriate code to describe the procedure is gingivectomy D4210 or D4211.

3. If the procedure involves soft tissue management, i.e., bony recontouring is not involved, see gingivectomy (D4210) for a quadrant (four or more teeth).

4. This procedure does not require a flap. A soft and/or hard tissue laser may also be utilized in helping to accomplish this procedure.

LIMITATIONS Current periodontal charting and a detailed narrative regarding the necessity for treatment may be required. Dental payers generally consider anatomic crown exposure (D4231) to be cosmetic in nature and not reimbursable.

NARRATIVES "Bone and enlarged gingival tissue were/will be removed to provide an anatomically correct gingival relationship. See attached periodontal chart."

D4240   GINGIVAL FLAP PROCEDURE, INCLUDING ROOT PLANING – FOUR OR MORE CONTIGUOUS TEETH OR TOOTH BOUNDED SPACES PER QUADRANT   CDT 2016

A soft tissue flap is reflected or resected to allow debridement of the root surface and the removal of granulation tissue. Osseous recontouring is not accomplished in conjunction with this procedure. May include open flap curettage, reverse bevel flap surgery, modified Kirkland flap procedure, and modified Widman surgery. This procedure is performed in the presence of moderate to deep probing depths, loss of attachment, need to maintain esthetics, need for increased access to the root surface and alveolar bone, or to determine the presence of a cracked tooth, fractured root, or external root resorption. Other procedures may be required concurrent to D4240 and should be reported separately using their own unique codes.

CODING WARNING CORRECTION

It is misleading to report D4240 for a "closed" soft tissue *laser* procedure. Use this code to describe a procedure where *a flap is reflected* with debridement of the root surface and granulation tissue removal. When reporting a "closed" soft tissue laser procedure, see Narrative #2.

COMMENTS

1. A gingival flap procedure reflects the periodontal tissue off the teeth and bone (a flap is laid) in order to have an unimpeded view and access to the root surfaces of the teeth. This allows the provider direct access for more effective removal of plaque and calculus from the roots of the teeth. Once the flap is laid and the teeth are root planed and polished, the dentist may also place a bone graft (D4263/D4264), place biologic materials to aid in soft and osseous tissue regeneration (D4265), and/or place a barrier membrane (D4266/D4267) as part of the treatment provided. Report D4240 if the bone around the teeth has not been reshaped (recontoured) during the procedure. If bone has been modified, report the procedure using the appropriate code for osseous surgery (D4260/D4261). Additionally, D4240 may be reported to describe a flap procedure used to diagnose external root resorption or to determine the presence of a cracked tooth or fractured root.

2. Scaling and root planing (SRP) does *not* precede this procedure. SRP is *included* with the gingival flap procedure.

3. D4241 can report LANAP®. See the author's comments at the first of the D4000 section.

LIMITATIONS

1. There is typically a 24 to 36 month exclusion period for another D4240 procedure provided in the same area of the mouth, on the same teeth.

2. Scaling and root planing is a part of D4240 and should not be submitted as a separate procedure. Dental plans typically consider three months of postoperative care and any other surgical treatment provided within three years to be a part of and included in the previous reimbursement. Current periodontal charting indicating at least Case Type II periodontal disease (early periodontitis) is typically required for reimbursement.

TIPS

Other separate procedures including, but not limited to, D3450, D3920, D4263, D4264, D4265, D4266 and D4267 may be performed along with D4240. Reimbursement will vary.

NARRATIVES

1. Submit a current dated (done within the previous 90 days), pre-operative periodontal charting with the claim. If the gingival flap on each tooth treated is related to pathology (not cosmetic) it may be reimbursed. Typically evidence of a 4mm or 5mm pocket depth on each tooth treated is required. The payer may want to know if a crown is involved. "See attached periodontal chart."

2. To describe a "closed" laser procedure (i.e., no flap has been reflected), report unspecified periodontal procedure, by report (D4999). Request an alternate benefit of D4240 when submitting D4999. D4999 requires an extensive narrative that may include objective findings, diagnosis, full periodontal charting, radiographic images, pretreatment photos (with probe in the sulcus documenting the pocket), photos taken during the treatment, and post treatment photos. "See attached periodontal chart."

D4241 GINGIVAL FLAP PROCEDURE, INCLUDING ROOT PLANING – ONE TO THREE CONTIGUOUS TEETH OR TOOTH BOUNDED SPACES PER QUADRANT CDT 2016

A soft tissue flap is reflected or resected to allow debridement of the root surface and the removal of granulation tissue. Osseous recontouring is not accomplished in conjunction with this procedure. May include open flap curettage, reverse bevel flap surgery, modified Kirkland flap procedure, and modified Widman surgery. This procedure is performed in the presence of moderate to deep probing depths, loss of attachment, need to maintain esthetics, need for increased access to the root surface and alveolar bone, or to determine the presence of a cracked tooth, fractured root, or external root resorption. Other procedures may be required concurrent to D4241 and should be reported separately using their own unique codes.

CODING WARNING CORRECTION

It is misleading to report D4241 for a "closed" soft tissue *laser* procedure. Use this code to describe a procedure where *a flap is reflected* with debridement of the root surface and granulation tissue removal. When reporting a "closed" soft tissue laser procedure, see Narrative #2.

COMMENTS

1. A gingival flap procedure reflects the periodontal tissue off the teeth and bone (a flap is laid) in order to have an unimpeded view and access to the root surfaces of the teeth. This allows the provider direct access for more effective removal of plaque and calculus from the roots of the teeth. Once the flap is laid and the teeth are root planed and polished, the dentist may also place a bone graft (D4263/D4264), place biologic materials to aid in soft and osseous tissue regeneration (D4265), and/or place a barrier membrane (D4266/D4267) as part of the treatment provided. Report D4241 if the bone around the teeth has not been reshaped (recontoured) during the procedure. If bone has been modified, report the procedure using the appropriate code for osseous surgery (D4260/D4261). Additionally, D4241 may be reported to describe a flap procedure used to diagnose external root resorption or to determine the presence of a cracked tooth or fractured root.

2. Scaling and root planing (SRP) does *not* precede this procedure. SRP is *included* with the gingival flap procedure.

3. D4241 can report LANAP®. See the author's comments at the first of the D4000 section.

LIMITATIONS

1. There is typically a 24 to 36 month exclusion period for another D4241 procedure provided in the same area of the mouth, on the same teeth.

2. Scaling and root planing is a part of D4241 and should not be submitted as a separate procedure. Dental plans typically consider three months of postoperative care and any other surgical treatment provided within three years to be a part of and included in the previous reimbursement. Current periodontal charting indicating at least Case Type II periodontal disease (early periodontitis) is typically required for reimbursement.

TIPS

Other separate procedures including, but not limited to, D3450, D3920, D4263, D4264, D4265, D4266, and D4267 may be performed along with D4241. Reimbursement will vary.

NARRATIVES

1. Submit a current dated (done within the previous 90 days), pre-operative periodontal charting with the claim. If the gingival flap procedure is related to pathology (not cosmetic) it may be reimbursed. Typically evidence of a 4mm or 5mm pocket depth on each tooth treated is required. The payer may want to know if a crown is involved. "See attached periodontal chart."

2. To describe a "closed" *laser* procedure (i.e., no flap has been reflected), report unspecified periodontal procedure, by report (D4999). Request an alternate benefit of D4241 when submitting D4999. D4999 requires an extensive narrative that may include objective findings, diagnosis, full periodontal charting, radiographic images, pretreatment photos (with probe in the sulcus documenting the pocket), photos taken during the treatment, and posttreatment photos. "See attached periodontal chart."

D4245 — APICALLY POSITIONED FLAP — CDT 2016

Procedure is used to preserve keratinized gingiva in conjunction with osseous resection and second stage implant procedure. Procedure may also be used to preserve keratinized/attached gingiva during surgical exposure of labially impacted teeth, and may be used during treatment of peri-implantitis.

COMMENTS

1. An apically positioned flap may be used to expose an impacted permanent tooth by laying a flap which includes the keratinized gingival tissue and repositioning the flap more apically (towards the root). This procedure preserves the attached keratinized tissue while allowing the exposure and eruption of the impacted permanent tooth. If the keratinized gum tissue is simply removed (gingivectomy D4210/D4211) the unkeratinized mucosal tissue next to the tooth will be left to reattach around the erupting tooth leading to insufficient attached gingiva.

2. D4245 may be reported during surgical exposure of labially impacted teeth. This procedure may be associated with surgical exposure of an unerupted tooth (D7280) and is generally related to orthodontic treatment. An orthodontic band, bracket, loop and/or cleat may be attached (D7283) during this procedure to aid in the eruption of the impacted tooth.

LIMITATIONS

1. Periodontal charting indicating moderate to severe periodontitis may be required. D4245 is not likely to be reimbursed if performed on the same date as, or within four weeks of, scaling and root planing. Most dental plans will consider D4245 a part of a frenectomy (D7960) and/or distal wedge (D4274) procedure performed in the same area on the same service date.

2. This procedure may be used with a second stage implant procedure or treatment of peri-implantitis. Refer to D6101 and D6102 for other peri-implantitis procedures. D4245 is not typically reimbursed if associated with implants unless the plan includes benefits for implant procedures.

3. There is typically a 24 to 36 month exclusion period for reimbursement for the same procedure performed on the same tooth/implant.

D4249 — CLINICAL CROWN LENGTHENING – HARD TISSUE — CDT 2016

This procedure is employed to allow a restorative procedure on a tooth with little or no tooth structure exposed to the oral cavity. Crown lengthening requires reflection of a full thickness flap and removal of bone, altering the crown to root ratio. It is performed in a healthy periodontal environment, as opposed to osseous surgery, which is performed in the presence of periodontal disease.

CODING CORRECTION WARNING

1. It is misleading to report D4249 for a "closed" hard tissue *laser* procedure unless a full thickness flap is reflected. (See the code's descriptor: "requires the reflection of a full thickness flap"). To appropriately report this code, a full thickness flap must be reflected and bone *removed* to expose more tooth structure. If using a laser for a portion of this procedure, be aware that payers reimburse according to the procedure performed, not based on the technique or technology used to perform the procedure. It appears that a "closed' hard tissue laser procedure would be reported as D4999. Ask for the alternate benefit of D4249.

2. It is improper/misleading to report "soft-tissue crown lengthening" as "hard-tissue crown lengthening." Any *soft tissue* crown lengthening is generally considered a part of the crown procedure and fee by insurance companies, however see D4212 for further information. D4212 reports a gingivectomy for restorative access, per tooth. Clinical crown lengthening – hard tissue (D4249) requires reflection of a *full thickness* flap (typically mesial and distal of the subject tooth) and removal of hard tissue (bone) to expose sound tooth structure. This procedure modifies the crown to root ratio. A healing period may be required by payers (typically at least six weeks) before a crown on the same tooth would be considered for reimbursement.

3. If a patient requires clinical crown lengthening – hard tissue (D4249) involving a *healthy site*, it is misleading to report osseous surgery (D4261). Osseous surgery (D4261) is used to describe the treatment of *periodontal* disease. Clinical crown lengthening (D4249) is performed in association with a healthy periodontal *site*.

COMMENTS

1. Per the descriptor, hard tissue crown lengthening is performed in a *healthy periodontal environment*. When treatment is provided in an area with periodontal disease (i.e., bone loss), the procedure should be described by reporting osseous surgery (D4260/D4261) codes.

3. State the periodontal prognosis and date(s) of prior scaling and root planing. If patient has had continuing periodontal maintenance (D4910), state that also and the dates of the procedures. "See attached periodontal chart and radiographic images."

D4261 OSSEOUS SURGERY (INCLUDING ELEVATION OF A FULL THICKNESS FLAP AND CLOSURE) – ONE TO THREE CONTIGUOUS TEETH OR TOOTH BOUNDED SPACES PER QUADRANT
CDT 2016

This procedure modifies the bony support of the teeth by reshaping the alveolar process to achieve a more physiologic form during the surgical procedure. This must include the removal of supporting bone (ostectomy) and/or non-supporting bone (osteoplasty). Other procedures may be required concurrent to D4261 and should be reported using their own unique codes.

CODING WARNING CORRECTION

1. Osseous surgery (D4261) now clarifies that the elevation of a full thickness flap is required. In addition, the alveolar process must be reshaped to provide a more physiologic form during the surgical procedure. That is, D4261 must include the removal of supporting bone (ostectomy) and/or non-supporting bone (osteoplasty). If a full thickness flap has not been reflected and bone reshaped to provide a more physiological form, then do not report D4261. D4999, by report, should be reported for a procedure that does not meet the criteria established in the nomenclature and descriptor of D4261.

2. LANAP is "Laser Assisted New Attachment Procedure." There is no current CDT Code that describes "LANAP" unless a full thickness flap has been reflected and bone reshaped to provide a more physiologic form during the surgical procedure. So, the dentist must determine if their LANAP procedure complies with the criterion established by D4261. If the dentist finds the LANAP procedure does not comply, then report D4999, by report. The dentist may ask for the alternate benefit of D4260 for reimbursement from the payer.

COMMENTS

1. Osseous surgery is performed to treat teeth with periodontal pocketing and bone loss to more effectively remove the plaque buildup that causes inflammation and continued attachment/bone loss. It involves removing some of the bone to create easier to clean contours and repositioning the gingival flaps more apically (closer to the root end of the tooth). While the tissue is reflected the dentist may also place a bone graft (D4263/D4264), place biologic materials to accelerate soft and hard tissue regeneration (D4265), place concentrated blood/growth factor PRP (D7921), and/or place a barrier membrane (D4266/D4267).

2. Other separate procedures that may be provided simultaneously can include, but not be limited to, D3450, D3920, D4263, D4264, D4265, D4266, D4267, D6010, D7140 and D7295.

3. The fee for D4261 (one to three contiguous teeth or tooth bounded spaces per quadrant) would typically be 50-60% of the fee for D4260 (four or more teeth per quadrant).

LIMITATIONS

1. Comprehensive periodontal charting showing pocket depths of 5mm or more on each tooth to be treated, areas of bleeding, and/or furcation involvement and radiographs indicating at least moderate periodontitis (Case Type III) may be required to justify reimbursement for osseous surgery. Payers may limit osseous surgery to once every 24 to 36 months. Payers may consider the fee reimbursed for D4261 to include scaling and root planing when the SRP is performed within four weeks of osseous surgery. Payers may consider any osseous contouring, distal or proximal wedge surgery, frenectomy, soft tissue grafts, gingivectomy, and/or flap procedures performed in the same quadrant on the same date as the osseous surgery as a part of the osseous surgery.

2. When multiple periodontal procedures are reported on the same service date, the highest UCR fee (most inclusive) may be the only procedure reimbursed. The other, less costly procedures are often considered a part of the more comprehensive procedure or these other procedures may be reimbursed at a lower than usual fee.

TIPS

Periodontal scaling and root planing (D4341/D4342), with a subsequent four to six week period for evaluation or a *continuous* period of periodontal maintenance (D4910) should *precede* osseous surgery.

NARRATIVES

1. Some payers limit reimbursement for D4261 to two quadrants per treatment visit. If there are extraordinary circumstances (medical conditions, travel, general anesthesia, etc.) making the treatment of three or all four quadrants more beneficial for the patient at one visit, write a narrative that describes the extraordinary circumstances that justifies the treatment of more than two quadrants on the same service date.

2. D4261 involves active treatment of periodontal disease. A narrative that addresses the type/status of the periodontal disease and the necessity of surgical modification is required. A current full and comprehensive probing and charting should be included that lists all pocket depths, areas of bleeding, furcation involvement, mucogingival defects, mobility, and bony pathology. There must be an elevation of a *full* thickness flap and removal of supporting bone (ostectomy) and/or non-supporting bone (osteoplasty) to report this code.

3. State the periodontal prognosis and date(s) of prior scaling and root planing. If the patient has had continuing periodontal maintenance (D4910), state this and dates of procedures. "See attached periodontal chart and radiographic images."

D4263 — BONE REPLACEMENT GRAFT – FIRST SITE IN QUADRANT — CDT 2016

This procedure involves the use of grafts to stimulate periodontal regeneration when the disease process has led to a deformity of the bone. This procedure does not include flap entry and closure, wound debridement, osseous contouring, or the placement of biologic materials to aid in osseous tissue regeneration or barrier membranes. Other separate procedures delivered concurrently are documented with their own codes.

CODING WARNING CORRECTION

1. It is an error to report D4263, if the bone replacement graft is placed in an extraction site for ridge preservation. The proper code to report a bone replacement graft placed in an extraction site for the purpose of ridge preservation is D7953.
2. See D3428, D3429, D7950, D7951, D7952, D7953, D6103, D6104, and D7955 for other types of bone grafts.

CODING WATCH CORRECTION

A bone replacement graft *stimulates periodontal regeneration* of bone. An *associated* natural tooth is required to report D4263.

COMMENTS

1. D4263 reports a bone replacement graft – delivered to the first site in a quadrant.
2. When bone loss results in deep, narrow pockets (i.e., vertical bone loss or infrabony pockets), a bone replacement graft may be placed to treat the bony defect. The bone replacement graft may be an autograft (from the patient's own body) or an allograft (human bone tissue from a commercially man made available source), a xenograft (tissue from another species, e.g., bovine bone) or an alloplastic graft, which are man made materials used for tissue grafting and augmentation. For access to the bony defect, a flap must be laid. When submitting a code for a bone replacement graft (D4263/D4264), either D4240/D4241 (gingival flap surgery) or D4260/D4261 (osseous surgery) should be reported in addition to the bone graft. Biologic materials (D4265) placed and/or barrier membrane (D4266/D4267) may also be reported separately.
3. The flap entry should always be coded separately using gingival flap procedure (D4240/D4241) or osseous surgery (D4260/D4261). Biologic materials (D4265) and barrier membranes (D4266/D4267), when used, should also be reported separately. Bone grafts placed for socket preservation should be reported as D7953, ridge augmentation for edentulous areas as D7950, and sinus lifts as D7951 and D7952. Also, see bone graft for repair of peri-implant defect(D6103) and bone graft at time of implant placement (D6104). In addition, there are bone grafts associated with periradicular surgery (D3428 and D3429).
4. Harvesting of bone (D7295) to provide the autograft material is reported separately.

LIMITATIONS

1. Payers may impose a 24 to 36 month exclusion period for the same procedure performed in the same area of the mouth.
2. A diagnosis of a type III or type IV periodontal disease is generally required for D4263 to be considered for reimbursement.
3. Bone replacement grafts, as reported by D4263 are limited to *periodontal* defects. A natural tooth must be associated for this procedure to apply. Grafts placed in an associated extraction site (D7953), defects from cyst removal, or an apicoectomy are *not* usually reimbursed, but should still be reported.

TIPS Associated procedures that may be performed with D4263 include, but are not limited to, D4240, D4241, D4260, D4261, D4265, D4266, D4267 and D7295.

NARRATIVES D4263 is used to report bone grafts placed to treat *periodontal* defects around natural teeth. A tooth number, surface, and current periodontal charting that support a diagnosis of moderate to severe periodontal disease (5mm pocket depths or greater) and a narrative indicating type of grafting material are typically required. Dental plans may limit payment for bone grafts to two sites in a quadrant.

D4264 BONE REPLACEMENT GRAFT – EACH ADDITIONAL SITE IN QUADRANT CDT 2016

This procedure involves the use of grafts to stimulate periodontal regeneration when the disease process has led to a deformity of the bone. This procedure does not include flap entry and closure, wound debridement, osseous contouring, or the placement of biologic materials to aid in osseous tissue regeneration or barrier membranes. This procedure is performed concurrently with one or more bone replacement grafts to document the number of sites involved.

CODING WARNING CORRECTION

1. It is an error to report D4264 if the bone replacement graft is placed in an extraction site for ridge preservation. The proper code to report a bone replacement graft placed in an extraction site for the purpose of ridge preservation is D7953.
2. See D3428, D3429, D7950, D7951, D7952, D7953, D6103, D6104 and D7955 for other types of bone grafts.

CODING WATCH CORRECTION

A bone replacement graft *stimulates periodontal regeneration* of bone. An *associated* natural tooth is required to report D4264.

COMMENTS
1. D4264 reports additional bone replacement graft(s) delivered to other sites in the same quadrant subsequent to D4263.
2. When bone loss results in deep, narrow pockets (i.e., vertical bone loss or infrabony pockets), a bone replacement graft may be placed to treat the bony defect. The bone replacement graft may be an autograft (from the patient's own body) or an allograft (human bone tissue from a commercially man made available source). A xenograft (tissue from another species, e.g., bovine bone) or an alloplastic graft, which are man made materials used for tissue grafting and augmentation. For access to the bony defect, a flap must be laid. When submitting a code for a bone replacement graft (D4363/D4364), either D4240/D4241 (gingival flap) or D4260/D4261 (osseous surgery) should be reported in addition to the bone graft. Biologic materials (D4265) placed and/or barrier membrane (D4266/D4267) may also be reported.
3. The flap entry should always be coded separately using gingival flap procedure (D4240/D4241) or osseous surgery (D4260/D4261). Biologic materials (D4265) and barrier membranes (D4266/D4267), when used, should also be reported separately. Bone grafts placed for socket preservation should be reported as D7953, ridge augmentation for edentulous areas as D7950, and sinus augmentations (lifts) as D7951 and D7952. Also, see bone graft for repair of peri-implant defect (D6103) and bone graft at time of implant placement (D6104). In addition, there are bone grafts associated with periradicular surgery (D3428 and D3429).
4. Harvesting of bone (D7295) to provide the autograft material is reported separately.

LIMITATIONS
1. Payers may impose a 24 to 36 month exclusion period for the same procedure performed in the same area of the mouth.
2. A diagnosis of a type III or type IV periodontal disease is generally required for D4264 to be considered for reimbursement.
3. Bone replacement grafts, as reported by D4264 are limited to *periodontal* defects. A natural tooth must be associated for this procedure to apply. Grafts placed in an extraction site (D7953), defects from cyst removal, or an apicoectomy are *not* usually reimbursed, but still should be reported.

TIPS Associated procedures that may be performed with D4264 include, but are not limited to, D4240, D4241, D4260, D4261, D4265, D4266, D4267 and D7295.

NARRATIVES D4264 is used to report bone grafts placed to treat *periodontal* defects around natural teeth. A tooth number, surface, and current periodontal charting that support a diagnosis of moderate to severe periodontal disease (5mm pocket depths or greater) and a narrative indicating type of grafting material are typically required. Dental plans may limit payment for bone grafts to two sites in a quadrant.

D4265 — BIOLOGIC MATERIALS TO AID IN SOFT AND OSSEOUS TISSUE REGENERATION
CDT 2016

Biologic materials may be used alone or with other regenerative substrates such as bone and barrier membranes, depending upon their formulation and the presentation of the periodontal defect. This procedure does not include surgical entry and closure, wound debridement, osseous contouring, or the placement of graft materials and/or barrier membranes. Other separate procedures may be required concurrent to D4265 and should be reported using their own unique codes.

CODING WARNING CORRECTION

1. Do not use D4265 to report Perio Protect®. Use D5994 to report Perio Protect®. See D5994 for comments on periodontal medicament payers (trays).
2. Platelet rich plasma (PRP) is also considered a biologic material. When using platelet rich plasma report D7921.

COMMENTS After laying a flap (D4240/D4241) and/or during osseous surgery (D4260/D4261), biologic materials may be placed in a periodontal defect to aid in the regeneration of soft and osseous tissue. These materials may include bone morphogenetic protein 2 [BMP-2], Emdogain®, etc. Graft materials and/or barrier membranes may also be placed at the same time and should be reported separately.

LIMITATIONS
1. Reimbursement for biologic materials used to aid in soft and osseous tissue regeneration (D4265) may be limited to periodontally related procedures. Ridge augmentation or implant related procedures are typically excluded from reimbursement.
2. Fibrin Glue®, PepGen®, and Emdogain® are all examples of biologic materials. Some payers limit reimbursement to specific materials such as Emdogain®.
3. D4265 is seldom reimbursed by payers. This procedure requires consultant review prior to reimbursement.
4. Some payers reimburse D4265 if used in *conjunction* with osseous surgery (D4260/D4261) or gingival flap procedures (D4240/D4241). In some cases, the amount reimbursed for D4265 is limited to the cost of the materials used.

TIPS Associated procedures that may be provided along with D4265 include but are not limited to D4240, D4241, D4260, D4261, D4263, D4264, D4266, and D4267.

NARRATIVES
1. A narrative is required to justify this procedure. The narrative should clearly describe the condition of the area being treated with the biologic materials and why the treatment was needed. The narrative should identify the material used for periodontal regenerative purposes.
2. Dental plans often limit reimbursement to one surgical procedure and one regenerative procedure for infrabony defects. For example, a plan may pay for osseous surgery (D4260/D4261) and guided tissue regeneration (D4266/D4267) but deny the biologic materials (D4265).

| D4266 | GUIDED TISSUE REGENERATION – RESORBABLE BARRIER, PER SITE | CDT 2016 |

This procedure does not include flap entry and closure, or, when indicated, wound debridement, osseous contouring, bone replacement grafts, and placement of biologic materials to aid in osseous regeneration. This procedure can be used for periodontal and peri-implant defects.

COMMENTS

1. The sequence of reattachment after flap and osseous surgery is important to the long term success of the procedure. Bone requires more time to generate and mature than soft tissue. Gingival tissues may attach to the tooth root more rapidly than bone can regenerate. A barrier membrane (GTR) is placed to prevent the fast growing gingiva from attaching to the root before the new bone can mature and attach to the root. The resorbable barrier membrane (D4266) is integrated into the regeneration site and/or resorbed or broken down by the body in the healing process. This type of barrier membrane does not require a second surgery for removal.
2. A bone graft is not always required when a barrier membrane is used. Some regeneration techniques encourage bone regrowth without the need for a bone graft.
3. Guided tissue regeneration (D4266) reports a "guided tissue regeneration – resorbable barrier." D4266 includes any follow up associated with this procedure.
4. Other procedures may be performed with D4266 and should be reported separately using their unique codes. These may include D4263, D4264, and D4265.

LIMITATIONS

1. Resorbable barrier membrane (D4266) should be reported separately when placed with periodontal bone replacement grafts, D4263 or D4264. Barrier membranes should also be reported separately when placed in concert with other grafts D7950, D7951, D7952, D7953 D6103, and D6104. Tooth number, surface/site, and current periodontal charting are typically required to be reported for reimbursement. Dental plans may reimburse barrier membranes when submitted with D4263/D4264 but deny them when associated with extractions/implants. Some contracts stipulate that only one regenerative procedure will be paid per infrabony defect. For example, D4266 or D4267 may be paid following osseous surgery but the biologic materials (D4265) denied. Additionally, payment for GTR is often limited to two sites per quadrant.
2. D4266, when provided in conjunction with sinus augmentation (D7951 or D7952), ridge augmentation (D7950) or bone replacement graft for ridge preservation (D7953, D6103, or D6104) may not be reimbursed when associated with an implant.
3. There typically is a 24 to 36 month exclusion period for the delivery of the same procedure to treat the same area of the mouth.
4. D4266 may be reimbursed in conjunction with osseous surgery. Reimbursement for this procedure may be limited to two sites per quadrant.
5. Reimbursement for D4266 may be limited to class II furcation involvement/infrabony defects. This code may not be reimbursed if associated with cyst removal, or the extraction of a tooth.

NARRATIVES The tooth number, surface, and a current periodontal charting indicating a diagnosis of moderate to severe periodontal disease (5mm pocket depths or greater) with treatable bony defects and a brief narrative indicating type of barrier material used are typically required before reimbursement will be considered. Including diagnostic radiographic images as well as treatment photos is helpful to document the need for this procedure.

| D4267 | GUIDED TISSUE REGENERATION – NON-RESORBABLE BARRIER, PER SITE (INCLUDES MEMBRANE REMOVAL) | CDT 2016 |

This procedure does not include flap entry and closure, or, when indicated, wound debridement, osseous contouring, bone replacement grafts, and placement of biologic materials to aid in osseous regeneration. This procedure can be used for periodontal and peri-implant defects.

COMMENTS

1. Non-resorbable barrier membranes prevent fast healing gingival tissues from encroaching on the surgical site until new bone has had time to fill in the periodontal defect. Filling in the periodontal defect with bone eliminate pockets where plaque and calculus accumulate. Placement of a non-resorbable membrane requires a second surgery to remove it. The membrane is removed four to six weeks after placement. The reimbursement for the second surgery is included in the reimbursement for D4267.
2. A bone graft is not always required when a barrier membrane is used. Some regeneration techniques encourage bone regrowth without the need for a bone graft.
3. Guided tissue regeneration D4267 reports a "guided tissue regeneration – nonresorbable barrier." D4267 includes any follow up and removal of the non-resorbable membrane.
4. Other procedures may be performed with D4267 and should be reported separately using their unique codes. These may include D4263, D4264, and D4265.

LIMITATIONS

1. Non-resorbable barrier membrane (D4267) should be reported separately when placed with periodontal bone replacement grafts, D4263 or D4264. Barrier membranes should be reported separately when placed in concert with other grafts D7950, D7951, D7952, D7953, D6103, or D6104. Tooth number, surface/site, and current periodontal charting are typically required to be reported for reimbursement. Dental plans may reimburse barrier membranes when submitted with D4263/D4264 but deny them when associated with extractions/implants. Some contracts stipulate that only one regenerative procedure will be paid per infrabony defect. For example, D4266 or D4267 may be paid following osseous surgery but the biologic materials (D4265) denied. Additionally, payment for GTR is often limited to two sites per quadrant.
2. D4267, when provided in conjunction with sinus augmentation (D7951 or D7952), ridge augmentation (D7950) or bone replacement graft for ridge preservation (D7953, D6103 or D6104) may not be reimbursed when associated with an implant.
3. There typically is a 24 to 36 month exclusion period for the delivery of the same procedure to treat the same area of the mouth.
4. D4267 may be reimbursed in conjunction with osseous surgery. Reimbursement for this procedure may be limited to two sites per quadrant.
5. Reimbursement for D4267 may be limited to class II furcation involvement/infrabony defects. This code may not be reimbursed if associated with cyst removal, or extraction of tooth.

NARRATIVES

The tooth number, surface, and a current periodontal charting indicating a diagnosis of moderate to severe periodontal disease (5mm pocket depths or greater) with treatable bony defects and a narrative indicating type of barrier material used are typically required before reimbursement will be considered. Including diagnostic radiographic images as well as treatment photos is helpful to document the need for this procedure.

D4268 SURGICAL REVISION PROCEDURE, PER TOOTH — CDT 2016

This procedure is to refine the results of a previously provided surgical procedure. This may require a surgical procedure to modify the irregular contours of hard or soft tissue. A mucoperiosteal flap may be elevated to allow access to reshape alveolar bone. The flaps are replaced or repositioned and sutured.

COMMENTS

1. Surgical revision procedure, per tooth (D4268) reports a surgical revision of a previously provided surgical procedure.
2. This procedure may involve either soft and/or hard tissue. A soft tissue flap/graft may need repositioning. When a soft tissue graft heals more apically than hoped and a flap procedure is used to reposition the tissue more coronally, use D4268 to describe this procedure. When a free soft tissue graft heals and the area is thicker than desired, if the area is thinned surgically, use D4268 to describe the thinning procedure.

LIMITATIONS

1. D4268 may be considered a part of other periodontal procedures. Plan limitations for this procedure are highly variable.

2. To receive reimbursement for D4268, at least three to six months must have elapsed since the original surgical procedure. Exclusions limits may be even as long as 24 to 36 months and greater.

NARRATIVES A narrative and supportive documentation (e.g., current periodontal charting, radiographs, photographs, etc.) should be submitted documenting the need for the revision. Dental plans often consider surgical periodontal follow up and revision a part of the initial procedure. This limit may apply for a period of three to six months following the surgical procedure. Plans may limit reimbursement for surgical re-entry for up to three years. Note: Individual consideration may be given in extraordinary circumstances.

D4270 — PEDICLE SOFT TISSUE GRAFT PROCEDURE — CDT 2016

A pedicle flap of gingiva can be raised from an edentulous ridge, adjacent teeth, or from the existing gingiva on the tooth and moved laterally or coronally to replace alveolar mucosa as marginal tissue. The procedure can be used to cover an exposed root or to eliminate a gingival defect if the root is not too prominent in the arch.

COMMENTS
1. Gingival grafts are typically performed to cover exposed roots where recession has occurred and/or to widen the zone of attached gingiva. Gingival grafts are performed to improve the topography making the tooth easier to clean and/or to decrease the sensitivity experienced while brushing/eating/drinking by increasing the zone of attached gingiva.

   A portion of the flap serves as a soft tissue graft. Part of the tissue remains attached to the host and therefore only a portion of the blood supply is compromised. The fact that part of the graft remains attached yields a very high success rate.

   Laterally: When a tooth with gingival recession has one or two teeth adjacent with adequate attached gingiva, a flap can be laid from the adjacent area and can be used to cover the adjacent site. This flap may be moved laterally to cover the neighboring tooth to cover the area of recession. A split thickness flap is laid, leaving the periosteum (a layer of connective tissue) attached to the bone in the donor area. New gingiva grows over the periosteum at the donor site. If the tooth with the gingival defect is adjacent to an edentulous space, a flap may be lifted from the edentulous area and moved laterally to cover the root.

   Coronally: If there is enough attached gingival tissue below the area of recession, a flap can be raised and moved coronally (towards the crown of the tooth) to cover the area of recession.

2. D4270 may be associated with surgical access of an unerupted tooth (D7280), related to orthodontics. Surgically uncovering the unerupted tooth (generally a canine) may require a pedicle soft tissue graft procedure.

3. D4270 may be used to report the Chao Pinhole® Technique (PST).

LIMITATIONS
1. Pedicle soft tissue graft (D4270) may be considered a part of osseous surgery (D4260/D4261). Pedicle soft tissue graft (D4270) may not be reimbursed if the procedure is performed in the same area and on the same date of service as osseous surgery. A frenectomy (D7960) or distal wedge procedure (D4274) performed on the same date of service and in the same area as a pedicle soft tissue graft is often considered a single service for reimbursement purposes.

2. There is typically a 24 to 36 month exclusion period for reimbursement for the same procedure performed in the same area of the mouth.

3. Soft tissue grafts are reimbursed per site or per tooth. Some payers limit reimbursement to two sites in a given quadrant.

NARRATIVES
1. Soft tissue grafts should be reported per tooth. Each graft should be reported on a separate line with tooth numbers and tooth surfaces identified. Despite the fact that the American Academy of Periodontology (AAP) maintains that radiographs and periodontal pocket measurements provide little value in documenting soft tissue pathology, some plans still request current periodontal charting with measurement of the amount of attached gingiva remaining for each tooth to be treated with D4270, before paying for soft tissue grafts. At least one plan currently requires a minimum of 3mm of recession to receive a benefit for a soft tissue graft and will pay one benefit for two contiguous grafts. Some payers require at least 4mm of recession with no attached gingiva and will only pay for one soft tissue graft when up to three contiguous teeth have been grafted. Dental plans often consider soft tissue grafts to include three months of post-operative care and surgical reentry for three years. According to the American Academy of Periodontology, claims for soft tissue grafts should ideally include a separate attachment that addresses the following:

- Tooth number and location of defect
- Amount of recession (in millimeters)
- Amount of attached gingiva remaining
- Amount of keratinized gingiva
- Statement concerning progressive recession
- Presence of marginal inflammation
- Influence of frenum
- Indications of root sensitivity
- Cervical caries
- Relationship to orthodontic care
- Relationship to existing restorations, e.g., recession on an existing bridge or subgingival restoration
- Statement that the procedure is not cosmetic

2. If the claim is related to hypersensitivity, document on the claim form that desensitizer (9910/D9911) had been used and failed.
3. At a minimum, the narrative must include the number of mm of remaining attached gingiva for each tooth that has been/will be grafted.

D4271 — PREVIOUSLY DELETED CODE FREE SOFT TISSUE GRAFT PROCEDURE (INCLUDING DONOR SITE SURGERY)

This is a previously deleted code. See D4277 for a free soft tissue graft procedure (first tooth) or D4278 free soft tissue graft procedure (each additional tooth).

D4273 — REVISED AUTOGENOUS CONNECTIVE TISSUE GRAFT PROCEDURE (INCLUDING DONOR AND RECIPIENT SURGICAL SITES) FIRST TOOTH, IMPLANT, OR EDENTULOUS TOOTH POSITION IN GRAFT — CDT 2016

There are two surgical sites. The recipient site utilizes a split thickness incision, retaining the overlapping flap of gingiva and/or mucosa. The connective tissue is dissected from a separate donor site leaving an epithelialized flap for closure.

REVISIONS AUTOGENOUS ~~SUBEPITHELIAL~~ CONNECTIVE TISSUE GRAFT PROCEDURE~~S~~ (INCLUDING DONOR AND RECIPIENT SURGICAL SITES)~~, PER~~ FIRST TOOTH, IMPLANT, OR EDENTULOUS TOOTH POSITION IN GRAFT

~~This procedure is performed to create or augment gingiva, to obtain root coverage to eliminate sensitivity and to prevent root caries, to eliminate frenum pull, to extend the vestibular fornix, to augment collapsed ridges, to provide an adequate gingival interface with a restoration or to cover bone or ridge regeneration sites when adequate gingival tissues are not available for effective closure.~~ There are two surgical sites. The recipient site utilizes a split thickness incision, retaining the ~~overlying~~ overlapping flap of gingiva and/or mucosa. The connective tissue is dissected from a separate ~~the~~ donor site leaving an epithelialized flap for closure. ~~After the graft is placed on the recipient site, it is covered with the retained overlying flap.~~

CODING WARNING CORRECTION: This code is used to describe the treatment provided at both the donor and recipient surgery site.

CODING CORRECTION MATCH — D4273 is used to report the first tooth, implant, or edentulous tooth position in the autogenous connective tissue graft. D4283 is used to report each additional contiguous tooth, implant, or edentulous tooth position in an autogenous connective tissue graft.

COMMENTS

1. D4273 reports a subepithelial connective tissue graft.
2. Most soft tissue grafts performed today are subepithelial connective tissue grafts, commonly referred to as "CT" grafts. They differ from free soft tissue grafts in that the graft material is taken from the layer of tissue just under the epithelium (the pink layer of soft tissue that you see when you look in the mouth). This graft is usually taken from the hard palate. A flap is raised in the area that needs coverage, the subepithelial connective tissue graft is placed under the flap, and the flap is sutured back in place. Placing the CT graft improves coverage of the exposed root.

LIMITATIONS

1. There is typically a 24 to 36 month exclusion period for the reimbursement for the same procedure performed on the same tooth or area.
2. A free soft tissue graft procedure (D4277) may be reimbursed as an alternate benefit for D4273/D4283.
3. D4273/D4283 may be considered an *integral* part of osseous surgery (D4260/D4261). D4273/D4283 may not be reimbursed if the procedure is performed in the same area, on same service date as osseous surgery. A frenectomy or distal wedge performed on the same service date as D4273/D4283 and in the same area is often considered a part of the D4273 procedure.
4. A surgical stent used to promote healing of the donor site is also considered a part of the D4273 procedure.
5. If D4273/D4283 is performed for cosmetic reasons, reimbursement may be denied.
6. Reimbursement may be limited two procedures per quadrant.
7. Although connective tissue grafts (D4273/D4283) are considered to be the "gold standard," some dental plans pay D4277 as an alternate benefit. Also note that a tunneling procedure is considered part of the D4273/D4283 procedure code, and when performed at the same appointment as a frenulectomy, only one benefit will likely be paid.

NARRATIVES **IMPORTANT!** See the D4270 Narrative section for recommendations regarding soft tissue grafts.

D4274 DISTAL OR PROXIMAL WEDGE PROCEDURE (WHEN NOT PERFORMED IN CONJUNCTION WITH SURGICAL PROCEDURES IN THE SAME ANATOMICAL AREA)
CDT 2016

This procedure is performed in an edentulous area adjacent to a periodontally involved tooth. Gingival incisions are utilized to allow removal of a tissue wedge to gain access and correct the underlying osseous defect and to permit close flap adaptation.

CODING CORRECTION WARNING — When a distal wedge procedure is performed at the same time and in the same area as a gingival flap procedure, a soft tissue graft, or an osseous surgery procedure, do not report D4274 as a *separate* procedure.

COMMENTS D4274, distal or proximal wedge procedure is performed on either the mesial or distal of a tooth. By definition, D4274 cannot be performed on the facial or lingual areas. D4274 is performed in an edentulous area adjacent to a periodontally involved tooth. The procedure involves the removal of a pie shape or rectangular wedge of gingival tissue. The remaining margins left after the wedge is removed are brought together and sutured. Removal of this gingival tissue is intended to reduce the depth of the pocket making the area easier to clean and maintain. If there is an underlying bony defect, treatment of the defect is accomplished while the area is open.

LIMITATIONS	1. Benefits are typically limited to treatment of areas where the distal of periodontally involved teeth are adjacent to edentulous areas.
	2. D4274 is considered a part of osseous surgery or soft tissue grafts when performed in the same area on the same date of service. Reimbursement is often limited to the most inclusive procedure. D4274's nomenclature states that the procedure is "not performed in conjunction with surgical procedures in the same anatomical area."
TIPS	If D4274 is a *stand-alone* procedure (not performed in conjunction with surgical procedures in the same anatomical area), some payers provide reimbursement equivalent to a gingivectomy (D4211), or a percentage of the osseous surgery (D4261) UCR fee.
NARRATIVES	Include a narrative fully explaining the procedure. Include photographs, current periodontal charting and a pretreatment radiographic image.

D4275 REVISED NON-AUTOGENOUS CONNECTIVE TISSUE GRAFT (INCLUDING RECIPIENT SITE AND DONOR MATERIAL) FIRST TOOTH, IMPLANT, OR EDENTULOUS TOOTH POSITION IN GRAFT — CDT 2016

There is only a recipient surgical site utilizing split thickness incision, retaining the overlying flap of gingiva and/or mucosa. A donor surgical site is not present.

REVISIONS NON-AUTOGENOUS CONNECTIVE ~~SOFT~~ TISSUE ~~ALLO~~GRAFT (INCLUDING RECIPIENT SITE AND DONOR MATERIAL) FIRST TOOTH, IMPLANT, OR EDENTULOUS TOOTH POSITION IN GRAFT

~~Procedure is performed to create or augment the gingiva, with or without root coverage. This may be used to eliminate the pull of the frena and muscle attachments, to extend the vestibular fornix, and correct localized gingival recession.~~ There is ~~no donor site.~~ only a recipient surgical site utilizing split thickness incision, retaining the overlying flap of gingiva and/or mucosa. A donor surgical site is not present.

CODING MATCH CORRECTION D4275 is used to report the first tooth, implant, or edentulous tooth position in the non-autogenous connective tissue graft. D4285 is used to report each additional contiguous tooth, implant, or edentulous tooth position in a non-autogenous connective tissue graft.

COMMENTS
1. A non-autogenous connective tissue graft procedure commonly known as a soft tissue allograft is similar to a free soft tissue graft and is performed in situations similar to those where an autogenous connective tissue graft procedure is performed. The difference is that the tissue graft material does not come from the patient. This tissue (allograft material) is available commercially and has been treated so that it will not be rejected by the patient's immune system and is free from pathogens. An allograft material is used in circumstances where the patient either does not have enough gingival tissue available to be used for a graft or when the patient does not want to use his/her tissue for a graft. The graft results are comparable to using the patient's tissue, but healing may take a few weeks longer. More than 50% of connective tissue grafts performed today are non-autogenous.
2. A material such as Alloderm®, Perioderm®, Mucoderm®, etc. may be used.

LIMITATIONS
1. Some plans do not provide reimbursement for D4275/D4285. Free soft tissue graft (D4277) may be reimbursed as an alternate benefit.
2. There is typically a 24 to 36 month exclusion period before reimbursement is available again for the same procedure in the same area/tooth.
3. Reimbursement may be limited to two procedures per quadrant.
4. If D4275 is reported for cosmetic reasons, reimbursement may be denied.

NARRATIVES
1. The narrative should report tooth number, any active recession, description of root exposure, amount of recession, frenum issues, pocket depth, and remaining keratinous tissue. It is recommended that photographs be included to support the need for treatment.
2. The allograft material (e.g., Dermis) is included in D4275/D4285. Some dental plans do not pay for non-autogenous connective tissue grafts but may provide an alternate benefit of a free soft tissue graft (D4277) if a narrative is sent indicating that adequate soft tissue was not available from the patient.
3. **IMPORTANT!** See D4270 for soft tissue graft narrative recommendations.

D4276 COMBINED CONNECTIVE TISSUE AND DOUBLE PEDICLE GRAFT, PER TOOTH   CDT 2016

Advanced gingival recession often cannot be corrected with a single procedure. Combined tissue grafting procedures are needed to achieve the desired outcome.

COMMENTS This procedure involves a connective tissue (CT) graft and two pedicle grafts. This procedure is indicated to treat areas of recession with root exposure. A small pedicle flap is lifted from both sides of the affected tooth. A CT graft is harvested (usually from the palate). The CT graft is placed on the root and the two pedicle grafts are positioned to cover the CT graft. Both pedicle flaps and the CT graft are sutured together and to the surrounding gum tissue to stabilize the flaps while the area heals.

LIMITATIONS
1. D4276 is seldom reimbursed.
2. A subepithelial connective tissue graft procedure (D4273) or free soft tissue graft (D4277) may be reimbursed as an alternate benefit.
3. There is typically a 24 to 36 month exclusion period for reimbursement for the same procedure provided on the same tooth.

NARRATIVES
1. The narrative should report tooth number, the presence of active recession, description of root exposure, amount of recession, frenum issues, pocket depth, remaining keratinized tissue and the number of mm of remaining attached gingiva. It is recommended that photographs be included with the claim.
2. If the claim is related to hypersensitivity, note on the claim form that conventional treatment (D9910/D9911) to reduce sensitivity had been used and failed.
3. **IMPORTANT!**   See D4270 for soft tissue graft narrative recommendations.

D4277 REVISED FREE SOFT TISSUE GRAFT PROCEDURE (INCLUDING RECIPIENT AND DONOR SURGICAL SITES) FIRST TOOTH, IMPLANT, OR EDENTULOUS TOOTH POSITION IN GRAFT   CDT 2016

REVISIONS FREE SOFT TISSUE GRAFT PROCEDURE (INCLUDING RECIPIENT AND DONOR SURGICAL SITES SURGERY) FIRST TOOTH, IMPLANT, OR EDENTULOUS TOOTH POSITION IN GRAFT

CODING CORRECTION WARNING The free soft tissue graft procedure (D4277) *includes* donor site surgery.

COMMENTS
1. Gingival grafts are typically performed to cover exposed roots where recession has occurred and/or to widen the zone of attached gingiva. Gingival grafts are intended to improve the topography making the tooth easier to clean, to decrease the sensitivity experienced by increasing the zone of attached gingiva, and to reduce the possibility of further gingival recession.

2. A free gingival graft refers to the fact that the gingival tissue being grafted is detached or "free" from the blood supply, i.e., excised from the body. The greatest benefit from the use of the free gingival graft technique is that the graft can be taken from a remote part of the mouth and placed in another independent location. A pedicle graft remains attached and must be reattached a few millimeters from where it is harvested. During the graft procedure, the tooth at the recipient site is root planed prior to attaching the graft. Most payers consider the root planing procedure a part of the graft procedure and not payable as a separate procedure. Free gingival grafts may be used to increase the width of the attached gingiva, but they can also be used to deepen the vestibule or eliminate frenum pulls.

3. D4277 may be associated with the surgical access of an unerupted tooth (D7280), related to orthodontics. Surgically uncovering the unerupted tooth may require a free soft tissue graft procedure, D4277.

LIMITATIONS

1. If a free soft tissue graft (D4277/D4278) is performed for cosmetic reasons, reimbursement is typically denied.

2. There is typically a 24 to 36 month exclusion period for reimbursement for the same procedure in the same area of the mouth or on the same tooth.

3. Free soft tissue graft procedure (D4277/D4278) may be considered a part of osseous surgery (D4260/D4261). Free soft tissue graft procedure may not be reimbursed in addition to osseous surgery if the graft procedure is performed in the same area on the same service date as the osseous surgery. A frenectomy or distal wedge procedure performed on the same service date in the same area as the free soft tissue graft is often considered a part of the graft procedure.

4. A surgical stent used to promote healing of the donor site is also considered a part of the free soft tissue graft procedure.

5. The preparation of the surgical site and harvesting the graft from the donor site is all a part of the global fee for the free soft tissue graft, D4277/D4278.

6. Soft tissue grafts should be reported per tooth. The first tooth in the graft site is reported as D4277. Each additional graft in the same graft site should be reported as D4278 on a separate line with tooth numbers and tooth surfaces identified.

NARRATIVES **IMPORTANT!** See D4270 for soft tissue graft narrative recommendations.

D4278 — REVISED FREE SOFT TISSUE GRAFT PROCEDURE (INCLUDING RECIPIENT AND DONOR SURGICAL SITES) EACH ADDITIONAL CONTIGUOUS TOOTH, IMPLANT, OR EDENTULOUS TOOTH POSITION IN SAME GRAFT SITE — CDT 2016

Used in conjunction with D4277.

REVISIONS FREE SOFT TISSUE GRAFT PROCEDURE (INCLUDING RECIPIENT AND DONOR SURGICAL SITES ~~SURGERY~~) EACH ADDITIONAL CONTIGUOUS TOOTH, IMPLANT, OR EDENTULOUS TOOTH POSITION IN SAME GRAFT SITE.

Used in conjunction with D4277.

CODING WARNING CORRECTION The free soft tissue graft procedure (D4278) *includes* donor site surgery.

COMMENTS

1. Gingival grafts are typically performed to cover exposed roots where recession has occurred and/or to widen the zone of attached gingiva. Gingival grafts are intended to improve the topography making the tooth easier to clean, to decrease the sensitivity experienced while brushing by increasing the zone of attached gingiva and to reduce the possibility of further gingival recession.

2. A free gingival graft refers to the fact that the gingival tissue being grafted is detached or "free" from the blood supply, i.e., excised from the body. The greatest benefit from the use of the free gingival graft technique is that the graft can be taken from a remote part of the mouth and placed in another independent location. A pedicle graft remains attached and must be sutured a few millimeters from where it is harvested. During the graft procedure, the tooth at the recipient site is root planed prior to attaching the graft. Most payers consider the root planing procedure to be included with the graft procedure and not payable as a separate procedure. Free gingival grafts may be used to increase the width of the attached gingiva, but they can also be used to deepen the vestibule or eliminate frenum pulls.

LIMITATIONS
1. If a free soft tissue graft (D4277/D4278) is performed for cosmetic reasons, reimbursement is usually denied.
2. There is typically a 24 to 36 month exclusion period for reimbursement for the same procedure in the same area of the mouth or on the same tooth.
3. Free soft tissue graft procedures (D4277/D4278) may be considered a part of osseous surgery (D4260/D4261). Free soft tissue graft procedure may not be reimbursed in addition to the osseous surgery if the graft procedure is performed in the same area on the same service date as the osseous surgery. A frenectomy or distal wedge procedure performed on the same service date as the free soft tissue graft is often considered a part of the graft procedure.
4. A surgical stent used to promote healing of the donor site is also considered a part of the free soft tissue graft procedure.
5. The preparation of the surgical site and harvesting the graft from the donor site is all a part of the overall global fee for the free soft tissue graft, D4277/D4278.
6. Soft tissue grafts should be reported per tooth. The first tooth in the graft site is reported as D4277. Each additional graft in the same graft site should be reported as D4278, on a separate line with tooth numbers and tooth surfaces identified.

NARRATIVES **IMPORTANT!** See D4270 for soft tissue graft narrative recommendations.

D4283 — NEW PROCEDURE AUTOGENOUS CONNECTIVE TISSUE GRAFT PROCEDURE (INCLUDING DONOR AND RECIPIENT SURGICAL SITES) – EACH ADDITIONAL CONTIGUOUS TOOTH, IMPLANT OR EDENTULOUS TOOTH POSITION IN SAME GRAFT SITE
CDT 2016

Used in conjunction with D4273.

CODING WARNING CORRECTION
D4273 reports the treatment provided to the donor and recipient surgical sites.

CODING WATCH CORRECTION
1. D4283 reports additional graft sites, following D4273, autogenous connective tissue graft procedures, per tooth, implant or edentulous tooth position when both a subepithelial connective tissue graft is performed and autogenous connective tissue is used to provide graft (filler) material.
2. D4283 includes the preparation, collection, and placement of the connective tissues used in the first graft site (D4273).

CODING MATCH CORRECTION
D4283 is used to report each additional contiguous tooth, implant, or edentulous tooth position in an autogenous connective tissue graft. The first tooth or tooth position in the autogenous connective tissue graft should be reported as D4273.

COMMENTS
1. D4273 and D4283 report subepithelial connective tissue grafts.
2. "CT" grafts differ from free soft tissue grafts in that the graft material is taken from the layer of tissue just under the epithelium (the layer of pink soft tissue) and is completely detached from the donor site before it is repositioned in the graft site.

   This graft is usually taken from the hard palate. A flap is raised in the area that needs coverage, the subepithelial connective tissue graft is placed under the flap is sutured back in place. CT grafts improve coverage of the exposed root.

LIMITATIONS
1. There is typically a 24 to 36 month exclusion period for reimbursement for the same procedure performed on the same tooth or position.
2. A free soft tissue graft procedure (D4277) may be reimbursed as an alternate benefit for D4273/D4283.
3. D4273/D4283 may be considered an integral part of osseous surgery (D4260/D4261). D4273/D4283 may not be reimbursed if the procedure is performed in the same area on same date service date as osseous surgery.

   A frenectomy or distal wedge performed on the same service date as D4273/D4283 and in the same area may be considered a part of the D4272/D4283 procedure.
4. A surgical stent used to promote healing of the donor site is considered part of the D4273/D4283 procedure.
5. If D4273/D4283 is performed for cosmetic reasons, reimbursement may be denied.
6. Reimbursement may be limited to two procedures per quadrant.
7. Although autogenous connective tissue grafts (D4273/D4283) are considered the "gold standard," some dental plans pay a free soft tissue graft procedure (D4277) as an alternate benefit. A tunneling procedure is considered part of the D4273/D4283 procedure code, and when performed at the same appointment as a frenulectomy, only one benefit will likely be paid.

NARRATIVES IMPORTANT! See the D4270 "Narrative" section for recommendations regarding soft tissue graft narratives.

D4285 — **NEW PROCEDURE** NON-AUTOGENOUS CONNECTIVE TISSUE GRAFT PROCEDURE (INCLUDING RECIPIENT SURGICAL SITE AND DONOR MATERIAL) – EACH ADDITIONAL CONTIGUOUS TOOTH, IMPLANT OR EDENTULOUS TOOTH POSITION IN SAME GRAFT SITE
CDT 2016

Used in conjunction with D4275.

CODING WARNING CORRECTION
D4285 is reported in conjunction with D4275, non-autogenous connective tissue graft, per tooth, implant or edentulous tooth position when both a subepithelial connective tissue graft is performed and non-autogenous connective tissue is used to provide graft (filler) material.

CODING WATCH CORRECTION
D4285 is to be reported in conjunction with D4275, non-autogenous connective tissue graft, per tooth, implant or edentulous tooth position when both a subepithelial connective tissue graft is performed and non-autogenous connective tissue is used to provide graft (filler) material.

CODING MATCH CORRECTION
D4285 reports each additional contiguous, tooth, implant or edentulous tooth position in a non-autogenous connective tissue graft. The first tooth, implant, or edentulous tooth position in the autogenous connective tissue graft should be reported as D4275.

COMMENTS

1. A non-autogenous connective tissue graft procedure commonly known as a soft tissue allograft is similar to a free soft tissue graft and is performed in situations similar to those where an autogenous connective tissue graft procedure is performed. The difference is that the tissue graft material does not come from the patient.

   Allograft material is available commercially. It has been treated so that it will not be rejected by the patient's immune system and is free from pathogens. An allograft material is used in circumstances where the patient either does not have enough gingival tissue available to be used for a graft or when the patient does not want to use his/her tissue for a graft. The graft results are comparable to using the patient's tissue, but healing may take a few weeks longer.

2. More than 50% of connective tissue grafts performed today are non-autogenous.

3. A material such as Alloderm®, Perioderm®, Mucoderm®, etc. may be used.

LIMITATIONS

1. Some plans do not provide reimbursement for D4275/D4285. Free soft tissue graft (D4277) may be reimbursed as an alternate benefit.

2. If D4275/D4285 is performed for cosmetic reasons, reimbursement may be denied.

3. Reimbursement may be limited to two procedures per quadrant.

4. There is typically a 24 to 36 month exclusion period before reimbursement is available again for the same procedure in the same area/tooth.

NARRATIVES

1. Document the tooth number, description of root exposure, any active recession, amount of recession, frenum issues, pocket depth, and remaining keratinous tissue. Photographs should be included to support the need for treatment.

2. The allograft material (e.g., Dermis) is included in the global fee for D4275/D4285. Some payers do not pay for non-autogenous connective tissue grafts but may provide an alternate benefit of a free soft tissue graft (D4277) if a narrative is sent indicating that adequate soft tissue was not available from the patient.

3. IMPORTANT! See D4270 "Narrative" section for recommendations regarding soft tissue graft narratives.

NON-SURGICAL PERIODONTAL SERVICE — CDT 2016

D4320 PROVISIONAL SPLINTING – INTRACORONAL — CDT 2016

This is an interim stabilization of mobile teeth. A variety of methods and appliances may be employed for this purpose. Identify the teeth involved.

CODING WARNING CORRECTION

1. It is misleading to report *individual* direct restorations (composites) as provisional splinting, even though interconnected, in order to gain reimbursement. Separate *necessary* restorations (in occlusion and with adjacent contacts) due to caries may be placed and finished, *prior* to the placement of a *separate* provisional splinting procedure.

2. For trauma related splinting, see D7270.

COMMENTS

1. D4320 is an interim procedure meant to stabilize periodontally involved teeth. While a variety of methods and appliances can be used to stabilize teeth, a common method involves cutting a horizontal groove/channel into the mobile teeth and into at least one stable tooth on either side. This groove/channel is filled with composite and either thin metal wire or polyethylene fibers. Think of a picket fence. When standing individually, the uprights of a fence are more easily tipped over. When the horizontal interconnective portion is added tying the uprights together the fence becomes much more stable. Even though the individual groove/channel cuts into the mobile teeth are filled with composite and may appear similar to individual composite restorations, they are *not* to be billed as restorations.

2. Do not confuse periodontal stabilization (D4320) with tooth reimplantation and/or stabilization of accidentally evulsed or displaced tooth (D7270). D4320 is used to describe splinting teeth that are mobile due to periodontal disease. D7270 is used to describe the stabilization of teeth that are mobile due to trauma.

3. Report D4320 for splinting *periodontally* compromised teeth (commonly periodontally involved lower anterior incisors).

LIMITATIONS
1. Relatively few dental plans cover provisional splinting. D4320 is used to stabilize teeth that are considered "hopeless" due to mobility caused by advanced periodontal disease.
2. The splinting of these teeth is considered a temporary splinting procedure with no long term value.

NARRATIVES For those plans that do offer a benefit, a current complete periodontal charting, current radiographic images and a diagnosis of moderate to severe periodontitis (Case type III or IV) is usually required. The teeth involved in the splint should be identified on the claim form.

D4321 PROVISIONAL SPLINTING – EXTRACORONAL CDT 2016

This is an interim stabilization of mobile teeth. A variety of methods and appliances may be employed for this purpose. Identify the teeth involved.

CODING CORRECTION WARNING
1. It is misleading to report *individual* direct restorations (composites) as provisional splinting, even though interconnected, in order to gain reimbursement. Separate *necessary* restorations (in occlusion and with adjacent contacts) due to caries may be placed and finished, *prior* to the placement of a *separate* provisional splinting procedure.
2. For trauma related splinting, see D7270.

COMMENTS
1. D4321 is an interim procedure meant to stabilize periodontally involved teeth. Appliances used for stabilizing the teeth either rest on the teeth or are bonded to them. Do not confuse periodontal stabilization (D4321) with tooth reimplantation and/or stabilization of accidentally evulsed or displaced tooth (D7270). D4321 is used to describe splinting teeth that are mobile due to periodontal disease. D7270 is used to describe stabilization of teeth that are mobile due to trauma.
2. Report D4321 for splinting periodontally compromised teeth (most commonly periodontally involved lower anterior incisors). The splinting medium may be placed on the *lingual or facial surface* of the splinted teeth.
3. D4321 can also report Essix® or Snap-On Smiles® retainers utilized as extracoronal stabilization of teeth with advanced periodontal disease.

LIMITATIONS Relatively few dental plans cover provisional splinting. D4321 is used to stabilize teeth that are considered "hopeless" due to advanced periodontal disease. They consider the splinting of these teeth a temporary procedure with no long term value.

NARRATIVES For those plans that do offer a benefit, a current complete periodontal charting, current periapical radiographic images and a diagnosis of moderate to severe periodontitis (Case type III or IV) is usually required. The teeth involved in the splint should be identified on the claim form.

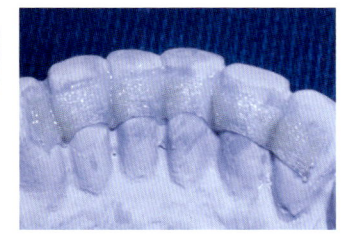

This is an example of extracoronal splinting using the Ribbond® splinting material.

Courtesy Ribbond®

D4341 — PERIODONTAL SCALING AND ROOT PLANING – FOUR OR MORE TEETH PER QUADRANT

CDT 2016

This procedure involves instrumentation of the crown and root surfaces of the teeth to remove plaque and calculus from these surfaces. It is indicated for patients with periodontal disease and is therapeutic, not prophylactic, in nature. Root planing is the definitive procedure designed for the removal of cementum and dentin that is rough, and/or permeated by calculus or contaminated with toxins or microorganisms. Some soft tissue removal occurs. This procedure may be used as a definitive treatment in some stages of periodontal disease and/or as a part of pre-surgical procedures in others.

Coding Warning/Correction

1. It is inappropriate to complete four quadrants of periodontal scaling and root planing (SRP) in one hour.

2. It is improper/misleading to report a "quadrant equivalent" (such as, a few teeth in different quadrants) for reimbursement using D4341. For each quadrant with one to three diseased teeth requiring scaling and root planing, report periodontal scaling and root planing – one to three teeth (D4342). Use D4341 to report scaling and root planing of *four or more* periodontally involved teeth in a given quadrant. There must be at least four teeth in the treated quadrant to report D4341 and those four or more teeth must have specific evidence of periodontal disease. To justify reimbursement the periodontally involved teeth must have radiographic bone loss and pockets of 4mm or more and bleeding on probing which indicates active periodontal disease. They may also have calculus on the radiographic image.

Coding Match/Correction

D4341 may be followed by either osseous surgery (D4260/D4261) *or* periodontal maintenance (D4910).

COMMENTS

1. SRP includes the instrumentation of both *crown* and *root* surfaces to remove plaque and calculus. See D1110 for preventive treatment and the removal of plaque, calculus, and stains. It is inappropriate to report D1110 with D4341 on the same service date. SRP (D4341) requires root planing that removes cementum and dentin that is rough, and/or permeated by calculus or contaminated with toxins or microorganisms. (Chart notes must indicate that root planing was performed, not just scaling.) Some soft tissue curettage will occur during the root planing process. A diagnosis of early, moderate, or advanced chronic periodontitis will include some level of clinical attachment loss (CAL). CAL may not be apparent from pocket depth measurements. CAL involves the loss of alveolar bone support and gingival attachment as the periodontal fibers migrate apically from the CEJ (cementoenamel junction) due to periodontal toxins in plaque. Attachment loss is measured from the CEJ to the bottom of the periodontal pocket.

   A periodontal pocket is a *pathologically deepened gingival sulcus* formed when toxins produced by plaque weaken the gingival attachment and connective tissues beneath the gum line. The gingival attachment pulls away from the teeth, forming a deeper pocket. As the disease progresses through the gingiva toward the bone, the pocket fills with plaque and the bacteria causes infection and inflammation. If not treated, the bone and connective tissue surrounding the tooth may become so severely damaged over time that the attachment is lost. If periodontitis continues untreated the tooth may become loose, fall out, or need to be extracted. Evidence of active disease may include bleeding on probing, increased pocket depth, continued attachment loss, purulent discharge, increased tooth mobility, high bacterial count, and/or evidence of sequential radiographic loss of the crestal bone.

2. Scaling and root planing provides *active therapy*. It is not prophylactic (preventive) in nature. Scaling and root planing can be a definitive treatment (followed by periodontal maintenance) for some patients or pre-surgical treatment (prior to osseous surgery) for other patients.

3. Use D4341 to report scaling and root planing for four or more diseased teeth in a given quadrant.

4. The code used to report the periodontal therapy should be based on the dentist's diagnosis and the service performed. For example, if the patient exhibits bleeding on probing and radiographic evidence of bone loss in two of the four quadrants, scaling and root planing (SRP) will likely be prescribed for the two affected quadrants. The remaining two quadrants may be treated with a prophylaxis (D1110). D1110 is provided to remove plaque, calculus and stains in areas where there is no evidence of periodontitis.

In this example, when sequencing treatment, it is often best to complete and report the prophylaxis (D1110) on the two healthy quadrants first and bring the patient back at a separate appointment to perform the two quadrants of SRP. This sequencing is beneficial in that it gives the hygiene team more time to educate the patient about periodontal disease, making it clear that more extensive therapy is needed to arrest the bacterial infection in the remaining two quadrants. After SRP has been completed, D4341 should be billed for each quadrant treated with SRP. If one to three teeth in a quadrant require SRP, D4342 (SRP one to three teeth) should be reported for that quadrant.

LIMITATIONS

1. For reimbursement of D4341, bleeding on probing which indicates active periodontal disease, 4 to 5mm pocket depth (plus presence of calculus), radiographic evidence of bone loss must be evident. Some payers do not require diagnostic images.

2. Some payers require that *five* teeth have evidence of periodontal disease for reimbursement of D4341. If less than five teeth are reported, some payers re-map this code to D4342, ignoring the nomenclature quadrant definition of "four or more" teeth. If four teeth are treated and the payer re-maps the reimbursement to D4342, ask the patient to request a copy of the plan document from their Human Resources department. Once a copy of the contract is received, review the language as to tooth count requirements and limitations pertaining to D4341 and respond accordingly.

3. Periodontal maintenance (D4910) should follow multi-quadrant (D4341) SRP (generally at least two quadrants). This may not apply for SRP when involving D4342 for a few, isolated teeth. See D4342 for details. Note that there is typically a ninety day exclusion period from the date of SRP and the date of D4910.

4. Scaling and root planing (D4341) usually has a 24 to 36 month exclusion period for retreatment (a few payers have a 12 month exclusion). Note: reimbursement for scaling and root planing is typically excluded for 24 to 36 months after a gingival flap procedure (D4240/D4241) or osseous surgery (D4260/D4261) provided in the same area.

TIPS

1. D4921 reports gingival irrigation. Payers typically consider gingival irrigation to be a component of D4341, D4342 or D4910. The PPO contract may prohibit charging a separate fee for irrigation. See D4921 for comments, regarding the clinical use of gingival irrigation.

2. Use D9910 to describe the application of desensitizing medicaments for one tooth or multiple teeth. Payers typically consider D9910 to be an integral part of D4341, D4342 or D4910. The PPO contract may prohibit charging a separate fee for the application of desensitizing medicaments. See D9910 for comments.

NARRATIVES

1. A narrative should document *active* disease. This may include, but is not limited to: 4mm or greater pockets that bleed on probing indicating active disease, loss of periodontal attachment, radiographic evidence of alveolar bone loss, gingival recession, furcation involvement, inflammation, tooth mobility, subgingival calculus, suppuration, etc. Enclose diagnostic radiographic images to document bone loss. Also send a current periodontal chart which includes the date(s) that the chart was recorded.

2. When scaling and root planing all four quadrants on the same day, include a narrative to document the treatment of all four quadrants in the same day. This may include time spent; anesthesia required; if pre-medication was necessary; apprehensiveness; medical conditions (i.e., taking blood thinner), extensive travel time, etc. Include any other supporting documentation that might justify the treatment of all four quadrants on the same service date. Generally speaking, forty-five to sixty minutes or more would be required per quadrant to report four quadrants of D4341.

D4342 PERIODONTAL SCALING AND ROOT PLANING – ONE TO THREE TEETH PER QUADRANT   CDT 2016

This procedure involves instrumentation of the crown and root surfaces of the teeth to remove plaque and calculus from these surfaces. It is indicated for patients with periodontal disease and is therapeutic, not prophylactic, in nature. Root planing is the definitive procedure designed for the removal of cementum and dentin that is rough, and/or permeated by calculus or contaminated with toxins or microorganisms. Some soft tissue removal occurs. This procedure may be used as a definitive treatment in some stages of periodontal disease and/or as a part of pre-surgical procedures in others.

CODING WARNING CORRECTION

1. The full mouth debridement code (D4355) should not be reported on *every* new patient, but only as indicated.

2. The full mouth debridement code (D4355) <u>does</u> not report "non-invasive chemical debridement." However, gingival irrigation – per quadrant is reported as D4921.

CODING WATCH CORRECTION

1. Full mouth debridement (D4355) is justified when the comprehensive oral evaluation (D0150) or comprehensive periodontal evaluation (D0180) *cannot* be performed due to excessive and bulky calculus, heavy plaque, and debris buildup.

2. A comprehensive oral evaluation (D0150 or D0180) should follow the full mouth debridement on a subsequent date giving the debrided area sufficient time to heal/react to the D4355 treatment so that an oral evaluation may be performed. The D0150 or D0180 would follow on the subsequent treatment date. D4355 is a paid benefit in only 25-33% of contracts even if sequenced *perfectly*.

3. D4355 is not a definitive treatment. It is *preparatory* in nature. The procedure is performed to clean the mouth enough so that the dentist can do a comprehensive oral evaluation (D0150) or a comprehensive periodontal evaluation (D0180) at a subsequent appointment. The patient may, or may not, be a patient that will require active periodontal treatment. *Either* a prophylaxis (D1110), scaling and root planing (D4341/D4342), or referral to a periodontist follows the D4355 procedure.

4. Do not report D4355 as a "first visit prophy." This *preliminary* procedure is provided so that a comprehensive oral evaluation (D0150/D0180) and diagnosis may be completed at the second visit. The patient could be *either* a periodontal or non-periodontal patient.

5. It is misleading to report D4355 following periodontal maintenance (D4910), unless the patient has been absent from the practice for such a long period that a new oral evaluation cannot be performed due to excessive plaque and calculus that interferes with the ability of the dentist to perform a comprehensive oral evaluation.

COMMENTS

1. Full mouth debridement is performed when heavy buildup of plaque and calculus makes the completion of a comprehensive oral evaluation (D0150 or D0180) impossible. It is important to note that D4355 is a *preliminary* procedure.

2. A definitive procedure, either D1110 or D4341/D4342, or referral to the periodontist will be necessary after the completion of a comprehensive oral evaluation (D0150 or D0180) at the second visit.

3. Palliative (D9110) may *possibly* be reimbursed for *partial* mouth debridement under an acute and spontaneous discomfort scenario. If reimbursed, it generally reimburses at a *lower* fee than D4355. The use of the palliative D9110 code may result in payment for non-PPO contracted offices, since the patient pays any balance of the fee. See D9110 for extensive comments.

4. D4355 is not a definitive treatment. It is preparatory in nature. The procedure is performed to clean the mouth enough so that the dentist can perform a comprehensive oral evaluation (D0150) or a comprehensive periodontal evaluation (D0180) on a subsequent appointment.

LIMITATIONS

1. The *sole* purpose of full mouth debridement (D4355) is to "pave the way" for the subsequent oral evaluation by removing the "roadblocks" and to allow for preliminary healing. The roadblocks being excessive plaque and calculus that interferes with the dentist's ability to perform a comprehensive oral evaluation. This *preliminary* debridement should be performed *prior* to the *comprehensive* oral evaluation (D0150) or *comprehensive periodontal* evaluation (D0180). If the evaluation *cannot* be completed due to the plaque and calculus buildup, an evaluation should not be submitted on the same service date as D4355. The evaluation would be completed on a *subsequent* date. *Preliminary* data may be gathered and recorded at the first visit. D4355 is not typically reimbursed by payers when submitted on the same service date as a comprehensive oral evaluation (D0150) or comprehensive periodontal evaluation (D0180). Note: A comprehensive oral evaluation (D0150/D0180) may be submitted on the same service date as the D4355 but D4355 will most likely not be reimbursed.

2. Proper *sequencing* of D4355 is very important for reimbursement. Improper sequencing results in either a *denial* or a re-mapping to a *different* code. For instance, many payers will remap the full mouth debridement (D4355) to a prophylaxis (D1110). In this scenario, when a subsequent prophylaxis (D1110) is submitted, the payer denies reimbursement, stating a prophylaxis within the typical "one per six-month" limitation period has already been reimbursed. If the comprehensive oral evaluation (D0150) or comprehensive periodontal evaluation (D0180) is performed *prior* to full mouth debridement, many payers will convert the D4355 to a prophylaxis (D1110) for reimbursement purposes and limitations apply.

3. When D4355 is reimbursed, it may be classified as preventive, basic, or major, but most often D4355 is classified as preventive. In some cases, a plan deductible may apply. Plan limitations are highly variable.

4. When a comprehensive oral evaluation (D0150 or D0180) cannot be performed due to plaque and calculus that interfere with the ability of the dentist to perform a comprehensive oral evaluation, a full mouth debridement and full series or panoramic diagnostic radiographic images (optional) are performed at the first visit. A healing period of fourteen to twenty one days should follow D4355 to allow resolution of the gingival tissue. The comprehensive oral evaluation is then *completed* at the second visit. Generally, diagnostic radiographic images (panoramic or full series) can be taken at the first visit in *conjunction* with the full mouth debridement (D4355) without affecting reimbursement. There may be exceptions.

5. Plan limitations regarding frequency of full mouth debridement (D4355) are highly variable. Limitations vary from "once per lifetime" to once per every three to five years.

6. Some payers will reimburse full mouth debridement (D4355) when reported as D4999. Some payers may reimburse D4355 by re-mapping the service as palliative (D9110). Refer to palliative (D9110) for further details.

7. Under current nomenclature, there is no *alternate* classification code for a *second* prophy or a "difficult" prophy. To report a "difficult" prophylaxis requiring additional time, simply report D1110 at a higher fee. Note that PPO contracts limit reimbursement for D1110 to the contracted fee regardless of the time required to complete a difficult prophylaxis.

NARRATIVES A narrative should be used when reporting D4355. That narrative might read: "Patient has not seen dentist in *three* years. A full mouth debridement is *necessary* for a *subsequent* comprehensive oral evaluation." The narrative should describe excessive plaque and calculus. The narrative should be specific as to how conditions were *preventing* an oral evaluation. Include photographs and radiographs showing heavy plaque and calculus.

Please see flow chart on page 176.

FLOW CHARTS

First Visit
Full mouth debridement
(D4355)

↓

PLUS
Intraoral – complete series (D0210)
may be taken at first or second visit
OR
Panoramic radiographic
image (D0330)

↓

Note: At first visit, preliminary oral evaluation data may be gathered but not reported since the comprehensive oral evaluation (D0150 or D0180) is still not complete.

Waiting Period Between Visits

→ Fourteen day wait suggested for healing

Second Visit
Comprehensive oral evaluation (D0150)
or comprehensive oral periodontal
evaluation (D0180) would be performed.

↓

There are three possible scenarios upon the completion of the comprehensive oral evaluation at the second visit:

1. A prophylaxis (D1110) is performed.

2. If periodontal problems exist, generally no prophylaxis is performed; fully document and proceed to root planing and scaling (D4341/D4342) for applicable quadrants.

3. Referral to a periodontist to treat a more complex case.

↓

Note: A panoramic radiographic image on the first visit and bitewings at the second visit (different service date) may result in a higher reimbursement than if both are taken on the same service date. See D0330 for further details.

Note:

1. If *unable* to perform a comprehensive oral evaluation (D0150/D0180) due to *excessive* buildup of calculus, plaque and debris, proceed to a gross debridement (D4355) to enable a comprehensive oral evaluation at that or a later visit.

2. Necessary diagnostic images may be taken on either gross debridement (D4355) or comprehensive oral evaluation (D0150/D0180) service dates. For instance, a panoramic image (D0330) on the gross debridement (D4355) service date and four bitewings (D0274) on the subsequent comprehensive oral evaluation (D0150/D0180) date may avoid "re-mapping" or down coding to a complete series (D0120) UCR fee.

3. The comprehensive oral evaluation (D0150 or D0180) should follow gross debridement (D4355) on a *subsequent* service date, with a suggested interval of 10-14 days or more for healing. Reimbursement for D4355 is only available from about 25-30% of insurance contracts, so inform the patient of potential responsibility for out of pocket costs. See also palliative D9110 as a possible alternative if the patient has discomfort at an emergency visit.

D4381 — LOCALIZED DELIVERY OF ANTIMICROBIAL AGENTS VIA CONTROLLED RELEASE VEHICLE INTO DISEASED CREVICULAR TISSUE, PER TOOTH — CDT 2016

FDA approved subgingival delivery devices containing antimicrobial medication(s) are inserted into periodontal pockets to suppress the pathogenic microbiota. These devices slowly release the pharmacological agents so they can remain at the intended site of action in a therapeutic concentration for a sufficient length of time.

CODING WARNING CORRECTION

1. Do not report D4381 to describe the use of Perio Protect®. D4381 reports the *localized* delivery of antimicrobial agents into the periodontal pocket. The Perio Protect® method utilizes custom trays to facilitate the delivery of antimicrobials to the *entire* upper and lower arches. Use D5994 to report Perio Protect®.
2. Do *not* use D4381 to report chlorhexidine or other irrigation. See D4921 to report gingival irrigation – per quadrant.

COMMENTS

1. Sustained or controlled releases LDAAs (local delivery antimicrobial agents) are placed in deep periodontal pockets in an attempt to reduce the bacterial load in the pocket area. Reducing the bacteria will reduce the inflammation. LDAAs come in the form of powders, gels, or thin wafer-like chips (e.g., Atridox, Arestin, PerioChip, etc.). The American Academy of Periodontology's position on LDAAs is contained in their "Statement on Local Delivery of Sustained or Controlled Release Antimicrobials as Adjunctive Therapy in the Treatment of Periodontics" (May 2006): "Clinicians may consider the use of LDAAs in chronic periodontitis patients as an adjunct to SRP when localized recurrent and/or residual pocket depth greater than or equal to 5mm with inflammation is still present following conventional therapies." The conventional therapies referred to in this quote are scaling and root planing (D4341/D4342).
2. D4381 is reported on a *per tooth* basis. The fee for each tooth should vary by the *number of sites* treated. A flat rate (per site) or sliding scale may be used to set the fee. For example, a fee for a tooth with two sites might be $55, or with three sites might be $75 or higher. The narrative should document that the fee is based on number of sites treated and amount of material used. Many payers limit the total UCR fee to one-half of a quadrant SRP reimbursement. Sometimes there is a reimbursement limitation to two or three teeth per quadrant.
3. Chemotherapeutic agents may be used as appropriate to reduce the quantity of microbial pathogens, or to alter the host response through local delivery. D4381 specifies a controlled release vehicle for the delivery of antimicrobial agents.

LIMITATIONS

1. Some plans do not provide benefits for local delivery of antimicrobial agents. Generally, to qualify for reimbursement, patients must have moderate to severe periodontal disease and a history of scaling and root planing (SRP) or current treatment of periodontal disease. Comparative periodontal charting can be helpful in demonstrating conventional therapy (SRP) has not been effective. Be aware that while some dental plans pay for D4381 when placed at the time of root planing and scaling (SRP), most limit reimbursement for D4381 to areas that continue to bleed on probing at least six weeks following SRP.
2. In some cases, D4381 may be considered a "take back" code by some payers. If osseous surgery (D4260/D4261) is initiated within 12 months of reporting D4341, the fee reimbursed for osseous surgery may be reduced by the amount previously reimbursed for D4381. Reimbursement for D4381 is highly variable among payers.
3. D4381 reimbursement for the same site may be denied for up to 24 months following the initial treatment. Some payers reimburse D4381 on an annual basis. Reimbursement for D4381 is highly variable.
4. When submitting D4381 with a pre-estimate, indicate the time interval anticipated between the SRP visit and proposed D4381 treatment date. A six-week minimum after SRP may be required.
5. The insured's pharmacy benefit may pay for the antimicrobial agent. Contact an Arestin® representative for further information.

6. Report D4381 for placement of FDA approved localized antimicrobial agents such as Arestin®, PerioChip®, and Atridox®. D4381 is an adjunct to D4341, D4342, or D4910. D4381 is also an adjunct to the prophylaxis (D1110) when used to treat a few isolated pockets. Note: D4381 may *not* be reimbursed if placed at the *initial* scaling and root planing (D4341/D4342) appointment. The patient is usually required to pay out of pocket for the first application, if placed at the initial scaling and root planing (D4341/D4342) appointment. D4381 is most often reimbursed when utilized at the four to six week evaluation appointment. D4381 may be reimbursed if placed at a subsequent ongoing periodontal maintenance (D4910) visit when provided in conjunction with selected scaling and root planing procedures performed to treat unresponsive pockets. Some payers require that the patient be six weeks post SRP before reimbursing D4381. It is recommended that coverage and limitations be verified with the payer before providing D4381.

NARRATIVES

1. The narrative should document that initial scaling and root planing *did not resolve* all the pockets. Also mention the actual medication, not the trade name (Minocycline HCL, not Arestin®.) Documentation such as SRP history, charting at all visits, diagnosis, loss of attachment, radiographic evidence of bone loss, bleeding on probing, dates of re-evaluation, etc., with ongoing periodontal charting is typically required. Also, document the desired outcome of the procedure, as well as including any contributing medical factors such as diabetes, heart disease, surgical candidate for hip replacement, etc. If D4381 is used in an attempt to avoid osseous surgery, also *indicate this intent* in the narrative.

2. A narrative should always be submitted when reporting D4381 in association with a periodontal abscess, for possible reimbursement. See table below for documenting on ADA Dental Claim Form.

   Documenting on ADA Dental Claim Form:

   Record of Services Provided

Procedure Date	Tooth Number	Procedure Code	Description	Fee
mm/dd/yy	13	D4381	Localized Delivery	$30
mm/dd/yy	14	D4381	Localized Delivery (2 sites)	$60
mm/dd/yy	15	D4381	Localized Delivery	$30
mm/dd/yy	30	D4381	Localized Delivery	$30

   Remarks: "6mm MB site of #13, 5mm DB and 7mm MB site of #14, 6mm ML site of #15 and 6mm DL site of #30. The fee listed reflects material costs and number of sites treated. Minocycline HCL micro spheres applied."

   Enclosures: Probing charts of mm/dd/yy and mm/dd/yy and radiographs.

3. Reimbursement for D4381 often requires *unresponsive* 5mm to 7mm pockets at least six weeks after SRP, loss of attachment or bone loss, bleeding on probing (BOP). This is indicative of *active* disease. These unresponsive areas should be limited to two to three specific teeth treated per quadrant. In addition, any increasing pocket depth readings after scaling and root planing (SRP) should be noted. "See attached pre-operative and post-operative periodontal charting." Be sure to document any systemic medical issues, such as diabetes, heart disease, etc.

4. If the Arestin® is furnished by the patient's pharmacy benefits, the dentist may charge a *placement* fee, reporting D4381. The placement (labor) fee would be less and typically limited to two teeth per quadrant. Full documentation would need to be provided as outlined in the narrative above.

FLOW CHARTS

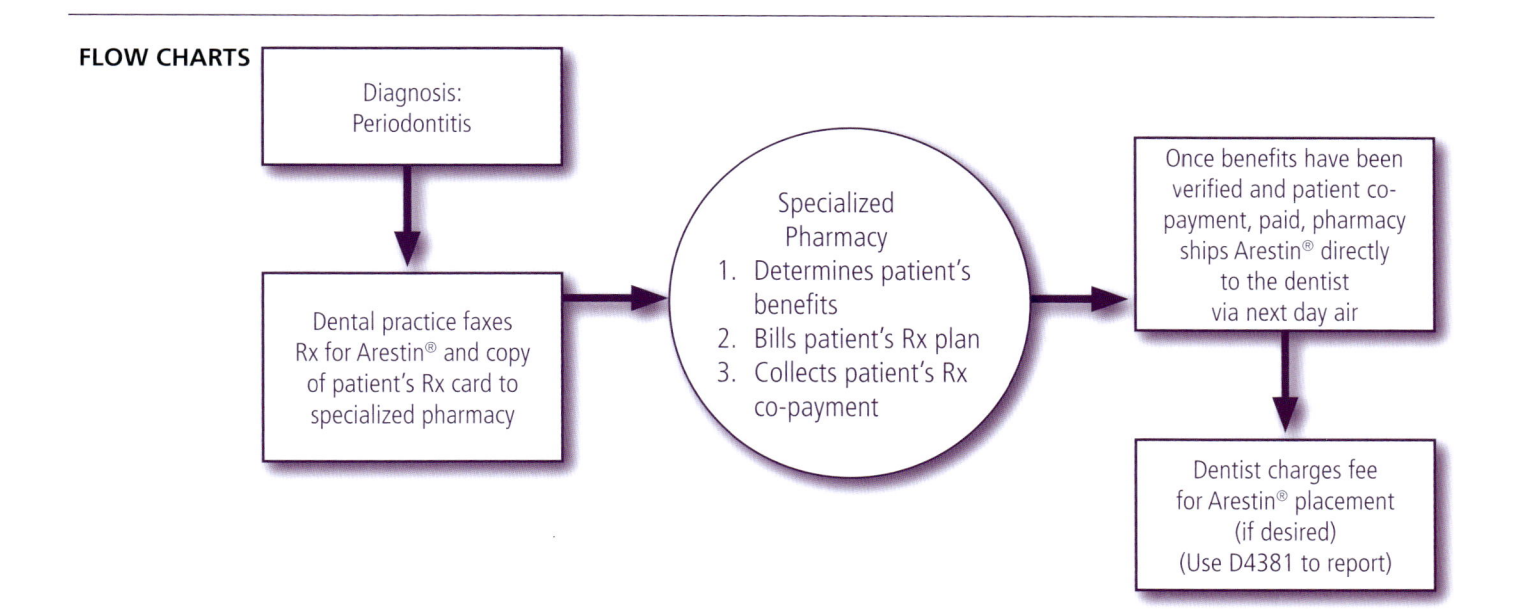

```
Diagnosis:
Periodontitis
    │
    ▼
Dental practice faxes          Specialized Pharmacy              Once benefits have been
Rx for Arestin® and copy   →   1. Determines patient's      →    verified and patient co-
of patient's Rx card to           benefits                        payment, paid, pharmacy
specialized pharmacy           2. Bills patient's Rx plan         ships Arestin® directly
                               3. Collects patient's Rx            to the dentist
                                  co-payment                       via next day air
                                                                        │
                                                                        ▼
                                                                  Dentist charges fee
                                                                  for Arestin® placement
                                                                  (if desired)
                                                                  (Use D4381 to report)
```

OTHER PERIODONTAL SERVICES — CDT 2016

D4910 PERIODONTAL MAINTENANCE — CDT 2016

This procedure is instituted following periodontal therapy and continues at varying intervals, determined by the clinical evaluation of the dentist, for the life of the dentition or any implant replacements. It includes removal of the bacterial plaque and calculus from supragingival and subgingival regions, site specific scaling and root planing where indicated, and polishing the teeth. If new or recurring periodontal disease appears, additional diagnostic and treatment procedures must be considered.

Coding Watch Correction

1. Ongoing periodontal maintenance (D4910) does *not* include a periodic oral evaluation (D0120) or comprehensive periodontal evaluation (D0180). The periodic evaluation (D0120) or D0180 is submitted as a separate procedure. The oral evaluation (D0120 or D0180) is generally provided twice per year, and is subject to the typical "one evaluation per six months" or "two evaluations per year" limitation. For a comprehensive periodontal evaluation of an *established periodontal* patient provided on a periodic basis consider reporting D0180. Note: The reimbursement for D0180 might be re-mapped as D0120. If the more extensive and time consuming D0180 is performed, report what you do.

2. Some offices report one D0180 and one D0120 per year for periodontal recall patients. Some offices have two consistent, but different, fee levels for D0180, depending on whether the procedure is provided for the new (entering the practice) or established (recall) D4910 patient. See D0180 for details.

Coding Match Correction

1. Periodontal maintenance (D4910) *follows* active periodontal therapy: scaling and root planing procedures (D4341/D4342), gingival flap surgery (D4240/D4241) or osseous surgery (D4260/D4261). The periodontal maintenance patient (D4910) must have undergone *either* SRP *or* periodontal surgery (gingival flap or osseous surgery) prior to periodontal maintenance (D4910). Periodontal maintenance (D4910) is *ongoing and therapeutic* in nature, not *preventive*. Typically there is a ninety day exclusion period following *active* treatment. Active periodontal treatment may be reported as D4341, D4342, D4240, D4241, D4260, D4261.

The ongoing periodontal maintenance (D4910) interval is typically ninety days but the frequency is determined by individual need. It is improper for the same practitioner to alternate D4910 with a prophylaxis (D1110). However, a patient alternating between the GP and periodontist might receive alternating D1110s and D4910s. The periodontist could provide ongoing periodontal maintenance (D4910) while the GP office provides prophylaxis. Be advised, however, that some payers *terminate* D4910 coverage if prophylaxis (D1110) is provided in the periodontal treatment sequence. Payers assert that the patient cannot be a periodontal patient one visit, and a prophy visit the next, alternating between a diseased and healthy state.

2. Once the patient is in ongoing periodontal maintenance (D4910) following active periodontal therapy, they could remain in D4910 status. Periodontal disease is *episodic*. If the patient's periodontal status improves (to good health), then prophylaxis (D1110) could be appropriate. This change may occur; however it may take one year for the issue to resolve following root planing and scaling (D4341) therapy. This change from periodontal disease to health is not the rule, but the exception. When the patient moves from periodontal disease to a condition of health and prophylaxis (D1110) is provided, then a sequence of SRP (D4341/D4342) would be required before D4910 would be reimbursed again. SRP (D4341 or D4342) typically has a twenty four or thirty six month frequency limitation with most plans.

3. Although most periodontal patients will require periodontal maintenance for a lifetime, the American Dental Association gives dentists some discretion when reporting D1110 and D4910. See page 157 of CDT 2009/2010: "Follow-up patients who have received active periodontal therapy (surgical or non-surgical) are appropriately reported using the periodontal maintenance code, D4910. However, if the treating dentist determines that a patient's oral condition can be maintained with a routine prophylaxis, delivery of this service and reporting with code D1110 may be appropriate."

COMMENTS Patients who need periodontal maintenance have periodontal disease and have been treated non-surgically (D4341/D4342) and/or surgically (D4240/D4241 or D4260/ D4261). Periodontal maintenance is performed in the presence of disease whereas a prophylaxis (D1110) is performed to *prevent* disease. D4910 is performed to maintain the periodontal condition of the patient as a result of nonsurgical and/or surgical periodontal treatment. Periodontal maintenance includes removing any new plaque and calculus that may have formed since the patient's last periodontal therapy appointment as well as site specific scaling and root planing where indicated, and polishing the teeth. The descriptor clearly states D4910 does not preclude the need for additional diagnostic and treatment procedures if new or recurring periodontal disease develops. Additional scaling and root planing, locally delivered antimicrobials (D4381), or periodontal surgery may be necessary when there is evidence of new disease.

LIMITATIONS
1. Reimbursement for ongoing periodontal maintenance D4910 is highly variable. Some payers may not reimburse D4910 at all or some may reimburse D4910 two to four times during a 12-month period. Some policies provide reimbursements for two D4910 *and* two prophylaxes (D1110) during a 12-month period. Even though the contract reimburses certain procedures at a frequency greater than every six months, you are bound to report **what you do**. Since plan limitations are highly variable when providing D4910, request an alternate benefit of a prophylaxis (D1110) in the event D4910 is not a covered benefit. Benefits are highly variable. Some plans will provide reimbursement more frequently for diabetic or pregnant patients.

2. D4910 may be reimbursed at a 50-80% fee (unlike the typical 100% reimbursement for a prophylaxis), and may also be subject to a deductible. Payers may reimburse D4910 as preventive, basic or major. Reimbursement for D4910 is highly variable.

3. A prophylaxis (D1110) is considered a part of D4910 by payers in the ongoing periodontal maintenance regime. The clinical record should reflect the fact that a prophylaxis was completed as part of the overall D4910 procedure.

4. Some payers require that osseous surgery (D4260/D4261) be completed to qualify for D4910 reimbursement. However, in general SRP treatment will justify ongoing periodontal maintenance (D4910).

5. D4921 reports periodontal pocket irrigation using medicinal agents, e.g., chlorhexidine. Payers typically consider gingival irrigation a part of D4910. PPO contracts may limit reimbursement for the use of gingival irrigation in periodontal maintenance. See D4921 for comments.

6. D9910 describes desensitizing medicaments applied to a single tooth or up to the entire mouth. Payers typically consider the application of desensitizing medicaments to the entire mouth a part of D4910. PPO contracts may limit reimbursement for the use of D9910 with periodontal treatments.

NARRATIVES
1. Consider filing a manual claim when reporting D4910 with the following narrative: "If periodontal maintenance (D4910) is denied, please provide the alternate benefit of a prophylaxis (D1110). The ongoing periodontal maintenance (D4910) visit included a prophylaxis (D1110)." The clinical notes should reflect the fact that a prophylaxis was provided as a part of D4910. Because payers consider D1110 a part of periodontal maintenance, expect reimbursement of the *alternate* benefit of a prophylaxis. Instruct the patient that you are bound by law to report D4910. Per HIPAA requirements, the government mandates it.

2. When submitting D4910 identify the date that active treatment SRP or osseous surgery was performed. Include a current periodontal chart with a claim of D4910. Consider a narrative: "This patient underwent SRP on mm/dd/yy" or "This patient underwent osseous surgery on mm/dd/yy at Dr. Smith's office." State which quadrants had SRP and on what date. "See attached periodontal chart."

3. If *benefit plans change or there is change in employment*, it is important to provide the new payer a narrative for the *first* D4910 claim (to turn the periodontal coverage switch "on") describing a history of scaling and root planing (SRP) or osseous surgery. Provide the same information from the patient's history when the patient returns from the periodontal office. When previous periodontal treatment history is not noted in the "remarks" section, D4910 may be *denied* by the subsequent plan. For documentation, submit current periodontal charting and a narrative stating that the patient is in ongoing periodontal maintenance therapy.

D4920 — UNSCHEDULED DRESSING CHANGE (BY SOMEONE OTHER THAN TREATING DENTIST OR THEIR STAFF) — CDT 2016

COMMENTS When periodontal surgery is performed, a periodontal dressing is often placed over the surgical area to protect the site while healing. The dressing may look like Silly Putty,® but it provides important protection to the surgical area for healing. The dressing is used to inhibit bacterial growth, prevent irritation of the area, and makes the surgical site more comfortable for the patient during the healing process. The surgical dressing is resilient and usually stays in place until removed by the dentist who performed the surgery. The dressing may loosen prematurely and need replacing. If the dentist who did the surgery (or the staff) is not available, another dentist, in another office, can replace the dressing and report D4920 to describe the procedure.

LIMITATIONS
1. This dressing change may be reimbursed if provided by an office other than the office that did the surgery and placed the dressing.
2. An alternate benefit of palliative (D9110) may be reimbursed. See D9110.

NARRATIVES When a dressing is changed by a different dentist (or staff) at a different location, a brief narrative should explain the circumstances.

D4921 — GINGIVAL IRRIGATION – PER QUADRANT — CDT 2016

Irrigation of gingival pockets with medicinal agent. Not to be used to report use of mouth rinses or non-invasive chemical debridement.

CODING WARNING CORRECTION
1. Non-invasive chemical debridement or mouth rinses should not be reported as D4921.
2. Therapeutic parenteral drug (D9610) should not be reported for gingival irrigation – per quadrant.
3. Other drugs and/or medicaments (D9630) should not be reported for gingival irrigation – per quadrant.

COMMENTS Gingival irrigation is used as an adjunct by many practitioners to assist in prophylaxis and periodontal treatment protocols. The procedure delivers a medicinal agent (such as chlorhexidine/Peridex®) into instrumented gingival pockets to help control periodontal disease and gingival inflammation.

LIMITATIONS
1. D4921 reports gingival irrigation, per quadrant. Payers typically consider gingival irrigation to be a part of the D4341, D4342, or D4910 procedures. The PPO contract may prohibit charging a separate fee for irrigation.
2. D4921 is a relatively new code, and may not be reimbursed by payers.

D4999	UNSPECIFIED PERIODONTAL PROCEDURE, BY REPORT	CDT 2016

Use for procedure that is not adequately described by a code. Describe procedure.

COMMENTS

1. Chlorhexidine used for gingival irrigation – per quadrant should be reported as D4921

2. D4999 reports procedures not adequately described by an existing code.

3. Use D4999, by report for the following periodontal-related procedures that have no specific reporting code:

   a. Complete periodontal charting and probing. At the charting visit, there is no oral evaluation (D0120 or D0180) performed by the dentist. D4999 may be reported to describe this charting procedure by a hygienist. However, D4999 is not usually reimbursed.

   b. Gross debridement to enable comprehensive oral evaluation. This procedure may not be recognized as D4355 but may be considered as D4999. Call the payer to see if D4355 is appropriate. A payer might reimburse D4999. Provide a comprehensive narrative that accurately describes the service provided. Always report **what you do**.

   c. Extended time required for the prophylaxis due to excessive calculus at a level that goes well above and beyond a routine prophylaxis (D1110). A prophylaxis (D1110) plus D4999 may be reported on the same day with full narrative. Generally this is not considered for reimbursement.

   d. A closed hard tissue laser procedure such as clinical crown lengthening. Report D4999 with full narrative. In this scenario, there is no flap access as D4249's descriptor requires reflection of a full thickness flap. Report D4999 for the laser procedure but ask for the alternate benefit of D4249. See D4249 for full details. Payers reimburse according to the procedures performed, not for specific equipment or technology used to perform the procedure.

   e. Gingival curettage. The former code for periodontal curettage D4220 was deleted January 1, 2008. D4999 would report curettage treatment. Gingival curettage is generally considered to be a part of the D4240, D4241, D4341 and D4342 procedures.

   f. LANAP (Laser Assisted New Attachment Procedure). The dentist must determine if their LANAP procedure complies with the criterion established by D4260. If the dentist finds that LANAP does not comply, then report D4999, by report. **IMPORTANT!** See D4260 and author's notes (located at start of 4000 section) for discussion of LANAP.

   g. Use D4999 to report adjunctive laser therapy (decontaminating periodontal pockets). Often described as laser curettage, laser debridement, or laser decontamination, dental practices are using laser therapy in conjunction with periodontal scaling and root planing to treat periodontal disease. Root planing has always been considered the gold standard for initial periodontal therapy as it involves removing diseased cementum, dentin, and calculus from the root surfaces of infected teeth. Laser therapy is focused on eliminating the diseased soft tissue inside the periodontal pocket. The laser destroys and cauterizes diseased soft tissue along the wall of the periodontal pocket. After laser treatment is completed, the periodontal pocket is typically irrigated with an antiseptic solution to flush away remaining debris. In theory, this protocol provides more thorough decontamination of the periodontal pocket, which facilitates improved healing.

What code is used for laser therapy? Today's dental codes do not differentiate between the various methods that may be used to perform a procedure. Other than code D7465, which is used to report the destruction of a lesion by cryo, laser, or electro surgery, lasers are not mentioned in CDT. One must report the code that reflects the procedure that was completed rather than the method used to perform the procedure. When a laser is used to decontaminate the soft tissue wall of a periodontal pocket, curettage is the procedure that has actually been performed. The glossary in CDT defines curettage as, "scraping and cleaning the walls of a real or potential space, such as a gingival pocket or bone, to remove pathologic material." When looking for "curettage" in the CDT index, we are referred to D3410, D3426 and D4240/D4241. Codes D3410-D3426 clearly do not apply as they are used when performing exploratory curettage to look for root fractures. While codes D4240 and D4241 appear to be appropriate because they include debridement of the root surface and the removal of granulation tissue, it is important to note that they also require the reflection of a flap. If a flap is not performed, then D4240/D4241 cannot be used to report periodontal laser therapy. Currently, when a laser has been used to perform periodontal curettage without the reflection of a flap, D4999 (unspecified periodontal procedure, by report) is the only code available to describe the procedure. D4999 can be used to report irrigation with an antiseptic solution. While it is well known that dental plans seldom provide a benefit for D4999, it is still important to submit the claim. Some dental plans provide a benefit for periodontal curettage even though the code for curettage (D4220) was deleted January 1, 2003. The narrative should describe the procedure, reference deleted code D4220, and ask the payer to check the contract language to see if curettage is a payable benefit.

4. D4999 is often used in error to report the following:

   a. Products that promote hemostasis by using a collagen matrix would be reported as D7999 or D4999.

   b. See prescription strength chlorhexidine dispensed for home use, D9630.

   c. Perio Protect Trays® utilizes a customized dental tray system used to direct medications (e.g., peroxide) into the gingival sulcus to help manage bioradiographic image. D5994 reports Perio Protect Trays®.

D5000-D5899 VI. PROSTHODONTICS (REMOVABLE) — CDT 2016

Local anesthesia is usually considered to be a part of removable prosthodontic procedures.

COMPLETE DENTURES (INCLUDING ROUTINE POST-DELIVERY CARE) — CDT 2016

D5110 COMPLETE DENTURE – MAXILLARY — CDT 2016

CODING WATCH CORRECTION

1. D5110 reports the delivery of a complete *maxillary* denture.
2. Do not use D5110 to report an *immediate* denture. An *immediate* complete denture (D5130) or *interim* complete denture (D5810) is inserted immediately after the extraction of the remaining teeth. See both D5130 and D5810 for further details.

CODING MATCH CORRECTION

1. For an *adjustment* of a complete maxillary denture, see D5410.
2. For a *repair* of a complete denture *base*, see D5510.
3. For a *replacement* of *missing or broken* teeth (each tooth), see D5520.
4. For a *rebase* of a complete maxillary denture, see D5710.
5. For a *chairside reline* of a complete maxillary denture, see D5730.
6. For a *laboratory* processed *reline* of a complete maxillary denture, see D5750.
7. For cleaning and inspection of a removable complete denture – maxillary, report D9932.

LIMITATIONS

1. Diagnostic casts (D0470) are considered part of the global fee for a maxillary complete denture (D5110).
2. There is typically a five to 10-year exclusion period for a replacement denture. To justify the replacement, the documentation (narrative/photos) must demonstrate why the existing prosthesis cannot be made serviceable.
3. Follow up adjustments within six months of delivery are typically included in the fee for D5110, and are not reimbursed separately. An adjustment made by an office not having delivered the denture might be reimbursed.
4. Replacement of a lost denture is not reimbursed.

TIPS

1. A patient covered by a PPO plan may choose to pay extra for a "characterized," or a metal base, denture. Generally, the patient must sign and agree with the treatment plan, listing a separate line item (D5899), explaining the additional procedure. Refer to your third party contract and their Processing Policy Manual to verify optional services and whether or not optional services are permitted. If there is a question, contact the payer for more information.
2. Use D5110 to report a complete upper denture with a cast metal palate.

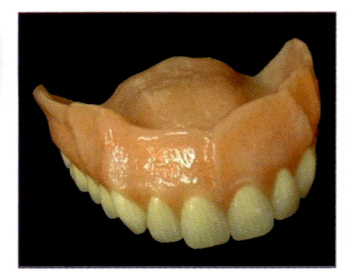

PHOTO

This is an upper (D5110) complete denture.

Courtesy Drake Dental Lab

D5120   COMPLETE DENTURE – MANDIBULAR   CDT 2016

CODING WATCH CORRECTION

1. D5120 reports the delivery of a complete *mandibular* denture.
2. Do not report D5120 for an immediate denture. An *immediate* complete mandibular denture (D5140), **or** *interim* complete denture (D5811) is inserted immediately after the extraction of the remaining teeth. See both D5140 and D5811 for further details.

CODING MATCH CORRECTION

1. For an *adjustment* of a complete mandibular denture, see D5411.
2. For a *repair* of a complete denture *base*, see D5510.
3. For a *replacement* of *missing or broken* teeth (each tooth), see D5520.
4. For a *rebase* of a complete mandibular denture, see D5711.
5. For a *chairside reline* of a complete mandibular denture, see D5731.
6. For a *laboratory* (processed) *reline* of a complete mandibular denture, see D5751.
7. For cleaning and inspection of a removable complete denture – mandibular, report D9932.

LIMITATIONS

1. Diagnostic casts (D0470) are considered part of the global fee for mandibular complete dentures (D5120).
2. There is typically a five to 10-year exclusion period for a replacement denture. To justify the replacement, the documentation (narrative/photos) must demonstrate why the existing prosthesis cannot be made serviceable.
3. Follow up adjustments within six months of delivery are typically included in the fee for D5120, and are not reimbursed separately. An adjustment made by an office not having delivered the denture might be reimbursed.
4. Replacement of a lost denture is not reimbursed.

TIPS

A patient covered by a PPO plan may choose to pay extra for a "characterized," or a metal base, denture. Generally, the patient must sign and agree with the treatment plan, listing a separate line item (D5899), explaining the additional procedure. Refer to your third party contract and their Processing Policy Manual to verify optional services and whether or not optional services are permitted. If there is a question, contact the payer for more information.

PHOTO

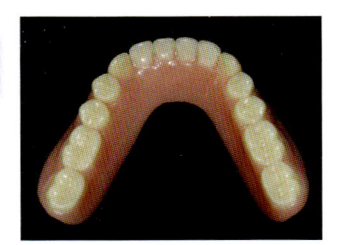

This is a mandibular (D5120) complete denture.

Courtesy Drake Dental Lab

D5130   REVISED IMMEDIATE DENTURE – MAXILLARY   CDT 2016

Includes limited follow-up care only; does not include required future rebasing/relining procedure(s)

REVISIONS   Includes limited follow-up care only; does not include future rebasing/relining procedure(s) ~~or a complete new denture~~.

CODING WATCH CORRECTION

1. It is proper to report an immediate denture (D5130) when extracting the remaining natural teeth and immediately inserting the newly fabricated denture. D5130 includes soft healing liners. D5130 is *followed*, at an additional fee, by one of these three procedures (*six month healing* is typically required by many payers before one of these subsequent services will be reimbursed):
    a. Reline (most common), chairside (D5730) or laboratory processed reline (D5750).
    b. Rebase (D5710) (reimbursement at a higher UCR fee than a reline).
    c. *New* complete maxillary denture (D5110).

2. *Interim* complete denture (maxillary) (D5810) can also be provided immediately after extractions. An Interim denture may also be provided for a patient with *an edentulous* arch for a *limited* period awaiting a more definitive restorative procedure, such as a maxillary complete denture (D5110) or an implant overdenture. Use caution when reporting D5810. See tip #2 below.

CODING MATCH CORRECTION

1. For an *adjustment* of an immediate maxillary denture, see D5410.
2. For a *repair* of an immediate denture *base*, see D5510.
3. For a *replacement* of *missing or broken* teeth (each tooth), see D5520.
4. For a *rebase* of an immediate maxillary denture, see D5710.
5. For a *chairside reline* of an immediate maxillary denture, see D5730.
6. For a *laboratory* processed *reline* of an immediate maxillary denture, see D5750.

COMMENTS

1. The fee for D5130 does not include the follow up hard acrylic reline (D5730 or D5750) or rebase (D5710) procedure or a new complete denture. Many payers will reimburse a reline or rebase six months or more after the delivery of the immediate denture. Note: An alternate benefit (reline/rebase) may be applied toward a subsequent (new) complete denture if the alternate benefit is requested.
2. A hard acrylic reline, rebase, or a completely new denture follows six months after the immediate denture is seated. The hard acrylic reline, rebase, or a completely new denture is reimbursable separately from the immediate denture. For the new denture, typically only an alternate benefit of a reline or rebase would be reimbursed.

LIMITATIONS

1. Diagnostic casts (D0470) are considered part of the global fee for (D5130).
2. Many payers require a six-month *healing* period after the insertion of an immediate maxillary denture before any subsequent prosthetic procedure is reimbursed for the upper arch. The healing interval begins with the *extraction* date. Normally the remaining teeth are extracted and the maxillary immediate denture is seated on the same appointment. The healing interval ends with the impression date for the subsequent reline, the rebase or for the completely new denture. Some payers require the reline be done within six months of the insertion date. Contact the payer regarding the reline policy for the plan.
3. Follow up adjustments within six months of delivery are typically included in the fee for D5130 and are not reimbursed separately. An adjustment made by an office not having delivered the denture might be reimbursed.
4. Immediate dentures may be reported on the impression date, but some payers will only reimburse the procedure on the delivery date (when the teeth are extracted) and the immediate denture is seated. Most contracted dentists must report D5130 on the delivery date.

TIPS

1. The immediate denture (D5130) is generally delivered immediately after the extraction of the remaining natural teeth. The fee for immediate dentures is typically $100 to $200 *higher* than a conventional denture. This fee includes healing relines and appropriate follow up care during the subsequent (up to) six-month healing phase. The reimbursement made by payers is typically higher for the immediate maxillary denture (D5130) than for the complete maxillary denture (D5110).
2. If both an immediate and a subsequent complete denture are fabricated, some payers will reimburse an alternate benefit fee of *either* a hard acrylic laboratory reline (D5750) or rebase (D5710) toward the *second* denture. If allowed, this scenario provides an overall higher reimbursement than the routine complete maxillary denture (D5110) reimbursed alone. Note: Many payers require that *at least* six months elapse between the service dates of the two dentures. The healing interval of the two service dates starts with the extraction (insertion) date and ends with the impression date for the subsequent reline or rebase of the immediate denture or a new complete denture. Reimbursement is maximized using this scenario rather than reporting the *interim* complete denture (D5810) first (with reimbursement), and then the complete denture (D5110) second (with no reimbursement). See also D5810.

FLOW CHARTS   **Immediate (Maxillary) Denture Scenario**

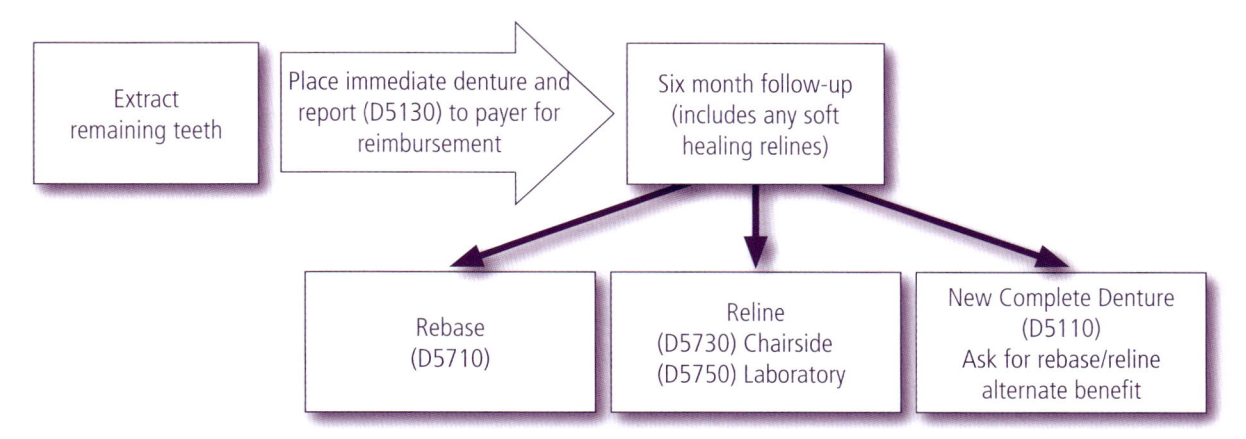

```
┌──────────────┐   Place immediate denture and   ┌──────────────────┐
│   Extract    │──▶ report (D5130) to payer for ─▶│ Six month follow-up│
│ remaining    │       reimbursement              │ (includes any soft │
│   teeth      │                                  │  healing relines)  │
└──────────────┘                                  └──────────────────┘
                                                    │      │      │
                          ┌─────────────────────────┘      │      └──────────────────────┐
                          ▼                                ▼                             ▼
                   ┌─────────────┐              ┌───────────────────────┐     ┌──────────────────────┐
                   │   Rebase    │              │        Reline         │     │ New Complete Denture │
                   │   (D5710)   │              │ (D5730) Chairside     │     │       (D5110)        │
                   │             │              │ (D5750) Laboratory    │     │ Ask for rebase/reline│
                   └─────────────┘              └───────────────────────┘     │  alternate benefit   │
                                                                              └──────────────────────┘
```

Steps:

1. An immediate denture (D5130) is inserted at the appointment when all remaining teeth are extracted. The immediate denture (D5130) fee is *inclusive* of six months of follow up care and includes any *healing* (soft) tissue relines.

2. The immediate denture is nearly *always* followed by *either* a rebase, reline, or a new complete denture (D5110). Some payers require a healing period of at least six months before any of these three procedures will be considered for reimbursement.

3. Always consider filing the higher UCR fee for an immediate denture (D5130) first. If a new complete denture is necessary after healing, ask for the alternate benefit of a reline or rebase fee toward the new denture. This approach reports "what you do" and often results in a higher reimbursement for the patient.

D5140   REVISED IMMEDIATE DENTURE – MANDIBULAR   CDT 2016

Includes limited follow-up care only; does not include required future rebasing/relining procedure(s).

REVISIONS   Includes limited follow-up care only; does not include required future rebasing/relining procedure(s) ~~or a complete new denture~~.

CODING WATCH CORRECTION

1. It is proper to report an immediate denture (D5140) when extracting the remaining natural teeth and immediately inserting the newly fabricated denture. D5140 includes soft healing liners. D5140 is *followed*, at an additional fee, by one of these three procedures (*six-month healing* is typically required):

   a. Reline (most common), chairside (D5731) or laboratory processed reline (D5751).

   b. Rebase (D5711) (reimbursement at a higher UCR fee than a reline).

   c. *New* complete mandibular denture (D5120).

2. *Interim* complete denture (mandibular) (D5811) can also be provided immediately after extractions. An interim denture may also be provided for a patient with *an edentulous* arch for a *limited* period awaiting a more definitive restorative procedure, such as a mandibular complete denture (D5120) or an implant overdenture. Use caution when reporting D5811. See tip #2 below.

CODING MATCH CORRECTION

1. For an *adjustment* of an immediate mandibular denture, see D5411.
2. For a *repair* of an immediate denture *base*, see D5510.
3. For a *replacement* of *missing or broken* teeth (each tooth), see D5520.
4. For a *rebase* of an immediate mandibular denture, see D5711.
5. For a *chairside reline* of an immediate mandibular denture, see D5731.
6. For a *laboratory* processed *reline* of an immediate mandibular denture, see D5751.

TIPS

1. Certain Delta Dental plans may reimburse a "stayplate" for a child (16 years of age and younger), when replacing permanent anterior teeth. Note: A stayplate could be reimbursed under *interim* partial denture (D5820). See D5820 for further details.
2. A resin base partial may be a "low cost" partial denture option for the patient and the cast partial a "higher cost" partial denture option.
3. D5211 reports a *unilateral* or bilateral maxillary resin base partial.

NARRATIVES A maxillary Cu-Sil® partial would be reported as D5211 that have a simple design. The ADA discusses how to code a Cu-Sil® partial denture on page 159 of CDT 2009/2010. It notes that D5211/D5212 are available (partial denture – resin base, including any conventional clasps, rests, and teeth) but also suggest billing D5899, by report if D5211/D5212 does not adequately describe the procedure. If the lab costs are considerably higher with a Cu-Sil® partial than a regular partial because the Cu-Sil® partial involves an unconventional clasping system, billing D5899 may be the better option. Send a copy of the laboratory bill along with a narrative describing the type of partial to justify a higher reimbursement.

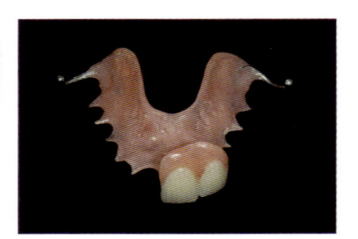

PHOTO This is an example of a maxillary acrylic partial denture with wire clasps. It is to be used as a permanent removable partial denture, if coded as D5211.

Courtesy Drake Dental Lab

D5212 — MANDIBULAR PARTIAL DENTURE – RESIN BASE (INCLUDING ANY CONVENTIONAL CLASPS, RESTS AND TEETH) — CDT 2016

Includes acrylic resin base denture with resin or wrought wire clasps.

CODING WATCH CORRECTION

1. It is misleading to report a mandibular (lower) partial denture (D5212) for a mandibular *interim* partial. D5212 should be used to report *a long term* (definitive) *resin* partial, including clasps. Use this code to report a "flipper," if the flipper is a definitive treatment.
   Note: Report D5821 for interim (temporary) partial dentures lasting generally less than one year. Interim (temporary) partials are followed by a more definitive restoration, such as a "regular" partial, fixed bridge, or implant restoration. See D5821 for further details.
2. For a flexible base (Valplast®/Proplast®) mandibular (lower) partial, see D5226.
3. For an immediate mandibular partial denture – resin base, see D5222.

CODING MATCH CORRECTION

1. For an *adjustment* of a resin mandibular partial denture, see D5422.
2. For a *repair* of a resin partial denture *base*, see D5610.
3. For a *repair* or to replace a *broken clasp*, see D5630.
4. For a *replacement* of *missing or broken* teeth (each tooth), see D5640.
5. For *adding a tooth* to an existing resin partial denture, see D5650.
6. For *adding a clasp* to an existing resin partial denture, see D5660.
7. For a *rebase* of a resin mandibular partial denture, see D5721.
8. For a *chairside reline* of a resin mandibular partial denture, see D5741.
9. For a *laboratory* processed reline of a *resin* mandibular partial denture, see D5761.

COMMENTS A Cu-Sil® partial is like a regular partial denture except that there are gaskets that fit over the patient's remaining teeth. Cu-Sil® uses elastomeric gaskets that adapt to the remaining teeth to stabilize and retain the partial denture. The gaskets "hug" the natural teeth, keeping the partial denture stable and preventing food from getting through the openings and under the partial denture. See the narrative section for code reporting guidelines.

LIMITATIONS
1. Diagnostic casts (D0470) are considered integral in the global fee for a mandibular partial denture (D5212).
2. There is typically a five to 10-year exclusion period for a replacement partial denture. To justify the replacement, the documentation (narrative/photos) must demonstrate why the existing prosthesis cannot be made serviceable.
3. Follow up adjustments within six months of delivery are also typically included in the fee for the prosthesis, and are not reimbursed separately. An adjustment made by an office not having delivered the denture might be reimbursed.
4. Replacement of a lost partial denture is not reimbursed.

TIPS
1. A resin base partial may be a "low cost" partial denture option for the patient and the cast partial a "higher cost" option.
2. D5212 reports a *unilateral* or a bilateral mandibular resin base partial.

NARRATIVES A mandibular Cu-Sil® partial would be reported as D5212 that have a simple design. The ADA discusses how to code a Cu-Sil® partial denture on page 159 of CDT 2009/2010. It notes that D5211/D5212 are available (partial denture – resin base, including any conventional clasps, rests, and teeth) but also suggests billing D5899, by report if D5211/D5212 does not adequately describe the procedure. If the lab costs are considerably higher with a Cu-Sil® partial than a regular partial because the Cu-Sil® partial involves an unconventional clasping system, billing D5899 may be the better option. Send a copy of the laboratory bill along with a narrative describing the type of partial to justify a higher reimbursement.

D5213 MAXILLARY PARTIAL DENTURE – CAST METAL FRAMEWORK WITH RESIN DENTURE BASES (INCLUDING ANY CONVENTIONAL CLASPS, RESTS AND TEETH) — CDT 2016

CODING MATCH CORRECTION
1. For an *adjustment* of a cast framework maxillary partial denture, see D5421.
2. For a *repair* of a *cast framework* for a cast framework partial, see D5620.
3. For a *repair* or to replace a *broken clasp*, see D5630.
4. For a *replacement* of *missing or broken* teeth (each tooth), see D5640.
5. For *adding a tooth* to an existing cast framework partial denture, see D5650.
6. For *adding a clasp* to an existing cast framework partial denture, see D5660.
7. For a *rebase* of a cast framework maxillary partial denture, see D5720.
8. For a *chairside reline* of a cast framework maxillary partial denture, see D5740.
9. For a *laboratory* processed *reline* of a cast framework maxillary partial denture, see D5760.
10. For replacing all teeth and acrylic on a cast framework maxillary partial denture see D5670.

COMMENTS
1. Maxillary partial denture (D5213) describes a bilateral partial denture with a cast metal framework.
2. For a *unilateral* cast metal partial denture, see D5281.
3. For an immediate partial denture – cast metal framework, see D5223.

LIMITATIONS
1. D5213 may be subject to age related exclusions (patients must be older than 12 to 16 depending on the plan). These age limitations vary among payers.

2. Diagnostic casts (D0470) are considered a part of the global fee for a maxillary partial denture (D5213).

3. There is typically a five to 10-year exclusion period for a replacement partial denture. To justify the replacement, the documentation (photo(s)/brief narrative) must demonstrate why the existing prosthesis cannot be made serviceable.

4. Follow up adjustments within six months of delivery are typically included in the fee for the prosthesis and are not reimbursed separately. An adjustment made by an office not having delivered the denture might be reimbursed.

5. Replacement of a lost partial denture is not reimbursed.

TIPS

1. If flexible Valplast® or Proplast® *clasps* are used in conjunction with a maxillary cast metal framework, report D5213.

2. For a precision partial, report each precision attachment separately. Use D5862 to describe each attachment which consists of a male-female pair.

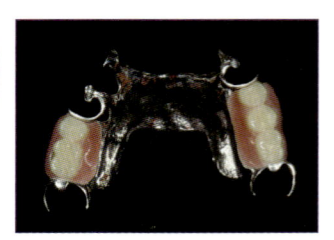

This is an example of a maxillary partial denture with a cast metal framework.

Courtesy Drake Dental Lab

D5214 MANDIBULAR PARTIAL DENTURE – CAST METAL FRAMEWORK WITH RESIN DENTURE BASES (INCLUDING ANY CONVENTIONAL CLASPS, RESTS AND TEETH) — CDT 2016

1. For an *adjustment* of a cast framework mandibular partial denture, see D5422.
2. For a *repair* of a *cast framework* for a cast framework partial, see D5620.
3. For a *repair* or to replace a *broken clasp*, see D5630.
4. For a *replacement* of *missing or broken* teeth (each tooth), see D5640.
5. For *adding a tooth* to an existing cast framework partial denture, see D5650.
6. For *adding a clasp* to an existing cast framework partial denture, see D5660.
7. For a *rebase* of a cast framework mandibular partial denture, see D5721.
8. For a *chairside reline* of a cast framework mandibular partial denture, see D5741.
9. For a *laboratory* processed *reline* of a cast framework mandibular partial denture, see D5761.
10. For *replacing all teeth* and acrylic on a cast framework mandibular partial denture, see D5671.

COMMENTS

1. Mandibular partial denture (D5214) describes a bilateral partial denture with cast metal framework.
2. For a *unilateral* cast metal partial denture, see D5281.
3. For an immediate partial denture – cast metal framework, see D5224.

LIMITATIONS

1. D5214 may be subject to age related exclusions (patients must be older than 12 to 16 depending on the plan). These age limitations vary among payers.

2. Diagnostic casts (D0470) are considered a part of the global fee for a mandibular partial denture (D5214).

3. There is typically a five to 10-year exclusion period for a replacement partial denture. To justify the replacement, the documentation (photo(s)/brief narrative) must demonstrate why the existing prosthesis cannot be made serviceable.

4. Follow up adjustments within six months of delivery are typically included in the fee for the prosthesis and are not reimbursed separately. An adjustment made by an office not having delivered the denture might be reimbursed.

5. Replacement of a lost partial denture is not reimbursed.

TIPS
1. If flexible Valplast® or Proplast® *clasps* are used in conjunction with a mandibular cast metal framework, report D5214.
2. For a precision partial, report each precision attachment separately. Use D5862 to describe each attachment which consists of a male-female pair.

D5221 — NEW PROCEDURE IMMEDIATE MAXILLARY PARTIAL DENTURE – RESIN BASE (INCLUDING ANY CONVENTIONAL CLASPS, RESTS AND TEETH) — CDT 2016

Includes limited follow-up care only; does not include future rebasing/relining procedure(s).

CODING WARNING CORRECTION

D5211 reports a conventional maxillary resin removable partial denture. D5221 describes the immediate resin base partial denture that is placed on the *same day as extractions*.

CODING WATCH CORRECTION

1. D5221 reports the immediate maxillary resin partial delivered on the same day the teeth are extracted.
2. Report an immediate partial (D5221) when extracting natural teeth and immediately placing the resin partial. D5221 may be followed, at an additional fee, by one of these procedures (six-month healing is typically required by many payers before one of these subsequent services will be reimbursed):
   a. Reline (most common), either chairside (D5740) or laboratory processed reline (D5760).
   b. Rebase (D5720) (generally reimbursed a higher UCR fee than a reline).

CODING MATCH CORRECTION

1. For an *adjustment* of an immediate resin maxillary partial denture, see D5421.
2. For a *repair* of an immediate resin partial denture base, see D5610.
3. For a *repair* or to *replace* a broken clasp, see D5630.
4. For a *replacement of missing or broken* teeth (each tooth), see D5640.
5. For *adding a tooth* to an existing immediate resin maxillary partial denture, see D5650.
6. For *adding a clasp* to an existing immediate resin maxillary partial denture, see D5660.
7. For a *rebase* of an immediate resin maxillary partial denture, see D5720.
8. For a *chairside reline* of an immediate resin maxillary partial denture, see D5740.
9. For a *laboratory processed reline* of an immediate maxillary partial denture, see D5760.

COMMENTS The fee for D5221 does not include subsequent hard acrylic relines (D5740 or D5760) or rebases (D5720). Many payers will reimburse a reline or rebase six months or more after delivery of the immediate partial denture.

LIMITATIONS
1. Many payers require a six-month healing period (to the day) following the placement of an immediate maxillary resin partial denture before any subsequent follow up procedures are reimbursed. The healing interval begins at the extraction/insertion date. The healing interval ends with the impression date for the subsequent reline or rebase. Contact the payer regarding the reline or rebase policy for the plan.
2. Follow up adjustments within six months of delivery are typically included in the fee for the D5221 and are not reimbursed. An adjustment made by an office not having delivered the immediate partial denture might be reimbursed.
3. Immediate resin partial dentures may be reported on the impression date, but some payers will only reimburse the procedure on the delivery date (when the teeth are extracted) and the immediate resin partial denture is delivered. Most PPO contracts require immediate resin partial dentures be submitted on the seat date, not the impression date.

D5222 — NEW PROCEDURE IMMEDIATE MANDIBULAR PARTIAL DENTURE – RESIN BASE (INCLUDING ANY CONVENTIONAL CLASPS, RESTS AND TEETH) — CDT 2016

Includes limited follow-up care only; does not include future rebasing/relining procedure(s).

CODING WARNING CORRECTION

D5212 reports a conventional mandibular resin removable partial denture. D5222 describes the immediate resin base partial denture that is placed on the same day as extractions.

CODING WATCH CORRECTION

1. D5222 reports the immediate mandibular resin partial delivered on the same day that teeth are extracted.
2. Report an immediate partial (D5222) when extracting natural teeth and immediately placing the resin partial. D5222 is followed, at an additional fee, by one of these procedures (six-month healing is typically required by many payers before one of these subsequent services will be reimbursed):
   a. Reline (most common), either chairside (D5741) or laboratory processed reline (D5761).
   b. Rebase (D5721) (generally reimbursed at a higher UCR fee than a reline).

CODING MATCH CORRECTION

1. For an *adjustment* of an immediate resin mandibular partial denture, see D5422.
2. For a *repair* of an immediate resin partial denture base, see D5610.
3. For a *repair* or to *replace* a broken clasp, see D5630.
4. For *replacement of missing or broken* teeth (each tooth), see D5640.
5. For *adding a tooth* to an existing immediate resin mandibular partial denture, see D5650.
6. For *adding a clasp* to an existing resin partial denture, see D5660.
7. For a *rebase* of an immediate resin mandibular partial denture, see D5721.
8. For a *chairside reline* of an immediate resin mandibular partial denture, see D5741.
9. For a *laboratory processed reline* of an immediate mandibular partial denture, see D5761.

COMMENTS The fee for D5222 does not include subsequent hard acrylic relines (D5741 or D5761) or rebases (D5721). Many payers will reimburse a reline or rebase six months or more after delivery of the immediate partial denture.

LIMITATIONS
1. Many payers require a six-month healing period (to the day) following the placement of an immediate mandibular resin partial denture before any subsequent follow up procedures are reimbursed. The healing interval begins at the extraction/insertion date. The healing interval ends with the impression date for the subsequent reline or rebase. Contact the payer regarding the reline or rebase policy for the plan.
2. Follow up adjustments within six months of delivery are typically included in the global fee for the D5222 and are not reimbursed. An adjustment made by an office not having delivered the immediate partial denture might be reimbursed.
3. Immediate resin partial dentures may be reported on the impression date, but some payers will only reimburse the procedure on the delivery date (when the teeth are extracted) and the immediate resin partial denture is delivered. Most PPO contracts require immediate resin partial dentures be submitted on the seat date, not the impression date.

D5223 — NEW PROCEDURE IMMEDIATE MAXILLARY PARTIAL DENTURE – CAST METAL FRAMEWORK WITH RESIN DENTURE BASES (INCLUDING ANY CONVENTIONAL CLASPS, RESTS AND TEETH)

CDT 2016

Includes limited follow-up care only; does not include future rebasing/relining procedure(s).

CODING CORRECTION — WARNING

D5213 reports a conventional maxillary partial denture – cast metal framework with resin denture base. D5223 describes the immediate partial denture with cast framework that is placed on the same day as extractions.

CODING CORRECTION — WATCH

1. D5223 reports the immediate maxillary partial denture – cast metal framework with resin bases delivered on the same day the teeth are extracted.

2. Report an immediate partial (D5223) when extracting natural teeth and immediately placing the cast framework partial. D5223 may be followed, at an additional fee, by one of these procedures (six-month healing is typically required by many payers before one of these subsequent services will be reimbursed):

    a. Reline (most common), either chairside (D5740) or laboratory processed reline (D5760).

    b. Rebase (D5720) (generally reimbursed a higher UCR fee than a reline).

CODING CORRECTION — MATCH

1. For an *adjustment* of an immediate cast metal framework with resin bases maxillary partial denture, see D5421.
2. For a *repair* of an immediate cast metal framework with resin bases maxillary partial denture, see D5610.
3. For a *repair* or to *replace* a broken clasp, see D5630.
4. For a *replacement of missing or broken* teeth (each tooth), see D5640.
5. For *adding a tooth* to an existing immediate cast metal framework with resin bases maxillary partial denture, see D5650.
6. For *adding a clasp* to an existing immediate cast metal framework with resin bases maxillary partial denture, see D5660.
7. For a rebase of an immediate cast metal framework with resin bases maxillary partial denture, see D5720.
8. For a *chairside reline* of an immediate cast metal framework with resin bases maxillary partial denture, see D5740.
9. For a *laboratory processed reline* of an immediate cast metal framework with resin bases maxillary partial denture, see D5760.

COMMENTS The fee for D5223 does not include subsequent hard acrylic relines (D5740 or D5760) or rebases (D5720). Many payers will reimburse a reline or rebase six months or more after delivery of the immediate partial denture.

LIMITATIONS

1. Many payers require a six-month healing period (to the day) following the placement of an immediate maxillary cast framework partial denture before any subsequent follow up procedures are reimbursed. The healing interval begins at the extraction/insertion date. The healing interval ends with the impression date for the subsequent reline or rebase. Contact the payer regarding the reline or rebase policy for the plan.

2. Follow up adjustments within six months of delivery are typically included in the fee for D5223 and are not reimbursed. An adjustment made by an office not having delivered the immediate partial denture might be reimbursed.

3. Immediate cast metal framework partial dentures may be reported on the impression date, but some payers will only reimburse the procedure on the delivery date (when the teeth are extracted) and the immediate partial denture is delivered. Most PPO contracts require immediate partial dentures be submitted on the seat date, not the impression date.

D5224 — IMMEDIATE MANDIBULAR PARTIAL DENTURE – CAST METAL FRAMEWORK WITH RESIN DENTURE BASES (INCLUDING ANY CONVENTIONAL CLASPS, RESTS AND TEETH)

NEW PROCEDURE — CDT 2016

Includes limited follow-up care only; does not include future rebasing/relining procedure(s).

CODING WARNING CORRECTION

D5214 reports a conventional mandibular partial denture – cast metal framework with resin denture base. D5224 describes the immediate partial denture with cast framework that is placed on the same day as extractions.

CODING WATCH CORRECTION

1. D5224 reports the immediate maxillary partial denture – cast metal framework with resin bases delivered on the same day the teeth are extracted.

2. Report an immediate partial (D5224) when extracting natural teeth and immediately placing the cast framework partial. D5224 may be followed, at an additional fee, by one of these procedures (six-month healing is typically required by many payers before one of these subsequent services will be reimbursed):

    a. Reline (most common), either chairside (D5741) or laboratory processed reline (D5761).

    b. Rebase (D5721) (generally reimbursed a higher UCR fee than a reline).

CODING MATCH CORRECTION

1. For an *adjustment* of an immediate cast metal framework with resin bases mandibular partial denture, see D5422.

2. For a *repair* of an immediate cast metal framework with resin bases mandibular partial denture, see D5610.

3. For a *repair* or to *replace* a broken clasp, see D5630.

4. For a *replacement of missing or broken* teeth (each tooth), see D5640.

5. For *adding a tooth* to an existing immediate cast metal framework with resin bases mandibular partial denture, see D5650.

6. For *adding a clasp* to an existing immediate cast metal framework with resin bases mandibular partial denture, see D5660.

7. For a *rebase* of an immediate cast metal framework with resin bases mandibular partial denture, see D5721.

8. For a *chairside reline* of an immediate cast metal framework with resin bases mandibular partial denture, see D5741.

9. For a *laboratory processed reline* of an immediate cast metal framework with resin bases maxillary partial denture, see D5761.

COMMENTS — The fee for D5224 does not include subsequent hard acrylic relines (D5741 or D5761) or rebases (D5721). Many payers will reimburse a reline or rebase six months or more after delivery of the immediate partial denture.

LIMITATIONS

1. Many payers require a six-month healing period (to the day) following the placement of an immediate mandibular partial denture before any subsequent follow up procedures are reimbursed. The healing interval begins at the extraction/insertion date. The healing interval ends with the impression date for the subsequent reline or rebase. Contact the payer regarding the reline or rebase policy for the plan.

2. Follow up adjustments within six months of delivery are typically included in the fee for D5224 and are not reimbursed. An adjustment made by an office not having delivered the immediate partial denture might be reimbursed.

3. Immediate cast metal framework partial dentures may be reported on the impression date, but some payers will only reimburse the procedure on the delivery date (when the teeth are extracted) and the immediate partial denture is delivered. Most PPO contracts require immediate partial dentures be submitted on the seat date, not the impression date.

D5225   MAXILLARY PARTIAL DENTURE – FLEXIBLE BASE (INCLUDING ANY CLASPS, RESTS AND TEETH)

CDT 2016

CODING MATCH CORRECTION

1. For an *adjustment* of a flexible base maxillary partial denture, see D5421.
2. For a *repair* of a flexible base partial denture *base*, see D5610.
3. For a *repair* or to replace a *broken clasp*, see D5630.
4. For a *replacement* of *missing or broken* teeth (each tooth), see D5640.
5. For *adding a tooth* to an existing flexible base partial denture, see D5650.
6. For *adding a clasp* to an existing flexible base partial denture, see D5660.
7. For a *rebase* of a flexible base maxillary partial denture, see D5720.
8. For a *chairside reline* of a flexible base maxillary partial denture, see D5740.
9. For *laboratory* processed reline of a flexible base maxillary partial denture, see D5760.

Note: Flexible base resin partials are difficult to adjust, and particularly, repair. Repairs for this type of partial would not be routine. *Confirm* with the doctor that the repairs are in fact for a flexible base resin partial. These would be unusual repairs.

COMMENTS
1. Maxillary partial denture – flexible base (D5225) is used to describe partials fabricated from materials such as Valplast® or Proplast® type materials.
2. Diagnostic casts (D0470) are included in the global fee for D5225.

LIMITATIONS
1. There is typically a five to 10-year exclusion period for a replacement partial denture. To justify the replacement, the documentation (photo(s)/brief narrative) must demonstrate why the existing prosthesis cannot be made serviceable.
2. Follow-up adjustments within six months of delivery are typically included in the fee for the prosthesis and are not reimbursed separately. An adjustment made by an office not having delivered the denture might be reimbursed.
3. Replacement of a lost partial denture is not reimbursed.
4. D5225 may be excluded if the patient is under 12 to 16 years of age. This varies according to the plan.
5. D5225 may be reimbursed with an alternate benefit of D5211. In some cases the reimbursement is equivalent to the fee for a cast metal framework (D5213). Some payers reimburse at a lower rate, 20% below the D5213 fee. Some payers may reimburse at a rate similar to the maxillary partial denture – resin base (D5211) partial denture fee.

TIPS
1. If Valplast® or Proplast® *flexible* clasps are used in conjunction with a cast metal framework partial denture, report D5213.
2. For a maxillary *unilateral* partial using Valplast® or Proplast® flexible base materials report D5225. Thus, the code is used to report *any* type of flexible base maxillary partial denture, whether it is bilateral or unilateral.

PHOTO

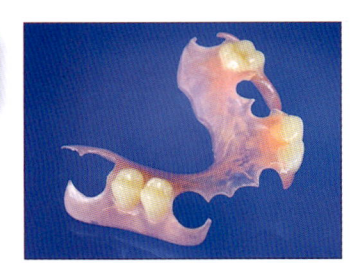

This is an example of a flexible base maxillary partial denture made of Valplast®.

Courtesy Keller Dental Lab

D5226 — MANDIBULAR PARTIAL DENTURE – FLEXIBLE BASE (INCLUDING ANY CLASPS, RESTS AND TEETH) — CDT 2016

CODING MATCH CORRECTION

1. For an *adjustment* of a flexible base mandibular partial denture, see D5422.
2. For a *repair* of a flexible base partial denture *base*, see D5610.
3. For a *repair* or to replace a *broken clasp*, see D5630.
4. For a *replacement* of *missing or broken* teeth (each tooth), see D5640.
5. For *adding a tooth* to an existing flexible base partial denture, see D5650.
6. For *adding a clasp* to an existing flexible base partial denture, see D5660.
7. For a *rebase* of a flexible base mandibular partial denture, see D5721.
8. For a *chairside reline* of a flexible base mandibular partial denture, see D5741.
9. For a *laboratory* processed *reline* of a flexible base mandibular partial denture, see D5761.

Note: Flexible base resin partials are difficult to adjust, and particularly, repair. Repairs for this type of partial would be very unusual. *Confirm* with the doctor that the repairs are in fact for a flexible base resin partial. These would not be routine.

COMMENTS

1. Mandibular partial denture – flexible base (D5226) is used to describe partials fabricated from materials such as Valplast® or Proplast® type materials.
2. Diagnostic casts (D0470) are included in the global fee for D5226.

LIMITATIONS

1. There is typically a five to 10-year exclusion period for a replacement partial denture. To justify the replacement, the documentation (photo(s)/brief narrative) must demonstrate why the existing prosthesis cannot be made serviceable.
2. Follow up adjustments within six months of delivery are typically included in the fee for the prosthesis and are not reimbursed separately. An adjustment made by an office not having delivered the denture might be reimbursed.
3. Replacement of a lost partial denture is not reimbursed.
4. D5226 may be excluded if the patient is under 12 to 16 years of age. This varies according to the plan.
5. D5226 may be reimbursed with an alternate benefit of code D5212. In some cases the reimbursement is equivalent to the fee for a cast metal framework (D5214). Some payers reimburse at a lower rate, 20% below the D5214 fee. Some payers may reimburse at a rate similar to the mandibular partial denture – resin base (D5212) partial denture fee.

TIPS

1. If Valplast® or Proplast® *flexible* clasps are used in conjunction with a cast metal framework partial denture, report D5214.
2. For a mandibular *unilateral* partial using Valplast® or Proplast® flexible base materials report D5226. Thus, the code is used to report *any* type of flexible base mandibular partial denture, whether it is bilateral or unilateral.

D5281 — REMOVABLE UNILATERAL PARTIAL DENTURE – ONE PIECE CAST METAL (INCLUDING CLASPS AND TEETH) — CDT 2016

CODING MATCH CORRECTION

1. For an *adjustment* of a unilateral maxillary cast partial denture, see D5421.
2. For an *adjustment* of a unilateral mandibular cast partial denture, see D5422.
3. For a *repair* of a *cast framework*, see D5620.
4. For a *repair* or to replace a *broken clasp*, see D5630.
5. For a *replacement of missing or broken* teeth (each tooth), see D5640.
6. For *adding a tooth* to an existing unilateral cast partial denture, see D5650.
7. For *adding a clasp* to an existing unilateral cast partial denture, see D5660.
8. For a *rebase* of a unilateral maxillary cast partial denture, see D5720.

9. For a *rebase* of a unilateral mandibular cast partial denture, see D5721.
10. For a *chairside reline* of a unilateral maxillary cast partial denture, see D5740.
11. For a *chairside reline* of a unilateral mandibular cast partial denture, see D5741.
12. For a *laboratory* processed *reline* of a unilateral maxillary cast partial denture, see D5760.
13. For a *laboratory* processed *reline* of a unilateral mandibular cast partial denture, see D5761.
14. For *replacing all teeth* and *acrylic* on a unilateral maxillary cast partial denture, see D5670.
15. For *replacing all teeth* and *acrylic* on a unilateral mandibular cast partial denture, see D5671.

COMMENTS
1. This one piece cast metal *unilateral* partial denture is also called a "Nesbit partial." It replaces a missing tooth/teeth on one side of the mouth in either the upper or lower arch.
2. Diagnostic casts (D0470) are included in the global fee for D5281.

LIMITATIONS
1. There is typically a five to 10-year exclusion period for a replacement partial denture. To justify the replacement, the documentation (photo(s)/brief narrative) must demonstrate why the existing prosthesis cannot be made serviceable.
2. Follow up adjustments within six months of delivery are typically included in the fee for the prosthesis and are not reimbursed separately. An adjustment made by an office not having delivered the denture might be reimbursed.
3. Reimbursement for D5281 may be excluded if the patient is under 12 to 16 years of age, depending on the plan.

TIPS
1. Use D5281 to report a one piece cast metal *unilateral* partial with Valplast® or Proplast® type clasps.
2. For a *unilateral* or bilateral Valplast® or Proplast® type flexible base partial, use D5225 or D5226 to describe this type of partial denture.
3. For a *unilateral* or bilateral resin base partial, report D5211 or D5212.

NARRATIVES Specify arch in the narrative.

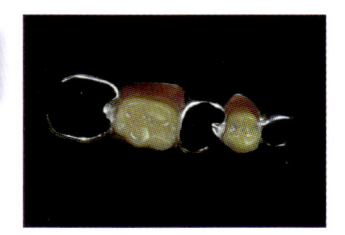

This is an example of a unilateral (only one side of the arch) partial denture.

Courtesy of Drake Dental Lab

ADJUSTMENTS TO DENTURES — CDT 2016

D5410 ADJUST COMPLETE DENTURE – MAXILLARY — CDT 2016

Use this code to report adjustments made to:

- Maxillary complete denture (D5110).
- Maxillary immediate denture (D5130).
- Maxillary interim complete denture (D5810).
- Maxillary complete (natural tooth) overdenture (D5863).
- Maxillary implant/abutment supported removable denture for completely edentulous arch (D6111).

LIMITATIONS 1. Any maxillary denture adjustments provided within six months of delivery of the prosthesis are typically included in the fee for the prosthesis and are not reimbursed separately. Adjustments provided six months *after* delivery may be reimbursed up to twice per 12-month period by some payers.

2. A complete denture adjustment provided by a *different* office than the fabricator of the denture may be reimbursable less than six months after delivery of the complete denture.

D5411 ADJUST COMPLETE DENTURE – MANDIBULAR — CDT 2016

Use this code to report adjustments made to:
- Mandibular complete denture (D5120).
- Mandibular immediate denture (D5140).
- Mandibular interim complete denture (D5811).
- Mandibular complete (natural tooth) overdenture (D5865).
- Mandibular implant/abutment supported removable denture for completely edentulous arch (D6112).

LIMITATIONS 1. Any mandibular denture adjustments provided within six months of delivery of the prosthesis are typically included in the fee for the prosthesis and are not reimbursed separately. Adjustments provided six months *after* delivery may be reimbursed up to twice per 12-month period by some payers.

2. A complete denture adjustment provided by a *different* office than the fabricator of the denture may be reimbursable less than six months after delivery of the complete denture.

D5421 ADJUST PARTIAL DENTURE – MAXILLARY — CDT 2016

Use this code to report adjustments made to maxillary resin base, cast metal framework, flexible base, unilateral, interim partial dentures and implant/abutment supported removable dentures for partially edentulous arches.

LIMITATIONS 1. Maxillary partial dentures (D5211/D5213/D5221/D5223/D5225/D5820/D5864/D6054): Any maxillary denture adjustments provided within six months of delivery of the prosthesis are typically included in the fee for the prosthesis and are not reimbursed separately. Adjustments provided six months *after* delivery may be reimbursed up to twice per 12-month period by some payers.

2. A denture adjustment provided by a *different* office than the fabricator of the denture may be reimbursable less than six months after delivery of the complete denture.

D5422 ADJUST PARTIAL DENTURE – MANDIBULAR — CDT 2016

Use this code to report adjustments provided for resin base, cast metal framework, flexible base, unilateral, interim partial dentures, and implant/abutment supported removable dentures for partially edentulous arches.

LIMITATIONS 1. Mandibular partial dentures (D5212/D5214/D5222/D5224/D5226/D5821/D5866/D6054): Any mandibular denture adjustments provided within six months of delivery of the prosthesis are typically included in the fee for the prosthesis and are not reimbursed separately. Adjustments provided six months *after* delivery may be reimbursed up to twice per 12-month period by some payers.

2. A denture adjustment provided by a *different* office than the fabricator of the denture may be reimbursable less than six months after delivery of the complete denture.

REPAIRS TO COMPLETE DENTURES — CDT 2016

D5510 — REPAIR BROKEN COMPLETE DENTURE BASE — CDT 2016

This code reports a repair of a broken upper (maxillary) or lower (mandibular) complete denture base.

LIMITATIONS
1. Some payers limit reimbursement for the repair fee to less than one half the fee normally reimbursed for a new removable prosthesis.
2. Providing a repair to a complete denture (D5110/D5120/D5130/D5140/D5863/D5865/D6110/D6111) base may extend the replacement limitation period of that prosthesis for two to five years. The repair may "reset" the limitation period (typically five to 10-years) for replacement of the repaired prosthesis with a new prosthesis. Some payers will reimburse a repair once per arch, per 12 months. The reimbursement for denture repairs (D5110/D5120/D5130/D5140/D5863/D5865/D6110/D6111) is highly variable. It is recommended that the coverage and limitations be verified before providing this service.

TIPS
Report the replacement/repair of missing or broken teeth (D5520) in addition to the repair of the denture base. Each tooth repaired/replaced (D5520) should be reported separately.

NARRATIVES
A brief narrative should describe the arch and the procedure performed, and identify the original delivery date of the prosthesis.

D5520 — REPLACE MISSING OR BROKEN TEETH – COMPLETE DENTURE (EACH TOOTH) — CDT 2016

This code is used to report the replacement of a missing or broken tooth for an upper (maxillary) or lower (mandibular) complete denture.

TIPS
Report the replacement/repair of missing or broken teeth (D5520) separately from the repair of base or framework. Each tooth repaired/replaced should be reported as a separate procedure.

NARRATIVES
A brief narrative should identify the arch, tooth number, the procedure performed, and the original delivery date of the prosthesis.

REPAIRS TO PARTIAL DENTURES — CDT 2016

D5610 — REPAIR RESIN DENTURE BASE — CDT 2016

Use this code to report a resin denture base repair for an upper (maxillary) or lower (mandibular) partial denture.

LIMITATIONS	1. Some payers limit reimbursement for the repair fee to less than one half the fee normally reimbursed for a new partial denture.
	2. Providing a repair to a partial denture base may extend the replacement limitation period of that prosthesis for two to five years. Depending on the cost, a repair may "reset" the limitation period (typically five to 10-years) for replacement of the repaired prosthesis with a new prosthesis. Some payers will reimburse a repair once per arch, per 12 months. The reimbursement for partial denture repairs is highly variable. Because of this variability, it is recommended that the coverage and limitations be verified before providing this service.
TIPS	Report the repair of the resin partial denture base separately from other repairs.
NARRATIVES	A brief narrative should identify the arch, the procedure performed, and the original delivery date of the prosthesis.

D5620 — REPAIR CAST FRAMEWORK — CDT 2016

(Coding Match Correction)

Use this code to report the repair of a cast framework for an upper or lower partial denture.

LIMITATIONS	1. Some payers limit reimbursement for the repair fee to less than one half the fee normally reimbursed for a new removable prosthesis.
	2. Providing a repair to a cast framework may extend the replacement limitation period of that prosthesis for two to five years. Depending on the cost, a repair may "reset" the limitation period (typically five to 10-years) for replacement of the repaired prosthesis with a new prosthesis. Some payers will reimburse a repair once per arch, per 12 months. The reimbursement for partial denture repairs is highly variable. Because of this variability, it is recommended that the coverage and limitations be verified before providing this service.
TIPS	Report the repair of the cast framework separately from other repairs.
NARRATIVES	A brief narrative should identify the arch, the procedure performed, and the original delivery date of the prosthesis.

D5630 — REVISED REPAIR OR REPLACE BROKEN CLASP – PER TOOTH — CDT 2016

REVISIONS	REPAIR OR REPLACE BROKEN CLASP – PER TOOTH

(Coding Match Correction)

Use this code to describe the repair or replacement of a broken clasp per tooth for a partial denture.

LIMITATIONS	1. Some payers limit reimbursement for the repair fee to less than one half the fee normally reimbursed for a new removable prosthesis.
	2. Providing a repair or replacement of a broken clasp may extend the replacement limitation period of that prosthesis for two to five years. Depending on the cost, a repair may "reset" the limitation period (typically five to 10-years) for replacement of the repaired prosthesis with a new prosthesis. Some payers will reimburse a repair once per arch, per 12 months. The reimbursement for partial denture repairs is highly variable. Because of this variability, it is recommended that the coverage and limitations be verified before providing this service.

TIPS	Report the repair or replacement of a broken clasp separately from other repairs.

NARRATIVES	A brief narrative should identify the procedure performed and identify the original delivery date of the prosthesis.

D5640 — REPLACE BROKEN TEETH – PER TOOTH — CDT 2016

CODING MATCH CORRECTION

1. Use this code to describe the replacement of a broken tooth on a partial denture.
2. Report the replacement of each tooth separately.

LIMITATIONS

1. Some payers may limit reimbursement for the repair fee to less than one half the fee originally reimbursed for a new prosthesis.
2. Replacing broken teeth on an existing partial may extend the replacement limitation period of that prosthesis for two to five years. Depending on the cost, a repair may "reset" the limitation period (typically five to 10-years) for replacement of the repaired prosthesis with a new prosthesis. Some payers will reimburse a repair once per arch, per 12 months. The reimbursement for broken tooth repairs is highly variable. Because of this variability, it is recommended that the coverage and limitations be verified before providing this service.

NARRATIVES A brief narrative should identify tooth number, the procedure performed, and note the original delivery date of the prosthesis.

D5650 — ADD TOOTH TO EXISTING PARTIAL DENTURE — CDT 2016

CODING MATCH CORRECTION

This code reports adding a tooth to an existing partial denture. Report each tooth separately.

LIMITATIONS Adding a tooth to an existing partial denture may extend the replacement limitation period of that prosthesis for two to five years. Depending on the cost, the addition of a tooth to an existing prosthesis may "reset" the limitation period (typically five to 10-years) for replacement of the repaired prosthesis with a new prosthesis. Some payers will reimburse a repair once per arch, per 12 months. The reimbursement for D5650 is highly variable. Because of this variability, it is recommended that the coverage and limitations be verified before providing this service.

NARRATIVES A brief narrative should identify the tooth number, the procedure performed, and the original delivery date of the prosthesis.

D5660 — REVISED ADD CLASP TO EXISTING PARTIAL DENTURE – PER TOOTH — CDT 2016

REVISIONS ADD CLASP TO EXISTING PARTIAL DENTURE – PER TOOTH

CODING MATCH CORRECTION

D5660 reports adding a clasp to an existing partial denture, per tooth.

LIMITATIONS Adding a clasp to an existing partial denture may extend the replacement limitation period of that prosthesis for two to five years. Depending on the cost, the addition of a clasp may "reset" the limitation period (typically five to 10-years) for replacement of the repaired prosthesis with a new prosthesis. Some payers will reimburse a repair once per arch, per 12 months. The reimbursement for D5660 is highly variable. Because of this variability, it is recommended that the coverage and limitations be verified before providing this service.

NARRATIVES A brief narrative should identify the tooth number and clasp position, the procedure performed, and the original delivery date of the prosthesis.

D5670 — REPLACE ALL TEETH AND ACRYLIC ON CAST METAL FRAMEWORK (MAXILLARY)
CDT 2016

CODING MATCH CORRECTION

D5670 describes the replacement of the existing teeth and acrylic (the pink part) on an existing maxillary cast metal framework with all new teeth and acrylic.

LIMITATIONS
1. D5670 may be covered once per five to 10-year period as per the contract's replacement language. Replacing all teeth and acrylic on a cast metal framework may "reset" the limitation period (typically five to 10-years) for replacement of the repaired prosthesis with a new prosthesis.
2. The replacement of all teeth and acrylic on a maxillary cast metal framework may be reimbursed at less than one half the fee normally reimbursed for a new prosthesis.

NARRATIVES A brief narrative should identify the arch, teeth numbers, the procedure performed, and the original delivery date of the prosthesis.

D5671 — REPLACE ALL TEETH AND ACRYLIC ON CAST METAL FRAMEWORK (MANDIBULAR)
CDT 2016

CODING MATCH CORRECTION

D5671 describes the replacement of the existing teeth and acrylic (the pink part) on an existing mandibular cast metal framework with all new teeth and acrylic.

LIMITATIONS
1. D5671 may be covered once per five to 10-year period as per the contract's replacement language. Replacing all teeth and acrylic on a cast metal framework may "reset" the limitation period (typically five to 10-years) for replacement of the repaired prosthesis with a new prosthesis.
2. The replacement of all teeth and acrylic on a maxillary cast metal framework may be reimbursed at less than one half the fee normally reimbursed for a new prosthesis.

NARRATIVES A brief narrative should identify the arch, teeth numbers, the procedure performed, and the original delivery date of the prosthesis.

DENTURE REBASE PROCEDURES
CDT 2016

Rebase – process of refitting a denture by replacing the base material.

D5710 REBASE COMPLETE MAXILLARY DENTURE — CDT 2016

CODING MATCH CORRECTION

This code reports rebasing a complete maxillary (upper) denture.

COMMENTS

1. "Rebase" is the process of removing the old denture base material (the pink part of a denture) and replacing it with new denture base material.
2. "Reline" is the process of resurfacing the tissue side of the denture with new denture base material. A rebase replaces the old denture base. A reline resurfaces the old base material.
3. Rebases are laboratory processed.

LIMITATIONS

1. Follow up adjustments within six months of the rebase are typically included in the fee for D5710 and are not reimbursed separately. If an adjustment is made by an office that did not deliver the denture, that office might be reimbursed. This should be noted in a brief narrative.
2. Providing a rebase to a maxillary denture may extend the replacement limitation period of that prosthesis for two to five years. The rebase may "reset" the limitation period (typically five to 10-years) for replacement of the rebased prosthesis with a new prosthesis. Some payers will reimburse a rebase once per arch, per 12 months. The reimbursement for the rebase of a complete denture is highly variable. It is recommended that the coverage and limitations be verified before providing this service.
3. A maxillary denture rebase may be denied when provided for cosmetic reasons, but may be approved when justified by alveolar ridge resorption and to treat changes in occlusion.

TIPS

Reimbursement for a rebase is typically higher than for a chairside or a laboratory processed reline.

D5711 REBASE COMPLETE MANDIBULAR DENTURE — CDT 2016

CODING MATCH CORRECTION

This code reports rebasing a complete mandibular (lower) denture.

COMMENTS

1. "Rebase" is the process of removing the old denture base material (the pink part of a denture) and replacing it with new denture base material.
2. "Reline" is the process of resurfacing the tissue side of the denture with new denture base material. A rebase replaces the old denture base. A reline resurfaces the old base material.
3. Rebases are laboratory processed.

LIMITATIONS

1. Follow up adjustments within six months of the rebase are typically included in the fee for D5711 and are not reimbursed separately. If an adjustment is made by an office that did not deliver the denture, that office might be reimbursed. This should be noted in a brief narrative.
2. Providing a rebase to a mandibular denture may extend the replacement limitation period of that prosthesis for two to five years. The rebase may "reset" the limitation period (typically five to 10-years) for replacement of the rebased prosthesis with a new prosthesis. Some payers will reimburse a rebase once per arch, per 12 months. The reimbursement for complete denture rebase is highly variable. It is recommended that the coverage and limitations be verified before providing this service.
3. A mandibular denture rebase may be denied when provided for cosmetic reasons, but may be approved when justified by alveolar ridge resorption and to treat changes in occlusion.

TIPS   Reimbursement for a rebase is typically higher than for a chairside or laboratory processed reline.

D5720 — REBASE MAXILLARY PARTIAL DENTURE   CDT 2016

This code reports the associated rebasing of a maxillary (upper) partial denture.

COMMENTS
1. "Rebase" is the process of removing the old denture base material (the pink part of a partial denture) and replacing it with new denture base material.
2. "Reline" is the process of resurfacing the tissue side of the denture with new denture base material. A rebase replaces the old denture base. A reline resurfaces the old base material.
3. Rebases are laboratory processed.

LIMITATIONS
1. Follow up adjustments within six months of the partial denture rebase are typically included in the fee for D5720 and are not reimbursed separately. If an adjustment is made by an office that did not deliver the denture, that office might be reimbursed. This should be noted in a brief narrative.
2. Providing a rebase to a maxillary partial denture may extend the replacement limitation period of that prosthesis for two to five years. The rebase may "reset" the limitation period (typically five to 10-years) for replacement of the rebased prosthesis with a new prosthesis. Some payers will reimburse a rebase once per arch, per 12 months. The reimbursement for the rebase of a mandibular partial denture repair is highly variable. It is recommended that the coverage and limitations be verified before providing this service.
3. A maxillary partial denture rebase may be denied when provided for cosmetic reasons, but may be approved when justified by alveolar ridge resorption and to treat changes in occlusion.

TIPS
1. Reimbursement for a rebase is typically higher than for a chairside or laboratory processed reline.
2. See D5670 for replacement of all teeth and acrylic base on an existing maxillary cast partial framework.

D5721 — REBASE MANDIBULAR PARTIAL DENTURE   CDT 2016

This code reports the associated rebasing of a mandibular (lower) partial denture.

COMMENTS
1. "Rebase" is the process of removing the old denture base material (the pink part of a partial denture) and replacing it with new denture base material.
2. "Reline" is the process of resurfacing the tissue side of the denture with new denture base material. A rebase replaces the old denture base. A reline resurfaces the old base material.
3. Rebases are laboratory processed.

LIMITATIONS
1. Follow up adjustments within six months of the partial denture rebase are typically included in the fee for D5721 and are not reimbursed separately. If an adjustment is made by an office that did not deliver the denture, that office might be reimbursed. This should be noted in a brief narrative.

2. Providing a rebase to a mandibular partial denture may extend the replacement limitation period of that prosthesis for two to five years. The rebase may "reset" the limitation period (typically five to 10-years) for replacement of the rebased prosthesis with a new prosthesis. Some payers will reimburse a rebase once per arch, per 12 months. The reimbursement for the rebase of a mandibular partial denture repair is highly variable. It is recommended that the coverage and limitations be verified before providing this service.

3. A mandibular partial rebase may be denied when provided for cosmetic reasons, but may be approved when justified by alveolar ridge resorption and to treat changes in occlusion.

TIPS
1. Reimbursement for a rebase is typically higher than for a chairside or laboratory processed reline.
2. See D5671 for replacement of all teeth and acrylic base on an existing mandibular cast partial framework.

DENTURE RELINE PROCEDURES — CDT 2016

Reline is the process of resurfacing the tissue side of a denture with new base material.

D5730 RELINE COMPLETE MAXILLARY DENTURE (CHAIRSIDE) — CDT 2016

Coding Watch Correction

1. Some practices err when reporting a *chairside* reline code instead of the in office *processed* (oven, pressure bath, etc.) *laboratory* reline. Report the laboratory reline code if the reline is *processed* either in the office *or* by an outside laboratory. A Triad® oven processed or a pressurized hot water bath is a laboratory reline and should be reported as D5750.

2. It is an error to report a chairside reline as tissue conditioning. Tissue conditioning is used to promote healing of unhealthy ridges prior to taking an impression for a final prosthesis or *prior* to a rebase or a reline. See D5850 for further details on tissue conditioning (maxillary).

Coding Match Correction

This code reports the associated chairside relining of a complete maxillary (upper) denture (D5110).

COMMENTS
1. "Rebase" is the process of removing the old denture base material (the pink part of a denture) and replacing it with new denture base material. See D5710.
2. "Reline" is the process of resurfacing the tissue side of the denture with new denture base material. A reline resurfaces the old base material.
3. Relines can be chairside or laboratory processed.

LIMITATIONS
1. Follow-up adjustments provided within six months of the reline are typically included in the fee for D5730 and are not reimbursed separately. Adjustment made by an office not having delivered the reline might be reimbursed.
2. Providing a reline to a denture may extend the replacement limitation period of that prosthesis two to five years. The reline may "reset" the limitation period (typically five to 10-years) for replacement of the relined prosthesis with a new prosthesis. Some payers will reimburse a reline once per arch, per 12 months. The reimbursement for relines is highly variable. Because of this variability, it is recommended that the coverage and limitations be verified before providing this service.
3. A reline may be denied when provided for cosmetic reasons, but may be approved when justified by alveolar ridge resorption and to treat changes in occlusion.

TIPS
1. Reimbursement for a laboratory processed reline is typically higher than for a chairside reline.
2. Reimbursement for a rebase is typically higher than for a chairside reline.

D5731   RELINE COMPLETE MANDIBULAR DENTURE (CHAIRSIDE)   CDT 2016

CODING WATCH CORRECTION

1. Some practices err when reporting a *chairside* reline code instead of the in office *processed* (oven, pressure bath, etc.) *laboratory* reline. Report the laboratory reline code if the reline is *processed* either in the office *or* by an outside laboratory. A Triad® oven processed or pressurized hot water bath is a laboratory reline and should be reported as D5751.

2. It is an error to report a chairside reline as tissue conditioning. Tissue conditioning is used to promote healing of an unhealthy ridge *prior* to taking an impression for a final prosthesis or prior to a rebase or a reline. See D5851 for further details on tissue conditioning (mandibular).

CODING MATCH CORRECTION

D5731 reports the chairside relining of a complete mandibular (lower) denture (D5120).

COMMENTS

1. "Rebase" is the process of removing the old denture base material (the pink part of a denture) and replacing it with new denture base material. See D5711.

2. "Reline" is the process of resurfacing the tissue side of the denture with new denture base material. A reline resurfaces the old base material.

3. Relines can be chairside or laboratory processed.

LIMITATIONS

1. Follow up adjustments provided within six months of the reline are typically included in the fee for D5731 and are not reimbursed separately. If an adjustment is made by an office that did not deliver the denture, that office might be reimbursed. This should be noted in a brief narrative.

2. Providing a reline to a denture may extend the replacement limitation period of that prosthesis for two to five years. The reline may "reset" the limitation period (typically five to 10-years) for replacement of the relined prosthesis with a new prosthesis. Some payers will reimburse a reline once per arch, per 12 months. The reimbursement for a reline is highly variable. Because of this variability, it is recommended that the coverage and limitations be verified before providing this service.

3. A reline may be denied when provided for cosmetic reasons, but may be approved when justified by alveolar ridge resorption and to treat changes in occlusion.

TIPS

1. Reimbursement for a laboratory processed reline is typically higher than for a chairside reline.

2. Reimbursement for a rebase is typically higher than for a chairside reline.

D5740   RELINE MAXILLARY PARTIAL DENTURE (CHAIRSIDE)   CDT 2016

CODING WATCH CORRECTION

1. Some practices err when reporting a *chairside* reline code instead of the in office *processed* (oven, pressure bath, etc.) *laboratory* reline. Report the laboratory reline code if the reline is *processed* either in the office *or* by an outside laboratory. A Triad® oven processed or pressurized hot water bath laboratory reline of a maxillary partial denture and should be reported as D5760.

2. It is an error to report a chairside reline as tissue conditioning. Tissue conditioning is used to promote healing of unhealthy ridges *prior* to taking an impression for a final prosthesis or prior to a rebase or a reline. See D5850 for further details on tissue conditioning (maxillary).

CODING MATCH CORRECTION

D5740 reports the chairside relining of a maxillary upper partial denture (D5211 or D5213).

COMMENTS

1. "Rebase" is the process of removing the old denture base material (the pink part of the partial denture) and replacing it with new denture base material.

2. "Reline" is the process of resurfacing the tissue side of the denture with new denture base material. A reline *resurfaces* the old base material.

3. Relines can be chairside or laboratory processed.

LIMITATIONS

1. Follow up adjustments provided within six months of the reline are typically included in the fee for D5740 and are not reimbursed separately. If an adjustment is made by an office that did not deliver the denture, that office might be reimbursed. This should be noted in a brief narrative.

2. Providing a reline to a partial denture may extend the replacement limitation period of that prosthesis for two to five years. The reline may "reset" the limitation period (typically five to 10-years) for replacement of the relined prosthesis with a new prosthesis. Some payers will reimburse a reline once per arch, per 12 months. The reimbursement for a reline is highly variable. Because of this variability, it is recommenced that the coverage and limitations be verified before providing this service.

3. A reline may be denied when provided for cosmetic reasons, but may be approved when justified by alveolar ridge resorption and to treat changes in occlusion.

TIPS

1. Reimbursement for a laboratory processed reline is typically higher than for a chairside reline.

2. Reimbursement for a rebase is typically higher than for a chairside reline.

D5741 — RELINE MANDIBULAR PARTIAL DENTURE (CHAIRSIDE) — CDT 2016

CODING WATCH CORRECTION

1. Some practices err when reporting a *chairside* reline code instead of the in office *processed* (oven, pressure bath, etc.) *laboratory* reline. Report the laboratory reline code if the reline is *processed* either in the office *or* by an outside laboratory. A Triad® oven processed or pressurized hot water bath laboratory reline of a mandibular partial denture should be reported as D5761.

2. It is an error to report a chairside reline as tissue conditioning. Tissue conditioning is used to promote healing of an unhealthy ridge *prior* to taking an impression for a final prosthesis or prior to a rebase or a reline. See D5851 for further details on tissue conditioning (mandibular).

CODING MATCH CORRECTION

D5741 reports the chairside relining of a mandibular (lower) partial denture (D5212 or D5214).

COMMENTS

1. "Rebase" is the process of removing the old denture base material (the pink part of a partial denture) and replacing it with new denture base material.

2. "Reline" is the process of resurfacing the tissue side of the denture with new denture base material. A reline resurfaces the old base material.

3. Relines can be chairside or laboratory processed.

LIMITATIONS

1. Follow up adjustments provided within six months of the reline are typically included in the fee for D5741 and are not reimbursed separately. If an adjustment is made by an office that did not deliver the denture, that office might be reimbursed. This should be noted in a brief narrative.

2. Providing a reline to a partial denture may extend the replacement limitation period of that prosthesis for two to five years. The reline may "reset" the limitation period (typically five to 10-years) for replacement of the relined prosthesis with a new prosthesis. Some payers will reimburse a reline once per arch, per 12 months. The reimbursement for a reline is highly variable. Because of this variability, it is recommended that the coverage and limitations be verified before providing this service.

3. A reline may be denied when provided for cosmetic reasons, but may be approved when justified by alveolar ridge resorption and to treat changes in occlusion.

TIPS
1. Reimbursement for a laboratory processed reline is typically higher than for a chairside reline.
2. Reimbursement for a rebase is typically higher than for a chairside reline.

D5750 RELINE COMPLETE MAXILLARY DENTURE (LABORATORY) — CDT 2016

Coding Watch Correction: Some practices err when reporting a *chairside* reline code instead of the in office *processed* (oven, pressure bath, etc.) *laboratory* reline. Report the laboratory reline code if the reline is *processed* either in the office *or* by an outside lab. A Triad® oven processed or pressurized hot water bath laboratory reline of a complete maxillary denture is reported as D5750.

Coding Match Correction: D5750 reports the laboratory processed reline of a complete maxillary (upper) denture (D5110).

COMMENTS
1. "Rebase" is the process of removing the old base material (the pink part of a denture) and replacing it with new base material.
2. "Reline," is the process of resurfacing the tissue side of the denture with new base material. A reline *resurfaces* the old base material.
3. D5750 is used to report *laboratory processed* (oven or pressurized hot water bath) maxillary complete denture hard acrylic relines. Laboratory processing can occur in office *or in* an outside laboratory.

LIMITATIONS
1. Follow up adjustments provided within six months of the reline are typically included in the fee for D5750 and are not reimbursed separately. If an adjustment is made by an office that did not deliver the denture, that office might be reimbursed. This should be noted in a brief narrative.
2. Providing a reline to a denture may extend the replacement limitation period of that prosthesis for two to five years. The reline may "reset" the limitation period (typically five to 10-years) for replacement of the relined prosthesis with a new prosthesis. Some payers will reimburse a reline once per arch, per 12 months. The reimbursement for a reline is highly variable. Because of this variability, it is recommended that the coverage and limitations be verified before providing this service.
3. A reline may be denied when provided for cosmetic reasons, but may be approved when justified by alveolar ridge resorption and to treat changes in occlusion.

TIPS
1. Reimbursement for a laboratory processed reline is typically higher than for a chairside reline.
2. Reimbursement for a laboratory processed reline is lower than for a rebase.

D5751 RELINE COMPLETE MANDIBULAR DENTURE (LABORATORY) — CDT 2016

Coding Watch Correction: Some practices err when reporting a *chairside* reline code instead of the in office *processed* (oven, pressure bath, etc.) laboratory reline. Report the laboratory reline code if the reline is *processed* either in the office *or* by an outside lab. A Triad® oven processed or pressurized hot water bath laboratory reline of a complete mandibular denture is reported as D5751.

CODING MATCH CORRECTION — D5751 reports the laboratory processed reline of a complete mandibular (lower) denture (D5120).

COMMENTS

1. "Rebase" is the process of removing the old base material (the pink part of a denture) and replacing it with new base material.

2. "Reline," is the process of resurfacing the tissue side of the denture with new base material. A reline *resurfaces* the old base material.

3. D5751 is used to report *laboratory processed* (oven or pressurized hot water bath) maxillary complete denture hard acrylic relines. Laboratory processing can occur in office *or in* an outside laboratory.

LIMITATIONS

1. Follow up adjustments provided within six months of the reline are typically included in the fee for D5751 and are not reimbursed separately. If an adjustment is made by an office that did not deliver the denture, that office might be reimbursed. This should be noted in a brief narrative.

2. Providing a reline to a denture may extend the replacement limitation period of that prosthesis for two to five years. The reline may "reset" the limitation period (typically five to 10-years) for replacement of the relined prosthesis with a new prosthesis. Some payers will reimburse a reline once per arch, per 12 months. The reimbursement for a reline is highly variable. Because of this variability, it is recommended that the coverage and limitations be verified before providing this service.

3. A reline may be denied when provided for cosmetic reasons, but may be approved when justified by alveolar ridge resorption and to treat changes in occlusion.

TIPS

1. Reimbursement for a laboratory processed reline is considerably higher than for a chairside reline.

2. Reimbursement for a laboratory processed reline is lower than for a rebase.

D5760   RELINE MAXILLARY PARTIAL DENTURE (LABORATORY)   CDT 2016

CODING WATCH CORRECTION — Some practices err when reporting a *chairside* reline code instead of the in office *processed* (oven, pressure bath, etc.) *laboratory* reline. Report the laboratory reline code if the reline is *processed* either in the office *or* by an outside laboratory. A Triad® oven processed or pressurized hot water bath laboratory reline of a maxillary partial denture is reported as D5760.

CODING MATCH CORRECTION — D5760 reports the laboratory processed reline of a maxillary (upper) partial denture (D5211 or D5213).

COMMENTS

1. "Rebase" is the process of removing the old base material (the pink part of a partial denture) and replacing it with new base material.

2. "Reline," is the process of resurfacing the tissue side of the denture with new base material. A reline *resurfaces* the old base material.

3. D5760 is used to report *laboratory processed* (oven or pressurized hot water bath) maxillary complete denture hard acrylic relines. Laboratory processing can occur in office *or in* an outside laboratory.

LIMITATIONS

1. Follow up adjustments provided within six months of the reline are typically included in the fee for D5760 and are not reimbursed separately. If an adjustment is made by an office that did not deliver the denture, that office might be reimbursed. This should be noted in a brief narrative.

2. Providing a reline to a partial denture may extend the replacement limitation period of that prosthesis for two to five years. The reline may "reset" the limitation period (typically five to 10-years) for replacement of the relined prosthesis with a new prosthesis. Some payers will reimburse a reline once per arch, per 12 months. The reimbursement for a reline is highly variable. Because of this variability, it is recommended that the coverage and limitations be verified before providing this service.

3. A reline may be denied when provided for cosmetic reasons, but may be approved when justified by alveolar ridge resorption and to treat changes in occlusion.

TIPS
1. Reimbursement for a laboratory processed reline is typically higher than for a chairside reline.
2. Reimbursement for a laboratory processed reline is typically lower than for a rebase.

D5761 — RELINE MANDIBULAR PARTIAL DENTURE (LABORATORY) — CDT 2016

CODING WATCH CORRECTION

Some practices err when reporting a *chairside* reline code instead of the in office *processed* (oven, pressure bath, etc.) *laboratory* reline. Report the laboratory reline code if the reline is *processed* either in the office *or* by an outside laboratory. A Triad® oven processed or pressurized hot water bath laboratory reline of a mandibular partial denture is reported as D5761.

CODING MATCH CORRECTION

D5761 reports the laboratory processed reline of a mandibular (lower) partial denture (D5212 or D5214).

COMMENTS
1. "Rebase" is the process of removing the old base material (the pink part of a partial denture) and replacing it with new base material.
2. "Reline," is the process of resurfacing the tissue side of the denture with new base material. A reline *resurfaces* the old base material.
3. D5761 is used to report *laboratory processed* (oven or pressurized hot water bath) maxillary complete denture hard acrylic relines. Processing can occur in office *or in* an outside laboratory.

LIMITATIONS
1. Follow up adjustments provided within six months of the reline are typically included in the fee for D5761 and are not reimbursed separately. If an adjustment is made by an office that did not deliver the denture, that office might be reimbursed. This should be noted in a brief narrative.

2. Providing a reline to a partial denture may extend the replacement limitation period of that prosthesis for two to five years. The reline may "reset" the limitation period (typically five to 10-years) for replacement of the relined prosthesis with a new prosthesis. Some payers will reimburse a reline once per arch, per 12 months. The reimbursement for a reline is highly variable. Because of this variability, it is recommended that the coverage and limitations be verified before providing this service.

3. A reline may be denied when provided for cosmetic reasons, but may be approved when justified by alveolar ridge resorption and to treat changes in occlusion.

TIPS
1. Reimbursement for a laboratory processed reline is typically higher than for a chairside reline.
2. Reimbursement for a laboratory processed reline is typically lower than for a rebase.

INTERIM PROSTHESIS — CDT 2016

A provisional prosthesis designed for use over a limited period of time, after which it is to be replaced by a more definitive restoration.

D5810   INTERIM COMPLETE DENTURE (MAXILLARY)   CDT 2016

CODING WATCH CORRECTION

1. Some practices opt to report a maxillary *interim* complete denture (D5810), rather than a maxillary *immediate* denture (D5130). When extracting the *remaining* natural teeth and *immediately* placing a maxillary denture, consider reporting an immediate denture (D5130) instead. D5130 is considered the most accurate code to describe this scenario and often results in a higher reimbursement. Note: An *interim* complete denture (D5810) may also be reported when the interim complete denture is inserted after extractions.

2. An interim complete denture (D5810) may be provided to rehabilitate an *already* edentulous arch for a limited period. The interim complete denture is provided for a time until a *definitive* prosthesis is fabricated, such as a maxillary complete denture (D5110), a natural tooth overdenture or an implant/abutment supported overdenture.

CODING MATCH CORRECTION

1. For an *adjustment* of an interim maxillary complete denture, see D5410.
2. For a *repair* of an interim complete denture *base*, see D5510.
3. For a *replacement of missing or broken teeth* (each tooth), see D5520.
4. For a *rebase* of an interim maxillary complete denture, see D5710.
5. For a *chairside reline* of an interim maxillary complete denture, see D5730.
6. For a laboratory processed *reline* of an interim maxillary complete denture, see D5750.

NOTE: Many of these procedures *would not* generally be associated with an interim complete denture.

LIMITATIONS

1. D5810 reports an interim *complete* denture (maxillary) following extractions, implant placement, or for restoration of an *already* edentulous mouth. The interim denture is followed by a long term definitive complete denture, natural tooth overdenture, or implant/abutment supported overdenture. Reporting the interim prosthesis may impact the reimbursement of the final definitive denture or overdenture. Many PPO contracts require all procedures to be billed (even non-covered procedures). The amount reimbursed for the interim complete denture will, in most cases, be deducted from the final denture. In some cases, reimbursement for the interim complete denture will subject the subsequent replacement denture to the five year limitation period for dentures.

2. When an interim complete denture is billed, it is commonly not reimbursed. If reimbursed, any amount paid by the payer may be deducted from the permanent (final) denture reimbursement. Interim dentures in service 12 months or longer are often viewed as permanent dentures by many payers. Thus, reimbursement for the permanent denture may be denied. Inform the patient of this possible limitation. It is important to verify payer policy prior to providing this treatment.

TIPS   When extracting the remaining natural teeth and immediately placing a denture, consider reporting an *immediate* denture (D5130), *not* an interim complete denture. Consider reporting an *immediate* denture even if the immediate denture will be replaced by a complete denture (D5110). See D5130.

FLOW CHARTS

Scenario #1

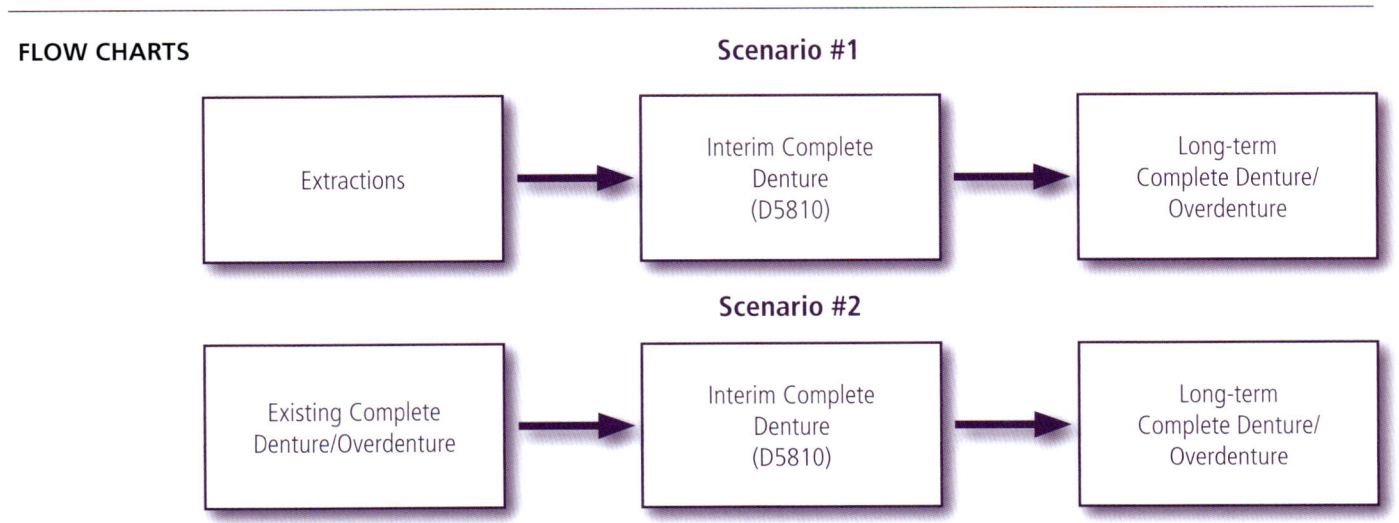

Extractions → Interim Complete Denture (D5810) → Long-term Complete Denture/Overdenture

Scenario #2

Existing Complete Denture/Overdenture → Interim Complete Denture (D5810) → Long-term Complete Denture/Overdenture

D5811 INTERIM COMPLETE DENTURE (MANDIBULAR) — CDT 2016

CODING WATCH CORRECTION

1. Some practices opt to report a mandibular *interim* complete denture (D5811), rather than a mandibular *immediate* denture (D5140). When extracting the *remaining* natural teeth and *immediately* placing a mandibular denture, consider reporting an immediate denture (D5140) instead. D5140 is considered the most accurate code to describe this scenario and often results in a higher reimbursement. Note: An *interim* complete denture (D5811) may also be reported when the interim complete denture is inserted after extractions.

2. An interim complete denture (D5811) may be provided to rehabilitate an *already* edentulous arch for a limited period. The interim complete denture is provided for a time until a *definitive* prosthesis is fabricated, such as a complete denture (D5120), a natural tooth overdenture, or an implant/abutment supported overdenture.

CODING MATCH CORRECTION

1. For an *adjustment* of an interim mandibular complete denture, see D5411.
2. For a *repair* of an interim complete denture *base*, see D5510.
3. For a *replacement of missing or broken teeth* (each tooth), see D5520.
4. For a *rebase* of an interim mandibular complete denture, see D5711.
5. For a *chairside reline* of an interim mandibular complete denture, see D5731.
6. For a *laboratory* processed *reline* of an interim mandibular complete denture, see D5751.

NOTE: Many of these procedures *would not* generally be associated with an interim complete denture.

LIMITATIONS

1. D5811 reports an interim *complete* denture (mandibular) following extractions, implant placement, or for restoration of an *already* edentulous mouth. The interim denture is followed by a long term definitive complete denture, natural tooth overdenture, or implant/abutment supported overdenture. Reporting the interim prosthesis may impact the reimbursement of the final, definitive denture or overdenture. Many PPO contracts require all procedures to be billed (even non-covered procedures). The amount reimbursed for the interim complete denture will, in most cases, be deducted from the final denture. In some cases, reimbursement for the interim complete denture will subject the subsequent replacement denture to the five year limitation period for dentures.

2. When an interim complete denture is billed, it is commonly not reimbursed. If reimbursed, any amount paid by the payer may be deducted from the permanent final denture reimbursement. Interim dentures in service 12 months or longer are often viewed as permanent dentures by many payers. Thus, reimbursement for the permanent denture may be denied. Inform the patient of this possible limitation. It is important to verify payer policy prior to providing this treatment.

TIPS

When extracting the remaining natural teeth and immediately placing a denture, consider reporting an *immediate* denture (D5140), *not* an interim complete denture. Consider reporting an immediate denture even if the *immediate* denture will be replaced by a complete denture (D5120). See D5140.

FLOW CHARTS

Scenario #1

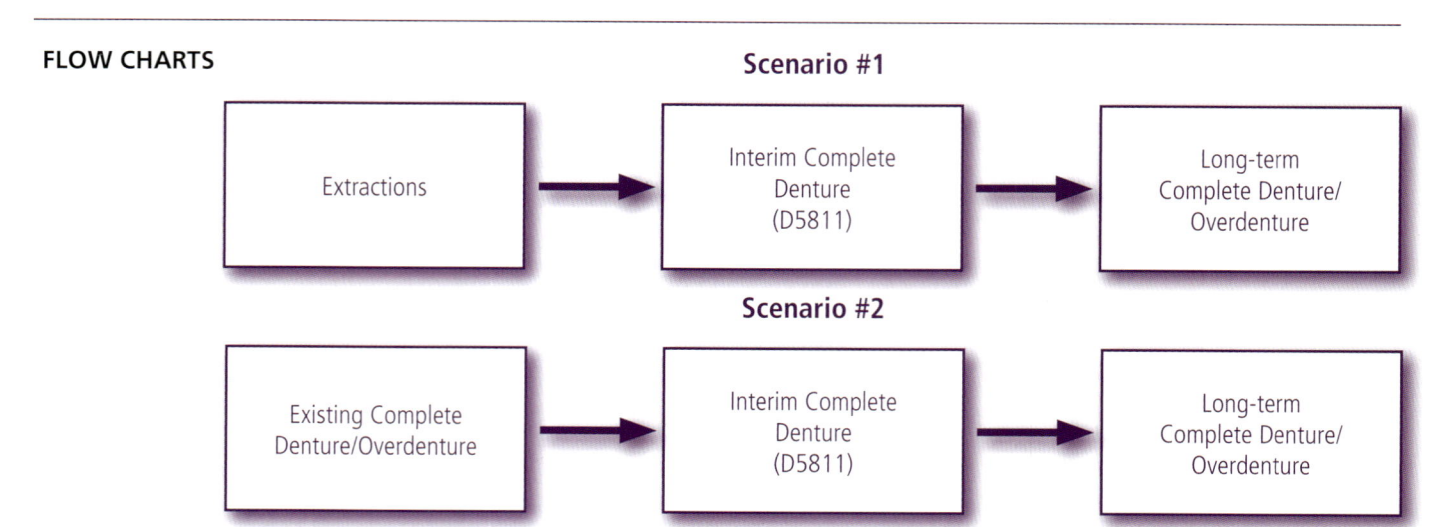

Extractions → Interim Complete Denture (D5811) → Long-term Complete Denture/Overdenture

Scenario #2

Existing Complete Denture/Overdenture → Interim Complete Denture (D5811) → Long-term Complete Denture/Overdenture

D5820   INTERIM PARTIAL DENTURE (MAXILLARY)   CDT 2016

Includes any necessary clasps and rests.

CODING WATCH CORRECTION

D5820 reports a *short term temporary* prosthesis, not a *long term* resin (acrylic) partial denture. A resin (acrylic) partial denture meant to be in service for a long lasting period should be reported as D5211. See D5211 for further details.

CODING MATCH CORRECTION

1. For an *adjustment* of an interim maxillary partial denture, see D5421.
2. For a *repair* of an interim partial denture *base*, see D5610.
3. For a *repair* or to replace a *broken clasp*, see D5630.
4. For a *replacement of missing or broken teeth* (each tooth), see D5640.
5. For *adding a tooth* to an existing interim maxillary partial denture, see D5650.
6. For *adding a clasp* to an existing interim maxillary partial denture, see D5660.
7. For a *rebase* of an interim maxillary partial denture, see D5720.
8. For a *chairside reline* of an interim maxillary partial denture, see D5740.
9. For a *laboratory* processed *reline* of an interim maxillary partial denture, see D5760.

NOTE: Many of these procedures would not generally be associated with an interim partial denture.

COMMENTS

1. Use D5820 to describe a "temp" or "flipper" maxillary resin (acrylic) partial denture which will be in service while *waiting* for a more definitive treatment. D5820 is meant to report an interim partial denture which is in place for one to 12 months. Many PPO contracts require all services to be billed (even non-covered procedures).
2. D5820 might report a Snap-On Smile® interim partial denture (maxillary).

LIMITATIONS

1. In a few cases an anterior "stay plate," placed after an extraction, is reimbursed in addition to a subsequent bridge. The interim partial denture is used to hold space and/or for esthetics while the extraction site heals.
2. A "stay plate" benefit may be limited to patients 16 years of age or younger and only for anterior permanent teeth. Reimbursement may be for D5820 (short term) in this situation, although D5211 may be more appropriate.
3. If the *interim* partial denture is submitted for reimbursement, the amount reimbursed for D5820 will typically be deducted from the subsequent reimbursement for the final restoration. Replacement of the interim partial may be with an implant, bridge, or cast partial denture. The delivery of the interim partial denture could trigger the limitation period (typically five to 10-years) for replacement of the interim prosthesis with a new prosthesis. The reimbursement for an interim partial denture is highly variable. It is recommended that the coverage and limitations be verified before providing this service.

D5821   INTERIM PARTIAL DENTURE (MANDIBULAR)   CDT 2016

Includes any necessary clasps and rests.

CODING WATCH CORRECTION

D5821 reports a *short term temporary* prosthesis, not a *long term* resin (acrylic) partial denture. A resin (acrylic) partial denture meant to be in service for long lasting period should be reported as D5212. See D5212 for further details.

CODING MATCH CORRECTION

1. For an *adjustment* of an interim mandibular partial denture, see D5422.
2. For a *repair* of an interim partial denture *base*, see D5610.
3. For a *repair* or to replace a *broken clasp*, see D5630.
4. For a *replacement of missing or broken teeth* (each tooth), see D5640.
5. For *adding a tooth* to an existing interim partial denture, see D5650.
6. For *adding a clasp* to an existing interim partial denture, see D5660.
7. For a *rebase* of an interim mandibular partial denture, see D5721.
8. For a *chairside reline* of an interim mandibular partial denture, see D5741.
9. For a *laboratory* processed *reline* of an interim mandibular partial denture, see D5761.

NOTE: Many of these procedures *would not* generally be associated with an interim partial denture.

COMMENTS

1. Use D5821 to describe a "temp" or "flipper" mandibular resin (acrylic) partial denture which will be in service while *waiting* for a more definitive treatment. D5821 is meant to report an interim partial denture which is in place for one to 12 months. Many PFO contracts require all services to be billed (even non-covered procedures).
2. D5821 might report a Snap-On Smile® interim partial denture (mandibular).

LIMITATIONS

1. In a few limited cases an anterior "stay plate," placed after an extraction, is reimbursed in addition to a subsequent bridge. The interim partial denture is used to hold space and/or for esthetics while the extraction site heals.
2. A "stay plate" benefit may be limited to patients 16 years of age or younger and only for anterior permanent teeth. Reimbursement may be for D5821 (short term) in this situation, although D5212 may be more appropriate.
3. If the *interim* partial denture is submitted for reimbursement, the amount reimbursed for D5821 will typically be deducted from the subsequent reimbursement for the final restoration. Replacement of the interim partial may be with an implant, bridge, or cast partial denture. The delivery of the interim partial denture could trigger the limitation period (typically five to 10-years) for replacement of the interim prosthesis with a new prosthesis. The reimbursement for an interim partial is highly variable. It is recommended that the coverage and limitations be verified before providing this service.

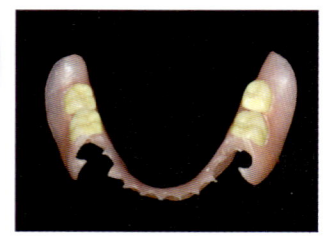

PHOTO

This is an example of an interim mandibular acrylic partial denture (without wire clasps). It is to be used for an interim (limited) period, and is to be replaced by a definitive restoration.

Courtesy Drake Dental Lab

OTHER REMOVABLE PROSTHETIC SERVICES — CDT 2016

D5850   TISSUE CONDITIONING, MAXILLARY   CDT 2016

Treatment reline using materials designed to heal unhealthy ridges prior to more definitive final restoration.

CODING WATCH CORRECTION

It is an error to report a maxillary chairside reline (typically acrylic) as tissue conditioning (D5850). The purpose of tissue conditioning treatment is to promote healing of unhealthy ridge tissues. The conditioner is placed in an *existing* denture, prior to a reline, or *prior* to fabrication of a new definitive, removable prosthesis. Tissue conditioning is not intended to be a long term service.

LIMITATIONS
1. Tissue conditioning is typically not reimbursed if done within six months of the delivery of a new prosthesis.
2. D5850 may be reimbursed twice per 12 to 36 month period. The frequency of reimbursement is dependent on plan limitations. Some payers do not reimburse tissue conditioning.

D5851	TISSUE CONDITIONING, MANDIBULAR	CDT 2016

Treatment reline using materials designed to heal unhealthy ridges prior to more definitive final restoration.

CODING WATCH CORRECTION

It is an error to report a mandibular chairside reline (typically acrylic) as tissue conditioning (D5851). The purpose of tissue conditioning treatment is to promote healing of unhealthy ridge tissues. The conditioner is placed in an *existing* denture, *prior* to a reline, or prior to fabrication of a new definitive, removable prosthesis. Tissue conditioning is not intended to be a long term service.

LIMITATIONS
1. Tissue conditioning is typically not reimbursed if used within six months of the delivery of a new prosthesis.
2. D5851 may be reimbursed twice per 12 to 36-month period. The frequency of reimbursement is dependent on plan limitations. Some payers do not reimburse tissue conditioning.

D5860	**PREVIOUSLY DELETED CODE** OVERDENTURE – COMPLETE, BY REPORT	

This is a deleted code. For maxillary complete overdenture, see D5863. For mandibular complete overdenture, see D5865.

D5861	**PREVIOUSLY DELETED CODE** OVERDENTURE – PARTIAL, BY REPORT	

This is a deleted code. For maxillary partial overdenture, see D5864. For mandibular partial overdenture, see D5866.

D5862	PRECISION ATTACHMENT, BY REPORT	CDT 2016

Each set of male and female components should be reported as one precision attachment. Describe the type of attachment used.

CODING WATCH CORRECTION

D5862 reports a "precision" attachment for a partial denture or an attachment (locator) associated with an overdenture (natural tooth or abutment/implant supported).

COMMENTS
1. The precision attachment described by this code consists of both male and female components. ERA, ZAAG or Zest attachments may be reported using D5862.
2. If the locator is attached directly to the *full size* implant (and there is a keeper assembly), see D6052 which is a semi-precision attachment abutment. This is the most common system. However, D5862 (two pieces) plus a D6056 or D6057 abutment (three pieces total) could report a locator system for a full size implant. This is not common now that D6052 is available to report a locator. See D6052.
3. With a natural tooth overdenture, D5862 could be reported as male-female attachment.
4. Sometimes the D5862 attachment could be connected to a coping, D2975.
5. When a mini implant (D6013) is used, D5862 reports the locator assembly (cap) that is embedded in the overdenture. Report mini implant (D6013) and D5862 separately.
6. D5862 reports the precision attachment used to affix a connector bar D6055 to the abutment/implant supported overdenture.

LIMITATIONS This code is not typically reimbursed.

NARRATIVES A narrative should be used when reporting D5862.

D5863 OVERDENTURE – COMPLETE MAXILLARY — CDT 2016

CODING WARNING CORRECTION Do not report D5863 for a maxillary abutment/implant supported complete overdenture. See D6110 for further details regarding an abutment/implant supported overdenture.

CODING MATCH CORRECTION
1. For an *adjustment* of a complete maxillary overdenture, see D5410.
2. For a *repair* of a complete maxillary overdenture *base*, see D5510.
3. For a *replacement* of *missing or broken teeth (each tooth), see D5520*.
4. *For a rebase of a complete maxillary overdenture,* see D5710.
5. For a *chairside reline* of a complete maxillary overdenture, see D5730.
6. For a *laboratory* processed *reline* of a complete maxillary overdenture, see D5750.

COMMENTS
1. D5863 reports a maxillary complete denture fabricated to fit over a retained, endodontically treated, natural tooth root(s). The complete maxillary overdenture may or may not be supported by the retained root(s).
2. For an *abutment/implant supported* complete maxillary overdenture, see D6110.

LIMITATIONS Reimbursement for a complete maxillary overdenture (D5863), when available, is typically limited by a five to 10-year replacement period.

TIPS
1. Other procedures may be required prior to the placement of a maxillary overdenture, D5863.   A root canal may be necessary on the retained natural tooth (teeth).
2. Precision attachment D5862 reports the ZAAG or ZEST locator attachment affixed to the retained root(s) beneath the overdenture.
3. D5862 could be connected to a coping, D2975.

NARRATIVES
1. An alternate benefit of a maxillary complete denture (D5110) may be reimbursed for the maxillary overdenture (D5863), unless specifically excluded by the contract. Request the alternate benefit of D5110 when fabricating a maxillary overdenture (D5863).
2. Submit a narrative justifying the retention of the natural tooth root(s) and the necessity of the tooth supported complete maxillary overdenture.

D5864 OVERDENTURE – PARTIAL MAXILLARY — CDT 2016

CODING WARNING CORRECTION Do not report D5864 for an abutment/implant-supported maxillary partial overdenture. See D6054 for further details regarding an abutment/implant-supported partial overdenture.

CODING MATCH CORRECTION
1. For an *adjustment* of a maxillary partial overdenture, see D5421.
2. For a *repair* of a resin maxillary partial overdenture *base*, see D5610.
3. For a *repair* or to replace a *broken clasp*, see D5630.
4. For a *replacement* of broken *teeth* (each tooth), see D5640.

5. For *adding a tooth* to an existing maxillary partial overdenture, see D5650.
6. For *adding a clasp* to an existing maxillary partial overdenture, see D5660.
7. For a *rebase* of a resin base maxillary partial overdenture, see D5720.
8. For a *chairside reline* of a maxillary partial overdenture, see D5740.
9. For a *laboratory* processed *reline* of a maxillary partial overdenture, see D5760.

COMMENTS
1. D5864 reports a maxillary partial overdenture fabricated to fit over natural teeth and/or retained tooth roots.
2. For an *abutment/implant supported* partial maxillary overdenture, see D6112.

LIMITATIONS Reimbursement for a natural tooth maxillary partial overdenture (D5864), when available, is typically limited by a five to 10-year period before a replacement overdenture would be considered for reimbursement.

TIPS
1. Other procedures may be required prior to the placement of a maxillary partial overdenture, D5864. A root canal may be necessary on the retained natural tooth (teeth).
2. Precision attachment D5862 reports a ZAAG or ZEST locator attachment affixed to the retained root(s) beneath the overdenture.
3. D5862 could be connected to a coping, D2975.

NARRATIVES
1. An alternate benefit of a conventional cast partial denture (D5213) may be reimbursed for the natural tooth maxillary partial overdenture (D5864), unless specifically excluded by the contract. If D5864 is denied, request the alternate benefit of D5213 on appeal.
2. Submit a narrative describing the necessity of the natural tooth supported maxillary partial overdenture.

D5865 OVERDENTURE – COMPLETE MANDIBULAR — CDT 2016

Do not report D5865 for a mandibular abutment/implant supported complete overdenture. See D6111 for further details regarding an abutment/implant supported mandibular overdenture.

1. For an *adjustment* of a complete mandibular overdenture, see D5411.
2. For a *repair* of a complete mandibular overdenture *base*, see D5510.
3. For a *replacement* of *missing or broken teeth* (each tooth), see D5520.
4. For a *rebase* of a complete mandibular overdenture, see D5711.
5. For a *chairside reline* of a complete mandibular overdenture, see D5731.
6. For a *laboratory* processed *reline* of a complete mandibular overdenture, see D5751.

COMMENTS
1. D5865 reports a mandibular complete denture fabricated to fit over a retained, endodontically treated, natural tooth root(s). The natural tooth mandibular overdenture may or may not be supported by the retained root(s).
2. For an *abutment/implant supported* complete mandibular overdenture, see D6111.

LIMITATIONS Reimbursement for a natural tooth mandibular overdenture (D5865), when available, is typically limited by a five to 10-year replacement period.

D5922　NASAL SEPTAL PROSTHESIS　　CDT 2016

Synonymous terminology: septal plug, septal button. Removable prosthesis to occlude (obturate) a hole within the nasal septal wall. Adverse chemical degradation in this moist environment may require frequent replacement. Silicone prostheses are occasionally subject to fungal invasion.

D5924　CRANIAL PROSTHESIS　　CDT 2016

Synonymous terminology: skull plate, cranioplasty prosthesis, cranial implant. A biocompatible, permanently implanted replacement of a portion of the skull bones; an artificial replacement for a portion of the skull bone.

D5925　FACIAL AUGMENTATION IMPLANT PROSTHESIS　　CDT 2016

Synonymous terminology: facial implant. An implantable biocompatible material generally onlayed upon an existing bony area beneath the skin tissue to fill in or collectively raise portions of the overlaying facial skin tissues to create acceptable contours. Although some forms of pre-made surgical implants are commercially available, the facial augmentation is usually custom made for surgical implantation for each individual patient due to the irregular or extensive nature of the facial deficit.

D5931　OBTURATOR PROSTHESIS, SURGICAL　　CDT 2016

Synonymous terminology: obturator, surgical stayplate, immediate temporary obturator. A temporary prosthesis inserted during or immediately following surgical or traumatic loss of a portion or all of one or both maxillary bones and contiguous alveolar structures (e.g., gingival tissue, teeth). Frequent revisions of surgical obturators are necessary during the ensuing healing phase (approximately six months). Some dentists prefer to replace many or all teeth removed by the surgical procedure in the surgical obturator, while others do not replace any teeth. Further surgical revisions may require fabrication of another surgical obturator (e.g., an initially planned small defect may be revised and greatly enlarged after the final pathology report indicates margins are not free of tumor).

D5936　OBTURATOR PROSTHESIS, INTERIM　　CDT 2016

Synonymous terminology: immediate postoperative obturator. A prosthesis that is made following completion of the initial healing after a surgical resection of a portion or all of one or both the maxillae; frequently many or all teeth in the defect area are replaced by this prosthesis. This prosthesis replaces the surgical obturator, which is usually inserted at, or immediately following the resection. Generally, an interim obturator is made to facilitate closure of the resultant defect after initial healing has been completed. Unlike the surgical obturator, which usually is made prior to surgery and frequently revised in the operating room during surgery, the interim obturator is made when the defect margins are clearly defined and further surgical revisions are not planned. It is a provisional prosthesis, which may replace some or all lost teeth, and other lost bone and soft tissue structures. Also, it frequently must be revised (termed an obturator prosthesis modification) during subsequent dental procedures (e.g., restorations, gingival surgery) as well as to compensate for further tissue shrinkage before a definitive obturator prosthesis is made.

D5932　OBTURATOR PROSTHESIS, DEFINITIVE　　CDT 2016

Synonymous terminology: obturator. A prosthesis, which artificially replaces part or all of the maxilla and associated teeth, lost due to surgery, trauma or congenital defects. A definitive obturator is made when it is deemed that further tissue changes or recurrence of tumor are unlikely and a more permanent prosthetic rehabilitation can be achieved; it is intended for long-term use.

D5933　OBTURATOR PROSTHESIS, MODIFICATION　　CDT 2016

Synonymous terminology: adjustment, denture adjustment, temporary or office reline. Revision or alteration of an existing obturator (surgical, interim, or definitive); possible modifications include relief of the denture base due to tissue compression, augmentation of the seal or peripheral areas to affect adequate sealing or separation between the nasal and oral cavities.

D5934 MANDIBULAR RESECTION PROSTHESIS WITH GUIDE FLANGE — CDT 2016

Synonymous terminology: resection device, resection appliance. A prosthesis that guides the remaining portion of the mandible, left after a partial resection, into a more normal relationship with the maxilla. This allows for some tooth-to-tooth or an improved tooth contact. It may also artificially replace missing teeth and thereby increase masticatory efficiency.

D5935 MANDIBULAR RESECTION PROSTHESIS WITHOUT GUIDE FLANGE — CDT 2016

A prosthesis which helps guide the partially resected mandible to a more normal relation with the maxilla allowing for increased tooth contact. It does not have a flange or ramp, however, to assist in directional closure. It may replace missing teeth and thereby increase masticatory efficiency. Dentists who treat mandibulectomy patients may prefer to replace some, all or none of the teeth in the defect area. Frequently, the defect's margins preclude even partial replacement. Use of a guide (a mandibular resection prosthesis with a guide flange) may not be possible due to anatomical limitations or poor patient tolerance. Ramps, extended occlusal arrangements and irregular occlusal positioning relative to the denture foundation frequently preclude stability of the prostheses, and thus some prostheses are poorly tolerated under such adverse circumstances.

D5937 TRISMUS APPLIANCE (NOT FOR TMD TREATMENT) — CDT 2016

Synonymous terminology: occlusal device for mandibular trismus, dynamic bite opener. A prosthesis, which assists the patient in increasing their oral aperture width in order to eat as well as maintain oral hygiene. Several versions and designs are possible, all intending to ease the severe lack of oral opening experienced by many patients immediately following extensive intraoral surgical procedures.

D5951 FEEDING AID — CDT 2016

Synonymous terminology: feeding prosthesis. A prosthesis, which maintains the right and left maxillary segments of an infant cleft palate patient in their proper orientation until surgery is performed to repair the cleft. It closes the oral-nasal cavity defect, thus enhancing sucking and swallowing. Used on an interim basis, this prosthesis achieves separation of the oral and nasal cavities in infants born with wide clefts necessitating delayed closure. It is eliminated if surgical closure can be affected or, alternatively, with eruption of the deciduous dentition a pediatric speech aid may be made to facilitate closure of the defect.

D5952 SPEECH AID PROSTHESIS, PEDIATRIC — CDT 2016

Synonymous terminology: nasopharyngeal obturator, speech appliance, obturator, cleft palate appliance, prosthetic speech aid, speech bulb. A temporary or interim prosthesis used to close a defect in the hard and/or soft palate. It may replace tissue lost due to developmental or surgical alterations. It is necessary for the production of intelligible speech. Normal lateral growth of the palatal bones necessitates occasional replacement of this prosthesis. Intermittent revisions of the obturator section can assist in maintenance of palatalpharyngeal closure (termed a speech aid prosthesis modification). Frequently, such prostheses are not fabricated before the deciduous dentition is fully erupted since clasp retention is often essential.

D5953 SPEECH AID PROSTHESIS, ADULT — CDT 2016

Synonymous terminology: prosthetic speech appliance, speech aid, speech bulb. A definitive prosthesis, which can improve speech in adult cleft palate patients either by obturating (sealing off) a palatal cleft or fistula, or occasionally by assisting an incompetent soft palate. Both mechanisms are necessary to achieve velopharyngeal competency. Generally, this prosthesis is fabricated when no further growth is anticipated and the objective is to achieve long-term use. Hence, more precise materials and techniques are utilized. Occasionally such procedures are accomplished in conjunction with precision attachments in crown work undertaken on some or all maxillary teeth to achieve improved aesthetics.

D5954 PALATAL AUGMENTATION PROSTHESIS — CDT 2016

Synonymous terminology: superimposed prosthesis, maxillary glossectomy prosthesis, maxillary speech prosthesis, palatal drop prosthesis. A removable prosthesis that alters the hard and/or soft palate's topographical form adjacent to the tongue.

D5955 — PALATAL LIFE PROSTHESIS, DEFINITIVE — CDT 2016

A prosthesis that elevates the soft palate superiorly and aids in restoration of soft palate functions that may be lost due to an acquired, congenital or developmental defect. A definitive palatal lift is usually made for patients whose experience with an interim palatal lift has been successful, especially if surgical alterations are deemed unwarranted.

D5958 — PALATAL LIFT PROSTHESIS, INTERIM — CDT 2016

Synonymous terminology: diagnostic palatal lift. A prosthesis that elevates and assists in restoring soft palate function that may be lost due to clefting, surgery, trauma or unknown paralysis. It is intended for interim use to determine its usefulness in achieving palatalpharyngeal competency or enhance swallowing reflexes. This prosthesis is intended for interim use as a diagnostic aid to assess the level of possible improvement in speech intelligibility. Some clinicians believe use of a palatal lift on an interim basis may stimulate an otherwise flaccid soft palate to increase functional activity, subsequently lessening its need.

D5959 — PALATAL LIFT PROSTHESIS, MODIFICATION — CDT 2016

Synonymous terminology: revision of lift, adjustment. Alterations in the adaptation, contour, form or function of an existing palatal lift necessitated due to tissue impingement, lack of function, poor clasp adaptation or the like.

D5960 — SPEECH AID PROSTHESIS, MODIFICATION — CDT 2016

Synonymous terminology: adjustment, repair, revision. Any revision of a pediatric or adult speech aid not necessitating its replacement. Frequently, revisions of the obturating section of any speech aid are required to facilitate enhanced speech intelligibility. Such revisions or repairs do not require complete remaking of the prosthesis, thus extending its longevity.

D5982 — SURGICAL STENT — CDT 2016

Synonymous terminology: periodontal stent, skin graft stent, columellar stent. Stents are utilized to apply pressure to soft tissues to facilitate healing and prevent cicatrization or collapse. A surgical stent may be required in surgical and post-surgical revisions to achieve close approximation of tissues. Usually such materials as temporary or interim soft denture liners, gutta percha, or dental modeling impression compound may be used.

CODING WARNING/CORRECTION: Surgical stent (D5982) does not report an implant surgical guide. See D6190 to report a radiographic/surgical implant index.

COMMENTS The surgical stent (D5982) applies pressure to soft tissues to facilitate healing and prevent collapse.

D5983 — RADIATION CARRIER — CDT 2016

Synonymous terminology: radiotherapy prosthesis, carrier prosthesis, radiation applicator, radium carrier, intracavity carrier, intracavity applicator.

A device used to administer radiation to confined areas by means of capsules, beads or needles of radiation emitting materials such as radium or cesium. Its function is to hold the radiation source securely in the same location during the entire period of treatment. Radiation oncologists occasionally request these devices to achieve close approximation and controlled application of radiation to a tumor deemed amiable to eradication.

Note: D5983 is listed here in numerical order. However, it is also listed below the "Carriers" heading following D5993.

D5984 — RADIATION SHIELD — CDT 2016

Synonymous terminology: radiation stent, tongue protector, lead shield.

An intraoral prosthesis designed to shield adjacent tissues from radiation during orthovoltage treatment of malignant lesions of the head and neck region.

D5985 — RADIATION CONE LOCATOR — CDT 2016

Synonymous terminology: docking device, cone locator.

A prosthesis utilized to direct and reduplicate the path of radiation to an oral tumor during a split course of irradiation.

D5986 — FLUORIDE GEL CARRIER — CDT 2016

Synonymous terminology: fluoride applicator.

A prosthesis, which covers the teeth in either dental arch and is used to apply topical fluoride in close proximity to tooth enamel and dentin for several minutes daily.

Note: D5986 is listed here in numerical order. However, it is also listed below the "Carriers" heading starting with D5993.

CODING WARNING CORRECTION: It is an error to report a fluoride gel carrier (D5986) to be reimbursed for at-home whitening bleaching trays (D9975) or Perio Protect Trays®. See D5994 to report Perio Protect Trays®.

COMMENTS
1. A fluoride gel carrier is fabricated for the daily application of fluoride to the teeth of high risk caries (or sensitivity) patients. These high risk patients may include seniors, pediatric patients or a patient receiving radiation treatment.
2. D5986 is reported on a "per arch" basis. Specify the arch on the claim form.

LIMITATIONS D5986 is typically not reimbursed.

D5987 — COMMISSURE SPLINT — CDT 2016

Synonymous terminology: lip splint.

A device placed between the lips, which assists in achieving increased opening between the lips. Use of such devices enhances opening where surgical, chemical or electrical alterations of the lips has resulted in severe restriction or contractures.

D5988 — SURGICAL SPLINT — CDT 2016

Synonymous terminology: Gunning splint, modified Gunning splint, labiolingual splint, fenestrated splint, Kingsley splint, cast metal splint. Splints are designed to utilize existing teeth and/or alveolar processes as points of anchorage to assist in stabilization and immobilization of broken bones during healing. They are used to re-establish, as much as possible, normal occlusal relationships during the process of immobilization. Frequently, existing prostheses (e.g., a patient's complete dentures) can be modified to serve as surgical splints. Frequently, surgical splints have arch bars added to facilitate intermaxillary fixation. Rubber elastics may be used to assist in this process. Circummandibular eyelet hooks can be utilized for enhanced stabilization with wiring to adjacent bone.

CODING WARNING CORRECTION:
1. This code *does not* report Perio Protect®. To report Perio Protect®, see D5994.
2. Many practices err by reporting surgical splint (D5988) to describe a radiographic/surgical implant index. See D6190 for reporting a radiographic/surgical implant index. D5988 is not related to implant procedures.

COMMENTS Surgical splints (D5988) use existing teeth and/or bone for anchorage to stabilize and immobilize broken bones during healing.

D5991 VESICULOBULLOUS DISEASE MEDICAMENT CARRIER — CDT 2016

A custom fabricated carrier that covers the teeth and alveolar mucosa, or alveolar mucosa alone, and is used to deliver prescription medicaments for treatment of immunologically mediated vesiculobullous disease.

Note: D5991 is listed here in numerical order. However, it is also listed below the "Carriers" heading starting with D5993.

CODING WARNING/CORRECTION This code *does not* report Perio Protect®. To report Perio Protect®, see D5994.

COMMENTS
1. This procedure describes a custom fabricated carrier that covers the teeth and alveolar mucosa, or alveolar mucosa alone. The carrier is used to deliver topical corticosteroids and similar prescription medicaments for maximum sustained contact with the alveolar ridge and/or attached gingival tissues.
2. The prescription medicaments treat and manage the immunologically mediated vesiculobullous mucosal, chronic recurrent ulcerative, and other desquamative diseases of the gingival and oral mucosa.

TIPS This service might be covered by a medical plan.

D5992 ADJUST MAXILLOFACIAL PROSTHETIC APPLIANCE, BY REPORT — CDT 2016

CODING WARNING/CORRECTION This code *does not* describe adjustments made to removable partial or full dentures. For adjustments to removable partial or full dentures, see D5410-D5422.

COMMENTS D5992 describes adjustments made to maxillofacial prosthetic appliances (such as an obturator).

LIMITATIONS This procedure would not generally be reimbursed by dental insurance.

TIPS
1. For *maintenance and cleaning* of a maxillofacial prosthesis (such as an obturator), see D5993.
2. It is appropriate to report both D5992, adjust maxillofacial prosthetic appliance, and maintenance and cleaning of a maxillofacial prosthesis (D5993) at the same appointment.

D5993 REVISED MAINTENANCE AND CLEANING OF A MAXILLOFACIAL PROSTHESIS (EXTRA- OR INTRA-ORAL) OTHER THAN REQUIRED ADJUSTMENTS, BY REPORT — CDT 2016

REVISIONS MAINTENANCE AND CLEANING OF A MAXILLOFACIAL PROSTHESIS (EXTRA- OR INTRA-ORAL) OTHER THAN REQUIRED ADJUSTMENTS, BY REPORT

~~Maintenance and cleaning of a maxillofacial prosthesis.~~

CODING WARNING CORRECTION: D5993 *may not* be reported for maintenance and cleaning of a removable partial or full denture. See D9932, D9933, D9934, D9935 to report cleaning and inspection of removable partial and complete dentures.

COMMENTS

1. Proper maintenance and cleaning of maxillofacial prostheses is critically important to minimize recurrent infections and to prevent tearing and/or breakdown of prostheses. D5993 can be used to describe the maintenance and cleaning of maxillofacial prostheses (intra and extra-oral) that have accumulated calculus and/or other foreign materials that patients cannot safely remove on their own. When a patient presents with hardened calculus on an obturator, hand instrumentation may be necessary in addition to using an ultrasonic cleaner. D5993 would be used to describe this procedure.

   Extra-oral prostheses are especially vulnerable to tearing, discoloration, and breakdown. The cleaning and maintenance of these appliances may require a professional's expertise to ensure the service is performed properly. The removal of adhesives and oils from facial prostheses may be necessary to extend their life. Report this cleaning service using D5993.

2. For adjustments to a maxillofacial prosthesis, see D5992.

3. D5993 and adjust maxillofacial prosthetic appliance (D5992) may be reported on the same date of service.

NARRATIVES A claim for D5993 is justified "by report." Include a narrative describing the service provided, whether the appliance is an extra oral or intraoral appliance, and include the method of cleaning used on the maxillofacial prosthesis.

D5994 — PERIODONTAL MEDICAMENT CARRIER WITH PERIPHERAL SEAL – LABORATORY PROCESSED — CDT 2016

Note: D5994 is listed here in numerical order. Find D5994 explanations in the next section, under "Carriers" prior to D5999.

CARRIERS — CDT 2016

D5983 — RADIATION CARRIER — CDT 2016

Synonymous terminology: radiotherapy prosthesis, carrier prosthesis, radiation applicator, radium carrier, intracavity carrier, intracavity applicator.

A device used to administer radiation to confined areas by means of capsules, beads or needles of radiation emitting materials such as radium or cesium. Its function is to hold the radiation source securely in the same location during the entire period of treatment. Radiation oncologists occasionally request these devices to achieve close approximation and controlled application of radiation to a tumor deemed amiable to eradication.

D5986 — FLUORIDE GEL CARRIER — CDT 2016

Synonymous terminology: fluoride applicator.

A prosthesis, which covers the teeth in either dental arch and is used to apply topical fluoride in close proximity to tooth enamel and dentin for several minutes daily.

Note: This code is placed here according to CDT. It is out of order numerically.

CODING WARNING CORRECTION: It is an error to report a fluoride gel carrier (D5986) to be reimbursed for at-home whitening bleaching trays (D9975) or Perio Protect Trays®. See D5994 to report Perio Protect Trays®.

COMMENTS 1. A fluoride gel carrier is fabricated for the daily application of fluoride to the teeth of patients with a high risk of caries (or sensitivity) patients. These high risk patients may include seniors, pediatric patients or a patient receiving radiation treatment.

2. D5986 is reported on a "per arch" basis. Specify the arch on the claim form.

LIMITATIONS D5986 is typically not reimbursed.

D5991   VESICULOBULLOUS DISEASE MEDICAMENT CARRIER   CDT 2016

A custom fabricated carrier that covers the teeth and alveolar mucosa, or alveolar mucosa alone, and is used to deliver prescription medicaments for treatment of immunologically mediated vesiculobullous disease.

Note: This code is placed in sequence here according to CDT. However, it is out of order numerically.

This code *does not* report Perio Protect®. To report Perio Protect®, see D4999.

COMMENTS 1. This procedure describes a custom fabricated carrier that covers the teeth and alveolar mucosa, or alveolar mucosa alone. The carrier is used to deliver topical corticosteroids and similar prescription medicaments for maximum sustained contact with the alveolar ridge and/or attached gingival tissues.

2. The prescription medicaments treat and manage the immunologically mediated vesiculobullous mucosal, chronic recurrent ulcerative, and other desquamative diseases of the gingival and oral mucosa.

TIPS This service might be covered by a medical plan.

D5994   PERIODONTAL MEDICAMENT CARRIER WITH PERIPHERAL SEAL – LABORATORY PROCESSED   CDT 2016

A custom fabricated, laboratory processed carrier that covers the teeth and alveolar mucosa. Used as a vehicle to deliver prescribed medicaments for sustained contact with the gingiva, alveolar mucosa, and into the periodontal sulcus or pocket.

Note: This code is placed in sequence here according to CDT. However, it is out of order numerically.

1. Some dental practices have mistakenly used D4381 (localized delivery of antimicrobial agents via a controlled release vehicle into diseased crevicular tissue) to describe the use of Perio Protect®. D4381 is intended to report the localized delivery of time-released antimicrobials such as Arestin®, Atridox®, or PerioChip®.

2. Do not use Topical Medicament Carrier D5991 to report Perio Protect Trays®. D5991 reports a topical medicament carrier that is useful in treating various desquamative diseases of the gingival and oral mucosa.

3. D5986 describes a custom tray used to apply topical fluoride gel. Do not report D5986 to describe the use of Perio Protect Trays®.

COMMENTS

1. D5994 reports a periodontal medicament carrier (tray) with a peripheral seal used in the Perio Protect® dental tray system. This medicament carrier has a peripheral seal, which is substantially different from other carriers due to the laboratory process. A vacuum formed tray does not seal to the tissue. The difference between a peripheral seal and a vacuum formed tray is similar to the difference between a shell crown and a cast crown, both of which are called crowns. One does not seal and has limited uses; the other has a seal and has broader applications. Thus, D5994 was created to distinguish this type of tray from others already in use for other purposes. Note that this is a laboratory processed carrier used to deliver prescribed medicaments for "sustained contact" with the gingiva, alveolar mucosa, and into the periodontal sulcus or pocket.

2. Insurance payers want to know what condition is being treated. Having a separate code makes it clear that this periodontal medicament carrier (D5994) is being used to treat periodontal disease. This type of tray is used to direct medications (e.g., peroxide) into the gingival sulcus to help manage biofilm. This type of tray directs prescribed solutions into periodontal pockets when used at home by the periodontal patient. Although a dentist must choose the most appropriate solution for individual patients, the most commonly prescribed solution with this type of tray has oxidizing and oxygenating agents. Oxidizing agents debride (chemically remove) the slimy coating of a biofilm and also cleanse the oral wounds.

LIMITATIONS The treatment of the periodontal patient using a periodontal medicament carrier with peripheral seal – laboratory processed (D5994) is seldom covered.

NARRATIVES The claim for D5994 should be supported by the periodontal diagnosis, an outline of the patient's periodontal history, including appropriate periodontal charting, methods previously implemented to control the periodontal condition, and the prescribed solution used in the tray(s).

D5999 — UNSPECIFIED MAXILLOFACIAL PROSTHESIS, BY REPORT — CDT 2016

Used for procedure that is not adequately described by a code. Describe procedure.

COMMENTS

1. See D5899 for reference of unspecified removable prosthodontic procedures.

2. Obstructive sleep apnea appliance – Typically not a covered dental benefit. This service may be reimbursed under a medical insurance plan when accompanied by sleep study and medical diagnosis.

3. Snore Guard Appliance – Typically not a covered dental benefit. Snoring is generally considered *social*, not medical.

SLEEPCOMPLETE™
Dental Sleep Medicine Program
www.sleepcomplete.com

NOTES

GENERAL COMMENTS FOR IMPLANT SERVICES — AUTHOR'S COMMENTS

Warning!

Many of the Implant Services codes in this section are not in numerical order, but are listed under various subcategory sections. Thumb through this implant section and the Index to look for the particular code you are seeking.

CODING WARNING CORRECTION

It is misleading to report "implant type" crowns (D60xx) as individual crowns (D27xx) restoring natural teeth, to gain reimbursement when implants are not a covered benefit.

CODING WATCH CORRECTION

1. Do not report <u>abutment</u> supported crowns as <u>implant</u> supported crowns or vice versa. If the crown is attached <u>directly</u> into an implant (no abutment involved), it is an <u>implant</u> <u>supported</u> crown. If an abutment is attached to the implant and the crown is attached to the abutment, the crown is considered an <u>abutment</u> <u>supported</u> crown. An abutment supported crown is the most common type of implant restoration.

2. Do not report implant/abutment supported complete or partial overdentures (D6110/D6111/D6112/D6113) as natural tooth complete and partial overdentures (D5863/D5864/D5865/D5866). Report the implant/abutment supported complete and partial overdenture as provided, then request the alternate benefit of a complete denture (D5110/D5120) or cast framework partial (D5213/D5214) as an alternate benefit.

3. Reporting the implant crown fee without separating the associated abutment is a common error. If submitting a claim to a PPO, the crown fee may be reduced to the negotiated PPO crown fee. If the implant abutment (D6051/D6056/D6057) is listed <u>separately</u> on the claim form, the patient would be responsible for payment since implants are not typically a covered benefit. Most PPO plans have a fee schedule for services that are not covered benefits. The contracted dentist must honor the PPO fees. Identifying the abutment as a separate service could increase reimbursement.

4. If reporting a fixed partial denture (bridge) the retainer crown material should be consistent with the pontic material reported (i.e. porcelain fused to metal (PFM), metal, ceramic, etc.).

COMMENTS

1. Reimbursement for "implant type" crowns, bridges or overdentures may be denied. <u>Always appeal</u> the denial. Ask the insured to obtain a copy of the plan document (not the benefits booklet) from their Human Resources department. Review the contract for language that excludes restorations placed on implants. Review the contract for limitations. Often an alternate benefit will be reimbursed upon appeal.

2. Some PPOs cover implants/implant crowns, subject to plan maximums.

3. There are <u>two</u> basic approaches for the coding/billing of *abutment supported* implant restorations. The fees, as mentioned, are illustrative only. Fees vary widely by location and individual practice:

    a. Scenario one: The implant surgeon inserts the implant, places the prefabricated abutment (D6056), and makes the temporary. The general practitioner removes the temporary, preps the abutment, takes an impression, and delivers the abutment supported crown. In many cases, the time involved with this scenario is typically less than the time taken to fabricate a conventional crown. The lab fee for the abutment supported crown may be higher than a "regular" crown. Most lab fees related to implant procedures are higher than non-implant crown fees. The general practitioner would report, for example, abutment supported porcelain fused to high noble metal crown (D6059) at $100 to $300 above the "regular" PFM high noble crown fee (D6750).

    The $100 to $300 differential covers the time needed for case presentation, communication with the surgeon, increased risk, additional lab fees, and follow up. The provider is "married" to the implant patient and long term customer service is important. The <u>pontic</u> of an implant type bridge is coded using the same pontic codes for a natural tooth bridge (D6205-D6253).

b. In a second, more complicated approach, the implant surgeon often places a "healing cap." The general practitioner places an interim abutment (D6051), a prefabricated (manufactured) abutment (D6056) or a custom abutment (D6057) cast by the laboratory before the crown is placed. If the GP places the healing cap, not the surgeon, report second stage implant surgery D6011. In some cases, the surgeon provides the prefabricated abutment. The surgeon who provides the prefabricated abutment <u>should not</u> report the abutment. The code's nomenclature includes the <u>placement of the abutment</u>. The surgeon should report D6199, by report, for "furnishing the prefabricated abutment" to the subsequent treating dentist. Report the implant crown fee at $100 to $300 above the standard crown fee for a crown on a natural tooth. Report the separate prefabricated abutment or custom abutment at a fee of $400 to $900. The custom abutment (D6057) is fabricated by the lab and the fee should be at least $100 to $200 higher than a prefabricated (manufactured) abutment (D6056).

4. Include the tooth number when reporting implant procedure codes, if applicable.

TIPS

The two scenarios below are for abutment supported crowns (porcelain fused to metal (PFM) high noble. The fees are illustrative only. Fees vary widely by location and by practice:

SCENARIO #1

The general practitioner removes the temporary, preps or does not prep the abutment, takes an impression, delivers the crown, and cements it to the abutment placed by the implant surgeon:

High noble abutment supported crown (D6059)   **$1,250 total implant crown fee**

(regular crown fee is $950 plus $300 surcharge for "implant-type" crown)

SCENARIO #2

The patient presents to the restorative dentist with the healing cap in place. The dentist places the implant abutment and the abutment supported crown.

High noble abutment supported crown (D6059)	$1,250	(See pricing example above).
Custom abutment (D6057) or prefabricated abutment (D6056)	$ 745	(Always charge separately for abutment).
	$1,995	**Total implant fee**

Note: The charge for the crown and the abutment are listed <u>separately</u> for the prefabricated or custom abutment. <u>Never</u> bundle the abutment fee into the implant type crown fee. The abutment may be billed to the patient. The PPO contract may control the fee charged, even though the implant or abutment is not a covered service. Often an alternate benefit of a gold crown is reimbursed for the abutment supported crown.

NARRATIVES

1. When submitting a claim for an implant crown, it is essential that a brief narrative be included. The narrative may help avoid delays and/or claim denials.
2. "See attached radiographic image" of the fully integrated implant.

D6000-D6199 VIII. IMPLANT SERVICES — CDT 2016

Local anesthesia is usually considered to be part of Implant Services procedures.

Warning!

Many of the Implant Services codes in this section are not in numerical order, but are listed under various subcategory sections. Thumb through this implant section and the Index to look for the particular code you are seeking.

PRE-SURGICAL SERVICES   CDT 2016

D6190 RADIOGRAPHIC/SURGICAL IMPLANT INDEX, BY REPORT   CDT 2016

An appliance, designed to relate osteotomy or fixture position to existing anatomic structures, to be utilized during radiographic exposure for treatment planning and/or during osteotomy creation for fixture installation.

Note: While out of numerical order, D6190 is correctly listed here under the Pre-surgical Services subcategory.

CODING WATCH CORRECTION

It is an error to report either a surgical stent (D5982) or surgical splint (D5988) when providing an implant index. D6190 is the correct code to report when a radiographic/surgical implant index (D6190) is provided to guide in the surgical placement of implants. Also use D6190 to report radiographic implant mapping or the implant template guide.

COMMENTS

1. D6190 is used to describe a radiographic index or a surgical guide used to assist in implant placement. The index is inserted in the patient's mouth while the radiograph is taken. The index is designed in such a manner that it can also be used during implant placement to guide the positioning of the implant. If this is the case, the radiographic index is also the surgical index.

2. When a surgical index is not also a radiographic index, the index may not be radiopaque. If the index is only a surgical index, it is used as a guide to the osteotomy or for ideal fixture positioning. In some cases, a radiographic index is sufficient. In other cases only the surgical index is needed. Some, more complex cases may require both.

3. A surgical index can be a suck down, acrylic guide or CAD/CAM fabricated (expensive). The patient fee for the implant index varies depending upon the laboratory fee.

LIMITATIONS

Typically, D6190 is not reimbursed unless the patient has a policy with an implant rider. This service is subject to any exclusions, limitations, or maximum reimbursements outlined in the plan.

TIPS

1. The surgeon may request the restorative dentist to make this radiographic/surgical index. The general practitioner might charge $150 to $400 for this procedure.

2. It is suggested that the surgical implant index (D6190) be billed as a separate component of the implant service. Many times the implant procedures are not a covered benefit (unless there is a rider). The index will generally be billable to, and the responsibility of, the patient.

NARRATIVES

A brief narrative should be provided when reporting D6190. The service will not be reimbursed unless there is an implant rider in the contract. Should the patient be covered by a policy with an implant rider, this procedure may be considered diagnostic and integral for the implant fee.

This is an example of a radiograph/surgical implant index to guide the surgeon to the proper site to place the implant(s).

Courtesy Drake Dental Lab

SURGICAL SERVICES   CDT 2016

Report surgical implant procedure using codes in this section.

D6010 — SURGICAL PLACEMENT OF IMPLANT BODY: ENDOSTEAL IMPLANT — CDT 2016

CODING WARNING CORRECTION

1. Do not report D6010 for interim (transitional) implant body, see D6012 instead.
2. Do not report D6010 to describe the surgical placement of a mini implant, see D6013 instead.
3. Do not report D6010 to report an anchorage device, see D7292/D7293/D7294 instead.

COMMENTS D6010 is the most commonly used code to report surgically placed (long term) implants into the alveolus or basal bone. D6010 reports most implant surgeries. Placement of the healing cap is NOT included in the surgical placement of implant body. Surgical exposure of the implant to enable placement of a healing cap is referred to as "second stage surgery" and is reported separately as D6011. Therefore, D6011 reports second stage surgery such as the placement of the healing cap or surgical access to enable placement of an implant abutment.

LIMITATIONS

1. While surgical placement of implant body (D6010) is not *typically* reimbursed by dental insurance, an implant or abutment supported crown may be reimbursed as an *alternate* benefit.
2. When D6010 is not reimbursed by dental insurance, the implant may be reimbursed by medical insurance in limited circumstances. Medical justification for an implant might be the treatment of health related digestive disorders by improving masticatory function. Another justification would be trauma.
3. Subject to the annual reimbursement limitation, the implant placement (D6010) may be paid if there is an implant rider to the policy.

PHOTO This is an example of a conventional full size implant

Courtesy Drake Dental Lab

D6011 — SECOND STAGE IMPLANT SURGERY — CDT 2016

Surgical access to an implant body for placement of a healing cap or to enable placement of an abutment.

COMMENTS

1. D6011 is used to describe the surgical process whereby the implant body, i.e., D6010, is exposed. Typically a healing cap is placed into the endosteal implant once the body of the implant is surgically exposed. The healing cap maintains an access opening through the gingiva to the endosteal implant body during the restorative phase of implant placement. D6011 also describes the surgical access to enable the placement of an abutment.
2. Second stage implant surgery (D6011) is a separate procedure performed at some time after the surgical placement of the implant body.
3. Not every implant case requires second stage surgery, or healing abutments. A different dentist from the one who placed the implant(s) may perform the second stage surgery, reporting D6011.

LIMITATIONS

1. D6011 is seldom reimbursed and is considered by payers to be a part of the implant placement service, i.e., D6010.
2. D6011 may be reimbursed if there is implant coverage, the body of the implant is exposed and the healing cap placed by a dentist other than the dentist who placed the endosteal implant body.
3. D6011 also may be considered for reimbursement if the patient has implant coverage, the original prosthesis was broken or was lost and the gingival tissue had overgrown the retained endosteal implant body.

NARRATIVES Support the submission of D6011 by identifying the circumstances in which the surgical access was necessary and that another practitioner placed the endosteal implant body, if applicable.

D6012 — SURGICAL PLACEMENT OF INTERIM IMPLANT BODY FOR TRANSITIONAL PROSTHESIS: ENDOSTEAL IMPLANT — CDT 2016

Includes removal during later therapy to accommodate the definitive restoration, which may include placement of other implants.

COMMENTS D6012 describes *interim* implants that will be placed and then removed when the permanent implants are placed. The interim implants are typically smaller in diameter and placed in areas apart from the future implant site. These implants support a temporary fixed prosthesis during the healing process in situations where the patients cannot tolerate a removable prosthesis.

LIMITATIONS
1. *Removal* of the interim implant body is included in the global fee for D6012.
2. Interim implants are generally not a covered benefit.

D6013 — SURGICAL PLACEMENT OF MINI IMPLANT — CDT 2016

CODING CORRECTION WARNING
1. Do not report mini implant (D6013) as an interim implant; the interim implant (D6012) functions as a component of an interim (transitional) implant system.
2. D6013 is NOT the correct code to describe a temporary anchorage device (TAD) for temporary orthodontic anchorage. The TAD type of implant is even smaller, often has an end for anchorage to attach an orthodontic wire, and should be described using codes D7292/D7293/D7294. Mini implants (D6013) are surgically placed (long term) implants.

COMMENTS
1. D6013 is used to describe the surgical placement of a long term mini implant. A mini implant is smaller than a full sized implant (D6010), and the fee is less.
2. Mini implants are typically used to support removable prostheses. The procedure involves drilling a pilot hole and placing the implant into the pilot hole. The healing period for mini implants is much shorter because osseointegration occurs more quickly.

LIMITATIONS
1. While surgical placement of the mini implant body (D6013) is not typically reimbursed by dental insurance (unless there is an implant rider), the implant supported prosthesis may be reimbursed as an alternate benefit of a denture in certain special circumstances.
2. Medical justification for a mini implant might be the treatment of health related digestive disorders by improving masticatory function. Another justification could be treatment for trauma.

PHOTO — This is an example of a mini implant

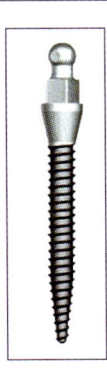

Courtesy Drake Dental Lab

D6020 — PREVIOUSLY DELETED CODE — ABUTMENT PLACEMENT OR SUBSTITUTION

This is a previously deleted code. The implant abutment global fee includes the "placement" labor. See D6051, D6052, D6056 and D6057 to report the various implant abutments, which include placement.

D6040   SURGICAL PLACEMENT: EPOSTEAL IMPLANT   CDT 2016

An eposteal (subperiosteal) framework of a biocompatible material designed and fabricated to fit on the surface of the bone of the mandible or maxilla with permucosal extensions which provide support and attachment of a prosthesis. This may be a complete arch or unilateral appliance. Eposteal implants rest upon the bone and under the periosteum.

COMMENTS
1. Report D6040 for a subperiosteal implant procedure. This type of implant is rarely done.
2. An eposteal implant is a metal framework surgically placed, resting on the mandible, with posts that protrude through the gum to support a prosthesis.
3. This type of implant is used in cases where inadequate ridge is available in the mandible to support an endosteal implant. Eposteal implants are typically used to support a complete mandibular overdenture.

D6050   SURGICAL PLACEMENT: TRANSOSTEAL IMPLANT   CDT 2016

A transosteal (transosseous) biocompatible device with threaded posts penetrating both the superior and inferior cortical bone plates of the mandibular symphysis and exiting through the permucosa providing support and attachment for a dental prosthesis. Transosteal implants are placed completely through the bone and into the oral cavity from extraoral or intraoral.

COMMENTS   A transosteal implant is also called a "staple implant." This type of implant often includes two to four long metal screws surgically placed through the mandible, starting under the chin and extending into the mouth. A plate is fastened to the base of the screws and over the jaw but under the gum. The two to four screws provide anchorage for a lower denture. This type of implant is rarely done.

D6100   IMPLANT REMOVAL, BY REPORT   CDT 2016

This procedure involves the surgical removal of an implant. Describe procedure.

Note: While out of numerical order, D6100 is correctly listed here in the Surgical Services subcategory.

COMMENTS   The average fee for implant removal is $250 – $300. Typically a bone graft is performed at the time of implant removal. Report bone grafting and barrier membrane separately.

LIMITATIONS   Implant removal (D6100) is typically not reimbursed.

NARRATIVES   A brief narrative should identify the arch/location of the implant removed and include a description of the procedure performed. Include the original delivery date of the implant to be removed in the narrative.

D6101   DEBRIDEMENT OF A PERI-IMPLANT DEFECT OR DEFECTS SURROUNDING A SINGLE IMPLANT, AND SURFACE CLEANING OF THE EXPOSED IMPLANT SURFACES, INCLUDING FLAP ENTRY AND CLOSURE   CDT 2016

Note: While out of numerical order, D6101 is correctly listed here under the Surgical Services subcategory.

CODING WATCH CORRECTION   If *osseous contouring* of the peri-implant defect area is provided, report D6102, not D6101.

COMMENTS
1. D6101 is used to describe the debridement of the area around an existing single implant where a bony defect has developed.

2. D6101 includes the cleaning of the exposed implant surfaces to eliminate bacterial pathogens. D6101 includes reflecting a surgical flap for access to the area of the defect(s) as well as the closure of the surgical flap once the debridement has been completed.

LIMITATIONS
1. Reimbursement may be available when there is implant coverage (a rider to the insurance contract) and the need for the procedure is appropriately supported.
2. If D6101 is performed less than a year after the implant has been placed, it is unlikely that the service would be considered for reimbursement. However, it should be reported.

NARRATIVES The reporting of D6101 should be supported by a narrative and documentation that includes:
1. Diagnosis and pretreatment radiographic images of the service area.
2. Photos of the service area after the flap has been laid and before the debridement begins.
3. Photos after the debridement have been provided.
4. Description of the procedure and prognosis.

D6102 DEBRIDEMENT AND OSSEOUS CONTOURING OF A PERI-IMPLANT DEFECT OR DEFECTS SURROUNDING A SINGLE IMPLANT AND INCLUDES SURFACE CLEANING OF THE EXPOSED IMPLANT SURFACES, INCLUDING FLAP ENTRY AND CLOSURE
CDT 2016

Note: While out of numerical order, D6102 is correctly listed here under the Surgical Services subcategory.

CODING WATCH CORRECTION
D6102 requires osseous contouring of the peri-implant defect. If no osseous contouring of the peri-implant defect area is provided, report D6101.

COMMENTS
1. D6102 reports the debridement and osseous contouring of the area around an existing single implant where a bony defect has developed.
2. D6102 includes the cleaning of the exposed implant surfaces to eliminate bacterial pathogens. D6102 includes reflecting a surgical flap for access to the area of the defect as well as the closure of the surgical flap once the debridement and osseous contouring has been completed.
3. If a bone graft is placed to repair the peri-implant defect as part of procedure D6102, report D6103 separately.
4. Report D4266 or D4267 for barrier membrane placement (GTR) and D4265 for biologic materials placement separately.

LIMITATIONS
1. Reimbursement may be available when there is implant coverage (a rider to the insurance contract) and the need for the procedure is appropriately supported.
2. If D6102 is performed less than a year after the implant has been placed, it is unlikely that the service would be considered for reimbursement. However, it should be reported.

NARRATIVES The reporting of D6102 should be supported by a brief narrative and documentation that includes:
1. Diagnosis and pretreatment radiographic images of the service area.
2. Photos of the service area after the flap has been laid and before the debridement and osseous contouring begins.
3. Photos after the debridement and osseous contouring has been provided and before the flap closure.
4. Description of the procedure and prognosis.

| **D6103** | **REVISED BONE GRAFT FOR REPAIR OF PERI-IMPLANT DEFECT – DOES NOT INCLUDE FLAP ENTRY AND CLOSURE** | **CDT 2016** |

Placement of a barrier membrane or biologic materials to aid in osseous regeneration are reported separately.

Note: While out of numerical order, D6103 is correctly listed here under the Surgical Services subcategory.

REVISIONS The descriptor had been inadvertently included in the nomenclature for D6103 in CDT 2015.

COMMENTS
1. D6103 reports the placement of a bone graft in the area around an existing implant where a bony defect exists. D6102 would report the debridement and osseous contouring of a peri-implant defect, while D6103 reports the placement of the bone graft.
2. D6103 does not include the placement of a barrier membrane. See D4266 or D4267 to describe the guided tissue regeneration (GTR) barrier membrane, per site, which is reported separately.
3. D4265 reports the use of biologic materials to aid in soft and osseous tissue regeneration, which is reported separately from D6103, D4266 or D4267.

LIMITATIONS
1. Reimbursement may be available when there is implant coverage (a rider to the insurance contract) and the need for the procedure is appropriately supported.
2. If D6103 is performed less than a year after the implant has been placed, it is unlikely that the service would be considered for reimbursement. However, it should be reported.

NARRATIVES The reporting of D6103 should be supported by a brief narrative and documentation that includes:
1. Diagnosis and pretreatment radiographic images of the service area.
2. Photos of the service area after the flap has been laid, bone contoured and before bone graft placement.
3. Photos after the bone graft for repair of peri-implant defect has been placed, but before the flap has been replaced.
4. Description of the procedures and prognosis.

| **D6104** | **BONE GRAFT AT TIME OF IMPLANT PLACEMENT** | **CDT 2016** |

Placement of a barrier membrane, or biologic materials to aid in osseous regeneration are reported separately

Note: While out of numerical order, D6104 is correctly listed here under the Surgical Services subcategory.

COMMENTS
1. D6104 is used to describe the placement of a bone graft at the same time the implant is placed. Report the surgical placement of the implant body separately.
2. D6104 does not include the placement of a guided tissue regeneration barrier membrane. See D4266 or D4267 to describe a guided tissue regeneration barrier membrane, per site.
3. D6104 does not include the use of biologic materials to aid in soft and osseous regeneration. See D4265 to report the use of biologic materials to aid in soft and osseous tissue regeneration.

LIMITATIONS Reimbursement may be available when there is implant coverage (a rider to the insurance contract) and the need for the procedure is appropriately supported.

NARRATIVES The reporting of D6104 should be supported by a narrative and documentation that includes:
1. Diagnosis and pretreatment radiographic images of the service area.
2. Photos of the service area prior to implant placement.

3. Photos after the implant and graft have been placed, but before the flap has been replaced.
4. Description of the procedures and prognosis.

IMPLANT SUPPORTED PROSTHETICS — CDT 2016

SUPPORTING STRUCTURES — CDT 2016

D6055 CONNECTING BAR – IMPLANT SUPPORTED OR ABUTMENT SUPPORTED — CDT 2016

Utilized to stabilize and anchor a prosthesis.

While out of numerical order, D6055 is correctly listed here under the Supporting Structures subcategory.

COMMENTS
1. Another option for stabilizing an implant overdenture is to use a connector bar (e.g., Hader® bar). The connector bar (D6055) attaches to implant abutments or to the implants themselves. The implant overdenture is fabricated to clip onto the connector bar. This attachment restricts movement of the prosthesis and makes the overdenture more secure. Each implant abutment is reported separately (D6056 or D6057).
2. Each of the implant components of the implant system are reported separately.
3. The connector bar may also be directly attached to the implants.
4. The connector bar should be reported just once, regardless of the number of abutments/implants to which it is attached. (Report D6920 when a connector bar is attached to fixed partial denture retainer crown or coping instead of being attached directly to the implants/abutments).
5. D5862 reports the attachments to the overdenture.

LIMITATIONS D6055 is not typically a covered benefit.

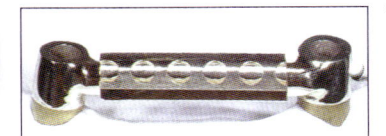

This is an example of a dental implant supported connecting bar – Dolder® type.

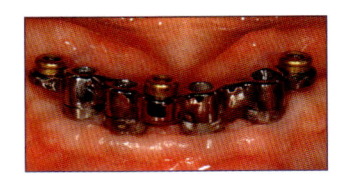

This is an example of a dental implant supported connecting bar – Hader® type.

Courtesy Drake Dental Lab

D6056 PREFABRICATED ABUTMENT – INCLUDES MODIFICATION AND PLACEMENT CDT 2016

Modification of a prefabricated abutment may be necessary.

Note: While out of numerical order, D6056 is correctly listed here under the Supporting Structures subcategory.

1. Do not solely report D6056 in conjunction with an abutment supported overdenture (D6110/D6111/D6112/D6113). See D6052 which describes a semi-precision attachment abutment which includes placement of keeper assembly in the removable overdenture, and is the most common procedure. D6052 is the locator for the full size implant and the overdenture.
2. Report both D6056 or D6057 and D5862 when separate abutment and locator assemblies are used (fairly rare).

CODING WATCH CORRECTION

1. Charge *separately* for a prefabricated implant abutment (D6056) when associated with an abutment supported crown. *Never* include the individual components of the implant "system" into the global implant crown fee. Reporting the components separately will correctly assign the fee for each component to the implant restoration. The implants are not a covered benefit under most contracts and reimbursement may be expected from the patient. Note, the PPO contract may dictate the fee charged for the implant and its components, even though it is not a covered benefit.

2. Do not report the prefabricated (manufactured) abutment (D6056), when a custom (cast or milled) abutment (D6057) is used. The custom abutment has a higher UCR fee assigned.

3. D6051 reports an *interim* abutment. See D6051 for details.

CODING MATCH CORRECTION

D6056 reports an abutment that is *prefabricated* or "manufactured" (may be used "out of the box"). See D6058-D6064 and D6094 that report the various associated abutment supported *single* crowns. See D6068-D6074 and D6194 that report the various associated abutment supported retainer crowns for fixed partial dentures (bridges).

COMMENTS

1. A prefabricated abutment (D6056) comes from the implant manufacturer and connects the abutment supported crown restoration to the surgically placed dental implant body (D6010).

2. D6052 reports a semi-precision attachment abutment placed in the full size implant which includes placement of a keeper assembly in the implant overdenture. It is a locator.

3. D5862 reports an ERA, ZAAG or Zest attachment for a root attachment with a natural tooth overdenture. D5862 would be reported with a natural tooth overdenture (D5863/D5864/D5865/D5866). Thus, D5862 is not reported with a removable *implant* overdenture except in the *rare* instance where a separate abutment (D6056/D6057) is used.

4. D6051 reports an interim abutment. See D6051 for details.

5. A prefabricated abutment is generally reported with All-on-4 or All-on-6.

LIMITATIONS

Only the implant surgeon or restorative dentist who *places the prefabricated abutment* may report this code. If the implant surgeon *provides* the abutment to the restorative dentist, the surgeon should not report D6056 since he/she did not place it. The implant surgeon could only report D6199, unspecified implant procedure.

PHOTO — D6056

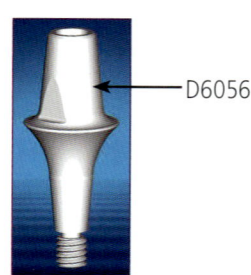

This is an example of a prefabricated abutment.

Courtesy Drake Dental Lab

D6057   CUSTOM FABRICATED ABUTMENT – INCLUDES PLACEMENT   CDT 2016

Created by a laboratory process, specific for an individual application.

Note: While out of numerical order, D6057 is correctly listed here under the Supporting Structures subcategory.

CODING WARNING CORRECTION

1. Do not report custom fabricated abutment (D6057) in conjunction with an abutment or implant supported overdenture (D6110/D6111/D6112/D6113). See D6052 which describes a semi-precision attachment abutment which includes placement of a keeper assembly in the removable overdenture, and is the most common procedure. D6052 is a locator.

2. Report D6056/D6057 and D5862 when separate abutment and locator assemblies are used (fairly rare).

CODING WATCH CORRECTION: Charge *separately* for the custom abutment (D6057) when associated with an abutment supported crown. *Never* include the individual components of the implant "system" into the global implant crown fee. Reporting the components separately will correctly assign the fee for each component to the global implant restoration. Implants are not a covered benefit under most contracts and reimbursement may be expected from the patient. Note, the PPO contract may dictate the fee charged for the implant and its abutment components, even though it is not a covered benefit. The fee dictated depends on either state law or if it is a self-funded plan, federal law will apply.

CODING MATCH CORRECTION: D6057 reports a *custom* abutment (cast or milled) by a laboratory. See D6058-D6064 and D6094 that report the various *associated* abutment supported *single* crowns. See D6068-D6074 and D6194 which report the various *associated* abutment supported retai*ner* crowns for fixed partial dentures (bridges).

COMMENTS
1. A casting or milling process is used to create a *custom* abutment (D6057) specific to an individual application.
2. D6052 reports a semi-precision attachment abutment which includes placement of a keeper assembly in the implant overdenture. It is a locator.
3. D5862 reports an ERA, ZAAG or Zest attachment for a root attachment with a natural tooth overdenture. D5862 would be reported with a natural tooth overdenture (D5863/D5864/D5865/D5866). D5862 is not reported with a removable *implant* overdenture except in the *rare* instance where a separate abutment (D6056/D6057) is used.
4. D6051 reports an interim abutment. See D6051 for details.

LIMITATIONS Only the implant surgeon or restorative dentist who *places* the custom abutment may report this code. If the implant surgeon *provides* a custom abutment to the restorative dentist, then the surgeon would report D6199 to describe this unspecified implant procedure scenario.

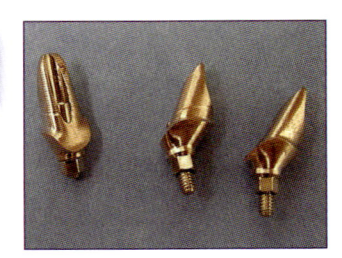

PHOTO: This is an example of several custom abutments.

Courtesy Drake Dental Lab

D6051 INTERIM ABUTMENT — CDT 2016

Includes placement and removal. A healing cap is not an interim abutment.

Note: While out of numerical order, D6051 is correctly listed here under the Supporting Structures subcategory.

CODING WATCH CORRECTION: Charge *separately* for an interim abutment (D6051). *Never* include the individual components of the implant "system" in the global implant crown fee. Reporting the components more accurately will correctly assign the fee and separate the charge for each component to the implant restoration. The implants are not a covered benefit under most contracts and reimbursement may be collected from the patient. Note, the PPO contract may dictate the fee charged for the implant and its components, even though it is not a covered benefit. The patient's responsibility to pay the non-covered amount depends on the state law or if it is a self-funded plan, federal law will apply.

COMMENTS The interim abutment D6051 would be placed while awaiting definitive treatment and would be replaced by either a prefabricated abutment D6056, custom abutment D6057, or a UCLA one piece (screw retained) crown.

LIMITATIONS The implant surgeon or restorative dentist who *places the interim abutment* may report this code. If the implant surgeon *provides* the interim abutment or the prefabricated abutment, D6056, to the restorative dentist, the surgeon should not report the abutment since he/she did not place it. The implant surgeon could only report D6199, unspecified implant procedure if the prefabricated abutment is furnished to the restoring dentist.

D6052   SEMI-PRECISION ATTACHMENT ABUTMENT   CDT 2016

Includes placement of keeper assembly.

Note: While out of numerical order, D6052 is correctly listed here under the Supporting Structures subcategory.

COMMENTS
1. D6052 describes the placement of a semi-precision attachment abutment in the body of an endosteal implant and includes the placement of the keeper assembly. D6052 should be used to report an implant locator abutment, which involves placement of a prefabricated abutment on an implant fixture and luting of the keeper assembly into the removable prosthesis.
2. If the patient has a complete maxillary or a complete mandibular *natural tooth* overdenture (D5863 or D5865), see D5862 to report a precision attachment (e.g., a locator).

LIMITATIONS Semi-precision attachment abutments may be reimbursed if the patient has implant coverage and there is sufficient justification for the use of the semi-precision attachment abutment.

NARRATIVES The narrative should establish the need for the semi-precision attachment abutment by describing the type of abutment used and how the keeper assembly was attached to the prosthesis along with appropriate radiographs and/or pictures.

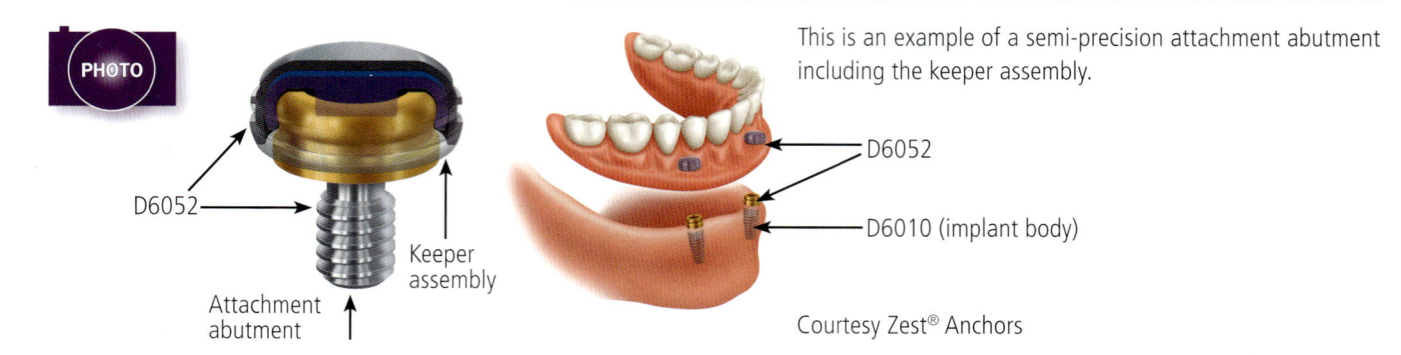

This is an example of a semi-precision attachment abutment including the keeper assembly.

D6052 — Attachment abutment, Keeper assembly
D6052
D6010 (implant body)

Courtesy Zest® Anchors

IMPLANT/ABUTMENT SUPPORTED REMOVABLE DENTURES   CDT 2016

D6053   PREVIOUSLY DELETED CODE IMPLANT/ABUTMENT SUPPORTED REMOVABLE DENTURE FOR COMPLETELY EDENTULOUS ARCH

This is a previously deleted code. See D6110 and D6111 for further details.

D6110   IMPLANT/ABUTMENT SUPPORTED REMOVABLE DENTURE FOR EDENTULOUS ARCH – MAXILLARY   CDT 2016

Note: While out of numerical order, D6110 is correctly listed here under the Implant/Abutment Supported Removable Dentures subcategory.

CODING WARNING CORRECTION
1. D6110 reports an *implant or abutment supported* maxillary removable overdenture for the *edentulous* arch.
2. The *natural* tooth supported maxillary overdenture – complete (D5863) is often erroneously reported when the *implant supported* removable denture for edentulous maxillary arch (D6110) is the correct code to describe the implant overdenture prosthesis. Use the correct *implant/abutment supported* removable overdenture code, D6110, to describe the maxillary prosthesis supported by an implant/abutment. For a natural tooth supported maxillary overdenture, see D5863.

3. You may report prefabricated abutment (D6056) or custom abutment (D6057) plus D5862 (two pieces) in conjunction with D6110. This is three pieces total. This is not common. See D6052.

COMMENTS
1. For a maxillary implant overdenture (D6110), report semi-precision abutment D6052 when a *full size* implant (D6010) is involved. To report this sequence properly, there must be a separate attachment abutment, and "keeper assembly" in the overdenture. Semi-precision attachment abutment (D6052) now reports the implant abutment semi-precision attachment which *includes* placement of the keeper assembly in the implant overdenture. This is a locator.
2. When a single piece mini-implant (D6013) is used, D5862 reports the "cap" that is embedded in the overdenture. Thus, report D6013 plus D5862.
3. ERA, ZAAG or Zest attachments may be reported using D5862.

LIMITATIONS Reimbursement for the implant or abutment supported removable overdenture is typically subject to the five to 10-year prosthetic replacement rule. An alternate benefit of a maxillary complete denture (D5110) may be reimbursed if no other denture (including immediate) has been reported within the period.

NARRATIVES Use D6110 to describe a complete removable maxillary overdenture supported by either abutments or implants. The claim should indicate if the prosthesis is the initial appliance or a replacement appliance and dates of the most recent extractions if this is the initial placement for the overdenture.

D6111 IMPLANT/ABUTMENT SUPPORTED REMOVABLE DENTURE FOR EDENTULOUS ARCH – MANDIBULAR   CDT 2016

Note: While out of numerical order, D6111 is correctly listed here under the Implant/Abutment Supported Removable Dentures subcategory.

1. D6111 reports an *implant or abutment supported* mandibular removable overdenture for the *edentulous* arch.
2. The *natural* tooth supported mandibular overdenture – complete (D5865) is often erroneously reported when the *implant supported* removable denture for completely edentulous mandibular arch (D6111) is the correct code to describe the implant overdenture prosthesis. Use the correct *implant/abutment supported* removable overdenture code, D6111, to describe the mandibular prosthesis supported by an implant/abutment. For a natural tooth supported mandibular overdenture, see D5865.
3. You may report prefabricated abutment (D6056) or custom abutment (D6057) plus D5862 (two pieces) in conjunction with D6111. This is three pieces total. This is not common. See D6052.

COMMENTS
1. For a mandibular implant overdenture (D6011), report semi-precision abutment D6052 when a *full size* implant D6010 is involved. To report this sequence properly, there must be a separate attachment abutment, and "keeper assembly" in the overdenture. Semi-precision attachment abutment (D6052) now reports the implant abutment semi-precision attachment which *includes* placement of the keeper assembly in the implant overdenture. This is a locator.
2. When a single piece mini-implant (D6013) is used, D5862 reports the "cap" that is embedded in the overdenture. Thus, report D6013 plus D5862.
3. ERA, ZAAG or Zest attachments may be reported using D5862.

LIMITATIONS Reimbursement for the implant or abutment supported removable overdenture is typically subject to the five to 10-year prosthetic replacement rule. An alternate benefit of a mandibular complete denture D5120 may be reimbursed if no other denture (including immediate) has been reported within the period.

NARRATIVES Use D6111 to describe a complete removable mandibular overdenture supported by either abutments or implants. The claim should indicate if the prosthesis is the initial appliance or a replacement appliance and dates of the most recent extractions if this is the initial placement for the overdenture.

D6054 — PREVIOUSLY DELETED CODE IMPLANT/ABUTMENT SUPPORTED REMOVABLE DENTURE FOR PARTIALLY EDENTULOUS ARCH

This is a previously deleted code. See D6112 and D6113 for further details.

D6112 — IMPLANT/ABUTMENT SUPPORTED REMOVABLE DENTURE FOR PARTIALLY EDENTULOUS ARCH – MAXILLARY — CDT 2016

Note: While out of numerical order, D6112 is correctly listed here under the Implant/Abutment Supported Removable Denture subcategory.

CODING WARNING CORRECTION

1. The *natural* tooth overdenture – maxillary partial (D5864) should not be used to describe *implant/abutment* supported removable denture for *partially edentulous* maxillary arch (D6112). If implants or abutments support the removable partial maxillary overdenture, then report a maxillary partially edentulous arch overdenture, (D6112).
2. You may report prefabricated abutment (D6056) or custom abutment (D6057) plus D5862 with D6112 – three pieces total. This is not common. See D6052.

COMMENTS

1. D6112 reports an *implant or abutment supported* removable overdenture for the partially edentulous maxillary arch. If the partially edentulous arch overdenture is supported/retained by *natural teeth*, see D5864.
2. For a maxillary implant overdenture (D6112), report semi-precision abutment D6052 when a *full size* implant (D6010) is involved. To report this sequence properly, there must be a separate attachment abutment, and "keeper assembly" in the overdenture. Semi-precision attachment abutment (D6052) now reports the implant abutment semi-precision attachment which *includes* placement of the keeper assembly in the implant overdenture. This is a locator.
3. When a single piece mini-implant (D6013) is used, D5862 reports the "cap" that is embedded in the overdenture. Thus, report D6013 plus D5862.
4. ERA, ZAAG or Zest attachments may be reported using D5862.

LIMITATIONS An alternate benefit of D5213 (maxillary partial denture) may be reimbursed if a partial denture has not been reported within five years (seven to 10 years for some dental plans). Any adjustments done within the first six months are included in the global fee.

NARRATIVES The claim should indicate, if the prosthesis is the initial appliance or a replacement appliance, and dates of most recent extractions if this is the initial placement for the overdenture.

D6113 — IMPLANT/ABUTMENT SUPPORTED REMOVABLE DENTURE FOR PARTIALLY EDENTULOUS ARCH – MANDIBULAR — CDT 2016

Note: While out of numerical order, D6113 is correctly listed here under the Implant/Abutment Supported Removable Denture subcategory.

CODING WARNING CORRECTION

1. The *natural* tooth overdenture – mandibular partial (D5866) should not be used to describe *implant/abutment* supported removable denture for *partially edentulous* mandibular arch (D6113). If implants or abutments support the removable partial mandibular overdenture, then report a mandibular partially edentulous arch overdenture, (D6113).
2. You may report the two piece precision attachment (D5862) plus the prefabricated abutment (D6056) or custom abutment (D6057) in conjunction with D6113. This is three pieces total. This is not common. See D6052.

COMMENTS

1. D6113 reports an *implant or abutment supported* removable overdenture for the partially edentulous mandibular arch. If the partially edentulous arch overdenture is supported/retained by *natural teeth*, see D5866.

2. For a mandibular implant overdenture (D6113), report semi-precision abutment D6052 when a *full size* implant (D6010) is involved. To report this sequence properly, there must be a separate attachment abutment, and "keeper assembly" in the overdenture. Semi-precision attachment abutment (D6052) now reports the implant abutment semi-precision attachment which *includes* placement of the keeper assembly in the implant overdenture. This is a locator.

3. When a single piece mini-implant (D6013) is used, D5862 reports the "cap" that is embedded in the overdenture. Thus, report D6013 plus D5862.

4. ERA, ZAAG or Zest attachments may be reported using D5862.

LIMITATIONS An alternate benefit of D5214 (mandibular partial denture) may be reimbursed if a partial denture has not been reported within five years (seven to 10 years for some dental plans). Any adjustments done within the first six months are included in the global fee.

NARRATIVES The claim should indicate if the prosthesis is the initial appliance or a replacement appliance, and dates of most recent extractions if this is the initial placement for the overdenture.

IMPLANT/ABUTMENT SUPPORTED FIXED DENTURES (HYBRID PROSTHESIS) — CDT 2016

D6078 — PREVIOUSLY DELETED CODE IMPLANT/ABUTMENT SUPPORTED FIXED DENTURE FOR COMPLETELY EDENTULOUS ARCH

This is a previously deleted code. See D6114 and D6115 for further details

D6114 — IMPLANT/ABUTMENT SUPPORTED FIXED DENTURE FOR EDENTULOUS ARCH – MAXILLARY — CDT 2016

Note: While out of numerical order, D6114 is correctly listed here under the Implant/Abutment supported fixed dentures (Hybrid Prosthesis) subcategory.

COMMENTS The maxillary "hybrid prosthesis" (D6114) completely replaces *all* the missing teeth via the use of a fixed denture. The implants do not necessarily have relative tooth positions. There may be implants any place in the alveolar ridge, wherever the restorative dentist deems necessary to place the implants. This horseshoe shaped substructure may have prosthetic teeth bonded to the framework via acrylic. There may be as few as four implants or as many as eight. This maxillary fixed prosthesis is for the edentulous arch. An All-on-4 hybrid is connected with prefabricated abutments (D6056).

LIMITATIONS
1. D6114 is typically not reimbursed.
2. A complete denture is subject to the five to 10 year replacement exclusion.

NARRATIVES
1. D6114 is used to report a fixed prosthesis in the maxillary arch. Specify if this is an initial fixed denture or a replacement. If it is a replacement, list the date that the initial denture was placed.
2. Request an alternate benefit of a maxillary complete denture (D5110) when providing an implant/abutment supported fixed maxillary denture (D6114).

D6115 — IMPLANT/ABUTMENT SUPPORTED FIXED DENTURE FOR EDENTULOUS ARCH – MANDIBULAR — CDT 2016

Note: While out of numerical order, D6115 is correctly listed here under the Implant/Abutment supported fixed dentures (Hybrid Prosthesis) subcategory.

COMMENTS — The mandibular "hybrid prosthesis" (D6115) completely replaces *all* the missing teeth via the use of a fixed denture. The implants do not necessarily have relative tooth positions. There may be implants any place in the alveolar ridge, wherever the restorative dentist deems necessary to place the implants. This horseshoe shaped substructure may have prosthetic teeth bonded to the framework via acrylic. There may be as few as four implants or as many as eight. This mandibular fixed prosthesis is for the edentulous arch. An All-on-4 hybrid is connected with prefabricated abutments (D6056).

LIMITATIONS
1. D6115 is typically not reimbursed.
2. An implant/abutment supported fixed partial denture is subject to the five to 10-year replacement limitation.

NARRATIVES
1. D6115 is used to report a fixed prosthesis in the mandibular arch. Specify if this is an initial fixed denture or a replacement. If it is a replacement, list the date that the initial denture was placed.
2. Request an alternate benefit of a mandibular complete denture (D5120) when providing an implant/abutment supported fixed mandibular denture (D6115).

D6079 — PREVIOUSLY DELETED CODE IMPLANT/ABUTMENT SUPPORTED FIXED DENTURE FOR PARTIALLY EDENTULOUS ARCH

This is a previously deleted code. See D6116 and D6117 for further details.

D6116 — IMPLANT/ABUTMENT SUPPORTED FIXED DENTURE FOR PARTIALLY EDENTULOUS ARCH – MAXILLARY — CDT 2016

Note: While out of numerical order, D6116 is correctly listed here under the Implant/Abutment supported fixed dentures (Hybrid Prosthesis) subcategory.

COMMENTS — The maxillary "hybrid prosthesis" (D6116) replaces some missing teeth via the use of a substructure. The implants do not necessarily have relative tooth positions, i.e., there may or may not be any implant in tooth #6 position. However, there may be implants any place in the alveolar ridge, wherever the restorative dentist deems necessary to place the implants. This substructure may have prosthetic teeth bonded to the framework via acrylic. This maxillary fixed prosthesis is for the partially edentulous arch.

LIMITATIONS
1. D6116 is typically not reimbursed.
2. An implant/abutment supported fixed partial denture is subject to the five to 10-year replacement exclusion.

NARRATIVES
1. D6116 is used to report a fixed prosthesis in the partially edentulous maxillary arch. Specify if this is an initial fixed denture or a replacement. If it is a replacement, list the date that the initial denture was placed.
2. Request an alternate benefit of a cast metal maxillary partial denture (D5213) when providing an implant/abutment supported maxillary fixed partial denture for a partially edentulous maxillary arch (D6116).

D6117 — IMPLANT/ABUTMENT SUPPORTED FIXED DENTURE FOR PARTIALLY EDENTULOUS ARCH – MANDIBULAR

CDT 2016

Note: While out of numerical order, D6117 is correctly listed here under the Implant/Abutment supported fixed dentures (Hybrid Prosthesis) subcategory.

COMMENTS The mandibular "hybrid prosthesis" (D6117) replaces some missing teeth via the use of a substructure. The implants do not necessarily have relative tooth positions, i.e., there may or may not be any implant in tooth #6 position. However, there may be implants any place in the alveolar ridge, wherever the restorative dentist deems necessary to place the implants. This substructure may have prosthetic teeth bonded to the framework via acrylic. This mandibular fixed prosthesis is for the partially edentulous arch.

LIMITATIONS
1. D6117 is typically not reimbursed.
2. An implant/abutment supported fixed partial denture is subject to the five to 10-year replacement limitation.

NARRATIVES
1. D6117 is used to report a fixed prosthesis in the partially edentulous mandibular arch. Specify if this is an initial fixed denture or a replacement. If it is a replacement, list the date that the initial denture was placed.
2. Request an alternate benefit of a cast metal mandibular partial denture (D5214) when providing an implant/abutment supported mandibular fixed partial denture for a partially edentulous arch.

SINGLE CROWNS, ABUTMENT SUPPORTED

CDT 2016

D6058 — ABUTMENT SUPPORTED PORCELAIN/CERAMIC CROWN

CDT 2016

A single crown restoration that is retained, supported and stabilized by an abutment on an implant.

CODING WARNING CORRECTION — It is misleading to report "implant type" crowns (D60xx) as "routine" individual crowns (D27xx) for natural teeth, solely to increase reimbursement. This may be considered a fraudulent act. Report exactly **what you do** rather than what may gain a higher reimbursement.

CODING WATCH CORRECTION — D6058 reports an "abutment supported" crown. It is an error to report an "implant supported" single tooth prosthesis when the crown is anchored to an *abutment*.

CODING MATCH CORRECTION — D6058 reports a porcelain/ceramic crown anchored to an implant abutment. This code describes an "abutment supported" crown anchored over either a prefabricated (D6056) or custom abutment (D6057). D6058 is not attached to the implant body.

LIMITATIONS
1. If an alternate benefit is provided or if covered by an implant policy rider, then reimbursement for "implant type" crowns is typically subject to the five to 10-year limitation period.
2. Age, waiting periods, missing tooth clauses, or other limitations may also apply.

NARRATIVES Ask for the alternate benefit of a similar material type crown if there is no implant coverage.

D6059 — ABUTMENT SUPPORTED PORCELAIN FUSED TO METAL CROWN (HIGH NOBLE METAL) — CDT 2016

A single metal-ceramic crown restoration that is retained, supported and stabilized by an abutment on an implant.

CODING WARNING CORRECTION: It is misleading to report "implant type" crowns (D60xx) as "routine" individual crowns (D27xx) for natural teeth, solely to increase reimbursement. This may be considered a fraudulent act. Report exactly **what you do** rather than what may gain a higher reimbursement.

CODING WATCH CORRECTION: D6059 reports an "abutment supported" crown. It is an error to report an "implant supported" single tooth prosthesis when the crown is anchored to an *abutment*.

CODING MATCH CORRECTION: D6059 reports a porcelain fused to high noble metal crown anchored to an implant abutment. This code describes an "abutment supported" crown anchored over either a prefabricated (D6056) or custom abutment (D6057). D6059 is not attached to the implant body.

LIMITATIONS
1. If an alternate benefit is provided or if covered by an implant policy rider, then reimbursement for "implant type" crowns is typically subject to a five to 10-year limitation period.
2. Age, waiting periods, missing tooth clause, or other limitations may also apply.

NARRATIVES Ask for the alternate benefit of a similar material type if there is no implant coverage.

D6060 — ABUTMENT SUPPORTED PORCELAIN FUSED TO METAL CROWN (PREDOMINANTLY BASE METAL) — CDT 2016

A single metal-ceramic crown restoration that is retained, supported and stabilized by an abutment on an implant.

CODING WARNING CORRECTION: It is misleading to report "implant type" crowns (D60xx) as "routine" individual crowns (D27xx) for natural teeth, solely to increase reimbursement. This may be considered a fraudulent act. Report exactly **what you do** rather than what may gain a higher reimbursement.

CODING WATCH CORRECTION: D6060 reports an "abutment supported" crown. It is an error to report an "implant supported" single tooth prosthesis when the crown is anchored to an *abutment*.

CODING MATCH CORRECTION: D6060 reports a PFM base metal crown anchored to an implant abutment. This code describes an "abutment supported" crown anchored over either a prefabricated (D6056) or custom abutment (D6057). D6060 is not attached to the implant body.

LIMITATIONS
1. If an alternate benefit is provided or if covered by an implant policy rider, then reimbursement for "implant type" crowns is typically subject to a five to 10-year limitation period.

2. Age, waiting periods, missing tooth clause, or other limitations may also apply.

NARRATIVES Ask for the alternate benefit of a similar material type if there is no implant coverage.

D6061 — ABUTMENT SUPPORTED PORCELAIN FUSED TO METAL CROWN (NOBLE METAL) — CDT 2016

A single metal-ceramic crown restoration that is retained, supported and stabilized by an abutment on an implant.

CODING CORRECTION — WARNING: It is misleading to report "implant type" crowns (D60xx) as "routine" individual crowns (D27xx) for natural teeth, solely to increase reimbursement. This may be considered a fraudulent act. Report exactly **what you do** rather than what may gain a higher reimbursement.

CODING CORRECTION — WATCH: D6061 reports an "abutment supported" crown. It is an error to report an "implant supported" single tooth prosthesis when the crown is anchored to an *abutment*.

CODING CORRECTION — MATCH: D6061 reports a PFM noble crown anchored to an implant abutment. This code describes an "abutment supported" crown anchored over either a prefabricated (D6056) or custom abutment (D6057). D6061 is not attached to the implant body.

LIMITATIONS
1. If an alternate benefit is provided or if covered by an implant policy rider, then reimbursement for "implant type" crowns is typically subject to a five to 10-year limitation period.
2. Age, waiting periods, missing tooth clause, or other limitations may also apply.

NARRATIVES Ask for the alternate benefit of a similar material type if there is no implant coverage.

D6062 — ABUTMENT SUPPORTED CAST METAL CROWN (HIGH NOBLE METAL) — CDT 2016

A single cast metal crown restoration that is retained, supported and stabilized by an abutment on an implant.

CODING CORRECTION — WARNING: It is misleading to report "implant type" crowns (D60xx) as "routine" individual crowns (D27xx) for natural teeth, solely to increase reimbursement. This may be considered a fraudulent act. Report exactly **what you do** rather than what may gain a higher reimbursement.

CODING CORRECTION — WATCH: D6062 reports an "abutment supported" crown. It is an error to report an "implant supported" single tooth prosthesis when the crown is anchored to an *abutment*.

CODING CORRECTION — MATCH: D6062 reports a high noble metal crown anchored to an implant abutment. This code describes an "abutment supported" crown anchored over either a prefabricated (D6056) or custom abutment (D6057). D6062 is not attached to the implant body.

D6069 — ABUTMENT SUPPORTED RETAINER FOR PORCELAIN FUSED TO METAL FPD (HIGH NOBLE METAL) CDT 2016

A metal-ceramic retainer for a fixed partial denture that gains retention, support and stability from an abutment on an implant.

CODING WARNING CORRECTION

1. It is an error to report "implant type" retainer crowns (D60xx) as "routine" retainer crowns (D67xx) attached to natural teeth, solely to increase reimbursement. This can be considered a fraudulent act. Always report exactly **what you do** not what may gain a higher reimbursement.
2. When providing a retainer crown (reimbursed at 50% of the UCR fee) it could be considered fraud to intentionally report the retainer crown as a single crown (sometimes reimbursed at 80% of the UCR fee) to gain a higher reimbursement. This could be considered upcoding, a fraudulent act.

CODING WATCH CORRECTION

D6069 reports an "abutment supported" porcelain fused to metal (high noble metal) retainer crown. It is an error to report the prosthesis as "implant supported" when the fixed partial denture (bridge) is supported by an abutment.

CODING MATCH CORRECTION

1. See the *regular* fixed partial denture (bridge) pontic codes that *match* the abutment supported retainer crown. See D6240 to report the correct pontic type for this abutment supported retainer, D6069.
2. D6069 reports the abutment supported (porcelain fused to metal) *retainer crown* for an "implant type" fixed partial denture (bridge) that is supported by either a prefabricated (D6056) or custom abutment (D6057).

LIMITATIONS

1. If an alternate benefit is provided or if covered by an implant policy rider, then reimbursement for "implant type" crowns is typically subject to a five to 10-year limitation period.
2. Age, waiting periods, missing tooth clause, or other limitations may also apply.

NARRATIVES Ask for the alternate benefit of a similar material type if there is no implant coverage.

D6070 — ABUTMENT SUPPORTED RETAINER FOR PORCELAIN FUSED TO METAL FPD (PREDOMINANTLY BASE METAL) CDT 2016

A metal-ceramic retainer for a fixed partial denture that gains retention, support and stability from an abutment on an implant.

CODING WARNING CORRECTION

1. It is misleading to report "implant type" retainer crowns (D60xx) as "routine" retainer crowns (D67xx) attached to natural teeth, solely to increase reimbursement. This can be considered a fraudulent act. Always report exactly **what you do** rather than what may gain a higher reimbursement.
2. When providing a retainer crown (reimbursed at 50% of the UCR fee) it could be considered fraud to intentionally report the retainer crown as a single crown (sometimes reimbursed at 80% of the UCR fee) to gain a higher reimbursement. This could be considered upcoding, a fraudulent act.

CODING WATCH CORRECTION

D6070 reports an "abutment supported" porcelain fused to metal (predominantly base metal) retainer crown. It is an error to report the prosthesis as "implant supported" when the fixed partial denture (bridge) is supported by an abutment.

CODING MATCH CORRECTION

1. See the *regular* fixed partial denture (bridge) pontic codes that *match* the abutment supported retainer crown. See D6241 to report the correct pontic type for this PFM base metal *abutment supported* retainer crown, D6070.
2. D6070 reports the abutment supported (porcelain fused to predominantly base metal) retainer crown for an "implant type" fixed partial denture (bridge) that is supported by either a prefabricated (D6056) or custom abutment (D6057).

LIMITATIONS
1. If an alternate benefit is provided or if covered by an implant policy rider, then reimbursement for "implant type" crowns is typically subject to a five to 10-year limitation period.
2. Age, waiting periods, missing tooth clause, or other limitations may also apply.

NARRATIVES Ask for the alternate benefit of a similar material type if there is no implant coverage.

D6071 — ABUTMENT SUPPORTED RETAINER FOR PORCELAIN FUSED TO METAL FPD (NOBLE METAL) — CDT 2016

A metal-ceramic retainer for a fixed partial denture that gains retention, support and stability from an abutment on an implant.

CODING WARNING CORRECTION
1. It is misleading to report "implant type" retainer crowns (D60xx) as "routine" retainer crowns (D67xx) attached to natural teeth, solely to gain reimbursement. Always report exactly **what you do** rather than what is reimbursed.
2. When providing a retainer crown (reimbursed at 50% of the UCR fee) it could be considered fraud to intentionally report the retainer crown as a single crown (reimbursed at 80% of the UCR fee) to gain a higher reimbursement. This could be considered upcoding, a fraudulent act.

CODING WATCH CORRECTION
D6071 reports an "abutment supported" porcelain fused to metal (noble metal) retainer crown. It is an error to report the prosthesis as "implant supported" when the fixed partial denture (bridge) is supported by an abutment.

CODING MATCH CORRECTION
1. See the *regular* fixed partial denture (bridge) pontic codes that *match* the abutment supported retainer crown. See D6242 to report the correct pontic type for this PFM noble metal *abutment supported* retainer crown, D6071.
2. D6071 reports the abutment-supported (porcelain fused to noble metal) retaine*r crown* for an "implant type" fixed partial denture (bridge) that is supported by either a prefabricated (D6056) or custom abutment (D6057).

LIMITATIONS
1. If an alternate benefit is provided or if covered by an implant policy rider, then reimbursement for "implant type" crowns is typically subject to a five to 10-year limitation period.
2. Age, waiting periods, missing tooth clause, or other limitations may also apply.

NARRATIVES Ask for the alternate benefit of a similar material type if there is no implant coverage.

D6072 — ABUTMENT SUPPORTED RETAINER FOR CAST METAL FPD (HIGH NOBLE METAL) — CDT 2016

A cast metal retainer for a fixed partial denture that gains retention, support and stability from an abutment on an implant.

CODING WARNING CORRECTION
1. It is misleading to report "implant type" retainer crowns (D60xx) as "routine" retainer crowns (D67xx) attached to natural teeth, solely to increase reimbursement. Always "report exactly **what you do** rather than what is reimbursed.
2. When providing a retainer crown (reimbursed at 50% of the UCR fee) it could be considered fraud to intentionally report the retainer crown as a single crown (reimbursed at 80% of the UCR fee) to gain a higher reimbursement. This could be considered upcoding, a fraudulent act.

CODING WATCH CORRECTION
D6072 reports an "abutment supported" metal (high noble metal) retaine*r crown*. It is an error to report the prosthesis as "implant supported" when the fixed partial denture (bridge) is supported by an abutment.

CODING MATCH CORRECTION

1. See the *regular fixed partial denture* (bridge) pontic codes that *match* the abutment supported retainer crown. See D6210 to report the correct pontic type for this high noble metal *abutment supported* retainer crown, D6072.
2. D6072 reports the abutment supported (high noble metal) retai*ner crown* for an "implant type" fixed partial denture (bridge) that is supported by either a prefabricated (D6056) or custom abutment (D6057).

LIMITATIONS
1. If reimbursed as an alternate benefit or as an implant when covered by an implant policy rider, reimbursement for "implant type" crowns is typically subject to a five to 10-year limitation period.
2. Age, waiting periods, missing tooth clause, or other limitations may also apply.

NARRATIVES Ask for the alternate benefit of a similar material type if there is no implant coverage.

D6073 ABUTMENT SUPPORTED RETAINER FOR CAST METAL FPD (PREDOMINANTLY BASE METAL) — CDT 2016

A cast metal retainer for a fixed partial denture that gains retention, support and stability from an abutment on an implant.

CODING WARNING CORRECTION

1. It is misleading to report "implant type" retainer crowns (D60xx) as "routine" retainer crowns (D67xx) attached to natural teeth, solely to increase reimbursement. Always report exactly **what you do** rather than what is reimbursed.
2. When providing a retainer crown (reimbursed at 50% of the UCR fee) it could be considered fraud to intentionally report the retainer crown as a single crown (reimbursed at 80% of the UCR fee) to gain a higher reimbursement. This could be considered upcoding, a fraudulent act.

CODING WATCH CORRECTION

D6073 reports an "abutment supported" metal (predominantly base metal) retai*ner crown*. It is an error to report the prosthesis as "implant supported" when the fixed partial denture (bridge) is supported by an abutment.

CODING MATCH CORRECTION

1. See the *regular fixed partial denture* (bridge) pontic codes that *match* the abutment supported retainer crown. See D6211 to report the correct pontic type for this base metal *abutment supported* retainer crown, D6073.
2. D6073 reports the abutment-supported (predominantly base metal) retai*ner crown* for an "implant type" fixed partial denture (bridge) that is supported by either a prefabricated (D6056) or custom abutment (D6057).

LIMITATIONS
1. If an alternate benefit is provided or if covered by an implant policy rider, then reimbursement for "implant type" crowns is typically subject to a five to 10-year limitation period.
2. Age, waiting periods, missing tooth clause, or other limitations may also apply.

NARRATIVES Ask for the alternate benefit of a similar material type if there is no implant coverage.

D6074 ABUTMENT SUPPORTED RETAINER FOR CAST METAL FPD (NOBLE METAL) — CDT 2016

A cast metal retainer for a fixed partial denture that gains retention, support and stability from an abutment on an implant.

CODING WARNING CORRECTION

1. It is misleading to report "implant type" retainer crowns (D60xx) as "routine" retainer crowns (D67xx) attached to natural teeth, solely to increase reimbursement. Always report exactly **what you do** rather than what is reimbursed.
2. When providing a retainer crown (reimbursed at 50% of the UCR fee) it could be considered fraud to intentionally report the retainer crown as a single crown (reimbursed at 80% of the UCR fee) to gain a higher reimbursement. This could be considered upcoding, a fraudulent act.

CODING WATCH CORRECTION — D6074 reports an "abutment supported" metal (noble metal) retainer crown. It is an error to report the prosthesis as "implant supported" when the fixed partial denture (bridge) is supported by an abutment.

CODING MATCH CORRECTION
1. See the *regular fixed partial denture* (bridge) pontic codes that *match* the abutment supported retainer crown. See D6212 to report the correct pontic type for this noble metal *abutment supported* retainer crown, D6074.
2. D6074 reports the abutment supported (noble metal) retainer crown for an "implant type" fixed partial denture (bridge) that is supported by either a prefabricated (D6056) or custom abutment (D6057).

LIMITATIONS
1. If an alternate benefit is provided or if covered by an implant policy rider, then reimbursement for "implant type" crowns is typically subject to a five to 10-year limitation period.
2. Age, waiting periods, missing tooth clause, or other limitations may also apply.

NARRATIVES Ask for the alternate benefit of a similar material type if there is no implant coverage.

D6194   ABUTMENT SUPPORTED RETAINER CROWN FOR FPD – (TITANIUM)   CDT 2016

A retainer for a fixed partial denture that gains retention, support and stability from an abutment on an implant. May be cast or milled.

Note: While out of numerical order, D6194 is correctly listed here under the Fixed Partial Denture, Abutment Supported subcategory.

CODING WARNING CORRECTION
1. It is misleading to report "implant type" retainer crowns (D60xx) as "routine" retainer crowns (D67xx) for *natural* teeth, solely to gain reimbursement. This can be considered a fraudulent act. Always report exactly what you do rather than what is reimbursed.
2. Single crowns may be reimbursed at 50-80% of the UCR fee. Retainer crowns may be reimbursed at a 50% UCR fee. It could be considered fraud to intentionally report retainer crowns as single crowns to increase the reimbursement rate for the service. This could be considered upcoding, a fraudulent act.

CODING WATCH CORRECTION — D6194 reports an "abutment supported" titanium retainer crown. It is an error to report the prosthesis as "implant supported" when the fixed partial denture (bridge) is supported by an abutment.

CODING MATCH CORRECTION
1. See the *regular fixed partial denture* (bridge) pontic codes that *match* the abutment supported retainer crown. See D6214 to report the *matching* titanium pontic for this titanium retainer crown, D6194.
2. D6194 reports the abutment supported titanium retainer crown for an "implant type" fixed partial denture (bridge) that is supported by either a prefabricated abutment (D6056) or custom abutment (D6057).

LIMITATIONS
1. If an alternate benefit is provided or if covered by an implant policy rider, then reimbursement for "implant type" crowns is typically subject to a five to 10-year limitation period.
2. Age, waiting periods, missing tooth clause, or other limitations may also apply.

NARRATIVES Request the alternate benefit of a similar retainer type material if there is no implant coverage.

FIXED PARTIAL DENTURE RETAINER, IMPLANT SUPPORTED — CDT 2016

D6075 — IMPLANT SUPPORTED RETAINER FOR CERAMIC FPD — CDT 2016

A ceramic retainer for a fixed partial denture that gains retention, support and stability from an implant.

CODING WARNING CORRECTION
1. It is misleading to report "implant type" retainer crowns (D60xx) as "routine" retainer crowns (D67xx) attached to natural teeth, solely to increase reimbursement. Always report exactly **what you do** rather than what is reimbursed.
2. When providing a retainer crown (reimbursed at 50% of the UCR fee) it could be considered fraud to intentionally report the retainer crown as a single crown (reimbursed at 80% of the UCR fee) to gain a higher reimbursement. This could be considered upcoding, a fraudulent act.

CODING WATCH CORRECTION
D6075 reports an "implant supported" ceramic retainer *crown*. It is an error to report the prosthesis as an "implant supported" retainer crown when the fixed partial denture (bridge) is supported by an abutment.

CODING MATCH CORRECTION
See the *regular fixed partial denture* (bridge) pontic codes that correctly *match* the *implant supported* ceramic retainer crown. See D6245 to report the *matching* ceramic pontic for this *implant supported* ceramic retainer crown (D6075).

COMMENTS D6075 reports the "implant supported" (ceramic) retai*ner crown* for an "implant type" fixed partial denture (bridge). The retainer crown attaches directly (cemented or screw retained) to the implant body. There is no associated abutment used to support the retainer crown.

LIMITATIONS
1. If an alternate benefit is provided or if covered by an implant policy rider, then reimbursement for "implant type" crowns is typically subject to a five to 10-year limitation period.
2. Age, waiting periods, missing tooth clause, or other limitations may also apply.

NARRATIVES Ask for the alternate benefit of a similar material type if there is no implant coverage.

D6076 — IMPLANT SUPPORTED RETAINER FOR PORCELAIN FUSED TO METAL FPD (TITANIUM, TITANIUM ALLOY, OR HIGH NOBLE METAL) — CDT 2016

A metal-ceramic retainer for a fixed partial denture that gains retention, support and stability from an implant.

CODING WARNING CORRECTION
1. It is misleading to report "implant type" retainer crowns (D60xx) as "routine" retainer crowns (D67xx) attached to natural teeth, solely to increase reimbursement. Always report exactly **what you do** rather than what is reimbursed.
2. When providing a retainer crown (reimbursed at 50% of the UCR fee) it could be considered fraud to intentionally report the retainer crown as a single crown (reimbursed at 80% of the UCR fee) to gain a higher reimbursement. This could be considered upcoding, a fraudulent act.

CODING WATCH CORRECTION
D6076 reports an "implant supported" porcelain fused to titanium, titanium alloy, or high noble metal retai*ner crown*. It is an error to report the prosthesis as an "implant supported" retainer crown when the fixed partial denture (bridge) is supported by an abutment.

CODING MATCH CORRECTION — See the *regular* fixed partial denture (bridge) pontic codes that correctly *match* the *implant supported* PFM retainer crown. See the appropriate titanium (D6214) or PFM high noble (D6240) code to report the *matching* pontic for this type of metal *implant supported* retainer crown, D6076.

COMMENTS D6076 reports the "implant-supported" (PFM titanium/PFM titanium alloy/PFM high-noble) retain*er crown* for an "implant-type" bridge. The retainer crown attaches directly (cemented or screw-retained) to the implant body. There is no associated abutment used to support the retainer crown.

LIMITATIONS
1. If an alternate benefit is provided or if covered by an implant policy rider, then reimbursement for "implant type" crowns is typically subject to a five to 10-year limitation period.
2. Age, waiting periods, missing tooth clause, or other limitations may also apply.

NARRATIVES Ask for the alternate benefit of a similar material type if there is no implant coverage.

D6077 — IMPLANT SUPPORTED RETAINER FOR CAST METAL FPD (TITANIUM, TITANIUM ALLOY, OR HIGH NOBLE METAL) — CDT 2016

A cast metal retainer for a fixed partial denture that gains retention, support and stability from an implant.

CODING WARNING CORRECTION
1. It is misleading to report "implant type" retainer crowns (D60xx) as "routine" retainer crowns (D67xx) attached to natural teeth, solely to increase reimbursement. Always report exactly **what you do** rather than what is reimbursed.
2. When providing a retainer crown (reimbursed at 50% of the UCR fee) it could be considered fraud to intentionally report the retainer crown as a single crown (reimbursed at 50% of the UCR fee) to gain a higher reimbursement. This is considered upcoding, a fraudulent act.

CODING WATCH CORRECTION — D6077 reports an "implant supported" titanium, titanium alloy, or high noble all metal retain*er crown*. It is an error to report the prosthesis as an "implant supported" retainer crown when the fixed partial denture (bridge) is supported by an abutment.

CODING MATCH CORRECTION — See the *regular fixed partial denture* (bridge) pontic codes that *match* the *implant supported* metal retainer crown. See the appropriate titanium (D6214) or cast high noble metal (D6210) code to report the *matching* pontic for this type of metal *implant supported* retainer crown, D6077.

COMMENTS D6077 reports the "implant supported" cast metal (titanium/titanium alloy/high noble) retain*er crown* for an "implant type" fixed partial denture (bridge). The retainer crown attaches directly (cemented or screw retained) to the implant body. There is no associated abutment used to support the retainer crown.

LIMITATIONS
1. If reimbursed as an alternate benefit or as an implant when covered by an implant policy rider, reimbursement for "implant type" crowns is typically subject to a five to 10-year limitation period.
2. Age, waiting periods, missing tooth clause, or other limitations may also apply.

NARRATIVES Ask for the alternate benefit of a similar material type if there is no implant coverage.

OTHER IMPLANT SERVICES — CDT 2016

D6080 — IMPLANT MAINTENANCE PROCEDURES WHEN PROSTHESES ARE REMOVED AND REINSERTED, INCLUDING CLEANSING OF PROSTHESES AND ABUTMENTS   CDT 2016

This procedure includes active debriding of the implant(s) and examination of all aspects of the implant system(s), including the occlusion and stability of the superstructure. The patient is also instructed in thorough daily cleansing of the implant(s). This is not a per implant code, and is indicated for implant supported fixed prostheses.

COMMENTS
1. D6080 reports the removal and maintenance of implant supported fixed prosthesis. Do not report D6080 when cleaning around an implant.
2. Implant maintenance procedures (D6080) *include* the active debridement of all the implant(s) as well as the other structures (prostheses) that are a part of the implant system. D6080 also includes hygiene instruction given to the patient on the importance of thorough daily cleansing of the implant(s) and the prostheses attached to them.
3. Diagnostic radiographic images, periodic oral evaluation (D0120), and prophylaxis (D1110) of natural teeth are not a part of the D6080 procedure and should be reported separately.
4. D6080 is reported on a per visit basis, not per prosthesis.
5. D6080 can be reported for any implant supported fixed prosthesis such as a hybrid or implant supported bridge, etc.

LIMITATIONS
1. When no implant benefits are available, there are no benefits available for implant maintenance procedures (D6080).
2. Note: Many payers require documentation and additional information when reporting D6080. D6080 can be billed *in addition* to a prophylaxis (with natural teeth present) when performed on the same day; however, this may not be a covered benefit. Reimbursement is subject to normal plan limitations and exclusions.
3. D6080 could be reported *in addition to* the prophylaxis (D1110) or periodontal maintenance (D4910) visit if the implant retained prosthesis was removed, inspected, cleaned, and reinserted. The implant maintenance procedure may be considered a part of the prophylaxis (D1110) or periodontal maintenance (D4910) service. D6080 is seldom reimbursed when reported with D1110 or D4910.

NARRATIVES
1. Ask for the alternate benefit of prophylaxis (D1110) and include a narrative if D6080 is not reimbursed for the *edentulous* mouth.
2. Many dental plans limit reimbursement for D6080 when an implant-supported superstructure is involved, i.e., a hybrid prosthesis/overdenture, implant-supported bridge, etc. Do not report this code when cleaning around an implant. The narrative should describe the service provided and that the prosthesis was removed, inspected, cleaned, and reinserted.

D6090 — REPAIR IMPLANT SUPPORTED PROSTHESIS, BY REPORT   CDT 2016

This procedure involves the repair or replacement of any part of the implant supported prosthesis.

COMMENTS
1. Repair implant supported prosthesis (D6090) is used to report the repair or replacement of any part of the implant supported prosthesis.
2. For repair or replacement of any part of the implant abutment, see D6095.
3. For replacement of a replaceable component of a semi-precision or precision attachment, see D6091.

LIMITATIONS
1. If a contract has no implant benefits there would be no benefit for the repair of an implant supported prosthesis.
2. D6090 may reset the five to 10-year exclusion period limitation for the implant supported prosthesis, if reimbursed.

NARRATIVES A brief narrative is required when reporting D6090. The narrative should identify the original date of placement, and a description of the repair provided.

| **D6095** | **REPAIR IMPLANT ABUTMENT, BY REPORT** | **CDT 2016** |

This procedure involves the repair or replacement of any part of the implant abutment.

Note: While out of numerical order, D6095 is correctly listed here under the Other Implant Services subcategory.

CODING MATCH CORRECTION — D6095 is used to describe the repair or replacement of any part of the prefabricated (D6056) or custom abutment (D6057).

COMMENTS D6095 is used to describe the replacement of a screw if the screw is used to affix the abutment. If the replacement screw is used to attach an implant-supported prosthesis, report unspecified implant procedure, by report (D6199) and include a narrative.

LIMITATIONS If a patient is covered under a contract with no implant benefits, there would generally be no benefit for the repair of an implant abutment.

NARRATIVES A brief narrative is required when reporting D6095. The narrative should report the original delivery date of the implant abutment to be repaired, the type of repair needed, and identify if the repair is provided for either a *prefabricated* (D6056) or a *custom* abutment (D6057).

| **D6091** | **REPLACEMENT OF SEMI-PRECISION OR PRECISION ATTACHMENT (MALE OR FEMALE COMPONENT) OF IMPLANT/ABUTMENT SUPPORTED PROSTHESIS, PER ATTACHMENT** | **CDT 2016** |

This procedure applies to the replaceable male or female component of the attachment.

CODING WATCH CORRECTION — When the replacement part of a semi-precision or precision attachment is associated with a *removable (natural)* tooth partial device, report D5867.

CODING MATCH CORRECTION — Use code D6091 to report the replacement of a semi-precision or precision attachment component of an associated implant/abutment supported prosthesis-overdenture (D6110/D6111) or partial overdenture (D6112/D6113).

NARRATIVES Identify the attachment type and delivery date of the original semi precision or precision attachment. D6091 is not typically reimbursed unless the replacement is due to damage. Reimbursement for replacement is not typically made for attachments worn out by normal wear and tear. When replacement is necessary due to damage request an alternate benefit of a repair (D6095).

| **D6092** | **RE-CEMENT OR RE-BOND IMPLANT/ABUTMENT SUPPORTED CROWN** | **CDT 2016** |

COMMENTS Re-cement or re-bond implant/abutment supported crown (D6092) reports re-cementing or re-bonding both implant and abutment supported *single* crowns.

LIMITATIONS 1. The exclusion period for re-cementation or re-bonding of an implant crown is typically six to 12 months following the initial placement of the restoration.

2. If re-cementation or re-bonding of the crown is performed in a different office within the exclusion period, the six to 12-month limitation period may not apply.

NARRATIVES Include a brief narrative that alerts the payer when the implant crown was originally seated. If re-cementation or re-bonding occurs in an office, by a dentist, that did not originally deliver the crown, note this in a brief narrative.

D6093 — RE-CEMENT OR RE-BOND IMPLANT/ABUTMENT SUPPORTED FIXED PARTIAL DENTURE (CDT 2016)

COMMENTS Re-cement or re-bond implant/abutment supported fixed partial denture (D6093) reports re-cementing or re-bonding both implant and abutment supported fixed partial dentures (bridges).

LIMITATIONS
1. The typical exclusion period for re-cementation or re-bonding of a fixed partial denture (bridge) is six to 12 months following initial placement of the fixed restoration.
2. If re-cementation or re-bonding of the fixed partial denture (bridge) is performed in a different office within the exclusion period, the six to 12-month limitation period may not apply.

NARRATIVES Include a brief narrative that alerts the payer when the implant/abutment supported fixed partial denture (bridge) was originally seated. If re-cementation or re-bonding occurs in an office, by a dentist, that did not originally deliver the prosthesis, note this in a brief narrative.

Note: D6110-D6117 codes are located under the Implant/Abutment supported removable dentures and Implant/Abutment supported fixed dentures (hybrid prosthesis) subcategories earlier in this section of the book. Many of the codes in this section are not in numerical order, but under various subcategory sections.

D6190 — RADIOGRAPHIC/SURGICAL IMPLANT INDEX, BY REPORT (CDT 2016)

An appliance, designed to relate osteotomy or fixture position to existing anatomic structures, to be utilized during radiographic exposure for treatment planning and/or during osteotomy creation for fixture installation.

Note: This code appears here in numerical order but it is properly situated at the start of the Implant Services, under the Pre-Surgical Services subcategory.

CODING WATCH CORRECTION — It is an error to report either a surgical stent (D5982) or surgical splint (D5988) when providing an implant index. D6190 is the correct code to report when a radiographic/surgical implant index (D6190) is provided to guide in the surgical placement of implants. Also use D6190 to report radiographic implant mapping or the implant template guide.

COMMENTS
1. D6190 is used to describe a radiographic index or a surgical guide used to assist in implant placement. The index is inserted in the patient's mouth while the radiograph is taken. The index is designed in such a manner that it can also be used during implant placement to guide the positioning of the implant. If this is the case, the radiographic index is also the surgical index.
2. When a surgical index is not also a radiographic index, the index may not be radiopaque. If the index is only a surgical index, it is used as a guide to the osteotomy or for ideal fixture positioning. In some cases, a radiographic index is sufficient. In other cases only the surgical index is needed. Some, more complex cases may require both.
3. A surgical index can be a suck down, acrylic guide or CAD/CAM fabricated (very expensive). The fee for the implant index varies depending upon the laboratory fee.

LIMITATIONS Typically, D6190 is not reimbursed unless the patient has a policy with an implant rider. This service is subject to any exclusions, limitations, or maximum reimbursements outlined in the plan.

TIPS
1. The surgeon may request the restorative dentist to make this radiographic/surgical index. The general practitioner might charge $150 to $400 for this procedure.
2. It is suggested that the surgical implant index (D6190) be billed as a separate component of the implant service. Many times the implant procedures are not a covered benefit (unless there is a rider). The index will generally be billable to, and the responsibility of the patient.

NARRATIVES A brief narrative should be provided when reporting D6190. The service will not be reimbursed unless there is an implant rider in the contract. Should the patient be covered by a policy with an implant rider, this procedure may be considered diagnostic and integral for the implant fee.

This is an example of a radiograph/surgical implant index to guide the surgeon to the proper site to place the implant.

Courtesy Drake Dental Lab

D6199 UNSPECIFIED IMPLANT PROCEDURE, BY REPORT   CDT 2016

Use for procedure that is not adequately described by a code. Describe procedure.

COMMENTS
1. For a provisional crown placed on an implant, see D2799.
2. Before you report D6199, look throughout this section and the index for the procedure you are looking for. A multitude of the implant services codes are not in numerical order.
3. D6199 is used to describe the replacement of a screw if the screw is used to attach an implant-supported prosthesis. If the screw is used to affix the abutment, report D6095.

NARRATIVES This is a by report code. Therefore, a brief narrative is always required when this code is submitted.

AUTHOR'S COMMENTS
GENERAL COMMENTS FOR FIXED PARTIAL DENTURE (BRIDGEWORK) SERVICES

1. The fixed partial denture (bridge) pontic metal-type must match the corresponding retainer crown metal type. Always use the matching code, according to its material classification.
2. The metal type used for crowns should be recorded in the clinical notes, entered on the treatment plan, and ordered on the laboratory slip to ensure the proper use and reporting of the metal for the fixed prosthesis.

Watch for any MATCH legends that relate to the corresponding fixed partial denture (bridgework) procedure.

LIMITATIONS
1. Payers may exclude reimbursement for Captek fixed partial dentures (bridges), due to the materials makeup.
2. Payers may exclude reimbursement for fixed partial dentures for patients under age sixteen.
3. Some plans have a six to 12-month waiting period for basic services. Longer limitations (12 to 36 months) may apply for major (fixed prosthetic) services. Plan limitations are highly variable as to what is considered basic or major coverage.
4. Some plans limit reimbursement of anterior fixed partial dentures (bridges) to three units (e.g., retainer crown, pontic, retainer crown).
5. Age, waiting periods, missing tooth, or other limitations may also apply.
6. If there are edentulous spaces in different quadrants in the same arch, alternate benefits may apply.

TIPS
1. Consider:
   a. The "missing tooth" clause may apply to the initial retainer crown placement; however, it may not apply to a replacement retainer crown or fixed partial denture (bridge). The "missing tooth" clause applies to teeth extracted (but not replaced) prior to the plan's current coverage.
   b. Some contracts have waiting periods. The placement of an original fixed partial denture (bridge) may be reimbursed after the current contract is in effect for one to three years.
   c. Benefits may apply if an additional tooth is extracted adjacent to the edentulous space while the contract is in place.
2. When there is more than one edentulous space in the arch, an alternate benefit of a removable partial denture is often applied. If, however, a fixed partial denture(s) has (have) been provided that restores all previous missing teeth in that arch, the narrative should communicate that the existing fixed partial denture(s) exist and the proposed fixed partial denture be reimbursed.

NARRATIVES
1. When submitting a crown claim, it is essential that appropriate documentation including a brief narrative be included to avoid delays and/or claim denials.
2. The payer may reimburse a retainer crown if the supporting abutment retainer qualifies for a crown.
3. If treating cracked tooth syndrome under palliative (D9110), indicate that the diagnosis for the full coverage crown was made by using a Tooth Slooth®, transillumination or seeing the crack into dentin.
4. The narrative should address the existence of caries or other pathology, condition and size of prior restoration, and the condition of the remaining tooth structure. Make note of any undermined, fractured or missing cusps and any symptoms the patient may be experiencing with the affected tooth.
5. "See attached radiographic image" (if tooth has RCT, send PA radiographic image).
6. List any missing cusps.
7. Estimate and state percentage of healthy tooth structure left after fracture, caries and/or any previous restoration is removed. If diagnosis is cracked tooth syndrome, state method of diagnosis, e.g. Tooth Slooth® positive on MF cusp.
8. State if tooth has existing or planned RCT (root canal therapy).
9. State if tooth has circumferential decay and amount of it, e.g. circumferential decay on M, L and D encompassing 270 degrees of tooth.
10. State endodontic and periodontal prognosis for tooth.
11. If this is a replacement crown, state date that the previous crown was seated.
12. If replacing an existing crown, state reason for replacement, e.g. tooth has caries, margins are open, porcelain is fractured off, poor contacts are causing food impactions, etc.

D6200-D6999 IX. PROSTHODONTICS, FIXED — CDT 2016

Each retainer and each pontic constitutes a unit in a fixed partial denture.

Local anesthesia is usually considered to be a part of Fixed Prosthodontic procedures.

The term "fixed partial denture" or FPD is synonymous with fixed bridge or bridgework.

Fixed partial denture prosthetic procedures include routine temporary prosthetics. When indicated, interim or provisional codes should be reported separately.

CLASSIFICATION OF MATERIALS — CDT 2016

Classification of Metals (Source: ADA Council on Scientific Affairs – online at ADA.org/2190.aspx**)**

The noble metal classification system has been adopted as a more precise method of reporting various alloys used in dentistry. The alloys are defined on the basis of the percentage of metal content:

high noble alloys - noble metal content >= 60% (gold+platinum group) and gold >= 40%;

titanium and titanium alloys – Titanium >= 85%;

noble alloys - noble metal content >= 25% (gold+platinum group);

predominantly base alloys - noble metal content < 25% (gold+platinum group);

*metals of the platinum group are platinum, palladium, rhodium, iridium, osmium and ruthenium.

Porcelain/ceramic - Refers to pressed, fired, polished or milled materials containing predominantly inorganic refractory compounds including porcelains, glasses, ceramics and glass-ceramics.

Resin - Refers to any resin-based composite, including fiber or ceramic reinforced polymer compounds, and glass ionomers.

FIXED PARTIAL DENTURE PONTICS — CDT 2016

D6205   PONTIC – INDIRECT RESIN BASED COMPOSITE — CDT 2016

Not to be used as a temporary or provisional prosthesis.

CODING WATCH CORRECTION
1. Be careful that the fixed partial (bridge) *pontic* material type matches the corresponding *retainer* crown material type. Always use the matching code, according to its material classification.
2. Pontic – indirect resin based composite (D6205) reports a permanent fixed partial denture (bridge) pontic. It is an error to report D6205 for a *provisional* prosthesis. D6253 should be reported for a *provisional* pontic.

CODING MATCH CORRECTION
When reporting D6205, pontic–indirect resin based composite, be careful that this code *matches* the corresponding permanent resin based composite retainer crown, D6710.

COMMENTS
1. D6205 describes Artglass®, Cristobel®, Belleglass®, etc., type resin based materials.
2. The pontic of a Hugger bridge is reported as D6205.

LIMITATIONS
1. Reimbursement for the replacement of a fixed partial denture (bridge) is typically subject to a five to 10-year limitation.
2. Age, waiting periods, missing tooth clause or other limitations may also apply to the placement of a fixed partial denture (bridge).

3. The permanent indirect resin fixed partial denture (bridge) pontic (D6205) may be reimbursed as, and subject to, the same exclusions/limitations as a cast fixed partial denture pontic.

NARRATIVES Non-metallic bridges may not be reimbursed. If reimbursement for D6205 is denied, appeal the denial and ask for an alternate benefit. It is recommended that the policy be reviewed to determine the contract language that identifies this exclusion. If reimbursed, this type of pontic would be paid at the D6251 UCR level.

D6210 PONTIC – CAST HIGH NOBLE METAL — CDT 2016

1. When reporting pontic-cast high noble metal (D6210), be careful that the materials reported to describe the pontic *match* the corresponding (cast high noble metal) retainer crown (D6790).
2. D6210 may also report the fixed partial denture (bridge) pontic to *match* the corresponding *abutment supported* implant retainer crown (D6072). D6210 may also report the fixed partial denture pontic that is a *match* to the corresponding *implant supported* retainer crown (D6077).

LIMITATIONS
1. Reimbursement for a fixed partial denture (bridge) is typically subject to a five to 10-year limitation.
2. Age, waiting periods, missing tooth clause or other limitations may also apply to the placement of a fixed partial denture (bridge).

D6211 PONTIC – CAST PREDOMINANTLY BASE METAL — CDT 2016

1. When reporting pontic-cast predominantly base metal (D6211), be careful that the materials reported to describe the pontic *match* the corresponding (cast base metal) retainer crown (D6791).
2. D6211 may also report the base metal bridge pontic that is supported by an *abutment supported* implant retainer crown (D6073).
3. D6211 bridge pontic *does not have a specific matching implant supported* retainer crown. Report D6199 with narrative to describe the *matching* (cast base metal) *implant supported* retainer crown.

LIMITATIONS
1. Reimbursement for a fixed partial denture is typically subject to a five to 10-year limitation.
2. Age, waiting periods, missing tooth clause, or other limitations may apply to the placement of a fixed partial denture.

D6212 PONTIC – CAST NOBLE METAL — CDT 2016

1. When reporting pontic-cast noble metal (D6212), be careful that the materials reported to describe the pontic *match* the corresponding (cast base metal) (D6792).
2. D6212 may also report the noble metal fixed partial denture (bridge) pontic that is supported by an *abutment supported* implant retainer crown (D6074).
3. D6212 bridge pontic *does not have a specific matching implant supported* retainer crown. Report D6199 with narrative to describe the *matching* (cast noble metal) *implant supported* retainer crown.

LIMITATIONS
1. Reimbursement for a fixed partial denture is typically subject to a five to 10-year limitation.
2. Age, waiting periods, missing tooth clause, or other limitations may apply to the placement of a fixed partial denture.

D6214 PONTIC – TITANIUM — CDT 2016

1. When reporting a titanium pontic (D6214), be careful that the materials reported to describe the pontic *match* the corresponding titanium crown retainer (D6794).
2. D6214 may also report the fixed partial denture (bridge) pontic that is supported by an *abutment supported* implant retainer crown (D6194).

3. D6214 may also report the fixed partial denture pontic that *matches* the corresponding *implant supported* PFM titanium retainer crown (D6076) or implant supported cast metal titanium retainer crown (D6077).

LIMITATIONS
1. Reimbursement for a fixed partial denture is typically subject to a five to 10-year limitation.
2. Age, waiting periods, missing tooth clause, or other limitations may apply to the placement of a fixed partial denture.

TIPS The nomenclature for pontic – titanium (D6214) is *broad* and reports *any* type of titanium pontic. D6214 includes a full metallic titanium pontic *or* a titanium pontic in association with a porcelain or resin composite coating.

D6240 — PONTIC – PORCELAIN FUSED TO HIGH NOBLE METAL — CDT 2016

1. When reporting pontic – porcelain fused to high noble metal (D6240), be careful to ensure this code *matches* the corresponding (PFM high noble metal) retainer crown (D6750).
2. D6240 may also be used to report the fixed partial denture (bridge) pontic that is a *match* to the corresponding *abutment supported* (PFM high noble metal) retainer crown, (D6069).
3. D6240 may also be used to report the fixed partial denture pontic that *matches* the corresponding *implant supported* (PFM high noble metal) retainer crown, (D6076).

LIMITATIONS
1. Reimbursement for a fixed partial denture is typically subject to a five to 10-year limitation.
2. Age, waiting periods, missing tooth clause, or other limitations may apply to the placement of a fixed partial denture.

D6241 — PONTIC – PORCELAIN FUSED TO PREDOMINANTLY BASE METAL — CDT 2016

1. When reporting pontic – porcelain fused to predominantly base metal (D6241), be careful to ensure this code used to describe the pontic *matches* the corresponding (PFM base metal) retainer crown (D6751).
2. D6241 may also be used to report the fixed partial denture (bridge) pontic that *matches* the corresponding *abutment supported* (PFM base metal) retainer crown, (D6070).
3. D6241 *does not have a matching implant supported* (PFM base metal) retainer crown code. Report D6199, with a brief narrative, to report the corresponding implant supported (PFM base metal) retainer crown.

LIMITATIONS
1. Reimbursement for a fixed partial denture is typically subject to a five to 10-year limitation.
2. Age, waiting periods, missing tooth clause, or other limitations may apply to the placement of a fixed partial denture.

D6242 — PONTIC – PORCELAIN FUSED TO NOBLE METAL — CDT 2016

1. When reporting pontic – porcelain fused to noble metal (D6242), be careful to ensure that this code *matches* the corresponding (PFM noble metal) retainer crown (D6752).
2. D6242 may also be used to report the fixed partial denture (bridge) pontic that *matches* the corresponding *abutment supported* (PFM noble metal) retainer crown (D6071).
3. D6242 *does not have a matching* "implant supported" (PFM noble metal) retainer crown code. Report D6199, with a brief narrative, to report the corresponding *implant supported* (PFM noble metal) retainer crown.

LIMITATIONS
1. Reimbursement for a fixed partial denture is typically subject to a five to 10-year limitation.
2. Age, waiting periods, missing tooth clause, or other limitations may apply to the placement of a fixed partial denture.

D6245   PONTIC – PORCELAIN/CERAMIC   CDT 2016

CODING MATCH CORRECTION

1. When reporting pontic – porcelain/ceramic (D6245), be careful to ensure that this code *matches* the corresponding (porcelain/ceramic) retainer crown (D6740).
2. D6245 may also be used to report the fixed partial denture (bridge) pontic that *matches* the corresponding *abutment supported* porcelain retainer crown (D6068).
3. D6245 may also be used to report the bridge pontic that *matches* the corresponding *implant supported* porcelain retainer crown (D6075).

LIMITATIONS

1. Reimbursement for a fixed partial denture is typically subject to a five to 10-year limitation.
2. Age, waiting periods, missing tooth clause, or other limitations may apply to the placement of a fixed partial denture.

NARRATIVES   All porcelain ceramic (non-metallic) fixed partial dentures (bridges) may be excluded from reimbursement. When reporting D6245, some payers may not reimburse an alternate benefit. However, always appeal if reimbursement for D6245 is initially denied, because the alternate benefit may be reimbursed. Ask the patient to obtain a copy of the full dental coverage contract from their Human Resources department. Review the policy to determine if there is a specific limitation. If all porcelain/ceramic pontics are excluded, ask for an alternate benefit.

PHOTO   The image depicts a three unit porcelain/ceramic bridge. The bridge is made up of the pontic (D6245) and two retainers (D6740).

Courtesy of Keller Dental Lab

D6250   PONTIC – RESIN WITH HIGH NOBLE METAL   CDT 2016

CODING MATCH CORRECTION

1. When reporting pontic – resin with high noble metal (D6250), be careful to ensure that this code *matches* the corresponding resin with high noble metal used in fabricating the retainer crown (D6720).
2. There are *no matching abutment supported* or *implant supported* resin with high noble metal retainer codes to report with high noble metal retainer crowns. Report D6199 with a brief narrative to describe this type of retainer crown.

LIMITATIONS

1. Reimbursement for a fixed partial denture (bridge) is typically subject to a five to 10-year limitation.
2. Age, waiting periods, missing tooth clause, or other limitations may apply to the placement of a fixed partial denture.

D6251   PONTIC – RESIN WITH PREDOMINANTLY BASE METAL   CDT 2016

CODING MATCH CORRECTION

1. When reporting pontic – resin with predominantly base metal (D6251), be careful to ensure this code *matches* the corresponding resin with base metal retainer crown (D6721).
2. There are *no matching abutment supported* or *implant supported* resin with base metal codes used to report resin with predominantly base metal retainer crowns. Report D6199 with a brief narrative to describe these retainer crowns.

LIMITATIONS

1. Reimbursement for a fixed partial denture (bridge) is typically subject to a five to 10-year limitation.
2. Age, waiting periods, missing tooth clause, or other limitations may apply to the placement of a fixed partial denture.

D6252 — PONTIC – RESIN WITH NOBLE METAL — CDT 2016

CODING CORRECTION (MATCH)
1. When reporting a pontic – resin with noble metal (D6252), be careful to ensure this code *matches* the corresponding resin with noble metal retainer crown (D6722).
2. There are *no matching abutment supported* or *implant supported* resin with noble metal retainer crown codes. Report D6199 to describe this type of retainer with a brief narrative.

LIMITATIONS
1. Reimbursement for a replacement fixed partial denture (bridge) is typically subject to a five to 10-year limitation.
2. Age, waiting periods, missing tooth clause, or other limitations may apply to the placement of a fixed partial denture.

D6253 — PROVISIONAL PONTIC – FURTHER TREATMENT OR COMPLETION OF DIAGNOSIS NECESSARY PRIOR TO FINAL IMPRESSION — CDT 2016

Not to be used as a temporary pontic for routine prosthetic fixed partial dentures.

CODING CORRECTION (WARNING)
1. Do not report provisional pontic (D6253) as a temporary pontic for routine fixed partial denture (bridge) procedures.
2. D6253 reports a *provisional* pontic to be in place for a limited period of time. For instance, during extended periodontal treatment. The length of time can vary and is not specified. A definitive (final) restoration would be placed later.

CODING CORRECTION (WATCH)
Be careful that the *pontic* material type matches the corresponding *retainer crown* material type. Always use the matching code, according to its material classification. The corresponding retainer crown code is D6793.

LIMITATIONS
Very few payers will reimburse D6253 and then, only if the provisional fixed partial denture is part of *a multistaged* treatment plan and anticipated to be in place for awhile.

NARRATIVES
1. "Provisional pontic will be utilized as interim restoration."
2. "Final impression has not been made."
3. State reason for provisional use – e.g. allow time for periodontal healing.

D6254 — PREVIOUSLY DELETED CODE INTERIM PONTIC

This is a previously deleted code. See Provisional Pontic D6253 for further details.

FIXED PARTIAL DENTURE RETAINERS – INLAYS/ONLAYS — CDT 2016

D6545 — RETAINER – CAST METAL FOR RESIN BONDED FIXED PROSTHESIS — CDT 2016

CODING CORRECTION (WATCH)
Be careful that the *pontic* material type matches the corresponding wing *retainer* material type. Always use the matching code, according to its material classification.

CODING MATCH CORRECTION

1. D6545 describes a "Maryland" type fixed partial denture (bridge) "wing" retainer. A "Maryland" fixed partial denture consists of two cast metal retainers (wings) which are resin bonded to retainer teeth *plus* the appropriate *matching* pontic(s).

2. For a "Maryland" type fixed partial denture with ceramic "wing" retainer crowns, see D6548.

3. If the retainer "wings" are resin, see D6549.

4. When the abutment tooth is prepared to receive an *inlay* instead of a conservative bonded "wing" retainer crown, report the appropriate *inlay* retainer code. If an inlay retainer code *does not exist that matches* the pontic, report D6999, by report.

COMMENTS

1. When reporting D6545, be careful to ensure this retainer code *matches* the corresponding material type pontic.

2. For re-cementing a Maryland bridge, report D6930.

LIMITATIONS

1. Age, waiting periods, missing tooth clause, or other limitations may apply to this service. Additionally, a Maryland type fixed partial denture is often *excluded* from reimbursement.

2. Most *payers* will not reimburse a "Maryland" or other fixed partial denture used to replace congenitally missing teeth (typically maxillary lateral incisors).

3. Reimbursement for replacement of fixed partial denture is typically subject to a five to 10-year limitation.

4. D6545 may not qualify as a fixed partial denture retainer with certain payers.

TIPS

Retainer – cast metal for resin bonded fixed prosthesis (D6545) describes the cast metal "wing" retainer of a Maryland type fixed partial denture. This type of fixed partial denture is used to conserve tooth structure of the retainers. The fee for *each* winged retainer is often equal to one-half to three-quarters of the pontic fee. The *total fee* for a Maryland type fixed partial denture is typically two to two and one-half times the pontic fee. Reimbursement for the "wings" of a Maryland fixed partial denture varies widely. Some plans do not cover Maryland type fixed partial dentures.

NARRATIVES

If the payer denies reimbursement for D6545, appeal the denial and request an alternate benefit of a conventional bridge. Ask the patient to obtain a copy of the full dental contract from Human Resources. Review the policy to determine if there is a specific limitation applicable to a Maryland bridge.

D6548 RETAINER – PORCELAIN/CERAMIC FOR RESIN BONDED FIXED PROSTHESIS CDT 2016

CODING WATCH CORRECTION

Be careful that the *pontic* material type matches the corresponding wing *retainer* material type. Always use the matching code, according to its material classification.

CODING MATCH CORRECTION

1. Two ceramic "wing retainers" (D6548) are resin bonded to retainer teeth, *plus* a matching ceramic pontic (D6245) reports a Maryland type fixed partial denture (bridge).

2. For cast metal "wing" retainers of a Maryland type fixed partial denture, see D6545.

3. If the retainer "wings" are made of resin or composite, report D6549. Do not report D6548 for fixed partial dentures that utilize resin or composite "wings."

4. If the tooth retainer is affixed into a prepared *inlay* prep instead of to a conservative bonded "wing" retainer, the retainer would be reported using inlay – porcelain/ceramic, two surfaces (D6600).

COMMENTS
1. When reporting D6548, be careful to ensure this retainer code *matches* the corresponding porcelain pontic (D6245).
2. For re-cementing a Maryland fixed partial denture, report D6930.

LIMITATIONS
1. Age, waiting periods, missing tooth clause, or other limitations may apply to this service. Additionally, a "Maryland" type fixed partial denture is often *excluded* from reimbursement.
2. Most payers will *not* reimburse a "Maryland" or other fixed partial denture used to replace congenitally missing teeth (typically maxillary lateral incisors).
3. Reimbursement for a bridge is typically subject to a five to 10-year limitation.
4. D6548 may not qualify as a fixed partial denture retainer with certain payers.

TIPS Retainer – porcelain/ceramic for resin bonded fixed prosthesis (D6548) is the porcelain/ceramic "wing retainer" of a Maryland type fixed partial denture. The Maryland type fixed partial denture is used in an effort to conserve the tooth structure of the tooth retainers. The fee for *each* winged retainer is often equal to one-half to three-quarters of the pontic fee. The *total fee* for a Maryland type fixed partial denture is typically two to two and one-half times the pontic fee. Reimbursement for the "wings" of a Maryland fixed partial denture varies widely. Some plans do not cover Maryland fixed partial dentures.

NARRATIVES If the payer denies reimbursement for D6548, appeal the denial and request an alternate benefit of a conventional bridge. Ask the patient to obtain a copy of the full dental contract from Human Resources. Review the policy to determine if there is a specific limitation applicable to a Maryland bridge.

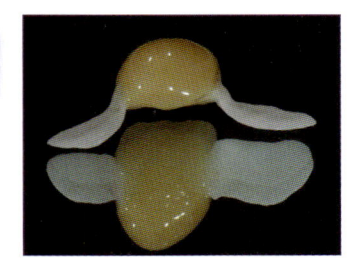

1. This is an example of a porcelain/ceramic Maryland fixed partial denture (bridge).
2. Each retainer tooth "wing" is reported as D6548 and the pontic is reported as D6245.

Courtesy Drake Dental Lab

D6549 RESIN RETAINER – FOR RESIN BONDED FIXED PROSTHESIS   CDT 2016

Be careful that the *pontic* material type matches the corresponding wing *retainer* material type. Always use the matching code, according to its material classification.

1. Two resin "wing retainers" (D6549) are resin bonded to retainer teeth, *plus* a matching resin pontic (D6205) reports a Maryland type fixed partial denture (bridge).
2. For cast metal "wing" retainers of a Maryland type fixed partial denture, see D6545.
3. If the retainer "wings" are made of porcelain or ceramic, report (D6548). Do *not* report D6548 for fixed partial dentures that utilize resin or composite "wings."
4. If the tooth retainer is affixed into a prepared *inlay* prep instead of to a conservative bonded "wing" retainer, the retainer would be reported using indirectly fabricated resin inlay, two surfaces (D2651).

COMMENTS
1. When reporting D6549, be careful that this resin retainer code *matches* the corresponding resin pontic (D6205).
2. For recementing a Maryland fixed partial denture, report D6930.

LIMITATIONS
1. Age, waiting periods, missing tooth clause, or other limitations may apply to this service. Additionally, a "Maryland" type fixed partial denture is often *excluded* from reimbursement.
2. Most payers will *not* reimburse a "Maryland" or fixed partial denture used to replace congenitally missing teeth (typically maxillary lateral incisors).
3. Reimbursement for a bridge is typically subject to a five to 10-year limitation.
4. D6549 may not qualify as a fixed partial denture retainer with certain payers.

TIPS
Resin retainer – for resin bonded fixed prosthesis (D6549) is the resin "wing retainer" portion of a Maryland type fixed partial denture. The Maryland type fixed partial denture is used in an effort to conserve the tooth structure of the tooth retainers. The fee for *each* winged retainer is often equal to one-half to three-quarters of the pontic fee. The *total fee* for a Maryland type fixed partial denture is typically two to two and one-half times the pontic fee. Reimbursement for the "wings" of a Maryland fixed partial denture varies widely. Some plans do not cover Maryland fixed partial dentures.

NARRATIVES
If the payer denies reimbursement for D6549, appeal the denial and request an alternate benefit of a conventional fixed partial denture. Ask the patient to obtain a copy of the full dental contract from their Human Resources department. Review the policy to determine if there is a specific limitation applicable to a Maryland fixed partial denture.

ADDITIONAL INFORMATION
Reporting the incorrect *type* of material (high noble, noble, base, ceramic, etc.) used in fabricating the wing retainer is a common coding error. Be careful to report the correct code based on the material classification. Document the correct material used in the pontic on the claim form as represented in the treatment plan, the lab prescription, and the documentation from the lab. Following this protocol should eliminate reporting errors.

D6600 REVISED RETAINER INLAY – PORCELAIN/CERAMIC, TWO SURFACES — CDT 2016

REVISIONS RETAINER INLAY – PORCELAIN/CERAMIC, TWO SURFACES

When reporting inlay – porcelain/ceramic, two surfaces (D6600), be careful to ensure the inlay material reported *matches* the corresponding porcelain/ceramic type pontic (D6245).

LIMITATIONS
1. Age, waiting periods, missing tooth, or other limitations may apply.
2. Reimbursement for a fixed partial denture (bridge) is typically subject to a five to 10-year limitation period.
3. D6600, which is an inlay, may not qualify as a fixed partial denture retainer with certain payers while an onlay could.

NARRATIVES
Non-metal bridges may be denied. Appeal the denial and request an alternate benefit of a conventional bridge. Ask the patient to obtain a copy of the full dental contract from Human Resources. Review the policy to determine if there is a specific limitation applicable either to a Maryland bridge or other inlay retainer-based bridge.

D6601 REVISED RETAINER INLAY – PORCELAIN/CERAMIC, THREE OR MORE SURFACES — CDT 2016

REVISIONS RETAINER INLAY – PORCELAIN/CERAMIC, THREE OR MORE SURFACES

When reporting inlay – porcelain/ceramic, three or more surfaces (D6601), be careful to ensure that this code *matches* the corresponding porcelain/ceramic pontic (D6245).

LIMITATIONS
1. Age, waiting periods, missing tooth, or other limitations may apply.
2. Reimbursement for replacement of a fixed partial denture bridge is typically subject to a five to 10-year limitation period.
3. D6601, which is an inlay, may not qualify as a fixed partial denture retainer with certain payers while an onlay could.
4. To receive reimbursement for an onlay retainer on a separate, stand-alone basis, the tooth must meet the same criterion that justifies the placement of a crown (missing a cusp, fractured cusp, extensive breakdown and/or decay).

NARRATIVES Non-metal bridges may be denied. Appeal the denial and request an alternate benefit of a conventional bridge. Ask the patient to obtain a copy of the full dental contract from Human Resources. Review the policy to determine if there is a specific limitation applicable either to a Maryland bridge or any other inlay-retained bridge.

D6602 — REVISED RETAINER INLAY – CAST HIGH NOBLE METAL, TWO SURFACES — CDT 2016

REVISIONS RETAINER INLAY – CAST HIGH NOBLE METAL, TWO SURFACES

CODING MATCH CORRECTION: When reporting inlay – cast high noble metal, two surfaces (D6602), be careful to ensure the inlay material *matches* the corresponding cast high noble metal pontic (D6210).

LIMITATIONS
1. Age, waiting periods, missing tooth, or other limitations may also apply.
2. Reimbursement for replacement of a fixed partial denture (bridge) is typically subject to a five to 10-year limitation period.
3. An inlay (D6602) might not qualify as a retainer, while an onlay could.
4. To receive reimbursement for an onlay retainer on a separate, stand-alone basis, the tooth must meet the same criterion that justifies the placement of a crown (missing a cusp, fractured cusp, extensive breakdown and/or decay).

NARRATIVES Inlay *retainer* claims could be reimbursed if accompanied with full documentation (proper narrative, pretreatment diagnostic radiographic image/photograph and photograph of the final preparation) to justify the need.

D6603 — REVISED RETAINER INLAY – CAST HIGH NOBLE METAL, THREE OR MORE SURFACES — CDT 2016

REVISIONS RETAINER INLAY – CAST HIGH NOBLE METAL, THREE OR MORE SURFACES

CODING MATCH CORRECTION: When reporting inlay – cast high noble metal, three or more surfaces (D6603), be careful to ensure the inlay material *matches* the corresponding cast high noble metal pontic (D6210).

LIMITATIONS
1. Age, waiting periods, missing tooth, or other limitations may apply.
2. Reimbursement for replacement of a fixed partial denture (bridge) is typically subject to a five to 10-year limitation period.
3. An inlay (D6603) might not qualify for reimbursement as a retainer, while an onlay could.
4. To receive reimbursement for an onlay retainer on a separate, stand-alone basis, the tooth must meet the same criterion that justifies the placement of a crown (missing a cusp, fractured cusp, fracture, extensive breakdown and/or decay).

NARRATIVES Inlay *retainer* claims could possibly be reimbursed if accompanied with full documentation (a brief narrative, pretreatment diagnostic radiographic image/photograph and photograph of the final preparation) to justify the need.

D6604 — REVISED RETAINER INLAY – CAST PREDOMINANTLY BASE METAL, TWO SURFACES
CDT 2016

REVISIONS RETAINER INLAY – CAST PREDOMINANTLY BASE METAL, TWO SURFACES

CODING MATCH CORRECTION
When reporting inlay – cast predominantly base metal, two surfaces (D6604), be careful that the inlay material *matches* the corresponding cast base metal type of pontic (D6211).

LIMITATIONS
1. Age, waiting periods, missing tooth, or other limitations may also apply.
2. Reimbursement for replacement of fixed partial denture (bridges) is typically subject to a five to 10-year limitation period.
3. An inlay (D6604) might not qualify for reimbursement as a retainer, while an onlay could.
4. To receive reimbursement for an onlay retainer on a separate, stand-alone basis, the tooth must meet the same criterion that justifies the placement of a crown (missing a cusp, fractured cusp, fracture, extensive breakdown and/or decay).

NARRATIVES Inlay *retainer* claims could be reimbursed if accompanied with full documentation (proper narrative, pretreatment diagnostic radiographic image/photograph and photograph of the final preparation) that justifies its placement.

D6605 — REVISED RETAINER INLAY – CAST PREDOMINANTLY BASE METAL, THREE OR MORE SURFACES
CDT 2016

REVISIONS RETAINER INLAY – CAST PREDOMINANTLY BASE METAL, THREE OR MORE SURFACES

CODING MATCH CORRECTION
When reporting inlay – cast predominantly base metal, three or more surfaces (D6605), be careful to ensure this code *matches* the corresponding cast base metal pontic (D6211).

LIMITATIONS
1. Age, waiting periods, missing tooth, or other limitations may apply.
2. Reimbursement for replacement of fixed partial dentures (bridges) is typically subject to a five to 10-year limitation period.
3. An inlay (D6605) might not qualify for reimbursement as a retainer, while an onlay could.
4. To receive reimbursement for an onlay retainer on a separate, stand-alone basis, the tooth must meet the same criterion that justifies the placement of a crown (missing a cusp, fractured cusp, extensive breakdown and/or decay).

NARRATIVES Inlay *retainer* claims could be reimbursed if accompanied with full documentation (proper narrative, pretreatment diagnostic radiographic image/photograph and photograph of the final preparation) that justifies its placement.

D6606 — REVISED RETAINER INLAY – CAST NOBLE METAL, TWO SURFACES — CDT 2016

REVISIONS — RETAINER INLAY – CAST NOBLE METAL, TWO SURFACES

CODING CORRECTION — MATCH: When reporting inlay – cast noble metal, two surfaces (D6606), be careful to ensure this code *matches* the corresponding cast noble metal pontic (D6212).

LIMITATIONS
1. Age, waiting periods, missing tooth, or other limitations may apply.
2. Reimbursement for replacement of fixed partial dentures (bridges) is typically subject to a five to 10-year limitation period.
3. An inlay (D6606) might not qualify for reimbursement as a retainer while an onlay could. To receive reimbursement for an onlay retainer, the tooth must meet the same criterion that justifies the placement of a crown (missing a cusp, fractured cusp, extensive breakdown and/or decay).

NARRATIVES — Inlay retainer claims could possibly be reimbursed if accompanied with full documentation (a brief narrative, pretreatment diagnostic radiographic image/photograph and photograph of the final preparation) that justifies the service.

D6607 — REVISED RETAINER INLAY – CAST NOBLE METAL, THREE OR MORE SURFACES — CDT 2016

REVISIONS — RETAINER INLAY – CAST NOBLE METAL, THREE OR MORE SURFACES

CODING CORRECTION — MATCH: When reporting inlay – cast noble metal, three or more surfaces (D6607), be careful to ensure that this code *matches* the corresponding cast noble metal pontic, D6212.

LIMITATIONS
1. Age, waiting periods, missing tooth, or other limitations may apply.
2. Reimbursement for replacement of bridges is typically subject to a five to 10-year limitation period.
3. An inlay (D6607) might not qualify for reimbursement as a retainer while an onlay could. To receive reimbursement for an onlay retainer, the tooth must meet the same criterion that justifies the placement of a crown (missing a cusp, fractured cusp, extensive breakdown and/or decay).

NARRATIVES — Inlay retainer claims could possibly be reimbursed if accompanied with full documentation (a brief narrative, pretreatment diagnostic radiographic image/photograph and photograph of the final preparation) that justifies the service.

D6624 — REVISED RETAINER INLAY – TITANIUM — CDT 2016

Note: While out of numerical order, D6624 is correctly listed here in the Prosthodontics, Fixed Category subcategory.

REVISIONS — RETAINER INLAY – TITANIUM

CODING CORRECTION — MATCH: When reporting inlay – titanium (D6624), be careful to ensure that this code *matches* the corresponding titanium pontic (D6214).

277

LIMITATIONS
1. If age limitations, waiting periods, missing tooth clause, least expensive alternate treatment (LEAT) clause, or prosthetic replacement clause does not apply, most dental plans will provide a benefit for inlay or onlay fixed partial denture (bridge) retainers as long as the supporting teeth are sound. Some plans provide an alternate base metal benefit when titanium inlay retainers are used.

2. Age, waiting periods, missing tooth, or other limitations may apply.

3. Reimbursement for replacement of fixed partial dentures is typically subject to a five to 10-year limitation period.

4. See D6602 Limitations #4.

TIPS The nomenclature used to describe inlay titanium restorations (D6624) is very broad. Titanium based codes report *all types of titanium inlays*, either metal, or coated with ceramic or resin. The titanium inlay code is used to report all surface classifications.

D6608 — REVISED RETAINER ONLAY – PORCELAIN/CERAMIC, TWO SURFACES — CDT 2016

REVISION RETAINER ONLAY – PORCELAIN/CERAMIC, TWO SURFACES

CODING WARNING CORRECTION Onlays must "cap" or "shoe" at least one cusp. If the onlay retainer restoration does not "cap" or "shoe" a cusp, reporting onlay porcelain/ceramic, two surfaces (D6608) is an error. The ADA Glossary of dental terms, when describing an onlay states: "Going up the incline more than one half of the distance from fossa to cusp tip *is not* an onlay." It further states that, "A restoration that restores one or more cusps and adjoining occlusal surfaces or the entire occlusal surface and is retained by mechanical or adhesive means." The Journal of Prosthodontic Dentistry, The Glossary of Prosthodontic Terms, July 2005, pg. 57).

CODING MATCH CORRECTION When reporting onlay porcelain/ceramic, two surfaces (D6608), be careful to ensure this code *matches* the corresponding porcelain/ceramic pontic (D6245).

COMMENTS It is important that at least one *buccal* or *lingual* surface be a part of the onlay restoration and reported on the claim form for reimbursement of an onlay retainer to be considered. An MO does not describe an onlay. An MOF, MOL, DOF, DOL, MODL, MODF or MODFL describes an onlay.

LIMITATIONS
1. If age limitations, waiting periods, missing tooth clause, least expensive alternate treatment (LEAT) clause, or prosthetic replacement clause does not apply, most dental plans will provide a benefit for onlay bridge retainers as long as the supporting teeth are sound. Some plans provide an alternate base metal benefit when porcelain/ceramic onlay retainers are used.

2. Age, waiting periods, missing tooth, or other limitations may apply.

3. Reimbursement for replacement of fixed partial dentures (bridges) is typically subject to a five to 10-year limitation period.

NARRATIVES Onlay claims are typically reimbursed if accompanied with full documentation (a brief narrative, pretreatment diagnostic radiographic image/photograph and photograph of the final preparation). To receive reimbursement for an onlay, the tooth must meet the same criterion that justifies the placement of a crown (missing a cusp, fractured cusp, extensive breakdown and/or decay). A narrative should be provided when reporting an onlay, stating that the onlay is a conservative option to a full crown.

D6609 REVISED RETAINER ONLAY – PORCELAIN/CERAMIC, THREE OR MORE SURFACES
CDT 2016

REVISION RETAINER ONLAY – PORCELAIN/CERAMIC, THREE OR MORE SURFACES

CODING WARNING CORRECTION Onlays must "cap" or "shoe" at least one cusp. If the onlay retainer restoration does not "cap" or "shoe" a cusp, reporting onlay porcelain/ceramic, three or more surfaces (D6609) is an error. The ADA Glossary of dental terms, when describing an onlay states: "Going up the incline more than one half of the distance from fossa to cusp tip *is not* an onlay." It further states that, "A restoration that restores one or more cusps and adjoining occlusal surfaces or the entire occlusal surface and is retained by mechanical or adhesive means." The Journal of Prosthodontic Dentistry, The Glossary of Prosthodontic Terms, July 2005, pg. 57).

CODING MATCH CORRECTION When reporting onlay – porcelain/ceramic, three or more surfaces (D6609), be careful to ensure that the onlay retainer code *matches* the corresponding porcelain/ceramic pontic (D6245).

COMMENTS It is important that at least one *buccal* and/or *lingual* surface be a part of the onlay restoration (capping one or more cusps) for reimbursement of an onlay retainer to be considered. An MOD does not describe an onlay. An MOF, MOL, DOF, DOL, MODL, MODF or MODFL describes an onlay.

LIMITATIONS
1. If age limitations, waiting periods, missing tooth clause, least expensive alternate treatment (LEAT) clause, or prosthetic replacement clause does not apply, most dental plans will provide a benefit for onlay bridge retainers as long as the supporting teeth are sound. Some plans provide an alternate base metal benefit when porcelain/ceramic onlay retainers are used.
2. Age, waiting periods, missing tooth, or other limitations may apply.
3. Reimbursement for replacement of fixed partial dentures is typically subject to a five to 10-year limitation period.

NARRATIVES Onlay claims are typically reimbursed if accompanied with full documentation (a brief narrative, pretreatment diagnostic radiographic image/photograph and photograph of the final preparation). To receive reimbursement for an onlay, the tooth must meet the same criterion that justifies the placement of a crown (missing a cusp, fractured cusp, extensive breakdown and/or decay). A narrative should be provided when reporting an onlay, stating that the onlay is a conservative option to a full crown.

D6610 REVISED RETAINER ONLAY – CAST HIGH NOBLE METAL, TWO SURFACES CDT 2016

REVISION RETAINER ONLAY – CAST HIGH NOBLE METAL, TWO SURFACES

CODING WARNING CORRECTION Onlays must "cap" or "shoe" at least one cusp. If the onlay retainer restoration does not "cap" or "shoe" a cusp, reporting onlay – cast high noble metal, two surfaces (D6610) is an error. The ADA Glossary of dental terms, when describing an onlay states: "Going up the incline more than one half of the distance from fossa to cusp tip *is not* an onlay." It further states that, "A restoration that restores one or more cusps and adjoining occlusal surfaces or the entire occlusal surface and is retained by mechanical or adhesive means." The Journal of Prosthodontic Dentistry, The Glossary of Prosthodontic Terms, July 2005, pg. 57).

CODING MATCH CORRECTION When reporting an onlay – cast high noble metal, two surfaces (D6610), be careful to ensure that the onlay retainer code *matches* the corresponding high noble metal pontic (D6210).

COMMENTS	It is important that at least one *buccal* and/or *lingual* surface be a part of the onlay restoration (capping one or more cusps) for reimbursement of an onlay retainer to be considered. An MOD does not describe an onlay. An MOF, MOL, DOF, DOL, MODL, MODF or MODFL describes an onlay.
LIMITATIONS	1. If age limitations, waiting periods, missing tooth clause, least expensive alternate treatment (LEAT) clause, or prosthetic replacement clause does not apply, most dental plans will provide a benefit for onlay bridge retainers as long as the supporting teeth are sound. Some plans provide an alternate base metal benefit when onlay retainers are used.
2. Age, waiting periods, missing tooth, or other limitations may apply.
3. Reimbursement for replacement of fixed partial dentures (bridges) is typically subject to a five to 10-year limitation period.
NARRATIVES	Onlay claims are typically reimbursed if accompanied with full documentation (a brief narrative, pretreatment diagnostic radiographic image/photograph and photograph of the final preparation). To receive reimbursement for an onlay, the tooth must meet the same criteria that justifies the placement of a crown (missing a cusp, fractured cusp, extensive breakdown and/or decay). A narrative should be provided when reporting an onlay, stating that the onlay is a conservative option to a full crown.

D6611 — REVISED RETAINER ONLAY – CAST HIGH NOBLE METAL, THREE OR MORE SURFACES
CDT 2016

REVISIONS	**RETAINER** ONLAY – CAST HIGH NOBLE METAL, THREE OR MORE SURFACES
CODING WARNING CORRECTION	Onlays must "cap" or "shoe" at least one cusp. If the onlay retainer restoration does not "cap" or "shoe" a cusp, reporting onlay – cast high noble metal, three or more surfaces (D6611) is an error. The ADA Glossary of dental terms, when describing an onlay states: "Going up the incline more than one half of the distance from fossa to cusp tip *is not* an onlay." It further states that, "A restoration that restores one or more cusps and adjoining occlusal surfaces or the entire occlusal surface and is retained by mechanical or adhesive means." The Journal of Prosthodontic Dentistry, The Glossary of Prosthodontic Terms, July 2005, pg. 57).
CODING MATCH CORRECTION	When reporting an onlay – cast high noble metal, three or more surfaces (D6611), be careful to ensure that the onlay retainer code *matches* the corresponding cast high noble metal pontic (D6210).
COMMENTS	It is important that at least one *buccal* and/or *lingual* surface be a part of the onlay restoration (capping one or more cusps) for reimbursement of an onlay retainer to be considered. An MOD does not describe an onlay. An MOF, MOL, DOF, DOL, MODL, MODF or MODFL describes an onlay.
LIMITATIONS	1. If age limitations, waiting periods, missing tooth clause, least expensive alternate treatment (LEAT) clause, or prosthetic replacement clause does not apply, most dental plans will provide a benefit for onlay bridge retainers as long as the supporting teeth are sound. Some plans provide an alternate base metal benefit when onlay retainers are used.
2. Age, waiting periods, missing tooth, or other limitations may apply.
3. Reimbursement for replacement of fixed partial dentures (bridges) is typically subject to a five to 10-year limitation period.
NARRATIVES	Onlay retainers are usually reimbursed when reported with full documentation (a brief narrative, beginning diagnostic radiographic image/photograph and photograph of preparation). To receive reimbursement for an onlay retainer, the tooth must meet the same criteria for a crown (missing a cusp, fractured cusp and breakdown), necessitated by fracture or decay. A brief narrative should be used when reporting an onlay retainer, stating that the onlay is a conservative option to a full crown.

D6612	**REVISED RETAINER ONLAY – CAST PREDOMINANTLY BASE METAL, TWO SURFACES**
	CDT 2016

REVISIONS RETAINER ONLAY – CAST PREDOMINANTLY BASE METAL, TWO SURFACES

CODING CORRECTION WARNING Onlays must "cap" or "shoe" at least one cusp. If the onlay retainer restoration does not "cap" or "shoe" a cusp, reporting onlay – cast predominantly base metal, two surfaces (D6612) is an error. The ADA Glossary of dental terms, when describing an onlay states: "Going up the incline more than one half of the distance from fossa to cusp tip *is not* an onlay." It further states that, "A restoration that restores one or more cusps and adjoining occlusal surfaces or the entire occlusal surface and is retained by mechanical or adhesive means." The Journal of Prosthodontic Dentistry, The Glossary of Prosthodontic Terms, July 2005, pg. 57).

CODING CORRECTION MATCH When reporting an onlay – cast predominantly base metal, two surfaces (D6612), be careful to ensure that the onlay retainer code *matches* the corresponding cast base metal type of pontic (D6211).

COMMENTS It is important that at least one *buccal* and/or *lingual* surface be a part of the onlay restoration (capping one or more cusps) for reimbursement of an onlay retainer to be considered. An MOD does not describe an onlay. An MOF, MOL, DOF, DOL, MODL, MODF or MODFL describes an onlay.

LIMITATIONS
1. If age limitations, waiting periods, missing tooth clause, least expensive alternate treatment (LEAT) clause, or prosthetic replacement clause does not apply, most dental plans will provide a benefit for onlay bridge retainers as long as the supporting teeth are sound. Some plans provide an alternate base metal benefit when onlay retainers are used.
2. Age, waiting periods, missing tooth, or other limitations may apply.
3. Reimbursement for replacement of bridges is typically subject to a five-to-10-year limitation period.

NARRATIVES Onlay retainers are usually reimbursed when reported with full documentation (a brief narrative, beginning diagnostic film/photograph and photograph of preparation). To receive reimbursement for an onlay retainer, the tooth must meet the same criteria for a crown (missing a cusp, fractured cusp and breakdown), necessitated by fracture or decay. A narrative should be used when reporting an onlay retainer, stating that the onlay is a conservative option to a full crown.

D6613	**REVISED RETAINER ONLAY – CAST PREDOMINANTLY BASE METAL, THREE OR MORE SURFACES**
	CDT 2016

REVISIONS RETAINER ONLAY – CAST PREDOMINANTLY BASE METAL, THREE OR MORE SURFACES

CODING CORRECTION WARNING Onlays must "cap" or "shoe" at least one cusp. If the onlay retainer restoration does not "cap" or "shoe" a cusp, reporting onlay – cast predominantly base metal, three or more surfaces (D6613) is an error. The ADA Glossary of dental terms, when describing an onlay states: "Going up the incline more than one half of the distance from fossa to cusp tip *is not* an onlay." It further states that, "A restoration that restores one or more cusps and adjoining occlusal surfaces or the entire occlusal surface and is retained by mechanical or adhesive means." The Journal of Prosthodontic Dentistry, The Glossary of Prosthodontic Terms, July 2005, pg. 57).

CODING CORRECTION MATCH When reporting an onlay – cast predominantly base metal, three or more surfaces (D6613), be careful to ensure that the onlay retainer code *matches* the corresponding cast base metal type of pontic (D6211).

281

COMMENTS It is important that at least one *buccal* and/or *lingual* surface be a part of the onlay restoration (capping one or more cusps) for reimbursement of an onlay retainer to be considered. An MOD does not describe an onlay. An MOF, MOL, DOF, DOL, MODL, MODF or MODFL describes an onlay.

LIMITATIONS
1. If age limitations, waiting periods, missing tooth clause, least expensive alternate treatment (LEAT) clause, or prosthetic replacement clause does not apply, most dental plans will provide a benefit for onlay bridge retainers as long as the supporting teeth are sound. Some plans provide an alternate base metal benefit when onlay retainers are used.
2. Age, waiting periods, missing tooth, or other limitations may apply.
3. Reimbursement for replacement of fixed partial dentures (bridges) is typically subject to a five to 10-year limitation period.

NARRATIVES Onlay retainers are usually reimbursed when reported with full documentation (a brief narrative, beginning diagnostic radiographic image/photograph and photograph of preparation). To receive reimbursement for an onlay retainer, the tooth must meet the same criteria for a crown (missing a cusp, undermined cusp, fractured cusp and breakdown), necessitated by fracture or decay. A narrative should be used when reporting an onlay retainer, stating that the onlay is a conservative option to a full crown.

D6614 REVISED RETAINER ONLAY – CAST NOBLE METAL, TWO SURFACES — CDT 2016

REVISIONS RETAINER ONLAY – CAST NOBLE METAL, TWO SURFACES

CODING WARNING CORRECTION Onlays must "cap" or "shoe" at least one cusp. If the onlay retainer restoration does not "cap" or "shoe" a cusp, reporting onlay porcelain/ceramic, two surfaces (D6614) is an error. The ADA Glossary of dental terms, when describing an onlay states: "Going up the incline more than one half of the distance from fossa to cusp tip *is not* an onlay." It further states that, "A restoration that restores one or more cusps and adjoining occlusal surfaces or the entire occlusal surface and is retained by mechanical or adhesive means." The Journal of Prosthodontic Dentistry, The Glossary of Prosthodontic Terms, July 2005, pg. 57).

CODING MATCH CORRECTION When reporting an onlay – cast noble metal, two surfaces, (D6614), be careful to ensure that the onlay code *matches* the corresponding cast noble metal type of pontic (D6212).

COMMENTS It is important that at least one *buccal* and/or *lingual* surface be a part of the onlay restoration (capping one or more cusps) for reimbursement of an onlay retainer to be considered.

LIMITATIONS
1. If age limitations, waiting periods, missing tooth clause, least expensive alternate treatment (LEAT) clause, or prosthetic replacement clause does not apply, most dental plans will provide a benefit for onlay bridge retainers as long as the supporting teeth are sound. Some plans provide an alternate base metal benefit when onlay retainers are used.
2. Age, waiting periods, missing tooth, or other limitations may apply.
3. Reimbursement for replacement of fixed partial dentures (bridges) is typically subject to a five to 10-year limitation period.

NARRATIVES Onlay retainers are usually reimbursed when reported with full documentation (a brief narrative, beginning diagnostic radiographic image/photograph and photograph of preparation). To receive reimbursement for an onlay retainer, the tooth must meet the same criteria for a crown (missing a cusp, undermined cusp, fractured cusp and breakdown), necessitated by fracture or decay. A narrative should be used when reporting an onlay retainer, stating that the onlay is a conservative option to a full crown.

D6615 — REVISED RETAINER ONLAY – CAST NOBLE METAL, THREE OR MORE SURFACES
CDT 2016

REVISIONS — RETAINER ONLAY – CAST NOBLE METAL, THREE OR MORE SURFACES

CODING WARNING CORRECTION

Onlays must "cap" or "shoe" at least one cusp. If the restoration does not "cap" or "shoe" a cusp, reporting onlay – cast noble metal, three or more surfaces (D6615) is an error. The ADA Glossary of dental terms, when describing an onlay states: "Going up the incline more than one half of the distance from fossa to cusp tip *is not* an onlay." It further states that, "A restoration that restores one or more cusps and adjoining occlusal surfaces or the entire occlusal surface and is retained by mechanical or adhesive means." (The Journal of Prosthodontic Dentistry, The Glossary of Prosthodontic Terms, July 2005, pg. 57).

CODING MATCH CORRECTION

When reporting onlay – cast noble metal, three or more surfaces (D6615), be careful to ensure that this code *matches* the corresponding cast noble metal pontic D6212.

COMMENTS — It is important that at least one *buccal* and/or *lingual* surface be a part of the onlay restoration (capping one or more cusps) for reimbursement of an onlay to be considered. An MOD does not describe an onlay. An MOF, MOL, DOF, DOL, MODL, MODF or MODFL describes an onlay.

LIMITATIONS
1. If age limitations, waiting periods, missing tooth clause, least expensive alternate treatment (LEAT) clause, or prosthetic replacement clause does not apply, most dental plans will provide a benefit for inlay or onlay bridge retainers as long as the supporting teeth are sound.
2. Age, waiting periods, missing tooth, or other limitations may apply.
3. Reimbursement for replacement of fixed partial denture (bridges) is typically subject to a five to 10- limitation period.

NARRATIVES — Onlay retainers are usually reimbursed when reported with full documentation (a brief narrative, beginning diagnostic radiographic image/photograph and photograph of preparation). To receive reimbursement for an onlay retainer, the tooth must meet the same criteria for a crown (missing a cusp, fractured cusp and breakdown), necessitated by fracture or decay. A narrative should be used when reporting an onlay retainer, stating that the onlay is a conservative option to a full crown.

D6624 — REVISED RETAINER INLAY – TITANIUM
CDT 2016

Note: D6624 appears here in numerical order. Its true location is after D6607 but the information for this code is printed in this location in its entirety.

REVISIONS — RETAINER INLAY – TITANIUM

CODING MATCH CORRECTION

When reporting inlay – titanium (D6624), be careful to ensure that this code *matches* the corresponding titanium pontic (D6214).

LIMITATIONS
1. If age limitations, waiting periods, missing tooth clause, least expensive alternate treatment (LEAT) clause, or prosthetic replacement clause does not apply, most dental plans will provide a benefit for inlay or onlay fixed partial denture (bridge) retainers as long as the supporting teeth are sound. Some plans provide an alternate base metal benefit when titanium inlay retainers are used.

2. Age, waiting periods, missing tooth, or other limitations may apply.

3. Reimbursement for replacement of fixed partial dentures is typically subject to a five to 10-year limitation period.

4. An inlay (D6624) might not qualify for reimbursement as a retainer while an onlay could. To receive reimbursement for an onlay retainer on a separate, stand-alone basis, the tooth must meet the same criterion that justifies the placement of a crown (missing a cusp, fractured cusp, extensive breakdown and/or decay).

TIPS The nomenclature use to describe inlay titanium restorations (D6624) is very broad. Titanium based codes report *all types of titanium inlays*, either metal, or coated with ceramic or resin. The titanium inlay code is used to report all surface classifications.

D6634 REVISED RETAINER ONLAY – TITANIUM — CDT 2016

REVISIONS RETAINER ONLAY – TITANIUM

CODING WARNING CORRECTION Onlays must "cap" or "shoe" at least one cusp. If the restoration does not "cap" or "shoe" a cusp, reporting onlay – titanium (D6634) is an error. The ADA Glossary of dental terms, when describing an onlay states: "Going up the incline more than one half of the distance from fossa to cusp tip *is not* an onlay." It further states that, "A restoration that restores one or more cusps and adjoining occlusal surfaces or the entire occlusal surface and is retained by mechanical or adhesive means." (The Journal of Prosthodontic Dentistry, The Glossary of Prosthodontic Terms, July 2005, pg. 57).

CODING MATCH CORRECTION When reporting onlay – titanium (D6634), be careful to insure that this code *matches* the corresponding titanium pontic, D6214.

COMMENTS It is important that at least one *buccal* and/or *lingual* surface be a part of the onlay restoration (capping one or more cusps) for reimbursement of an onlay to be considered. An MOD does not describe an onlay. An MOF, MOL, DOF, DOL, MODL, MODF or MODFL describes an onlay.

LIMITATIONS
1. If age limitations, waiting periods, missing tooth clause, least expensive alternate treatment (LEAT) clause, or prosthetic replacement clause does not apply, most dental plans will provide a benefit for inlay or onlay bridge retainers as long as the supporting teeth are sound.

2. Age, waiting periods, missing tooth, or other limitations may apply.

3. Reimbursement for replacement of fixed partial dentures (bridges) is typically subject to a five to 10-year limitation period.

TIPS The nomenclature used to describe titanium restorations (D6634) is very broad. Titanium based codes report *all types of titanium onlay*, either metal, or coated with ceramic or resin. The titanium onlay code is used to report all surface classifications, i.e., whether it is two, three or more surfaces.

NARRATIVES Onlays are usually reimbursed when reported with full documentation (a brief narrative, beginning diagnostic radiographic image/photograph and photograph of preparation). To receive reimbursement for an onlay, the tooth must meet the same criteria for a crown (missing a cusp, undermined cusp, fractured cusp and breakdown), necessitated by fracture or decay. A narrative should be used when reporting an onlay, stating that the onlay is a conservative option to a full crown.

FIXED PARTIAL DENTURE RETAINERS – CROWNS — CDT 2016

| D6710 | REVISED RETAINER CROWN – INDIRECT RESIN BASED COMPOSITE | CDT 2016 |

Not to be used as a temporary or provisional prosthesis.

REVISIONS RETAINER CROWN – INDIRECT RESIN BASED COMPOSITE

CODING CORRECTION WARNING: This code is not intended to describe a temporary or provisional prosthesis.

CODING CORRECTION WATCH: Crown – indirect resin based composite (D6710) reports a permanent indirect retainer crown (resin based composite). It is an error to use D6710 to describe a *provisional* prosthesis. D6793 may be used to report a *provisional* retainer crown.

CODING CORRECTION MATCH: When reporting crown – indirect resin based composite (D6710), be careful to ensure that this retainer crown code *matches* the corresponding indirect resin based composite pontic (D6205).

COMMENTS
1. When reporting the supporting retainer crowns of a fixed partial denture (bridge), note that the term used in current CDT is "fixed partial denture retainer crowns." While many dental practices still use the term "abutment" to identify the retainer crown units of a fixed partial denture (bridge), the use of the term retainer can be confusing. The term "abutment" refers to the connection piece that attaches a prosthetic device to a root form implant (see D6056/D6057). To avoid billing errors, the components of a three unit fixed partial denture should be identified as retainer-pontic-retainer, rather than abutment-pontic-abutment.
2. D6710 is used to describe resin based retainer crowns made of Artglass®, Belleglass®, Cristobel®, etc. type materials.

LIMITATIONS
1. Age restrictions, waiting periods, missing tooth clause, or other limitations may apply to the reimbursement for this service.
2. Reimbursement for replacement of fixed partial dentures is typically subject to a five to 10-year limitation period.
3. D6710 may be reimbursed according to the same exclusions/limitations as a cast fixed partial denture retainer crown.

NARRATIVES Non-metal bridges may be denied. Appeal the denial of the indirect resin based composite fixed partial denture and request an alternate benefit of a conventional fixed partial denture. Ask the patient to obtain a copy of the full dental coverage contract from their Human Resources department. Review the policy to determine if there is a specific limitation applicable to an indirect resin based composite fixed partial denture and appeal appropriately. If reimbursed, this service may be paid at the D6721 UCR fee level.

| D6720 | REVISED RETAINER CROWN – RESIN WITH HIGH NOBLE METAL | CDT 2016 |

REVISIONS RETAINER CROWN – RESIN WITH HIGH NOBLE METAL

CODING CORRECTION MATCH: When reporting crown – resin with high noble (D6720), be careful to ensure that this retainer crown code *matches* the corresponding resin with high noble metal pontic (D6250).

COMMENTS When reporting the supporting retainer crowns of a fixed partial denture bridge, note that the term used in current CDT is "fixed partial denture retainer crowns." While many dental practices still use the term "abutment" to identify the retainer crown units of a fixed partial denture, the use of the term retainer can be confusing. The term "abutment" refers to the connection piece that attaches a prosthetic device to a root form implant (see D6056/D6057). To avoid billing errors, the components of a three unit fixed partial denture should be identified as retainer-pontic-retainer, rather than abutment-pontic-abutment.

LIMITATIONS
1. Age restrictions, waiting periods, missing tooth clause, or other limitations may apply to the reimbursement for this service.
2. Reimbursement for replacement of fixed partial dentures is typically subject to a five to 10-year limitation period.

D6721 REVISED RETAINER CROWN – RESIN WITH PREDOMINANTLY BASE METAL CDT 2016

REVISIONS RETAINER CROWN – RESIN WITH PREDOMINANTLY BASE METAL

CODING CORRECTION MATCH

When reporting crown – resin with predominantly base metal (D6721), be careful to ensure that this retainer crown code *matches* the corresponding resin with base metal pontic (D6251).

COMMENTS When reporting the supporting retainer crown of a fixed partial denture (bridge), note that the term used in current CDT is "fixed partial denture retainer crowns." While many dental practices still use the term "abutment" to identify the retainer crown units of a fixed partial denture, the use of the term retainer can be confusing. The term "abutment" refers to the connection piece that attaches a prosthetic device to a root form implant (see D6056/D6057). To avoid billing errors, the bridge components of a three-unit fixed partial denture should be identified as retainer-pontic-retainer, rather than abutment-pontic-abutment.

LIMITATIONS
1. Age restrictions, waiting periods, missing tooth clause, or other limitations may apply to the reimbursement for this service.
2. Reimbursement for replacement of fixed partial dentures is typically subject to a five to 10-year limitation period.

D6722 REVISED RETAINER CROWN – RESIN WITH NOBLE METAL CDT 2016

REVISIONS RETAINER CROWN – RESIN WITH PREDOMINANTLY BASE METAL

CODING CORRECTION MATCH

When reporting crown – resin with noble metal (D6722), be careful to ensure that the retainer crown code *matches* the corresponding resin with noble metal pontic (D6252).

COMMENTS When reporting the supporting retainer crown of a fixed partial denture (bridge), note that the term used in current CDT is "fixed partial denture retainer crowns." While many dental practices still use the term "abutment" to identify the retainer crown units of a fixed partial denture, the use of the term retainer can be confusing. The term "abutment" refers to the connection piece that attaches a prosthetic device to a root form implant (see D6056/D6057). To avoid billing errors, the components of a three-unit fixed partial denture should be identified as retainer-pontic-retainer, rather than abutment-pontic-abutment.

LIMITATIONS
1. Age restrictions, waiting periods, missing tooth clause, or other limitations may apply to the reimbursement for this service.

2. Reimbursement for replacement of fixed partial dentures is typically subject to a five to 10-year limitation period.

D6740 — REVISED RETAINER CROWN – PORCELAIN/CERAMIC — CDT 2016

REVISIONS RETAINER CROWN – PORCELAIN/CERAMIC

CODING CORRECTION — MATCH

When reporting crown – porcelain/ceramic (D6740), be careful to ensure that this retainer crown code *matches* the corresponding porcelain/ceramic pontic (D6245).

COMMENTS When reporting the supporting retainer crown of a fixed partial denture (bridge), note that the term used in current CDT is "fixed partial denture retainer crowns." While many dental practices still use the term "abutment" to identify the retainer crown units of a fixed partial denture, the use of the term retainer can be confusing. The term "abutment" refers to the connection piece that attaches a prosthetic device to a root form implant (see D6056/D6057). To avoid billing errors, the components of a three-unit fixed partial denture should be identified as retainer-pontic-retainer, rather than abutment-pontic-abutment.

LIMITATIONS
1. Age restrictions, waiting periods, missing tooth clause, or other limitations may apply to the reimbursement for this service.
2. Reimbursement for replacement of fixed partial dentures is typically subject to a five-to-10-year limitation period.
3. D6740 is used to report fixed partial denture retainers made of materials such as Procera®, Empress® and LavaUltimate®.

PHOTO

The image depicts a three unit porcelain/ceramic bridge. The bridge is made up of the pontic (D6245) and two retainer crowns (D6740).

Courtesy of Keller Dental Lab

D6750 — REVISED RETAINER CROWN – PORCELAIN FUSED TO HIGH NOBLE METAL — CDT 2016

REVISIONS RETAINER CROWN – PORCELAIN FUSED TO HIGH NOBLE METAL

CODING CORRECTION — MATCH

When reporting crown – porcelain fused to high noble metal (D6750), be careful to ensure that the retainer crown code *matches* the corresponding PFM high noble metal pontic (D6240).

COMMENTS When reporting the supporting retainer crowns of a fixed partial denture (bridge), note that the term used in current CDT is "fixed partial denture retainer crowns." While many dental practices still use the term "abutment" to identify the retainer crown units of a fixed partial denture, the use of the term retainer can be confusing. The term "abutment" refers to the connection piece that attaches a prosthetic device to a root form implant (see D6056/D6057). To avoid billing errors, the components of a three unit fixed partial retainer should be identified as retainer-pontic-retainer, rather than abutment-pontic-abutment.

LIMITATIONS
1. Age restrictions, waiting periods, missing tooth clause, or other limitations may apply to the reimbursement for this service.
2. Reimbursement for replacement of fixed partial dentures is typically subject to a five to 10-year limitation period.

D6751 — REVISED RETAINER CROWN – PORCELAIN FUSED TO PREDOMINANTLY BASE METAL — CDT 2016

REVISIONS RETAINER CROWN – PORCELAIN FUSED TO PREDOMINANTLY BASE METAL

Coding Match Correction: When reporting crown – porcelain fused to predominantly base metal (D6751), be careful to ensure that the retainer crown code *matches* the corresponding PFM base metal pontic (D6241).

COMMENTS When reporting the supporting retainer crowns of a fixed partial denture (bridge), note that the term used in current CDT is "fixed partial denture retainer crowns." While many dental practices still use the term "abutment" to identify the retainer crown units of a fixed partial denture, the use of the term retainer can be confusing. The term "abutment" refers to the connection piece that attaches a prosthetic device to a root form implant (see D6056/D6057). To avoid billing errors, the components of a three unit fixed partial denture should be identified as retainer-pontic-retainer, rather than abutment-pontic-abutment.

LIMITATIONS
1. Age restrictions, waiting periods, missing tooth clause, or other limitations may apply to the reimbursement for this service.
2. Reimbursement for replacement of fixed partial dentures is typically subject to a five to 10-year limitation period.

D6752 — REVISED RETAINER CROWN – PORCELAIN FUSED TO NOBLE METAL — CDT 2016

REVISIONS RETAINER CROWN – PORCELAIN FUSED TO NOBLE METAL

Coding Match Correction: When reporting crown – porcelain fused to noble metal (D6752), be careful to ensure that this code *matches* the corresponding PFM noble metal pontic (D6242).

COMMENTS When reporting the supporting retainer crowns of a fixed partial denture (bridge), note that the term used in current CDT is "fixed partial denture retainer crowns." While many dental practices still use the term "abutment" to identify the retainer crown units of a fixed partial denture, the use of the term retainer can be confusing. The term "abutment" refers to the connection piece that attaches a prosthetic device to a root form implant (see D6056/D6057). To avoid billing errors, the components of a three unit fixed partial denture should be identified as retainer-pontic-retainer, rather than abutment-pontic-abutment.

LIMITATIONS
1. Age restrictions, waiting periods, missing tooth clause, or other limitations may apply to the reimbursement for this service.
2. Reimbursement for replacement of fixed partial dentures is typically subject to a five to 10-year limitation period.

D6780 — REVISED RETAINER CROWN – 3/4 CAST HIGH NOBLE METAL — CDT 2016

REVISIONS RETAINER CROWN – ¾ CAST HIGH NOBLE METAL

CODING MATCH CORRECTION

When reporting crown – ¾ cast high noble metal (D6780), be careful to ensure that the code reported for the retainer *matches* the corresponding cast high noble metal pontic (D6210).

COMMENTS
1. When reporting the retainer crowns of a fixed partial denture (bridge), note that the term used in current CDT is "fixed partial denture retainer crowns." While many dental practices still use the term "abutment" to identify the retainer crown units of a fixed partial denture, the use of the term retainer can be confusing. The term "abutment" refers to the connection piece that attaches a prosthetic device to a root form implant (see D6056/D6057). To avoid billing errors, the components of a three unit fixed partial denture should be identified as retainer-pontic-retainer, rather than abutment-pontic-abutment.
2. ¾ crowns are most often placed on first molars with the mesio-buccal surfaces left intact for esthetics.

LIMITATIONS
1. Age restrictions, waiting periods, missing tooth clause, or other limitations may apply to the reimbursement for this service.
2. Reimbursement for replacement of fixed partial dentures is typically subject to a five to 10-year limitation period.

TIPS A ¾ crown covers the occlusal surface in addition to three of the four remaining sides of the tooth.

D6781 — REVISED RETAINER CROWN – 3/4 CAST PREDOMINANTLY BASE METAL — CDT 2016

REVISIONS RETAINER CROWN – ¾ CAST PREDOMINANTLY BASE METAL

CODING MATCH CORRECTION

When reporting crown – ¾ cast predominantly base metal (D6781), be careful to ensure that this code *matches* the corresponding cast base metal pontic (D6211).

COMMENTS
1. When reporting the retainer crowns of a fixed partial denture (bridge), note that the term used in current CDT is "fixed partial denture retainer crowns." While many dental practices still use the term "abutment" to identify the retainer crown units of a fixed partial denture, the use of the term retainer can be confusing. The term "abutment" refers to the connection piece that attaches a prosthetic device to a root form implant (see D6056/D6057). To avoid billing errors, the components of a three unit fixed partial denture should be identified as retainer-pontic-retainer, rather than abutment-pontic-abutment.
2. ¾ crowns are most often placed on first molars with the mesio-buccal surfaces left intact for esthetics.

LIMITATIONS
1. Age restrictions, waiting periods, missing tooth clause, or other limitations may apply to the reimbursement for this service.
2. Reimbursement for replacement of fixed partial dentures is typically subject to a five to 10-year limitation period.

TIPS A ¾ crown covers the occlusal surface in addition to three of the four remaining sides of the tooth.

D6782 — REVISED RETAINER CROWN – 3/4 CAST NOBLE METAL — CDT 2016

REVISIONS RETAINER CROWN – ¾ CAST NOBLE METAL

CODING MATCH CORRECTION

When reporting crown – ¾ cast noble metal (D6782), be careful to ensure that this code *matches* the corresponding cast noble metal pontic (D6212).

COMMENTS

1. When reporting the retainer crowns of a fixed partial denture (bridge), note that the term used in current CDT is "fixed partial denture retainer crowns." While many dental practices still use the term "abutment" to identify the retainer crown units of a fixed partial denture, the use of the term retainer can be confusing. The term "abutment" refers to the connection piece that attaches a prosthetic device to a root form implant (see D6056/D6057). To avoid billing errors, the components of a three unit fixed partial denture should be identified as retainer-pontic-retainer, rather than abutment-pontic-abutment.

2. ¾ crowns are most often placed on first molars with the mesio-buccal surfaces left intact for esthetics.

LIMITATIONS

1. Age restrictions, waiting periods, missing tooth clause, or other limitations may apply to the reimbursement for this service.

2. Reimbursement for replacement of fixed partial dentures is typically subject to a five to 10-year limitation period.

TIPS A ¾ crown covers the occlusal surface in addition to three of the four remaining sides of the tooth.

D6783 — REVISED RETAINER CROWN – 3/4 PORCELAIN/CERAMIC — CDT 2016

REVISIONS RETAINER CROWN – ¾ PORCELAIN/CERAMIC

Coding Match Correction

When reporting crown – ¾ porcelain/ceramic (D6783), be careful that the corresponding porcelain/ceramic pontic (D6245) material matches the retainer crown.

COMMENTS

1. When reporting the retainer crowns of a fixed partial denture (bridge), note that the term used in current CDT is "fixed partial denture retainer crowns." While many dental practices still use the term "abutment" to identify the retainer crown units of a fixed partial denture, the use of the term retainer can be confusing. The term "abutment" refers to the connection piece that attaches a prosthetic device to a root form implant (see D6056/D6057). To avoid billing errors, the components of a three unit fixed partial denture should be identified as retainer-pontic-retainer, rather than abutment-pontic-abutment.

2. ¾ crowns are most often placed on first molars with the mesio-buccal surfaces left intact or anterior teeth for esthetics.

3. D6783 is used to report ¾ crowns fabricated of materials such as Empress® and Procera® and includes Lava Ultimate®.

LIMITATIONS

1. Age restrictions, waiting periods, missing tooth clause, or other limitations may apply to the reimbursement for this service.

2. Reimbursement for replacement of fixed partial dentures is typically subject to a five to 10-year limitation period.

TIPS

1. A ¾ crown covers the occlusal surface in addition to three of the four remaining sides of the tooth.

2. D6783 is used to report a restoration placed on an anterior tooth with the lingual or the facial surface of enamel intact.

D6790 — REVISED RETAINER CROWN – FULL CAST HIGH NOBLE METAL — CDT 2016

REVISIONS RETAINER CROWN – FULL CAST HIGH NOBLE METAL

Coding Match Correction

When reporting crown – full cast high noble metal (D6790), report the corresponding cast high noble pontic (D6210).

COMMENTS	When reporting the retainer crowns of a fixed partial denture (bridge), note that the term used in current CDT is "fixed partial denture retainer crowns." While many dental practices still use the term "abutment" to identify the retainer crown units of a fixed partial denture, the use of the term retainer can be confusing. The term "abutment" refers to the connection piece that attaches a prosthetic device to a root form implant (see D6056/D6057). To avoid billing errors, the components of a three unit fixed partial denture should be identified as retainer-pontic-retainer, rather than abutment-pontic-abutment.
LIMITATIONS	1. Age restrictions, waiting periods, missing tooth clause, or other limitations may be applied to the reimbursement for this service. 2. Reimbursement for replacement of fixed partial dentures is typically subject to a five to 10-year limitation period.

D6791 — REVISED RETAINER CROWN – FULL CAST PREDOMINANTLY BASE METAL — CDT 2016

REVISIONS	RETAINER CROWN – FULL CAST PREDOMINANTLY BASE METAL
CODING CORRECTION MATCH	When reporting crown – full cast predominantly base metal (D6791), be careful to ensure that the code *matches* the corresponding cast base metal pontic (D6211).
COMMENTS	When reporting the retainer crowns of a fixed partial denture (bridge), note that the term used in current CDT is "fixed partial denture retainer crowns." While many dental practices still use the term "abutment" to identify the retainer crown units of a fixed partial denture, the use of the term retainer can be confusing. The term "abutment" refers to the connection piece that attaches a prosthetic device to a root form implant (see D6056/D6057). To avoid billing errors, the components of a three unit fixed partial denture should be identified as retainer-pontic-retainer, rather than abutment-pontic-abutment.
LIMITATIONS	1. Age restrictions, waiting periods, missing tooth clause, or other limitations may be applied to the reimbursement for this service. 2. Reimbursement for replacement of fixed partial dentures is typically subject to a five to 10-year limitation period.

D6792 — REVISED RETAINER CROWN – FULL CAST NOBLE METAL — CDT 2016

REVISIONS	RETAINER CROWN – FULL CAST NOBLE METAL
CODING CORRECTION MATCH	When reporting crown – full cast noble metal (D6792), be careful to ensure that the code *matches* the corresponding cast noble metal pontic (D6212).
COMMENTS	When reporting the retainer crowns of a fixed partial denture (bridge), note that the term used in current CDT is "fixed partial denture retainer crowns." While many dental practices still use the term "abutment" to identify the retainer crown units of a fixed partial denture, the use of the term retainer can be confusing. The term "abutment" refers to the connection piece that attaches a prosthetic device to a root form implant (see D6056/D6057). To avoid billing errors, the components of a three unit fixed partial denture should be identified as retainer-pontic-retainer, rather than abutment-pontic-abutment.
LIMITATIONS	1. Age restrictions, waiting periods, missing tooth clause, or other limitations may be applied to the reimbursement for this service. 2. Reimbursement for replacement of fixed partial dentures is typically subject to a five to 10-year limitation period.

D6794 — REVISED RETAINER CROWN – TITANIUM — CDT 2016

Note: While out of numerical order, this code is correctly listed here within the Fixed Partial Denture Retainers-Crowns subcategory.

REVISIONS RETAINER CROWN – TITANIUM

CODING MATCH CORRECTION

When reporting D6794, the retainer crown (titanium) code should *match* the corresponding titanium pontic (D6214).

COMMENTS

1. When reporting the retainer crowns of a fixed partial denture (bridge), note that the term used in current CDT is "fixed partial denture retainer crowns." While many dental practices still use the term "abutment" to identify the retainer crown units of a fixed partial denture, the use of the term retainer can be confusing. The term "abutment" refers to the connection piece that attaches a prosthetic device to a root form implant (see D6056/D6057). To avoid billing errors, the components of a three unit fixed partial denture should be identified as retainer-pontic-retainer, rather than abutment-pontic-abutment.

2. The nomenclature for an abutment supported retainer crown titanium (D6794) is broad and may be used to report any type of titanium crown, including full metallic or titanium crowns with a surface coating of ceramic or resin.

LIMITATIONS

1. Reimbursement for the replacement of a fixed partial denture is typically subject to a five to 10-year limitation.
2. Age, waiting periods, missing tooth, or other limitations may apply to the reimbursement of fixed partial dentures.

D6793 — PROVISIONAL RETAINER CROWN – FURTHER TREATMENT OR COMPLETION OF DIAGNOSIS NECESSARY PRIOR TO FINAL IMPRESSION — CDT 2016

Not to be used as a temporary retainer crown for routine prosthetic fixed partial dentures.

CODING WARNING CORRECTION

1. Do not report provisional retainer crown (D6793) as a temporary provisional retainer for routine fixed partial denture (bridge) procedures.

2. Crown – indirect resin based composite (D6710) reports a permanent indirect retainer (resin based composite). It is an error to report D6710 for a *provisional* prosthesis. D6793 should be reported for a *provisional* retainer crown. Do not report D6710 to describe a *provisional* retainer crown.

CODING MATCH CORRECTION

When reporting the *provisional* retainer crown (D6793), *match* the corresponding provisional pontic (D6253) with the *provisional* retainer crown.

COMMENTS D6793 reports a *provisional* retainer crown placed temporarily (i.e., during extended periodontal treatment).

LIMITATIONS Very few payers will reimburse D6793 and then, only if the provisional fixed partial denture is part of a *multistaged* treatment plan and anticipated to be in place for awhile.

NARRATIVES

1. "Provisional retainer crown will be utilized as extended time interim restoration."
2. "Final impression has not been made."
3. State reason for provisional use – e.g. allow time for periodontal healing.

| D6794 | REVISED RETAINER CROWN – TITANIUM | CDT 2016 |

Note: D6794 appears here in numerical order. Its true location is after D6792 but the information for this code is printed in this location in its entirety.

REVISIONS — RETAINER CROWN – TITANIUM

CODING CORRECTION — MATCH

When reporting D6794, the retainer crown (titanium) code should *match* the corresponding titanium pontic (D6214).

COMMENTS

1. When reporting the retainer crowns of a fixed partial denture, note that the term used in current CDT is "fixed partial denture retainer crowns." While many dental practices still use the term "abutment" to identify the retainer crown units of a fixed partial denture, the use of the term retainer can be confusing. The term "abutment" refers to the connection piece that attaches a prosthetic device to a root form implant (see D6056/D6057). To avoid billing errors, the components of a three unit fixed partial denture should be identified as retainer-pontic-retainer, rather than abutment-pontic-abutment.

2. The nomenclature for an abutment supported retainer crown titanium (D6794) is broad and may be used to report any type of titanium retainer crown, including full metallic or titanium crowns with a surface coating of ceramic or resin.

LIMITATIONS

1. Reimbursement for the replacement of a fixed partial denture is typically subject to a five to 10-year limitation.
2. Age, waiting periods, missing tooth, or other limitations may apply to the reimbursement of fixed partial dentures.

| D6795 | PREVIOUSLY DELETED CODE INTERIM RETAINER CROWN |

This code is a previously deleted code. See D6793 for further details.

OTHER FIXED PARTIAL DENTURE SERVICES — CDT 2016

| D6920 | CONNECTOR BAR | CDT 2016 |

A device attached to fixed partial denture retainer or coping which serves to stabilize and anchor a removable overdenture prosthesis.

COMMENTS

1. D6920 reports a "connector bar," such as Hader® bar or Dolder® bar, that connects the fixed partial denture retainer crowns or copings (D2975) together and supports and anchors a removable overdenture or a removable partial overdenture (D5863-D5866).

2. The bar connects to each abutment coping (D2975) or each fixed partial denture retainer crown. A removable overdenture or a removable partial overdenture (D5863-D5866) "snaps" over the connector bar (D6920).

3. Fees for the connector bar vary with the length/size/complexity of the bar.

LIMITATIONS D6920 is seldom reimbursed and if reimbursed the coverage is highly variable among payers.

| D6930 | RE-CEMENT OR RE-BOND FIXED PARTIAL DENTURE | CDT 2016 |

COMMENTS D6930 is used to report the re-cementation or re-bonding of a conventional fixed partial denture (bridge) and includes Maryland bridges.

LIMITATIONS
1. Some payers will not reimburse a re-cementation or re-bonding provided by the same provider within six to 12 months of delivery. If re-cementation or re-bonding is necessary within six to 12 months of delivery, the service is considered a part of the initial procedure.
2. Some payers reimburse the re-cementation or re-bonding of a bridge once per lifetime.
3. The re-cementation or re-bonding of a bridge may not be subject to the typical limitation period if re-cemented or re-bonded by a different dentist in a different office.
4. The reimbursement for re-cementing or re-bonding a bridge is typically higher than the re-cementation or re-bonding of a single crown unit.

NARRATIVES Include a brief narrative that alerts the payer when the fixed partial denture (bridge) was originally seated. If re-cementation or re-bonding occurs in an office, by a dentist that did not originally deliver the bridge, note this in a brief narrative.

ADDITIONAL INFORMATION
1. For re-cementing or re-bonding a *single* unit natural tooth restoration, see D2910 and D2920.
2. For re-cementing or re-bonding a *single* unit *abutment* or *implant supported* restoration, see D6092.
3. D6093 describes the re-cementation or re-bonding of an *abutment* or *implant supported* fixed partial denture (bridge).

D6940 STRESS BREAKER — CDT 2016

A non-rigid connector.

COMMENTS D6940 is used to report a "stress breaker" for a fixed partial denture (bridge), such as a "keyway." The purpose of a stress breaker is to relieve harmful stresses on the crown retainer teeth. It is a non-rigid connector.

LIMITATIONS D6940 is not typically reimbursed. Reimbursement is highly variable among payers.

NARRATIVES Submit D6940 with a narrative that explains why the stress breaker is necessary.

D6950 PRECISION ATTACHMENT — CDT 2016

A male and female pair constitutes one precision attachment, and is separate from the prosthesis.

COMMENTS This type of precision attachment (D6950) is used to report the male and female component of a "precision" partial. The precision attachment connects the prosthesis to a fixed retainer crown.

LIMITATIONS D6950 is typically not reimbursed. Reimbursement is highly variable among payers.

NARRATIVES Submit D6950 with a narrative that explains why the precision attachment is necessary. If the precision attachment is used for cosmetic reasons, the service will not be reimbursed.

D6970 PREVIOUSLY DELETED CODE POST AND CORE IN ADDITION TO FIXED PARTIAL DENTURE RETAINER, INDIRECTLY FABRICATED

This is a previously deleted code. See D2952 to report an indirectly fabricated post and core for a crown or retainer crown.

D6971 — PREVIOUSLY DELETED CODE CAST POST AS PART OF FIXED PARTIAL DENTURE RETAINER

This is a previously deleted code. See D6999 to report this procedure since it is deleted.

D6972 — PREVIOUSLY DELETED CODE PREFABRICATED POST AND CORE IN ADDITION TO FIXED PARTIAL DENTURE RETAINER

This is a previously deleted code. See D2954 to report prefabricated post and core for a crown or retainer crown.

D6973 — PREVIOUSLY DELETED CODE CORE BUILD UP FOR RETAINER, INCLUDING ANY PINS

This is a previously deleted code. See D2950 to report a core buildup for a crown or retainer crown.

D6975 — PREVIOUSLY DELETED CODE COPING

This is a previously deleted code. See D2975 for further details.

D6976 — PREVIOUSLY DELETED CODE EACH ADDITIONAL INDIRECTLY FABRICATED POST - SAME TOOTH

This is a previously deleted code. See D2953 for further details.

D6977 — PREVIOUSLY DELETED CODE EACH ADDITIONAL PREFABRICATED POST - SAME TOOTH

This is a previously deleted code. See D2957 for further details.

D6980 — FIXED PARTIAL DENTURE REPAIR, NECESSITATED BY RESTORATIVE MATERIAL FAILURE   CDT 2016

COMMENTS
1. Fixed partial denture repair (D6980) requires a restorative material failure (fracture).
2. Do not report D6980 for a composite or amalgam placed to restore a tooth due to decay. Report a composite or amalgam code depending on the type of restoration done.

LIMITATIONS Some payers limit the reimbursement for the repair to no more than one half of the fee allowed for a new fixed partial denture (bridge) and if paid, is 50% of the UCR fee. Note, a repair may "reset" the exclusion period of five, seven or 10 years for the reimbursement of the replacement of the old prosthesis with a new fixed prosthesis.

NARRATIVES
1. The narrative should describe the procedure and original placement date. The narrative should indicate the time involved in the repair and a copy of the laboratory bill should be included.
2. For endodontic access closure (through an existing cemented or bonded bridge) consider a single surface composite (D2391) or single surface amalgam (D2140) to report this type of service, typically paid at 80% of the UCR fee. A narrative could state, "An occlusal retainer was placed for endodontic access hole closure."

D6985 — PEDIATRIC PARTIAL DENTURE, FIXED — CDT 2016

This prosthesis is used primarily for aesthetic purposes.

CODING CORRECTION WARNING

1. It could be considered fraud to report a pediatric partial denture, fixed (D6985) situation, which is really utilized for aesthetic purposes (pediatric partial), when replacing the central and lateral incisors and canines as a space maintainer. For instance, fixed bilateral (D1515). The narrative should disclose the true nature of the prosthesis which is aesthetic.
2. A space maintainer is not considered dentally necessary when only replacing central and/or lateral incisors and/or canines.

COMMENTS Pediatric partial denture, fixed (D6985), reports a fixed partial prosthesis that may replace extracted primary or permanent teeth. This aesthetic service is generally provided as a result of the parent's insistence.

LIMITATIONS
1. The code descriptor states that D6985 is used "primarily for aesthetic purposes." Most payers will not reimburse D6985 since is it considered cosmetic in nature. If the primary canines have been lost, the payer might reimburse a space maintainer as an alternate benefit.
2. Most payers require the loss of a primary first or second molar for reimbursement of D6985. Plan limitations and reimbursement is highly variable.

D6999 — UNSPECIFIED FIXED PROSTHODONTIC PROCEDURE, BY REPORT — CDT 2016

Used for procedure that is not adequately described by a code. Describe procedure.

COMMENTS Report unspecified fixed prosthodontic procedure, by report (D6999) for fixed prosthodontic related procedures. This list is not exhaustive. There may be other unspecified fixed prosthodontic procedures not included in this list:

1. For recementing a Maryland type fixed partial denture (bridge), see D6930.
2. The cast post as part of a fixed partial denture retainer (D6791) is deleted. Use D6999, by report, to file this procedure.
3. For sectioning a fixed bridge and retaining a portion of it, intact and serviceable in the mouth, see D9120.
4. Describing a fixed partial denture retainer crown material for which there is no code.
5. Use D6999, by report, to describe surveying a *new* retainer crown (as extra charge in addition to crown) to receive a clasp assembly of a *new* partial denture framework.
6. Use D6999 to report *each* wing type retainer of a Hugger® bridge.
7. Use D6999 to report *each* "Talon" retainer of a Monodont® bridge.
8. Custom staining of a bridge with the patient presenting to an outside laboratory for a color and characterization evaluation, report the fee for custom staining separately as D6999.

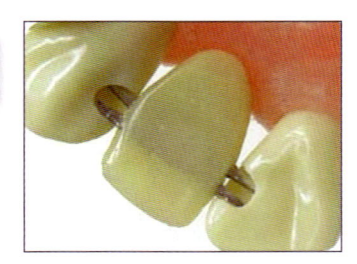

PHOTO
1. This is an example of a Monodont® bridge.
2. Each retainer wing (Talon) is reported as D6999 and the pontic as D6251.

Courtesy Drake Dental Lab

NOTES

Go to www.practicebooster.com to learn about the Revenue Enhancement Program, a coding and fee positioning consultation for you and your staff.
Cut coding errors and maximize legitimate reimbursement!
Tel: (866) 858-7596; Fax: (855) 825-3960; info@drcharlesblair.com

D7000-D7999 X. ORAL AND MAXILLOFACIAL SURGERY — CDT 2016

Local anesthesia is usually considered to be part of Oral and Maxillofacial Surgical procedures.

For dental benefit reporting purposes a quadrant is defined as four or more contiguous teeth and/or teeth spaces distal to the midline.

EXTRACTIONS (INCLUDES LOCAL ANESTHESIA, SUTURING, IF NEEDED, AND ROUTINE POSTOPERATIVE CARE) — CDT 2016

D7111 EXTRACTION, CORONAL REMNANTS – DECIDUOUS TOOTH — CDT 2016

Removal of soft tissue-retained coronal remnants.

CODING WATCH CORRECTION

1. It is a common coding error to report extraction, *coronal remnants* – deciduous tooth (D7111), for *"routine"* deciduous (baby) tooth extractions. If any deciduous *root* structures remain, report the "routine" extraction (D7140) for a primary tooth. See D7140 for further details.

COMMENTS

1. A coronal remnant's removal is described using D7111. *Be careful* to bill primary tooth extractions using code D7140 if a portion of the root remains. Most payers reimburse D7140 for a primary tooth extraction at a higher rate than for extraction of coronal remnants (D7111). Most dental plans provide the same reimbursement for primary and permanent extractions. Note: some dentists charge a lower fee for primary extractions than for permanent extractions.
2. Report extraction, coronal remnants – deciduous tooth (D7111), for primary teeth that are held in by soft-tissue, *without roots*. Only the primary crown (or fragments of it) remains and is held in by soft tissue.
3. "Routine" primary tooth extractions with full crown and some root structure present should be reported as D7140.

LIMITATIONS

1. The reimbursement for D7111 is typically at 80% of the UCR fee for D7140.
2. Some payers have an exclusion for reimbursement of D7111 if an extraction is performed in conjunction with other surgery performed at the same site on the same day. For instance, when deciduous coronal remnants and an underlying permanent bicuspid are extracted on the same service date, some payers would reimburse the underlying permanent bicuspid tooth only, but not the primary tooth remnant.

    If the extraction is for orthodontics, answer the question, "Is this for orthodontics?" on the claim form, "yes." If orthodontic benefits are available, orthodontic extractions for orthodontic reasons are generally reimbursed at 50% of the UCR fee, subject to the typical $1,500 lifetime orthodontic benefit. Sometimes an "orthodontic extraction" is reimbursed from the general dental benefits. If this is the case, reimbursement is usually made at 80% of the UCR fee. A deductible and other plan limitations may apply. Plan limitations are variable.

TIPS

1. Extraction, coronal remnants – deciduous tooth (D7111) could be used to report a child's emergency visit, when the primary tooth remnant is "hanging." The fee for extraction of a coronal remnant (D7111) may represent an "office visit" fee to remove the coronal remnant and consult with the parent.
2. When extracting several primary teeth on the same service date where some are classified as D7111 and others as D7140, (if you choose to "discount" the fee in these situations) report each extraction at a discounted fee. Do not charge the full fee for some of the extractions and not report other teeth that were extracted. Always report "what you do." This approach will work for contracted providers.

D7140 EXTRACTION, ERUPTED TOOTH OR EXPOSED ROOT (ELEVATION AND/OR FORCEPS REMOVAL) — CDT 2016

Includes routine removal of tooth structure, minor smoothing of socket bone, and closure, as necessary.

CODING WATCH CORRECTION

1. It is a common coding error to report extraction, coronal remnants – deciduous tooth (D7111), for "routine" deciduous (baby) tooth extractions. If some primary deciduous root structures and crown remains, report the "routine" extraction (D7140) for a primary tooth. See D7111 for further details regarding extraction of soft tissue retained coronal remnants.

2. D7140 is used to describe a routine "exposed root" removal, where the coronal portion of the tooth has broken or decayed at or near the gum line. If the exposed root remnant can be accessed without laying a flap, removing bone, or sectioning the root, report D7140.

3. If bone is removed and/or the exposed tooth root is sectioned for removal, see surgical removal of erupted tooth (D7210). D7210 is a more complicated procedure than D7140 for removal of the exposed root and is reimbursed at a higher UCR fee.

4. See surgical removal of residual (not exposed root) tooth roots (D7250) to describe procedures where a flap is laid and bone is surgically removed in the extraction process.

5. If the extraction is a part of orthodontic treatment, answer the question, "Is this for orthodontics?" on the claim form, "yes." If orthodontic benefits are available, extractions for orthodontic reasons are generally reimbursed at 50% of the UCR fee, subject to the lifetime orthodontic benefit. Sometimes an "orthodontic extraction" is reimbursed from the general dental benefits. If this is the case, reimbursement is usually made at 80% of the UCR fee. A deductible and other plan limitations may apply.

6. Do not report surgical removal of residual tooth roots (D7250) for the routine extraction of exposed roots of an erupted tooth. See D7250 to report surgical removal of residual roots.

COMMENTS

1. Reimbursement for the extraction of an erupted tooth (D7140) is generally considered a "basic service" and paid at 80% of UCR.

2. D7140 is used to describe the "*routine*" removal of an erupted tooth (both primary *and* permanent) or *exposed roots* of an erupted tooth. Since this code is used to report "multiple extractions" on the same service date, the D7140 code may be used to report each *additional* tooth or exposed root extraction extracted on the same date of service.

3. Payers typically reimburse the *same* UCR fee for primary *or* permanent tooth extraction.

4. For *surgical* removal of an erupted tooth, requiring *removal of bone* and/or *sectioning of the tooth*, see D7210. To report D7210, laying a flap is not required, and is only done if surgically indicated.

LIMITATIONS

1. Most payers consider alveoloplasty in *conjunction* with extractions to be a part of the *global* extraction fee. The description of D7140 indicates some *minor* removal/smoothing of bone is included. This minor removal/smoothing of bone should not be reported as an alveoloplasty in addition to the extraction. If significant bony recontouring is required and involves *multiple adjacent* sites, see alveoloplasty (D7310/D7311).

2. Suture removal, minor smoothing of bone, closure, and follow up is included in the global fee for an erupted tooth extraction. The treatment of infection after extractions can be reported. See treatment of complications (post surgical) – unusual circumstances (D9930). This code may be used to report treatment of a dry socket or removal of a bony sequestrum. See D9930 for common limitations.

TIPS

Some doctors, for multiple extractions, will charge for *fewer* extractions than were actually performed, when some extractions may have been "easy," and they want to reduce the patient's expense. By reducing the true extraction count and then charging the full fee for fewer extractions than were actually done, the overall reimbursement will be *less* when participating in a low UCR fee plan. For better reimbursement, charge a lower fee for *each* extraction, rather than reduce the true extraction count. The total fee charged is the same with either approach, but if the patient has a low UCR fee plan, charging a fee on each extraction performed and reporting all the extractions will result in higher reimbursement. Always report the exact number of teeth extracted and the actual fee charged for each extraction. There is no rule that requires every extraction to be charged at the same fee.

SURGICAL EXTRACTIONS (INCLUDES LOCAL ANESTHESIA, SUTURING, IF NEEDED, AND ROUTINE POSTOPERATIVE CARE) — CDT 2016

D7210 SURGICAL REMOVAL OF ERUPTED TOOTH REQUIRING REMOVAL OF BONE AND/OR SECTIONING OF TOOTH, AND INCLUDING ELEVATION OF MUCOPERIOSTEAL FLAP, IF INDICATED — CDT 2016

Includes related cutting of gingiva and bone, removal of tooth structure, minor smoothing of socket bone and closure.

CODING WARNING CORRECTION

1. When an *erupted* tooth is extracted without removal of bone and/or sectioning of the tooth and only a suture is placed, it is misleading to report surgical removal of an erupted tooth. D7210 requires removal of bone and/or sectioning of the tooth. When bone is not removed and/or the tooth is not sectioned, *do not* report D7210. Placing suture(s) does not elevate the routine extraction to the level of a *surgical* extraction of an erupted tooth (D7210). The removal of bone and/or "sectioning of tooth" are required to report D7210. Sectioning the tooth does elevate the service to that described by D7210. The elevation of a mucoperiosteal flap is included as part of D7210, if indicated. Note: the elevation of a mucoperiosteal flap is no longer required to report D7210.

2. Reporting D7210 is considered "upcoding" which could be considered a fraudulent act when actually performing routine extractions (D7140).

COMMENTS If the extraction of an erupted tooth requires the removal of bone and/or sectioning of the tooth, report D7210, not D7140. D7210 is typically reimbursed at a level of 150-180% higher than D7140. The increased fee/reimbursement is justified by the fact that the surgical removal procedure requires increased time and because of the increased difficulty of the procedure. Some general practitioners do not utilize the surgical extraction code, D7210, when justified. The procedure counts for D7210 generally make up a *fraction* of the "routine" extraction (D7140) counts in a general dental office.

LIMITATIONS

1. Suture placement and removal, minor smoothing of bone, closure, and routine follow up is included in the global surgical fee for D7210. Treatment for extensive infection after tooth removal could be a reimbursable service (see D9930). Alveoloplasty in conjunction with an extraction is generally considered a part of the extraction when performed on the same service date. Incidental bone removal during a single surgical extraction (D7210) is not considered a separate billable alveoloplasty service. If multiple adjacent extractions are performed or if significant bony recontouring is required, see alveoloplasty in conjunction with extractions (D7310/D7311).

2. D7210 is used to report a *surgical* extraction. Some payers require that the procedure be submitted to the patient's medical payer before reimbursement is considered under the dental plan. If the claim has been submitted to the medical payer, attach the medical explanation of benefits to the dental claim form.

3. The descriptor for D7210 indicates that either "removal of bone" *or* "sectioning of the tooth" is justification for reporting D7210. Note: Some payers may require *both* removal of bone and sectioning of the tooth to qualify for reimbursement. Some payers require that laying a mucoperiosteal flap be done to be considered for reimbursement even though the elevation of a mucoperiosteal flap is no longer required to report D7210, according to the code's descriptor.

4. See D9930 to report treatment of complicated (post-surgical) situations. Most payers consider D9930 (by the same office) to be a part of the global extraction fee.

NARRATIVES

1. D7210 should not be overutilized. Accurately describe the procedure in the clinical notes. A typical note might read: "elevated flap (if applicable) and removed bone and/or sectioned tooth. These procedures were necessary to extract the tooth." An intraoral camera photo of the sectioned tooth is recommended as proof that the procedure was provided and qualifies as a "surgical" extraction.

2. State if bone was removed during the extraction and why it was necessary, e.g., tooth was fractured off below bone level. "See attached image."

3. State if tooth was sectioned during extraction and why, e.g., tooth had curved roots, sectioning was necessary to remove tooth as atraumatically as possible. "See attached image."

4. A current diagnostic radiographic image should be sent as part of the documentation and any supporting photographs.

| D7220 | REMOVAL OF IMPACTED TOOTH – SOFT TISSUE | CDT 2016 |

Occlusal surface of tooth covered by soft tissue; requires mucoperiosteal flap elevation.

COMMENTS
1. Suture removal and follow up is considered a part of the global surgical fee for removal of an impacted tooth – soft tissue (D7220). Extensive infection after an impacted tooth removal, can be reported separately on a subsequent service date.
2. See D9930 to report treatment of complicated (post-surgical) situations. Most payers consider D9930 (by the same office) to be a part of the global extraction fee.

LIMITATIONS
1. Reimbursement of D7220 is typically based on the payer's assessment of the narrative and the anatomical position of the impacted tooth from submitted diagnostic radiographic images. The surgical technique necessary for removal is not considered. This procedure requires the elevation of a mucoperiosteal flap for access as the tooth is located beneath soft tissue. When reporting D7220, the coronal portion of the tooth is not submerged in bone.
2. Some payers require that the medical plan be billed *before* consideration of the service under the dental plan. If medical billing is required, attach the medical explanation of benefits to the subsequent dental claim form.
3. Sectioning the tooth is not a requirement to submit this procedure (D7220) for payment, but it does require mucoperiosteal flap elevation.
4. In some cases, D7220 may be subject to age limitations. Some plans limit coverage to patients who are 15 to 30 years of age.

NARRATIVES
1. A brief narrative should describe the anatomical position of the tooth and should indicate that the occlusal surface of the tooth was covered by soft tissue.
2. The narrative should explain that a mucoperiosteal flap was elevated.
3. A current diagnostic radiographic image of the pretreatment area should be sent as part of the documentation. "See attached radiographic images(s) and operative notes." A pretreatment photograph of the surgical area may also be sent.

| D7230 | REMOVAL OF IMPACTED TOOTH – PARTIALLY BONY | CDT 2016 |

Part of crown covered by bone; requires mucoperiosteal flap elevation and bone removal.

COMMENTS
1. Suture removal and follow up is considered a part of the global surgical fee for removal of an impacted tooth – partially bony (D7230). Extensive infection after an impacted tooth removal can be reported separately.
2. See D9930 to report treatment of complicated (post-surgical) situations. Most payers consider D9930 (by the same office) to be a part of the global extraction fee.

LIMITATIONS
1. D7230 reports removal of impacted tooth – partially bony where "part of" the crown is covered by bone. "Part of" the crown covered by bone implies that less than 50% of the crown is covered by bone. The surgical technique necessary for removal is not considered for reimbursement. This code requires that both a mucoperiosteal flap be elevated and that pericoronal bone be removed in order to access the tooth for extraction.
2. Some payers require that the medical plan be billed *before* consideration of the service under the dental plan. If medical billing is required, attach the medical explanation of benefits to the subsequent dental claim form.
3. Sectioning the tooth is not a requirement to submit this procedure (D7230) for payment, but it does require a mucoperiosteal flap elevation and bone removal to access the tooth.
4. In some cases, D7230 may be subject to age limitations. Some plans limit coverage to patients who are 15 to 30 years of age.

NARRATIVES 1. A brief narrative should describe the anatomical position of the tooth and should indicate that a portion of the crown was covered by soft tissue and bone and that there was some bone removed to allow access for the extraction.

2. The narrative should explain that a mucoperiosteal flap was elevated and that pericoronal bone was removed.

3. A current diagnostic radiographic image of the pretreatment area should be sent as part of the documentation. "See attached image(s) and operative notes."

D7240 REMOVAL OF IMPACTED TOOTH – COMPLETELY BONY — CDT 2016

Most or all of crown covered by bone; requires mucoperiosteal flap elevation and bone removal.

COMMENTS 1. Suture removal and follow up is considered a part of the global surgical fee for removal of an impacted tooth – completely bony (D7240). Extensive infection after an impacted tooth removal can be reported separately on a subsequent service date.

2. See D9930 to report treatment of complicated (post-surgical) situations. Most payers consider D9930 (by the same office) to be a part of the global extraction fee.

LIMITATIONS 1. D7240 reports removal of impacted tooth – completely bony where "most *or* all" of the crown is covered by bone. "Most" of the crown covered by bone implies that more than 50% of the crown is covered by bone. The surgical technique necessary for removal is not considered for reimbursement. This code requires that both a mucoperiosteal flap be elevated and that pericoronal bone be removed in order to access the tooth for extraction.

2. Some payers require that the medical plan be billed *before* consideration of the service under the dental plan. If medical billing is required, attach the medical explanation of benefits to the subsequent dental claim form.

3. Sectioning the tooth is not a requirement to submit this procedure (D7240) for payment, but it does require a mucoperiosteal flap elevation and bone removal to access the tooth.

4. In some cases, D7240 may be subject to age limitations. Some plans limit coverage to patients who are 15 to 30 years of age.

NARRATIVES 1. A brief narrative should describe the anatomical position of the tooth and should indicate that a portion of the crown was covered by soft tissue and that more than 50% of the crown was covered by bone.

2. The narrative should explain that a mucoperiosteal flap was elevated and that pericoronal bone was removed.

3. A current diagnostic radiograph of the pretreatment area should be sent as part of the documentation. "See attached image(s) and operative notes."

D7241 REMOVAL OF IMPACTED TOOTH – COMPLETELY BONY, WITH UNUSUAL SURGICAL COMPLICATIONS — CDT 2016

Most or all of crown covered by bone; unusually difficult or complicated due to factors such as nerve dissection required, separate closure of maxillary sinus required or aberrant tooth position.

COMMENTS 1. This code is used to describe the removal of a completely bony impaction which is "unusually difficult or complicated." Factors that may justify the use of this code are: Nerve dissection required, separate closure of maxillary sinus, or difficult access due to aberrant tooth position." The reimbursement for this service is higher than for a "routine" completely bony impaction. This code is used infrequently and is designed to describe particularly exceptional circumstances.

2. Suture removal and follow up is considered a part of the global surgical fee for removal of an impacted tooth – completely bony with unusual surgical complication (D7241). Extensive infection after an impacted tooth removal, could be reported separately. See D9930 to report treatment of complicated (post-surgical) situations. Most payers consider D9930 (by the same office) to be a part of the global extraction fee.

LIMITATIONS

1. D7241 reports removal of impacted tooth – completely bony where "most *or* all" of the crown is covered by bone and the procedure was unusually complicated. "Most" is defined as more than 50% of the crown is covered by bone. The surgical technique necessary for removal is not considered for reimbursement. This code requires that both a mucoperiosteal flap be elevated and that pericoronal bone be removed in order to access the tooth for extraction.

2. Some payers require that the medical plan be billed *before* consideration of the service under the dental plan. If medical billing is required, attach the medical explanation of benefits to the subsequent dental claim form.

3. Sectioning the tooth is not a requirement to submit this procedure (D7241) for payment.

4. In some cases, D7241 may be subject to age limitations. Some plans limit coverage to patients who are 15 to 30 years of age.

NARRATIVES

1. A brief narrative should describe the anatomical position of the tooth and should indicate that a portion of the crown was covered by soft tissue and more than 50% of the crown was covered by bone.

2. The narrative should explain that a mucoperiosteal flap was elevated and that pericoronal bone was removed and how the procedure was unusually complicated. Mention nerve dissection, separate closure of maxillary sinus required, or aberrant tooth position as may apply.

3. A current diagnostic radiograph of the pretreatment area should be sent as part of the documentation. "See attached image(s) and operative notes."

D7250 SURGICAL REMOVAL OF RESIDUAL TOOTH ROOTS (CUTTING PROCEDURE) CDT 2016

Includes cutting of soft tissue and bone, removal of tooth structure, and closure.

CODING WATCH CORRECTION

1. D7250, surgical removal of residual tooth roots (cutting procedure) does not describe "difficult" extractions of an erupted tooth (D7140) or the removal of the exposed root (D7140). If removing bone or sectioning the erupted tooth or exposed root is required to extract the erupted tooth/root, report D7210.

2. "Residual tooth roots" refers to roots remaining after an extraction visit. D7250 should not be used to describe the removal of a root fractured at the extraction appointment. D7250 does describe the removal of a root at a subsequent appointment, on a different treatment date, or by a different provider. The initial extraction occurred sometime before removal of the *residual* root. In this case, reporting D7250 might evoke the "missing tooth" clause. The tooth was "extracted" (although partially) at an earlier appointment. The missing tooth clause might limit the reimbursement for a new bridge, implant or partial if the initial extraction was done before the patient was covered under the existing dental plan.

3. If a retained root is *exposed* (visible in the mouth), then the routine removal of the exposed root should be reported as extraction of *exposed roots*, D7140. If the exposed root requires removal of bone or sectioning to remove, report D7210.

LIMITATIONS

1. The D7250 descriptor describes the "cutting of the soft tissue and *bone*, removal of tooth structure, and closure." This code is appropriate to use when removing *residual* root fragments remaining in the bone left from a previous *incomplete* extraction. Some payers require a diagnostic image to confirm that the residual root is completely embedded in bone.

2. D7250 would be used to describe the situation where a general practitioner attempts the extraction of a tooth, cannot remove all the root structure and refers the patient for completion of the procedure, removal of the residual tooth root(s) to an oral surgeon. The oral surgeon would use D7250 to describe the procedure. The GP would report a partial extraction, D7999, by report.

3. Suture removal and follow up is included in the global fee for D7250. Treatment of extensive infection after this procedure removal would be reported separately. See D9930 to report treatment of complications (post-surgical) – unusual circumstances. However, most payers consider D9930 to be in the global extraction fee.

4. The reporting of surgical removal of residual tooth roots (D7250) may invoke the "missing tooth" limitation. Clearly explain the circumstances in a brief narrative and appeal the denial.

5. Some payers require that the medical plan be billed *before* consideration of this service under the dental plan. If medical billing is required, attach the medical explanation of benefits to the subsequent dental claim form.

NARRATIVES A brief narrative should describe the position of the *residual* tooth roots, the required cutting of soft tissue and bone, removal of the tooth structure, and closure. A current diagnostic radiographic image of the residual roots should also be included with the claim.

D7251 CORONECTOMY – INTENTIONAL PARTIAL TOOTH REMOVAL — CDT 2016

Intentional partial tooth removal is performed when a neurovascular complication is likely if the entire impacted tooth is removed.

CODING CORRECTION — WARNING

1. D7251 reports an *intended* partial removal of an impacted tooth leaving residual root(s) on purpose.
2. Do not use D7251 to report an unintended, incomplete extraction of an erupted tooth leaving residual root structures. See unspecified oral procedure, by report (D7999), to report an incomplete extraction of a tooth.

COMMENTS
1. D7251 reports a procedure where the coronal portion of the impacted tooth is removed while some root structure is intentionally left.
2. This intentional procedure (D7251) should have the pretreatment consent of the patient.
3. The residual root structures are not disturbed in this procedure.

NARRATIVES
1. A brief narrative should reflect that a neurovascular complication is likely if the entire impacted tooth is removed.
2. "Intentionally removed only part of tooth due to proximity of neurovascular bundle. See attached radiographic images(s) and operative notes."
3. A current diagnostic radiographic image of the tooth should be included with the claim.

OTHER SURGICAL PROCEDURES — CDT 2016

D7260 OROANTRAL FISTULA CLOSURE — CDT 2016

Excision of fistulous tract between maxillary sinus and oral cavity and closure by advancement flap.

NARRATIVES A detailed narrative is often required for consultant review before this procedure will be considered for reimbursement.

D7261 PRIMARY CLOSURE OF A SINUS PERFORATION — CDT 2016

Subsequent to surgical removal of tooth, exposure of sinus requiring repair, or immediate closure of oroantral or oralnasal communication in absence of fistulous tract.

NARRATIVES A detailed narrative is often required for consultant review before this procedure will be considered for reimbursement.

D7270 TOOTH REIMPLANTATION AND/OR STABILIZATION OF ACCIDENTALLY EVULSED OR DISPLACED TOOTH — CDT 2016

Includes splinting and/or stabilization.

CODING CORRECTION — WATCH

1. D7270 reports reimplanting and/or stabilization of an accidentally *evulsed* or *displaced* tooth. Report D7270 for "each" evulsed or displaced tooth. D7270 is a *trauma related* code. In some cases, the tooth (teeth) is (are) stabilized with a bonded wire to anchor the teeth (splinted).
2. If the alveolus is fractured, see alveolus-closed reduction (D7670).
3. Do not report intraoral placement of a fixation device (D7998) in addition to D7270. A fixation device would be considered integral with tooth reimplantation and/or stabilization (D7270).
4. For splinting/stabilizing of mobile, periodontally involved teeth, see provisional splinting-intracoronal (D4320) and provisional splinting-extracoronal (D4321).

COMMENTS Any adjustments, removal of splint, or follow up visits, are included in the initial global fee. These procedures should be considered in the overall treatment fee.

LIMITATIONS
1. This procedure may also be reimbursed under medical or accident insurance. Most payers process medical claims for accident and trauma and consider the medical plan as primary for reimbursement purposes. The 2012 ADA Dental Claim Form should be accompanied by the medical or accident insurance EOB.
2. Attach the medical explanation of benefits to the dental claim form. Some dental payers have a six to 12-month filing limitation.
3. File a dental claim form (with all pertinent information) within this limitation period, even if medical has not responded within the established period. This locks up the initial filing limitation.

NARRATIVES Write a detailed narrative and include radiographs and the tooth numbers involved.

D7272 TOOTH TRANSPLANTATION (INCLUDES REIMPLANTATION FROM ONE SITE TO ANOTHER AND SPLINTING AND/OR STABILIZATION) CDT 2016

1. D7272, tooth *transplantation* does not describe a tooth *reimplantation* related to an accident. D7272 is *not* accident related. D7272 is an intentional tooth transplantation. See tooth reimplantation and/or stabilization of accidentally evulsed or displaced tooth (D7270) or alveolus-closed reduction (D7670) to report situations regarding trauma.
2. It is an error to report D7272 as an intentional reimplantation (D3470), which is an endodontic related procedure. See D3470 for further details.
3. Do not report intraoral placement of a fixation device (D7998) in addition to reporting D7272. A fixation device would be considered integral with the tooth transplantation (D7272).

COMMENTS Tooth transplantation (D7272) describes the transplanting (extracting and moving) of a tooth from one site to another site. An example of this procedure is transplanting a third molar to a second molar socket. *(This is not a common procedure.)*

LIMITATIONS Tooth transplantation (D7272) is not generally reimbursed. If tooth transplantation is reimbursed, the associated extraction may be considered in the global fee for D7272.

D7280 SURGICAL ACCESS OF AN UNERUPTED TOOTH CDT 2016

An incision is made and the tissue is reflected and bone removed as necessary to expose the crown of an impacted tooth not intended to be extracted.

Surgical access of an unerupted tooth to expose the crown is often orthodontically related. The ADA claim form has a question, "Is this for orthodontics?" Most software programs, by default, answer this "no." It is an error to answer "no" if the service is in fact related to orthodontic treatment. Reimbursement for D7280, when performed with orthodontic treatment, may be applied toward the "lifetime orthodontic benefit" which is typically a $1,500 lifetime benefit.

D7280 describes the surgical access of an impacted/unerupted tooth. Note: If placing an attachment (button, ectopic pin, band or, bracket) report this procedure *separately*. See D7283 for further details regarding the placement of a device to facilitate eruption of an impacted tooth.

COMMENTS
1. D7283 is often reported in association with the "uncovering" of an unerupted/impacted tooth for placement of an orthodontic "button," band, ectopic pin or bracket placement.

2. D7280 is *not* limited to use with patients undergoing orthodontic treatment. For instance, D7280 could report uncovering bone for a second molar to erupt.

3. A pedicle graft (D4270) or a free soft tissue graft (D4277) may also be required as a separate procedure. See D4270 and D4277 for further details.

LIMITATIONS D7280 will generally require an orthodontic rider for reimbursement. The claim form question, "Is this for orthodontics?" usually must be answered "yes" for D7280 to be considered for reimbursement.

NARRATIVES A brief narrative should describe the tooth number and location of the unerupted tooth. Describe that an incision was made, tissue reflected, and any bone that was removed to expose the crown of the impacted tooth.

D7281 PREVIOUSLY DELETED CODE SURGICAL EXPOSURE OF IMPACTED OR UNERUPTED TOOTH TO AID ERUPTION

This is a previously deleted code. See D7280 for further details.

D7282 MOBILIZATION OF ERUPTED OR MALPOSITIONED TOOTH TO AID ERUPTION — CDT 2016

To move/luxate teeth to eliminate ankylosis; not in conjunction with an extraction.

COMMENTS
1. D7280 reports the mobilization of an erupted or malpositioned tooth to aid eruption.
2. The purpose of the mobilization procedure is to eliminate ankylosis (the union of the root of the tooth to the surrounding bone). By "breaking loose" or "mobilizing" the tooth from the bone, the tooth is free to erupt normally.
3. D7282 is not associated with an extraction.

D7283 PLACEMENT OF DEVICE TO FACILITATE ERUPTION OF IMPACTED TOOTH — CDT 2016

Placement of an orthodontic bracket, band or other device on an unerupted tooth, after its exposure, to aid in its eruption. Report the surgical exposure separately using D7280.

CODING WARNING CORRECTION Placement of device to facilitate eruption of impacted tooth (D7283) is orthodontically related. The ADA claim form has a related question, "Is this for orthodontics?" Most software programs, by default, answer this "no." It is an error to answer "no", if the procedure is an *orthodontic related* procedure. Reimbursement for D7283 may be applied to the "lifetime orthodontic benefit" (typically $1,500) and be reimbursed at 50% of the UCR fee.

CODING MATCH CORRECTION Placement of a bracket or device to facilitate eruption of impacted tooth (D7283) reports placing a "button," bracket, ectopic pin, or band on an unerupted tooth, after the surgical exposure of the crown (D7280). Thus, D7283 is associated with surgical access of an unerupted tooth (D7280) and is reported separately.

LIMITATIONS
1. D7283 may be eligible for reimbursement *if* surgical access of an unerupted tooth (D7280) procedure is also reimbursed. See D7280.
2. D7283 will generally require an orthodontic rider for reimbursement. The claim form question, "Is this for orthodontics?" usually must be answered "yes" for D7283 to be considered for reimbursement.

NARRATIVES Briefly describe the placement of a device (orthodontic bracket, pin, band or other device) on an unerupted tooth, after the tooth has been surgically exposed. Describe the device.

| **D7285** | **INCISIONAL BIOPSY OF ORAL TISSUE – HARD (BONE, TOOTH)** | **CDT 2016** |

For partial removal of specimen only. This procedure involves biopsy of osseous lesions and is not used for apicoectomy/periradicular surgery. This procedure does not entail an excision.

CODING WATCH CORRECTION D7285, incisional biopsy of oral tissue – hard (bone, tooth) is used to describe an incisional biopsy of oral *osseous* or *bone* tissue. A biopsy is the surgical removal of a *specimen* of tissue for histologic evaluation. The microscopic examination is a separate procedure.

COMMENTS A biopsy describes the *removal* of a specimen, not the entire lesion, not the *microscopic examination* of the specimen. This code does not report the total excision of a hard tissue lesion.

LIMITATIONS
1. D7285, biopsy of oral tissue – hard (bone, tooth) is not typically reimbursed without an accompanying pathology report.
2. Biopsies may be considered a part of other associated procedures performed in the same area, on the same service date when processed for reimbursement. D7285 should not be reported in conjunction with apicoectomy or periradicular surgery.
3. For medical insurance reimbursement, a "referral" may be required from the patient's primary care physician.

TIPS If the entire lesion is excised, report the appropriate lesion code, not D7285.

NARRATIVES
1. Remit the hard tissue biopsy specimen for analysis. After receiving the pathology report prepare the dental claim form. Make a copy of the pathology report and attach the pathology report to the dental claim form. Unless the pathology report accompanies the dental claim form, D7285 will probably not be reimbursed by dental insurance. The narrative should describe the location of the lesion, procedures used for the *hard* tissue removal, and a differential diagnosis.
2. "See attached copy of pathology report."

| **D7286** | **INCISIONAL BIOPSY OF ORAL TISSUE – SOFT** | **CDT 2016** |

For partial removal of an architecturally intact specimen only. This procedure is not used at the same time as codes for apicoectomy/periradicular curettage. This procedure does not entail an excision.

CODING WATCH CORRECTION
1. An incisional biopsy consists of removing part of the lesion for histologic evaluation.
2. Biopsy of oral tissue – soft (D7286) should not be used to describe the "OralCDx® brush biopsy" procedure. Report the brush biopsy as: transepithelial sample collection (D7288), for the OralCDx® brush biopsy.

COMMENTS
1. Report D7286 for an incisional soft-tissue biopsy. An incisional biopsy consists of removing part of the lesion for a histologic evaluation. By definition the specimen is architecturally intact. Architecturally intact refers to the fact that the sample is three dimensional.
2. A biopsy describes the *removal* of a specimen, not the microscopic examination of the specimen. This code *does not* report the total removal of the soft tissue lesion.
3. A soft tissue laser could be used as an adjunct to perform this procedure provided the specimen removed is architecturally intact.

LIMITATIONS
1. The soft tissue biopsy will not typically be reimbursed by dental insurance without an accompanying pathology report.
2. A biopsy may be considered to be a part of other associated procedures performed in the same area, on the same service date. D7286 should not to be reported in conjunction with apicoectomy (D3410, D3421, D34245, D3426) or periradicular surgery (D3427).

TIPS If the entire lesion is excised, report the appropriate lesion code (D7410-D7415), not D7286.

NARRATIVES
1. Send the soft tissue biopsy specimen to a pathologist for analysis. After receiving the pathology report, prepare the dental claim form. Make a copy of the pathology report and attach it to the dental claim form. Unless the pathology report accompanies the dental claim form, D7286 will probably not be reimbursed by the payer. A brief narrative should describe the location of the lesion, procedures used for the *soft* tissue removal, and a differential diagnosis.
2. "See attached copy of pathology report."

D7287 EXFOLIATIVE CYTOLOGICAL SAMPLE COLLECTION — CDT 2016

For collection of non-transepithelial cytology sample via mild scraping of the oral mucosa.

CODING WATCH CORRECTION
Do not report exfoliative cytological sample collection (D7287) for a "OralCDx® brush biopsy." For the OralCDx® brush biopsy, report brush biopsy – transepithelial sample collection (D7288).

COMMENTS Report D7287 for a non-transepithelial cytology sample, or smear. A smear often involves swabbing an area with a cotton swab and submitting the cells that have adhered to the swab for microscopic evaluation.

LIMITATIONS
1. D7287 will not typically be reimbursed without an accompanying pathology report attached to the dental claim form.
2. Biopsies may be considered a part of associated procedures performed in the same area, on the same service date.

NARRATIVES
1. Send the exfoliative cytological sample to a pathologist for analysis. After receiving the pathology report prepare the dental claim form. Make a copy of the pathology report and attach it to the dental claim form. Unless the pathology report accompanies the dental claim form, D7287 will probably not be reimbursed by the payer.
2. A brief narrative should describe the location of the lesion, procedures used for the sample removal, and a differential diagnosis.
3. "See attached copy of pathology report."

D7288 BRUSH BIOPSY – TRANSEPITHELIAL SAMPLE COLLECTION — CDT 2016

For collection of oral disaggregated transepithelial cells via rotational brushing of the oral mucosa.

CODING WATCH CORRECTION
Use brush biopsy – transepithelial sample collection (D7288) to report the OralCDx® brush biopsy. Do *not* report biopsy of oral tissue – soft (D7286) or exfoliative cytological sample collection (D7287) for the OralCDx® transepithelial sample collection.

COMMENTS
1. The brush biopsy (D7288) sample includes more cell layers than an exfoliative cytological sample (D7287). A brush biopsy scrapes the mucosa exposing the subcutaneous layer and creates bleeding. A cytology sample does not puncture the mucosa. A brush biopsy is like *scraping* into the floor, whereas a cytology sample (D7287) is more like *sweeping* the floor.
2. See D0486 for the associated oral pathology laboratory procedure.
3. A biopsy describes the removal of the specimen, not the microscopic examination of the specimen.

LIMITATIONS
1. D7288 will not typically be reimbursed without including a copy of the pathology report with the claim form.
2. D7288 reports the "sample collection" of transepithelial cells. The OralCDx® laboratory fee is reported *separately* through medical insurance.

NARRATIVES
1. Send the brush biopsy specimen to a pathologist for analysis. After receiving the pathology report prepare the dental claim form. Make a copy of the pathology report and attach it to the dental claim form. Unless the pathology report accompanies the dental claim form, D7288 will probably not be reimbursed by the payer.
2. A brief narrative should describe the location of the lesion, procedures used for the transepithelial sample removal, and a differential diagnosis.

D7290 SURGICAL REPOSITIONING OF TEETH — CDT 2016

Grafting procedure(s) is/are additional.

COMMENTS D7290, surgical repositioning of teeth is not limited to orthodontic treatment.

LIMITATIONS
1. Surgical repositioning of teeth (D7290) may be reimbursed and subject to the orthodontic lifetime maximum limitation when associated with orthodontic treatment. Reimbursement for D7290 is highly variable among payers.
2. The ADA claim form has a question, "Is this for orthodontics?" Most software programs, by default, answer this "no." It is an error to answer "no" if the service is in fact related to the orthodontic treatment. Reimbursement for D7290, when performed with the orthodontics, may be applied toward the "lifetime orthodontic benefit," which is typically $1500.

NARRATIVES A brief narrative should identify the tooth number (or letter) and include pre-operative radiographs. Explain why the procedure was necessary, the technique used and include radiographic image and pre-operative photographs.

D7291 TRANSSEPTAL FIBEROTOMY/SUPRA CRESTAL FIBEROTOMY, BY REPORT — CDT 2016

The supraosseous connective tissue attachment is surgically severed around the involved teeth. Where there are adjacent teeth, the transseptal fiberotomy of a single tooth will involve a minimum of three teeth. Since the incisions are within the gingival sulcus and tissue and the root surface is not instrumented, this procedure heals by the reunion of connective tissue with the root surface on which viable periodontal tissue is present (reattachment).

COMMENTS Report each target tooth (not adjacent teeth) involved for each transseptal fiberotomy/supra crestal fiberotomy.

CODING MATCH CORRECTION Transseptal fiberotomy/supra crestal fiberotomy (D7291) is typically associated with orthodontic treatment and at its completion after the active tooth movement phase is complete.

LIMITATIONS
1. Reimbursement for D7291 is subject to the plan's limitations and may be limited to the anterior permanent teeth and bicuspids.
2. The ADA claim form has a question, "Is this for orthodontics?" If the procedure is associated with orthodontic treatment, answer "yes" to the question on the ADA form "Is this for orthodontics?" Most software programs, by default, answer this "no." It is an error to answer "no" if the service is in fact related to the orthodontic treatment. Reimbursement for D7291, when performed with the orthodontics, may be applied toward the "lifetime orthodontic benefit," which is typically $1500.

D7292 — SURGICAL PLACEMENT OF TEMPORARY ANCHORAGE DEVICE (SCREW RETAINED PLATE) REQUIRING FLAP; INCLUDES DEVICE REMOVAL — CDT 2016

COMMENTS

1. Temporary skeletal anchorage devices are used in orthodontics. They are devices temporarily fixed in bone to provide a stationary anchorage point to attach appliances to orthodontically move teeth. They may be used to intrude or extrude teeth, to treat anterior cross bites or open bites, to move teeth distally or mesially, etc. These devices may be also used as part of orthognathic treatment. Because D7292 may be used with orthognathics, the codes have been listed in the oral and maxillofacial surgery category of codes. These anchorage devices are not intended to be permanent. In most instances, the device (plate/screw) is placed underneath the alveolar mucosa.
2. D7292 reports the placement of a temporary anchorage device which requires a surgical flap. Its purpose is for temporary skeletal anchorage. D7292 is used to specifically report a *screw retained plate*. This may be an orthodontic related procedure.
3. Removal of the temporary anchorage device is included in the global fee for D7292.
4. See also D7293 and D7294 for other types of temporary anchorage devices.

LIMITATIONS

1. D7292 is generally not a reimbursed procedure.
2. The ADA claim form has a question, "Is this for orthodontics?" If the procedure is associated with orthodontic treatment, answer "yes" to the question on the ADA form "Is this for orthodontics?" Most software programs, by default, answer this "no." It is an error to answer "no" when the service is in fact related to the orthodontic treatment. Reimbursement for D7292, when performed in conjunction with orthodontics, may be applied toward the "lifetime orthodontic benefit," which is typically $1500.

D7293 — SURGICAL PLACEMENT OF TEMPORARY ANCHORAGE DEVICE REQUIRING FLAP; INCLUDES DEVICE REMOVAL — CDT 2016

COMMENTS

1. Temporary skeletal anchorage devices are used in orthodontics. They are devices temporarily fixed in bone to provide a stationary anchorage point to attach appliances to orthodontically move teeth. They may be used to intrude or extrude teeth, to treat anterior cross bites or open bites, to move teeth distally or mesially, etc. These devices are also used as part of orthognathic treatment. Because D7293 have been used with orthognathics, the codes have been listed in the oral and maxillofacial surgery category of codes. These anchorage devices are not intended to be permanent. In most instances, the device is placed underneath the alveolar mucosa making the long term integration of the device unlikely.
2. D7293 reports the placement of a temporary anchorage device which *requires* a surgical flap. Its purpose is for temporary skeletal anchorage. This may be an orthodontic related procedure.
3. Removal of the temporary anchorage device is included in the global fee for D7293.
4. See also D7292 and D7294 for other types of temporary anchorage devices.

LIMITATIONS

1. D7293 is generally not a reimbursed procedure.
2. The ADA claim form has a question, "Is this for orthodontics?" If the procedure is associated with orthodontic treatment, answer "yes" to the question on the ADA form "Is this for orthodontics?" Most software programs, by default, answer this "no." It is an error to answer "no" when the service is in fact related to the orthodontic treatment. Reimbursement for D7293, when performed in conjunction with orthodontics, may be applied toward the "lifetime orthodontic benefit," which is typically $1500.

D7294 — SURGICAL PLACEMENT OF TEMPORARY ANCHORAGE DEVICE WITHOUT FLAP; INCLUDES DEVICE REMOVAL — CDT 2016

NARRATIVES 1. A brief narrative is generally required when reporting D7411. The narrative should describe the location of the lesion, procedures used for the tissue removal, and a differential diagnosis.

2. "See attached copy of pathology report."

D7412 — EXCISION OF BENIGN LESION, COMPLICATED — CDT 2016

Requires extensive undermining with advancement or rotational flap closure.

LIMITATIONS 1. Excision of benign lesion, complicated (D7412) may be excluded from consideration for reimbursement if associated with another surgical procedure or biopsy procedure performed at the same site, on the same service date.

2. When D7412 is reported as a stand-alone procedure of the excision of a complete lesion, a pathology report describing the lesion as benign should be attached and submitted for dental reimbursement.

3. If the lesion is not benign, report D7415.

4. D7412 may not be a covered dental benefit; however, the procedure may be considered for reimbursement through medical insurance.

NARRATIVES 1. A brief narrative is generally required when reporting D7412. The narrative should describe the location of the lesion, procedures used for the tissue removal, a differential diagnosis, and identify that extensive undermining with advancement or a rotational flap closure was performed as part of the procedure.

2. "See attached copy of pathology report."

D7413 — EXCISION OF MALIGNANT LESION UP TO 1.25 CM — CDT 2016

LIMITATIONS 1. Excision of malignant lesion up to 1.25 cm (D7413) may be excluded from consideration for reimbursement if associated with another surgical procedure or biopsy procedure performed at the same site, on the same service date.

2. When D7413 is reported as a stand-alone procedure of the excision of a complete lesion, a pathology report describing the lesion as malignant should be attached and submitted for dental reimbursement.

3. If the lesion is not malignant, report D7410.

4. D7413 may not be a covered dental benefit; however, the procedure may be considered for reimbursement through medical insurance.

NARRATIVES 1. A brief narrative and pathology report is required when reporting this code. After receiving the pathology report, prepare the dental claim form. Make a copy of the pathology report and attach it to a dental claim form. Unless the pathology report accompanies the dental claim form, this code may not be reimbursed by the payer. The narrative should describe the location of the lesion, procedures used for the tissue removal, and a differential diagnosis of the lesion.

2. "See attached copy of pathology report."

D7414 — EXCISION OF MALIGNANT LESION GREATER THAN 1.25 CM — CDT 2016

LIMITATIONS 1. Excision of malignant lesion greater than 1.25 cm (D7414) may be excluded from consideration for reimbursement if associated with another surgical procedure or biopsy procedure performed at the same site, on the same service date.

2. When D7414 is reported as a stand-alone procedure of the excision of a complete lesion, a pathology report describing the lesion as malignant should be attached and submitted for dental reimbursement.

3. If the lesion is not malignant, report D7411.

4. D7414 may not be a covered dental benefit; however, the procedure may be considered for reimbursement through medical insurance.

NARRATIVES 1. A brief narrative and pathology report is required when reporting D7414. After receiving the pathology report, prepare the dental claim form. Make a copy of the pathology report and attach it to a dental claim form. Unless the pathology report accompanies the dental claim form, this code may not be reimbursed by the payer. The narrative should describe the location of the lesion, procedures used for the tissue removal, and a differential diagnosis of the lesion.

2. "See attached copy of pathology report."

D7415 — EXCISION OF MALIGNANT LESION, COMPLICATED — CDT 2016

Requires extensive undermining with advancement or rotational flap closure.

LIMITATIONS 1. Excision of malignant lesion, complicated (D7415) may be excluded from consideration for reimbursement if associated with another surgical procedure or biopsy procedure performed at the same site, on the same service date.

2. When D7415 is reported as a stand-alone procedure of the excision of a complete lesion, a pathology report describing the lesion as malignant should be attached and submitted for dental reimbursement.

3. If the lesion is not malignant, report D7412.

4. D7415 may or may not be a covered dental benefit; however, the procedure may be considered for reimbursement through medical insurance.

NARRATIVES 1. A brief narrative and pathology report is required generally when reporting D7415. After receiving the pathology report, prepare the dental claim form. Make a copy of the pathology report and attach it to the dental claim form. Unless the pathology report accompanies the dental claim form, D7415 will probably not be reimbursed by the payer. The narrative should describe the location of the lesion, procedures used for the tissue removal, a differential diagnosis, and should explain that extensive undermining with advancement or a rotational flap closure was performed as part of the procedure.

2. "See attached copy of pathology report."

D7465 — DESTRUCTION OF LESION(S) BY PHYSICAL OR CHEMICAL METHOD, BY REPORT — CDT 2016

Examples include using cryo, laser or electro surgery.

Note: While out of numerical order, D7465 is correctly listed here under the surgical excision of soft tissue lesions category.

COMMENTS 1. The descriptor of destruction of lesion(s) by physical or chemical method (D7465) gives examples of specific technologies (cryo, laser, electro surgery) to perform this procedure.

2. This is the *only* descriptor that specifically mentions a laser. Keep in mind that insurance payers reimburse for the procedure being performed rather than for the device used to perform it.

3. The technology used to perform a procedure provides increased efficiency by reducing procedure time and clinical benefits such as faster healing time, better results, etc. The technology used does not increase the reimbursement for the procedure performed.

NARRATIVES This is a "by report" code and a brief narrative is required. Describe the lesion and the method used to obliterate the lesion.

SURGICAL EXCISION OF INTRA-OSSEOUS LESIONS — CDT 2016

D7440 — EXCISION OF MALIGNANT TUMOR – LESION DIAMETER UP TO 1.25 CM — CDT 2016

LIMITATIONS 1. Excision of malignant tumor – lesion diameter up to 1.25 cm (D7440) may be excluded from consideration for reimbursement if associated with another surgical procedure or biopsy procedure performed at the same site, on the same service date.

2. When D7440 is reported as a stand-alone procedure of the excision of a tumor, a pathology report describing the tumor as malignant should be attached and submitted for dental reimbursement.

3. D7440 may not be a covered dental benefit; however, the procedure may be considered for reimbursement through medical insurance.

NARRATIVES
1. A brief narrative and pathology report is required when reporting D7440. Send the tissue biopsy specimen for analysis. After receiving the pathology report, prepare the dental claim form. Make a copy of the pathology report and attach it to the dental claim form. Unless the pathology report accompanies the dental claim form, D7440 will probably not be reimbursed by the payer. The brief narrative should describe the location of the lesion, procedures used for the tissue removal, and a differential diagnosis.
2. "See attached copy of pathology report."

D7441 EXCISION OF MALIGNANT TUMOR – LESION DIAMETER GREATER THAN 1.25 CM — CDT 2016

LIMITATIONS
1. Excision of malignant tumor – lesion diameter greater than 1.25 cm (D7441) may be excluded from consideration for reimbursement if associated with another surgical procedure or biopsy procedure performed at the same site, on the same service date.
2. When D7441 is reported as a stand-alone procedure of the excision of a tumor, a pathology report describing the tumor as malignant should be attached and submitted for dental reimbursement.
3. D7441 may, or may not be a covered dental benefit; however, the procedure may be considered for reimbursement through medical insurance.

NARRATIVES
1. A brief narrative and pathology report is required when reporting D7441. Send the tissue biopsy specimen for analysis. After receiving the pathology report, prepare the dental claim form. Make a copy of the pathology report and attach it to a dental claim form. Unless the pathology report accompanies the dental claim form, D7441 will probably not be reimbursed by the payer. The brief narrative should describe the location of the lesion, procedures used for the tissue removal, and a differential diagnosis.
2. "See attached copy of pathology report."

D7450 REMOVAL OF BENIGN ODONTOGENIC CYST OR TUMOR – LESION DIAMETER UP TO 1.25 CM — CDT 2016

LIMITATIONS
1. Removal of benign odontogenic cyst or tumor – lesion diameter up to 1.25 cm (D7450) may be excluded from consideration for reimbursement if associated with another surgical procedure or biopsy procedure performed at the same site, on the same service date.
2. When D7450 is reported as a stand-alone procedure, a pathology report should be attached describing the cyst or tumor as benign and submitted for dental reimbursement.
3. D7450 may not be a covered dental benefit; however, the procedure may be considered for reimbursement through medical insurance.

NARRATIVES
1. A brief narrative is required when reporting D7450. Send the tissue biopsy specimen for analysis. After receiving the pathology report, prepare the dental claim form. Make a copy of the pathology report and attach it to the dental claim form. Unless the pathology report accompanies the dental claim form, D7450 will probably not be reimbursed by the payer. The brief narrative should describe the location of the lesion, procedures used for the tissue removal, and a differential diagnosis.
2. "See attached copy of pathology report."

D7451 REMOVAL OF BENIGN ODONTOGENIC CYST OR TUMOR – LESION DIAMETER GREATER THAN 1.25 CM — CDT 2016

LIMITATIONS
1. Removal of benign odontogenic cyst or tumor – lesion diameter greater than 1.25 cm (D7451) may be excluded from consideration for reimbursement if associated with another surgical procedure or biopsy procedure performed at the same site, on the same service date.

2. When D7451 is reported as a stand-alone procedure, a pathology report should be attached describing the cyst or tumor as benign and submitted for dental reimbursement.

3. D7451 may not be a covered dental benefit; however, the procedure may be considered for reimbursement through medical insurance.

NARRATIVES
1. A brief narrative and pathology report is highly recommended when reporting D7451. After receiving the pathology report prepare the dental claim form. Make a copy of the pathology report and attach it to the dental claim form. Unless the pathology report accompanies the dental claim form, D7451 will probably not be reimbursed by the payer. The brief narrative should describe the location of the lesion, procedures used for the tissue removal, and a differential diagnosis.

2. "See attached copy of pathology report."

D7460 REMOVAL OF BENIGN NONODONTOGENIC CYST OR TUMOR – LESION DIAMETER UP TO 1.25 CM — CDT 2016

LIMITATIONS
1. Removal of benign nonodontogenic cyst or tumor – lesion diameter up to 1.25 cm (D7460) may be excluded from consideration for reimbursement if associated with another surgical procedure or biopsy procedure performed at the same site, on the same service date.

2. When D7460 is reported as a stand-alone procedure, a pathology report should be attached describing the cyst or tumor as benign and submitted for dental reimbursement.

3. D7460 may not be a covered dental benefit; however, the procedure may be considered for reimbursement through medical insurance.

NARRATIVES
1. A brief narrative and pathology report is highly recommended when reporting D7460. After receiving the pathology report, prepare the dental claim form. Make a copy of the pathology report and attach it to the dental claim form. Unless the pathology report accompanies the dental claim form, D7460 will probably not be reimbursed by the payer. The brief narrative should describe the location of the lesion, procedures used for the tissue removal, and a differential diagnosis.

2. "See attached copy of pathology report."

D7461 REMOVAL OF BENIGN NONODONTOGENIC CYST OR TUMOR – LESION DIAMETER GREATER THAN 1.25 CM — CDT 2016

LIMITATIONS
1. Removal of benign nonodontogenic cyst or tumor – lesion diameter greater than 1.25 cm (D7461) may be excluded from consideration for reimbursement if associated with another surgical procedure or biopsy procedure performed at the same site, on the same service date.

2. When D7461 is reported as a stand-alone procedure, a pathology report should be attached describing the cyst or tumor as benign and submitted for dental reimbursement.

3. D7461 may not be a covered dental benefit; however, the procedure may be considered for reimbursement through medical insurance.

NARRATIVES
1. A brief narrative and pathology report is highly recommended when reporting D7461. After receiving the pathology report prepare the dental claim form. Make a copy of the pathology report and attach it to the dental claim form. Unless the pathology report accompanies the dental claim form, D7461 will probably not be reimbursed by the payer. The brief narrative should describe the location of the lesion, procedures used for the tissue removal, and a differential diagnosis.

2. "See attached copy of pathology report."

D7465 DESTRUCTION OF LESION(S) BY PHYSICAL OR CHEMICAL METHOD, BY REPORT — CDT 2016

Examples include using cryo, laser or electro surgery.

This code's actual position is not in numerical order here. It actually follows D7415. However, D7465 is printed here in its entirety.

COMMENTS
1. The descriptor of destruction of lesion(s) by physical or chemical method (D7465) gives examples of specific technologies (cryo, laser, electro surgery) to perform this procedure.
2. This is the *only* descriptor that specifically mentions a laser. Keep in mind that insurance payers reimburse for the procedure being performed rather than for the device used to perform it.
3. The technology used to perform a procedure provides increased efficiency by reducing procedure time and clinical benefits such as faster healing time, better results, etc. The technology used does not increase the reimbursement for the procedure performed.
4. D7465 reports aphthous ulcer treatment performed with a laser.

NARRATIVES This is a "by report" code and a brief narrative is required. Describe the lesion and the method used to obliterate the lesion.

EXCISION OF BONE TISSUE — CDT 2016

D7471 REMOVAL OF LATERAL EXOSTOSIS (MAXILLA OR MANDIBLE) — CDT 2016

COMMENTS A lateral exostosis is a bony growth on the cheek facing side of the maxilla or cheek facing of the mandible.

LIMITATIONS Although this is a *per site* code used for the removal of tori, osseous tuberosities, or any other bony protuberances, some payers pay only once per arch per lifetime. When submitting a claim, identify the arch treated and include current pre-operative radiographs of the area. It can also be helpful to send a pretreatment photograph. Be aware that reimbursement for removal of lateral exostosis is unlikely if performed on the same day as osseous surgery.

NARRATIVES
1. A brief narrative is required when reporting D7471. Report if the procedure is done in conjunction with the reline or construction of a removable prosthesis. Photos and/or models may be required.
2. Claims for the services should indicate the site treated. If multiple sites are involved, use separate lines to report each site. Benefits are often limited to one arch per lifetime.
3. Some dental plans require that the patient's medical payer be billed first before considering payment under dental. Include the EOB from the medical payer with the claim to the dental payer as documentation that the medical plan was billed first.

D7472 REMOVAL OF TORUS PALATINUS — CDT 2016

COMMENTS A torus palatinus is a bony growth which develops on the midline of the roof of the mouth, and is slow-growing.

LIMITATIONS Removal of torus palatinus (D7472), if a covered benefit, is often reimbursed only once per lifetime.

NARRATIVES
1. A brief narrative is required when reporting D7472. Report if the procedure is done in conjunction with the reline or construction of a removable prosthesis. Photos and/or models may be required.
2. Claims for the service should indicate the site treated. If multiple sites are involved, use separate lines to report each site. Benefits are often limited to one per lifetime.
3. Some dental plans require that the patient's medical payer be billed first before considering payment under dental. Include the EOB from the medical payer with the claim to the dental payer as documentation that the medical plan was billed first.

D7473 REMOVAL OF TORUS MANDIBULARIS — CDT 2016

COMMENTS A torus mandibularis is a bony growth which develops on the lingual of the mandible, and is slow-growing.

| LIMITATIONS | Removal of torus mandibularis (D7473), if a covered benefit, is often reimbursed only once per arch, per lifetime. |

| NARRATIVES | 1. A brief narrative is required when reporting D7473. Report if the procedure is done in conjunction with the reline or construction of a removable prosthesis. Photos and/or models may be required.
2. Claims for the services should indicate the site treated. If multiple sites are involved, use separate lines to report each site. Benefits are often limited to one arch per lifetime.
3. Some dental plans require that the patient's medical payer be billed first before considering payment under dental. Include the EOB from the medical payer with the claim to the dental payer as documentation that the medical plan was billed first. |

D7485 SURGICAL REDUCTION OF OSSEOUS TUBEROSITY — CDT 2016

| LIMITATIONS | Surgical reduction of osseous tuberosity (D7485), if a covered benefit, is often reimbursed only once per arch, per lifetime. |

| NARRATIVES | 1. A narrative is required when reporting D7485. Note: If the procedure is done in conjunction with the reline or construction of a removable prosthesis, photos and/or models may be required.
2. Claims for the services should indicate the site treated. If multiple sites are involved, use separate lines to report each site. Benefits are often limited to one per arch per lifetime.
3. Some dental plans require that the patient's medical payer be billed before considering payment under dental. Include the EOB from the medical payer with the claim to the dental payer as documentation that the medical plan was billed first. |

D7490 RADICAL RESECTION OF MAXILLA OR MANDIBLE — CDT 2016

Partial resection of maxilla or mandible; removal of lesion and defect with margin of normal appearing bone. Reconstruction and bone grafts should be reported separately.

| COMMENTS | Reconstruction procedures and bone grafts should be reported separately. |

| LIMITATIONS | 1. Radical resection of maxilla or mandible (D7490) is not typically reimbursed by dental insurance.
2. Specify the arch.
3. This is typically considered for reimbursement through medical insurance. |

SURGICAL INCISION — CDT 2016

D7510 INCISION AND DRAINAGE OF ABSCESS – INTRAORAL SOFT TISSUE — CDT 2016

Involves incision through mucosa, including periodontal origins.

| COMMENTS | 1. The incision and drainage of abscess (D7510) may be accomplished through an incision in the gingival sulcus.
2. Incision and drainage of abscess – intraoral soft tissue (D7510) includes the incision and drainage of a periodontal abscess. |

| LIMITATIONS | 1. Payers will consider post-operative visits a part of the incise and drainage global fee.
2. D7510 is considered to be a global component of an extraction, apicoectomy, excision of foreign body, root canal procedure, palliative procedure, or any definitive (final in nature) procedure on the same service date.
3. If the intraoral abscess extends beyond the alveolus, D7510 may not be reimbursed by the dental plan. However, the procedure may be considered for reimbursement through the medical plan. |

TIPS	1. Incision and drainage of abscess – intraoral soft tissue (D7510) is often reimbursed. Palliative (D9110) should not be used to describe this *type* of procedure since the UCR fee for D9110 is generally lower. D7510 is a better description of the procedure and D7510 has a higher UCR fee than D9110.
	2. If the "incision and drainage" is accomplished during a *single* appointment, consider charging a *lower* fee. If *two* visits are required, i.e., procedure is more complicated and/or a rubber dam drain is placed, then consider a *higher* fee for D7510.
NARRATIVES	Identify the quadrant and include a brief clinical description for the dental consultant's review. D7510 is often disallowed if done on the same date and by the same provider who performed endodontics, extractions, palliative treatment, or other definitive treatment. A pretreatment photograph and radiographic image of the area can be helpful in documenting the need for the procedure.

D7511 — INCISION AND DRAINAGE OF ABSCESS – INTRAORAL SOFT TISSUE – COMPLICATED (INCLUDES DRAINAGE OF MULTIPLE FASCIAL SPACES)   CDT 2016

Incision is made intraorally and dissection is extended into adjacent fascial space(s) to provide adequate drainage of abscess/cellulitis.

COMMENTS	This incision and drainage procedure is associated with an acute abscess with facial swelling. D7511 is used to describe the situation where the infection has spread into adjacent fascial spaces and treatment requires intraoral drainage of one or more fascial spaces.
LIMITATIONS	1. Payers will consider post-operative visits a part of the incise and drain global fee.
	2. If the intraoral abscess extends beyond the alveolus, then D7511 may be excluded by dental insurance, but reimbursed through a medical insurance plan.
NARRATIVES	A brief narrative is required and should be very specific as to the appearance of the area treated, procedures used to accomplish the drainage, and the fascial spaces involved. A pretreatment photograph and radiographic image of the area can be helpful in documenting the need for the procedure.

D7520 — INCISION AND DRAINAGE OF ABSCESS – EXTRAORAL SOFT TISSUE   CDT 2016

Involves incision through skin.

CODING WATCH CORRECTION: Report D7520 for the incision and draining of an abscess through an *external* access opening. That is, the access to the abscess is made *extraorally* (not in the mouth but somewhere on the face) and through soft tissue. For incision and drainage *intraoral* soft tissue, report D7510.

COMMENTS	D7520 is used to describe a procedure performed in an acute situation of facial swelling. The spread of infection into adjacent fascial spaces requires drainage and is most easily accessed from an area outside the oral cavity. It requires additional expertise and time. D7520 is more likely considered for reimbursement under a medical plan.
LIMITATIONS	Typically not a covered dental benefit; possibly considered for reimbursement through medical insurance.
NARRATIVES	A brief narrative is required and should be very specific as to the appearance of the area treated, procedures used to accomplish the drainage, and the fascial spaces involved. Pretreatment photographs and possibly radiographic images can be helpful in documenting the need for this procedure.

D7521 — INCISION AND DRAINAGE OF ABSCESS – EXTRAORAL SOFT TISSUE – COMPLICATED (INCLUDES DRAINAGE OF MULTIPLE FASCIAL SPACES)   CDT 2016

Incision is made extraorally and dissection is extended into adjacent fascial space(s) to provide adequate drainage of abscess/cellulitis.

CODING WATCH CORRECTION: Report D7521 for the incision and draining of an abscess through an *external access* opening. That is, the access to the abscess is made *extraorally* (not in the mouth but somewhere on the face) and through soft tissue. For incision and drainage – *intraoral* soft tissue, report D7510.

COMMENTS D7521 is used to describe a complicated procedure performed in medically acute situations of facial swelling. The spread of infection into adjacent fascial spaces requires drainage and is most appropriately accessed from an area outside the oral cavity. It requires additional expertise and time. D7521 is more likely a covered benefit under a medical plan.

LIMITATIONS Typically not a covered dental benefit; could possibly be considered for reimbursement through medical insurance.

NARRATIVES A brief narrative is required and should be very specific as to the appearance of the area treated, procedures used to accomplish the drainage, and the fascial spaces involved. Pretreatment photographs and possibly radiographic images can be helpful in documenting the need for this procedure.

D7530 REMOVAL OF FOREIGN BODY FROM MUCOSA, SKIN, OR SUBCUTANEOUS ALVEOLAR TISSUE — CDT 2016

COMMENTS
1. D7530 could include the removal of splinters (foreign body) embedded in soft tissue.
2. If the foreign body is embedded in muscle and/or bone, report D7540.

LIMITATIONS Removal of foreign body from mucosa, skin, or subcutaneous alveolar tissue (D7530) may be reimbursed under dental insurance. If not, D7530 could possibly be considered for reimbursement through medical insurance.

NARRATIVES A brief narrative is required and should be very specific as to the appearance of the area treated, procedures used to accomplish the drainage, and the fascial spaces involved. Pretreatment photographs and possibly radiographic images can be helpful in documenting the need for this procedure.

D7540 REMOVAL OF REACTION PRODUCING FOREIGN BODIES, MUSCULOSKELETAL SYSTEM — CDT 2016

May include, but is not limited to, removal of splinters, pieces of wire, etc., from muscle and/or bone.

COMMENTS
1. D7540 includes removal of splinters, wire, etc. from muscle and/or bone.
2. For removal of a foreign body from soft tissue, report D7530.

LIMITATIONS Removal of reaction producing foreign bodies, musculoskeletal system (D7540) may be reimbursed under dental insurance. If not, D7540 could possibly be considered for reimbursement through medical insurance.

NARRATIVES A brief narrative is required and should be very specific as to the appearance of the area treated, procedures used to accomplish the drainage, and the fascial spaces involved. Pretreatment photographs and possibly radiographic images can be helpful in documenting the need for this procedure.

D7550 PARTIAL OSTECTOMY/SEQUESTRECTOMY FOR REMOVAL OF NON-VITAL BONE — CDT 2016

Removal of loose or sloughed-off dead bone caused by infection or reduced blood supply.

COMMENTS Partial ostectomy/sequestrectomy for removal of non-vital bone (D7550) reports the removal of loose or denuded (sloughed off) non-vital bone from surrounding healthy bone.

LIMITATIONS
1. If D7550 is used to describe a follow up procedure provided by the *same* provider, many payers may consider this procedure a part of the *global* extraction fee. The payer may deny reimbursement for D7550. If a *different* office (other than the office performing the initial procedure) performs this procedure, D7550 may be reimbursed.
2. Some payers may "remap" D7550 to palliative (D9110) for reimbursement. See D9110 for further details.

NARRATIVES For the *simple* removal of a sliver of loose or denuded non-vital bone at the emergency visit, consider reporting a palliative procedure (D9110). Include a brief narrative with the claim that describes the location and includes a description of foreign body. See D9110 for further details.

D7560 MAXILLARY SINUSOTOMY FOR REMOVAL OF TOOTH FRAGMENT OR FOREIGN BODY — CDT 2016

LIMITATIONS This is typically considered for reimbursement through medical insurance.

TREATMENT OF FRACTURES – SIMPLE — CDT 2016

D7610 MAXILLA – OPEN REDUCTION (TEETH IMMOBILIZED, IF PRESENT) — CDT 2016

Teeth may be wired, banded or splinted together to prevent movement. Surgical incision required for interosseous fixation.

LIMITATIONS This is typically considered for reimbursement through medical insurance.

D7620 MAXILLA – CLOSED REDUCTION (TEETH IMMOBILIZED, IF PRESENT) — CDT 2016

No incision required to reduce fracture. See D7610 if interosseous fixation is applied.

LIMITATIONS This is typically considered for reimbursement through medical insurance.

D7630 MANDIBLE – OPEN REDUCTION (TEETH IMMOBILIZED, IF PRESENT) — CDT 2016

Teeth may be wired, banded, or splinted together to prevent movement. Surgical incision required to reduce fracture.

LIMITATIONS This is typically considered for reimbursement through medical insurance.

D7640 MANDIBLE – CLOSED REDUCTION (TEETH IMMOBILIZED, IF PRESENT) — CDT 2016

No incision required to reduce fracture. See D7630 if interosseous fixation is applied.

LIMITATIONS This is typically considered for reimbursement through medical insurance.

D7650 MALAR AND/OR ZYGOMATIC ARCH – OPEN REDUCTION — CDT 2016

LIMITATIONS This is typically considered for reimbursement through medical insurance.

D7660 MALAR AND/OR ZYGOMATIC ARCH – CLOSED REDUCTION — CDT 2016

LIMITATIONS This is typically considered for reimbursement through medical insurance.

| **D7670** | **ALVEOLUS – CLOSED REDUCTION, MAY INCLUDE STABILIZATION OF TEETH CDT 2016** |

Teeth may be wired, banded, or splinted together to prevent movement.

LIMITATIONS This is typically considered for reimbursement through medical insurance.

| **D7671** | **ALVEOLUS – OPEN REDUCTION, MAY INCLUDE STABILIZATION OF TEETH** | **CDT 2016** |

Teeth may be wired, banded or splinted together to prevent movement.

LIMITATIONS This is typically considered for reimbursement through medical insurance.

| **D7680** | **FACIAL BONES – COMPLICATED REDUCTION WITH FIXATION AND MULTIPLE SURGICAL APPROACHES** | **CDT 2016** |

Facial bones include upper and lower jaw, cheek, and bones around eyes, nose, and ears.

LIMITATIONS This is typically considered for reimbursement through medical insurance.

NARRATIVES If covered by a dental plan, an operative report is required for consultant review of the services provided. Some dental plans require that the patient's medical payer be billed first before considering payment under dental. Include the EOB from the medical payer with the claim to the dental payer as documentation that the medical plan was billed first.

TREATMENT OF FRACTURES – COMPOUND   CDT 2016

| **D7710** | **MAXILLA – OPEN REDUCTION** | **CDT 2016** |

Surgical incision required to reduce fracture.

LIMITATIONS This is typically considered for reimbursement through medical insurance.

| **D7720** | **MAXILLA – CLOSED REDUCTION** | **CDT 2016** |

LIMITATIONS This is typically considered for reimbursement through medical insurance.

| **D7730** | **MANDIBLE – OPEN REDUCTION** | **CDT 2016** |

Surgical incision required to reduce fracture.

LIMITATIONS This is typically considered for reimbursement through medical insurance.

| **D7740** | **MANDIBLE – CLOSED REDUCTION** | **CDT 2016** |

LIMITATIONS This is typically considered for reimbursement through medical insurance.

| **D7750** | **MALAR AND/OR ZYGOMATIC ARCH – OPEN REDUCTION** | **CDT 2016** |

Surgical incision required to reduce fracture.

LIMITATIONS This is typically considered for reimbursement through medical insurance.

D7760 — MALAR AND/OR ZYGOMATIC ARCH – CLOSED REDUCTION — CDT 2016

LIMITATIONS This is typically considered for reimbursement through medical insurance.

D7770 — ALVEOLUS – OPEN REDUCTION STABILIZATION OF TEETH — CDT 2016

Fractured bone(s) are exposed to mouth or outside the face. Surgical incision required to reduce fracture.

LIMITATIONS This is typically considered for reimbursement through medical insurance.

D7771 — ALVEOLUS, CLOSED REDUCTION STABILIZATION OF TEETH — CDT 2016

Fractured bone(s) are exposed to mouth or outside the face.

LIMITATIONS This is typically considered for reimbursement through medical insurance.

D7780 — FACIAL BONES – COMPLICATED REDUCTION WITH FIXATION AND MULTIPLE SURGICAL APPROACHES — CDT 2016

Surgical incision required to reduce fracture. Facial bones include upper and lower jaw, cheek, and bones around eyes, nose, and ears.

LIMITATIONS This is typically considered for reimbursement through medical insurance.

REDUCTION OF DISLOCATION AND MANAGEMENT OF OTHER TEMPOROMANDIBULAR JOINT DYSFUNCTIONS — CDT 2016

Procedures that are an integral part of a primary procedure should not be reported separately.

D7810 — OPEN REDUCTION OF DISLOCATION — CDT 2016

Access to TMJ via surgical opening.

LIMITATIONS This is typically considered for reimbursement through medical insurance.

D7820 — CLOSED REDUCTION OF DISLOCATION — CDT 2016

Joint manipulated into place; no surgical exposure.

LIMITATIONS This is typically considered for reimbursement through medical insurance.

D7830 — MANIPULATION UNDER ANESTHESIA — CDT 2016

Usually done under general anesthesia or intravenous sedation.

LIMITATIONS This is typically considered for reimbursement through medical insurance.

D7840 CONDYLECTOMY — CDT 2016

Surgical removal of all or portion of the mandibular condyle (separate procedure).

LIMITATIONS This is typically considered for reimbursement through medical insurance.

D7850 SURGICAL DISCECTOMY, WITH/WITHOUT IMPLANT — CDT 2016

Excision of the intra-articular disc of a joint.

LIMITATIONS This is typically considered for reimbursement through medical insurance.

D7852 DISC REPAIR — CDT 2016

Repositioning and/or sculpting of disc; repair of perforated posterior attachment.

LIMITATIONS This is typically considered for reimbursement through medical insurance.

D7854 SYNOVECTOMY — CDT 2016

Excision of a portion or all of the synovial membrane of a joint.

LIMITATIONS This is typically considered for reimbursement through medical insurance.

D7856 MYOTOMY — CDT 2016

Cutting of muscle for therapeutic purposes (separate procedure).

LIMITATIONS This is typically considered for reimbursement through medical insurance.

D7858 JOINT RECONSTRUCTION — CDT 2016

Reconstruction of osseous components including or excluding soft tissues of the joint with autogenous, homologous, or alloplastic materials.

LIMITATIONS This is typically considered for reimbursement through medical insurance.

D7860 ARTHROTOMY — CDT 2016

Cutting into joint (separate procedure).

LIMITATIONS This is typically considered for reimbursement through medical insurance.

D7865 ARTHROPLASTY — CDT 2016

Reduction of osseous components of the joint to create a pseudoarthrosis or eliminate an irregular remodeling pattern (osteophytes).

LIMITATIONS This is typically considered for reimbursement through medical insurance.

D7870 ARTHROCENTESIS — CDT 2016

Withdrawal of fluid from a joint space by aspiration.

LIMITATIONS This is typically considered for reimbursement through medical insurance.

D7871 NON-ARTHROSCOPIC LYSIS AND LAVAGE — CDT 2016

Inflow and outflow catheters are placed into the joint space. The joint is lavaged and manipulated as indicated in an effort to release minor adhesions and synovial vacuum phenomenon as well as to remove inflammation products from the joint space.

COMMENTS Non-arthroscopic lysis and lavage is typically used to describe the debridement and irrigation for removal of inflammatory products (scar tissue) from the joint space.

LIMITATIONS D7871 is usually reported to the medical payer and will require an operative report.

D7872 ARTHROSCOPY – DIAGNOSIS, WITH OR WITHOUT BIOPSY — CDT 2016

LIMITATIONS This is typically considered for reimbursement through medical insurance.

D7873 ARTHROSCOPY – SURGICAL: LAVAGE AND LYSIS OF ADHESIONS — CDT 2016

Removal of adhesions using the arthroscope and lavage of the joint cavities.

LIMITATIONS This is typically considered for reimbursement through medical insurance.

D7874 ARTHROSCOPY – SURGICAL: DISC REPOSITIONING AND STABILIZATION — CDT 2016

Repositioning and stabilization of disc using arthroscopic techniques.

LIMITATIONS This is typically considered for reimbursement through medical insurance.

D7875 ARTHROSCOPY – SURGICAL: SYNOVECTOMY — CDT 2016

Removal of inflamed and hyperplastic synovium (partial/complete) via an arthroscopic technique.

LIMITATIONS This is typically considered for reimbursement through medical insurance.

D7876 ARTHROSCOPY – SURGICAL: DISCECTOMY — CDT 2016

Removal of disc and remodeled posterior attachment via the arthroscope.

LIMITATIONS This is typically considered for reimbursement through medical insurance.

D7877 ARTHROSCOPY – SURGICAL: DEBRIDEMENT — CDT 2016

Removal of pathologic hard and/or soft tissue using the arthroscope.

LIMITATIONS This is typically considered for reimbursement through medical insurance.

D7880 OCCLUSAL ORTHOTIC DEVICE, BY REPORT — CDT 2016

Presently includes splints provided for treatment of temporomandibular joint dysfunction.

CODING WARNING CORRECTION: Occlusal orthotic device (D7880) does not describe tooth whitening trays (D9972) or an occlusal guard (D9940).

CODING WATCH CORRECTION: It is wrong to report an occlusal orthotic device (D7880) as an occlusal guard (D9940). D7880 reports a device to alleviate *pain/clicking in the jaw* joint(s) associated with TMJ dysfunction and typically involves multiple follow up treatment visits. D9940 is used to describe an occlusal guard which minimizes the effects of bruxism (grinding) and other occlusal factors.

COMMENTS
1. D7880 is used to report a TMJ dysfunction treatment device. The majority of general dental plans exclude all diagnostic and treatment of TMJ dysfunction related services.
2. An occlusal splint is considered an "occlusal orthotic device." D7880 is not typically a covered dental benefit. The procedure may be considered for reimbursement through the medical insurance plan.
3. An Aqualizer® is a specific type of appliance that can be described using D7880 for the patient that has a documented issue with TMJ. If the patient only grits, grinds, and/or clinches without associated TMD symptoms, the appliance would be described using code D9940.

LIMITATIONS
1. Some payers require preauthorization *prior* to treatment of TMJ dysfunction.
2. Payers maintain that the global fee for occlusal orthotic device (D7880) includes multiple visits and all occlusal adjustments, no matter how many follow up visits are required.
3. If the patient's dental plan includes a separate TMJ rider, D7880 may be reimbursed. The TMJ rider may cover a complete occlusal adjustment and a removable hard acrylic splint. The TMJ rider may include coverage for an occlusal guard (D9940). If D7880 is a covered benefit through the TMJ rider, reimbursement may have a lifetime maximum and/or be subject to a deductible. Call the payer to verify specific coverage. Reimbursement is highly variable.

NARRATIVES
1. The narrative should include a description of the signs, symptoms, prognosis of treatment, estimated treatment duration, and type of orthotic device and materials used.
2. The narrative should include the diagnosis i.e., temporomandibular joint dysfunction, and a brief description of the patient's symptoms. "See attached radiographic image(s) and TMJ workup notes and diagnosis."

PHOTO
1. This is an example of a device/appliance/splint to treat temporomandibular joint dysfunction (NTI-tss).

Courtesy Keller Dental Laboratory

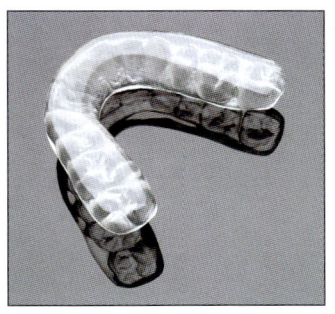

2. The appliances used to treat TMJ dysfunction and bruxism can appear to be similar. The occlusal orthotic device treatment (D7880) would involve a series of occlusal adjustments.

Courtesy Keller Dental Laboratory

D7881 NEW PROCEDURE OCCLUSAL ORTHOTIC DEVICE ADJUSTMENT — CDT 2016

CODING WATCH CORRECTION

D7881 does not report adjustments made to the occlusal orthotic device at delivery. Adjustments made within six months of delivery are included in the *global* fee for the occlusal orthotic device, by report (D7880).

COMMENTS D7880/D7881 reports TMJ related treatment and is typically not reimbursed by dental payers. These procedures may be considered for reimbursement through a medical insurance plan.

LIMITATIONS
1. Occlusal orthotic device (D7880) reports the delivery of a device to alleviate pain/clicking in the jaw/joint(s) due to TMJ dysfunction. It typically involves multiple follow up visits as part of the overall treatment. Some payers maintain that the global fee for the occlusal orthotic device includes multiple visits and *all* occlusal adjustments, no matter how many follow up visits are required. Some payers have a limitation period of six months following the initial delivery of the device when adjustments are included in the global fee.

2. Reimbursement for TMJ related treatment such as occlusal orthotic device, by report (D7880) and occlusal orthotic device adjustment (D7881) may be available when a dental plan includes a separate TMJ rider, which is not a common rider. If there is a TMJ rider, benefits for the device and any adjustments may have a separate lifetime maximum and/or may be subject to a deductible.

NARRATIVES Note the initial delivery date of the occlusal orthotic device (D7880) on claims submitted for adjustments.

D7899 UNSPECIFIED TMD THERAPY, BY REPORT — CDT 2016

Used for procedure that is not adequately described by a code. Describe procedure.

COMMENTS D7899 can be used to report TMD laser therapy.

NARRATIVES TMJ dysfunction appliance adjustment would be reported as D7899, by report. By report means that a brief narrative is required when this code is reported.

REPAIR OF TRAUMATIC WOUNDS — CDT 2016

Excludes closure of surgical incisions.

D7910 — SUTURE OF RECENT SMALL WOUNDS UP TO 5 CM — CDT 2016

CODING WATCH CORRECTION — It is wrong to use D7910 to report the routine closure of a surgical incision that is *inclusive* in another procedure.

COMMENTS This code is used to describe the repair of a laceration (trauma) and should be reported when closing a wound.

LIMITATIONS
1. Suture of small wounds up to 5 cm (D7910) may be covered under dental benefits, limited to the repair of oral related structures.
2. Suture of recent small wounds may be covered under medical insurance.

COMPLICATED SUTURING (RECONSTRUCTION REQUIRING DELICATE HANDLING OF TISSUES AND WIDE UNDERMINING FOR METICULOUS CLOSURE) — CDT 2016

Excludes closure of surgical incisions.

D7911 — COMPLICATED SUTURE – UP TO 5 CM — CDT 2016

COMMENTS This code reports complicated suturing in an emergency setting. This procedure is more complicated than the routine suture of recent small wounds up to 5 cm (D7910). It requires delicate handling and meticulous closure of tissues.

LIMITATIONS This is typically considered for reimbursement through medical insurance.

D7912 — COMPLICATED SUTURE – GREATER THAN 5 CM — CDT 2016

COMMENTS This code is used to describe complicated suturing in an emergency setting. This procedure is more complicated than either D7910 or D7911. It requires delicate handling and meticulous closure of tissues.

LIMITATIONS This is typically considered for reimbursement through medical insurance.

OTHER REPAIR PROCEDURES — CDT 2016

D7920 — SKIN GRAFT (IDENTIFY DEFECT COVERED, LOCATION AND TYPE OF GRAFT) CDT 2016

LIMITATIONS This is typically considered for reimbursement through medical insurance.

D7921 — COLLECTION AND APPLICATION OF AUTOLOGOUS BLOOD CONCENTRATE PRODUCT — CDT 2016

COMMENTS
1. D7921 reports the utilization of platelet rich plasma (PRP) to enhance the success of sinus grafting, ridge augmentation, osseous integration of implants, some endodontic procedures and some periodontal procedures. It can improve wound healing, tissue regeneration and can help augment bone graft procedures.
2. The patient's blood is drawn and centrifuged to separate and highly concentrate the red blood cells and platelets with growth factors.
3. The autologous blood concentrate product is derived from the patient's own blood, reducing the risk of disease transmission.

4. The time needed to prepare and place platelet rich plasma (PRP) adds only a little additional time to the overall bone graft procedure.

LIMITATIONS
1. D7921 is not generally reimbursed.
2. Some policies with an implant rider may reimburse D7921.

D7940 OSTEOPLASTY – FOR ORTHOGNATHIC DEFORMITIES — CDT 2016

Reconstruction of jaws for correction of congenital, developmental or acquired traumatic or surgical deformity.

LIMITATIONS This is typically considered for reimbursement through medical insurance.

D7941 OSTEOTOMY – MANDIBULAR RAMI — CDT 2016

LIMITATIONS This is typically considered for reimbursement through medical insurance.

D7943 OSTEOTOMY – MANDIBULAR RAMI WITH BONE GRAFT; INCLUDES OBTAINING THE GRAFT — CDT 2016

LIMITATIONS This is typically considered for reimbursement through medical insurance.

D7944 OSTEOTOMY – SEGMENTED OR SUBAPICAL — CDT 2016

Report by range of tooth numbers within segment.

COMMENTS An osteotomy involves the surgical sectioning of bone. A segmental osteotomy is used to correct skeletal dental malocclusions that would otherwise be unmanageable with conventional orthodontic care.

LIMITATIONS This is typically considered for reimbursement through medical insurance.

NARRATIVES Report the range of tooth numbers within the segment sectioned.

D7945 OSTEOTOMY – BODY OF MANDIBLE — CDT 2016

Surgical section of lower jaw. This includes the surgical exposure, bone cut, fixation, routine wound closure and normal post-operative follow-up care.

LIMITATIONS This is typically considered for reimbursement through medical insurance.

D7946 LEFORT I (MAXILLA – TOTAL) — CDT 2016

Surgical section of the upper jaw. This includes the surgical exposure, bone cuts, downfracture, repositioning, fixation, routine wound closure and normal post-operative follow-up care.

LIMITATIONS This is typically considered for reimbursement through medical insurance.

D7947 LEFORT I (MAXILLA – SEGMENTED) — CDT 2016

When reporting a surgically assisted palatal expansion without downfracture, this code would entail a reduced service and should be "by report."

LIMITATIONS This is typically considered for reimbursement through medical insurance.

D7948 — LEFORT II OR LEFORT III (OSTEOPLASTY OF FACIAL BONES FOR MIDFACE HYPOPLASIA OR RETRUSION) – WITHOUT BONE GRAFT — CDT 2016

Surgical section of upper jaw. This includes the surgical exposure, bone cuts, downfracture, segmentation of maxilla, repositioning, fixation, routine wound closure and normal post-operative follow-up care.

LIMITATIONS This is typically considered for reimbursement through medical insurance.

D7949 — LEFORT II OR LEFORT III – WITH BONE GRAFT — CDT 2016

Includes obtaining autografts.

LIMITATIONS This is typically considered for reimbursement through medical insurance.

D7950 — OSSEOUS, OSTEOPERIOSTEAL, OR CARTILAGE GRAFT OF THE MANDIBLE OR MAXILLA – AUTOGENOUS OR NONAUTOGENOUS, BY REPORT — CDT 2016

This procedure is for ridge augmentation or reconstruction to increase height, width and/or volume of residual alveolar ridge. It includes obtaining graft material. Placement of a barrier membrane, if used, should be reported separately.

CODING WARNING CORRECTION

1. This graft procedure *includes* the harvesting of the graft material. Do not report the harvest of bone (D7295) in conjunction with this procedure.
2. D7950 does *not* report grafting procedures related to *periodontal* or other *disease conditions*. See D4263/D4264 to describe periodontal grafting procedures associated with periodontally related osseous surgery.

CODING WATCH CORRECTION

1. It is an error to report D7950 to describe a "socket graft" in conjunction with an *extraction*. D7950 does *not* involve an extraction site. The maxillary or mandibular is edentulous. See D7953 for further details regarding a routine "socket graft" associated with an *extraction* for ridge *preservation*.
2. If there is an extraction, and an implant is immediately placed with a bone graft, report the bone graft at time of implant placement (D6104) separately.

CODING MATCH CORRECTION

Placement of a barrier membrane (in addition to the graft procedure) should be reported as a separate procedure. See the guided tissue regeneration codes (D4266/D4267) for further details on reporting the placement of a barrier membrane with a graft.

COMMENTS The goal for D7950 is to increase the height, width and/or volume of the existing alveolar ridge. D7950 reports a ridge *augmentation* with a bone graft *not* associated with an extraction performed on the same service date.

D7950 is used to report a block graft as well as a particulate graft in an edentulous area of the maxilla or mandible.

LIMITATIONS
1. If implant related, this procedure is not a covered dental benefit, unless the policy has an implant rider. Reimbursement is subject to plan limitations.
2. The flap is a part of the ridge augmentation (D7950) procedure and should not be billed separately.

TIPS Terms you should know:

Allogenic graft – usually freeze dried cells transferred from another human being that are used to repair a defect or supplement a deficiency. Demineralized bone graft products are an example of this (allograft bone material).

Alloplastic — refers to inorganic bone substitute materials used for tissue grafting and augmentation. Hydroxylapatite bone graft is an example of this type of graft (e.g., OsteoGraft®, Bio-oss®, PepGen®, etc.).

Autogenous — a graft taken from one part of a patient's body and transferred to another. Chin, hip, and rib grafts would be examples of an autogenous graft.

Guided tissue regeneration — used to enhance and promote bone growth by placing a barrier membrane D4266/D4267 under gingival tissue and over remaining bone, e.g., Gore-tex®, BioMend®, etc.

NARRATIVES D7950 may be reimbursed for a graft placed in the *anterior* area to provide support for a pontic of an anterior bridge. It is recommended that a brief narrative be provided to justify the service associated with the fabrication of an anterior bridge.

D7951 SINUS AUGMENTATION WITH BONE OR BONE SUBSTITUTES VIA A LATERAL OPEN APPROACH — CDT 2016

The augmentation of the sinus cavity to increase alveolar height for reconstruction of edentulous portions of the maxilla. This procedure is performed via a lateral open approach. This includes obtaining the bone or bone substitutes. Placement of a barrier membrane, if used, should be reported separately.

CODING WARNING CORRECTION

1. This procedure describes a "sinus lift" via a lateral open approach and *includes* the harvesting of the autograft or obtaining the allograft material. Do not report harvest of bone for use in autogenous grafting procedure (D7295) in conjunction with D7951.
2. An alternate "sinus lift" procedure is achieved via a "vertical approach." D7952 reports the other sinus lift technique utilizing the vertical approach, or "punch method."

CODING WATCH CORRECTION

1. It is wrong to report D7951 for a bone "socket graft" in conjunction with an extraction. D7951 is *not* associated with the preservation of bone after an extraction. A bone socket graft (associated with the extraction) for ridge preservation is described by D7953.
2. D7951 should not be used to report grafting related to periodontally involved teeth. See D4263 or D4264 to report periodontally related grafting procedures, associated with periodontal osseous surgery (D4260 or D4261).

CODING MATCH CORRECTION

Placement of a barrier membrane used in conjunction with sinus augmentation (D7951) should be reported separately. See the guided tissue regeneration codes (D4266 or D4267) for further details on reporting the placement of a resorbable or non-resorbable membrane as a separate procedure.

COMMENTS

1. Sinus augmentations (lifts) are used to enhance alveolar height for implant placement within edentulous portions of the maxilla. The procedure includes the harvesting of the bone graft material but does not include a barrier membrane. D7951 reports a sinus augmentation (lift) utilizing a lateral open approach ("window") technique. The flap is included and is not billed separately.
2. The global fee for D7951 includes obtaining the bone (from the patient) or the use of bone substitutes.

TIPS The sinus augmentation via a lateral open approach procedure is usually not a covered dental benefit unless covered by an implant rider. Reimbursement is limited by the plan's deductibles and annual maximums.

D7952 SINUS AUGMENTATION VIA A VERTICAL APPROACH — CDT 2016

The augmentation of the sinus to increase alveolar height by vertical access through the ridge crest by raising the floor of the sinus and grafting as necessary. This includes obtaining the bone or bone substitutes.

CODING WARNING CORRECTION

1. This procedure describes a "punch method" or "sinus lift" via a vertical approach and *includes* the harvesting of the autograft or obtaining the allograft material. Do not report harvest of bone for use in autogenous grafting procedure (D7295) in conjunction with D7952.

2. An alternate "sinus lift" procedure is achieved via a lateral open "window." D7951 reports this technique utilizing a lateral open approach.

CODING WATCH CORRECTION

1. It is wrong to report D7952 for a bone "socket graft" in conjunction with an extraction. D7952 is *not* associated with the preservation of bone after an extraction. A bone socket graft (associated with the extraction) for ridge preservation is described by D7953.

2. D7952 should not be used to report grafting related to periodontally involved teeth. See D4263 or D4264 to report periodontally related grafting procedures associated with osseous surgery (D4260 or D4261).

CODING MATCH CORRECTION

Placement of a barrier membrane used in conjunction with sinus augmentation (D7952) should be reported separately. See the guided tissue regeneration codes (D4266 or D4267) for further details on reporting the placement of a resorbable or non-resorbable barrier membrane as a separate procedure.

COMMENTS

1. Sinus augmentations (lifts) are used to enhance alveolar height for implant placement within edentulous portions of the maxilla. The procedure includes the harvesting of the bone graft material but does not include a barrier membrane (D4266 or D4267). D7952 reports a sinus augmentation (lift) utilizing a vertical approach osteotome technique. The flap is included and is not billed separately.

2. The global fee for D7952 includes obtaining the bone (from the patient) or the use of bone substitutes.

TIPS

The sinus augmentation via a vertical approach procedure is usually not a covered dental benefit unless covered by an implant rider. Reimbursement is limited by the plan's deductibles and annual maximums.

D7953 BONE REPLACEMENT GRAFT FOR RIDGE PRESERVATION – PER SITE CDT 2016

Graft is placed in an extraction or implant removal site at the time of the extraction or removal to preserve ridge integrity (e.g., clinically indicated in preparation for implant reconstruction or where alveolar contour is critical to planned prosthetic reconstruction). Does not include obtaining graft material. Membrane, if used, should be reported separately.

CODING WATCH CORRECTION

1. Bone replacement graft (D7953) is used to describe any type of bone graft placed in a "fresh" *extraction* site or *implant removal site* where there will be healing prior to implant placement on a later service date. *Do not* use periodontal osseous surgery bone replacement grafts codes (D4263 or D4264) to report a bone replacement graft for an *extraction* or *implant removal site*. D4263 or D4264 reports osseous surgery related bone replacement grafts to stimulate periodontal (around a tooth) regeneration when the disease process has led to a deformity of the bone.

2. D7950 reports the ridge augmentation of an *existing* edentulous ridge (not at a fresh extraction site). A ridge augmentation (D7950) does not describe a bone replacement graft (D7953), which is placed in the fresh socket after an extraction or implant removal.

3. D6104 reports the bone graft placed at the same time as implant placement.

4. This code does not report bone grafting after a third molar removal.

CODING MATCH CORRECTION

If a membrane is placed, the membrane would be reported separately with a guided tissue regeneration code (D4266 or D4267).

COMMENTS

1. The extraction of a tooth often results in loss of alveolar ridge volume. Significant bone loss can hinder and complicate the placement of an implant and/or compromise the function and esthetics of a fixed partial denture. A bone graft for ridge preservation preserves the ideal anatomy of the extraction site. D7953 is reported when performing a socket preservation graft at the time of the extraction or implant removal. D7953 includes bone replacement materials. Guided tissue regeneration barriers D4266 or D4267 or biologic materials (D4265), when placed are reported separately.

2. If an implant rider *is* available, a bone replacement graft may be reimbursed for anterior *or* posterior teeth. Reimbursement is subject to the need and benefit availability. Reimbursement for this procedure is inconsistent. Some payers may require the bone graft be done on the same service date as the implant placement. It is recommended that the payer be contacted for specific coverage information/limitations prior to providing this treatment for the patient.

LIMITATIONS

1. The procedure is not typically reimbursed unless an implant rider is available. The reimbursement is subject to the plan's limitations.

2. If no implant rider is available, D7953 will usually not be reimbursed for a bone replacement graft for *posterior* teeth as it is associated with an implant.

3. For anterior teeth, a benefit may be reimbursed as the procedure may benefit a conventional bridge. If so, a brief narrative should be included documenting the necessity of the bone graft. Pre-operative photos and radiographic images should also be included.

TIPS

1. The material cost of grafts varies widely. The fee charged should be the actual material cost of the graft plus a "labor" charge to place the graft.

2. Terms you should know:

    Allogenic graft – usually freeze dried cells from another human being that are used to repair a defect or supplement a deficiency. Demineralized bone graft products are an example of this (allograft bone material).

    Alloplastic – refers to inorganic bone substitute materials used for tissue grafting and augmentation. Hydroxylapatite bone graft is an example of this type of graft (e.g., OsteoGraft®, Bio-oss®, PepGen®, etc.).

    Autogenous – a graft taken from one part of a patient's body and transferred to another. Chin, hip, and rib grafts would be examples of an autogenous graft.

    Guided tissue regeneration – used to enhance and promote bone growth by placing a barrier membrane D4266/D4267 under gingival tissue and over remaining bone, e.g., Gore-tex®, BioMend®, etc.

D7955 REPAIR OF MAXILLOFACIAL SOFT AND/OR HARD TISSUE DEFECT — CDT 2016

Reconstruction of surgical, traumatic, or congenital defects of the facial bones, including the mandible, may utilize graft materials in conjunction with soft tissue procedures to repair and restore the facial bones to form and function. This does not include obtaining the graft and these procedures may require multiple surgical approaches. This procedure does not include edentulous maxilla and mandibular reconstruction for prosthetic considerations.

CODING CORRECTION — WARNING

1. Do not use this code to describe the reconstruction and grafting of the edentulous maxilla and mandible for prosthetic reasons. See D7950.

2. The harvesting of bone (D7295) would be reported separately, in addition to D7955.

CODING CORRECTION — WATCH

1. Do not report the repair of maxillofacial soft and/or hard tissue defect (D7955) for a bone "socket graft" in conjunction with an *extraction* for ridge preservation. D7955 *does not* pertain to a fresh extraction site. See bone replacement graft for ridge preservation – per site (D7953) for further details.

2. D7955 *does not* describe ridge augmentation. For bone socket ridge preservation, see D7950.

3. Any type of bone graft may be used for D7955.

| COMMENTS | The revised descriptor clarifies that D7955 should not be used to report ridge augmentation in preparation for an implant or prosthesis. D7955 is typically billed to the patient's medical plan and is used to describe the repair of residual defects resulting from resection of tumors, defects related to traumatic injuries, or congenital defects that limit the form or function of the facial bones. This procedure may be used to describe situations where the repair involves the treatment of a defect found anywhere in the facial bones. |

D7960 FRENULECTOMY – ALSO KNOWN AS FRENECTOMY OR FRENOTOMY – SEPARATE PROCEDURE NOT INCIDENTAL TO ANOTHER PROCEDURE CDT 2016

Surgical removal or release of mucosal and muscle elements of a buccal, labial or lingual that is associated with a pathological condition, or interferes with proper oral development or treatment.

| COMMENTS | 1. D7960 can be used to report the excision of a frenum that *restricts the ability to function normally*. D7960 has no age restriction and may be performed using any of several techniques. The frenulum labii inferioris (between the lower lip and gum), frenulum labii superiorus (between upper gum and lip), or the frenulum linguae (below the tongue) may be involved. Sutures may or may not be placed during the frenectomy procedure.
| | 2. Frenectomy, (D7960), may be used to prevent the progression of gingival recession, eliminate large diastemas between teeth, or eliminate interference with a prosthetic appliance. An unusually strong frenum can affect speech and mastication. |

| LIMITATIONS | 1. Frenulectomy (frenectomy or frenotomy) D7960, may be a contract benefit as a stand-alone procedure.
| | 2. Many payers deny D7960 when performed on the same day at the same site as other surgical procedures, such as a gingivectomy, soft tissue graft, osseous surgery, alveoloplasty, or vestibuloplasty. They consider a frenectomy integral to any of these procedures. Documentation supporting the fact that the doctor performed this separate service, that it required significant effort, and that the procedure was a separate service from any of the above listed surgeries should be contained in the patient's record. |

| TIPS | D7960 often has a lower UCR fee than frenuloplasty (D7963). Frenuloplasty is a more complicated procedure with "repositioning of aberrant muscle and z-plasty or other local flap closure." It's not a "clip and snip." |

| NARRATIVES | A brief narrative should describe the frenum location and the pathological condition it caused which interferes with proper oral development or function. If the frenectomy was associated with another procedure requiring significant effort, so state it. |

D7963 FRENULOPLASTY CDT 2016

Excision of frenum with accompanying excision or repositioning of aberrant muscle and z-plasty or other local flap closure.

| COMMENTS | Frenuloplasty, also known as "Z-plasty," is a more complex procedure than D7960. The "Z-plasty" is named as a result of the "Z" shaped incision associated with a frenuloplasty. The frenum is released from the underlying muscle and sutured. A "Z" shaped closure is made. This type of surgical approach is often used in cosmetic surgery and reconstructive surgery. It allows greater flexibility of the skin and underlying structure during the healing process. |

| LIMITATIONS | 1. It should also be noted that many payers deny frenuloplasty (D7963) when performed on the same day in the same site area as other surgical procedures, such as a gingivectomy, soft tissue graft, osseous surgery, alveoloplasty, or vestibuloplasty. Documentation supporting the fact that the doctor performed these services, that they required significant effort, and that the procedure was a separate service should be contained in the patient's record.
| | 2. D7963 is reported as a per site procedure. |

| TIPS | Frenuloplasty (D7963) may have a higher UCR fee than frenulectomy (D7960). Frenuloplasty is a more complicated procedure with "repositioning of aberrant muscle and z-plasty or other local flap closure." |

NARRATIVES A brief narrative should describe the frenum location, the necessity of the excision and repositioning of the aberrant muscle, and local flap closure. If the frenuloplasty was associated with another procedure requiring significant effort, state this in the narrative.

D7970 — EXCISION OF HYPERPLASTIC TISSUE – PER ARCH — CDT 2016

COMMENTS
1. D7970 is used to describe the removal of an epulis. An epulis is typically caused by an ill-fitting denture. The denture irritates the underlying tissue causing the hyperplasia. The area may be asymptomatic and the size of the epulis and resulting symptoms can increase significantly if not treated. This hyperplastic tissue may affect the fit of the denture. D7970 is used to report the excision of this "flabby" tissue.
2. Hyperplastic gingival tissue may result from orthodontic treatment. D7970 reports the excision of the overgrowth of gingival tissue around the teeth and orthodontic appliances. This hyperplastic tissue may be excised before or after the removal of the orthodontic appliances. The claim form question, "Is this for orthodontics?" must be answered "yes."

LIMITATIONS
1. Excision of hyperplastic tissue (D7970) may be a covered benefit and subject to policy limitations.
2. D7970 may not be reimbursed if other surgical procedures are performed at the same site on the same service date.

NARRATIVES
1. The narrative should identify the specific arch when reporting D7970. This procedure is reported on a "per arch" basis. Identify if the procedure is due to an ill-fitting denture.
2. In cases of drug related hyperplastic tissue, (such as with Dilantin®, etc.) submit a narrative. Identify the arch. If drug related, D7970 may be reimbursed under the patient's medical insurance.

D7971 — EXCISION OF PERICORONAL GINGIVA — CDT 2016

Surgical removal of inflammatory or hypertrophied tissues surrounding partially erupted/impacted teeth.

CODING CORRECTION – WARNING
1. D7971 is only reported in association with *partially* erupted or impacted teeth. Generally D7971 is used to describe the excision of pericoronal gingiva in the child or young adult cutting a first, second, or third molar. In addition, D7971 could report cutting a "facial window" on erupting central or lateral incisors in a young child.
2. Do not report D7971 for routine soft tissue management of a fully erupted tooth associated with an amalgam or composite restorations or crown preparation. See gingivectomy to allow for restorative access, D4212 for further details.

CODING CORRECTION – WATCH
Do not report a gingivectomy (D4210 or D4211) when excising periocoronal gingiva (D7971) of a partially erupted tooth. Gingivectomy is associated with a fully *erupted tooth* while excision of pericoronal gingiva is associated with *partially erupted/impacted tooth*. Gingivectomy (D4210 or D4211) is a *periodontal* procedure (removing pockets) associated with a fully erupted tooth.

COMMENTS Report D7971 for "removing inflamed or thickened tissue" around a partially erupted or impacted primary or permanent tooth. D7971 may also report an operculectomy (removal of a mucosal flap that partially or completely covers a partially erupted/impacted tooth).

LIMITATIONS A partially erupted tooth with surrounding inflamed or hypertrophied tissue may require access for a restoration (sealant/composite/amalgam). If performed on the same service date as the restoration, D7971 may be considered a part of the restoration and not reimbursed.

TIPS The excision of pericoronal gingiva (D7971) on previous service date with the restorative procedure on a subsequent restorative service date will improve reimbursement odds.

NARRATIVES A brief narrative should identify the tooth number and explain why the procedure was necessary.

| D7972 | **SURGICAL REDUCTION OF FIBROUS TUBEROSITY** | CDT 2016 |

COMMENTS D7972 is used to describe pre-prosthetic surgery where fibrous tissue creates an unstable base to support a removable complete denture or a removable partial denture or where the tuberosity is so large that there is inadequate space between the tuberosity and the opposing arch for the prosthesis.

LIMITATIONS
1. Surgical reduction of fibrous tuberosity (D7972) may be reimbursed if necessary for the success of the prosthetic appliance. If reimbursed, the procedure is subject to a once per lifetime limitation for the same treatment location.
2. D7972 may be considered a part of a gingivectomy (D4210 or D4211) or periodontal osseous surgery (D4260 or D4261) when performed in the same area on the same date.

NARRATIVES The narrative should identify the quadrant and explain the necessity of the pre-prosthetic surgery. Describe how the fibrous tuberosity is creating an unstable base or how it may interfere with the delivery of a removable complete denture or a removable partial denture.

| D7980 | **SIALOLITHOTOMY** | CDT 2016 |

Surgical procedure by which a stone within a salivary gland or its duct is removed, either intraorally or extraorally.

LIMITATIONS This is typically considered for reimbursement through medical insurance.

| D7981 | **EXCISION OF SALIVARY GLAND, BY REPORT** | CDT 2016 |

LIMITATIONS This is typically considered for reimbursement through medical insurance.

| D7982 | **SIALODOCHOPLASTY** | CDT 2016 |

Surgical procedure for the repair of a defect and/or restoration of a portion of a salivary gland duct.

LIMITATIONS This is typically considered for reimbursement through medical insurance.

| D7983 | **CLOSURE OF SALIVARY FISTULA** | CDT 2016 |

Surgical closure of an opening between a salivary duct and/or gland and the cutaneous surface, or an opening into the oral cavity through other than the normal anatomic pathway.

LIMITATIONS This is typically considered for reimbursement through medical insurance.

| D7990 | **EMERGENCY TRACHEOTOMY** | CDT 2016 |

Surgical formation of a tracheal opening usually below the cricoid cartilage to allow for respiratory exchange.

LIMITATIONS This is typically considered for reimbursement through medical insurance.

| D7991 | **CORONOIDECTOMY** | CDT 2016 |

Surgical removal of the coronoid process of the mandible.

LIMITATIONS This is typically considered for reimbursement through medical insurance.

| **D7995** | **SYNTHETIC GRAFT – MANDIBLE OR FACIAL BONES, BY REPORT** | **CDT 2016** |

Includes allogenic material.

LIMITATIONS This is typically considered for reimbursement through medical insurance.

| **D7996** | **IMPLANT-MANDIBLE FOR AUGMENTATION PURPOSES (EXCLUDING ALVEOLAR RIDGE), BY REPORT** | **CDT 2016** |

LIMITATIONS This is typically considered for reimbursement through medical insurance.

| **D7997** | **APPLIANCE REMOVAL (NOT BY DENTIST WHO PLACED APPLIANCE), INCLUDES REMOVAL OF ARCH BAR** | **CDT 2016** |

CODING WATCH CORRECTION

1. D7997 appliance removal (not by dentist who placed appliance) reports the removal of an arch bar, which was placed as a part of a surgical procedure.
2. D7997 *does not* describe the removal of *orthodontic appliances*.
3. For the removal of orthodontic appliances after active treatment, see orthodontic retention (D8680).

COMMENTS D7997 reports the removal of a surgery related arch bar by a provider who did not place the appliance.

LIMITATIONS Do not expect reimbursement.

| **D7998** | **INTRAORAL PLACEMENT OF A FIXATION DEVICE NOT IN CONJUNCTION WITH A FRACTURE** | **CDT 2016** |

The placement of intermaxillary fixation appliance for documented medically accepted treatments not in association with fractures.

COMMENTS
1. D7998 reports the intraoral placement of a fixation device not in conjunction with the treatment of a fracture.
2. Do not use this code to describe tooth reimplantation and/or stabilization of accidentally evulsed or displaced tooth (D7270) or tooth transplantation (includes reimplantation from one site to another and splinting and/or stabilization) (D7272). Any fixation provided with D7998 is considered to be a part of the procedure.
3. D7998 includes a device used for stabilization of the TMJ during a CT scan.

LIMITATIONS This is typically considered for reimbursement through medical insurance.

| **D7999** | **UNSPECIFIED ORAL SURGERY PROCEDURE, BY REPORT** | **CDT 2016** |

Used for procedure that is not adequately described by a code. Describe procedure.

CODING WATCH CORRECTION

1. D7999 may be used to describe the *unintended* partial extraction of a tooth, with referral to oral surgeon for removal of the root fragment and may be reported as D7999.
2. See D7251 for an *intentional* partial removal of an impacted tooth's crown or coronectomy. D7251 applies to situations where when a neurovascular complication is likely if the entire *impacted* tooth is removed.
3. Biopsy in conjunction with apicoectomy or periradicular surgery procedures should be reported as D7999. The biopsy descriptors for D7285 and D7286 prohibit its use with procedures reported for apicoectomy (D3410, D3421, D3425, and D3426) or periradicular surgery without apicoectomy (D3427).

NOTES

Go to www.practicebooster.com to learn about the Revenue Enhancement Program, a coding and fee positioning consultation for you and your staff.
Cut coding errors and maximize legitimate reimbursement!
Tel: (866) 858-7596; Fax: (855) 825-3960; info@drcharlesblair.com

GENERAL INFORMATION REGARDING ORTHODONTICS — AUTHOR'S COMMENTS

It is important to have a clear understanding of orthodontic coding requirements to minimize coding errors. Comprehensive orthodontics includes a coordinated diagnosis, which would include, but not be limited to, a cephalometric radiographic image with analysis, photographs, and diagnostic casts.

Additionally, comprehensive orthodontics includes treatment of the entire mouth that leads to the improvement of a patient's craniofacial dysfunction and/or dentofacial deformity which may include anatomical, functional and/or esthetic relationships. The treatment should result in a functional and ideal occlusion to create a class I molar/canine relationship. If the orthodontic treatment being provided does not meet this definition of comprehensive orthodontics from both the diagnostic and treatment aspects, consider reporting limited orthodontic treatment.

D8040 reports limited orthodontic treatment of the adult dentition. Limited treatment might include the treatment of one arch and/or segments of both arches, closing open spaces, crossbite correction or uprighting a tooth for a fixed partial denture, etc. D8030 or D8040 may be used to report a case where the treatment if limited in scope or where the entire dentition may not be engaged. Because limited orthodontic treatment does not involve the entire dentition, PPO fees are typically less than fees offered for treatment of a comprehensive case. Refer to page 345 for additional information regarding comprehensive orthodontic treatment.

Receiving payment for orthodontic claims can be challenging because each insurance payer has its own way of structuring payments. With orthodontic claims in particular, it is essential to contact the payer directly to find out its payment schedule, limitations, and restrictions. Some make monthly payments while others pay quarterly. Some will not pay unless monthly claims are submitted, while others automatically remit quarterly or monthly payments once they approve the initial claim. Once the patient's dental plan describes how they structure their orthodontic payments, create a spreadsheet or a tickler file to keep track of how each plan pays claims.

As an example, one plan will pay 50% of its allowable fee when orthodontic treatment begins, another 25% five months later, and the remaining 25% as a final payment six months later. Regardless of how many months the patient will be in treatment, this plan pays off its portion within 12 months. This is just an example of how one major payer structures its orthodontic payments. There are as many variations as there are payers, which is why it is so important to know up front how each patient's plan is structured before initiating treatment.

Submitting each component of orthodontic records (e.g., D0330, D0340, D0350, D0470) (separately) up-front can not only increase the cash flow for your practice, it may also act as an early indication to the provider on exactly how the case will be paid. Some payers will reimburse records in addition to the typical lifetime maximum benefits of $1,500.

D8000-D8999 XI. ORTHODONTICS — CDT 2016

DENTITION — CDT 2016

Primary Dentition: Teeth developed and erupted first in order of time.

Transitional Dentition: The final phase of the transition from primary to adult teeth, in which the deciduous molars and canines are in the process of shedding and the permanent successors are emerging.

Adolescent Dentition: The dentition that is present after the normal loss of primary teeth and prior to cessation of growth that would affect orthodontic treatment.

Adult Dentition: The dentition that is present after the cessation of growth that would affect orthodontic treatment.

All of the following orthodontic treatment codes may be used more than once for the treatment of a particular patient depending on the particular circumstance. A patient may require more than one interceptive procedure or more than one limited procedure depending on their particular problem.

LIMITED ORTHODONTIC TREATMENT — CDT 2016

Orthodontic treatment with a limited objective, not necessarily involving the entire dentition. It may be directed at the only existing problem, or at only one aspect of a larger problem in which a decision is made to defer or forego more comprehensive therapy.

COMMENTS

1. D8070 reports "comprehensive orthodontic treatment of the transitional dentition." It may be considered "Phase I" of continuing comprehensive treatment. Basically, comprehensive orthodontic treatment is often started with the transitional dentition if the treatment plan is comprehensive.

2. Transitional dentition is a term used to describe the final phase of the transition from primary to permanent teeth in which most primary teeth have been lost or are in the process of shedding and permanent successors are not yet in function (Mosby's Dental Dictionary, © 2008). In other words, the patient has both primary and permanent teeth.

3. Comprehensive orthodontic treatment always involves both the upper and lower arches. But, all teeth do not necessarily need to be banded for a case to be considered comprehensive. For example, the second molars may not need to be banded, but the end result of a comprehensive case involves the proper alignment and function of all teeth in both arches.

4. None of CDT's orthodontic treatment codes specify that orthodontic brackets or bands are required. In other words, orthodontic cases using traditional orthodontic brackets and wires are coded the same as orthodontic cases using a series of removable appliances.

5. There is no standard that establishes how long active treatment must last for a case to be considered comprehensive. More complex cases typically take longer than simpler cases. Typically, the cost of orthodontic treatment varies depending on the complexity of the case and the length of active treatment. Likewise, most third party payers adjust their payments based on the provider's anticipated length of active treatment, prior to retention.

LIMITATIONS This procedure is typically reimbursed if there are orthodontic benefits available.

TIPS Do not "save" the orthodontic lifetime benefits. Many times the dental insurance benefits change if the parent's employment changes. The change in employment and coverage may reset the lifetime maximum. That new maximum (if available) can be applied to subsequent orthodontic treatment.

NARRATIVES The initial claim should include an identification of the occlusion type (I, II, III), overall charge, banding fee (typically $1/3$-$1/2$ of the total fee), the estimated number of months in treatment, and the remaining monthly charge.

D8080 — COMPREHENSIVE ORTHODONTIC TREATMENT OF THE ADOLESCENT DENTITION
CDT 2016

IMPORTANT: See general orthodontic comments located prior to D8000.

COMMENTS

1. D8080 reports "comprehensive orthodontic treatment of the adolescent dentition." It may be considered "Phase I" of continuing comprehensive treatment. Basically, comprehensive orthodontic treatment is often started with the adolescent dentition if the treatment plan is comprehensive.

2. With the *adolescent* dentition (all permanent teeth erupted with the normal loss of primary teeth), the mandible and maxilla are still growing and growth that would affect orthodontic treatment is not complete.

3. Comprehensive orthodontic treatment involves both the upper and lower arches. But, all teeth do not necessarily need to be banded ultimately for a case to be considered comprehensive. For example, the second molars may not need to be banded, but the end result of a comprehensive case involves the proper alignment and function of all teeth in both arches.

4. None of CDT's orthodontic treatment codes specify that orthodontic brackets or bands are required. In other words, orthodontic cases using traditional orthodontic brackets and wires are coded the same as orthodontic cases using a series of removable appliances.

5. There is no standard that establishes how long active treatment must last for a case to be considered comprehensive. More complex cases typically take longer than simpler cases. Typically, the cost of orthodontic treatment varies depending on the complexity of the case and the length of active treatment. Likewise, most third party payers adjust their payments based on the provider's anticipated length of active treatment, prior to retention.

LIMITATIONS	This procedure is typically reimbursed if there are orthodontic benefits available.
TIPS	Do not "save" the orthodontic lifetime benefit. Many times the dental insurance benefits change if the parent's employment changes. The change in employment and coverage may reset the lifetime maximum. That new maximum (if available) can be applied to subsequent orthodontic treatment.
NARRATIVES	The initial claim should include an identification of the occlusion type (I, II, III), overall charge, banding fee (typically $1/3$-$1/2$ of the total fee), the estimated number of months in treatment, and the remaining monthly charge.

D8090 — COMPREHENSIVE ORTHODONTIC TREATMENT OF THE ADULT DENTITION — CDT 2016

IMPORTANT: See general orthodontic comments located prior to D8000.

COMMENTS

1. Comprehensive orthodontic treatment involves both the upper and lower arches. But, all teeth do not necessarily need to be banded ultimately for a case to be considered comprehensive. For example, the second molars may not need to be banded, but the end result of a comprehensive case involves the proper alignment and function of all teeth in both arches.

2. When reporting treatment for the *adult* dentition, the maxillary and mandibular growth is *complete* before treatment is started.

3. None of CDT's orthodontic treatment codes specify that orthodontic brackets or bands are required. In other words, orthodontic cases using traditional orthodontic brackets and wires are coded the same as orthodontic cases using a series of removable devices.

4. There is no standard that establishes how long active treatment must last for a case to be considered comprehensive. More complex cases typically take longer than simpler cases. Typically, the cost of orthodontic treatment varies depending on the complexity of the case and the length of active treatment. Likewise, most third party payers adjust their payments based on the provider's anticipated length of active treatment, prior to retention.

LIMITATIONS	This procedure is typically reimbursed if there are orthodontic benefits available.
TIPS	Do not "save" the orthodontic lifetime benefit. Many times the dental insurance benefits change if the adult's employment changes. The change in employment and coverage could possibly reset the lifetime maximum. That new maximum (if available) can be applied to subsequent orthodontic treatment.
NARRATIVES	The initial claim should include an identification of the occlusion type (I, II, III), overall charge, banding fee (typically $1/3$-$1/2$ of the total fee), the estimated number of months in treatment, and the remaining monthly charge.

MINOR TREATMENT TO CONTROL HARMFUL HABITS — CDT 2016

D8210 — REMOVABLE APPLIANCE THERAPY — CDT 2016

Removable indicates patient can remove; includes appliances for thumb sucking and tongue thrusting.

IMPORTANT: See general orthodontic comments located prior to D8000.

CODING WATCH CORRECTION

1. It is wrong to report removable appliance therapy (D8210) for active minor tooth movement using Hawley/springs to correct a crossbite for a child. D8050 and D8060 reports interceptive treatment. D8210 may be used to report removable appliances used to control *harmful habits*. Habit appliances are not intended to move teeth, but to break a harmful habit.

2. D8210 reports a removable appliance designed to prevent a growth and development related condition created by a harmful habit.

3. D8210 should not be used to report an occlusal guard, occlusal orthotic device, periodontal guard, bite guard, or occlusal splint. See D9940 for an occlusal guard (bruxism) appliance and occlusal orthotic device (D7880) regarding a TMJ dysfunction appliance.

COMMENTS

1. Removable appliance therapy (D8210) reports "removable" appliances designed to treat harmful habits such as thumb sucking and tongue thrusting. D8210 (removable appliance therapy) is seldom used to treat a thumb sucking habit as the child can remove it.

2. If the appliance does not treat a "harmful habit," consider reporting the appropriate "limited orthodontic treatment" or "interceptive orthodontic treatment" procedures to describe the procedure.

LIMITATIONS

1. This procedure may be reimbursed if there are orthodontic benefits available. The reimbursement is generally made at 50% of the UCR fee and is applied to the orthodontic lifetime maximum (typically $1,500 to $2,000).

2. Harmful habit appliances may not be covered by some plans with orthodontic coverage.

TIPS

Do not "save" the orthodontic lifetime benefits. Many times the dental insurance benefits change if the parent's employment changes. The change in employment and coverage may reset the lifetime maximum. That new maximum can be applied to subsequent orthodontic treatment.

NARRATIVES

A brief narrative should describe the "harmful habit."

D8220 FIXED APPLIANCE THERAPY — CDT 2016

Fixed indicates patient cannot remove appliance; includes appliances for thumb sucking and tongue thrusting.

IMPORTANT: See general orthodontic comments located prior to D8000.

CODING WATCH CORRECTION

1. It is wrong to report fixed appliance therapy (D8220) for active minor tooth movement. D8220 is used to describe a fixed (cemented/bonded) appliance provided to control *harmful habits*, such as thumb sucking and tongue thrusting. Habit appliances are not intended to move teeth but to break a harmful habit.

2. D8220 reports a fixed appliance designed to prevent a growth and development related condition created by a harmful habit.

3. D8220 should not be used to report an occlusal guard, occlusal orthotic device, periodontal guard, bite guard, or occlusal splint. See occlusal guard (D9940) regarding a bruxism appliance and occlusal orthotic device (D7880) regarding a TMJ dysfunction appliance.

COMMENTS

1. Fixed appliance therapy (8220) is used to describe a *fixed* "harmful habit" appliance, i.e., for thumb sucking, tongue thrusting, etc.

2. If the appliance does not treat the "harmful habit," but is an active appliance, consider reporting the appropriate "limited orthodontic treatment" or "interceptive orthodontic treatment" procedures to describe the procedure.

LIMITATIONS

1. This procedure is typically reimbursed if there are orthodontic benefits available. The reimbursement is generally made at 50% of the UCR fee and is applied to the orthodontic lifetime maximum (typically $1,500 to $2,000).

2. Harmful habit appliances may not be covered by some plans with orthodontic coverage.

TIPS

Do not "save" the orthodontic lifetime benefits. Many times the dental insurance benefits change if the parent's employment changes. The change in employment and coverage may reset the lifetime maximum. That new maximum (if available) can be applied to subsequent orthodontic treatment.

NARRATIVES A brief narrative should describe the "harmful habit."

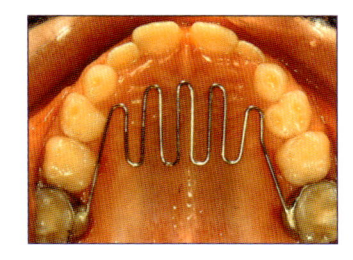

This is a maxillary fixed appliance to control harmful habits.

Courtesy Drake Dental Lab

OTHER ORTHODONTIC SERVICES — CDT 2016

D8660 PRE-ORTHODONTIC TREATMENT EXAMINATION TO MONITOR GROWTH AND DEVELOPMENT — CDT 2016

Periodic observation of patient dentition, at intervals established by the dentist, to determine when orthodontic treatment should begin. Diagnostic procedures are documented separately.

COMMENTS
1. Pre-orthodontic treatment examination to monitor growth and development (D8660) may be used to report a visit (prior to initiation of active orthodontic treatment) where growth and development of the patient is monitored to determine when active treatment should begin.
2. Case presentation (D9450) could also be reported for presenting an orthodontic case after a periodic oral evaluation (D0120) or comprehensive oral evaluation (D0150) visit. Typically, there is no charge or reimbursement for D9450.
3. D8660 *does not* include orthodontic records (D0330, D0340, D0350 and D0470). These records should be reported separately from the case, upfront, *before* the case begins.

LIMITATIONS
1. Pre-orthodontic treatment examination to monitor growth and development (D8660) is seldom charged to the patient and the courtesy is used as an incentive to treat the case later. The pre-orthodontic treatment examination, if reimbursed, is typically re-mapped to one of the oral evaluation codes and is subject to either the "one evaluation per year" or "two evaluations per year" limitation. Some payers will reimburse a more liberal "three evaluations per year" if an evaluation is done at a different provider's office. D8660 may be re-mapped by some payers to some type of oral evaluation (such as D0150 or D0140).
2. The consultation-diagnostic service provided by dentist or physician other than the requesting dentist or physician (D9310) may possibly be reimbursed. See D9310 for details.

D8670 PERIODIC ORTHODONTIC TREATMENT VISIT — CDT 2016

COMMENTS
1. Periodic orthodontic treatment visit (D8670) reports monthly or quarterly active orthodontic treatment adjustments and/or visits. Some payers require the submission of monthly or quarterly claims to disburse payments for ongoing active treatment. Other payers automatically make monthly or quarterly payments.
2. Periodic orthodontic treatment visits (D8670) are often part of the global (case) treatment fee paid by the payer during the course of active orthodontic treatment and are subject to the contract limitations.

D8680 — ORTHODONTIC RETENTION (REMOVAL OF APPLIANCES, CONSTRUCTION AND PLACEMENT OF RETAINER(S)) — CDT 2016

CODING WATCH CORRECTION

1. D8680 is used to describe *orthodontic* retention appliances (retainers) delivered immediately after the active orthodontic phase of treatment has been completed.
2. It is an error to report (D7997) for removal of orthodontic appliances. D7997 includes the *surgical* removal of an arch bar and is an *oral surgery* code.
3. For the replacement of a lost or broken retainer previously placed, see D8692.

COMMENTS D8681 is used to describe an adjustment of an existing removable retainer not performed on the delivery date of the retainer placed for retention. See D8681 for removable orthodontic retainer adjustment.

LIMITATIONS Orthodontic retention (D8680) is used to describe: *Removing* braces or other active appliances as well as the fabrication and delivery of *removable or fixed* orthodontic retainers. Most payers consider retention a part of the orthodontic case fee. Even so, retention may be separately reported.

TIPS If a *different* provider other than the provider who placed the active appliances removes the active appliances, report D8680 and submit a brief narrative describing the retainers placed. D8680 might be reimbursed if the orthodontic lifetime benefits have not been exhausted.

NARRATIVES Occasionally, a general practitioner will remove a *fixed* retention appliance e.g., for the six mandibular anterior teeth, previously placed by an orthodontist. If another practitioner removes the fixed mandibular retainer and delivers a bilateral removable retainer, then space maintainer – removable (D1525) would be used to report this procedure. The removal of the first retainer, and the delivery of the second retainer, would not generally be reimbursed unless orthodontic benefits are available when the retainer is removed and the new retainer delivered. Write a brief narrative.

D8681 — NEW PROCEDURE REMOVABLE ORTHODONTIC RETAINER ADJUSTMENT — CDT 2016

CODING WATCH CORRECTION

D8681 does not report the adjustment of an appliance for a patient in active removable appliance therapy. An appliance adjustment for a patient in active removable appliance therapy is included in the global fee of the active therapy.

COMMENTS D8681 reports the adjustment of an existing removable retainer *after* active treatment is complete and retention placed, if applicable.

LIMITATIONS D8681 is not typically reimbursed.

TIPS D8681 may be reimbursed if the orthodontic lifetime benefits have not been exhausted or the patient has a new insurance plan with orthodontic benefits.

NARRATIVE If the provider adjusting the retainer did not place the retainer, indicate as such.

D8690 — ORTHODONTIC TREATMENT (ALTERNATIVE BILLING TO A CONTRACT FEE) — CDT 2016

Services provided by dentist other than original treating dentist. A method of payment between the provider and the responsible party for services that reflect an open-ended fee arrangement.

COMMENTS
1. Orthodontic treatment (alternative billing to a contract fee), D8690 reports *ongoing* (open ended) fees assessed during treatment by a subsequent treating dentist.
2. D8690 is reported by the subsequent treating dentist for reimbursement for services provided. The fee reported is separate and apart from the fee submitted by the previous dentist.
3. See periodic treatment visit (as part of a contract), D8670 for further comments.

D8691 — REPAIR OF ORTHODONTIC APPLIANCE — CDT 2016

Does not include bracket and standard fixed orthodontic appliances. It does include functional appliances and palatal expanders.

COMMENTS
1. Repair of orthodontic appliance (D8691) *includes repair of functional appliances* and *palatal expanders*.
2. D8691 *does not* include the replacement of brackets and standard fixed orthodontic appliances.
3. See D8693 for re-bonding or re-cementing *fixed* orthodontic retainers.
4. See D8694 for repair of fixed retainers, including reattachment.
5. Answer the claim form question, "Is this for orthodontics?" "Yes."

LIMITATIONS
1. D8691 is not typically reimbursed.
2. Any repair of an appliance during active treatment is generally included in the global orthodontic case fee.

D8692 — REPLACEMENT OF LOST OR BROKEN RETAINER — CDT 2016

COMMENTS
1. D8692 is used to describe the "replacement of lost or broken retainer," previously placed – post-orthodontics. The retainer can be fixed or removable.
2. The common scenario for reporting D8692 is when the patient has completed orthodontic treatment, had retainers placed, but has lost subsequent contact with the orthodontist. Consequently, a general practitioner replaces the lost or broken retainer.
3. For re-bonding or re-cementing a *fixed* retainer, see D8693.
4. Answer the claim form question, "Is this for orthodontics?" "Yes." Use D8692 to describe the replacement.
5. D8681 is used to describe an adjustment made to an existing orthodontic retainer, which is not performed on the delivery date of the retainer.

LIMITATIONS
1. D8692 is not typically reimbursed unless part of the lifetime orthodontic maximum remains and the patient still has orthodontic coverage.
2. Reimbursement for lost or broken retainers (fixed or removable) is often excluded under most orthodontic riders.

TIPS Occasionally, a general practitioner will remove a *fixed* retention appliance, e.g., for the six mandibular anterior teeth, previously placed by an orthodontist. If another practitioner removes the fixed mandibular retainer and delivers a bilateral removable retainer, then space maintainer – removable (D1525) would be used to report this procedure. The removal of the first retainer and the delivery of the second retainer would not generally be reimbursed unless orthodontic benefits are available when the retainer is removed and the new retainer delivered. Write a brief narrative.

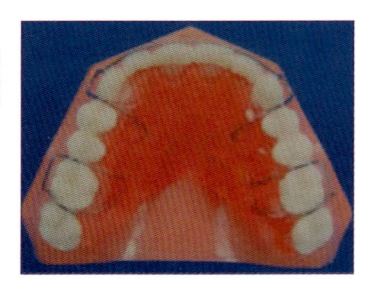

This is a replacement appliance (Hawley) for a broken retainer (placed post orthodontics).

Courtesy Space Maintainers Lab

D8693 RE-CEMENT OR RE-BOND FIXED RETAINER — CDT 2016

COMMENTS
1. D8693 may be used to report the re-cementing or re-bonding of a *fixed* orthodontic retainer.
2. The *fixed* retainer (placed after the completion of active orthodontic treatment) may become loose. An example of a fixed retainer is one that connects to the lower permanent canines. A button is cemented to the linguals of the lower canines with a connecting heavy wire that provides retention of the lower anterior teeth's position.

LIMITATIONS
1. D8693 is not reimbursed when the lifetime orthodontic maximums have been exhausted and/or if orthodontic coverage is not available.
2. If *a different* dentist or office, other than the original treating dentist, re-cements or re-bonds the retainer, it may be reimbursed.

NARRATIVES
1. Ask for an alternate benefit of palliative (D9110) if the re-cementing or re-bonding was performed at an emergency visit where the patient presented with discomfort. See D9110 for further details.
2. Occasionally, a general practitioner will remove a *fixed* retention appliance, e.g., for the six mandibular anterior teeth, previously placed by an orthodontist. If another practitioner removes the fixed mandibular retainer and delivers a bilateral removable retainer, then space maintainer – removable (D1525) could be used to report this procedure. The removal of the first fixed retainer and the delivery of the second removable retainer would not generally be reimbursed unless orthodontic benefits are available when the retainer is removed and the new retainer delivered. Write a brief narrative identifying what was done and why the treatment was necessary.

ADDITIONAL INFORMATION
1. D8691 is reported when repairing *removable* orthodontic appliances, including retainers. See D8691 for details.
2. D8694 may be reported when repairing *fixed* orthodontic appliances including reattachment. See D8694 for details.
3. If the fixed retainer is not re-bonded but removed, and replaced by a removable space maintenance appliance, then report D1525.
4. Answer the claim form question, "Is this for orthodontics?," "Yes."

D8694 REPAIR OF FIXED RETAINERS, INCLUDES REATTACHMENT — CDT 2016

When reporting D8694, the repair of fixed retainers, including reattachment, be sure to answer, "Is this for orthodontics on the claim form?," "Yes."

COMMENTS
1. Repair of fixed orthodontic retainer (D8694) includes the reattachment/re-cementation of the repaired fixed retainers into proper position.
2. The fixed retainer (placed after the completion of active orthodontic treatment for retention) may become broken or damaged. An example of a fixed retainer is one that connects to the lower permanent canines. A bar or wire is cemented to the linguals of the lower six anterior teeth.

3. D8691 may be reported when repairing *removable* orthodontic appliances, including retainers. See D8691 for details.

4. For *re-cementation* of a fixed retainer see D8693.

LIMITATIONS

1. D8694 is not typically reimbursed unless there is an orthodontic rider. D8694 is not reimbursed when the lifetime orthodontic maximums have been exhausted and/or if orthodontic coverage is not available.

2. Any repair of an appliance during active treatment is generally included in the global orthodontic case fee.

3. If the fixed (retention) retainer breaks while the patient is still covered by orthodontic insurance but the lifetime maximum has not been exhausted, then the repair might be reimbursed.

D8999 UNSPECIFIED ORTHODONTIC PROCEDURE, BY REPORT — CDT 2016

Used for procedure that is not adequately described by a code. Describe procedure.

COMMENTS

1. D8999 is used to report a procedure not adequately described by an existing code.

2. Unspecified orthodontic procedure, by report (D8999) may be used to describe the following orthodontic related procedures:

    a. Removal of *residual* bonding "flash" after the debanding appointment. D8999 would be reported as an additional procedure in addition to the prophylaxis by the general practitioner, typically at a recall visit subsequent to orthodontic debanding. See prophylaxis – adult (D1110) for details.

    b. If used, ceramic brackets may be an additional fee.

    c. If used, Invisalign® aligners may be an additional fee.

    d. If used, lingual brackets may be an additional fee.

    Note: PPO contracts control the fee of an orthodontic case. Call the payer and ask how to report and charge (with the patient's written consent) the "extra fee" for the optional services listed above. Some payers may not allow the surcharge. PPO contracts generally require ALL services be submitted, even "non-covered" procedures for which there is a charge.

D9000-D9999 XII. ADJUNCTIVE GENERAL SERVICES — CDT 2016

UNCLASSIFIED TREATMENT

D9110 PALLIATIVE (EMERGENCY) TREATMENT OF DENTAL PAIN – MINOR PROCEDURE

This is typically reported on a "per visit" basis for emergency treatment of dental pain.

Author's Comments:

It is important to always report "what you do" using the CDT code that best describes the procedure performed. At the emergency visit, there may be coding options available. The information below discusses some minor procedures that may be performed to alleviate the patient's pain/discomfort at the emergency visit as reported by palliative, D9110. Some of these procedures may be considered definitive procedures, meaning the procedure performed resolved the patient's pain without subsequent treatment. As long as the patient's record states the issues of the patient's complaint or discomfort, describes the minor procedure performed to alleviate the pain/discomfort, then D9110 may be used at the dentist's discretion. As always, the dentist should determine the current CDT code that best describes overall the context of the procedure and the patient's record must support the procedure performed and reported.

The insurance industry considers certain procedures "integral" to the procedure and those procedures reported as separate codes may not be reimbursed (re-bonding of an appliance while under active treatment, desensitizing, adjustments, follow-up, treatment of dry socket, etc.). For instance, desensitizing at the SRP visit or at recall may not be reimbursed, while desensitizing a "hot tooth" with discomfort at the D9110 emergency visit may be reimbursed. Therefore, always provide a truthful narrative with the reporting of D9110.

CODING CORRECTION WARNING

D9110 is not reported when only writing a prescription. D9110 is reported when the patient is treated with a minor procedure to alleviate discomfort. For proper compliance, the palliative treatment must include the treatment of pain or discomfort which includes the performance of a minor procedure.

CODING CORRECTION WATCH

1. D9110 is reported on a "per *visit*" basis *regardless* of the *number* of procedures rendered on the same service date.
2. The palliative (D9110) code is used to report a *minor procedure* performed to alleviate acute symptoms of pain/discomfort.
3. Palliative (D9110) should not be used to describe the start of a root canal when measuring length using an apex locator and then starting instrumentation of the canal(s). Opening the tooth and debriding a *portion* of the pulpal tissue (to relieve pain) may be reported by D9110. Report the chief complaint and the treatment provided at the emergency visit in a brief narrative.

COMMENTS

1. Palliative (D9110) should not be used to describe *definitive* treatment (extractions, endodontics, crowns, fillings, surgery, etc.). Palliative generally means to ease symptoms without curing the underlying disease. But, sometimes a palliative treatment eliminates the problem. For instance, smoothing a tooth might not require any subsequent treatment. Palliative treatment describes a *minor* procedure performed to alleviate the patient's *acute* and/or *spontaneous* complaint/problem. The service is performed at an emergency visit. Most plans exclude reimbursement for palliative procedures when other, definitive treatment procedures are reported on the same service date. Thus, palliative treatment (D9110) should not be reported in conjunction with *definitive* treatment provided on the same service date. Note: The descriptor of the code does not prohibit reporting D9110, palliative treatment, with other treatment or a problem focused oral evaluation (D0140) performed on the same service date.

2. D9110 is an *under utilized* code. The reporting of D9110 is appropriate for minor non-definitive procedures, reducing discomfort and/or sensitivity, or relief of acute and/or spontaneous pain at an *emergency visit*. The patient who is complaining of spontaneous discomfort always *initiates* the palliative visit and would present complaining of spontaneous discomfort/pain.

3. Palliative (D9110) can be reported in *conjunction* with an office visit – after regularly scheduled hours (D9440). The patient would generally be responsible for payment of the after hours visit (D9440) out-of-pocket.

LIMITATIONS
1. An emergency, problem focused oral evaluation (D0140) is an "evaluation or exam" while palliative (D9110) is "performing" a procedure to alleviate pain/discomfort. Palliative treatment is *initiated* by the patient. The problem focused oral evaluation (D0140) is generally limited by the "one evaluation per six months" or "two evaluations per year" exclusion. The problem focused evaluation (D0140) is *stand-alone* and may always be reported in conjunction with D9110. However many payers will not reimburse D0140 in conjunction with D9110 if performed on the same service date. See D0140 for further details.

2. Some payers will reimburse palliative (D9110), the problem focused oral evaluation (D0140), and diagnostic pulp tests, i.e., pulp vitality test (D0460) performed on the same service date. However, even though this is seldom the case, **always report what you do**.

3. Reimbursement is variable. Palliative (D9110) may be classified as preventive and reimbursed at 100% of the UCR fee or palliative may be considered a basic service and reimbursed at 80% of the UCR fee. In some cases palliative (D9110) may have a deductible applied before reimbursement is forthcoming.

4. Palliative (D9110) *should not* be reported *in conjunction* with an office visit for observation (during regularly scheduled hours), D9430. The descriptor of D9430 stipulates that no other services are performed on the same service date.

TIPS
1. Consider D9110 in situations where D0140 may also apply. Note: D0140 is an evaluation code and evaluation codes are generally limited to "one evaluation per six months" or "two evaluations per 12 months." The reporting of D9110 is not generally limited as D0140. Read this section for explanation and comments regarding the application of palliative (D9110) and compare the problem focused oral *evaluation* (D0140) code as to their applicability. See D0140 for details.

2. Palliative (D9110) and one or two periapical diagnostic image(s) could be performed for the patient of record who presents with acute pain/discomfort *between* recall visits, where a minor, non-definitive service is performed. *The fee reported for palliative treatment should vary according to the time spent and the complexity of the procedure. The fee charged should be consistent for both non-insured and insured patients.* Local anesthesia related palliative (D9110) procedures could be reported with a higher fee than shorter procedures performed with no anesthesia. The UCR fee for palliative is usually *fixed* by the payer.

3. *Periapical radiographic images are often taken in conjunction with the palliative procedure and both codes are generally reimbursed.* Two or three periapical radiographic images may be reimbursed at an emergency visit. If a bitewing is reported at the emergency visit, it may affect bitewing reimbursement at the subsequent *recall visit*. Bitewings may be limited to "once a year." *One* bitewing may be subject to the bitewing limitation with some payers. *Periapicals, taken at emergency visits, typically are not associated with the bitewing limitation.* However, periapicals may be subject to a deductible and may be paid at 80% of the UCR fee in some situations.

NARRATIVES
1. Palliative (D9110) *requires* a brief narrative. *Always* submit a narrative, reporting "what you do," with full disclosure regarding the reporting of D9110. *Always* mention the tooth number or area of mouth, if applicable. The narrative, if applicable, should state "patient will return for more definitive treatment." This indicates *definitive* treatment was not performed during the palliative visit. Palliative (D9110) is generally *not reimbursed in conjunction* with definitive treatment (extraction, filling, etc.) performed on the same service date. However, the descriptor of D9110 *does not* restrict the delivery of other services performed on the same service date.

2. The following are possible *palliative* procedures provided to relieve acute and spontaneous pain, discomfort, or sensitivity. These procedures are performed *at an emergency visit* and *initiated* by the patient. Identify the tooth number, if one was treated. Note: Electronic claims software may limit narratives to 80 characters in the "remarks" section of the claim form. If so, you need to shorten the narratives listed below or file with an electronic attachment:

    a. <u>Fractured tooth:</u> "Mesio-buccal cusp of tooth #3 was fractured. Area was smoothed for patient comfort." Add "To be followed by subsequent visit," if the situation requires a subsequent visit.

    b. <u>Fractured tooth:</u> "Gluma was applied to mesio-buccal cusp area to relieve discomfort, tooth #19." Add "To be followed by subsequent visit," if the situation requires a subsequent visit.

c. Open tooth for relief of pain only, no endo instrumentation sequence initiated: "Acute pain with tooth #3. #3 was opened only *(partial pulpal debridement)* for drainage and patient relief. To be followed by subsequent visit." Full endodontic benefits (when initiated subsequently) typically remain under this scenario. See pulpal debridement (D3221) for comments regarding referral to an endodontist (another billing office), when a *complete* pulpal debridement is reported. D3221 may have a higher UCR fee than palliative (D9110). Some payers consider D3221 to be a "take back" code if the same office does the subsequent endodontic treatment.

d. Temporary placement of IRM for discomfort associated with heat and/or cold: "Patient had sensitivity with tooth #3. Caries was excavated and IRM placed. To be followed by subsequent visit for further evaluation."

e. Sensitive individual tooth upon biting: "#6 was adjusted slightly out of occlusion for relief of pain/sensitivity upon biting. To be followed at subsequent visit."

f. Examine/write prescription in conjunction with relief of discomfort and pain: "Upon biting, tooth #3 was painful. Tooth #3 was adjusted out of occlusion for patient's comfort/relieve bite. Patient will return for further evaluation." A prescription is written and the patient is to be seen later in the GP office or the patient is referred to a specialist for treatment. However, note that D9110 is not to be reported just for writing a prescription. Some treatment must actually be performed before D9110 can be reported.

g. Discomfort with inflammation, heavy calculus buildup, debris: "Patient presented with heavy calculus, debris, and gingival inflammation. Calculus and debris removed from *some areas* (partial debridement) for patient comfort, relief, and healing. To be followed by subsequent visit." Also refer to gross debridement to enable comprehensive oral evaluation and diagnosis (D4355), which is only reimbursed about 30% of the time.

h. Diagnostic at emergency visit: "Patient has previously been seen for pain and diagnosis of tooth #3. Patient was in pain upon biting, with a tentative diagnosis of cracked tooth syndrome. Tooth taken out of occlusion for diagnostic purposes; to be followed by subsequent visit for further evaluation."

i. Anesthetic for acute pain relief: "Patient was in severe pain and long lasting anesthetic was administered for temporary relief. Patient was referred to endodontist for further treatment later in the day."

ADDITIONAL INFORMATION Discussion of related codes and use

1. Protective Restoration (D2940) A protective restoration (D2940) may be placed at the emergency visit for treatment of dental pain or D9110 may be applicable. Either could apply. Protective restorations (D2940) may be payable or a "take back" code — the fee previously paid for the protective restoration may be subtracted from the fee of the final restoration. Review the protective restoration (D2940) code. Determine which code best describes a given scenario.

2. Full Mouth Debridement To Enable Comprehensive Evaluation and Diagnosis (D4355) — The sole purpose for D4355 is to debride (**full mouth**) the patient (of calculus and plaque) since a proper *comprehensive oral evaluation (D0150 or D0180) cannot* be performed due to the level and extent of gross and excessive calculus and plaque. The *full mouth* debridement is to be performed *prior* to the comprehensive oral evaluation (D0150) or comprehensive periodontal *evaluation* (D0180). The patient *may or may not* be a periodontal patient. The comprehensive oral evaluation (D0150 or D0180) is not generally completed on the *same* service date, but at a *subsequent* visit and reported then. With perfect sequence and clinical protocol, D4355 is only reimbursed by contracts about 25% to 30% of the time. See D4355 for proper reporting.

3. Certain scenarios will arise when the patient presents with *acute* discomfort from gingival inflammation, excessive calculus, and bleeding or generalized discomfort in a given area(s) of the mouth and *less* than the full mouth is debrided. *See item (2g) in the Narratives section above for an appropriate narrative for the use of D9110* for a *partial* debridement of calculus and debris.

4. Office Visit for Observation – No Other Services Performed (D9430) – Often reported for "no-charge" office visits. This code is generally *not* reimbursed. Some offices use this code internally for "work in process" visits (such as multiple ongoing visits for a partial fabrication or a no charge post-operative visit) and it is not charged out or reported for payment. *If a minor, non-definitive procedure is actually performed as a result of spontaneous discomfort/ sensitivity/pain, palliative (D9110), or another code should be considered, as discussed above.*

5. Limited Occlusal Adjustment (D9951) – Associated with equilibration, discing, odontoplasty, and enameloplasty. D9951 is not typically reimbursed except when associated with periodontal treatment. Always use a brief narrative to describe the procedure. For instance, discing primary canines to allow proper alignment of the permanent incisors would report D9971, odontoplasty. See D9971 for further information.

6. If the patient presents with discomfort at an *emergency* visit with a fractured tooth, "sharp to the tongue," then palliative (D9110) could also be considered. See (2a) in the Narratives section above for an appropriate narrative for D9110.

D9120 — FIXED PARTIAL DENTURE SECTIONING — CDT 2016

Separation of one or more connections between abutments and/or pontics when some portion of a fixed prosthesis is to remain intact and serviceable following sectioning and extraction or other treatment. Includes all recontouring and polishing of retained portions.

COMMENTS
1. D9120 is used to report the sectioning of a fixed bridge between the retainer crown (abutment crown) and/or pontic(s). Some portion of the existing fixed bridge is retained.
2. The procedure includes all recontouring and polishing of the remaining retainer crown (abutment crown)
3. An extraction, if done, would be reported *separately* and apart from D9120.

LIMITATIONS
1. If the sectioning of the fixed bridge is part of a transitional/provisional procedure, D9120 may be considered a part of the global fee for the definitive treatment, and therefore not reimbursed.
2. Some payers include the sectioning of the bridge as part of the extraction fee for a failed retainer, if done on the same date of service as the extraction and by the same provider.

NARRATIVES
1. "See attached pre-operative radiographic image."
2. State which part(s) of bridge were removed and which part(s) remained intact, e.g., "removed retainer crown #30 due to caries and pontics #28 and #29. Crown on #27 remains."

ANESTHESIA — CDT 2016

D9210 — LOCAL ANESTHESIA NOT IN CONJUNCTION WITH OPERATIVE OR SURGICAL PROCEDURES — CDT 2016

LIMITATIONS
1. Local anesthesia is not generally reimbursed separately from a clinical procedure. However, D9120 may be reimbursed when anesthesia is administered to help determine a definitive *diagnosis*.
2. Local anesthesia may be administered to aid with a definitive *diagnosis* (to identify a pain source). Local anesthesia not in conjunction with operative or surgical procedures (D9210) may be reported for this diagnostic procedure.
3. D9210 may be reported in conjunction with a limited oral evaluation – problem focused (D0140). Note: There may be frequency limitations applied to D0140.
4. Palliative treatment (D9110) involving the administration of anesthesia for discomfort may be reimbursed at the emergency visit. See D9110 for details.
5. If D9210 is reported, a participating PPO provider may be contractually obligated to write off the additional costs. Most payers include local anesthesia in the global procedure fee of all the procedures where it is normally used.

NARRATIVES
1. If a patient requests local anesthesia in conjunction with a routine prophylaxis, consider reporting D9210 (with narrative) when an extra fee is charged. The anesthesia may be the patient's responsibility, depending on the PPO provider contract. For non-contracted dentists, D9210 would be the patient's responsibility.
2. D9210 may be used to report Oraqix® used prior to prophylaxis (D1110) or SRP (D4341/D4342). However, D9999 is recommended. When using Oraqix®, report D9999 and include a brief note, "Patient requested needle free Oraqix®." If D9210 is reported, EOBs may instruct contracted providers to write off the additional costs. Payers may maintain that any local anesthesia administered is a part of the global fee for the definitive procedure.

D9211 — REGIONAL BLOCK ANESTHESIA — CDT 2016

LIMITATIONS Regional block anesthesia (D9211) may be used to report local anesthesia administered to aid in making a diagnosis during a problem focused oral evaluation (D0140) during a recall evaluation (D0120). Generally, local anesthesia is not reimbursed, but may be reimbursed when necessary to determine a definitive *diagnosis*.

TIPS See palliative D9110 for information related to emergency treatment of acute and spontaneous dental pain.

NARRATIVES Include a brief narrative that indicates the procedure was performed to diagnose the trigger area for spontaneous/acute pain.

D9212 — TRIGEMINAL DIVISION BLOCK ANESTHESIA — CDT 2016

LIMITATIONS Trigeminal division block anesthesia (D9212) may be used to report the administration of local anesthesia to help in the diagnostic process during a problem focused oral evaluation (D0140) or during a recall evaluation (D0120). Generally, local anesthesia is not reimbursed unless the administration is necessary to make a diagnosis.

TIPS See palliative (D9110) for treatment/diagnosis of acute and spontaneous dental pain.

NARRATIVES Include a brief narrative to explain that the procedure was necessary to diagnose the cause and location of pain.

D9215 — LOCAL ANESTHESIA IN CONJUNCTION WITH OPERATIVE OR SURGICAL PROCEDURES — CDT 2016

LIMITATIONS Most payers consider local anesthesia (D9215) to be a part of the treatment fee. Note: The descriptors for various operative, endodontic and surgical procedures use the word "usually" as it applies to anesthesia. These descriptors state that local anesthesia is usually considered to be a part of the various clinical procedures." Local anesthesia *may* be reported *separately* from the clinical procedure; however, most payers consider local anesthesia an integral part of the *global* procedure." D9215 is rarely reimbursed.

If D9215 is reported, the contracted provider may be obligated to write off the additional costs. Most payers hold that local anesthesia is included in the global procedure fee.

TIPS
1. Do not routinely charge a separate fee for local anesthesia.
2. See palliative (D9110) for treatment/diagnosis of acute and spontaneous dental pain.
3. If a patient requests local anesthesia in conjunction with a routine prophylaxis or SRP, consider reporting D9210 (with narrative) if an extra fee is charged. D9210 reports local anesthesia not in conjunction with operative or surgical procedures. The anesthesia may be the patient's responsibility or the provider may be contractually obligated to write off the additional costs. See D9210.

D9219 — EVALUATION FOR DEEP SEDATION OR GENERAL ANESTHESIA — CDT 2016

D9219 consists of a review of the patient's current medical history and medication use and NPO status. However, patients with significant medical considerations (e.g., ASA III or IV) may require consultation with their primary care physician or consulting medical specialist. The same guidelines define the term "must" as "indicates an imperative need and/or duty; an essential or indispensable item."

CODING CORRECTION WATCH — Although some payers argue that the pre-anesthesia evaluation is part of D9223, the descriptor for D9223 states that anesthesia begins when the doctor administering the anesthetic agent initiates the appropriate anesthesia and non-invasive monitoring protocol and remains in continuous attendance of the patient. It does not refer to any evaluation that occurs prior to the administration of the anesthetic. Because of this, the Code Maintenance Committee (CMC) considers this stand-alone evaluation to be separate from existing deep sedation/anesthesia procedure codes (D9223).

COMMENTS — If the anesthesiologist is an independent provider, he/she may not have an established relationship with the patient and would need to spend additional time before the procedure to review the patient's chart and medical history.

LIMITATIONS — Reimbursement for (D9219) will likely be poor.

D9220 DELETED DEEP SEDATION/GENERAL ANESTHESIA – FIRST 30 MINUTES   CDT 2016

This is a deleted code. See D9223.

D9221 DELETED DEEP SEDATION/GENERAL ANESTHESIA – EACH ADDITIONAL 15 MINUTES   CDT 2016

This is a deleted code. See D9223.

D9223 NEW PROCEDURE DEEP SEDATION/GENERAL ANESTHESIA – EACH 15 MINUTE INCREMENT   CDT 2016

Anesthesia time begins when the doctor administering the anesthetic agent initiates the appropriate anesthesia and non-invasive monitoring protocol and remains in continuous attendance of the patient. Anesthesia services are considered completed when the patient may be safely left under the observation of trained personnel and the doctor may safely leave the room to attend to other patients or duties.

The level of anesthesia is determined by the anesthesia provider's documentation of the anesthetics effects upon the central nervous system and not dependent upon the route of administration.

CODING CORRECTION WATCH — D9223 is measured in 15 minute increments. Any period of less than 15 minutes should not be submitted for reimbursement. This 15 minute increment mirrors the medical coding guidelines.

COMMENTS — The period of anesthesia starts when the doctor begins to administer the anesthetic agent and ends when the doctor may safely leave the room; leaving the patient with trained personnel to be monitored during the recovery period.

LIMITATIONS
1. Deep sedation/general anesthesia – each 15 minute increment (D9223) may be reimbursed in connection with qualified oral surgery, endodontic, or periodontal *surgical* procedures. Dental and medical plan limitations relating to sedation vary widely.
2. Payers may require the patient's medical plan to be billed before submitting the claim to the dental plan
3. It is common for payers to limit reimbursements to two hours of general anesthesia.

TIPS — General anesthesia is typically only covered when provided in conjunction with a qualified oral surgery procedure and is medically necessary, not as an elective procedure to make the patient comfortable or the procedure easier for the dentist. Anesthesia records and an anesthesia permit number are typically required.

NARRATIVES
1. A report is required that establishes medical necessity for deep sedation/general anesthesia. Deep sedation, general anesthesia, and intravenous moderate (conscious) sedation are reimbursed only when deemed medically necessary. Documentation may include the fact that the patient is handicapped, uncontrollable, or has other qualifying medical or dental conditions, such as:
   a. The removal of bony impacted third molars.
   b. Six or more teeth in various quadrants extracted on the same date of service.
   c. Patients allergic to local anesthetic.
   d. High risk medical patients requiring surgical or multiple extractions.
   e. Patients with cerebral palsy, epilepsy, Down Syndrome, hyperactivity, etc.
   f. Patients under six years of age who require multiple extractions and/or restorations.
   g. Infection causing local anesthesia to be ineffective.
   h. Three or more surgical flaps reflected in a single appointment.
2. Include the general anesthesia permit number on the claim form in the remarks section. Some payers require the permit number.
3. See D9219 to report evaluation for deep sedation or general anesthesia.

D9230 INHALATION OF NITROUS OXIDE/ANALGESIA, ANXIOLYSIS — CDT 2016

COMMENTS
1. D9230 is used to report the administration of N_2O without regard to the length of administration.
2. Report behavior management (D9920) when provided in *addition* to D9230.

LIMITATIONS
1. Nitrous oxide (N_2O) is reported as inhalation of nitrous oxide/analgesia, anxiolysis (D9230). A fee should be charged for N_2O. Nitrous oxide is typically a non-covered service.
2. Some Medicaid plans and a few other programs reimburse nitrous oxide or reimburse behavior management (D9920) as an alternate benefit. Special consideration may be given for more complex treatment visits or for young or phobic patients.
3. Most payers will not pay for the administration of nitrous oxide. If administered under an emergency trauma related scenario, request special consideration for management of anxiety.
4. Plan limitations and reimbursement, if any, for D9230 are highly variable.

NARRATIVES While nitrous oxide may not be a covered benefit, submitting a brief narrative that outlines the extra time for the procedure may result in a higher UCR fee reimbursement for the procedure itself. If administered as part of an operative procedure, submit a brief narrative to support the medical necessity stating, "The patient's level of anxiety and the patient's ability to cooperate made extra time and the administration of N_2O necessary to complete the three surface MOD composite procedure, #J. Please consider reimbursement at a higher UCR fee than for the normal pediatric related procedure." Be sure the clinical notes reflect the medical necessity of the nitrous oxide.

D9241 DELETED INTRAVENOUS MODERATE (CONSCIOUS) SEDATION/ANALGESIA – FIRST 30 MINUTES — CDT 2016

This is a deleted code. See D9243

D9242 ~~DELETED~~ INTRAVENOUS MODERATE (CONSCIOUS) SEDATION/ANALGESIA – EACH ADDITIONAL 15 MINUTES — CDT 2016

This is a deleted code. See D9243

D9243 NEW PROCEDURE INTRAVENOUS MODERATE (CONSCIOUS) SEDATION/ANALGESIA – EACH 15 MINUTE INCREMENT — CDT 2016

Anesthesia time begins when the doctor administering the anesthetic agent initiates the appropriate anesthesia and non-invasive monitoring protocol and remains in continuous attendance of the patient. Anesthesia services are considered completed when the patient may be safely left under the observation of trained personnel and the doctor may safely leave the room to attend to other patients or duties.

The level of anesthesia is determined by the anesthesia provider's documentation of the anesthetics effects upon the central nervous system and not dependent upon the route of administration.

CODING WATCH CORRECTION: IV sedation is measured in 15 minute increments. Any period of less than 15 minutes should not be submitted for reimbursement. This 15 minute increment mirrors the medical coding guidelines.

COMMENTS
1. The period of anesthesia starts when the doctor begins to administer the anesthetic agent and ends when the doctor may safely leave the room; leaving the patient with trained personnel to be monitored during the recovery period.
2. Some payers provide reimbursement for general anesthesia, but not IV sedation. If reimbursed, anesthesia records and an anesthesia permit number are typically required and must be noted on the claim to qualify for reimbursement of D9243.
3. Report D9243 for each fifteen minute increment.

LIMITATIONS
1. Intravenous moderate (conscious) sedation/analgesia– each 15 minute increment (D9223) may be reimbursed when provided with certain oral surgery, endodontic, or periodontal surgery procedures. Dental and medical plan limitations related to sedation are highly variable.
2. Payers may require that the patient's medical plan be billed before submitting the claim to the dental plan.

NARRATIVES
1. *Describe* the need for intravenous moderate (conscious) sedation/analgesia. Deep sedation, general anesthesia, and intravenous moderate (conscious) sedation are reimbursed only when deemed medically necessary. Documentation of need may include the fact that the patient is handicapped, uncontrollable, or has other qualifying medical or dental conditions, such as:
   a. The removal of bony impacted third molars.
   b. Six or more teeth in various quadrants extracted on the same date of service.
   c. Patients allergic to local anesthetic.
   d. High risk medical patients requiring surgical or multiple extractions.
   e. Patients with cerebral palsy, epilepsy, Down Syndrome, hyperactivity, etc.
   f. Patients under six years of age who require multiple extractions and/or restorations.
   g. Infection causing local anesthesia to be ineffective.
   h. Three or more surgical flaps reflected in a single appointment.
2. The time for recovery and monitoring after the doctor has left the room by trained personnel should not be billed as deep sedation or general anesthesia time.
3. Include the anesthesia permit number on the claim form in the remarks section. Some payers require the permit number.

ADDITIONAL INFORMATION While some plans consider reimbursement for IV sedation in conjunction with qualifying oral surgery procedures, coverage for IV sedation varies widely among dental plans. Plans may reimburse D9243 if two or more teeth are extracted at a single visit. Other plans may require the extraction of eight or more teeth at a single visit before IV sedation will be considered for reimbursement. D9243 may be reimbursed for periodontal surgery procedures under some dental plans.

Although D9243 is not a "by report" procedure, it may be helpful to note if the patient is allergic to local anesthesia, has a severe infection, is less than six years old, or is medically impaired or compromised. An anesthesia report should be included. If reimbursement is not available under the dental plan, IV sedation may be covered by the patient's medical plan, in some circumstances. If the dental procedure being performed is a covered benefit of the medical plan then IV sedation may be covered by the medical plan. In addition, if the patient's medical condition meets the criteria necessitating IV sedation then a benefit may be available. For example, a child with severe intellectual disabilities, etc. may receive benefit for IV sedation from the medical plan. Always verify coverage with the medical payer prior to treatment. Medical benefits are always primary to any dental benefits. A medical preauthorization may be required for reimbursement.

D9248   REVISED NON-INTRAVENOUS CONSCIOUS SEDATION   CDT 2016

This includes non-IV minimal and moderate sedation.

A medically controlled state of depressed consciousness while maintaining the patient's airway, protective reflexes and the ability to respond to stimulation or verbal commands. It includes non-intravenous administration of sedative and/or analgesic agent(s) and appropriate monitoring.

The level of anesthesia is determined by the anesthesia provider's documentation of the anesthetic's effects upon the central nervous system and not dependent upon the route of administration.

REVISIONS   NON-INTRAVENOUS ~~MODERATE (~~CONSCIOUS~~)~~ SEDATION

COMMENTS
1. D9248 is reported when performing non-intravenous conscious sedation (D9248). The duration of sedation does not affect billing. D9248 is billed per session, just like nitrous oxide (N_2O).

2. Non-intravenous conscious sedation (oral and by injection) reports administration and *monitoring* of sedation with agents such as Valium®, Ativan®, Halcion®, and chloral hydrate. Thus, it can include liquid, tablets and intramuscular injection of sedative (e.g., Ketamine®).

LIMITATIONS
1. D9248 may occasionally be reimbursed when administered with qualifying oral surgery, endodontic, or periodontal *surgical* procedures. Dental and medical plan limitations for D9248 are highly variable. Dental plans may require a medical claim be submitted before a dental claim.

2. Non-intravenous conscious sedation (D9248) is typically a non-covered service. Certain Medicaid or other programs may reimburse D9248 or reimburse behavior management (D9920) as an alternate benefit. Consult the state's Medicaid Processing Policy manual. Reimbursement for D9248 is highly variable.

NARRATIVES
1. A report is required that outlines the reasons why non-intravenous conscious sedation is necessary. Reasons that may justify the administration of non-intravenous conscious sedation might include the treatment of a handicapped patient, or one that has mitigating medical problems, has multiple impactions, is less than three to four years old, etc. A brief narrative should include a copy of the doctor's conscious sedation certificate with the claim.

2. While non-intravenous conscious sedation may not be a covered benefit, writing a narrative that outlines the extra time and effort expended to provide the procedure may result in a higher reimbursement for the procedure. Submit a narrative that describes why the extra time for the procedure was needed. The request may result in a higher UCR fee reimbursement for the procedure itself. Submit a narrative with the restorative procedure stating, "The patient's level of anxiety and the patient's ability to cooperate made extra time and the administration of non-intravenous conscious sedation was necessary to complete the three surface MOD composite procedure, #J. Please consider reimbursement at a higher UCR fee than for the normal pediatric related procedure."

PROFESSIONAL CONSULTATION   CDT 2016

D9310   CONSULTATION – DIAGNOSTIC SERVICE PROVIDED BY DENTIST OR PHYSICIAN OTHER THAN REQUESTING DENTIST OR PHYSICIAN   CDT 2016

A patient encounter with a practitioner whose opinion or advice regarding evaluation and/or management of a specific problem; may be requested by another practitioner or appropriate source. The consultation includes an oral evaluation. The consulted practitioner may initiate diagnostic and/or therapeutic services.

CODING WATCH CORRECTION

1. It is an error to report a consultation (D9310) for treatment plan presentations. Use case presentation (D9450) to describe treatment plan presentations given on a subsequent service date after the comprehensive oral evaluation (D0150/D0180). See D9450.

2. D9310 would be reported by a consulting doctor, when rendering an opinion, to whom the patient has been referred. D9310 requires a requesting dentist, physician, or other appropriate source. The doctor who renders the second opinion may or may not provide the clinical treatment. The consulting dentist (often a specialist) may initiate *diagnostic* and/or *therapeutic services. D9310 includes an oral evaluation*. A general practitioner does not routinely report D9310, although any dentist can report D9310.

3. The general practitioner should consider reporting D0140 or D0150/D0180 when the patient (not a physician or dentist) requests a second opinion. The general practitioner may report a problem focused evaluation (D0140) or comprehensive evaluation (D0150/D0180) for the patient requested second opinion.

COMMENTS

1. D9310 should only be reported if the doctor is giving an *opinion or advice* for a patient specifically referred by a physician, dentist, or other appropriate source. The consulting dentist may initiate *diagnostic* and/or *therapeutic* services under D9310. This code always includes an oral evaluation related to the specific request for the opinion or advice. The specialist should consider reporting the consultation (D9310) code for second opinions. The doctor providing the consultation should send (and maintain a copy of) written communication to the referring dentist or physician about his/her findings during the consultation.

2. A *new* patient presenting to a general practitioner for a second opinion with a *complete treatment plan* from a previous dentist should report a comprehensive oral evaluation (D0150/D0180). If the *new* patient requests a consultation regarding a *single* or limited service (example: evaluating a tooth for a crown), the general practitioner should consider reporting a limited oral evaluation – problem focused (D0140).

LIMITATIONS

1. D9310 may not be reimbursed by certain payers. The reimbursement for D9310, if paid, is typically higher than the comprehensive oral evaluation (D0150/D0180).

2. Some payers consider the consultation an *alternate b*enefit to an oral evaluation and will reimburse the consultation subject to the typical "one evaluation per year" or "two evaluations per year" limitation. Some payers reimburse a "third" evaluation performed in a different office if the third evaluation is performed by a specialist. Coverage is plan specific.

3. If the consultation (D9310) is directed toward a non-covered procedure (for instance, TMJ dysfunction or implants), the consultation may not be reimbursed.

4. D9310 is not reimbursed on the same service date in conjunction with a comprehensive oral evaluation (exam) (D0150/D0180). The consultation code (D9310) *includes* an oral evaluation.

5. If D9310 is denied as a non-covered benefit, then submit an appeal and ask for an alternate benefit of D0120, D0150 or D0180 as may apply.

TIPS

1. If the purpose of the visit is for a case presentation after the comprehensive evaluation (D0150/D0180), report case presentation (D9450), not consultation (D9310).

2. If the purpose of the visit is to give a second opinion, at the patient's request – not at the request of a dentist or physician, report evaluation, problem focused D0140 for a particular patient complaint or report D0150/D0180 (comprehensive evaluation) for a general second opinion. The *self-referred* patient is classified as a new patient and the appropriate comprehensive oral evaluation is reported, *not a* consultation (D9310) which specifically requires a referral from a dentist, physician, or another appropriate source.

PROFESSIONAL VISITS — CDT 2016

D9410 HOUSE/EXTENDED CARE FACILITY CALL — CDT 2016

Includes visits to nursing homes, long-term care facilities, hospice sites, institutions, etc. Report in addition to reporting appropriate code numbers for actual services performed.

COMMENTS Report D9410 for *each* patient visited.

LIMITATIONS House/extended care facility call (D9410) is not typically reimbursed.

D9420 HOSPITAL OR AMBULATORY SURGICAL CENTER CALL — CDT 2016

Care provided outside the dentist's office to a patient who is in a hospital or ambulatory surgical center. Services delivered to the patient on the date of service are documented separately using the applicable procedure codes.

COMMENTS
1. Hospital or ambulatory surgical center call (D9420) is used to report an *additional* fee for providing a clinical procedure in a hospital or surgical center setting.
2. D9420 is reported for *each* patient seen in the hospital or ambulatory surgical call center.

LIMITATIONS D9420 is typically a non-covered service. Some medical plans may provide reimbursement.

TIPS It is suggested that prepayment for hospital or ambulatory surgical center call (D9420) be obtained from the patient or parent *before* scheduling hospital time for the operating room. In lieu of that, at a minimum, a predetermination of benefits for the proposed treatment should be obtained from the dental insurance payer.

D9430 OFFICE VISIT FOR OBSERVATION (DURING REGULARLY SCHEDULED HOURS) – NO OTHER SERVICES PERFORMED — CDT 2016

1. Office visit for observation – no other services performed (D9430) is not typically reimbursed. Consider reporting problem focused oral evaluation (D0140), or the oral re-evaluation (D0170), if an oral evaluation is performed. See D0140 and D0170 for further details.
2. Follow up observation appointments (after specific treatment) are typically included in the *global* fee for the procedure performed. D9430 is not typically reimbursed. D0171 is available to report a re-evaluation – post-operative visit, generally not reimbursed.
3. The oral re-evaluation (D0170) is inappropriate if it follows a specific treatment. D0170 is a follow-up monitoring of continuing pain or soft tissue lesion.

COMMENTS	1. D9430 may be reported for *observing* the patient during regular hours, *without performing any clinical services*. Office visit for observation (D9430) is not generally reimbursed. If the office visit for observation is reimbursed the benefit will generally be classified as an "oral evaluation" and subject to the "one evaluation per six months" or "two evaluations per year" limitation. If the observation visit is a follow up to a problem focused (emergency) oral evaluation (D0140), D0170 or D0171 may apply. See D0170 and D0171 for further details.
	2. If a minor, non-definitive procedure is actually performed at the office as a result of spontaneous discomfort/sensitivity/pain, then consider using palliative (D9110). Report any radiographic images taken in addition to the palliative treatment provided. See palliative D9110, for further details.
TIPS	D9430 is often used to report a "no charge" office visit. Some offices use this code internally for "work in progress" visits (such as multiple visits for constructing a partial denture). Under this scenario, the D9430 code is not charged or filed for reimbursement. For internal office codes such as work in progress, crown delivery, broken appointment, etc., assign codes in the D0000-D0119 range to prevent confusion or improper billing/coding.

D9440 OFFICE VISIT – AFTER REGULARLY SCHEDULED HOURS   CDT 2016

COMMENTS	The fee charged for an office visit – after regularly scheduled hours (D9440) is typically in a range of $75 to $150 *plus* the treatment fee for the specific services rendered.
TIPS	If the doctor and staff leave the office on Friday at noon and are called back Friday afternoon for an emergency, D9440 would apply.
NARRATIVES	D9440 is typically a non-covered service. Always submit a brief narrative when reporting D9440 as it may be reimbursed by some payers. Some Medicaid programs reimburse the doctor for the D9440 visit. The narrative should identify the time of day, day of the week, and circumstances necessitating an office visit after regularly scheduled hours.

D9450 CASE PRESENTATION, DETAILED AND EXTENSIVE TREATMENT PLANNING CDT 2016

Established patient. Not performed on same day as evaluation.

CODING WATCH CORRECTION: Many practices err by reporting a consultation (D9310) for a treatment plan case presentation. Use D9450 to report the case presentation. See consultation (D9310) for further details on proper use of the consultation code.

COMMENTS	1. Report case presentation (D9450) for a case presentation performed on a date *after* the comprehensive oral evaluation (D0150), comprehensive periodontal evaluation (D0180), or detailed and extensive oral evaluation (D0160) was performed. D9450 is not typically reimbursed but may be used to "track" the office's formal case presentations. Generally there is no charge or reimbursement. If a lab bill is incurred, usually there is a charge.
	2. Once an orthodontic workup is completed then the patient can return for a case presentation (D9450) on a subsequent service date.
LIMITATIONS	If the case presentation (D9450) is reimbursed, the payers generally treat the D9450 as a periodic oral evaluation (D0120) or comprehensive oral evaluation (D0150 or D0180) and make the case presentation (D9450) subject to the "one evaluation per six months" or "two evaluations per 12 months" frequency limitation.
TIPS	A fee is not generally charged for the case presentation (D9450); however, if the doctor incurs a fee (typically a laboratory fee) related to the case presentation, it would be appropriate to assign a fee to D9450. Some offices will credit all or a part of any related case presentation fee toward the total case fee, if treatment is accepted and completed.

DRUGS — CDT 2016

D9610 THERAPEUTIC PARENTERAL DRUG, SINGLE ADMINISTRATION — CDT 2016

Includes single administration of antibiotics, steroids, anti-inflammatory drugs, or other therapeutic medications. This code should not be used to report administration of sedative, anesthetic or reversal agents.

CODING WARNING/CORRECTION

1. Do not use D9610 to report the administration of sedatives, anesthetic or reversal agents. For deep sedation/general anesthesia, see D9223; for intravenous moderate (conscious) sedation/analgesia, see D9243. For non-intravenous conscious sedation, including tablets, liquids and intramuscular injections, see D9248. For nitrous oxide, see D9230.
2. Do not use D9610 to report gingival irrigation. D4921 reports gingival irrigation – per quadrant.

COMMENTS

1. Therapeutic parenteral drug injection (D9610) includes a *single* drug injected (subcutaneous, intramuscular, or intravenous). These injections are generally administered for the treatment of infection or anti-inflammatory therapeutic purposes.
2. Sedative agents should be reported as D9223, D9230, D9243 or D9248.
3. D9610 reports the administration of a single therapeutic drug. When two or more different medications are administered, report D9612.

LIMITATIONS Therapeutic parenteral drug injection (D9610) is not typically a covered benefit.

NARRATIVES A brief narrative should identify the drug name, dosage, type of injection (subcutaneous, intramuscular or intravenous), and the therapeutic purpose of the drug administered.

D9612 THERAPEUTIC PARENTERAL DRUGS, TWO OR MORE ADMINISTRATIONS, DIFFERENT MEDICATIONS — CDT 2016

Includes multiple administrations of antibiotics, steroids, anti-inflammatory drugs or other therapeutic medications. This code should not be used to report administration of sedatives, anesthetic or reversal agents.

CODING WARNING/CORRECTION

1. Do not report this code to describe the administration of sedatives, anesthetic or reversal agents. For deep sedation/general anesthesia, see D9223; for intravenous moderate (conscious) sedation/analgesia, see D9243; and for non-intravenous conscious sedation, see D9248. For nitrous oxide, see D9230.
2. This code reports two or more different therapeutic parenteral drugs. Do not report D9612 in conjunction with single administration, D9610. For a *single* injection of just *one* drug, report D9610.
3. Do not use D9612 to report gingival irrigation. D4921 reports gingival irrigation – per quadrant.

COMMENTS

1. Therapeutic parenteral drug injection (D9612) describes the injection of *two or more* drugs (subcutaneous, intramuscular, or intravenous). These injections are typically administered for the treatment of infection or for anti-inflammatory therapeutic purposes.
2. Sedative agents should be reported as D9223, D9230, D9243 or D9248.
3. D9612 reports the administration of two or more therapeutic parenteral drugs. When a single therapeutic drug is administered, report D9610.

LIMITATIONS Therapeutic parenteral drugs (D9612) are not typically a covered benefit.

NARRATIVES A brief narrative should identify the drug name, dosage, type of injection (subcutaneous, intramuscular or intravenous), and the therapeutic purpose of the drug administered.

| **D9630** | **OTHER DRUGS AND/OR MEDICAMENTS, BY REPORT** | **CDT 2016** |

Includes, but is not limited to oral antibiotics, oral analgesics, and topical fluoride dispensed in the office for home use; does not include writing prescriptions.

CODING WATCH CORRECTION

This code should not be used to report the writing of prescriptions. See problem focused evaluation (D0140) or pulp vitality test (D0460) for use of these codes.

COMMENTS
1. Do not report D9630 for chlorhexidine or Peridex® used in *clinical* treatment in the office. See gingival irrigation – per quadrant (D4921) to report the clinical use of chlorhexidine and/or Peridex® as a gingival irrigant.
2. For internal office use, an alternative approach is to assign tooth whitening refills or other take home products/drugs a numerical code *less* than D0120 (since the official CDT code range starts with D0120).
3. See gingival irrigation – per quadrant (D4921) for further details in reporting medicaments such as chlorhexidine or Peridex® used as an irrigant in conjunction with scaling and root planing clinical services.
4. There is not a specific code for MI Paste™ or MI Paste Plus.™ Use D9630 if dispensed in the office for *home* use of these pastes. For in office treatment of white spots after orthodontic treatment, report this procedure as unspecified adjunctive procedure, by report (D9999). For use as a preventive treatment of white spots during orthodontic treatment, report unspecified preventive procedure, by report (D1999).
5. See D1999, by report for reporting fluoride toothpaste, xylitol products and floss. Also report D1999 for cleaning devices such as toothbrushes, inter-dental cleaners, and floss threaders.

TIPS D9630 may be used to report prescription strength products dispensed in the office for *at home* use. For tracking purposes, consider assigning subcategories to this code, such as D9630A, D9630B, D9630C, etc., to account for the various drugs and/or medicaments. Typical *take home* products include, but are not limited to, prescription strength topical fluoride, chlorhexidine rinses, oral antibiotics, oral analgesics, remineralization products, MI Paste™, MI Paste Plus™, PreviDent®, Fluoridex®, gel refill for Perio Protect Trays® etc.

LIMITATIONS D9630 is not typically reimbursed.

NARRATIVES Include a brief narrative to document the need for the take home drug and/or medicament and the quantity dispensed. This code is "by report." Reimbursement is poor.

ADDITIONAL INFORMATION Dental practices should use D9630 to report a variety of products dispensed for home use, including oral antibiotics, oral analgesics, chlorhexidine rinses, prescription strength topical fluorides, and remineralization products. Here are some examples of the type of products that may be reported using D9630:

Oral antibiotics Instead of writing a prescription, some dentists dispense oral antibiotics in the office for certain patients (e.g., to prevent infective endocarditis, for patients who have had total joint replacement, or for patients with an oral infection requiring antibiotic therapy, etc.). Justification for this protocol may be when emergency treatment is being rendered during hours in which pharmacies are closed, there is no pharmacy nearby, or when the dentist wants to confirm that the patient actually took the medication.

Oral analgesics Oral analgesics are medications that block pain or raise the patient's pain tolerance. The more familiar analgesics are aspirin, acetaminophen, codeine, etc. Debacterol® is a medication that is also considered to be an oral analgesic in that it is used to treat and relieve the pain associated with aphthous stomatitis (canker sores). In the past, D9630 has been used to report oral analgesics whether administered in the dental office or dispensed for home use. However, effective January 1, 2009, D9630 can only be used to report oral analgesics dispensed for use at home.

Chlorhexidine rinses Chlorhexidine rinses are often used in the dental office to irrigate inflamed and bleeding gums when curetting a periodontal abscess or performing a prophylaxis, full mouth debridement, periodontal scaling and root planing (SRP), etc. Some dental plans now provide a benefit for antimicrobial rinses such as Peridex®, PerioGard®, PerioRx®, etc., when initially administered at the time of SRP and dispensed for patients to use at home. D9630 should only be reported for chlorhexidine rinses that are dispensed for use at home. In office gingival irrigation with a chlorhexidine rinse should be reported as D4921.

Topical home fluoride gels/rinses D9630, by report, can also be used to report prescription strength topical fluoride gels, prescription strength fluoride rinses, etc., when dispensed for use by the patient at home. Some dental plans now provide coverage for products such as PreviDent®, Fluoridex®, etc., for patients who have an increased risk of developing root caries following gingival recession. When fluoride is used to treat root sensitivity, D9910 should be billed on a "per visit" basis, and when fluoride varnish is used therapeutically to prevent caries, D1206 should be billed. Topical fluoride applied as a preventive protocol (whether gel, foam, or swish) should be reported using D1208. See D1206 and D1208 for details.

Note: For fluoride toothpaste, xylitol products and floss, toothbrushes, inter-dental cleaners, and floss threaders, report D1999, by report.

MRS. SMITH NEEDS HOME TOPICAL FLUORIDE "Mrs. Smith, you have a high risk of developing caries, and we do not have fluoridated water here in our community. This is a fluoride gel for you to use daily after brushing and flossing to help prevent cavities. Be sure to spit out the excess after brushing. Please remember that this is a prescription strength medication, not toothpaste, and must be kept out of reach of young children."

Remineralization products Decalcified "white spots" (typically seen in moderate to high caries risk patients, such as those with orthodontic appliances, high sugar diet, heavy plaque buildup, etc.) are caused when acid producing bacteria attack tooth enamel. When this occurs, the goal is to remineralize the tooth before a cavity develops. MI Paste™, MI Paste Plus™, and ReNew Remineralizing Paste® are examples of remineralization products that may be applied in the office with a prophy cup or dispensed for home use (e.g., custom tray application or Q-tip application). When dispensed for home use, remineralization products can be reported using D9630. When fluoride varnish is used for remineralization (in office) for caries risk patients, report D1206. See D1206 and D1208 for distinction in reporting.

MISCELLANEOUS SERVICES — CDT 2016

D9910 APPLICATION OF DESENSITIZING MEDICAMENT — CDT 2016

Includes in-office treatment for root sensitivity. Typically reported on a "per visit" basis for application of topical fluoride. This code is not to be used for bases, liners or adhesives used under restorations.

CODING WATCH CORRECTION

1. It is an error to report the application of a desensitizing medicament (D9910) for *caries related, preventive* fluoride application. Report D1206 or D1208 for *caries reduction related fluoride application*, not D9910.

2. Do not report D9910 in conjunction with routine crown delivery to reduce subsequent sensitivity. The fluoride application under this scenario is considered *integral to* the crown procedure. In this scenario D9910 should not be reported *separately*. D9910 should not be used to report the use of a base, liner, or adhesive applied under restorations. The D9910 descriptor states "this code is not to be used for bases, liners or adhesives used under restorations." The restorative codes are *inclusive* of all bases, liners, adhesives and desensitizers.

3. Desensitizing *resins* are not to be reported as D9910. Desensitizing resins are reported separately using D9911, on a "per tooth" basis. The objective is to apply a resin to the cervical and/or root surface to desensitize the tooth.

COMMENTS

1. Report application of desensitizing medicament (D9910) at checkups and *regularly* scheduled clinical visits when treating tooth sensitivity with a medicament. D9910 is reported on a "per visit" basis and may be applied to one tooth, some teeth or all of the teeth in the mouth.

2. D9910 may be used to report the application of a desensitizing medicament as an *adjunct* to prophylaxis or periodontal treatment. D9910 may be reported in conjunction with osseous surgery, SRP or at a periodontal maintenance (D4910) visit. D9910 is *not* generally reimbursed. The patient may be billed and is expected to pay out of pocket if the procedure is not reimbursed. An exception may apply for contracted PPO dentists who are prohibited from charging a separate fee for the application of a desensitizing medicament.

3. D9910 is not limited to fluoride, however fluoride is commonly used.

LIMITATIONS D9910 is excluded for reimbursement by most dental plans.

TIPS
1. Consider charging a lower fee for a desensitizing treatment (D9910) if reported in connection with a recall visit. A higher fee should be considered for desensitizing treatment provided at a *stand-alone* appointment (D9110), due to operatory setup time and performance of OSHA procedures.
2. Also refer to palliative (D9110)

NARRATIVES Although D9910 is not a "by report" code, a brief narrative citing the details of the patient's sensitivity is suggested.

ADDITIONAL INFORMATION How can different CDT codes be reported to describe essentially the same procedure? When reporting the application of fluoride varnish (e.g., Duraflor, Duraphat, CavityShield, etc.), the patient's diagnosis determines the code. Why was fluoride varnish used? Was it used to remineralize incipient carious lesions, or was it used to treat root sensitivity at a regularly scheduled or emergency visit?

1. D1206 is used to report the application of fluoride varnish to reduce caries risk (generally at recall) – child or adult.
2. D1208 is used to report the administration of topical fluoride preparations (other than varnish) to reduce caries risk – child or adult.
3. If fluoride varnish is used to treat tooth sensitivity, report D9910. D9910 (application of desensitizing medicament) is billed "per visit." The treatment could be done on one tooth or the whole mouth.

D9911 — APPLICATION OF DESENSITIZING RESIN FOR CERVICAL AND/OR ROOT SURFACE, PER TOOTH
CDT 2016

Typically reported on a "per tooth" basis for application of adhesive resins. This code is not to be used for bases, liners, or adhesives used under restorations.

CODING WATCH CORRECTION

1. It is an error to report D9911 for bases, liners, or adhesives when used under a restoration. The D9911 descriptor prohibits the reporting of the use of desensitizing resins for restorations. Restorative procedure codes *include* the use of all bases, liners, and adhesives with the procedure.
2. Do not report D9911 in conjunction with routine crown delivery to reduce subsequent sensitivity. The desensitizing resin under this scenario is considered *a part of* the crown procedure. In this case D9911 should not be reported *separately*.
3. If *caries* is involved and the preparation extends into the *dentin* (or fracture is involved), report an anterior or a posterior resin/composite direct restoration that includes any bases, liners, or adhesives placed. DO NOT report D9911 as a separate procedure.

COMMENTS D9911 is reported on a "per tooth" basis.

LIMITATIONS Application of desensitizing resin (D9911) is used to report the application of adhesive resins to desensitize the "cervical and/or root surface" of a tooth and is reported "per tooth." *D9911 may or may not be reimbursed*.

TIPS	1. Some payers will re-map D9911 as a resin-based composite – one surface, anterior (D2330), or to a resin-based composite – one surface, posterior (D2391). In some cases it is re-mapped to palliative, D9110. Report D9911 even though a payer may re-map this code to an alternative code. Always "report **what you do**." Let the payer remap to an alternative code according to the contract language.
	2. Also refer to palliative (D9110).

NARRATIVES	The key word is a desensitizing "resin." D9911 would be used for those patients presenting with root sensitivity. Narratives should emphasize the pain/sensitivity reported by the patient.

D9920 BEHAVIOR MANAGEMENT, BY REPORT CDT 2016

May be reported in addition to treatment provided. Should be reported in 15-minute increments.

COMMENTS	1. The use of a papoose board would be a form of behavior management. Other types of behavior management may also be reported with this code.
	2. D9920 treatment is billed separately. Additional treatment may include N_2O (D9230) and/or non-intravenous conscious sedation (D9248).
	3. D9920 can be reported when other procedures cannot. For example, the dentist spends a considerable amount of time trying to get the child to cooperate, however no procedure was able to be performed.

LIMITATIONS	Behavior management (D9920) is not typically reimbursed, except through certain government funded programs.

NARRATIVES	1. When reporting D9920, note the extra time taken to complete the procedure (in addition to the normal procedure time) and describe the need for behavior management. Outline the nature of the patient's behavior (young unruly child, etc.). Consult with the payer regarding the reporting of D9920. Determine the applicability of the service to the individual situation and the coverages available. Plan limitations are highly variable.
	2. In some cases, a narrative may yield a higher UCR fee for the procedure. Submit a narrative with the restorative procedure stating "extra time required for three surface MOD composite, #J. Please consider a higher UCR fee for the pediatric restorative procedure." Plan limitations are highly variable.

D9930 TREATMENT OF COMPLICATIONS (POST-SURGICAL) – UNUSUAL CIRCUMSTANCES, BY REPORT CDT 2016

For example, treatment of a dry socket following extraction or removal of bony sequestrum.

LIMITATIONS	1. Treatment of complications (post-surgical), D9930 may not be reimbursed when performed by the *same* office that provided the original surgical service. A thirty day follow up is typically considered *a part of the original* surgical service and not reimbursed separately by many payers. Most surgical codes indicate that "routine post-operative care" is included. Follow up and suture removal *would be considered* routine under this scenario. Treatment of a dry socket or removal of a bony sequestrum is considered by many payers as *routine* post-surgical care.
	2. If a *different* billing office treats a dry socket, removes a bony sequestrum, or controls bleeding, D9930 may be reimbursed under that scenario.

TIPS	A follow up visit could be reported as re-evaluation – post operative office visit (D0171).

NARRATIVES	1. Include a brief narrative that explains the circumstances of the office visit and who originally provided the surgical treatment. If the extraction was performed by a different provider, be sure to indicate that in the narrative.
	2. "See attached copy of operative notes."

D9931 ~~DELETED~~ CLEANING AND INSPECTION OF A REMOVABLE APPLIANCE — CDT 2016

This is a deleted code. See D9932, D9933, D9934, and D9935

D9932 **NEW PROCEDURE** CLEANING AND INSPECTION OF REMOVABLE COMPLETE DENTURE, MAXILLARY — CDT 2016

This procedure does not include any adjustments.

CODING WATCH CORRECTION — Adjustments of removable prosthesis done in *addition* to the cleaning and inspection of the prosthesis are reported as D5410 adjust complete denture – maxillary.

COMMENTS
1. D9932 is used to report the cleaning and inspection of a removable maxillary complete denture. Dentures that have accumulated calculus and other foreign materials require professional cleaning. For example, a patient presents with hardened calculus on his/her denture, which is removed by an ultrasonic cleaner and/or dental hand instrument.
2. Report each complete denture separately.

LIMITATIONS
1. Payers may require verification that an inspection is performed by a dentist (i.e., inspection by a dentist) rather than a dental team member who puts the appliance in an ultrasonic cleaner.
2. Document that the dentist inspected the appliance and recommended that D9932 be performed. The clinical notes should describe the inspection by the dentist and the cleaning.

D9933 **NEW PROCEDURE** CLEANING AND INSPECTION OF REMOVABLE COMPLETE DENTURE, MANDIBULAR — CDT 2016

This procedure does not include any adjustments.

CODING WATCH CORRECTION — Adjustments of removable prosthesis done in *addition* to the cleaning and inspection of the prosthesis are reported as D5411 adjust complete denture – mandibular.

COMMENTS
1. D9933 is used to report the cleaning and inspection of a removable mandibular complete denture. Dentures that have accumulated calculus and other foreign materials require professional cleaning. For example, a patient presents with hardened calculus on his/her denture, which is removed by an ultrasonic cleaner and/or dental hand instrument.
2. Report each complete denture separately.

LIMITATIONS
1. Payers may require verification that an inspection is performed by a dentist (i.e., inspection by a dentist) rather than a dental team member who puts the appliance in an ultrasonic cleaner.
2. Document that the dentist inspected the appliance and recommended that D9933 be performed. The clinical notes should describe the inspection by the dentist and the cleaning.

D9934 — NEW PROCEDURE CLEANING AND INSPECTION OF REMOVABLE PARTIAL DENTURE, MAXILLARY — CDT 2016

This procedure does not include any adjustments.

CODING WATCH CORRECTION

Adjustments of removable prosthesis done in *addition* to the cleaning and inspection of the prosthesis are reported as D5421 adjust partial denture – maxillary.

COMMENTS
1. D9934 is used to report the cleaning and inspection of a maxillary removable partial denture. Dentures that have accumulated calculus and other foreign materials require professional cleaning. For example, a patient presents with hardened calculus on his/her partial denture, which is removed by an ultrasonic cleaner and/or dental hand instrument.
2. Report each partial denture separately.

LIMITATIONS
1. Payers may require verification that an inspection is performed by a dentist (i.e., inspection by a dentist) rather than a dental team member who puts the appliance in an ultrasonic cleaner.
2. Document that the dentist inspected the appliance and recommended that D9934 be performed. The clinical notes should describe the inspection by the dentist and the cleaning.

D9935 — NEW PROCEDURE CLEANING AND INSPECTION OF REMOVABLE PARTIAL DENTURE, MANDIBULAR — CDT 2016

This procedure does not include any adjustments.

CODING WATCH CORRECTION

Adjustments of removable prosthesis done in *addition* to the cleaning and inspection of the prosthesis are reported as D5422 adjust partial denture – mandibular.

COMMENTS
1. D9935 is used to report the cleaning and inspection of a mandibular removable partial denture. Dentures that have accumulated calculus and other foreign materials require professional cleaning. For example, a patient presents with hardened calculus on his/her partial denture, which is removed by an ultrasonic cleaner and/or dental hand instrument.
2. Report each partial denture separately.

LIMITATIONS
1. Payers may require verification that an inspection is performed by a dentist (i.e., inspection by a dentist) rather than a dental team member who puts the appliance in an ultrasonic cleaner.
2. Document that the dentist inspected the appliance and recommended that D9935 be performed. The clinical notes should describe the inspection by the dentist and the cleaning performed.

D9940 — OCCLUSAL GUARD, BY REPORT — CDT 2016

Removable dental appliances, which are designed to minimize the effects of bruxism (grinding) and other occlusal factors.

CODING WARNING CORRECTION

It is misleading to report the delivery of an occlusal guard (D9940) to describe tooth whitening trays (D9975) or for TMJ treatment to increase reimbursement. Tooth whitening trays are provided for cosmetic purposes and are not a covered service. TMJ dysfunction treatment is typically not reimbursed unless there is a TMJ dysfunction rider attached to the dental insurance policy and it is reported as D7880.

CODING WATCH CORRECTION: The occlusal guard (D9940) and the occlusal orthotic device (D7880) are often confused. Report D9940 to describe an occlusal guard for minimizing the effects of "bruxism" and "clenching of teeth." Report D7880 to describe an appliance provided to treat TMJ dysfunction.

COMMENTS

1. Bruxism is the parafunctional or habitual "grinding" of teeth, often nocturnal.
2. There are three basic, broad types of bruxism appliances:
   a. Soft suck down appliance, typically fabricated in the dental office.
   b. Laboratory made hard acrylic appliance with or without soft liner.
   c. The NTI-tss, an anterior appliance, generally worn at night.

   The occlusal guard fee will typically vary from $250 to $595, depending on the type of appliance. Factors such as the laboratory bill, the clinical technique used, and the total number of visits for impressions, delivery and follow up may affect the fee charged. Occlusal guards may require two or more visits to deliver the appliance.
3. There is a code to report an adjustment of an occlusal guard. See D9943 to report an adjustment of an occlusal guard. Adjusting an occlusal guard is usually not reimbursed.

LIMITATIONS

1. If the occlusal guard (D9940), also known as a night guard, perio guard, or bite guard is reimbursed, it is generally reimbursed under dental, not medical insurance.
2. Reimbursement for an occlusal guard (D9940) may be subject to an age exclusion for children 12 years of age or younger.
3. Some payers only reimburse for bruxism; others require periodontal treatment (SRP or in some cases osseous surgery) to justify reimbursement.
4. Occlusal guards may be reimbursed under "preventive," "basic," or "major" classifications. Classification is highly variable. Waiting periods may apply for basic and major coverage.
5. After delivery of the occlusal appliance, six months of follow up care (including adjustments) is typically considered *integral* in the global occlusal guard fee. For an occlusal guard adjustment, see D9943.
6. Although the occlusal orthotic device, by report (D7880) is generally considered to be for TMJ dysfunction, few payers *will* reimburse the occlusal guard (for bruxism) as an alternate benefit of the TMJ dysfunction appliance code D7880.
7. Pretreatment authorization may be required.

Note: D9940 does *not* report a TMJ dysfunction appliance or active TMJ dysfunction treatment. TMJ dysfunction is *not* typically a covered dental benefit without a TMJ dysfunction rider; however, it may be reimbursed through medical insurance. TMJ dysfunction treatment (for pain, symptoms) involves a splint, multiple visits, and occlusal adjustments. The dental code for an appliance used to treat TMJ dysfunction is occlusal orthotic device (D7880). See D7880 for further details.

NARRATIVES

1. To determine if a splint or occlusal guard is covered by a patient's dental plan, one must determine the purpose of the appliance. Is it needed to minimize the effects of bruxism? Is periodontal mobility a part of the diagnosis, or is the patient experiencing headaches and pain in the temporomandibular joint area?
2. If there is a *history* of scaling and root planing (D4341/D4342) or periodontal osseous surgery (D4260/D4261), note this in the narrative when reporting an occlusal guard. The narrative might read "This patient has undergone periodontal therapy on (date), with description of the case type." Coverage for D9940 may vary based on whether the policy includes a supplemental "periodontal rider." The rider could make a difference in coverage if there is a supplemental "periodontal rider" on the contract. Even so, some payers make a distinction between case types and will only reimburse for the more serious osseous surgery. SRP (D4341/D4342) treatment may not suffice. Some plans require the occlusal guard be placed within six months of active periodontal treatment. If D9940 is reimbursed under a periodontal rider, the benefit may be available only once every five years or be limited to a lifetime maximum. The annual maximum will generally apply. Reimbursement is highly variable.

3. Include a narrative as indicated below:

   a. If the diagnosis is bruxism, state "Diagnosis = Bruxism." An occlusal guard is necessary to minimize the effects of bruxism and clenching of teeth."

   b. If the diagnosis is periodontitis, state case type, state periodontal treatment that has been performed, and include current periodontal chart. If treatment is provided for a patient with periodontal treatment, state: "This patient has undergone active periodontal therapy (or osseous surgery, for chronic periodontitis) on mm/dd/yy and is a case Type III. If an occlusal guard (D9940) is not available for reimbursement, please consider an alternate benefit, if available."

   c. Some plans require the occlusal guard be placed within six months of the active periodontal treatment (SRP or osseous surgery). If the occlusal guard is required to address periodontal mobility, include a periodontal diagnosis, current periodontal charting, and radiographs.

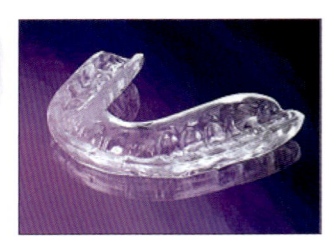

1. This is an example of a hard acrylic occlusal guard (D9940).
2. Occlusal guards can be fabricated as soft suck-down, hard acrylic or NTI-tss appliances. Go to the D7880 code to view a NTI-tss appliance. The NTI-tss can function as an occlusal guard and also be used in the treatment of TMJ.

Courtesy Drake Dental Lab

D9941 FABRICATION OF ATHLETIC MOUTHGUARD — CDT 2016

CODING WARNING CORRECTION

It is misleading to report diagnostic casts (D0470), fluoride gel carrier (D5986), occlusal orthotic device (TMJ dysfunction appliance) (D7880), or occlusal guard (D9940) solely to increase reimbursement for fabrication of athletic mouthguard (D9941).

LIMITATIONS
1. Fabrication of athletic mouthguard (D9941) is not generally reimbursed.
2. Always submit a claim for D9941. Some payers may reimburse this service.

D9942 REPAIR AND/OR RELINE OF OCCLUSAL GUARD — CDT 2016

CODING WATCH CORRECTION

It is inappropriate and misleading to report repair and/or reline of occlusal guard (D9942) for *adjusting* an occlusal guard. After delivery, six months of follow up adjustments are generally considered by payers to be a part of the *global fee* for the occlusal guard (D9940). See D9943, for an adjustment to an occlusal guard.

COMMENTS
1. Occlusal guards may break or no longer fit after long term use. They may be relined or repaired at less expense to the patient than a replacement. The occlusal guard that is repaired and/or relined is reported as D9942.
2. For *adjusting* an occlusal guard more than six months after delivery, see D9943.

LIMITATIONS
1. When benefits are available, the fee reimbursed for a repair or reline may be limited to less than 50% of a new occlusal guard fee. In some cases the reimbursement of the repair/reline may "reset" the five year limitation period.
2. In certain cases, the repair/reline may be reimbursed if the fabrication of the occlusal guard is reimbursed. Reimbursement for the repair and/or reline of an occlusal guard is highly variable among payers.

NARRATIVES Include the date of the original delivery of the occlusal guard and the reason for the repair and/or reline of the guard.

D9943 — NEW PROCEDURE OCCLUSAL GUARD ADJUSTMENT — CDT 2016

CODING WATCH CORRECTION D9943 does not report occlusal guard adjustments at the delivery. Adjustments made on the date of the delivery are included in the global fee for the occlusal guard.

COMMENTS After delivery, six months of follow up adjustments are generally considered to be part of the global fee for the occlusal guard (D9940).

LIMITATIONS This is a new code that will not be reimbursed by most plans.

NARRATIVES Document the original delivery date of the occlusal guard on the claim.

D9950 — OCCLUSION ANALYSIS – MOUNTED CASE — CDT 2016

Includes, but is not limited to, facebow, interocclusal records tracings, and diagnostic wax-up; for diagnostic casts, see D0470.

COMMENTS
1. D9950 is a mounted case and the diagnostic casts (D0470) would be reported separately.
2. D9950 includes a diagnostic wax-up.

LIMITATIONS Occlusion analysis – mounted case (D9950) is not generally reimbursed.

TIPS Some offices choose to credit the occlusal analysis – mounted case plus diagnostic cast fees by 50-100% toward the overall case fee, particularly if it's associated with a preliminary wax-up.

D9951 — OCCLUSAL ADJUSTMENT – LIMITED — CDT 2016

May also be known as equilibration; reshaping the occlusal surfaces of teeth to create harmonious contact relationships between the maxillary and mandibular teeth. Presently includes discing/odontoplasty/enamoplasty. Typically reported on a "per visit" basis. This should not be reported when the procedure only involves bite adjustment in the routine post-delivery care for a direct/indirect restoration or fixed/removable prosthodontics.

CODING WATCH CORRECTION D9951 "should not be reported when the procedure involves minor bite adjustments in the routine post-delivery care for a direct/indirect restoration or fixed/removable prosthodontics."

COMMENTS
1. If an occlusal adjustment is required within a short period of completion of a restorative procedure, it is considered a part of the restorative procedure and D9951 should not be reported.
2. Occlusal adjustment- limited (D9951) is typically reported on a "per visit" basis. This procedure is not generally reimbursed.
3. If the occlusal adjustment is deemed necessary at an emergency visit for the treatment of acute pain, see palliative (D9110). Provide an appropriate narrative to justify the submission of the D9110 code. See D9110 for details.
4. A fissurotomy is a mechanical component of a sealant placement. See sealant (D1351), which includes fissurotomy.
5. For removal of enamel projections or odontoplasty for 1-2 teeth, see D9971. This is not related to an occlusal adjustment for equilibration.

2. Many PPO contracts require reporting all procedures performed, even if it is a non-covered procedure. Contracted PPO offices may have tooth whitening procedure fees controlled when submitted. To not submit a procedure (if charged) is typically a violation of the PPO contract.

LIMITATIONS 1. Certain dental policies include a "periodontal rider," which may reimburse occlusal adjustments. The occlusal adjustment may be considered an "adjunct" to periodontal therapy (SRP) or osseous surgery. Occlusal adjustment may improve the prognosis of the periodontal treatment. However, a periodontal surgical case may be required for reimbursement.

CODING WATCH CORRECTION

1. D9972 External bleaching reports in office bleaching only, **per arch**.
2. For take home bleaching treatments e.g., (trays or strips), report D9975 **per arch**.

COMMENTS

1. D9972 is used to describe external bleaching performed in office only.
2. Diagnostic casts D0470 are considered integral to the in office tooth whitening service code, D9972 and should not be reported separately.
3. D9972 is reported on a per arch basis. If treating the whole mouth, cut in half the total whitening fee and report it for each arch reporting D9972. Correctly reporting external bleaching per arch (at one-half fee per arch) may limit a PPO's fee controls for non-covered procedures.

LIMITATIONS As a general rule, tooth whitening (bleaching) is not reimbursed. Some payers may offer "cosmetic riders," which cover the bleaching of severe tetracycline staining or severe fluorosis of anterior permanent teeth. The benefit, if available, may be subject to frequency or lifetime maximums.

TIPS

1. For in office "power bleaching" D9972, consider a total fee of $395 to $695. In office bleaching D9972 is generally $200 to $300 greater than the fee for home application bleaching tray systems (D9975). The bleaching fee for most offices typically *includes* the at home trays to enhance whitening effects, or for "touch up," after the in office bleaching has been performed. Split the total fee in *half* and report the upper and lower arch separately as D9972.

2. Consider this type of pricing:

    (D9972A) Bleaching – Whitening (upper arch) – $195 and up.

    (D9972B) Bleaching – Whitening (lower arch) – $195 and up.

    Compare fees in your local area and consider the cost of the time and materials required to perform this procedure in your office before establishing your office fee.

D9973 EXTERNAL BLEACHING – PER TOOTH — CDT 2016

CODING WARNING CORRECTION

1. It is misleading to report diagnostic casts (D0470), fluoride gel carrier (D5986), occlusal orthotic device (TMJ dysfunction treatment appliance) (D7880), or occlusal guard (D9940) when providing external bleaching for tooth whitening in the dental office to increase reimbursement.
2. Many PPO contracts require reporting all procedures performed, even if it is a non-covered procedure. Contracted PPO offices may have tooth whitening procedure fees controlled when submitted. To not submit a procedure (if charged) is typically a violation of the PPO contract.

COMMENTS

1. D9973 is used to describe external bleaching on a per tooth basis and is performed in the office.
2. Diagnostic casts D0470 are considered a part of the tooth whitening service code, D9973, and should not be reported separately.
3. See D9972 for external bleaching-per arch in office. See D9975 for take home bleaching trays and strips. See D9974 for internal bleaching-per tooth (bleaching an endodontically treated tooth).

LIMITATIONS As a general rule, tooth whitening (bleaching) is not reimbursed. Some payers may offer "cosmetic riders," which cover the bleaching of severe tetracycline staining or severe fluorosis of anterior permanent teeth. The benefit, if available, may be subject to frequency or lifetime maximums.

D9974 INTERNAL BLEACHING – PER TOOTH — CDT 2016

CODING WARNING CORRECTION

For endodontic access closure after internal bleaching of a natural tooth, it is improper to report a core buildup (D2950). A core buildup is specifically for securing the *retention of a crown* on a fully prepared tooth. See D2950 for specific reporting requirements of a core buildup.

CODING WATCH CORRECTION

1. It is an error to report D3960 to describe internal bleaching of an endodontically treated tooth. D3960 is a previously deleted code. Report the current code, internal bleaching – per tooth (D9974).
2. It is an error to report *external* bleaching (D9972, D9973 or D9975) as internal bleaching of an endodontically treated tooth.

COMMENTS

1. Internal bleaching – per tooth (D9974) is used to describe the internal bleaching (whitening) of an endodontically treated tooth that is not crowned. D9974 reports a series of treatment visits to bleach a tooth from the inside. Two or more treatment visits may be required to complete the bleaching process.
2. D9974 *does not* include the closure of the endodontic access opening. Reporting a single surface anterior (D2330) or posterior resin composite (D2391) would be appropriate for reporting the endodontic access closure performed on a *natural* tooth, after the internal bleaching treatment is completed. D9974 is generally performed on anterior teeth.

LIMITATIONS

If reimbursement is available, it may be subject to a three year or five year limitation. Generally internal bleaching (D9974) is a patient expense.

TIPS

One approach would be to quote a flat fee for two or three internal bleaching visits. Any additional visits would be quoted as $X per visit extra.

NARRATIVES

D9974 may occasionally be reimbursed. Submit a photograph and a brief narrative describing the initial endodontic treatment date, with a before and final diagnostic image demonstrating the completed internal bleaching procedure.

D9975 EXTERNAL BLEACHING FOR HOME APPLICATION – PER ARCH; INCLUDES MATERIALS AND FABRICATING OF CUSTOM TRAYS — CDT 2016

CODING WARNING CORRECTION

1. It is misleading to report diagnostic casts (D0470), fluoride gel carrier (D5986), occlusal orthotic device (TMJ dysfunctional treatment appliance) (D7880), or occlusal guard (D9940) when providing external bleaching for tooth whitening, to increase reimbursement.
2. Many PPO contracts require reporting all procedures performed, even if it is a non-covered procedure. Contracted PPO offices may have tooth whitening procedure fees controlled when submitted. To not submit a procedure (if charged) is typically a violation of the PPO contract.

CODING WATCH CORRECTION

For in office bleaching report D9972, per arch.

COMMENTS

1. D9975, external bleaching reports home bleaching only. The home bleaching application can be accomplished using custom trays or strips.
2. Diagnostic casts D0470 are considered inclusive of the home application tooth whitening service code, D9975, and should not be reported separately.

3. D9975 is reported on a per arch basis. If treating the whole mouth, report each upper and lower arch separately, at one-half of the full fee. Reporting external bleaching-per arch (at one-half of the full fee per arch) may be important, if an insured plan that is written in a state without non-covered legislation or if the plan is self-funded under ERISA then this could be beneficial by improving the allowable fee in some cases. D9974 is generally performed on anterior teeth.

LIMITATIONS As a general rule, tooth whitening (bleaching) is not reimbursed. Some payers may offer "cosmetic riders," which cover the bleaching of severe tetracycline staining or severe fluorosis of anterior permanent teeth. The benefit, if available, may be subject to frequency or lifetime maximums.

TIPS
1. $99 "tooth whitening for life" has gained some popularity as a marketing tool. This is a program that includes free bleaching refills as an incentive if the patient keeps recall appointments.

2. Consider this type of pricing:

   (D9975A) Home Application Whitening, first arch – upper – $100 or higher.

   (D9975B) Home Application Whitening, second arch – lower – $100 or higher.

   (D9975C) Whitening Strips (Crest White Strips®/Ultradent's Tres White®) – $65 to $95 or higher.

   Compare fees in your local area and consider the cost of the time and materials required to perform this procedure before establishing your fee.

NON-CLINICAL PROCEDURES   CDT 2016

D9985   SALES TAX   CDT 2016

CODING CORRECTION WARNING

Sales and use tax is NOT a Medical Device Tax. A medical device tax is a federal tax. Only sales tax should be reported with D9985.

COMMENTS
1. The lack of a sales/service tax CDT code creates significant processing and financial balancing issues with amounts submitted in the "Other Fees" box on the ADA Claim Form. With the eventual conversion to the HIPAA standard electronic claim form in the future, it is essential that this be made easier. Creating a code for Sales Tax (D9985) will alleviate some of these reporting problems.

2. Sales tax is reported with Sales Tax (D9985) and describes the application of sales tax to dental services and/or products provided to the patient. The sales tax amount, if any, is directed by local and state law.

3. The majority of states have a sales and use tax on products separately sold by dentists, but only a few states have a tax on dental services. For instance, a toothbrush included in a prophylaxis appointment would be included in the dental service fee, and would be exempt from product sales tax, as it is not separately stated in most states. But, if the patient wanted to buy extra toothbrushes for the family, there would be sales tax on the tooth brush purchase. There are at least three states that have a sales tax on dental services, and several others are considering legislation. Sometimes, just cosmetic procedures are taxed such as cosmetic dentistry and tooth whitening trays. Without this sales tax code, it may appear a provider's charges for certain procedures are higher than intended and thus artificially inflate fee rates and potential tax liability.

4. A sales/service/product tax code is necessary to properly record transactions in the patient record and invoicing. Consult your CPA as to the specifics of your state.

LIMITATIONS Sales Tax (D9985) is not reimbursed by dental payers and must be paid by the patient (or the practice can pay the sales tax).

D9986 MISSED APPOINTMENT — CDT 2016

COMMENTS

1. Centers for Medicare and Medicaid Services (CMS) asserts that it is illegal to charge (by statute) for missed appointments (and those cancelled without sufficient notice), but dentists could benefit from having a way to electronically document (and track) patient missed appointments. According to the National Association of Dental Plans' CDT Workgroup, a missed appointment code is needed for compliance with certain state and federally funded programs and to allow the electronic health record to accurately reflect patient behavior related to dental care.

2. It is common knowledge that a patient who does not arrive for scheduled care adds to the cost of dental care because both administrative staff and clinical staff must prepare for the delivery of the patient's scheduled services and the loss of productive time. Patients who miss their appointments undermine both the efficiency and productivity of the entire dental practice.

3. Until now, there has been no specific CDT code for reporting a missed appointment, whether a provider intends to charge a fee or not.

4. D9986 allows a provider to document and more easily track his/her inability to provide services when a patient fails to attend a scheduled appointment.

LIMITATIONS

1. There will be no reimbursement by payers for a missed appointment.

2. For private pay patients, with a prior written agreement, missed appointments and those cancelled (without sufficient notice) might be charged.

3. For patients of government programs, it is illegal to charge for a missed appointment according to Centers for Medicare and Medicaid Services (CMS).

ADDITIONAL INFORMATION A typical coding scenario involves a patient who does not show up for a scheduled appointment to be treated by the dentist, hygienist, or other professional. There is no record of the patient's intent to cancel or reschedule the appointment. The unanticipated void in the schedule disrupts the practice workflow and requires adjustment to the schedule for delivery of services to other patients who arrive on time. D9986 describes this missed appointment.

D9987 CANCELLED APPOINTMENT — CDT 2016

COMMENTS

1. D9987 may be used to document a patient who cancels a previously scheduled appointment without adequate notice (creating an unanticipated void in the provider's schedule), to track a patient who cancels an appointment without rescheduling, or to simply document in the patient's electronic record that he/she cancelled an appointment.

2. Tracking cancelled appointments is important to document continuity of care in the patient's electronic health record. The addition of administrative code D9987 will be particularly helpful for identifying and tracking patients who frequently cancel appointments.

3. Although traditional dental plans do not provide a benefit for broken appointments or cancellations without adequate notice, having the ability to codify/document a broken, cancelled, or late appointment on a patient's billing statement may improve compliance, even when no fee is assessed.

4. This may also help providers track patients who have not yet rescheduled their appointment following a cancellation.

LIMITATIONS

1. There will be no reimbursement by payers for a cancelled appointment.

2. For private pay patients, with a prior written agreement, a cancelled appointment (without sufficient notice) might incur a fee.

3. For patients of government programs, it is illegal to charge for a cancelled appointment according to the Centers for Medicare and Medicaid Services (CMS).

ADDITIONAL INFORMATION It was the National Association of Dental Plans' CDT Workgroup that requested this new administrative based code stating that it is needed for compliance with certain state and federally funded programs and to allow for the electronic health record to accurately reflect patient behavior related to dental care. Having a code would allow a provider to document that s/he was unable to provide services because the patient cancelled his/her scheduled appointment.

D9999	UNSPECIFIED ADJUNCTIVE PROCEDURE, BY REPORT	CDT 2016

Used for procedure that is not adequately described by a code. Describe procedure.

COMMENTS
1. D9999 reports a procedure not adequately described by an existing code in any other category.
2. Unspecified adjunctive procedure, by report (D9999) may be used to describe the following procedures. The list is not exhaustive and D9999 may be used to report any type of unspecified adjunctive procedure, by report.

    a. For reporting Oraqix®, consider D9999. Having a needle free option for anesthesia removes a major obstacle to initial periodontal therapy for patients fearful of injections. Oraqix®, an FDA approved local anesthetic gel, was developed for adults requiring local anesthesia during scaling and root planing. Hygienists love its quick 30 second onset, and patients like the fact that they are only numb for 20 minutes instead of two to three hours following treatment. Since Oraqix® anesthetizes only the nerves in the gingival margin and periodontal pockets where it is applied, dentists have also found it useful for other procedures such as gingivectomies, packing cord, etc.

    Oraqix® is more expensive than conventional anesthesia. Based on the current descriptor, D9215 can be used to report Oraqix®. D9215 does not indicate that local anesthesia must be injected. However, only a few dental plans pay for local anesthesia separately. Most include anesthesia in their allowable fee for root planing and scaling. Unfortunately, most PPO contracts often instruct contracted providers to write off the additional costs. To avoid this, consider billing D9999 with a brief note: "Patient requested needle free Oraqix®." While it is not likely to be paid by the dental plan, some plans consider Oraqix® an optional service and this will allow contracted providers to charge their patients. Be sure the patient agrees to the charge in writing.

    b. Report D9999 to describe the in office treatment using MI Paste® or MI Paste Plus® to treat white spots after orthodontic treatment. This is typically not reimbursed. This treatment may involve multiple visits and some practices may charge one fee ($150 – $200) for up to x number of visits.

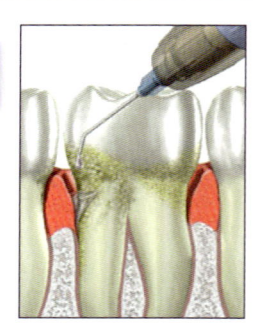

Oraqix® is applied to the gingiva to relieve the discomfort of SRP.

Courtesy DENTSPLY Pharmaceutical

GLOSSARY

A

AAE – American Academy of Endodontics.

AAO – American Academy of Orthodontics.

AAOMS – American Association of Oral Maxillofacial Surgeons.

AAP – American Academy of Periodontology.

AAPD – American Academy of Pediatric Dentistry.

Abutment – An abutment supports a prosthesis; a component of an implant system that is used to affix the crown to the implant.

Adjudication – Refers to the processing of a claim.

Adjunct/Adjunctive – Describes a treatment that is performed following the primary treatment.

Allowable Charge – The maximum amount of benefit allowed for a dental procedure per the indemnity or the PPO plan contract.

Alternate Benefit – A provision of a dental plan allowing the payer to provide a less expensive benefit, or an alternate benefit for a non-covered procedure, such as molar composite restorations. An alternate benefit of an amalgam may be applied for a composite restoration performed on a molar.

Auto Adjudication – The payer automatically processes the claim without review.

B

By Report – A brief narrative describing the dental procedure performed, required when reporting certain procedures.

C

CAL – Clinical Attachment Loss – involves the loss of alveolar bone support and gingival attachment as the periodontal fibers migrate apically from the CEJ due to periodontal toxins in plaque.

CBCT – Cone Beam CT imaging technology (3D radiographic image).

CEJ – Cementoenamel junction – the area of the tooth where the enamel covering the crown of the tooth and the cementum that covers the root of the tooth meet.

Claim – A written request to an insurance plan for benefit payment. A claim form may be submitted by the patient or the provider to the payer.

Claim Form – The paper form or electronic format used to submit the claim. These forms are specific to dental and medical claims and the appropriate form must be used. The 2012 ADA Dental Claim Form is the current claim form version.

Clinical – Refers to direct patient care (i.e., the diagnosis and treatment of the patient).

Connective Tissue Grafts (CT) – Donor tissue is taken usually from the patient and is placed in the area of gingival recession to obtain root coverage. Sometimes the tissue is from a donor other than the patient. Materials such as Allograft® may be used.

Current Dental Terminology (CDT) – A code set defined by the American Dental Association that the dentist is required to report for services rendered, as outlined in the summary plan description and the plan document.

D

Debridement – The gross removal of supra and subgingival calculus.

Dental Benefits Consultant – The dentist who reviews dental claims for insurance companies in order to determine benefits per the established criteria of the dental plan document.

Diastema – A space between two adjacent teeth, usually a large space between anterior teeth.

Digital Imaging and Communication in Medicine (DICOM-) – refers to the set of rules followed when exchanging a digital image to other providers.

Discing Teeth – A term used to describe an orthodontic procedure where a disc is used to remove a small amount of enamel from primary teeth to create adequate space for the eruption of the permanent teeth. Discing is also performed to make space for orthodontic aligners for permanent tooth movement.

Downcoding – The practice by payers to change a procedure from the one reported for benefit determination only. Typically, this results in a less expensive benefit allowed for, than the actual procedure performed, as stated in the plan document.

E

ECC – Early Childhood Caries.

EOB – Explanation of benefits – explains the plan's benefit and how it is calculated.

Epulis – An oral tumor typically benign often caused by ill-fitting dentures.

Exposed Roots – The crown of the tooth is missing and the exposed root is above or at the gum line.

F

Fixed Partial Denture (FPD) (also known as a bridge) – May consist of retainer crowns and a pontic(s) to replace a missing tooth and is permanently affixed to the teeth on either side of the missing tooth, usually with the retainer affixed with a dental cement or bonding material. The FPD may be supported by natural teeth or implants.

Flipper – Common term used to describe an interim removable partial denture. It is used typically for a short time period such as during the healing phase after implant placement.

Fraud – A benefit received when a false claim, inflated claim or billing of services not actually performed has taken place (determined by a court of law).

Furcation – The area of a multi rooted tooth where the roots separate from one another.

G

General Practitioner (GP) – General dentist.

Gingivectomy – The surgical removal of gingiva (soft tissue) from around a fully erupted tooth.

Gingivoplasty – A surgical procedure that reshapes the gingiva (soft tissue) around a tooth.

Global Fee – The fee for a procedure that includes all necessary procedures prior to, during, and following the procedure (e.g., bases, liners, and etching are considered part of the global fee for an operative procedure).

Guided Tissue Regeneration (GTR) – Also known as a barrier membrane – placed under the tissue and over the bone to aid in the regeneration of new bone.

H

Hugger Bridge – Consists of two resin retainer "wings" and one pontic (Maryland Bridge).

I

Iatrogenic – Trauma or condition created by the dentist's treatment.

Incision and Drainage (I&D) – The surgical incision in order to drain an area of infection.

Indirect Restoration – A restoration fabricated outside of the mouth, i.e., a lab fabricated or CAD/CAM made crown or onlay.

Interim – Short-term use – typically refers to a denture or other appliance used during the healing phase of treatment or to allow further needed treatment to be completed.

IRM – Intermediate Restorative Material – A medicative material typically used after removing extensive decay and remains until the patient returns for a definitive treatment.

ITR – Interim Therapeutic Restoration – A medicative restoration placed until a definitive restorative can be placed. This procedure is typically performed on primary teeth with decay and may last the lifetime of the primary tooth.

L

LDA/LDAA – Local Delivery Antimicrobial Agents – such as Atridox®, Arestin®, PerioChip®, etc.

Least Expensive Alternative Treatment (LEAT) – A clause within a dental plan that allows the payer to pay a benefit for the least expensive treatment option when multiple options of treatment are available (e.g., benefits of a removable partial denture in lieu of a benefit for implants or fixed partial dentures when multiple teeth are missing throughout the arch being restored).

M

Mandible – The lower jaw.

Maryland Bridge – Refers to a resin bonded bridge fabricated to replace a missing tooth and consists of two retainer wings bonded to the lingual of the teeth adjacent to the missing tooth and attached to the pontic replacing the missing tooth. This bridge is named for the University of Maryland, where it was developed.

Maxilla – The upper jaw.

Maximum Plan Allowance (MPA) – A benefit allowance for a procedure.

Mineral Trioxide Aggregate (MTA) – Describes a filling material that creates a plug for the apex of a tooth as part of repairing a perforated root, treatment for apexogenesis, or is used to treat internal root resorption.

MRI – Magnetic Resonance Imaging – A technique used in dentistry for the purpose of diagnosing and evaluating soft tissue.

Multi-Slice Computer Tomography (MSCT) – A scan that captures an image of a specific part of the body.

N

Narrative – A written report describing the dental procedure performed with the goal of proving medical/dental necessity.

O

Occlusal – The biting surface of posterior teeth, i.e., premolars and molars.

Occlusal Guard – A removable appliance placed to protect against bruxism, and clinching or grinding of teeth.

Occupational Health and Safety Administration (OSHA) – A set of federal laws and regulations enforced by OSHA to ensure safety and health in the workplace.

P

Payer (carrier) – A third party company who administers plan benefits.

Porcelain Fused to Metal (PFM) – A crown fabricated with porcelain fused to a metal coping (various metals) resulting in a tooth colored restoration.

PPO – Preferred Provider Organization – A plan that allows the patient to seek treatment from the dentist of his/her choice. If the chosen provider participates with the patient's PPO network then the patient's out-of-pocket expense is less. The participating provider agrees to only charge the patient the lowest contracted amount.

PRP – Platelet Rich Plasma – The process of spinning the patient's blood and using the growth factors when performing bone graft procedures in order to boost bone growth.

PRR – Preventive Resin Restoration – Restoration of an active carious lesion in a pit and fissure (enamel) where the preparation does not extend into the dentin.

Pulp – Blood vessels and tissue inside the pulp cavity of a tooth.

R

Re-mapping or Downcoding – A practice by payers whereby the benefit has been provided for a less expensive alternate treatment (LEAT).

Residual Tooth Roots – Root tips remaining after the extraction or loss of the crown of a tooth. A surgical procedure is required to remove residual tooth roots.

Rider – An amendment within a dental plan that can add or delete benefits and/or limitations of the plan (e.g., implant rider).

Root Canal Therapy (RCT) – Treatment that consists of removing the damaged or diseased pulp from the root of the tooth, obturating the canals, and sealing the canals with a non-resorbable material.

S

Scaling and Root Planing (SRP) – Treatment procedure for periodontal disease. The removal of plaque and calculus from around the teeth and the root surfaces where pocketing has occurred due to the loss of bone. It also involves the smoothing of the root.

Snap-on-Smile – A custom-made set of teeth that fit over the existing teeth of the arch. It is made of a thin material and looks like natural teeth. In addition to using this appliance as a cosmetic appliance, it can be used to stabilize mobile teeth, act as an interim partial, or as a retainer after the completion of active orthodontics such as to maintain space until an implant can be placed.

Stainless Steel Crown (SSC) – A type of crown fabricated using nickel chrome commonly used as a restoration for primary teeth with a large amount of decay and not enough tooth structure for a conventional (filling) restoration. An SSC can also be used for permanent tooth restorations in some situations.

Stayplate – Sometimes, referred to as a "flipper" – A temporary appliance that replaces a missing tooth or multiple missing teeth and functions until a definitive procedure can be performed. Typically fabricated out of acrylic and may not have clasps.

Surgical Splint – A splint which assists in the stabilization and immobilization of broken bones during healing.

Surgical Stent – A custom made clear mold of the arch that has been modified to be used as a guide for the dentist to know where to adjust bone after extractions.

T

Take Back Code – Used to describe when a payer reduces the benefit of a definitive procedure after paying a benefit for another procedure previously done at a different date of service. This is usually when both procedures are performed by the same billing office.

Temporomandibular Disorder (TMD) – A disorder of the joint often caused by bruxism, clenching and grinding of the teeth.

Temporomandibular Joint (TMJ) – The hinge part of the jawbone which connects the jaw to the skull.

Third-Party – Also known as the payer, carrier, or the insurer. The third party is responsible for the collection of premium payments, determines benefits and processes the benefit payments for claims. For insured plans, the third party assumes financial risks and for self-funded plans the third party only performs administration services on behalf of the self-funded plan, and provides a provider network.

TMJ Dysfunction – A syndrome affecting the joint most often caused by bruxism, clenching and grinding of the teeth.

Torus/Tori – Protrusion of bone.

U

Upcoding – The reporting of a more complex procedure than actually performed with a higher fee (i.e., a surgical extraction).

Usual, Customary, and Reasonable (UCR) Fees – A method used by payers to set average fees based upon the fee submission of dentists in a defined zip code area.

INDEX

A	Code	Page
Abscess, incision and drainage, all types	D7510-D7521	320-321
Abutments		
Custom abutment (implant) – includes placement	D6057	242
Interim abutment (implant) – includes placement	D6051 (includes removal)	243
Locator abutment (implants)	D5862	217
Place abutment (previously deleted)	D6020 (previously deleted)	237
Prefabricated abutment (implant) – includes placement	D6056	241
Semi-precision attachment abutment	D6052	244
Retainer crown (bridgework)	D6710-D6794	284-293
Retainer crown for resin bonded "Maryland Bridge"	D6545/D6548/D6549	271/272/273
Retainer crown (implant/abutment supported bridgework)	D6068-D6074; D6194	255-258;259
Accession of tissue	D0472-D0485; D0486	47-49;48
Access closure (after endodontic treatment) – (Do not report crown repair)		
Direct restoration (endodontic access closure)	D2140/D2330/D2391	65/68/73
Accident		
Avulsed tooth	D7270/D7670	304/324
Displaced tooth	D7270/D7670	304/324
Evulsed tooth	D7270/D7670	304/324
Palliative (emergency) treatment (minor procedure)	D9110	354
Problem focused evaluation (exam)	D0140	9
Re-evaluation (follow up) limited evaluation	D0170 (should follow D0120/D0140/D0150/D0180)	15
Suture lip/other (small wound)	D7910-D7912	330
Acid etch, integral to direct resin procedure	No separate code – integral to procedure	
Acrylic hard splint		
Occlusal or perio guard (bruxism)	D9940	372
Occlusal orthotic device (TMJ dysfunction/TMD)	D7880	328
Acrylic (resin) partial (immediate)	D5221/D5222	193/194
Acrylic (resin) partial (long-lasting, not temporary)	D5211/D5212	189/190
Acrylic (resin) partial (temporary flipper)	D5820/D5821	215
Acute pain relief		
Palliative (emergency) treatment (minor procedure)	D9110	354
Problem focused (emergency) evaluation (exam)	D0140	9
Pulpal debridement (open prior to endodontic treatment visit)	D3221	118
Pulpotomy (primary tooth generally)	D3220	117
Sedative filling now termed "protective restoration"	D2940	102
Adhesives, bonding agents (resin and amalgam)	No separate code – integral to procedure	
Adjunctive general services (category of service)	D9000-D9999	354-382
Adjunctive pre-diagnostic test (cancer screening) ViziLite®/VELscope™/ Microlux DL, Identafi® 3000/ OralID®	D0431	43

Adjustments

Complete occlusal adjustment (includes multiple visits)	D9952	376
Denture (complete) adjustment	D5410/D5411	199/200
Emergency visit (isolated occlusal adjustment, one or several teeth)	D9110	354
Limited occlusal adjustment (includes discing/enamoplasty)	D9951	375
Maxillofacial prosthetic appliance adjustment	D5992	228
Occlusal guard adjustment	D9943	375
Occlusal orthotic device (TMJ) adjustment	D7881	329
Partial denture adjustment	D5421/D5422	200
Removable orthodontic retainer adjustment	D8681	350

Adult services (common names)

"Difficult" prophylaxis (higher fee)	D1110	51
Periodontal (recall) maintenance	D4910	179
Periodontal prophylaxis (recall maintenance)	D4910	179
Prophylaxis (adult)	D1110	51

Agents, chemotherapeutic	See Index, "Chemotherapeutic agents"	
Allograft, soft tissue	D4275/D7955	163/335
Alveolar segment fracture (accident)	D7670/D7671	324

Alveoloplasty (preparation for prosthesis)

In conjunction with extractions	D7310/D7311	311/312
Not in conjunction with extractions	D7320/D7321	313

Alveolus, fracture	D7670/D7671	324
Amalgam and resin bonding agents	No separate code – integral to procedure	
Amalgam restorations	D2140-D2161	65-68
Ambulatory surgical center call or hospital call	D9420	364

Analgesia

I.V. conscious sedation/analgesia	D9243	361
Nitrous oxide (N_2O)/anxiolysis, analgesia	D9230	360
Non-intravenous conscious sedation analgesia	D9248	362

Anchorage device (temporary skeletal) (TAD) – orthodontic anchorage procedure

Anchorage device requiring surgical flap	D7293	310
Anchorage device with no flap required	D7294	310
Screw retained plate requiring flap	D7292	310

Anesthesia

Evaluation for deep sedation or general anesthesia	D9219	358
General anesthesia/deep sedation	D9223	359
I.V conscious sedation/analgesia	D9243	361
Local anesthesia in conjunction with operative or surgical procedures	D9215	358
Local anesthesia not with operative/surgical procedure	D9210	357
Regional block anesthesia	D9211	358
Trigeminal division block anesthesia	D9212	358

Ankyloglossia (tongue-tie)	See Index, "Frenulectomy"	

Antimicrobial agent

Arestin® (antimicrobial agent)	D4381	177
Atridox® (antimicrobial agent)	D4381	177
PerioChip® (antimicrobial agent)	D4381	177

Apexification/recalcification (not pulpal regeneration)	D3351-D3353	128-129
Apexogenesis (partial pulpotomy to form root)	D3222	119
Apically positioned flap	D4245	151
Apicoectomy/periradicular surgery services	D3410-D3432	133-139

Appliance adjustment

Maxillofacial prosthetic	D5992	228
Orthodontic retainer adjustment (removable)	D8681	350

Application

Desensitizing medicament (one tooth or mouth)	D9910	368
Desensitizing resin (root) report per tooth	D9911	369
Interim caries arresting medicament application	D1354	59
Topical fluoride application (not fluoride varnish)	D1208	55
Topical fluoride varnish application	D1206	55

Appointment

Cancelled appointment	D9987	381
Missed appointment	D9986	381

Arestin® (antimicrobial agent)	D4381	177
Arthrocentesis	D7870	327
Arthroplasty	D7865	326
Arthroscopy	D7872-D7877	327
Arthrotomy	D7860	326
Assessment of a Patient (pre-diagnostic service)	D0191	19
Athletic mouthguard	D9941	374
Atridox® (antimicrobial agent)	D4381	177

Attachments

Fixed bridgework related attachment (precision)	D6950	294
Locator implant attachment (mini implant)	D5862	217
Locator root attachment for natural tooth overdenture	D5862	217
Orthodontic attachment (place button/pin/bracket)	D7283	306
Precision attachment (removable/fixed partial denture)	D5862/D6950	217/294
Semi precision attachment abutment (full size implant)	D6052	244

Augmentation (see also Graft procedures)

Bone graft at time of implant placement	D6104	240
Bone socket graft for ridge preservation	D7953	334
Ridge augmentation (graft in edentulous area)	D7950	332
Sinus augmentation via a lateral (window) approach	D7951	333
Sinus augmentation via a vertical approach	D7952	333

Author's services		439

Autogenous procedures

Autogenous connective tissue graft procedure (including donor and recipient surgical sites)	D4283	166
Collection and application of autologous blood concentrate product – platelet rich plasma (PRP)	D7921	330
Harvest of bone for use in autogenous grafting procedure	D7295	311
Avulsed or displaced tooth (emergency visit) – per tooth	D7270	304

B	**Code**	**Page**
Bacteriologic studies	D0415	40
Band and loop (space maintainer – unilateral)	D1510	59
Barrier membranes		
Guided Tissue Regeneration (GTR) resorbable	D4266 (perio/implant)	158
Guided Tissue Regeneration (GTR) non-resorbable	D4267 (perio/implant)	158
Guided Tissue Regeneration (GTR) resorbable	D3432 (endo)	139
Base (integral to direct restorative procedure)	No separate code	
Base (restorative foundation for indirect restoration)	D2949	103
Behavior management (extra time/management)	D9920	370
Benign lesion (various)	D7410-D7412/D7450-D7461	314-315/317-318
BioLase® soft tissue laser	D7465 (also see "Laser Comments")	318
Biologic materials (periodontal or implant)	D4265	157
Biologic materials (periradicular surgery)	D3431	138
Biopsy (excise specimen of lesion) – not a microscopic exam		
Brush biopsy – OralCDx®	D7288	308
Excisional – hard tissue biopsy	D7285	307
Excisional – soft tissue biopsy	D7286	307
Exfoliative cytological sample biopsy	D7287	308
OralCDx® brush biopsy	D7288	308
Bitewing radiographic images		
Four bitewing images (horizontal or vertical)	D0274	27
Seven to eight vertical bitewing images (vertical only)	D0277	28
Single bitewing images (horizontal or vertical)	D0270	24
Three bitewing images (horizontal or vertical)	D0273	26
Two bitewing images (horizontal or vertical)	D0272	24
Bleaching (whitening)		
External – per arch (bleaching performed in office)	D9972	377
External – per tooth whitening (bleaching performed in office)	D9973	378
Internal – per tooth whitening (endodontic non-vital tooth)	D9974	379
External bleaching for home application (trays/strips)	D9975	379
Blood Products – platelet rich plasma (PRP)		
Collection and application of autologous blood concentrate product (PRP) – platelet rich plasma	D7921	330
Bonding agents (adhesives integral to resin and amalgam procedure)	No separate procedure code	
Bone, augmentation		
Bone graft in conjunction with periradicular surgery	D3428 (single site)	136

Bone graft in conjunction with periradicular surgery	D3429 (each additional contiguous tooth)	137
Bone socket graft for ridge preservation (implant)	D7953	334
Collection and application of autologous blood concentrate product (PRP) – platelet rich plasma	D7921	330
Periodontal (bone) graft (with osseous surgery)	D4263/D4264 (not associated with implants)	155/156
Ridge augmentation (graft) – edentulous area	D7950	332
Sinus (lift) augmentation via a lateral (window) approach	D7951	333
Sinus augmentation (lift) via a vertical approach	D7952	333

Bone fragment (post-surgical removal of bony sequestrum) — D9930 — 370

Bone graft

Bone graft in conjunction with periradicular surgery	D3428 (per tooth, single site)	136
Bone graft in conjunction with periradicular surgery	D3429 (additional contiguous tooth in same site)	137
Bone graft inserted at same time as implant placement	D6104	240
Extraction site "bone socket graft" (ridge preservation)	D7953	334
Peri-implant defect bone graft (at debridement/osseous contouring visit)	D6103 (in conjunction with D6102)	240
Periodontally-related bone graft with osseous surgery	D4263/D4264	155/156
Ridge augmentation (graft) – edentulous area (onlay graft)	D7950	332
Sinus augmentation (lift) via a lateral (window) approach	D7951	333
Sinus augmentation (lift) via a vertical approach (punch method)	D7952	333

Bone, harvest of (from body) — D7295 — 311

Bone, smoothing — See Index, "Extraction or alveoloplasty"

Bone tissue, excision — D7471-D7490 — 319-320

Bridge procedure — Also see Index, "Fixed partial dentures"

Bridge pontics (report same code for natural tooth or implant bridge pontic)	D6205-D6254	267-271
Bridge re-cementation	D6930	293
Bridge removal (complete removal)	D6999 (unspecified procedure, by report)	296
Bridge repair (necessitated by restorative material failure)	D6980	295
Bridge retainer buildups (various types)	D6970/D6971/D6972/D6973 PREVIOUSLY DELETED CODES	294/295
Bridge retainer crown (implant bridge)	D6068-D6074/D6194	255-258/259
Bridge retainer crown (natural tooth)	D6545-D6795	271-293
Bridge sectioning (retain good portion of bridge in mouth/polish)	D9120	357
Cantilever Bridge	Use D62xx pontic plus D67xx retainer crown	
Hugger Bridge	See Index, "Hugger Bridge"	
Maryland Bridge	See Index, "Maryland Bridge"	
Monodont® Bridge	See Index, "Monodont® Bridge"	

Broken instrument (endodontic)

Treatment of root canal obstruction (could be due to broken instrument or calcified canal))	D3331	125

Broken or lost orthodontic appliance replacement — D8692 (post orthodontics placement) — 351

Brush biopsy (OralCDx®) — D7288 — 308

Bruxism/clenching appliance (for TMJ dysfunction appliance, see D7880) — D9940 (also known as perio guard) — 372

	Code	Page
Buildups (for retention of crown)		
Bridge retainer crown buildups (various – all <u>deleted</u>) (now see D2950/D2952/D2954)	D6970/D6971/D6972/D6973	(294/295/295/295) 104/106/107
Cast or indirect (CAD/CAM) post (crown or retainer crown)	D2952	106
Core buildup (crown or retainer crown)	D2950	104
"Filler" (not a core build up)	D2949	103
Indirect fabricated post (crown or retainer crown)	D2952	106
Pre-fab post and core (crown or retainer crown)	D2954	107
Button/pin/bracket placement (typically for orthodontics)	D7283	306

C	Code	Page
Calcified canals		
Treatment of root canal obstruction due to calcified canal(s)	D3331	125
Cancelled appointment	D9987	381
Cancer Detection		
Cancer screening adjunct (ViziLite®, VELscope™, Microlux DL, Identafi® 3000, OralID™)	D0431	43
Excisional biopsy (hard tissue) – lesion specimen	D7285	307
Excisional biopsy (soft tissue) – lesion specimen	D7286	307
Exfoliative cytological sample (cell sample)	D7287	308
OralCDx® biopsy (brush biopsy sample)	D7288	308
Canine, primary tooth stripping/discing	D9951 (to make room for permanent incisors)	375
Cantilever (fixed) bridge	Use D62xx pontic plus D67xx retainer crown	
Caregiver counseling (child under age three evaluation)	D0145	11
Caries arresting medicament application	D1354 (silver diamine, etc.)	59
Caries detectability test (presence of caries)	D0999	50
Caries infiltrant (DMG-ICON)	D2990	113
Caries risk assessment and documentation	D0601-D0603 (low, moderate, and high caries risk)	44-46
Caries susceptibility test (diagnostic)	D0425	42
Carrier		
Carrier, fluoride gel	D5986	227
Carrier, periodontal medicament	D5994	229
Carrier, radiation	D5983	226
Carrier, topical medicament (vesiculobullous disease)	D5991	230
Case presentation (on date after oral evaluation appointment)	D9450	365
Cast post and core (indirectly fabricated by lab) – either crown or retainer crown		
Each additional indirect fabricated post (same tooth)	D2953	106
Indirect fabricated post and core (crown or retainer crown)	D2952	106
Casts, diagnostic (study models)	D0470 (can be component of orthodontic record)	44
Casts, mounted case (occlusion analysis)	D9950	375
Cementation		
Re-cement crown or ¾ crown	D2920	99
Re-cement fixed bridge (fixed partial denture)	D6930	293
Re-cement implant/abutment supported crown	D6092	263

Re-cement implant/abutment supported fixed bridge	D6093	264
Re-cement indirect or prefabricated post and core	D2915	98
Re-cement inlay/onlay/veneer	D2910	98
Re-cement Maryland Bridge (wings re-cemented)	D6930	293
Re-cement or re-bond fixed orthodontic retainer (post orthodontics)	D8693	352
Re-cement space maintainer	D1550	62
Repair of fixed retainers, includes reattachment	D8694	352

Cephalometric radiographic image (component of orthodontic records) D0340 — 31

CEREC®/E4D®/PlanScan® Restorations – CAD/CAM

¾ crown ceramic/resin	D2783/D2712	94/88
Crown ceramic/resin	D2740/D2710	90/87
Endodontic crown (one piece crown with "foot" into pulp chamber)	D2999 (unspecified procedure, by report)	113
Inlay ceramic/resin	D2610-D2630; D2650-D2652	80-81;83-84
Onlay ceramic/resin	D2642-D2644; D2662-D2664	81-83;84-86
Veneer ceramic/resin	D2962/D2961	109

Chairside relines (not lab processed)

Complete denture reline (chairside cure)	D5730/D5731	207/208
Partial denture reline (chairside cure)	D5740/D5741	208/209

Characterization (special lab service)

Bridge characterization/ceramic margin	D6999 (unspecified procedure, by report)	296
Crown characterization/ceramic margin	D2999 (unspecified procedure, by report)	113
Denture characterization	D5899 (unspecified procedure, by report)	221

Charting and probing (periodontal) – generally integral D4999 (unspecified procedure, by report) — 182

Chemotherapeutic agents (adjuncts)

Arestin®	D4381	177
Atridox®	D4381	177
PerioChip®	D4381	177

Child Procedures

Assessment of a patient (pre-diagnostic service)	D0191	19
Evaluation, comprehensive oral (three years and older)	D0150	12
Evaluation under three years of age, includes counseling	D0145	11
Extraction, coronal remnant (deciduous tooth)	D7111	298
Extraction, exposed root (not a surgical extraction)	D7140 (primary or permanent tooth)	298
Extraction, routine erupted tooth (primary or permanent)	D7140	298
Fluoride application excluding varnish	D1208 (includes various types of fluoride treatment)	55
Fluoride varnish application	D1206 (same code reports adult and child)	55
Interim caries arresting medicament application	D1354	59
Interim therapeutic restoration – primary dentition	D2941	103
Prophylaxis (child)	D1120	54
Screening of a patient (pre-diagnostic service)	D0190	19
Topical fluoride application (includes child prophylaxis)	D1201 (previously deleted) – see D1206 or D1208	54
Topical fluoride application (child)	D1203 (previously deleted) – see D1206 or D1208	54

Chlorhexidine rinse

Gingival irrigation (adjunct to scaling and root planing clinical procedure)	D4921	181

Take home product dispensed for home use	D9630	367
Cleaning and inspection of removable complete denture	D9932/D9933	371
Cleaning and inspection of removable partial denture	D9934/D9935	372
Cleaning (prophylaxis)		
Adult prophylaxis	D1110	51
Child prophylaxis	D1120	54
"Difficult" adult prophylaxis (higher fee)	D1110	51
"Orthodontic" prophylaxis (removal of "flashing")	D8999 (in addition report prophylaxis)	353
"Teenage" prophylaxis (lower fee than adult)	D1110	51
Closure (of access hole) – endo related (don't report crown repair)	D2140/D2330/D2391	65/68/73
Collagen wound dressing products (integral to procedure)	No separate code	
Collection and application of autologous blood concentrate – platelet rich plasma (PRP)	D7921	330
Collection and preparation of genetic sample material for laboratory analysis and report	D0422	41
Combined connective tissue and double pedicle graft	D4276	164
Complete occlusal adjustment (includes multiple visits)	D9952 (for limited occlusal adjustment, see D9951)	376
Complete x-ray series – intraoral radiographic images	D0210	20
Complications, post-surgical (not routine follow-up)	D9930	370
Composite resin (resin-based composite) – direct restorations		
Anterior composites (primary and permanent)	D2330-D2390	68-73
Composite crown, anterior (primary and permanent)	D2390	72
Preventive Resin Restoration (PRR) – dentist procedure	D1352	57
Posterior composites (primary and permanent)	D2391-D2394	73-76
Veneer composite – direct restoration	D2960	108
Comprehensive oral evaluation/comprehensive periodontal evaluation	D0150/D0180	12/18
Comprehensive orthodontic case	D8070-D8090	345-347
Condylectomy	D7840	326
Cone Beam CT, (CBCT) diagnostic imaging	See Index, "Radiographs"	
Connective tissue grafts (various)	See Index, "Grafts"	
Connector bar		
Bridgework connector bar	D6920	293
Dental implant/abutment supported connector bar (Hader® Bar)	D6055	241
Conscious sedation/analgesia (intravenous)	D9243	361
Conscious sedation/analgesia (non-intravenous)	D9248	362
Consultations (evaluations/exams)		
Case presentation (booked after oral evaluation), established patient	D9450	365
Comprehensive oral (initial) evaluation	D0150	12
Comprehensive periodontal oral evaluation (perio patient)	D0180 (mandatory probing and charting)	18
Consultation (patient specifically referred by dentist or physician)	D9310 (typically reported by specialist)	363
Detailed and extensive evaluation (may follow D0150/D0180)	D0160 (by report)	14
Detailed treatment (case) presentation (following D0150/D0180 evaluation, established patient)	D9450	365
Problem focused (emergency) evaluation	D0140	9
Re-evaluation – limited, problem focused	D0170 (may follow D0120/D0170/D0150/D0180)	15

Re-evaluation – post-operative office visit	D0171	17
Consultation type visit		
Case presentation (follows D0150/D0180 oral evaluation, at subsequent date)	D9450	365
Consultation (referred by dentist or physician – typically reported by a specialist)	D9310 (patient must be referred to report this code)	363
Coping (single tooth or as part of a fixed prosthesis)	D2975 (definitive procedure)	111
Core buildup (single tooth or bridge retainer crown)	D2950	104
Coronectomy (intentional partial tooth removal)	D7251	304
Coronoidectomy (mandible)	D7991	338
Counseling		
Nutritional counseling	D1310	56
Oral hygiene counseling	D1330	56
Tobacco cessation counseling	D1320	56
Counseling, caregiver (child under three) oral evaluation	D0145	11
Crevicular antimicrobial agents (various)	D4381 (such as Arestin®)	177
Crown exposure		
Anatomical crown exposure (requires soft and hard tissue removal)	D4230/D4231 (typically esthetic procedure)	147/148
Clinical crown lengthening (requires bone removal)	D4249	151
Operculectomy (excision of pericoronal gingiva)	D7971	337
Unerupted tooth crown exposure (surgical bone removal)	D7280 (may or may not be orthodontic related)	305
Crowns (single)		
Abutment supported crowns (on implant)	D6058-D6064/D6094	249-252/253
BruxZir® (report as porcelain/ceramic)	D2740	90
Coping (definitive restoration or under telescopic crown)	D2975	111
Custom staining (crown, onlay, etc.)	D2999	113
Extra lab procedure under existing partial denture framework	D2971	110
Fractured tooth (temporary crown)	D2799/D9110	97/354
Gramm crown (report as PFM high noble)	D2750	91
Implant supported individual crown	D6065-D6067	253-254
Individual crown restorations (indirect)	D2710-D2799	87-97
Prefabricated crown (various)	D2929-D2934	99-102
Prefabricated porcelain/ceramic crown – primary tooth	D2929	99
Provisional crown (any time duration)	D2799	97
Re-cement crown or ¾ crown	D2920	99
Re-cement implant/abutment supported crown	D6092	263
Repair crown (necessitated by materials failure)	D2980	111
Resin-based composite crown, anterior, direct restoration	D2390	72
Resin-based composite crown, indirect	D2710	87
Splinting individual crowns together (two or more)	**Report as single crowns – not retainer crowns**	
Stainless steel crown (various)	D2930/D2931/D2933/D2934	100/100/101/101
Telescopic crown (coping under crown or retainer crown)	D2975	111
Temporary crown (fractured tooth)	D2799/D9110	97/354
Zirconium substrate crown (report as porcelain/ceramic)	D2740	90

¾ Crown

¾ Base metal crown	D2781	93
¾ Ceramic/porcelain crown	D2783	94
¾ High noble metal crown	D2780	93
¾ Noble metal crown	D2782	94
¾ Resin based composite crown (indirect)	D2712	88

Crown lengthening procedure

Gingivectomy or gingivoplasty to allow restorative access	D4212	147
Hard tissue crown lengthening (requires bone removal)	D4249	151

Crown or bridge repair (necessitated by restorative material failure)	D2980/D6980	111/295
Crown splinting (two or more splinted crowns)	Report as single crowns – not retainer crowns	
Crown survey (bill in addition to crown)	D2999/D6999	113/296
Cryosurgery (destruction of soft tissue lesion)	D7465	316
CT Cone Beam (X-ray)	D0364-D0368/D0393-D0394	34-35/37-38
Culture and sensitivity test (periodontal – related bacteria)	D0415	40
Culture, viral (diagnostic test)	D0416	40

Curettage

Apical/periradicular (endodontic)	D3410-D3426	133-136
Gingival curettage (no current code)	D4999 (unspecified procedure, by report)	182
Open flap surgery (periodontal curettage)	D4240/D4241	149/150
Without flap (includes incidental periodontal curettage)	D4341/D4342	170/171

CU-SIL® partial denture	D5211/D5212	189
Custom abutment, implant (includes placement)	D6057	242
Custom staining (bridge)	D6999	296
Custom staining (crown, onlay, etc.)	D2999 (unspecified procedure, by report)	113
Cvek pulpotomy (trauma related)	D3222	119
Cysts, removal of	D7410-D7415; D7465	314-316;316
Cytologic smears	D0480	48
Cytology exfoliative sample collection (biopsy)	D7287	308

D	**Code**	**Page**
Debacterol® (oral analgesic)		
In office palliative treatment (at emergency visit)	D9110	354
Debridement		
Debridement of a peri-implant defect and surface cleaning of exposed implant surfaces, including flap entry and closure	D6101	238
Debridement and osseous contouring of a peri-implant defect; includes surface cleaning of exposed implant surfaces and flap entry and closure	D6102	239
Endodontic debridement (remove pulpal tissue to relieve pain)	D3221 (prior to endodontic treatment)	118
Full mouth debridement to enable comprehensive oral evaluation	D4355 (<u>not</u> a periodontal treatment)	173
Gross debridement (calculus removal to enable oral evaluation)	D4355 (preliminary treatment)	173
Gross pulpal debridement (endodontic) – open tooth	D3221 (root canal next visit)	118
Partial pulpal debridement at emergency visit (palliative)	D9110 (root canal next visit)	354
Pulpal debridement (relief of pain, open tooth)	D3221 (root canal next visit)	118

Deciduous (primary) tooth extraction

Coronal remnant only (no root present)	D7111	298
Primary tooth extraction with some or all root structure left	D7140	298

"Deep" cleaning (perio procedure) – SRP (scaling and root planing)   D4341/D4342   170/171

Deep sedation/general anesthesia – each 15 minute increment   D9223   359

Deep sedation/general anesthesia evaluation   D9219   358

Deleted Codes

Cast post as part of fixed partial denture retainer	D6971 (previously deleted code, see D6999)	295
Cleaning and inspection of removable device	D9931 (deleted)	371
Cone Beam CT – craniofacial data capture	D0360 (previously deleted code, see CBCT codes)	34
Cone Beam three-dimensional image	D0363 (previously deleted, see CBCT codes)	34
Cone Beam two-dimensional image	D0362 (previously deleted code, see CBCT codes)	34
Coping	D6975 (previously deleted code, see D2975)	295
Core buildup for retainer, including any pins bridge abutment	D6973 (previously deleted code, see D2950)	295
Deep sedation/general anesthesia	D9220/D9221 (deleted)	359
Each additional indirectly fabricated post – same tooth	D6976 (previously deleted code, see D2953)	295
Each additional prefabricated post – same tooth	D6977 (previously deleted code, see D2957)	295
Extraoral – each additional radiographic image	D0260 (deleted)	24
Free sort tissue graft procedure (including donor site surgery)	D4271 (previously deleted code, see D4277/D4278)	161 (164/165)
Genetic test for susceptibility to oral diseases	D0421 (deleted)	41
Interim Pontic	D6254 (previously deleted code, see D6253)	271
Interim retainer crown	D6795 (previously deleted code, see D6793)	293
Intravenous moderate (conscious) sedation/analgesia	D9241/D9242 (deleted)	360/361
Place abutment	D6020 (previously deleted code, see D6056/D6057)	237
Post and core (indirectly fabricated)	D6970 (previously deleted code, see D2952)	294
Post and core (prefabricated)	D6972 (previously deleted code, see D2954)	295
Pulpal regeneration	D3354 (previously deleted code, see D3357)	131
Overdenture – complete (natural tooth)	D5860 (previously deleted code, see D5863 and D5865)	217
Overdenture – implant/abutment related – fixed	D6078/D6079 (previously deleted code, see D6114/D6115 and D6116/D6117)	247/248
Overdenture – implant/abutment related – removable	D6053/D6054 (previously deleted code, see D6110/D611 and D6112/D6113	244/246
Overdenture – partial (natural tooth)	D5861 (previously deleted code, see D5864 and D5866)	217
Temporary crown (fractured tooth)	D2970 (deleted)	110
Topical application of fluoride – child	D1203 (previously deleted code, see D1206 or D1208)	54
Topical application of fluoride – adult	D1204 (previously deleted code, see D1206 or D1208)	54
Topical fluoride including prophylaxis – adult	D1205 (previously deleted code)	55
Topical fluoride including prophylaxis – child	D1201 (previously deleted code)	54

Dentures (removable)

Adjustments (complete/partial)	D5410-D5422	199-200
Characterization of denture acrylic (custom denture)	D5899 (unspecified procedure, by report)	221
Cleaning and inspection of removable complete denture	D9932/D9933	371

Cleaning and inspection of removable partial denture	D9934/D9935	372
Complete denture (including cast metal plate type)	D5110/D5120	184/185
Complete denture (immediate) heal six months before reline	D5130/5140	185/187
Complete denture (interim denture)	D5810/D5811	213/214
Duplicate denture (duplicate existing denture)	D5899 (unspecified procedure, by report)	221
Full denture (complete denture)	D5110/D5120	184/185
Immediate, complete denture – placement after extractions	D5130/D5140	185/187
Immediate, partial denture – cast metal framework	D5223/D5224	195/196
Immediate, partial denture – resin	D5221/D5222	193/194
Implant overdenture/abutment supported, complete denture		
Mandibular arch	D6111	245
Maxillary arch	D6110	244
Implant overdenture/abutment supported, partial denture		
Mandibular arch	D6113	246
Maxillary arch	D6112	246
Interim complete denture (temporary denture)	D5810/D5811	213/214
Interim partial denture (temporary partial denture)	D5820/D5821 (includes "flipper")	215
Modification of removable prosthesis (after implant surgery)	D5875	221
Overdenture (complete) – implant type overdenture		
Mandibular arch	D6111	245
Maxillary arch	D6110	244
Overdenture (partial) – implant type overdenture		
Mandibular arch	D6113	246
Maxillary arch	D6112	246
Overdenture (complete) – natural tooth type overdenture	D5863 (maxillary) D5865 (mandibular)	218
Overdenture (partial) – natural tooth type overdenture	D5864 (maxillary) D5866 (mandibular)	218
Partial denture (various types)	D5211-D5281; D5221/D5222 D5223/D5224; D5820/D5821	189-198;193/194 195/196;215
Precision attachment (removable denture/mini implant locator)	D5862	217
Rebase denture (complete/partial)	D5710-D5721	205-207
Reline denture (complete/partial)	D5730-D5761	207-212
Repair (complete denture)	D5510/D5520	201
Repair (partial denture)	D5610-D5671	201-204
Stayplate partial denture (interim partial denture)	D5820/D5821	215/216

Dentures (fixed) – could be All-on-4

Implant/abutment supported, complete denture (fixed denture)		
Mandibular arch	D6115	248
Maxillary arch	D6114	247
Implant/abutment supported, partial denture (fixed partial denture)		
Mandibular arch	D6117	249
Maxillary arch	D6116	248

Desensitizing medicament application

Desensitizing application (in office procedure) maybe with SRP	D9910 (single tooth or whole mouth application)	368

Emergency visit application (palliative treatment)	D9110	354
Resin application (cervical/roots) – report "per tooth"	D9911 (per tooth)	369
Scaling and root planing or osseous surgery adjunct	D9630 (home use after in office treatment)	367
Desensitizing resin (cervical or root sensitivity), per tooth	D9911	369
Destruction of lesion (cryo, laser, electro surgery)	D7465 (only soft tissue laser mentioned code)	316
Detailed and extensive evaluation (after D0120/D0150/D0180)	D0160	14
Diagnostic services		
Diagnostic casts (study model) – can be part of orthodontic record	D0470	44
Diagnostic crown – cracked tooth (emergency visit)	D9110	354
Diagnostic photographs (oral/facial images)	D0350/D0351 (2D and 3D images)	32/33
Diagnostic radiographic images (various)	D0210-D0368/D0380-D0384	20-35/36
Diagnostic services	D0100-D0999	8-50
Diagnostic waxup		
For occlusion analysis--mounted case (waxup with facebow, interocclusal records, etc.)	D9950	375
Waxup (only) on model	D9999 (unspecified procedure, by report)	382
Dietary planning (nutritional counseling)	D1310	56
"Difficult" adult prophy (extended appointment – higher fee visit)	D1110	51
Digital subtraction of two or more images	D0394	38
Direct composites (resin restorations)	D1352; D2330-D2394	57;68-76
Direct composite crown (anterior) – primary or permanent tooth	D2390	72
Direct pulp cap (exposed pulp)	D3110	116
Disc repair (TMJ dysfunction)	D7852	326
Discing (enamel) to make room for tooth alignment	D9951	375
Distal/proximal wedge procedure	D4274	162
DMG America (Icon product – caries infiltrant)	D2990	113
Dolder bar (implant supported connecting bar)	D6055	241
Dressing change, periodontal, unscheduled	D4920	181
Drugs		
Injection (antibiotic, sedative, steroids, etc.)	D9610/D9612 (single; two or more injections)	366
Other drugs (take home products dispensed by office)	D9630	367
Dry socket/localized osteitis (unusual circumstances)	D9930	370
Durafluor® and Duraphat® (desensitizing agent)	D9110/D9910	354/368

E	**Code**	**Page**
Ectopic eruption device (interceptive growth and development)	D8050/D8060	344
Electrosurgery (destruction of soft tissue lesion)	D7465	316
Emdogain®	D4265	157
Emergency "accident" visit	See also Index, "Accident"	
Emergency (evaluation) problem focused exam	D0140	9
Emergency treatment (palliative)	D9110	354
Emergency visit – after regular hours	D9440	365
Emergency visit – periodontal dressing change	D4920	181
Enamel fissurotomy	D9971	377

Enamel fracture/smoothing of tooth (emergency visit)	D9110	354
Enamel microabrasion	D9970	377
Enameloplasty	D9951/D9971	375-377

Endodontics

Access closure (after endodontic treatment) – Do not report crown repair for access closure – use restoration		
Amalgam restoration for access closure	D2140	65
Composite restoration for access closure	D2330/D2391	68/73
Anterior root canal	D3310	121
Apexification		
Initial visit – apexification	D3351	128
Interim visit – apexification	D3352	129
Final visit – apexification	D3353	130
Apexogenesis (partial pulpotomy)	D3222	119
Apicoectomy/periradicular surgery		
Anterior (first root)	D3410	133
Bicuspid (first root)	D3421	134
Each additional root (typically for bicuspid and molars)	D3426	135
Molar (first root)	D3425	135
Bicuspid root canal (includes all multiple root configurations)	D3320	122
Canal preparation/fitting performed dowel/post	D3950	141
Endodontic access closure (use direct restoration, not crown repair)	D2140/D2330/D2391	65/68/73
Endodontic bleaching (non-vital) – single tooth	D9974	379
Endodontic endosseous implant	D3460	140
Hemisection, not including root canal therapy	D3920	141
Incomplete treatment (endodontic)	D3332	125
Intentional re-implantation (endodontic reason)	D3470	140
Internal root repair of perforation defects	D3333	126
Molar root canal (includes all multiple root configurations)	D3330	124
Partial pulpotomy (apexogenesis)	D3222	119
Pulpal regeneration – initial visit	D3355	131
Pulpal regeneration – interim visit	D3356	132
Pulpal regeneration – completion of treatment	D3357	132
Pulpotomy (to maintain vitality) – typically primary tooth	D3220 (not the first stage of root canal)	117
Recalcification – initial visit	D3351	128
Recalcification – interim visit	D3352	129
Recalcification – final visit	D3353	130
Retreatment (root canal)		
Anterior root canal	D3346	127
Bicuspid root canal	D3347	127
Molar root canal	D3348	128
Retrograde filling	D3430	138
Root amputation – per root	D3450	139
Surgical procedure for isolation of tooth with rubber dam	D3910	140
Treatment of root canal obstruction	D3331	125

Eposteal implant (surgical placement)	D6040	238
Epulis removal	D7970	337
Equilibration (occlusal adjustment)	D9951/D9952 (limited and complete)	375-376
ERA (precision attachment/implant locator)	D5862	217
Eruption of teeth		
Mobilization, surgical	D7282	306
Operculectomy (excision of pericoronal gingiva)	D7971	337
Pericoronal gingival excision (operculectomy)	D7971	337
Placement of device to aid eruption (orthodontic related)	D7283	306
Surgical access of an unerupted tooth (could be orthodontic related)	D7280	305
Surgical exposure of impacted or unerupted tooth (orthodontic related) to aid eruption	D7281 (previously deleted code, see D7280))	306
Etching (integral to restorative procedure)	No separate code	
Evaluations (exams)		
Assessment of a patient (pre-diagnostic service)	D0191	19
Comprehensive oral evaluation (exam)	D0150	12
Comprehensive periodontal oral evaluation (exam)	D0180 (mandatory probing and charting)	18
Consultation (generally reported by specialist)	D9310 (patient referred by physician or dentist)	363
Detailed and extensive evaluation, problem focused	D0160 (by report)	14
Detailed treatment case presentation (follows oral evaluation visit)	D9450	365
Evaluation for deep sedation or general anesthesia	D9219	358
Follow-up re-evaluation, problem focused visit	D0170 (after D0120/D0140/D0150/D0180)	15
Oral evaluation and counseling the caregiver (under three years)	D0145	11
Problem focused evaluation (exam) – emergency visit	D0140	9
Re-evaluation – limited, problem focused	D0170	15
Re-evaluation – post-operative office visit	D0171	17
Screening of a patient (pre-diagnostic service)	D0190	19
Evolution E4D®/ CEREC®/PlanScan™ Restorations		
¾ crown ceramic/resin	D2783/D2712	94/88
Crown ceramic/resin	D2740/D2710	90/87
Inlay ceramic/resin	D2610-D2630; D2650-D2652	80-81;83-84
Onlay ceramic/resin	D2642-D2644; D2662-D2664	81-83;84-86
Veneer ceramic/resin	D2961/D2962	109
Evulsed (avulsed) tooth		
Alveolus closed reduction (alveolus not intact)	D7670	324
Stabilization of evulsed/avulsed tooth (alveolus intact)	D7270	304
Exams (evaluations)	See Index, "Evaluations"	
Excision of soft tissue		
Benign lesion excision	D7410-D7412	314-315
Hyperplastic tissue excision – per arch	D7970	337
Malignant lesion/tumor excision	D7413-D7415	315-316
Pericoronal gingival excision (operculectomy)	D7971	337
Exfoliative cytological sample collection	D7287	308
Exostosis (tuberosity), removal of		
Lateral exostosis removal	D7471	319

Osseous tuberosity reduction	D7485	320
Surgical reduction of fibrous tuberosity	D7972	338
Torus mandibularis removal	D7473	319
Torus palatinus removal	D7472	319

Exposure of tooth

Anatomical crown exposure (hard and soft tissue requirement)	D4230/D4231	147/148
Operculectomy (excision of pericoronal gingiva)	D7971	337
Unerupted tooth, surgical access	D7280	305

External bleaching (whitening) – vital teeth

Per arch bleaching (home application) – trays, strips	D9975	379
Per arch bleaching (performed in office) – vital	D9972	377
Per tooth bleaching (external) – vital	D9973	378

Extracoronal splinting (periodontally related, not trauma)	D4321	169

Extractions

Coronal remnants, deciduous tooth – <u>no</u> root remains	D7111	298
Coronectomy (intentional <u>partial</u> tooth removal)	D7251	304
Deciduous tooth coronal remnant – <u>no</u> root remains	D7111	298
Deciduous tooth extraction (routine) – <u>some</u> root remains	D7140 (includes primary teeth)	298
Erupted tooth extraction	D7140	298
Exposed root extraction (non-surgical removal of exposed root)	D7140	298
Impacted – bony impactions	D7230-D7241	301-302
Impacted – soft tissue removal	D7220	301
<u>Partial</u> extraction (intentional) – coronectomy	D7251	304
Partial extraction (unintended)	D7999 (unspecified procedure, by report)	339
Primary tooth – coronal remnants only – no root remaining	D7111	298
Primary tooth (routine) crown with <u>some</u> root remaining	D7140	298
Residual tooth roots – surgical removal	D7250	303
Routine primary tooth extraction with <u>some</u> root remaining	D7140	298
Single and multiple tooth extractions, erupted tooth	D7140	298
Surgical extraction, erupted tooth (bone removal/sectioning required)	D7210	300
Surgical removal of residual tooth roots (surgical cutting procedure)	D7250	303
Unintended <u>partial</u> extraction of tooth	D7999 (unspecified procedure, by report)	339

Extraoral photographic image

2D photo images	D0350	32
3D photo images	D0351	33

Extra-oral posterior dental radiographic image	D0251	23
Extraoral radiographic image	D0250	23

F	**Code**	**Page**
Facial bone survey	D0290	29
Facial/oral photographic images	D0350 (can be part of orthodontic records)	32
Fiberotomy, transseptal (orthodontic related procedure)	D7291	309
Fibroma removal (benign lesion)	D7410/D7411	314
"Filler" buildup (foundation)	D2949 (foundation, not a core buildup)	103

Filling

Amalgam restorations	D2140-D2161	65-67
Resin composite restorations	D1352/D2330-D2394	57/68-76
Sedative filling (now reported as "protective restoration")	D2940	102

Fine scale and polish (prophylaxis) — D1110 — 51

Fissurotomy — D9971 — 377

Fissurotomy (as part of sealant procedure) — D1351 — 56

Fistula closure

Oroantral fistula closure	D7260	304
Salivary fistula closure	D7983	338

Fixation device not in conjunction with a fracture — D7998 — 339

Fixed appliance therapy (harmful habit) – thumb sucking — D8220 — 348

Fixed partial dentures (bridges) — Also see Index, "Bridge"

Bridge sectioning (retainer crown remains)	D9120	357
Implant/abutment supported retainers	D6075-D6077; D6068-D6074 D6194	260-261;255-258 259
Inlay/onlay retainers	D6600-D6634	274-284
"Maryland" retainer crowns (ceramic/metal/resin)	D6545/D6548/D6549	271/272/273
Pediatric fixed bridge (for esthetics not space maintainer)	D6985	296
Pontics (various)	D6205-D6254	267-271
Re-cement implant/abutment supported bridge	D6093	264
Re-cementation of bridge (fixed partial denture)	D6930	293
Repair of bridge (fixed partial denture)	D6980	295
Retainer crowns (implant/abutment supported)	D6068-D6077; D6194	255-261;259
Retainer crowns (natural tooth)	D6545-D6794	271-293
Section bridge (at a minimum the retainer crown remains)	D9120	357

Flaps

Apically positioned flap	D4245	151
Gingival flap procedure, includes root planing	D4240/D4241	149/150

Flexible base partial denture (Valplast®/Proplast®) — D5225/D5226 (unilateral or bilateral) — 197/198

"Flipper," interim partial denture

Removable partial denture prosthesis (temporary use)	D5820/D5821	215

"Flipper," resin (long term use) partial denture — D5211/D5212 — 189-190

Fluoride treatment

Adult or child fluoride varnish application	D1206	55
Adult fluoride application – <u>not</u> fluoride varnish	D1204 (previously deleted code, D1208)	54
Child fluoride application – <u>not</u> fluoride varnish	D1203 (previously deleted code, D1208)	54
Child fluoride varnish application (also adult)	D1206	55
Desensitizing application in office as fluoride	D9910 (single tooth or whole mouth application)	368
Dispensing for home use (caries prevention or as desensitizer)	D9630	367
Emergency treatment visit (palliative D9110)	D9110 (desensitizing use of fluoride application)	354
Fluoride (child or adult) – any type other than fluoride varnish	D1208	55
Fluoride varnish (child or adult) – regardless of caries risk	D1206	55

	Code	Page
Gel carrier for fluoride application (tray)	D5986	227
Includes prophylaxis (plus fluoride) (previously deleted)	D1201/D1205 (previously deleted codes)	54/55
Interim caries arresting medicament application	D1354	59
Paint-on fluoride application or fluoride varnish application	D1208 or D1206	55
Rinse/swish fluoride application – regardless of caries risk	D1208 (child or adult)	55
Varnish (fluoride) – regardless of caries risk	D1206 (child or adult)	55
Foreign bodies, removal of	D7530/D7540	322
Foundation for an indirect restoration	D2949 (not a core buildup)	103
Fractured tooth (temporary crown)	D2970 (deleted)	110
Fractures, treatment of		
Alveolus fracture	D7670/D7671; D7770/D7771	324;325
Closed reduction-mandible	D7640/D7740	323/324
Closed reduction-maxilla	D7620/D7720	323/324
Facial bones fracture – complicated	D7680/D7780	324/325
Malar/zygomatic arch (open/closed)	D7650/D7660;D7750/D7760	323;324-325
Open reduction-mandible – simple fracture	D7630/D7730	323/324
Open reduction-maxilla	D7610/D7710	323/324
Fragment of tooth – reattachment	D2921	99
Frenulectomy/frenectomy/frenotomy (separate procedure)	D7960 (less complicated)	336
Frenuloplasty (separate procedure)	D7963 (more complicated)	336
Full mouth series images (radiographs) – intraoral images	D0210	20

G	Code	Page
General anesthesia/deep sedation – each 15 minute increment	D9223	359
General anesthesia/deep sedation (evaluation for procedure)	D9219	358
Genetic test for susceptibility to diseases – specimen analysis	D0423	42
Gingiva, pericoronal, removal of (operculectomy)	D7971	337
Gingival flap procedure (active periodontal therapy)	D4240/D4241	149/150
Gingival irrigation – per quadrant	D4921	181
Gingivectomy/gingivoplasty		
Gingivectomy (to allow restorative access)	D4212	147
Partial quadrant (one to three contiguous teeth) – periodontal issue only	D4211	145
Pericoronal gingival excision (operculectomy)	D7971	337
Gingivectomy quadrant (four or more contiguous teeth) Gingivectomy – periodontal issue only	D4210	144
Gingivitis (inflammation) – see prophylaxis for treatment	D1110 (removal of irritational factors)	51
Glass ionomers (reported as direct resin restorations)	D2330-D2394	68-76
Gluma® (resin application)		
Emergency visit application to desensitize	D9110	354
"Per tooth" desensitizing application (in office treatment)	D9911	369
Gold foil restorations	D2410-D2430	77
Graft Procedures		
Autogenous connective tissue graft procedure (including donor and recipient surgical sites)	D4283	166

Autogenous graft (harvesting)	D7295	311
Bone graft at same time as implant placement	D6104	240
Bone graft in conjunction with periradicular surgery	D3428 (per tooth, single site)	136
Bone graft in conjunction with periradicular surgery	D3429 (additional contiguous tooth in same site)	137
Bone replacement graft (with periodontal osseous surgery)	D4263/D4264	155/156
Bone replacement (socket graft) – for ridge preservation	D7953 (extraction site graft)	334
Combined connective tissue and double pedicle graft	D4276	164
Free soft tissue graft	D4271 (previously deleted code)	161
Free soft tissue graft procedure, first tooth	D4277	164
Free soft tissue graft procedure, each additional tooth	D4278	165
Harvesting, autogenous graft (bone from patient)	D7295	311
Maxillofacial soft/hard tissue defect repair	D7955	335
Non-autogenous connective tissue graft procedure (including recipient surgical site and donor material)	D4285	167
Osseous, osteoperiosteal, or cartilage graft (ridge augmentation)	D7950 (edentulous area graft)	332
Pedicle soft tissue graft (periodontal)	D4270	160
Peri-implant defect bone graft (for repair of peri-implant defect)	D6103 (in conjunction with D6102)	240
Ridge augmentation graft (edentulous area)	D7950 (edentulous area graft)	332
Ridge preservation (bone socket graft)	D7953 (extraction site graft)	334
Sinus lift augmentation via a lateral (window) approach	D7951	333
Sinus lift augmentation via a vertical approach	D7952	333
Skin graft	D7920	330
Soft tissue grafts (periodontal)	D4270-D4273, D4275-D4278	160-162;163-166
Subepithelial connective soft tissue graft (periodontal)	D4273	161
With implant placement (graft at same time as implant placement)	D6104	240
Gramm crown (Report as PFM – high noble metal)	D2750	91
Gross debridement		
Calculus removal to <u>enable</u> comprehensive oral evaluation	D4355	173
Pulpal debridement (endodontic related) – open tooth	D3221	118
Guard, occlusal – adjustment	D9943	375
Guard, occlusal (bruxism/perioguard)	D9940	372
Guided tissue regeneration (related to periodontal surgery, implant placement, and periradicular surgery procedures)		
Guided tissue regeneration – non-resorable barrier (membrane)	D4267	158
Guided tissue regeneration – resorbable barrier (membrane)	D4266	158
Guided tissue regeneration – resorbable barrier (membrane)	D3432 (periradicular surgery)	139

H	**Code**	**Page**
Habit appliance (harmful) – thumb sucking habit		
Fixed appliance therapy (to control harmful habit)	D8220	348
Removable appliance therapy (to control harmful habit)	D8210	347
Hader® Bar (implant supported connecting bar)	D6055	241
Hard acrylic splint appliance		
Athletic mouth guard	D9941	374
Occlusal guard adjustment	D9943	375

Occlusal guard (bruxism/clenching)/perio guard	D9940	372
Occlusal orthotic device (TMJ/TMD) adjustment	D7881	329
Occlusal orthotic device (TMJ/TMD) appliance	D7880	328
Harmful habit appliance – thumb sucking habit		
Fixed appliance therapy (to control harmful habit)	D8220	348
Removable appliance therapy (to control harmful habit)	D8210	347
Harvest of bone (from patient)	D7295	311
Hawley (orthodontic appliance)		
Harmful habit appliance (removable) – thumb sucking	D8210	347
Interceptive tooth movement appliance (child)	D8050/D8060	344
Minor tooth movement appliance	D8010-D8040; D8050/D8060	342-343;344
Removable orthodontic retainer adjustment	D8681	350
Repair orthodontic appliance	D8691	350
Replacement lost/broken retainer (post orthodontic treatment)	D8692	351
Retention (remove active fixed appliances, place retainer)	D8680	350
Retention (remove braces, place retainer)	D8680	350
Hemisection (section tooth – endodontic related)	D3920	141
Hospital call (hospital or ambulatory surgical center visit)	D9420	364
House call (nursing home visit)	D9410	364
Hugger Bridge (two resin retainer wings plus resin pontic)		
Resin pontic (True Vitality® resin)	D6205	267
Resin wing retainer – see illustration	D6549	273
Hybrid prosthesis – fixed (implant related)		
Implant/abutment supported (edentulous)	D6114/D6115	247/248
Implant/abutment supported (partially edentulous)	D6116/D6117	248/249
Hygiene instructions, oral	D1330	56
Hyperplastic tissue, excision (report per arch)	D7970	337

I	**Code**	**Page**
I-CAT® (Cone Beam 3-D x-ray) – CBCT	See index "Radiographs"	
Icon (DMG America – caries infiltrant)	D2990	113
Identafi® 3000 (Trimira) – oral cancer screening adjunct	D0431	43
Image, 3D simulation	D0393	37
Image, oral/facial photographs (can be component of orthodontic records)		
2D photographic image	D0350	32
3D photographic image	D0351	33
Images, X-rays, radiographs	See Index, "Radiographs"	
Immediate (complete) denture (placed after extractions)	D5130/D5140	185/187
Immediate (partial) denture – cast base framework	D5223/D5224	195/196
Immediate (partial) denture – resin	D5222/D5223	194/195
Impacted tooth, removal of	D7220-D7241; D7251	301-302;304
Implants		
Abutment		
Custom abutment (lab or CAD/CAM fabricated)	D6057	242

Interim abutment (not healing cap – includes removal)	**D6051**	243
Place abutment (previously deleted)	**D6020 (previously deleted code)**	237
Prefabricated abutment (manufactured)	**D6056**	241
Abutment supported retainer crown (bridge)		
Base metal retainer	**D6073**	258
High noble metal retainer	**D6072**	257
Noble metal retainer	**D6074**	258
PFM base metal retainer	**D6070**	256
PFM high noble metal retainer	**D6069**	256
PFM noble metal retainer	**D6071**	257
Porcelain/ceramic retainer	**D6068**	255
Titanium metal retainer	**D6194**	259
Abutment supported crowns (single)		
Cast metal (base) crown	**D6063**	252
Cast metal (high noble) crown	**D6062**	251
Cast metal (noble) crown	**D6064**	252
Cast metal (titanium) crown	**D6094**	253
PFM base metal crown	**D6060**	250
PFM high noble crown	**D6059**	250
PFM noble crown	**D6061**	251
Porcelain/ceramic crown	**D6058**	249
Titanium crown (any type including coated)	**D6094**	253
Attachment (locator) – typically for mini implant	**D5862 (see also D6052)**	217
Bone graft at same time as implant placement	**D6104**	240
Bone graft for repair of peri-implant defect	**D6103 (reported in conjunction with D6102)**	240
Bridge pontics (includes implant/abutment supported bridge)	D6205-D6254	267-271
Chin implant graft (synthetic)	**D7995**	339
Connecting bar (implant/abutment supported)	**D6055**	241
Debridement (soft tissue) of a peri-implant defect (no graft is placed)	**D6101**	238
Debridement and osseous contouring of a peri-implant defect	**D6102 (graft separately reported as D6103)**	239
Endodontic endosseous implant (surgical placement)	**D3460**	140
Endosteal implant (full size surgical placement)	**D6010 (most common implant placement code)**	236
Endosteal implant (mini) (surgical placement)	**D6013**	237
Eposteal (subperiosteal) implant (surgical placement)	**D6040 (not common procedure)**	238
Guide/radiographic index/surgical guide	**D6190 (guide for implant surgery placement)**	264
Hader® Bar (implant/abutment supported)	**D6055 (associated with overdenture)**	241
Healing cap – second stage implant surgery	**D6011**	245
Implant supported crowns (single) – no abutment involved		
Metal crown (high noble metal, titanium), implant supported	**D6067**	254
PFM high noble/titanium crown, implant supported	**D6066**	254
Porcelain/ceramic crown, implant supported	**D6065**	253
Index, surgical/radiographic guide	**D6190 (guide for implant surgery placement)**	264
Locator (implant) – mini implant	**D5862 (see also D6052)**	217

Maintenance, implant		
Implant prosthesis removal, cleaning, reinsertion	D6080	262
Repair implant abutment (repair/replace any part)	D6095	263
Repair implant supported prosthesis	D6090	262
Replacement of attachment (replaceable component)	D6091	263
Mandible, implant for augmentation purposes	D7996	339
Mini implant placement	D6013	246
Modification of removable prosthesis following implant surgery	D5875	221
Other implant services	D6080-D6199	262-265
Overdenture – complete (implant/abutment supported)	D6110/D6111	244/245
Overdenture partial denture (implant/abutment supported)	D6112/D6113	246
Pontic (implant pontic is same as tooth bridge pontic)	D6205-D6253	267-271
Provisional crown on implant	D2799	97
Radiographic/surgical index guide for implant placement	D6190	264
Re-cement implant/abutment supported bridge (FPD)	D6093	264
Re-cement implant/abutment supported crown	D6092	263
Removal of implant	D6100	238
Second stage implant surgery (place healing cap/abutment placement)	D6011	236
Semi-precision attachment abutment with keeper assembly	D6052	244
Surgery (implant)		
Endosteal implant (most common procedure)	D6010	244
Eposteal implant (not common procedure)	D6040	238
Interim implant body (for transitional prosthesis)	D6012	237
Second stage implant surgery	D6011	236
Temporary anchorage device (TAD) (for orthodontics)	D7292/D7293/D7294	310
Surgical implant index/radiographic index guide	D6190 (guide for implant placement)	264
Implant Services	D6000-D6199	234-265
Implantation/reimplantation of tooth		
Intentional reimplantation (after endodontic therapy in hand)	D3470	140
Reimplantation (accident related – evulsed or displaced)	D7270	304
Incipient smooth surface lesions, resin infiltration (Icon®)	D2990	113
Incision and drainage (abscess)	D7510/D7511/D7520/D7521	320-321
Incomplete endodontic procedure	D3332	125
Indirect pulp cap (all caries not removed)	D3110	116
Indirect restoration foundation – "filler"	D2949	103
Infant (under age three) oral evaluation and caregiver counseling	D0145	11
Infiltrant, caries resin (ICON-DMG America) not a restoration	D2990	113
Inflammation (gingivitis) treatment (prophylaxis)	D1110	51
Inhalation of nitrous oxide (N_2O)	D9230	360
Inlay		
Ceramic/porcelain inlay (single tooth)	D2610-D2630	80-81
Fixed partial denture inlay retainers	D6600-D6624	274-277
Metallic inlay (retainer)	D6602-D6624	275-277
Metallic inlay (gold) (single tooth)	D2510-D2530	77

Porcelain/ceramic inlay (retainer)	D6600/D6601	274
Porcelain/ceramic inlay (single tooth)	D2610-D2630	80-81
Re-cement inlay	D2910	98
Resin-based composite inlay	D2650-D2652	83-84
Titanium inlay (bridge retainer)	D6624	277
In-office bleaching (power) – per arch	D9972 (for home application trays – see D9975)	377
In-office desensitizing		
Emergency visit desensitizing	D9110	354
Resin application (cervical/roots)	D9911 (per tooth)	369
Up to whole mouth, regular treatment visit	D9910 (desensitizing medicament)	368
In-office fluoride application	D1206 or D1208 (child or adult)	55
Instruction, oral hygiene	D1330	56
Intentional partial tooth removal (coronectomy)	D7251	304
Intentional reimplantation of tooth	D3470	140
Interceptive orthodontics (child)	D8050/D8060	344
Interim caries arresting medicament application	D1354	59
Interim Restorative Procedure		
Complete denture (interim denture)	D5810/D5811	213/214
Interim abutment (implant)	D6051	243
Interim pontic (less than six months duration)	D6254 (previously deleted code)	271
Interim retainer crown (less than six months duration)	D6795 (previously deleted code)	293
Interim therapeutic restoration – primary dentition	D2941	103
Palliative (emergency) treatment in office	D9110	354
Partial denture (interim) flipper	D5820/D5821	215
Protective restoration (formerly termed "sedative filling")	D2940	102
Provisional bridge (pontic)	D6253	271
Provisional bridge (retainer)	D6793	292
Provisional crown (single)	D2799	97
Sedative filling (now termed "protective restoration") – IRM	D2940	102
Internal bleaching (endodontic tooth) – single tooth	D9974	379
Internal root repair (endodontic procedure)	D3333	126
Interpretation of diagnostic image (by provider who did not take image)	D0391	37
Interproximal reduction (enamel/discing)	D9951/D9971	375/377
Intracoronal splinting (periodontal-related splinting)	D4320	168
Intraoral – complete series of radiographic images	D0210	20
Intraoral photographic image (could be component of orthodontic records)		
2D image	D0350	32
3D image	D0351	33
Intravenous conscious sedation/analgesia		
I.V. moderate (conscious) sedation (each 15 minute increment)	D9243	361
Non-intravenous conscious sedation	D9248	362
Invisalign® (orthodontic) case types		
Anterior case (adolescent/adult) – front teeth	D8030/D8040	342/343

	Comprehensive case (adolescent/adult)	D8080/D8090 (requires comprehensive diagnosis (ceph) and treatment to ideal occlusion)	346/347
	Limited case	D8030/D8040 (adolescent/adult) most common Invisalign® case	342/343
Ionomers, glass (report as direct composite restoration)		D2330-D2394	68-76
IRM restoration (now termed "protective restoration")		D2940 (formerly termed "sedative filling")	102
IRM (Intermediate restorative material)		D2940/D9110	102/354
Irrigation (using medicinal agent following SRP) – in office		D4921 (per quadrant)	181

J	Code	Page
Joint reconstruction	D7858	326

K	Code	Page
No "K" terms		

L	Code	Page
Labial veneer		
Direct restoration (chairside) – "free-hand" composite veneer	D2960	108
Lab (ceramic) veneer (indirect) – lab or CAD/CAM fabricated	D2962	109
Lab (resin) veneer (indirect) – lab or CAD/CAM fabricated	D2961	109
Laboratory (oral pathology) procedures	D0472-D0502	47-50
Lab relines (processed in office or outside lab)		
Complete denture reline	D5750/D5751	210
Partial denture reline	D5760/D5761	211/212
Laminate (veneer)	See Index, "Labial Veneer"	
LANAP (laser periodontal procedure)	D4999 (IMPORTANT! See D4260)	182 (152)
Laser (destruction of soft tissue lesion)	D7465 (see other laser comments at D4999)	318 (182)
Lateral exostosis removal	D7471	319
LED Dental Identafi® – oral cancer screening adjunct	D0431	43
LeFort (various procedures)	D7946-D7949	331-332
Legend explanation	See "Legends"	
Lesions, surgical excision		
Bone tissue excision	D7471-D7490	319-320
Destruction of soft tissue (cryo, laser, electro surgery)	D7465	318
Intra-osseous lesions	D7440-D7461	316-318
Soft tissue excision	D7410-D7415/D7465	314-316
Limited orthodontic treatment	D8010-D8040	342-343
Liner (integral to direct restorative procedure)	No separate code	
Lingual (bilateral) space maintainer (fixed)	D1515	60
Local anesthesia		
Local anesthesia in conjunction with operative or surgical procedures	D9215	358
Non-operative or non-surgical related local anesthesia	D9210	357
Oraqix® (see D9999 for comments)	D9215/D9999	358/382
Regional block anesthesia	D9211	358
Trigeminal division block anesthesia	D9212	358

	Code	Page
Localized osteitis/dry socket complications treatment	D9930	370
Locator attachments		
Locator implant attachment (interim, prefabricated, or custom abutment)	D6051/D6056/D6057	243/241/242
Locator attachment (precision attachment)	D5862 (associated with mini implant)	217
Semi-precision implant abutment (locator) with keeper assembly	D6052 (associated with full size implant)	244
Lost or broken orthodontic appliance (replacement) – per arch	D8692	351

M	Code	Page
Maintainer, space	See "Space maintainer"	
Maintenance		
Complete denture maintenance (cleaning and inspection)	D9932/D9933	371
Implant maintenance (prosthesis removal, cleaning, reinsertion)	D6080	262
Maxillofacial prosthesis maintenance	D5993	228
Partial denture maintenance (cleaning and inspection)	D9934/D9935	372
Periodontal maintenance (recall visit)	D4910	179
Space maintenance (passive "holding" appliance)	D1510-D1525	59-61
Malar bone, repair of fracture (simple and compound)	D7650/D7660;D7750/D7760	323;324/325
Malocclusion, correction of	D8000-D8999	341-353
Mandible, fracture of	D7630/D7640;D7730/D7740	323;324
Mandibular advancement device (MAD)		
Sleep apnea device (if billing dental plan for medical problem)	D5999 (unspecified, by report)	231
Snoreguard (social issue)	D5999 (unspecified, by report)	231
TMJ dysfunction/TMD (if billing dental plan)	D7880	328
Maryland Bridge (two retainer crown "wings" plus pontic)		
Ceramic/porcelain "wing" retainer (Maryland Bridge)	D6548	272
Composite or resin "wing" retainer (Maryland retainer)	D6549	273
Metal "wing" retainer (Maryland Bridge)	D6545	271
Pontics for Maryland Bridge (match materials)	D6205-D6252	267-271
Re-cement Maryland Bridge	D6930	293
Maxilla, repair of fracture	D7610/D7620;D7710/D7720	323;324
Maxillofacial defect repair	D7955	335
Maxillofacial MRI (capture and interpretation/or just capture)	D0369/D0385	35/37
Maxillofacial prosthesis (this is not a removable partial or full denture)		
Adjustment of maxillofacial prosthesis	D5992	228
Maintenance and cleaning of maxillofacial prosthesis	D5993	228
Maxillofacial prosthetics	D5900-D5999	222-231
Maxillofacial ultrasound (capture and interpretation or just capture)	D0370/D0386	35/37
Medical device tax (not a sales tax)	D9985 (See "Sales tax")	380
Medicament carrier (topical) – vesiculobullous disease	D5991	230
Medicaments		
Arestin® – chemotherapeutic agent	D4381	177
Atridox® – chemotherapeutic agent	D4381	177
Chemotherapeutic agents	See Index, "Chemotherapeutic agents"	
Chlorhexidine (take home)	D9630	367

Chlorhexidine (gingival irrigation) – per quadrant	D4921	181
Debacterol® (in-office treatment to relieve pain from canker sores)	D9110 (emergency visit)	354
Desensitizing agent (up to full mouth) – in-office	D9910 (one tooth or whole mouth)	368
Emergency visit- application of desensitizing agent	D9110 (one tooth or whole mouth)	354
Fluoride (as desensitizing agent) – reported "per visit"	D9910 (one tooth or whole mouth)	368
Gingival irrigation (quadrant)	D4921	181
Periochip® chemotherapeutic agent	D4381	177
Resin (desensitizing agent) – cervical and/or root surface	D9911 (per tooth)	369
Viroxyn® (Dispensed for at home treatment of cold sores)	D9630 (at home use)	367
Viroxyn® (in office emergency treatment to relieve pain from cold sores)	D9110 (emergency treatment)	354

MI Paste™ or MI Paste Plus™

In-office treatment as a preventive procedure during ortho	D1999	63
In-office treatment for desensitization (emergency visit)	D9110	354
In-office treatment for white spots after ortho	D9999	382
Remineralization – dispensed for at-home treatment	D9630 (take home use)	367

Microabrasion, enamel — D9970 — 377

Microlux DL® (adjunct cancer screening device) — D0431 — 43

Microorganisms, culture and sensitivity test — D0415 — 40

Mini implant related services

Complete overdenture (implant related) – upper/lower arch	D6110/D6111	244/245
Mini implant placement	D6013	246
Partial overdenture (implant related) – upper/lower arch	D6112/D6113	246
Precision attachments (mini implant related) – locator	D5862	217

Missed appointment — D9986 — 381

Models

Diagnostic casts (models) – can be orthodontic records	D0470	44
Mounted case – occlusion analysis (includes waxup)	D9950	375
Waxup only	D9999	382

Moderate (conscious) sedation/analgesia

Intravenous moderate (conscious) sedation (each 15 minutes)	D9223	359
Non-intravenous (conscious) sedation	D9248	362

Monodont® bridge (two retainer "talons" plus pontic)

Pontic (resin with base metal)	D6251	270
"Talon" retainer (report two retainers) – see illustration after D6999	D6999 (unspecified, by report)	296

Moulage, facial — D5911/D5912 — 222

Mounted case – occlusion analysis (includes waxup) — D9950 — 375

Mouthguard, athletic — D9941 — 374

MRI, maxillofacial (capture and interpretation/or just capture) — D0369/D0385 — 35/37

Mucocele removal — D7410 — 314

Mucosal abnormalities, pre-diagnostic test — D0431 — 43

Myotomy — D7856 — 326

MyPerioID℠PST® (Oral DNA® Labs) — D0417 — 40

MyPerioPath℠ (Oral DNA® Labs) — D0417/D0418 — 40/41

N	Code	Page
Neoplasms, removal of	D7410-D7465	314-316
Nesbit (unilateral) one piece cast metal partial	D5281	198
Nightguard (bruxism and clenching) – also known as perio guard	D9940 (for adjustment, see D9943)	372
Nitrous oxide (N$_2$0), analgesia	D9230	360
Non-I.V. (conscious) sedation	D9248	362
Non-odontogenic cyst	D7460/D7461	318
Non-vital tooth whitening (endodontic treated single tooth)	D9974 (internal bleaching)	379
NTI appliance		
Occlusal guard adjustment	D9943	375
Occlusal guard (bruxism) appliance	D9940	372
Occlusal orthotic device (TMJ dysfunction/TMD) adjustment	D7881	329
Occlusal orthotic device (TMJ dysfunction/TMD)	D7880	328
Nursing home, (house/extended care facility visit)	D9410	364
Nutritional counseling	D1310	56

O	Code	Page
Obsolete/deleted codes	See Index, "Deleted Codes"	
Obturator		
Post-surgical obturator (definitive)	D5932	224
Refitting obturator	D5933	224
Surgical obturator (immediate temporary)	D5931	224
Occlusal adjustment (equilibration of teeth)		
Complete occlusal adjustment (includes mulitple visits)	D9952	376
Emergency visit (limited tooth adjustment to relieve pain at visit)	D9110	354
Limited occlusal adjustment (up to 6-8 teeth) – single visit	D9951	375
Occlusal radiographic image		
Extraoral, radiographic image	D0250	23
Intraoral, occlusal radiographic image	D0240	22
Occlusal guards		
Adjustment of occlusal guard	D9943	375
Bruxism and clenching appliance (also perio guard)	D9940	372
Occlusal orthotic device (TMJ dysfunction/TMD)	D7880	328
Occlusion analysis-mounted case (includes wax-up)	D9950	375
Perio guard appliance (reported as occlusal guard)	D9940	372
Reline or repair occlusal guard	D9942	374
Occlusal orthotic device (TMJ dysfunction/TMD) adjustment	D7881	329
Occlusal orthotic device (TMJ dysfunction/TMD) – not for bruxism	D7880	328
Odontogenic cyst (benign)	D7450/D7451	317
Odontoplasty (enameloplasty)		
Odontoplasty 1-2 teeth, includes removal of enamel projections	D9971	377
Odontoplasty (as part of limited occlusal adjustment) – up to 6 to 8 teeth	D9951	375

Office visit

After hours visit (doctor returns to office to see patient)	D9440	365
Observation visit – no other services performed	D9430	364
Re-evaluation post-operative office visit	D0171	17

Onlay

Fixed partial denture retainers		
Metallic onlay (retainer)	D6610-D6615	279-282
Titanium onlay (retainer)	D6634	284
Metallic onlays	D2542-D2544	78-80
Porcelain/ceramic onlays	D2642-D2644	81-83
Resin-based composite onlays	D2662-D2664	84-86

Open tooth to relieve pain (prior to endodontic therapy)

Emergency visit (open tooth to relieve pain prior to endodontics)	D9110 (root canal is on later date)	354
Pulpal debridement (open tooth prior to endodontic treatment)	D3221 (root canal is on later date)	118
Vital pulpotomy (do not do prior to endodontic therapy)	D3220 (typically primary teeth)	117

Operculectomy (excision of pericoronal gingiva)   D7971   337

OralCDx® brush biopsy   D7288   308

Oral and maxillofacial surgery procedures   D7000-D7999 (unspecified procedure by report)   298-339

Oral DNA® Labs

MyPerioID® PST® Test	D0417	40
MyPerioPath® Test	D0417/D0418	40/41
OraRisk℠ HPV Test	D0416-D0418/D0431	40-41/43

Oral evaluation (exam)   See Index, "Evaluations"

Oral/facial photographic images (can be orthodontic record)   D0350/D0351 (2D and 3D images)   32/33

Oral hygiene instructions   D1330   56

OralID™ (oral cancer adjunct)   D0431   43

Oral pathology laboratory procedures   D0472-D0502   47-50

OraPharma (Arestin®)   D4381   177

Oraqix® (D9999 is recommended, see narrative)   D9210/D9999 (unspecified, by report)   357/382

OraRisk℠ HPV test (Oral DNA® Labs)   D0416-D0418/D0431   40-41/43

Oraverse® (anesthesia reversal agent)   D9999 (unspecified, by report)   382

Orthodontics

Case presentation (follows oral evaluation appointment)	D9450	365
Comprehensive case orthodontic treatment	D8070-D8090	345-347
Consultation (typically by orthodontist after dentist referral)	D9310 (requires referral by dentist/physician)	363
Fixed retainer (orthodontic) repair	D8694	352
Fixed retainer (orthodontic) re-bonding/re-cementing	D8693	352
Inman Aligner™	D8040	343
Invisalign®	See Index, "Invisalign®"	
Minor case appliances (limited treatment)		
Adolescent dentition	D8030	342
Adult dentition	D8040	343
Periodic orthodontic visit	D8670	349
Primary dentition	D8010	342

Transitional dentition	D8020	342
Place device to facilitate eruption (button/pin/bracket)	D7283	306
Pre-treatment orthodontic visit (to evaluate orthodontic readiness)	D8660	349
Prophylaxis (after removal of braces) – flashing remains	D1110 (report D8999 plus prophylaxis D1110)	51
Records, orthodontic		
Cephalometric radiographic image	D0340	31
Diagnostic casts (study models)	D0470	44
Evaluation, comprehensive/detailed, problem focused	D0150/D0160	12/14
Oral/facial photo images	D0350/D0351 (2D and 3D images)	32/33
Panoramic radiographic image	D0330	30
Replace lost or broken retainer	D8692	351
Retainer (removable) adjustment	D8681	350
Retention (remove active appliances, immediately place retention)	D8680	350
Six Month Smiles®	D8030/D8040	342/343
Smart Moves®	D8040	343
Uncovering impacted or unerupted tooth (can be pre-orthodontic)	D7280	305
Orthodontic appliance		
Fixed retainer (orthodontic) repair	D8694	352
Fixed retainer (orthodontic) re-bonding/re-cementing	D8693	352
Harmful habit appliance (removable) – thumb sucking	D8210	347
Harmful habit appliance (fixed) – thumb sucking	D8220	348
Interceptive tooth movement appliance (child)	D8050/D8060	344
Minor tooth movement appliance	D8010-D8040; D8050/D8060	342-343;344
Repair orthodontic appliance	D8691	351
Replacement of lost or broken retainer (post orthodontic treatment)	D8692	351
Retainer (removable) adjustment	D8681	350
Retention (remove active appliances, place retainer)	D8680	350
Orthodontic retainer adjustment (removable)	D8681	350
Orthodontic treatment visit	D8670	349
Orthodontic workup (radiographs, photographs, study models)	D0340/D0350/D0470	31/32/44
Orthotic device appliance (TMJ dysfunction/TMD)	D7880	328
Orthotic device adjustment	D7881	329
Osseous graft (bone socket extraction site)	D7953	334
Osseous graft (edentulous area)	D7950	332
Osseous graft (related to periodontal surgery with teeth present)	D4263/D4264	155/156
Osseous graft (related to graft at same time as implant placement)	D6104	240
Osseous surgery (periodontal) – requires reshaping alveolar process		
1-3 contiguous teeth per quadrant	D4261	154
Quadrant – 4 or more contiguous teeth	D4260	152
Ostectomy, partial	D7550	322
Osteitis, localized; dry socket (post-surgical complications)	D9930	370
Osteoplasty	D7940	331
Osteotomy	D7941-D7945	331

Overdenture

Complete (full denture) implant overdenture (upper/lower)	D6110/D6111	244/245
Complete (full denture) natural tooth overdenture		
Maxillary overdenture	D5863	218
Mandibular overdenture	D5865	219
Fixed implant supported full overdenture (upper/lower)	D6114/D6115 (hybrid prosthesis)	247/248
Fixed implant supported partial overdenture (upper/lower)	D6116/D6117 (hybrid prosthesis)	248/249
Implant/abutment supported complete overdenture		
Cap embedded in overdenture (mini implant supported overdenture)	D5862 (with mini implant)	217
Semi-precision implant abutment with keeper assembly	D6052 (with full size implant)	244
Partial (implant supported) overdenture – removable	D6112/D6113	246
Partial overdenture – implant overdenture – removable	D6112/D6113	246
Partial overdenture (root retained natural tooth overdenture)		
Maxillary partial overdenture – natural tooth	D5864	218
Mandibular partial overdenture – natural tooth	D5866	220

P	Code	Page

Pain relief

Emergency visit (open and drain prior to endodontics) palliative	D9110	354
Incise and drain abscess	D7510/D7511/D7520/D7521	320/321
Pulpal debridement (open and drain prior to endo treatment later)	D3221	118
Pulpotomy (vital tooth) – not first step of root canal treatment	D3220 (generally primary teeth)	117
Sedative filling (now termed "protective restoration")	D2940	102

Paint on fluoride application (in office)	D1208	55
Palatal tissue – removal of excess formation	D7970	337
Palliative treatment (minor treatment for pain relief)	D9110	354
Panoramic radiographic image	D0330	30
Parenteral drug administration (in office)	D9610/D9612	366
Partial dentures, fixed (bridgework)	See Index, "Fixed partial dentures"	

Partial dentures, removable

Adjustments to partial denture	D5421/D5422	200
Cast metal framework, resin base partial denture	D5213/D5214	191/192
Cu-Sil® partial denture	D5211/D5212	189/190
Fixed (bridge) – child – esthetic partial (fixed)	D6985 (not a space maintainer)	296
Flexible resin base (Valplast®, Proplast®, etc.) partial denture	D5225/D5226	197/198
Flexible unilateral resin base (Valplast®, Proplast®, etc.) partial	D5225/D5226	197/198
Immediate partial denture – cast metal framework	D5223/D5224	195/196
Immediate partial denture – resin	D5221/D5222	193/194
Implant/abutment supported partial denture overdenture	D6112/D6113	246
Interim partial denture (upper/lower) – temporary only	D5820/D5821	215
Nesbitt type (unilateral) partial denture (cast framework)	D5281	198
Overdenture (implant/abutment supported) partial overdenture	D6054 (Previously deleted code)	246
Overdenture (natural tooth) partial overdenture	D5864 (maxillary); D5866 (mandibular)	218;220

Rebase partial denture	D5720/D5721	206
Reline partial denture (chairside or laboratory processed)	D5740/D5741;D5760/D5761	208/209;211/212
Repair partial denture (various repairs)	D5610-D5660	201-204
Resin base partial denture (long term acrylic)	D5211/D5212	189/190
Unilateral partial denture (cast metal framework) – Nesbit	D5281	198
Unilateral partial denture (Valplast®, Proplast®, etc.) long term	D5225/D5226	197/198

Partial pulpotomy for apexogenesis (permanent tooth) — D3222 — 119

Partial tooth removal

<u>Intentional</u> partial tooth extraction (coronectomy)	D7251	304
<u>Unintentional</u> partial extraction (not all of tooth removed)	D7999 (unspecified procedure, by report)	339

Pathology (oral) laboratory procedures — D0472-D502 — 47-50

Pediatric partial denture (fixed) – for esthetics only — D6985 (not a space maintainer) — 296

Pedicle graft — D4270 — 160

Perforation defect, internal repair (endodontic) — D3333 — 126

Periapical radiographic images (first, additional images) — D0220/D0230 — 21/22

Pericoronal gingival excision (operculectomy) — D7971 — 337

Peri-implant procedures

Bone graft at same time as implant placement	D6104	240
Bone graft for repair of peri-implant defect	D6103 (in conjunction with D6102)	240
Debridement and osseous contouring of a peri-implant defect	D6102 (see D6103 for associated bone graft)	239
Debridement of a peri-implant defect (soft tissue only)	D6101 (debridement with no osseous contouring)	238

PerioChip® (antimicrobial agent) — D4381 — 177

Periodontal abscess (incise and drain) — D7510 — 320

Periodontal comprehensive oral evaluation (exam) — D0180 (must be perio patient or have perio risk factors) — 18

Periodontal maintenance (recall visit) — D4910 — 179

Periodontal medicament carrier with seal – per arch — D5994 (Perio Protect Tray®) — 229

Periodic oral evaluation (recall exam) — D0120 — 8

Periodic orthodontic treatment visit — D8670 — 349

Periodontal probing and charting (as separate procedure) — D4999 (typically reported by hygienist) — 182

Periodontal probing and charting (inclusive in a procedure)

Comprehensive oral evaluation	D0150 (may include probing and charting)	12
Comprehensive periodontal oral evaluation	D0180 (mandatory probing and charting)	18
Periodic evaluation (recall visit)	D0120 (may include probing and charting)	8
Unspecified periodontal procedure (by hygienist)	D4999	182

Periodontal prophylaxis (periodontal maintenance visit) — D4910 — 179

Periodontal splinting (not trauma related)

Extracoronal splinting (not trauma related)	D4321	177
Intracoronal splinting (not trauma related)	D4320	168

Perio guard (occlusal guard) – bruxism — D9940 — 372

PerioLase (soft tissue laser) — D7465 (see laser comments after D4999) — 318

Perio Protect Trays® (do not use D4265, D4381, or D5986) — D5994 (per arch) — 229

Periradicular services

Apicoectomy	D3410-D3426	133-135

Feriradicular services without apicoectomy	D3427-D3432	136-139
Feriradicular surgery without apicoectomy	D3427	136

Pharmacologic agents

Therapeutic parenteral drug (administered in office)	D9610/D9612	366
Other drugs and/or medicaments – take home products	D9630	367

Photographic images, diagnostic (can be orthodontic records)	D0350/D0351 (2D or 3D images)	32/33
Photographs, oral/facial (diagnostic) (can be orthodontic records)	D0350/D0351 (2D or 3D images)	32/33
Pinhole technique	D4270	160
Pin retention (report in addition to amalgam/composite restoration)	D2951 (pins are included in core buildup procedure)	106
Pit and fissure sealant (not preventative resin restoration D1352)	D1351 (can be applied by hygienist)	56
Place abutment	D6020 (previously deleted code)	237
Placement of device to facilitate eruption of impacted tooth	D7283	306
Plasma rich protein (PRP) – platelet rich plasma	D7921	330
Plates (dentures)	See Index, "Dentures"	
Pontics, bridgework (various) – also applies to implant bridge	D6205-D6253	267-271
Porcelain/ceramic crown	D2740	90
Porcelain/ceramic prefabricated crown, primary tooth	D2929	99

Post and core (various)

Frefabricated post and core	D2954 (either for a crown or retainer crown)	107
Indirectly fabricated post and core (lab or CAD/CAM)	D2952 (either for a crown or retainer crown)	106

Post-operative office visit, re-evaluation	D0171	17
Post, removal of	D2955 (separate procedure)	108
Power bleach (external bleaching) – in office procedure	D9972 (for take home trays – see D9975)	377
Practice Booster Code software	Go to www.practicebooster.com	

Precision attachment

Locator (implant – overdenture or precision partial denture)	D5862 (associated with mini implant)	217
Precision attachment (fixed denture)	D6950	294
Removable precision attachment/mini implant locator	D5862	217
Replacement of replaceable part of precision attachment	D5867	221
Replacement of replaceable part (implant prosthesis)	D6091	263
Semi precision attachment abutment (with keeper assembly)	D6052 (associated with full size implant)	244

Prefabricated abutment (implant) – includes placement	D6056	241

Prefabricated crowns

Prefabricated porcelain/ceramic crown – primary tooth only	D2929	99
Prefabricated resin crown (primary or permanent tooth)	D2932	100
Stainless steel crown, esthetic coated – primary tooth only	D2934	101
Stainless steel crown, permanent tooth only	D2931	100
Stainless steel crown, primary tooth only	D2930	100
Stainless steel crown, resin window (primary or permanent tooth)	D2933	101

Prefabricated post and core

Bridge retainer crown prefab post and core	D6972 (previously deleted code) – see D2954	295
Each additional prefab post and core (same tooth)	D2957	108
Prefab post and core (crown and retainer crown)	D2954	107

Pre-orthodontic treatment exam	D8660	349

Preventive (direct) resin options

If caries and preparation extends into <u>dentin</u> – a resin-based composite restoration	D2391	73
If in enamel surface, pits and fissures – a sealant	D1351	56
If preparation (by doctor) is in cavitated pits and fissures of enamel – preventative resin <u>restoration</u>	D1352 (prep in enamel but does not extend into dentin)	57
Resin infiltration (ICON – DMG America)	D2990	113

Preventive procedure, unspecified — D1999 (toothpaste, toothbrush) — 63

Preventive services — D1000-D1999 — 51-63

Preventative resin restoration (PRR) — D1352 (doctor procedure, not hygienist) — 57

Primary (deciduous) tooth procedures

Anterior crown (direct composite)	D2390	100
Extractions		
Coronal remnant extraction, deciduous tooth	D7111	298
Extraction, deciduous tooth with some root remaining	D7140	298
Primary tooth crowns		
Esthetic coated SSC – primary tooth only	D2934	100
Permanent tooth SSC – permanent tooth only	D2931	100
Porcelain, prefabricated ceramic crown, primary tooth only	D2929	99
Primary tooth SSC – primary tooth only	D2930	100
Resin window SSC (primary or permanent tooth)	D2933	101
Pulpal therapy (deciduous tooth) – resorbable material (not gutta percha)		
Anterior tooth (deciduous) – non-vital tooth	D3230	120
Posterior tooth (deciduous) – non-vital tooth	D3240	120
Pulpotomy (vital tooth) – to maintain vitality of tooth	D3220 (not first step of root canal therapy)	117
Restorations (direct placement)		
Amalgam restoration	D2140-D2161	65-66
Anterior composite restorations	D2330-D2390	68-73
Anterior composite crown (primary or permanent tooth)	D2390	72
Posterior composite restorations	D2391-D2394	73-76
Preventative resin restoration (PRR) – dentist procedure	D1352	57

Primer (integral to restorative procedure) — No separate code

Probing, periodontal (and charting)

Evaluation (probing and charting included, if applicable)		
Comprehensive oral evaluation	D0150 ("may" include probing and charting)	12
Comprehensive periodontal evaluation	D0180 (mandatory probing and charting)	18
Extensive, detailed evaluation (follows oral evaluation visit)	D0160 (by report)	14
Periodic (recall) evaluation (exam)	D0120 ("may" include probing and charting)	8
Unspecified periodontal procedure by hygienist	D4999 (unspecified procedure, by report)	182

Problem focused evaluation (exam) — D0140 (can be emergency exam) — 9

Prophylaxis

Adult prophylaxis (standard fee)	D1110	51
Child prophylaxis	D1120	54
"Difficult" prophylaxis (higher fee)	D1110	51
"Extended visit" prophylaxis (higher fee)	D1110	51

Gingivitis (Type I) treatment is by prophylaxis	D1110	51
"Orthodontic" prophylaxis after fixed appliance removal	D8999 (report in addition to prophylaxis D1110)	353
"Teenage" prophylaxis (lower adult prophy fee)	D1110	51
"Short visit" prophylaxis for limited teeth (lower fee)	D1110	51
Proplast® or Valplast® (flexible) base partial denture		
Mandibular flexible partial denture	D5226	198
Maxillary flexible partial denture	D5225	197
Prosthesis (maxillofacial prosthetics)		
Adjust maxillofacial prosthesis	D5992	228
Auricular	D5914	223
Cranial	D5924	224
Maintenance and cleaning	D5993	228
Mandibular resection prosthesis	D5934/D5935	225
Ocular	D5916	223
Orbital	D5915	223
Palatal	D5954-D5959	225-226
Speech aid	D5952/D5953/D5960	225/226
Prosthodontics		
Fixed bridgework	D6200-D6999	267-296
Implant services	D6000-D6199	234-265
Maxillofacial prosthesis	D5900-D5999	222-231
Removable prosthodontics	D5000-D5899	184-221
Protective restoration (formally "sedative filling")	D2940	102
Provisional		
Single crown provisional	D2799	97
Pontic (FPD) provisional – any time length	D6253	271
Retainer crown (FPD) provisional – any time length	D6793	292
Provisional splinting		
Periodontal (not trauma) splinting – bone loss		
Provisional splinting – extracoronal	D4321 (could be Ribbond®)	169
Provisional splinting – intracoronal	D4320	168
Splinting/stabilization of evulsed or displaced tooth (trauma related)	D7270 (report per tooth)	304
Proximal/distal wedge (periodontal procedure)	D4274	162
Pulp cap		
Direct pulp cap (pulpal exposure)	D3110	116
Indirect pulp cap (all caries is not removed)	D3120	116
Pulp vitality tests	D0460	44
Pulpal debridement (endodontic related)	D3221 (root canal performed later)	118
Pulpal regeneration (not apexification/recalcification)		
Pulpal regeneration – initial visit	D3355	131
Pulpal regeneration – interim medication visit	D3356	132
Pulpal regeneration – final visit (new code)	D3357	132
Pulpal therapy, primary teeth (root canal)		
Anterior tooth – pulpal therapy	D3230	120

Posterior tooth – pulpal therapy	D3240	120
Pulpotomy (to maintain vitality and generally is a primary tooth)	**D3220 (not first stage of root canal treatment)**	117
Pulpotomy (partial) – apexogenesis of permanent tooth	D3222	119

Q	**Code**	**Page**

No "Q" terms

R	**Code**	**Page**
Radiation		
Carrier	D5983	226
Cone locator	D5985	227
Shield	D5984	227
Radiographic/surgical implant index guide	D6190	264
Radiographs, diagnostic imaging (X-rays)		
Bitewings		
Bitewings – four radiographic Images (horizontal or vertical)	D0274	27
Bitewing – single radiographic image (horizontal or vertical)	D0270	24
Bitewings – three radiographic images (horizontal or vertical)	D0273	26
Bitewings – two radiographic images (horizontal or vertical)	D0272	24
Bitewings – vertical bitewings – 7 to 8 radiographic images	D0277	28
Cephalometric radiographic image	D0340	31
Complete series of radiographic images (intraoral)	D0210	20
Cone Beam CT – Image capture and interpretation		
Cone Beam CT – Data capture	D0360 (previously deleted code)	34
Cone Beam CT – 2D reconstruction	D0362 (previously deleted code)	34
Cone Beam – 3D image reconstruction using existing data, includes multiple images	D0363 (previously deleted code)	34
Cone Beam CT capture and interpretation with limited field of view – less than one whole jaw	D0364	34
Cone Beam CT capture and interpretation with field of view of one full dental arch – mandible	D0365	34
Cone Beam CT capture and interpretation with field of view of one full dental arch – maxilla, with or without cranium	D0366	34
Cone Beam CT capture and interpretation with field of view of both jaws, with or without cranium	D0367	35
Cone Beam CT capture and interpretation for TMJ series including two or more exposures	D0368	35
Sialoendoscopy capture and interpretation	D0371	35
Cone Beam CT – Image capture only interpretation and report performed by a practitioner not associated with the capture		
Cone Beam CT image capture with limited field of view - less than one whole jaw	D0380	36
Cone Beam CT image capture with field of view of one full dental arch – mandible	D0381	36
Cone Beam CT image capture with field of view of one full dental arch – maxilla, with or without cranium	D0382	36
Cone Beam CT image capture with field of view of both jaws, with or without cranium	D0383	36

Cone Beam CT image capture for TMJ series including two or more exposures	D0384	36
Cone Beam CT – Interpretation and report only		
Interpretation of diagnostic image by a practitioner not associated with capture of the image	D0391	37
Cone Beam CT – Post processing of images or image sets		
Digital subtraction of two or more images or image volumes of the same modality	D0394	38
Fusion of two or more 3D image volumes of one or more modalities	D0395	39
Treatment simulation using 3D image volumes	D0393	37
Extraoral image	D0250	23
Maxillofacial MRI image capture	D0385	35
Maxillofacial ultrasound image capture	D0386	35
Maxillofacial MRI capture and interpretation	D0369	35
Maxillofacial ultrasound capture and interpretation	D0370	35
Occlusal radiographic image (intraoral)	D0240	22
Panoramic radiographic image	D0330	30
Periapical images (intraoral)		
Periapical radiographic image (first)	D0220	21
Periapical radiographic image (each additional)	D0230	22
Posterior – anterior or lateral skull and facial bone surgery	D0290	29
Sialography	D0310	29
TMJ arthrogram	D0320	29
Tomographic survey radiographic image	D0322	30
Vertical bitewings (7 to 8 images) – typically perio patient	D0277	28
Reattachment of tooth fragment, incisal edge or cusp	D2921	99
Rebase procedures	See Index, "Relines and tissue conditioning"	
Full denture rebase (save teeth, all new acrylic)	D5710/D5711	205/206
Partial denture rebase (save teeth, all new acrylic)	D5720/D5721	206/207
Re-bond procedures		
Maryland bridge re-bond	D6930	293
Orthodontic fixed retainer re-bond	D8693	352
Re-bond tooth fragment (incisal edge or cusp)	D2921	99
Recalcification/apexification	D3351-D3353	128-130
Recall procedures		
Adult prophylaxis	D1110	51
Child prophylaxis	D1120	54
Periodontal maintenance (recall) visit	D4910	179
Recall oral evaluation	D0120/D0180	8/18
Re-cement procedures		
¾ crown re-cementation	D2920	99
Bridge re-cementation (natural teeth)	D6930	293
Crown (single crown) re-cementation	D2920	99
Implant bridge re-cementation	D6093	264
Implant crown re-cementation (single crown)	D6092	263

Inlay re-cementation	D2910	98
Maryland Bridge re-cementation (wing retainer(s))	D6930	293
Onlay re-cementation	D2910	98
Orthodontic fixed retainer re-cementation (post orthodontic)	D8693	352
Post and core (cast, indirect, or prefabricated) re-cementation	D2915	98
Space maintainer re-cementation	D1550	62
Veneer re-cementation	D2910	98
Records, orthodontic (individual codes listed below report orthodontic records)		
Cephalometric radiographic image	D0340	31
Complete radiographic image series (intraoral)	D0210	20
Diagnostic casts/models	D0470	44
Diagnostic oral/facial photos	D0350/D0351 (2D or 3D images)	32/33
Panoramic radiographic image	D0330	30
Pre-orthodontic treatment visit (to evaluate orthodontic readiness)	D8660	349
Reduction, interproximal (enamel) – discing for tooth alignment	D9951	375
Re-evaluation (typically follows D0140/D0150/D0180)	D0170	15
Re-evaluation – post operative office visit	D0171	17
Regeneration (pulpal)	D3355-D3357	131-132
Reimplantation		
Accidentally evulsed or displaced tooth (trauma related)	D7270;D7670/D7671	304;324
Intentional reimplantation (endodontic procedure)	D3470	140
Relief of pain/pain relief		
Emergency visit (palliative) to relieve pain/discomfort	D9110	354
Pulpal debridement (endodontic)	D3221 (not first step of endodontics)	118
Pulpotomy (to maintain vitality of tooth)	D3220 (typically primary teeth)	117
Sedative filling (now termed "protective restoration")	D2940	102
Relines	See also "Rebases" and "Tissue conditioning"	
Chairside reline (polymerizes at chair)		
Full denture reline (chairside reline)	D5730/D5731	207/208
Partial denture reline (chairside reline)	D5740/D5741	208/209
Laboratory (processed) reline (in office or outside laboratory)		
Full denture reline (in office or outside laboratory)	D5750/D5751	210/211
Partial denture reline (in office or outside laboratory)	D5760/D5761	211/212
Removable appliance		
Harmful habit appliance (removable) – thumb sucking	D8210	347
Minor tooth movement		
Adult dentition (partial arch adult treatment)	D8040	343
Primary dentition minor tooth movement	D8010/D8050	342/344
Removable space maintainer	D1520/D1525	61
Removable orthodontic retainer adjustment	D8681	350
Repair orthodontic appliance	D8691	351
Replace lost/broken retainer	D8692	351
Retention, orthodontic (place retention after active appliance removal)	D8680	350

Removable partial denture	See Index, "partial dentures, removable"	
Remove fixed space maintainer (not by provider placing maintainer)	D1555	62
Repair procedures		
Complete denture repair	D5510/D5520	201
Crown repair necessitated by restorative material failure	D2980	111
Fixed partial denture repair (bridge)	D6980	295
Fixed retainer (orthodontic) re-bonding/re-cementing	D8693	352
Implant abutment repair	D6095	263
Implant-supported prosthesis repair	D6090	262
Inlay repair necessitated by restorative material failure	D2981	112
Maxillofacial defect repair	D7955	335
Occlusal guard repair	D9942	374
Onlay repair necessitated by restorative material failure	D2982	112
Orthodontic appliance repair (includes functional)	D8691	351
Orthodontic fixed retainer re-bonding/re-cementing	D8693	352
Orthodontic fixed retainer repair (after ortho treatment)	D8694	352
Partial denture repair	D5610-D5671	201-204
Precision or semi-precision attachment component replacement	D5867	221
Sealant repair	D1353	58
Veneer repair necessitated by restorative material failure	D2983	113
Replace lost or broken retainer (previous orthodontic treatment)		
Hawley retainer replacement (lost or broken)	D8692	351
Orthodontic retainer replacement (previous orthodontic treatment)	D8692	351
Replacement of semi-precision or precision attachment	D6091 (implant related)	263
Resin-based composite (direct restoration)		
Anterior composites	D2330-D2335	68-72
Crown composite (anterior composite crown)	D2390	72
Posterior composite (back teeth)	D2391-D2394	73-76
Preventive resin restoration (PRR)	D1352 (doctor procedure, not hygienist)	57
Veneer (direct) resin composite restoration	D2960	108
Resin-based composite, indirect (Lab fabricated/milled/CAD/CAM)		
¾ crown (resin)	D2712	88
Crown (resin)	D2710	87
Fixed partial denture (bridge) abutment (resin)	D6710	284
Inlay/onlay (resin)	D2650-D2664	83-86
Pontic (resin)	D6205	267
Veneer (resin)	D2961	109
Resin-based acrylic removable partial denture		
Resin-based partial denture (long term acrylic partial)	D5211/D5212	189/190
Resin-based partial denture (temporary acrylic partial)	D5820/D5821	215/216
Resin-based composites		
Anterior and posterior composite restorations	D2330-D2394	68-76
Preventive resin restoration (PRR)	D1352 (doctor procedure, not hygienist)	57

Resin infiltration of incipient smooth surface lesions (Icon)	D2990	113
Resin bonded bridge	See Index, "Maryland Bridge"	
Resin window SSC (stainless steel crown) – primary or permanent	D2933	101
Restorations		
Amalgam restorations	D2140-D2161	65-68
Composite restorations	D2330-D2394	68-76
Gold foil	D2410-D2430	77
Inlay/onlay	D2510-D2664; D6600-D6615 D6624/D6634	77-86;274-282 277/284
Interim therapeutic restoration – primary dentition	D2941	103
Preventive resin restoration (PRR)	D1352 (doctor procedure, not hygienist)	57
Protective restoration (formerly termed "sedative filling")	D2940	102
Restorative foundation for an indirect restoration	D2949	103
Restorative codes	D2000-D2999	65-114
Restorative foundation for an indirect restoration	D2949	103
Retainers		
Fixed partial denture retainer crown	D6710-D6794	284-293
Fixed retainer repair (post ortho)	D8694	352
Interceptive orthodontic appliance	D8050/D8060	344
Implant/abutment supported retainer crown	D6068-D6077/D6194	255-261/259
Orthodontic retention (place retention after active appliance removal)	D8680	350
Re-bond fixed retainer	D8693	352
Removable orthodontic retainer adjustment	D8681	350
Remove active appliances, then immediately place retainers	D8680	350
Replace lost or broken retainer	D8692	351
Retention (remove active appliances, immediately place retainer)	D8680	350
Retreatment, endodontic	D3346-D3348	127-128
Retrofitting a removable prosthesis for implants	D5875	221
Retrograde filling (endodontic procedure)	D3430	138
Reversal agent (Oraverse®, etc.)	D9999 (unspecified procedure, by report)	382
Revision, periodontal surgery	D4268	159
Ribbond® (perio splinting – not trauma related) – extracoronal	D4321	169
Ridge augmentation/sinus augmentation	D7950/D7951/D7952	332/333
Ridge preservation		
Bone graft (at same time as implant placement)	D6104	240
Socket graft (at the time of extraction) – not perio osseous graft	D7953	334
Risk assessment and documentation (caries)	D0601-D0603	45-47
Root		
Amputation, root (endodontic procedure)	D3450	139
Apexogenesis (to form root)	D3222	119
Erupted tooth extraction		
Exposed root extraction (not surgical extraction)	D7140 (primary and permanent tooth)	298
Routine extraction, erupted tooth/exposed root removal	D7140 (primary and permanent tooth)	298

	Code	Page
Surgical extraction, erupted tooth (remove bone and/or section tooth)	D7210 (primary and permanent tooth)	300
Surgical removal of residual tooth roots (flap/remove bone)	D7250 (primary and permanent tooth)	303
Root Canal (other procedures)	See Index, "Endodontics"	
Root canal, incomplete inoperable, unrestorable or fractured tooth	D3332	125
Root canal obstruction	D3331	125
Root canal (permanent tooth)		
Anterior root canal	D3310	121
Anterior (retreat) root canal	D3346	127
Bicuspid root canal	D3320	122
Bicuspid (retreat) root canal	D3347	127
Closure of endodontic access hole (place occlusal or lingual restoration)	D2140/D2330/D2391	65/68/73
Molar root canal	D3330	124
Molar (retreat) root canal	D3348	128
Root canal (primary/deciduous teeth) – resorbable material – not gutta percha		
Pulpal therapy (anterior primary)	D3230	120
Pulpal therapy (posterior primary)	D3240	120
Root planing and scaling (SRP) – quadrant/partial quadrant	D4341/D4342	170/171
Root removal		
Exposed root, erupted tooth	D7140	298
Surgical removal of residual tooth roots (surgical cutting procedure)	D7250 (primary and permanent tooth)	303
Root amputation/resection	D3450	139
Rubber dam, surgical isolation of tooth	D3910	140

S

	Code	Page
Sales tax	D9985	380
Saliva (analysis of sample collected)	D0418	41
Saliva (sample collection)	D0417	40
Salivary gland		
Excision	D7981	338
Fistula closure	D7983	338
Scaling and root planing (SRP)	D4341/D4342	170/171
Screening of a patient (pre-diagnostic service)	D0190	19
Sealant (remains in enamel surface)	D1351 (see also D1352 for preventative resin)	56
Sealant repair	D1353	58
Search for a given code, directions		438
Second stage implant surgery (placing healing cap/abutment)	D6011	236
Section bridge	D9120	357
Sedation		
Deep sedation, general anesthesia – each 15 minute increment	D9223	359
Intravenous moderate (conscious) sedation/analgesia - each 15 minute increment	D9243	361
Non-intravenous conscious sedation	D9248	362
Sedative filling (now termed "protective restoration")	D2940	102
Semi precision attachment abutment (with keeper assembly)	D6052	244

Sequestrum, bony	D9930	370
Sequestrectomy (for removal of non-vital bone)	D7550	322
Services – Author's		437
Sialodochoplasty (salivary duct repair)	D7982	338
Sialography (image)	D0310	29
Sialolithotomy	D7980	338
Simulation of treatment using 3D image volume	D0393	37
Single crown and retainer crown build up (various procedures)		
Core buildup (for crown and retainer crown)	D2950	104
Post and core, indirectly fabricated (cast or CAD/CAM), for a crown or retainer crown	D2952	106
Pre-fabricated post and core (crown and retainer crown)	D2954	107
Sinus augmentation (sinus lift for implant placement)		
Sinus augmentation via a lateral open approach (window)	D7951	333
Sinus augmentation via a vertical approach	D7952	333
Sinus perforation, closure	D7261	304
Sinusotomy	D7560	323
Six Month Smiles® (orthodontic)	D8030/D8040	342/343
Skin graft	D7920	330
Sleep apnea appliance (submit to medical)	D5999 (unspecified procedure, by report)	231
Smart Moves® orthodontics	D8040	343
Smear (biopsy)	D7287	308
Smooth bone associated with extractions	See Index, "Alveoloplasty"	
Snap-On Smile® (multiple purpose appliance – see various codes)	D9999/D5820/D5821/D5225 D5226/D4321/D7270/D8680	382/215/215/197 198/169/304/350
Snore guard (social problem, not medical)	D5999 (unspecified procedure, by report)	231
Soft splint appliance		
Athletic mouth guard	D9941	374
Occlusal guard (bruxism/clenching); perio guard	D9940	372
Occlusal orthotic device (TMJ dysfunction/TMD)	D7880	328
Soft-suck-down appliance		
Athletic mouth guard	D9941	374
Occlusal guard (bruxism/clenching); perio guard	D9940	372
Occlusal orthotic device (TMJ dysfunction/TMD)	D7880	328
Soft tissue allograft	D4275	163
Software		
Coding system software	See www.practicebooster.com	
Space maintainer		
Fixed (esthetic) appliance (not for space maintenance) – Pediatric partial denture	D6985	296
Fixed space maintainer (space holding – not active appliance)		
Bilateral (lingual arch) – fixed	D1515	60
Unilateral (band and loop) – fixed	D1510	59
Re-cement space maintainer	D1550	62
Removal of fixed space maintainer (removed by different office)	D1555	62

Removable space maintainer		
Bilateral removable space maintainer	D1525	61
Unilateral removable space maintainer	D1520	61

Special characterization (lab characterization)

Bridge characterization	D6999 (unspecified procedure, by report)	206
Crown characterization	D2999 (unspecified procedure, by report)	113
Denture characterization	D5899 (unspecified procedure, by report)	221
Porcelain margin option for crown and fixed bridge	D2999/D6999 (unspecified procedure, by report)	113/296

Speech aid

Adult speech aid	D5953	225
Pediatric speech aid	D5952	225

Splint

Hard/soft splint (bruxism – occlusal guard and perio guard)	D9940	372
Occlusal orthotic appliance (TMJ dysfunction/TMD)	D7880	328

Splinted crowns — Report as individual crowns, not as retainer crowns

Splinting/splint

Commissure splint	D5987	227
Occlusal (bruxism) guard or perio guard	D9940	372
Occlusal orthotic (TMJ dysfunction/TMD) device appliance	D7880	328
Periodontal provisional splinting (not trauma related)		
Extracoronal splinting (Ribbond® on lower linguals)	D4321	169
Intracoronal splinting (groove/composite between teeth)	D4320	168
Provisional splinting (periodontal, not trauma related)	D4320/D4321	168/169
Surgical splint	D5988 (for implant surgical guide, see D6190)	227
Trauma splinting (stabilization after trauma) – per tooth	D7270	304
Two or more crowns (all splinted together)	Report as <u>individual</u> crowns, not as retainer crowns	

Stainless steel crown (SSC)

Esthetic coated SSC – primary tooth only	D2934	101
Permanent SSC – permanent tooth	D2931	100
Primary SSC – primary tooth only	D2930	100
Resin window SSC – primary or permanent tooth	D2933	101

Stayplate (flipper as temporary partial denture)	D5820/D5821	215/216
Stent, surgical	D5982 (see D6190 for implant surgical guide/index)	226
Stress breaker (fixed)	D6940 (bridge related)	294
Strip (disc) to provide room for tooth alignment	D9951/D9971	375/377
Study models (diagnostic cast)	D0470 (can be component of orthodontic records)	44
Subepithelial connective tissue graft	D4273	161
Supra crestal fiberotomy (transseptal) (orthodontic-related)	D7291	309
Surgical access, unerupted tooth (generally orthodontic-related)	D7280	305
Surgical/ambulatory center call	D9420	364
Surgical exposure of impacted tooth (generally orthodontic-related)	D7280	305
Surgical or radiographic guide/index for implant placement	D6190	264
Surgical or radiographic revision (periodontal procedure)	D4268	159

Survey crown (extra charge in addition to crown or retainer crown)

	Code	Page
Crown survey	D2999	113
Retainer crown survey	D6999	296
Suture procedures		
Complicated suture	D7911/D7912	330
Recent small wound suture	D7910	330
Swish fluoride application in office – (not fluoride varnish)	D1208	55
Syndrome, cracked tooth (minor emergency treatment)	D9110	354
Synovectomy	D7854	326

T	Code	Page
Tax, sales	D9985	380
"Teen Adult" Prophylaxis (lower teen fee)	D1110	51
Telescopic crown (coping under crown or FPD)	D2975	111
Temporary crown (fractured tooth)	D2970 (deleted code)	110
Temporary (interim) procedure – not long lasting		
Denture (complete) – temporary denture	D5810/D5811	213/214
Interim caries arresting medicament application	D1354	59
Interim crown – not routine	D2799 (any time duration)	97
Partial denture (temporary partial)	D5820/D5821	215/216
Provisional bridge (pontic) – less than six months' duration	D6254 (previously deleted code)	271
Provisional bridge (pontic) – not routine	D6253 (any time duration)	271
Provisional bridge (retainer) – less than six months' duration	D6795 (previously deleted code)	293
Provisional bridge (retainer) – not routine	D6793 (any time duration)	292
Provisional crown – not routine	D2799 (any time duration)	97
Temporary crown (fractured tooth)	D2970 (deleted code)	110
Temporary skeletal anchorage device (TAD)		
Anchorage device requiring surgical flap	D7293	310
Anchorage device with no flap required	D7294	310
Screw retained plate requiring flap	D7292	310
Temporomandibular joint (TMJ dysfunction/TMD)		
TMJ appliance	D7880	328
TMJ radiograph images	D0320/D0321/D0330	29/29/30
TMJ treatment (various)	D7810-D7899	325-329
Tests (Also see OralDNA® Labs in Index)		
Biopsy procedures		
Brush biopsy (OralCDx®)	D7288	308
Exfoliative cytologic sample (cells)	D7287	308
Hard tissue biopsy	D7285	307
Soft tissue biopsy (excisional)	D7286	307
Cancer screening (Vizilite®, VELscope®, Microlux DL, Identafi®, OralID™)	D0431 (adjunct procedure)	42
Caries susceptibility tests	D0425	42
Collection of microorganisms for culture and sensitivity	D0415	40
DNA probe (genetic test)	D0421	41

Genetic test for susceptibility to diseases	D0423	42
Pulp test – pulp vitality test	D0460	44
Saliva sample analysis	D0418	41
Viral culture	D0416	40
Therapeutic parenteral drug administration	D9610/D9612 (single drug, two or more drugs)	366
Therapeutic interim restoration – primary dentition	D2941	103
Thumb sucking/habit appliance		
Fixed appliance therapy (harmful habit)	D8220	348
Removable appliance therapy (harmful habit)	D8210	347
Tissue conditioning (see also "Rebases" and "Relines")	D5850/D5851	216/217
Tissue, excision of hyperplastic – per arch	D7970	337
Tissue, excision of pericoronal gingiva (operculectomy)	D7971	337
Titanium		
Crown, FPD retainer	D6794	293
Crown, single unit	D2794	96
Implant, abutment supported crown	D6094	253
Implant, abutment supported retainer for FPD	D6194	259
Implant supported crown (single) – metal	D6067	254
Implant supported crown (single) – PFM	D6066	254
Implant supported retainer for FPD	D6076/D6077	260/261
Inlay, FPD retainer	D6624	277
Onlay, FPD retainer	D6634	284
Pontic (titanium)	D6214	268
Tissue, accession of	D0472-D0480/D0486	47-48/48
TMJ/TMD appliance	D7880	328
TMJ/TMD appliance adjustment	D7881	329
Tobacco counseling	D1320	56
Tomographic survey (radiographic images)	D0322	30
Tongue thrusting (harmful habit) appliance (also harmful thumb sucking)		
Fixed appliance (habit)	D8220 (placed in roof of mouth)	348
Removable appliance (habit)	D8210	347
Tooth brush instruction (oral hygiene)	D1330	56
Tooth fragment reattachment (incisal edge or cusp)	D2921	99
Tooth removal (partial extraction of tooth)		
<u>Intentional</u> partial extraction – coronectomy	D7251	304
<u>Unintentional</u> partial extraction – roots remain	D7999 (unspecified procedure, by report)	339
Tooth uprighting (adult dentition) – partial case	D8040	343
Tooth whitening/bleaching	See Index, "Bleaching (whitening)"	
Topical anesthetic application (pain at emergency visit)	D9110	354
Topical fluoride application (see codes for explanation)	D1206/D1208 (child or adult)	55
Topical medicament carrier		
Fluoride gel carrier	D5986	227
Periodontal carrier	D5994	229

	Code	Page
Vesiculobullous disease medicament carrier	D5991	228
Torus (removal of)		
Lateral exostosis (maxilla or mandible)	D7471	319
Mandibularis	D7473	319
Palatinus	D7472	319
Tracheotomy, emergency	D7990	338
Transplantation, tooth (intentional transplantation)	D7272	305
Transseptal fiberotomy (cutting procedure after ortho completion)	D7291 (cutting fibers around tooth)	309
Tray, fluoride gel carrier	D5986	227
Tray, Perio Protect®	D5994	229
Tray, topical medicament carrier	D5991	228
Treatment simulation 3D images volume	D0393	37
Trimira (Identafi®) – oral cancer screening adjunct	D0431	43
Trismus appliance	D5937	225
Tuberosity		
Fibrous tuberosity reduction	D7972	338
Surgical reduction of osseous tuberosity	D7485	320
Tumor, (removal of)	D7440-D7461	316-318

U	Code	Page
Ultrasound, maxillofacial (capture and interpretation or capture)	D0370/D0386	35/37
Uncovering implant (second stage implant surgery)	D6011	236
Unerupted tooth, surgical access, typically an orthodontic procedure	D7280	305
Unerupted tooth, surgical exposure – orthodontic procedure	D7281 (previously deleted)	306
Unilateral removable partial denture (Nesbit cast partial denture)	D5281	198
Unscheduled dressing change (periodontal)	D4920	181
Unspecified preventive procedure	D1999	63

V	Code	Page
Valplast® (flexible) resin partial (upper/lower)	D5225/D5226	197/198
Valplast® (flexible) unilateral or bilateral resin partial	D5225/D5226	197/198
Varnish fluoride application (child or adult)	D1206	55
VELscope™/Vizilite® /Microlux DL/ Identafi®/ OralID™	D0431 (adjunct cancer screening device)	43
Veneer repair	D2983	113
Veneers (various types of materials and techniques)	D2960-D2962	108-109
Vertical bitewings (7 to 8 radiographic images) – typically perio patient	D0277	28
Vesiculobullous disease medicament carrier	D5991	228
Vestibuloplasty	D7340/D7350	314
Viral culture diagnostic kit	D0416	40
Viroxyn®		
Dispensed for home treatment of cold sores/fever blisters	D9630	367
In office palliative treatment of cold sores/fever blisters	D9110 (emergency visit)	354

	Code	Page
Vital tooth bleaching (whitening)	D9972/D9973/D9975	377-379
Vizilite®/VELscope™ /Microlux DL/Identafi®/OralID™	D0431 (adjunct cancer screening test)	43

W	Code	Page
Wax-up (diagnostic)		
Wax-up	D9999 (unspecified procedure, by report)	382
Wax-up when part of occlusion analysis--mounted case	D9950	375
Wing retainer, Maryland Bridge (report pontic separately)		
Ceramic/porcelain wing	D6548	272
Metal wing	D6545	271
Resin wing	D6549	273
Whitening (bleaching)		
Non-vital tooth (endodontically treated) single tooth whitening	D9974	379
Vital tooth		
External (in office) tooth whitening	D9972	377
External per tooth whitening	D9973	378
External (home application) – trays, strips	D9975	379
Wounds, treatment of	D7910-D7912	330

X	Code	Page
X-rays – See Index, "Radiographs"		

Y		
No "Y" terms		

Z	Code	Page
ZAAG (precision attachment) – locator on overdenture	D5862 (typically mini implant)	217
Zest anchors – semi-precision attachment abutment	D6052 (typically full size implant)	244
Zirconium substrate crowns (reported as porcelain/ceramic material)	D2740	90
Zygomatic arch		
Compound fracture treatment		
Closed reduction	D7760	325
Open reduction	D7750	324
Simple fracture treatment		
Closed reduction	D7660	323
Open reduction	D7650	323

NOTES

Go to www.practicebooster.com to learn about the Revenue Enhancement Program, a coding and fee positioning consultation for you and your staff.
Cut coding errors and maximize legitimate reimbursement!
Tel: (866) 858-7596; Fax: (855) 825-3960; info@drcharlesblair.com

NOTES

Go to www.practicebooster.com to learn about the Revenue Enhancement Program, a coding and fee positioning consultation for you and your staff.
Cut coding errors and maximize legitimate reimbursement!
Tel: (866) 858-7596; Fax: (855) 825-3960; info@drcharlesblair.com

CODING COMPLIANCE

The Four Levels of Coding Compliance

Dentists are obligated, legally and morally, to observe four levels of code reporting and clinical protocol compliance. Compliance may be:

1. **Legal** in nature and involve reporting under CDT 2016 (federal and state law).
2. Required by a third-party's contract provisions between dentist and payer.
3. Required for maintaining membership in the American Dental Association by the ADA's Principle of **Ethics** and **Code** of **Professional Conduct**.
4. Adherence to a fundamental **moral standard** of fairness.

Noncompliance with legal and third-party contract stipulations may result in restitution, fines, suspension and forfeiture of license, and incarceration. **In simple terms, noncompliance from a legal or contract perspective is very serious business!**

I. Here is a sample of what the Federal Government has to say about compliance and reporting by the dentist:

False claims Act 31 U.S.C.

§3729. False claims

LIABILITY FOR CERTAIN ACTS. Any person who:

(A) Knowingly presents, or causes to be presented, a false or fraudulent claim for payment or approval.

(B) Knowingly makes, uses, or causes to be made or used, a false record or statement material to a false or fraudulent claim.

II. Comments concerning compliance with a typical third-party contract and the provider's manual:

The agreement between the dentist provider and the third-party payer is a legally enforceable contract. The dentist must be in compliance with the contract to maintain the contractual relationship. Furthermore, the dentist agrees to be subject to audit regarding any provision of the contract and the proper reporting of CDT 2016 codes. Generally the dentist is warned first, and may be placed on probation if he/she has violated the contract. The third party (and patient, if applicable) is entitled to recovery for any noncompliance with the contract or provider manual. In addition to civil remedies, the third party may make a criminal referral to state and federal authorities if fraud is alleged.

The signed contract between the dentist provider and third party (insurance company) controls, through the provider manual, how charges and fee write offs are handled, charges that are not permitted (i.e., local anesthetic, periodontal charting, submission of radiographs, intraoral photographs, etc.), procedures not covered or considered integral to a procedure, repayments and refunds, and coordination or duplication of benefits, etc. The dental provider's manual (provided by the third party) spells out these details.

The manual's guidelines are wide ranging and cover both clinical and some financial criteria. When the dentist signs the contract, the dentist is agreeing with all limitations outlined in the provider manual, often received at a later time. The third party may unilaterally change the contract or manual at any time, and after a grace period elapses (typically 30 or 60 days), the amended manual is enforceable (unless the dentist provider gives proper notice and resigns from the plan).

III. Compliance with ADA ethics is required to maintain membership in the ADA.

IV. A moral standard of fairness/compliance also comes into play.

"Always do right. This will gratify some people – and astonish the rest." Mark Twain

The vast majority of dentists adhere to code reporting and clinical protocol compliance simply because it is morally and ethically the right thing to do.

When the words "misleading," "improper," "miscoding," or "fraud" are used in this manual, they are referring to one or more, or all, of these four basic levels of compliance, as outlined above.

Why Compliance Can Be Painful

After reading this manual some practices may find that correction of the miscoding and misreporting errors, and adjusting clinical protocols, may actually result in decreased revenues. It is obviously painful to decrease revenues as a result of compliance, but compliance is well worth it. Some dentists and staff are cavalier, even arrogant, about coding and record keeping compliance, assuming they will never be audited or "found out." However, audits can and DO occur! Just because a practice does not participate and has not signed a contract with a given payer DOES NOT mean the practice cannot be audited. Any payer (federal or state government program, patient, administrator, or insurance company) of a claim has the direct or indirect right to verify that the submitted procedure was:

- Actually performed.
- Medically necessary.
- Reported accurately, using the correct CDT 2016 code set.
- Performed to meet at least the basic clinical standards of practice.
- Billed at the same fee and used the same clinical protocol for both insurance and non-insurance patients if performed by a contract dentist. A third-party contract will require a write off of the practice's unrestricted fee, if greater than the contracted fee.
- Not improperly "upcoded" or "unbundled," according to the CDT 2016 nomenclature and descriptor.

The third party payer can also ask for verification that:

- The office did not forgive the patient's obligation without notifying the third party (fee forgiveness notification). If fee forgiveness applies very infrequently, always describe it in the narrative as such: "The patient will not contribute to the cost of care."
- The total fee reported on the claim form was the actual fee obligation to be paid by the patient. For instance, if the patient's treatment costs $1,000 and a 5% cash discount is offered for prepayment, $950 must be reported or noted on the claim form as the actual fee charged and collected from the patient, not $1,000.

Finally, f chosen, the dentist must also answer to state dental board scrutiny.

Why Compliance Can Be Profitable

Alternatively, in many cases thousands of dollars are realized when the codes are used properly. Both the practice and the patient "win" through proper documentation and accurate reporting for maximum legal reimbursement! Many offices will find that they are leaving "money on the table" by not understanding the proper application of the official CDT 2016 code set or providing the necessary documentation for the adjudication of the claim. Overall, compliance results in a positive, economic result for most offices.

Proper documentation may be burdensome, but should be considered a necessary cost of doing business.

Surviving an Audit: The Importance of Good Records and Documentation

Some offices keep poor or non-existent records and have non-diagnostic radiographic images. By doing so, they leave themselves wide open to malpractice claims, state board actions, and third party action. Documentation that is complete and accurate truly affects all aspects of the practice. Documentation is the cornerstone of diagnosis for indicating the need for treatment and forms the foundation for proper CDT 2016 reporting. Documentation should record treatment history in a complete way. The clinical and financial record serves to validate the appropriateness of treatment, and of the billing history.

For each visit, the patient's documentation should include some or all, (but not be limited to), the following elements:

1. Date of evaluation/treatment.
2. Relevant history and signs/symptoms.
3. Assessment of findings and clinical impression.
4. Diagnosis and treatment plan.
5. Description of service performed (CDT 2016).
6. Narrative and documentation for the claim form, if any.
7. Supporting diagnostic quality radiographic images, photographs, and diagnostic study models, if appropriate.
8. Informed consent.

The dental chart should **not** be a "ledger" of treatment performed and sequence, listing the individual procedures down the page with no other comments. For instance, the following entry is inadequate:

Crown and core buildup, #3 – no other entry.

This kind of inadequate record keeping leaves the dentist defenseless against legal action or auditor. Lightning can, and does, strike! Keep good records.

INSURANCE ISSUES

Why the Insurance Companies "March to the Beat of a Different Drummer"

Dental offices are bound by federal, state, and contract law when reporting dental services rendered, using official CDT (Current Dental Terminology) codes. CDT 2016 requires that the procedures accurately be reported by the dental office, not "an equivalent procedure." For instance, a panoramic radiographic image and bitewing images must be reported as a panorex and bitewings, not an equivalent, full series radiographic images.

It is a **felony** to intentionally miscode a claim form or file misleading information in order to increase reimbursement. If a code does not exist, or does not accurately describe a given procedure, an unspecified procedure code should be reported. The narrative, by report, would then be used to describe the procedure. For example, a periodontally related procedure with no specific code description would be reported as D4999, with a narrative. The various unspecified codes are reported and end in the digits 99 or 999. The payer of the claim would then review the contract for any reimbursement due for the procedure. In some cases, an "alternate benefit" may be reimbursed by the payer. Obviously, this works to the patient's benefit.

Just because there is a descriptive, official code for a given procedure, does not assure reimbursement. Contracts have many exclusions, limitations, and deductibles. Unfortunately, many patients believe… "If I need it, my insurance should cover it." Dental procedures – even when necessary – are not always reimbursed. Your practice should communicate the limitations of dental benefits to your patients!

Always refer to dental "insurance" as dental "benefits". It is not insurance (for calamity) as there is typically only a $1,500 maximum annual reimbursement.

It is required, by law, to report exactly what is performed. The payer can "change" or "remap" the code for reimbursement purposes. This occurs because the payer of the claim adjudicates reimbursement in accordance with the contract plan language, often allowing the payer to "re-map" the submitted code to a different, "payment" code. The patient may benefit from this "re-mapping" versus a strict contract interpretation when otherwise the carrier would totally deny the claim.

Do not Try to 'Get Back' at the Insurance Company

Many doctors and staff are angered and frustrated by the insurance company's exclusions, limitations, deductibles and waiting periods, etc. Inherent in this anger and frustration is the natural desire to "get 'em back." The *degree* of the limitations is determined by the dental plan that the employer chose to buy and is driven by the changing reimbursement marketplace.

Remember, the "wiggle" clauses control or diminish the dental policy premium paid by the employer. The payer has a legal right to restrict reimbursement, according to the plan document. The contract is "king," and is contractually binding. The bottom line is: the office must report exactly "what they do" according to CDT 2016. That is the way it is. The successful dental team must learn to work within the system and legitimately adhere to the contract's rules. Be grateful that the availability of dental benefits drives demand for dental services. Indeed, the dental profession should appreciate the benefits of third-party reimbursement. Reread "Why Compliance Can Be Profitable" on the preceding page.

The Insurance Independent Practice

"We're an insurance independent practice. Why do, or should we, care about coding?"

It is true that being "insurance independent" offers certain perks. The patient pays you up front, and you give them an insurance form reporting the procedures provided, and they are then "on their own." The practice is not subject to any third party contract. While many perceive this to be the optimum practice, (assuming you're still at maximum production capacity), it is not a green light to miscode, misreport, or engage in practice protocols or philosophies that do not comply with CDT 2016 and/or with state or federal law. It should be considered a **serious error in judgment** for insurance-independent practices to believe they are somehow "above the law" and to routinely disregard the rules. They must report what they do exactly as the insurance-driven practice and comply with all reporting rules and regulations mandated under CDT 2016.

Can an insurance independent practice be audited? Absolutely! As mentioned earlier, anyone who pays a claim can audit a practice regarding that particular claim. The dental profession is quickly shifting to PPOs just like medicine. Less than 15% are still out-of-network, and the percentage of insurance independent practices continues to decrease.

CODING AND EXPLANATIONS IN THIS MANUAL

The "F" Word (FRAUD!)

The most common term mentioned under the "warning" and "coding watch" legends for the various codes is "misleading." In many of these cases, "fraud" could easily replace the word "misleading." However, the author is not an attorney and decides against "splitting hairs" as to the exact legal definition for every comment under each and every scenario. Thus, "misleading" has been used throughout the manual except in a very few instances. **Remember, fraud does apply under the "warning" legend if done with intent to deceive in order to receive a reimbursement not legitimately earned.**

Let us look at some examples of dental insurance fraud as outlined by the United Concordia Insurance Companies, Inc., on their website:

"Dental fraud is any crime where an individual receives insurance money for filing a false claim, inflating a claim or billing for services not rendered. Fraud is sometimes called the "hidden" crime because we are all victims without even knowing it.

Dental fraud takes many forms. Examples include:

- Billing for services not provided.
- Reporting a higher level of dental service than was actually performed. This is often called "upcoding."
- Submitting a dental claim under one patient's name when services were provided to another person.
- Altering claim forms and dental records.
- Billing for non-covered services as if they were covered services.
- Changing the date of service on a claim form so that it falls within a patient's benefit period.
- Routinely waiving a patient's co-payment or deductible.
- Performing services that are not suitable or "necessary."

The Importance of Using Current CDT Codes and The Future

HIPAA (the Health Insurance Portability and Accountability Act) requires the proper reporting of dental codes using the current, mandated CDT 2016 code set. Under HIPAA, the Code Maintenance Committee (CMC) is the keeper of the codes. The current CDT 2016 codes are the "law." Each specific insurance contract, or self-funded plan, defines what is, or is not, reimbursed. Reporting a valid CDT code does not assure a given procedure will be reimbursed under a given contract. A typical contract is written with numerous "wiggle" clauses in order to reduce overall reimbursement and to hold down the premium costs for the employer. The payer is permitted, by the employer's contract, to "map" one procedure code to another payment code. For example, bitewing images plus a panoramic image on the same service date often "maps" the services to a lesser, complete series, (D0210) MPA (maximum plan allowance) or UCR payment. Like it or not, this is how the system works.

Your practice MUST adapt to changes in the insurance (dental benefits) system as they occur by assisting your patients to the best of your ability with insurance matters, to provide explanation of benefits (EOBs), and with proper adjudication of the claim to maximize legitimate reimbursement. Whether you like it or not, the insurance market is dominated by PPOs and they will continue to dramatically increase market share. At the same time, patients must also be educated as to their responsibility for payment of any fees not reimbursed by their particular plan — whether they like it or not.

A Simple Guide to Using this Manual to Search for a Given CDT Code

Step 1: Use the Index at the back of this manual if you do not know the specific code. If you know the proper code, go directly to the official CDT 2016 code listings that are "tabbed." The manual has search tabs for the reader's convenience — one for the index, and one for the CDT 2016 codes.

Step 2: First, read the official CDT 2016 code, nomenclature, and descriptor. Next, read any associated legends such as Coding Warning, Coding Watch, Coding Match, Comments/Limitations, Tips/Narratives, and Clinical Flow Chart. Note if the code is new, revised, deleted or previously deleted (as printed in red). Read about the legend definitions that are described on the page prior to code D0120.

Step 3: Refer to any *alternate* code(s) cross-referenced and read all related information for further details or ideas.

Step 4: Apply the knowledge! Improve your accuracy!

ACKNOWLEDGEMENTS

The author wishes to thank the following persons for their assistance in reviewing and assistance in editing this edition of the manual. A thousand thanks for the professional assistance of:

Margaret Macknelly – design/layout, Margaret Macknelly Design, England, design@macknelly.co.uk

Roy Shelburne, DDS, Appalachian Dental Group, roy_shelburne@yahoo.com

Christina Gore, DMD, FAGD, CDC

The entire staff of *Insurance Solutions Newsletter*: Vicki Anderson, Denise Connett, Dilaine Gloege, Debbie Hains, Glenda Hood, Sara Jordan, Penny McClure and Julie Devinney.

A personal thank you to my wife, Maryvan, and her father, Mr. Charles Sawyer, for their endless support and encouragement.

I want to thank my children, my daughter-in-law, and son-in-law for their many hours of assistance in reviewing and editing the manuscript. They are as follows: Janet Blair, Mason Blair, Trip Blair (MBA) and Leigh Blair (CPA), Susan Jordan and Joe Jordan, Esq.

ABOUT THE AUTHOR

Dr. Charles Blair is President of Dr. Charles Blair & Associates, Inc. and publisher of multiple publications including *Administration with Confidence Insurance Guide* and *Insurance Solutions Newsletter*, located in Belmont, North Carolina. He also founded PracticeBooster.com, a dental coding support website. A graduate of Erskine College, he earned his Doctorate of Dental Surgery at the University of North Carolina at Chapel Hill. Dr. Blair holds degrees in Accounting, Business Administration, Mathematics, and Dental Surgery.

In this publication, Dr. Blair continues the use and application of **Predictive Error Correction**[SM] technology – a simple and easy to follow system designed to identify and correct coding and clinical protocol errors made by the typical dental office.

Dr. Blair is a highly sought after speaker for national, state and local dental groups, study clubs and other organizations. His leading edge presentations in the business/finance and dental insurance coding arena of dentistry are revolutionary. In addition, he has assisted thousands of practices across the country to maximize their profits through his tested and proven **Revenue Enhancement Program and Clinical Treatment Analyzer**[SM].

Dr. Blair is the author or coauthor of multiple publications. His latest manuals are **Coding with Confidence: The "Go-To" Dental Coding Guide for CDT 2016** and **Administration with Confidence: The "Go-To" Guide for Insurance Administration 2016** and **Diagnostic Coding for Dental Claim Submission 2015-2016**.

AUTHOR'S SPEAKING

For more information about the author's lectures for organizations, contact Susan Jordan for information or visit the website:

www.practicebooster.com
Dr. Charles Blair & Associates, Inc.
(866) 858-7596

PRACTICEBOOSTER® SERVICES – ATTENTION DOCTORS AND STAFF

Go to **www.practicebooster.com** to learn all about the website tools and consulting services that are available.

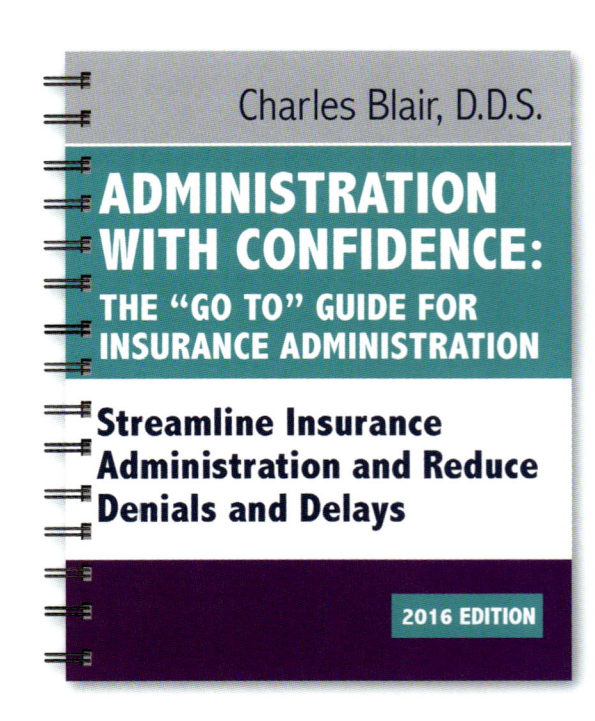

ADMINISTRATION WITH CONFIDENCE:

The "Go To" Insurance Administration Guide

Charles Blair, D.D.S.

ADMINISTRATION WITH CONFIDENCE: THE "GO TO" GUIDE FOR INSURANCE ADMINISTRATION

Streamline Insurance Administration and Reduce Denials and Delays

2016 EDITION

Administration with Confidence provides dental practice team members with need-to-know information to successfully navigate the challenging ins and outs of dental insurance administration.

Proper insurance administration is key for maintaining a profitable practice and this Guide offers solutions for both the common and complex problems facing practices today. Additionally, the new 2016 edition includes over 10 new chapters including the Affordable Care Act, Medicaid Contract Provisions, Recovery Audit Contractor Program and much more!

TOP REASONS this Guide is a *must-have for every practice*:

- PPOs – Joining/Dropping/Negotiating Fees
- Affordable Care Act and Dentistry
- Navigating Medicaid and Medicare
- Top Administrative Q&As – Solutions for Your Most Common Issues
- Maximizing Legitimate Reimbursement
- Properly Calculate Write-Offs (COB) – Get Your Full Fee!
- Discounting and Copay Forgiveness – Stay Out of Jail
- Scenarios for New CDT 2016 Codes

ORDER FORM

☐ Administration with Confidence $99.95* + $10 S/H

☐ Bundle with Coding with Confidence $189.95* + $15 S/H

*Plus applicable sales tax for NC only.

Practice Information:

Practice Name _____

Attn. _____

Address _____

City _____ State _____ ZIP _____

Phone (_____) _____

Email _____

Order Online at:
www.practicebooster.com

Method of Payment:
SEND TO: American Dental Support, LLC
P.O. Box 986, Belmont, NC 28012-0986
FAX TO: (855) 825-3960

☐ Check # _____ Amt. _____
Payable to American Dental Support, LLC

☐ Visa   ☐ MasterCard   ☐ AMEX   ☐ Discover

Card # _____

Exp. Date _____ Security # _____

Signature _____

P.O. Box 986 Belmont, NC 28012-0986 ▪ (866) 858-7596 ▪ Fax (855) 825-3960 ▪ www.practicebooster.com ▪ email: info@practicebooster.com

ENHANCE YOUR CODING EXPERIENCE
with **Practice Booster** and Insurance Solutions Newsletter!

Available anytime, anywhere on your desktop or iPad

Practice Booster

Practice Booster is the key to maximizing legitimate reimbursement and minimizing coding risk in your practice! Practice Booster's breakthrough online system is a complete resource for your dental practice to eliminate costly coding errors and recover lost revenue.

Your annual subscription to Practice Booster includes:

- Access to Code Advisor
- Call center support to assist you with your difficult dental and medical coding issues
- A subscription to Insurance Solutions Newsletter
- Access to the online resource center featuring Q & As, coding forum, and much more!

Insurance Solutions Newsletter

Insurance Solutions Newsletter covers a wide range of topics relating to dental insurance coding and administration to enhance your practice's productivity and profitability. Dental practices nationwide rely on *Insurance Solutions Newsletter* to help them fully understand CDT Codes, insurance administration, and many other industry trends.

Your annual subscription to Insurance Solutions Newsletter includes:

- Six bi-monthly issues of the newsletter
- Access to our online database of previous issues
- Access to our online forum
- Call center support to assist you with your difficult dental and medical coding issues

ORDER FORM

☐ **Practice Booster - $297/year***
  *Includes Insurance Solutions Newsletter

☐ **Insurance Solutions Newsletter - $169/year**

Practice Information:

Practice Name _____

Attn. _____

Address _____

City _____ State _____ ZIP _____

Phone (_____) _____

Email _____
*Email address required for online access

Order Online at:
www.practicebooster.com

Method of Payment:
SEND TO: American Dental Support, LLC
P.O. Box 986, Belmont, NC 28012-0986
FAX TO: (855) 825-3960

☐ Check # _____ Amt. _____
Payable to American Dental Support, LLC

☐ Visa ☐ MasterCard ☐ AMEX ☐ Discover

Card # _____

Exp. Date _____ Security # _____

Signature _____

P.O. Box 986 Belmont, NC 28012-0986 ▪ (866) 858-7596 ▪ Fax (855) 825-3960 ▪ www.practicebooster.com ▪ email: info@practicebooster.com

Order Your ICD-9-CM and ICD-10-CM Edition of Diagnostic Coding for Dental Claim Submission *Today!*

Diagnostic Coding for Dental Claim Submission provides today's practice with a "go to" resource for understanding the implementation of diagnostic coding on the 2012 ADA Dental Claim Form. This new, in-depth Guide helps dental team members who need guidance on the proper use of diagnoses codes in the dental practice.

Many states' Medicaid programs are now requiring the use of ICD (diagnosis) codes when reporting dental procedures. In addition, many Affordable Care Act (ACA) plans with mandated pediatric dental benefits are also requiring the use of ICD codes. This is a trend we expect to continue among other dental payers.

Different practices have different levels of understanding and experience with ICD coding. This Guide is a comprehensive resource for team members submitting ICD codes on the 2012 ADA Dental Claim Form.

Dental coding is challenging, but medical coding is even more complex. With this Guide, you will be able to break down the complexities of diagnoses codes and successfully file your dental claims. You will not only improve your practice's efficiency, you will also increase profitability and reduce risk!

Diagnostic Coding for Dental Claims

- Reviews both ICD-9-CM and ICD-10-CM as they relate to dental procedures
- Uses a Scenario-Based Teaching Method to help team members quickly identify and select the appropriate diagnoses codes for specific dental procedures
- Provides a listing of ICD-9-CM and ICD-10-CM codes, broken down by procedure type
- Enables your practice to increase claim submissions and processing efficiencies while reducing denials and delays

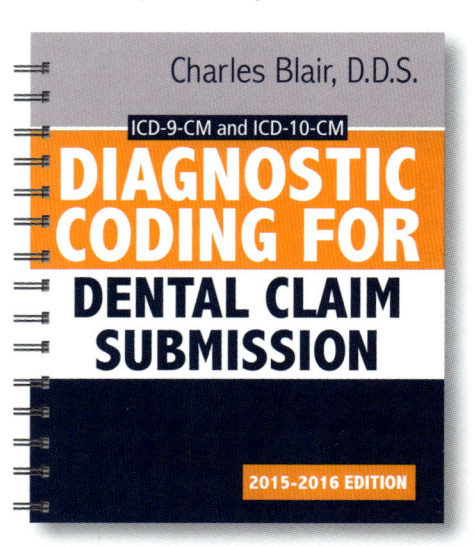

ORDER FORM

☐ **Diagnostic Coding for Dental Claim Submission**
$169.95* + $10 S/H
Plus applicable sales tax for NC only.

Practice Information:

Practice Name _____
Attn. _____
Address _____
City _____ State _____ ZIP _____
Phone (_____) _____
Email _____

Order Online at:
www.practicebooster.com

Method of Payment:
SEND TO: American Dental Support, LLC
P.O. Box 986, Belmont, NC 28012-0986
FAX TO: (855) 825-3960

☐ Check # _____ Amt. _____
Payable to American Dental Support, LLC

☐ Visa ☐ MasterCard ☐ AMEX ☐ Discover

Card # _____
Exp. Date _____ Security # _____
Signature _____

P.O. Box 986 Belmont, NC 28012-0986 ▪ (866) 858-7596 ▪ Fax (855) 825-3960 ▪ www.practicebooster.com ▪ email: info@practicebooster.com